Antiquities of the Jews

Antiquities of the Jews

Volume 1

Flavius Josephus

Waking Lion Press

ISBN 978-1-4341-1504-1

Published by Waking Lion Press, an imprint of The Editorium

The Editorium, LLC
West Valley City, UT 84128-3917
wakinglionpress.com
wakinglion@editorium.com

Contents

Contents

Preface

1. THOSE who undertake to write histories,[1] do not, I perceive, take that trouble on one and the same account, but for many reasons, and those such as are very different one from another. For some of them apply themselves to this part of learning to show their skill in composition, and that they may therein acquire a reputation for speaking finely: others of them there are, who write histories in order to gratify those that happen to be concerned in them, and on that account have spared no pains, but rather gone beyond their own abilities in the performance: but others there are, who, of necessity and by force, are driven to write history, because they are concerned in the facts, and so cannot excuse themselves from committing them to writing, for the advantage of posterity; nay, there are not a few who are induced to draw their historical facts out of darkness into light, and to produce them for the benefit of the public, on account of the great importance of the facts themselves with which they have been concerned. Now of these several reasons for writing history, I must profess the two last were my own reasons also; for since I was myself interested in that war which we Jews had with the Romans, and knew myself its particular actions, and what conclusion it had, I was forced to give the history of it, because I saw that others perverted the truth of those actions in their writings.

2. Now I have undertaken the present work, as thinking it will appear to all the Greeks[2] worthy of their study; for it will contain all our antiquities, and the constitution of our government, as interpreted out of the Hebrew Scriptures. And indeed I did formerly intend, when

---

1. This preface of Josephus is excellent in its kind, and highly worthy the repeated perusal of the reader, before he set about the perusal of the work itself.

2. That is, all the Gentiles, both Greeks and Romans.

I wrote of the war,[3] to explain who the Jews originally were,—what fortunes they had been subject to,—and by what legislature they had been instructed in piety, and the exercise of other virtues,—what wars also they had made in remote ages, till they were unwillingly engaged in this last with the Romans: but because this work would take up a great compass, I separated it into a set treatise by itself, with a beginning of its own, and its own conclusion; but in process of time, as usually happens to such as undertake great things, I grew weary and went on slowly, it being a large subject, and a difficult thing to translate our history into a foreign, and to us unaccustomed language. However, some persons there were who desired to know our history, and so exhorted me to go on with it; and, above all the rest, Epaphroditus,[4] a man who is a lover of all kind of learning, but is principally delighted with the knowledge of history, and this on account of his having been himself concerned in great affairs, and many turns of fortune, and having shown a wonderful rigor of an excellent nature, and an immovable virtuous resolution in them all. I yielded to this man's persuasions, who always excites such as have abilities in what is useful and acceptable, to join their endeavors with his. I was also ashamed myself to permit any laziness of disposition to have a greater influence upon me, than the delight of taking pains in such studies as were very useful: I thereupon stirred up myself, and went on with my work more cheerfully. Besides the foregoing motives, I had others which I greatly reflected on; and these were, that our forefathers were willing to communicate such things to others; and that some of the Greeks took considerable pains to know the affairs of our nation.

3. I found, therefore, that the second of the Ptolemies was a king who was extraordinarily diligent in what concerned learning, and the collection of books; that he was also peculiarly ambitious to procure a translation of our law, and of the constitution of our government

---

3. We may seasonably note here, that Josephus wrote his Seven Books of the Jewish War long before he wrote these his Antiquities. Those books of the War were published about A.D. 75, and these Antiquities, A. D. 93, about eighteen years later.

4. This Epaphroditus was certainly alive in the third year of Trajan, A.D. 100. See the note on the First Book Against Apion, sect. 1. Who he was we do not know; for as to Epaphroditus, the freedman of Nero, and afterwards Domitian's secretary, who was put to death by Domitian in the 14th or 15th year of his reign, he could not be alive in the third of Trajan.

therein contained, into the Greek tongue. Now Eleazar the high priest, one not inferior to any other of that dignity among us, did not envy the forenamed king the participation of that advantage, which otherwise he would for certain have denied him, but that he knew the custom of our nation was, to hinder nothing of what we esteemed ourselves from being communicated to others. Accordingly, I thought it became me both to imitate the generosity of our high priest, and to suppose there might even now be many lovers of learning like the king; for he did not obtain all our writings at that time; but those who were sent to Alexandria as interpreters, gave him only the books of the law, while there were a vast number of other matters in our sacred books. They, indeed, contain in them the history of five thousand years; in which time happened many strange accidents, many chances of war, and great actions of the commanders, and mutations of the form of our government. Upon the whole, a man that will peruse this history, may principally learn from it, that all events succeed well, even to an incredible degree, and the reward of felicity is proposed by God; but then it is to those that follow his will, and do not venture to break his excellent laws: and that so far as men any way apostatize from the accurate observation of them, what was practical before becomes impracticable[5] and whatsoever they set about as a good thing, is converted into an incurable calamity. And now I exhort all those that peruse these books, to apply their minds to God; and to examine the mind of our legislator, whether he hath not understood his nature in a manner worthy of him; and hath not ever ascribed to him such operations as become his power, and hath not preserved his writings from those indecent fables which others have framed, although, by the great distance of time when he lived, he might have securely forged such lies; for he lived two thousand years ago; at which vast distance of ages the poets themselves have not been so hardy as to fix even the generations of their gods, much less the actions of their men, or their own laws. As I proceed, therefore, I shall accurately describe what is contained in our records, in the order of time that belongs to them; for I have already promised so to do throughout this undertaking; and

---

5. Josephus here plainly alludes to the famous Greek proverb, If God be with us, every thing that is impossible becomes possible.

this without adding any thing to what is therein contained, or taking away any thing therefrom.

4. But because almost all our constitution depends on the wisdom of Moses, our legislator, I cannot avoid saying somewhat concerning him beforehand, though I shall do it briefly; I mean, because otherwise those that read my book may wonder how it comes to pass, that my discourse, which promises an account of laws and historical facts, contains so much of philosophy. The reader is therefore to know, that Moses deemed it exceeding necessary, that he who would conduct his own life well, and give laws to others, in the first place should consider the Divine nature; and, upon the contemplation of God's operations, should thereby imitate the best of all patterns, so far as it is possible for human nature to do, and to endeavor to follow after it: neither could the legislator himself have a right mind without such a contemplation; nor would any thing he should write tend to the promotion of virtue in his readers; I mean, unless they be taught first of all, that God is the Father and Lord of all things, and sees all things, and that thence he bestows a happy life upon those that follow him; but plunges such as do not walk in the paths of virtue into inevitable miseries. Now when Moses was desirous to teach this lesson to his countrymen, he did not begin the establishment of his laws after the same manner that other legislators did; I mean, upon contracts and other rights between one man and another, but by raising their minds upwards to regard God, and his creation of the world; and by persuading them, that we men are the most excellent of the creatures of God upon earth. Now when once he had brought them to submit to religion, he easily persuaded them to submit in all other things: for as to other legislators, they followed fables, and by their discourses transferred the most reproachful of human vices unto the gods, and afforded wicked men the most plausible excuses for their crimes; but as for our legislator, when he had once demonstrated that God was possessed of perfect virtue, he supposed that men also ought to strive after the participation of it; and on those who did not so think, and so believe, he inflicted the severest punishments. I exhort, therefore, my readers to examine this whole undertaking in that view; for thereby it will appear to them, that there is nothing therein disagreeable either to the majesty of God, or to his love to mankind; for all things have here a reference to the nature of the universe; while our legislator speaks

some things wisely, but enigmatically, and others under a decent allegory, but still explains such things as required a direct explication plainly and expressly. However, those that have a mind to know the reasons of every thing, may find here a very curious philosophical theory, which I now indeed shall wave the explication of; but if God afford me time for it, I will set about writing it[6] after I have finished the present work. I shall now betake myself to the history before me, after I have first mentioned what Moses says of the creation of the world, which I find described in the sacred books after the manner following.

---

6. As to this intended work of Josephus concerning the reasons of many of the Jewish laws, and what philosophical or allegorical sense they would bear, the loss of which work is by some of the learned not much regretted, I am inclinable, in part, to Fabricius's opinion, ap. Havercamp, p. 63, 61, That "we need not doubt but that, among some vain and frigid conjectures derived from Jewish imaginations, Josephus would have taught us a greater number of excellent and useful things, which perhaps nobody, neither among the Jews, nor among the Christians, can now inform us of; so that I would give a great deal to find it still extant."

Book 1

Containing the Interval of Three Thousand Eight Hundred and Thirty-Three Years, from the Creation to the Death of Isaac

1 *The Constitution of the World and the Disposition of the Elements*

1. In the beginning God created the heaven and the earth. But when the earth did not come into sight, but was covered with thick darkness, and a wind moved upon its surface, God commanded that there should be light: and when that was made, he considered the whole mass, and separated the light and the darkness; and the name he gave to one was *Night,* and the other he called *Day:* and he named the beginning of light, and the time of rest, *The Evening* and *The Morning,* and this was indeed the first day. But Moses said it was one day; the cause of which I am able to give even now; but because I have promised to give such reasons for all things in a treatise by itself, I shall put off its exposition till that time. After this, on the second day, he placed the heaven over the whole world, and separated it from the other parts, and he determined it should stand by itself. He also placed a crystalline [firmament] round it, and put it together in a manner agreeable to the earth, and fitted it for giving moisture and rain, and for affording the advantage of dews. On the third day he appointed the dry land to appear, with the sea itself round about it; and on the very same day he made the plants and the seeds to spring out of the earth. On the fourth day he adorned the heaven with the sun, the moon, and the other stars, and appointed them their motions and courses, that the vicissitudes of the seasons might be clearly signified. And on the

fifth day he produced the living creatures, both those that swim, and those that fly; the former in the sea, the latter in the air: he also sorted them as to society and mixture, for procreation, and that their kinds might increase and multiply. On the sixth day he created the four-footed beasts, and made them male and female: on the same day he also formed man. Accordingly Moses says, That in just six days the world, and all that is therein, was made. And that the seventh day was a rest, and a release from the labor of such operations; whence it is that we Celebrate a rest from our labors on that day, and call it the Sabbath, which word denotes *rest* in the Hebrew tongue.

2. Moreover, Moses, after the seventh day was over[1] begins to talk philosophically; and concerning the formation of man, says thus: That God took dust from the ground, and formed man, and inserted in him a spirit and a soul.[2] This man was called Adam, which in the Hebrew tongue signifies *one that is red,* because he was formed out of red earth, compounded together; for of that kind is virgin and true earth. God also presented the living creatures, when he had made them, according to their kinds, both male and female, to Adam, who gave them those names by which they are still called. But when he saw that Adam had no female companion, no society, for there was no such created, and that he wondered at the other animals which were male and female, he laid him asleep, and took away one of his ribs, and out of it formed the woman; whereupon Adam knew her when she was brought to him, and acknowledged that she was made out of himself.

---

1. Since Josephus, in his Preface, sect. 4, says that Moses wrote some things enigmatically, some allegorically, and the rest in plain words, since in his account of the first chapter of Genesis, and the first three verses of the second, he gives us no hints of any mystery at all; but when he here comes to ver. 4, etc. he says that Moses, after the seventh day was over, began to talk philosophically; it is not very improbable that he understood the rest of the second and the third chapters in some enigmatical, or allegorical, or philosophical sense. The change of the name of God just at this place, from Elohim to Jehovah Elohim, from God to Lord God, in the Hebrew, Samaritan, and Septuagint, does also not a little favor some such change in the narration or construction.

2. We may observe here, that Josephus supposed man to be compounded of spirit, soul, and body, with St. Paul, 1 Thessalonians 5:23, and the rest of the ancients: he elsewhere says also, that the blood of animals was forbidden to be eaten, as having in it soul and spirit, Antiq. B. III. ch. 11. sect. 2.

Now a woman is called in the Hebrew tongue *Issa;* but the name of this woman was Eve, which signifies *the mother of all living.*

3. Moses says further, that God planted a paradise in the east, flourishing with all sorts of trees; and that among them was the tree of life, and another of knowledge, whereby was to be known what was good and evil; and that when he brought Adam and his wife into this garden, he commanded hem to take care of the plants. Now the garden was watered by one river,[3] which ran round about the whole earth, and was parted into four parts. And Phison, which denotes a multitude, running into India, makes its exit into the sea, and is by the Greeks called Ganges. Euphrates also, as well as Tigris, goes down into the Red Sea.[4] Now the name Euphrates, or Phrath, denotes either a dispersion, or a flower: by Tiris, or Diglath, is signified what is swift, with narrowness; and Geon runs through Egypt, and denotes what arises from the east, which the Greeks call Nile.

4. God therefore commanded that Adam and his wife should eat of all the rest of the plants, but to abstain from the tree of knowledge; and foretold to them, that if they touched it, it would prove their destruction. But while all the living creatures had one language,[5] at

---

3. Whence this strange notion came, which yet is not peculiar to Joseph,, but, as Dr. Hudson says here, is derived from older authors, as if four of the greatest rivers in the world, running two of them at vast distances from the other two, by some means or other watered paradise, is hard to say. Only since Josephus has already appeared to allegorize this history, and take notice that these four names had a particular signification; Phison for Ganges, a multitude; Phrath for Euphrates, either a dispersion or a flower; Diglath for Tigris, what is swift, with narrowness; and Geon for Nile, what arises from the east,—we perhaps mistake him when we suppose he literally means those four rivers; especially as to Geon or Nile, which arises from the east, while he very well knew the literal Nile arises from the south; though what further allegorical sense he had in view, is now, I fear, impossible to be determined.

4. By the Red Sea is not here meant the Arabian Gulf, which alone we now call by that name, but all that South Sea, which included the Red Sea, and the Persian Gulf, as far as the East Indies; as Reland and Hudson here truly note, from the old geographers.

5. Hence it appears, that Josephus thought several, at least, of the brute animals, particularly the serpent, could speak before the fall. And I think few of the more perfect kinds of those animals want the organs of speech at this day. Many inducements there are also to a notion, that the present state they are in, is not their original state; and that their capacities have been once much greater than we now see them, and are capable of being restored to their former condition. But as to this

that time the serpent, which then lived together with Adam and his wife, shewed an envious disposition, at his supposal of their living happily, and in obedience to the commands of God; and imagining, that when they disobeyed them, they would fall into calamities, he persuaded the woman, out of a malicious intention, to taste of the tree of knowledge, telling them, that in that tree was the knowledge of good and evil; which knowledge, when they should obtain, they would lead a happy life; nay, a life not inferior to that of a god: by which means he overcame the woman, and persuaded her to despise the command of God. Now when she had tasted of that tree, and was pleased with its fruit, she persuaded Adam to make use of it also. Upon this they perceived that they were become naked to one another; and being ashamed thus to appear abroad, they invented somewhat to cover them; for the tree sharpened their understanding; and they covered themselves with fig-leaves; and tying these before them, out of modesty, they thought they were happier than they were before, as they had discovered what they were in want of. But when God came into the garden, Adam, who was wont before to come and converse with him, being conscious of his wicked behavior, went out of the way. This behavior surprised God; and he asked what was the cause of this his procedure; and why he, that before delighted in that conversation, did now fly from it, and avoid it. When he made no reply, as conscious to himself that he had transgressed the command of God, God said, "I had before determined about you both, how you might lead a happy life, without any affliction, and care, and vexation of soul; and that all things which might contribute to your enjoyment and pleasure should grow up by my providence, of their own accord, without your own labor and pains-taking; which state of labor and pains-taking would soon bring on old age, and death would not be at any remote distance: but now thou hast abused this my good-will, and hast disobeyed my commands; for thy silence is not the sign of

---

most ancient, and authentic, and probably allegorical account of that grand affair of the fall of our first parents, I have somewhat more to say in way of conjecture, but being only a conjecture, I omit it: only thus far, that the imputation of the sin of our first parents to their posterity, any further than as some way the cause or occasion of man's mortality, seems almost entirely groundless; and that both man, and the other subordinate creatures, are hereafter to be delivered from the curse then brought upon them, and at last to be delivered from that bondage of corruption, Romans 8:19–22.

thy virtue, but of thy evil conscience." However, Adam excused his sin, and entreated God not to be angry at him, and laid the blame of what was done upon his wife; and said that he was deceived by her, and thence became an offender; while she again accused the serpent. But God allotted him punishment, because he weakly submitted to the counsel of his wife; and said the ground should not henceforth yield its fruits of its own accord, but that when it should be harassed by their labor, it should bring forth some of its fruits, and refuse to bring forth others. He also made Eve liable to the inconveniency of breeding, and the sharp pains of bringing forth children; and this because she persuaded Adam with the same arguments wherewith the serpent had persuaded her, and had thereby brought him into a calamitous condition. He also deprived the serpent of speech, out of indignation at his malicious disposition towards Adam. Besides this, he inserted poison under his tongue, and made him an enemy to men; and suggested to them, that they should direct their strokes against his head, that being the place wherein lay his mischievous designs towards men, and it being easiest to take vengeance on him, that way. And when he had deprived him of the use of his feet, he made him to go rolling all along, and dragging himself upon the ground. And when God had appointed these penalties for them, he removed Adam and Eve out of the garden into another place.

2 Concerning the Posterity of Adam, and the Ten Generations from Him to the Deluge

1. ADAM and Eve had two sons: the elder of them was named Cain; which name, when it is interpreted, signifies *a possession:* the younger was Abel, which signifies *sorrow.* They had also daughters. Now the two brethren were pleased with different courses of life: for Abel, the younger, was a lover of righteousness; and believing that God was present at all his actions, he excelled in virtue; and his employment was that of a shepherd. But Cain was not only very wicked in other respects, but was wholly intent upon getting; and he first contrived to plough the ground. He slew his brother on the occasion following— They had resolved to sacrifice to God. Now Cain brought the fruits of the earth, and of his husbandry; but Abel brought milk, and the

first-fruits of his flocks: but God was more delighted with the latter oblation,[6] when he was honored with what grew naturally of its own accord, than he was with what was the invention of a covetous man, and gotten by forcing the ground; whence it was that Cain was very angry that Abel was preferred by God before him; and he slew his brother, and hid his dead body, thinking to escape discovery. But God, knowing what had been done, came to Cain, and asked him what was become of his brother, because he had not seen him of many days; whereas he used to observe them conversing together at other times. But Cain was in doubt with himself, and knew not what answer to give to God. At first he said that he was himself at a loss about his brother's disappearing; but when he was provoked by God, who pressed him vehemently, as resolving to know what the matter was, he replied, he was not his brother's guardian or keeper, nor was he an observer of what he did. But, in return, God convicted Cain, as having been the murderer of his brother; and said, "I wonder at thee, that thou knowest not what is become of a man whom thou thyself hast destroyed." God therefore did not inflict the punishment [of death] upon him, on account of his offering sacrifice, and thereby making supplication to him not to be extreme in his wrath to him; but he made him accursed, and threatened his posterity in the seventh generation. He also cast him, together with his wife, out of that land. And when he was afraid that in wandering about he should fall among Wild beasts, and by that means perish, God bid him not to entertain such a melancholy suspicion, and to go over all the earth without fear of what mischief he might suffer from wild beasts; and setting a mark upon him, that he might be known, he commanded him to depart.

2. And when Cain had traveled over many countries, he, with his wife, built a city, named Nod, which is a place so called, and there he settled his abode; where also he had children. However, he did not accept of his punishment in order to amendment, but to increase

---

6. St. John's account of the reason why God accepted the sacrifice of Abel, and rejected that of Cain; as also why Cain slew Abel, on account of that his acceptance with God, is much better than this of Josephus: I mean, because "Cain was of the evil one, and slew his brother. And wherefore slew he him? Because his own works were evil, and his brother's righteous," 1 John 3:12. Josephus's reason seems to be no better than a pharisaical notion or tradition.

his wickedness; for he only aimed to procure every thing that was for his own bodily pleasure, though it obliged him to be injurious to his neighbors. He augmented his household substance with much wealth, by rapine and violence; he excited his acquaintance to procure pleasures and spoils by robbery, and became a great leader of men into wicked courses. He also introduced a change in that way of simplicity wherein men lived before; and was the author of measures and weights. And whereas they lived innocently and generously while they knew nothing of such arts, he changed the world into cunning craftiness. He first of all set boundaries about lands: he built a city, and fortified it with walls, and he compelled his family to come together to it; and called that city Enoch, after the name of his eldest son Enoch. Now Jared was the son of Enoch; whose son was Malaliel; whose son was Mathusela; whose son was Lamech; who had seventy-seven children by two wives, Silla and Ada. Of those children by Ada, one was Jabal: he erected tents, and loved the life of a shepherd. But Jubal, who was born of the same mother with him, exercised himself in music;[7] and invented the psaltery and the harp. But Tubal, one of his children by the other wife, exceeded all men in strength, and was very expert and famous in martial performances. He procured what tended to the pleasures of the body by that method; and first of all invented the art of making brass. Lamech was also the father of a daughter, whose name was Naamah. And because he was so skillful in matters of divine revelation, that he knew he was to be punished for Cain's murder of his brother, he made that known to his wives. Nay, even while Adam was alive, it came to pass that the posterity of Cain became exceeding wicked, every one successively dying, one after another, more wicked than the former. They were intolerable in war, and vehement in robberies; and if any one were slow to murder people, yet was he bold in his profligate behavior, in acting unjustly, and doing injuries for gain.

3. Now Adam, who was the first man, and made out of the earth, (for our discourse must now be about him,) after Abel was slain, and Cain fled away, on account of his murder, was solicitous for posterity,

---

7. From this Jubal, not improbably, came Jobel, the trumpet of jobel or jubilee; that large and loud musical instrument, used in proclaiming the liberty at the year of jubilee.

and had a vehement desire of children, he being two hundred and thirty years old; after which time he lived other seven hundred, and then died. He had indeed many other children,[8] but Seth in particular. As for the rest, it would be tedious to name them; I will therefore only endeavor to give an account of those that proceeded from Seth. Now this Seth, when he was brought up, and came to those years in which he could discern what was good, became a virtuous man; and as he was himself of an excellent character, so did he leave children behind him who imitated his virtues.[9] All these proved to be of good dispositions. They also inhabited the same country without dissensions, and in a happy condition, without any misfortunes falling upon them, till they died. They also were the inventors of that peculiar sort of wisdom which is concerned with the heavenly bodies, and their order. And that their inventions might not be lost before they were sufficiently known, upon Adam's prediction that the world was to be destroyed at one time by the force of fire, and at another time by the violence and quantity of water, they made two pillars,[10] the one of brick, the other of stone: they inscribed their discoveries on them both, that in case the pillar of brick should be destroyed by the flood, the pillar of stone might remain, and exhibit those discoveries to mankind; and also inform them that there was another pillar of brick erected by them. Now this remains in the land of Siriad to this day.

---

8. The number of Adam's children, as says the old tradition was thirty-three sons, and twenty-three daughters.

9. What is here said of Seth and his posterity, that they were very good and virtuous, and at the same time very happy, without any considerable misfortunes, for seven generations, [see ch. 2. sect. 1, before; and ch. 3. sect. 1, hereafter,] is exactly agreeable to the state of the world and the conduct of Providence in all the first ages.

10. Of Josephus's mistake here, when he took Seth the son of Adam, for Seth or Sesostris, king of Egypt, the erector of this pillar in the land of Siriad, see Essay on the Old Testament, Appendix, p. 159, 160. Although the main of this relation might be true, and Adam might foretell a conflagration and a deluge, which all antiquity witnesses to be an ancient tradition; nay, Seth's posterity might engrave their inventions in astronomy on two such pillars; yet it is no way credible that they could survive the deluge, which has buried all such pillars and edifices far under ground in the sediment of its waters, especially since the like pillars of the Egyptian Seth or Sesostris were extant after the flood, in the land of Siriad, and perhaps in the days of Josephus also, as is shown in the place here referred to.

3   *Concerning the Flood; and After What Manner Noah Was Saved in an Ark, with His Kindred, and Afterwards Dwelt in the Plain of Shinar,*

1. NOW this posterity of Seth continued to esteem God as the Lord of the universe, and to have an entire regard to virtue, for seven generations; but in process of time they were perverted, and forsook the practices of their forefathers; and did neither pay those honors to God which were appointed them, nor had they any concern to do justice towards men. But for what degree of zeal they had formerly shown for virtue, they now showed by their actions a double degree of wickedness, whereby they made God to be their enemy. For many angels[11] of God accompanied with women, and begat sons that proved unjust, and despisers of all that was good, on account of the confidence they had in their own strength; for the tradition is, that these men did what resembled the acts of those whom the Grecians call giants. But Noah was very uneasy at what they did; and being displeased at their conduct, persuaded them to change their dispositions and their acts for the better: but seeing they did not yield to him, but were slaves to their wicked pleasures, he was afraid they would kill him, together with his wife and children, and those they had married; so he departed out of that land.

2. Now God loved this man for his righteousness: yet he not only condemned those other men for their wickedness, but determined to destroy the whole race of mankind, and to make another race that should be pure from wickedness; and cutting short their lives, and making their years not so many as they formerly lived, but one hundred and twenty only,[12] he turned the dry land into sea; and thus

---

11. This notion, that the fallen angels were, in some sense, the fathers of the old giants, was the constant opinion of antiquity.

12. Josephus here supposes that the life of these giants, for of them only do I understand him, was now reduced to 120 years; which is confirmed by the fragment of Enoch, sect. 10, in Authent. Rec. Part I. p. 268. For as to the rest of mankind, Josephus himself confesses their lives were much longer than 120 years, for many generations after the flood, as we shall see presently; and he says they were gradually shortened till the days of Moses, and then fixed [for some time] at 120, ch. 6. sect. 5. Nor indeed need we suppose that either Enoch or Josephus meant to interpret these 120 years for the life of men before the flood, to be different from the 120 years of

were all these men destroyed: but Noah alone was saved; for God suggested to him the following contrivance and way of escape—That he should make an ark of four stories high, three hundred cubits[13] long, fifty cubits broad, and thirty cubits high. Accordingly he entered into that ark, and his wife, and sons, and their wives, and put into it not only other provisions, to support their wants there, but also sent in with the rest all sorts of living creatures, the male and his female, for the preservation of their kinds; and others of them by sevens. Now this ark had firm walls, and a roof, and was braced with cross beams, so that it could not be any way drowned or overborne by the violence of the water. And thus was Noah, with his family, preserved. Now he was the tenth from Adam, as being the son of Lamech, whose father was Mathusela; he was the son of Enoch, the son of Jared; and Jared was the son of Malaleel, who, with many of his sisters, were the children of Cainan, the son of Enos. Now Enos was the son of Seth, the son of Adam.

3. This calamity happened in the six hundredth year of Noah's government, [age,] in the second month,[14] called by the Macedonians *Dius,* but by the Hebrews *Marchesuan:* for so did they order their year in Egypt. But Moses appointed that · *Nisan,* which is the same with Xanthicus, should be the first month for their festivals, because he brought them out of Egypt in that month: so that this month began the year as to all the solemnities they observed to the honor of God, although he preserved the original order of the months as to selling and buying, and other ordinary affairs. Now he says that this flood began on the twenty-seventh [seventeenth] day of the forementioned month; and this was two thousand six hundred and fifty-six [one thousand six hundred and fifty-six] years from Adam, the first man; and the time is written down in our sacred books, those who then

---

God's patience [perhaps while the ark was preparing] till the deluge; which I take to be the meaning of God when he threatened this wicked world, that if they so long continued impenitent, their days should be no more than 120 years.

13. A cubit is about 21 English inches.

14. Josephus here truly determines, that the year that the Flood began, our Hebrew and Samaritan, and perhaps Josephus's own copy, more rightly placed it on the 17th day, instead of the 27th, as here; for Josephus agrees with them, as to the distance of 150 days to the 17th day of the 7th month, as Genesis 7. ult. with 8:3.

lived having noted down,[15] with great accuracy, both the births and deaths of illustrious men.

4. For indeed Seth was born when Adam was in his two hundred and thirtieth year, who lived nine hundred and thirty years. Seth begat Enos in his two hundred and fifth year; who, when he had lived nine hundred and twelve years, delivered the government to Cainan his son, whom he had in his hundred and ninetieth year. He lived nine hundred and five years. Cainan, when he had lived nine hundred and ten years, had his son Malaleel, who was born in his hundred and seventieth year. This Malaleel, having lived eight hundred and ninety-five years, died, leaving his son Jared, whom he begat when he was in his hundred and sixty-fifth year. He lived nine hundred and sixty-two years; and then his son Enoch succeeded him, who was born when his father was one hundred and sixty-two years old. Now he, when he had lived three hundred and sixty-five years, departed and went to God; whence it is that they have not written down his death. Now Mathusela, the son of Enoch, who was born to him when he was one hundred and sixty-five years old, had Lamech for his son when he was one hundred and eighty-seven years of age; to whom he delivered the government, when he had retained it nine hundred and sixty-nine years. Now Lamech, when he had governed seven hundred and seventy-seven years, appointed Noah, his son, to be ruler of the people, who was born to Lamech when he was one hundred and eighty-two years old, and retained the government nine hundred and fifty years. These years collected together make up the sum before set down. But let no one inquire into the deaths of these men; for they extended their lives along together with their children and grandchildren; but let him have regard to their births only.

5. When God gave the signal, and it began to rain, the water poured down forty entire days, till it became fifteen cubits higher than the earth; which was the reason why there was no greater number

---

15. Josephus here takes notice, that these ancient genealogies were first set down by those that then lived, and from them were transmitted down to posterity; which I suppose to be the true account of that matter. For there is no reason to imagine that men were not taught to read and write soon after they were taught to speak; and perhaps all by the Messiah himself, who, under the Father, was the Creator or Governor of mankind, and who frequently in those early days appeared to them.

preserved, since they had no place to fly to. When the rain ceased, the water did but just begin to abate after one hundred and fifty days, (that is, on the seventeenth day of the seventh month,) it then ceasing to subside for a little while. After this, the ark rested on the top of a certain mountain in Armenia; which, when Noah understood, he opened it; and seeing a small piece of land about it, he continued quiet, and conceived some cheerful hopes of deliverance. But a few days afterward, when the water was decreased to a greater degree, he sent out a raven, as desirous to learn whether any other part of the earth were left dry by the water, and whether he might go out of the ark with safety; but the raven, finding all the land still overflowed, returned to Noah again. And after seven days he sent out a dove, to know the state of the ground; which came back to him covered with mud, and bringing an olive branch: hereby Noah learned that the earth was become clear of the flood. So after he had staid seven more days, he sent the living creatures out of the ark; and both he and his family went out, when he also sacrificed to God, and feasted with his companions. However, the Armenians call this place[16] *The Place of Descent*; for the ark being saved in that place, its remains are shown there by the inhabitants to this day.

6. Now all the writers of barbarian histories make mention of this flood, and of this ark; among whom is Berosus the Chaldean. For when he is describing the circumstances of the flood, he goes on thus: "It is said there is still some part of this ship in Armenia, at the mountain of the Cordyaeans; and that some people carry off pieces of the bitumen, which they take away, and use chiefly as amulets for the averting of mischiefs." Hieronymus the Egyptian also, who wrote the Phoenician

---

16. "Place of Descent" is the proper rendering of the Armenian name of this very city. It is called in Ptolemy Naxuana, and by Moses Chorenensis, the Armenian historian, Idsheuan; but at the place itself Nachidsheuan, which signifies The first place of descent, and is a lasting monument of the preservation of Noah in the ark, upon the top of that mountain, at whose foot it was built, as the first city or town after the flood. See Antiq. B. XX. ch. 2. sect. 3; and Moses Chorenensis, who also says elsewhere, that another town was related by tradition to have been called Seron, or, The Place of Dispersion, on account of the dispersion of Xisuthrus's or Noah's sons, from thence first made. Whether any remains of this ark be still preserved, as the people of the country suppose, I cannot certainly tell. Mons. Tournefort had, not very long since, a mind to see the place himself, but met with too great dangers and difficulties to venture through them.

Antiquities, and Mnaseas, and a great many more, make mention of the same. Nay, Nicolaus of Damascus, in his ninety-sixth book, hath a particular relation about them; where he speaks thus: "There is a great mountain in Armenia, over Minyas, called Baris, upon which it is reported that many who fled at the time of the Deluge were saved; and that one who was carried in an ark came on shore upon the top of it; and that the remains of the timber were a great while preserved. This might be the man about whom Moses the legislator of the Jews wrote."

7. But as for Noah, he was afraid, since God had determined to destroy mankind, lest he should drown the earth every year; so he offered burnt-offerings, and besought God that nature might hereafter go on in its former orderly course, and that he would not bring on so great a judgment any more, by which the whole race of creatures might be in danger of destruction: but that, having now punished the wicked, he would of his goodness spare the remainder, and such as he had hitherto judged fit to be delivered from so severe a calamity; for that otherwise these last must be more miserable than the first, and that they must be condemned to a worse condition than the others, unless they be suffered to escape entirely; that is, if they be reserved for another deluge; while they must be afflicted with the terror and sight of the first deluge, and must also be destroyed by a second. He also entreated God to accept of his sacrifice, and to grant that the earth might never again undergo the like effects of 'his wrath; that men might be permitted to go on cheerfully in cultivating the same; to build cities, and live happily in them; and that they might not be deprived of any of those good things which they enjoyed before the Flood; but might attain to the like length of days, and old age, which the ancient people had arrived at before.

8. When Noah had made these supplications, God, who loved the man for his righteousness, granted entire success to his prayers, and said, that it was not he who brought the destruction on a polluted world, but that they underwent that vengeance on account of their own wickedness; and that he had not brought men into the world if he had himself determined to destroy them, it being an instance of greater wisdom not to have granted them life at all, than, after it was granted, to procure their destruction; "But the injuries," said he, "they offered to my holiness and virtue, forced me to bring this

punishment upon them. But I will leave off for the time to come to require such punishments, the effects of so great wrath, for their future wicked actions, and especially on account of thy prayers. But if I shall at any time send tempests of rain, in an extraordinary manner, be not affrighted at the largeness of the showers; for the water shall no more overspread the earth. However, I require you to abstain from shedding the blood of men, and to keep yourselves pure from murder; and to punish those that commit any such thing. I permit you to make use of all the other living creatures at your pleasure, and as your appetites lead you; for I have made you lords of them all, both of those that walk on the land, and those that swim in the waters, and of those that fly in the regions of the air on high, excepting their blood, for therein is the life. But I will give you a sign that I have left off my anger by my bow [whereby is meant the rainbow, for they determined that the rainbow was the bow of God]. And when God had said and promised thus, he went away.

9. Now when Noah had lived three hundred and fifty years after the Flood, and that all that time happily, he died, having lived the number of nine hundred and fifty years. But let no one, upon comparing the lives of the ancients with our lives, and with the few years which we now live, think that what we have said of them is false; or make the shortness of our lives at present an argument, that neither did they attain to so long a duration of life, for those ancients were beloved of God, and [lately] made by God himself; and because their food was then fitter for the prolongation of life, might well live so great a number of years: and besides, God afforded them a longer time of life on account of their virtue, and the good use they made of it in astronomical and geometrical discoveries, which would not have afforded the time of foretelling [the periods of the stars] unless they had lived six hundred years; for the great year is completed in that interval. Now I have for witnesses to what I have said, all those that have written Antiquities, both among the Greeks and barbarians; for even Manetho, who wrote the Egyptian History, and Berosus, who collected the Chaldean Monuments, and Mochus, and Hestieus, and, besides these, Hieronymus the Egyptian, and those who composed the Phoenician History, agree to what I here say: Hesiod also, and Hecatseus, Hellanicus, and Acusilaus; and, besides these, Ephorus and

Nicolaus relate that the ancients lived a thousand years. But as to these matters, let every one look upon them as he thinks fit.

4 Concerning the Tower of Babylon, and the Confusion of Tongues

1. Now the sons of Noah were three,—Shem, Japhet, and Ham, born one hundred years before the Deluge. These first of all descended from the mountains into the plains, and fixed their habitation there; and persuaded others who were greatly afraid of the lower grounds on account of the flood, and so were very loath to come down from the higher places, to venture to follow their examples. Now the plain in which they first dwelt was called Shinar. God also commanded them to send colonies abroad, for the thorough peopling of the earth, that they might not raise seditions among themselves, but might cultivate a great part of the earth, and enjoy its fruits after a plentiful manner. But they were so ill instructed that they did not obey God; for which reason they fell into calamities, and were made sensible, by experience, of what sin they had been guilty: for when they flourished with a numerous youth, God admonished them again to send out colonies; but they, imagining the prosperity they enjoyed was not derived from the favor of God, but supposing that their own power was the proper cause of the plentiful condition they were in, did not obey him. Nay, they added to this their disobedience to the Divine will, the suspicion that they were therefore ordered to send out separate colonies, that, being divided asunder, they might the more easily be Oppressed.

2. Now it was Nimrod who excited them to such an affront and contempt of God. He was the grandson of Ham, the son of Noah, a bold man, and of great strength of hand. He persuaded them not to ascribe it to God, as if it was through his means they were happy, but to believe that it was their own courage which procured that happiness. He also gradually changed the government into tyranny, seeing no other way of turning men from the fear of God, but to bring them into a constant dependence on his power. He also said he would be revenged on God, if he should have a mind to drown the world again; for that he would build a tower too high for the waters to be able to reach! and that he would avenge himself on God for destroying their forefathers !

3. Now the multitude were very ready to follow the determination of Nimrod, and to esteem it a piece of cowardice to submit to God; and they built a tower, neither sparing any pains, nor being in any degree negligent about the work: and, by reason of the multitude of hands employed in it, it grew very high, sooner than any one could expect; but the thickness of it was so great, and it was so strongly built, that thereby its great height seemed, upon the view, to be less than it really was. It was built of burnt brick, cemented together with mortar, made of bitumen, that it might not be liable to admit water. When God saw that they acted so madly, he did not resolve to destroy them utterly, since they were not grown wiser by the destruction of the former sinners; but he caused a tumult among them, by producing in them divers languages, and causing that, through the multitude of those languages, they should not be able to understand one another. The place wherein they built the tower is now called *Babylon*, because of the confusion of that language which they readily understood before; for the Hebrews mean by the word *Babel*, confusion. The Sibyl also makes mention of this tower, and of the confusion of the language, when she says thus: "When all men were of one language, some of them built a high tower, as if they would thereby ascend up to heaven, but the gods sent storms of wind and overthrew the tower, and gave every one his peculiar language; and for this reason it was that the city was called *Babylon*." But as to the plan of Shinar, in the country of Babylonia, Hestiaeus mentions it, when he says thus: "Such of the priests as were saved, took the sacred vessels of Jupiter Enyalius, and came to Shinar of Babylonia."

5   *After What Manner the Posterity of Noah Sent Out Colonies, and Inhabited the Whole Earth*

1. AFTER this they were dispersed abroad, on account of their languages, and went out by colonies every where; and each colony took possession of that land which they light upon, and unto which God led them; so that the whole continent was filled with them, both the inland and the maritime countries. There were some also who passed over the sea in ships, and inhabited the islands: and some of those nations do still retain the denominations which were given them by their first

founders; but some have lost them also, and some have only admitted certain changes in them, that they might be the more intelligible to the inhabitants. And they were the Greeks who became the authors of such mutations. For when in after-ages they grew potent, they claimed to themselves the glory of antiquity; giving names to the nations that sounded well (in Greek) that they might be better understood among themselves; and setting agreeable forms of government over them, as if they were a people derived from themselves.

6 *How Every Nation Was Denominated from Their First Inhabitants*

1. Now they were the grandchildren of Noah, in honor of whom names were imposed on the nations by those that first seized upon them. Japhet, the son of Noah, had seven sons: they inhabited so, that, beginning at the mountains Taurus and Amanus, they proceeded along Asia, as far as the river Tansis, and along Europe to Cadiz; and settling themselves on the lands which they light upon, which none had inhabited before, they called the nations by their own names. For Gomer founded those whom the Greeks now call Galatians, [Galls,] but were then called Gomerites. Magog founded those that from him were named Magogites, but who are by the Greeks called Scythians. Now as to Javan and Madai, the sons of Japhet; from Madai came the Madeans, who are called Medes, by the Greeks; but from Javan, Ionia, and all the Grecians, are derived. Thobel founded the Thobelites, who are now called Iberes; and the Mosocheni were founded by Mosoch; now they are Cappadocians. There is also a mark of their ancient denomination still to be shown; for there is even now among them a city called Mazaca, which may inform those that are able to understand, that so was the entire nation once called. Thiras also called those whom he ruled over Thirasians; but the Greeks changed the name into Thracians. And so many were the countries that had the children of Japhet for their inhabitants. Of the three sons of Gomer, Aschanax founded the Aschanaxians, who are now called by the Greeks Rheginians. So did Riphath found the Ripheans, now called Paphlagonians; and Thrugramma the Thrugrammeans, who, as the Greeks resolved, were named Phrygians. Of the three sons of Javan also, the son of Japhet, Elisa gave name to the Eliseans, who were his subjects; they are now the Aeolians. Tharsus to the Tharsians, for so

was Cilicia of old called; the sign of which is this, that the noblest city they have, and a metropolis also, is Tarsus, the *tau* being by change put for the *theta*. Cethimus possessed the island Cethima: it is now called Cyprus; and from that it is that all islands, and the greatest part of the sea-coasts, are named Cethim by the Hebrews: and one city there is in Cyprus that has been able to preserve its denomination; it has been called Citius by those who use the language of the Greeks, and has not, by the use of that dialect, escaped the name of Cethim. And so many nations have the children and grandchildren of Japhet possessed. Now when I have premised somewhat, which perhaps the Greeks do not know, I will return and explain what I have omitted; for such names are pronounced here after the manner of the Greeks, to please my readers; for our own country language does not so pronounce them: but the names in all cases are of one and the same ending; for the name we here pronounce Noeas, is there Noah, and in every case retains the same termination.

2. The children of Ham possessed the land from Syria and Amanus, and the mountains of Libanus; seizing upon all that was on its sea-coasts, and as far as the ocean, and keeping it as their own. Some indeed of its names are utterly vanished away; others of them being changed, and another sound given them, are hardly to be discovered; yet a few there are which have kept their denominations entire. For of the four sons of Ham, time has not at all hurt the name of Chus; for the Ethiopians, over whom he reigned, are even at this day, both by themselves and by all men in Asia, called Chusites. The memory also of the Mesraites is preserved in their name; for all we who inhabit this country [of Judea] called Egypt Mestre, and the Egyptians Mestreans. Phut also was the founder of Libya, and called the inhabitants Phutites, from himself: there is also a river in the country of Moors which bears that name; whence it is that we may see the greatest part of the Grecian historiographers mention that river and the adjoining country by the apellation of Phut: but the name it has now has been by change given it from one of the sons of Mesraim, who was called Lybyos. We will inform you presently what has been the occasion why it has been called Africa also. Canaan, the fourth son of Ham, inhabited the country now called Judea, and called it from his own name Canaan. The children of these [four] were these: Sabas, who founded the Sabeans; Evilas, who founded the Evileans, who are

called Getuli; Sabathes founded the Sabathens, they are now called by the Greeks Astaborans; Sabactas settled the Sabactens; and Ragmus the Ragmeans; and he had two sons, the one of whom, Judadas, settled the Judadeans, a nation of the western Ethiopians, and left them his name; as did Sabas to the Sabeans: but Nimrod, the son of Chus, staid and tyrannized at Babylon, as we have already informed you. Now all the children of Mesraim, being eight in number, possessed the country from Gaza to Egypt, though it retained the name of one only, the Philistim; for the Greeks call part of that country Palestine. As for the rest, Ludieim, and Enemim, and Labim, who alone inhabited in Libya, and called the country from himself, Nedim, and Phethrosim, and Chesloim, and Cephthorim, we know nothing of them besides their names; for the Ethiopic war[17] which we shall describe hereafter, was the cause that those cities were overthrown. The sons of Canaan were these: Sidonius, who also built a city of the same name; it is called by the Greeks Sidon

Amathus inhabited in Amathine, which is even now called Amathe by the inhabitants, although the Macedonians named it Epiphania, from one of his posterity: Arudeus possessed the island Aradus: Arucas possessed Arce, which is in Libanus. But for the seven others, [Eueus,] Chetteus, Jebuseus, Amorreus, Gergesus, Eudeus, Sineus, Samareus, we have nothing in the sacred books but their names, for the Hebrews overthrew their cities; and their calamities came upon them on the occasion following.

3. Noah, when, after the deluge, the earth was resettled in its former condition, set about its cultivation; and when he had planted it with vines, and when the fruit was ripe, and he had gathered the grapes in their season, and the wine was ready for use, he offered sacrifice, and feasted, and, being drunk, he fell asleep, and lay naked in an unseemly manner. When his youngest son saw this, he came laughing, and showed him to his brethren; but they covered their father's nakedness.

---

17. One observation ought not here to be neglected, with regard to that Ethiopic war which Moses, as general of the Egyptians, put an end to, Antiq. B. II. ch. 10., and about which our late writers seem very much unconcerned; viz. that it was a war of that consequence, as to occasion the removal or destruction of six or seven nations of the posterity of Mitzraim, with their cities; which Josephus would not have said, if he had not had ancient records to justify those his assertions, though those records be now all lost.

And when Noah was made sensible of what had been done, he prayed for prosperity to his other sons; but for Ham, he did not curse him, by reason of his nearness in blood, but cursed his prosperity: and when the rest of them escaped that curse, God inflicted it on the children of Canaan. But as to these matters, we shall speak more hereafter.

4. Shem, the third son of Noah, had five sons, who inhabited the land that began at Euphrates, and reached to the Indian Ocean. For Elam left behind him the Elamites, the ancestors of the Persians. Ashur lived at the city Nineve; and named his subjects Assyrians, who became the most fortunate nation, beyond others. Arphaxad named the Arphaxadites, who are now called Chaldeans. Aram had the Aramites, which the Greeks called Syrians; as Laud founded the Laudites, which are now called Lydians. Of the four sons of Aram, Uz founded Trachonitis and Damascus: this country lies between Palestine and Celesyria. Ul founded Armenia; and Gather the Bactrians; and Mesa the Mesaneans; it is now called Charax Spasini. Sala was the son of Arphaxad; and his son was Heber, from whom they originally called the Jews Hebrews.[18] Heber begat Joetan and Phaleg: he was called Phaleg, because he was born at the dispersion of the nations to their several countries; for Phaleg among the Hebrews signifies *division*. Now Joctan, one of the sons of Heber, had these sons, Elmodad, Saleph, Asermoth, Jera, Adoram, Aizel, Decla, Ebal, Abimael, Sabeus, Ophir, Euilat, and Jobab. These inhabited from Cophen, an Indian river, and in part of Asia adjoining to it. And this shall suffice concerning the sons of Shem.

5. I will now treat of the Hebrews. The son of Phaleg, whose father Was Heber, was Ragau; whose son was Serug, to whom was born Nahor; his son was Terah, who was the father of Abraham, who accordingly was the tenth from Noah, and was born in the two

---

18. That the Jews were called Hebrews from this their progenitor Heber, our author Josephus here rightly affirms; and not from Abram the Hebrew, or passenger over Euphrates, as many of the moderns suppose. Shem is also called the father of all the children of Heber, or of all the Hebrews, in a history long before Abram passed over Euphrates, Genesis 10:21, though it must be confessed that, Genesis 14:13, where the original says they told Abram the Hebrew, the Septuagint renders it "the passenger": but this is spoken only of Abram himself, who had then lately passed over Euphrates, and is another signification of the Hebrew word, taken as an appellative, and not as a proper name.

hundred and ninety-second year after the deluge; for Terah begat Abram in his seventieth year. Nahor begat Haran when he was one hundred and twenty years old; Nahor was born to Serug in his hundred and thirty-second year; Ragau had Serug at one hundred and thirty; at the same age also Phaleg had Ragau; Heber begat Phaleg in his hundred and thirty-fourth year; he himself being begotten by Sala when he was a hundred and thirty years old, whom Arphaxad had for his son at the hundred and thirty-fifth year of his age. Arphaxad was the son of Shem, and born twelve years after the deluge. Now Abram had two brethren, Nahor and Haran: of these Haran left a son, Lot; as also Sarai and Milcha his daughters; and died among the Chaldeans, in a city of the Chaldeans, called Ur; and his monument is shown to this day. These married their nieces. Nabor married Milcha, and Abram married Sarai. Now Terah hating Chaldea, on account of his mourning for Ilaran, they all removed to Haran of Mesopotamia, where Terah died, and was buried, when he had lived to be two hundred and five years old; for the life of man was already, by degrees, diminished, and became shorter than before, till the birth of Moses; after whom the term of human life was one hundred and twenty years, God determining it to the length that Moses happened to live. Now Nahor had eight sons by Milcha; Uz and Buz, Kemuel, Chesed, Azau, Pheldas, Jadelph, and Bethuel. These were all the genuine sons of Nahor; for Teba, and Gaam, and Tachas, and Maaca, were born of Reuma his concubine: but Bethuel had a daughter, Rebecca, and a son, Laban.

7   *How Abram Our Forefather Went Out of the Land of the Chaldeans, and Lived in the Land Then Called Canaan but Now Judea*

1. Now Abram, having no son of his own, adopted Lot, his brother Haran's son, and his wife Sarai's brother; and he left the land of Chaldea when he was seventy-five years old, and at the command of God went into Canaan, and therein he dwelt himself, and left it to his posterity. He was a person of great sagacity, both for understanding all things and persuading his hearers, and not mistaken in his opinions; for which reason he began to have higher notions of virtue than

21

others had, and he determined to renew and to change the opinion all men happened then to have concerning God; for he was the first that ventured to publish this notion, That there was but one God, the Creator of the universe; and that, as to other [gods], if they contributed any thing to the happiness of men, that each of them afforded it only according to his appointment, and not by their own power. This his opinion was derived from the irregular phenomena that were visible both at land and sea, as well as those that happen to the sun, and moon, and all the heavenly bodies, thus:—"If [said he] these bodies had power of their own, they would certainly take care of their own regular motions; but since they do not preserve such regularity, they make it plain, that in so far as they co-operate to our advantage, they do it not of their own abilities, but as they are subservient to Him that commands them, to whom alone we ought justly to offer our honor and thanksgiving." For which doctrines, when the Chaldeans, and other people of Mesopotamia, raised a tumult against him, he thought fit to leave that country; and at the command and by the assistance of God, he came and lived in the land of Canaan. And when he was there settled, he built an altar, and performed a sacrifice to God.

2. Berosus mentions our father Abram without naming him, when he says thus: "In the tenth generation after the Flood, there was among the Chaldeans a man righteous and great, and skillful in the celestial science." But Hecatseus does more than barely mention him; for he composed, and left behind him, a book concerning him. And Nicolaus of Damascus, in the fourth book of his History, says thus: "Abram reigned at Damascus, being a foreigner, who came with an army out of the land above Babylon, called the land of the Chaldeans: but, after a long time, he got him up, and removed from that country also, with his people, and went into the land then called the land of Canaan, but now the land of Judea, and this when his posterity were become a multitude; as to which posterity of his, we relate their history in another work. Now the name of Abram is even still famous in the country of Damascus; and there is shown a village named from him, *The Habitation of Abram.*"

8   That When There Was a Famine in Canaan, Abram Went Thence into Egypt; and After He Had Continued There a While He Returned Back Again

1. NOW, after this, when a famine had invaded the land of Canaan, and Abram had discovered that the Egyptians were in a flourishing condition, he was disposed to go down to them, both to partake of the plenty they enjoyed, and to become an auditor of their priests, and to know what they said concerning the gods; designing either to follow them, if they had better notions than he, or to convert them into a better way, if his own notions proved the truest. Now, seeing he was to take Sarai with him, and was afraid of the madness of the Egyptians with regard to women, lest the king should kill him on occasion of his wife's great beauty, he contrived this device—he pretended to be her brother, and directed her in a dissembling way to pretend the same, for he said it would be for their benefit. Now, as soon as he came into Egypt, it happened to Abram as he supposed it would; for the fame of his wife's beauty was greatly talked of; for which reason Pharaoh, the king of Egypt, would not be satisfied with what was reported of her, but would needs see her himself, and was preparing to enjoy her; but God put a stop to his unjust inclinations, by sending upon him a distemper, and a sedition against his government. And when he inquired of the priests how he might be freed from these calamities, they told him that this his miserable condition was derived from the wrath of God, upon account of his inclinations to abuse the stranger's wife. He then, out of fear, asked Sarai who she was, and who it was that she brought along with her. And when he had found out the truth, he excused himself to Abram, that supposing the woman to be his sister, and not his wife, he set his affections on her, as desiring an affinity with him by marrying her, but not as incited by lust to abuse her. He also made him a large present in money, and gave him leave to enter into conversation with the most learned among the Egyptians; from which conversation his virtue and his reputation became more conspicuous than they had been before.

2. For whereas the Egyptians were formerly addicted to different customs, and despised one another's sacred and accustomed rites, and were very angry one with another on that account, Abram conferred with each of them, and, confuting the reasonings they made use of,

every one for their own practices, demonstrated that such reasonings were vain and void of truth: whereupon he was admired by them in those conferences as a very wise man, and one of great sagacity, when he discoursed on any subject he undertook; and this not only in understanding it, but in persuading other men also to assent to him. He communicated to them arithmetic, and delivered to them the science of astronomy; for before Abram came into Egypt they were unacquainted with those parts of learning; for that science came from the Chaldeans into Egypt, and from thence to the Greeks also.

3. As soon as Abram was come back into Canaan, he parted the land between him and Lot, upon account of the tumultuous behavior of their shepherds, concerning the pastures wherein they should feed their flocks. However, he gave Lot his option, or leave, to choose which lands he would take; and he took himself what the other left, which were the lower grounds at the foot of the mountains; and he himself dwelt in Hebron, which is a city seven years more ancient than Tunis of Egypt. But Lot possessed the land of the plain, and the river Jordan, not far from the city of Sodom, which was then a fine city, but is now destroyed, by the will and wrath of God, the cause of which I shall show in its proper place hereafter.

9   The Destruction of the Sodomites by the Assyrian Wall

AT this time, when the Assyrians had the dominion over Asia, the people of Sodom were in a flourishing condition, both as to riches and the number of their youth. There were five kings that managed the affairs of this county: Ballas, Barsas, Senabar, and Sumobor, with the king of Bela; and each king led on his own troops: and the Assyrians made war upon them; and, dividing their army into four parts, fought against them. Now every part of the army had its own commander; and when the battle was joined, the Assyrians were conquerors, and imposed a tribute on the kings of the Sodomites, who submitted to this slavery twelve years; and so long they continued to pay their tribute: but on the thirteenth year they rebelled, and then the army of the Assyrians came upon them, under their commanders Amraphel, Arioch, Chodorlaomer, and Tidal. These kings had laid waste all Syria, and overthrown the offspring of the giants. And when they were come over against Sodom, they pitched their camp at the vale called the

Slime Pits, for at that time there were pits in that place; but now, upon the destruction of the city of Sodom, that vale became the Lake Asphaltites, as it is called. However, concerning this lake we shall speak more presently. Now when the Sodomites joined battle with the Assyrians, and the fight was very obstinate, many of them were killed, and the rest were carried captive; among which captives was Lot, who had come to assist the Sodomites.

10   How Abram Fought with the Assyrians, and Overcame Them, and Saved the Sodomite Prisoners, and Took from the Assyrians the Prey They Had Gotten

1. WHEN, Abram heard of their calamity, he was at once afraid for Lot his kinsman, and pitied the Sodomites, his friends and neighbors; and thinking it proper to afford them assistance, he did not delay it, but marched hastily, and the fifth night fell upon the Assyrians, near Dan, for that is the name of the other spring of Jordan; and before they could arm themselves, he slew some as they were in their beds, before they could suspect any harm; and others, who were not yet gone to sleep, but were so drunk they could not fight, ran away. Abram pursued after them, till, on the second day, he drove them in a body unto Hoba, a place belonging to Damascus; and thereby demonstrated that victory does not depend on multitude and the number of hands, but the alacrity and courage of soldiers overcome the most numerous bodies of men, while he got the victory over so great an army with no more than three hundred and eighteen of his servants, and three of his friends: but all those that fled returned home ingloriously.

2. So Abram, when he had saved the captive Sodomites, who had been taken by the Assyrians, and Lot also, his kinsman, returned home in peace. Now the king of Sodom met him at a certain place, which they called The King's Dale, where Melchisedec, king of the city Salem, received him. That name signifies, *the righteous king:* and such he was, without dispute, insomuch that, on this account, he was made the priest of God: however, they afterward called Salem *Jerusalem.* Now this Melchisedec supplied Abram's army in an hospitable manner, and gave them provisions in abundance; and as they were feasting, he began to praise him, and to bless God for subduing his enemies under

him. And when Abram gave him the tenth part of his prey, he accepted of the gift: but the king of Sodom desired Abram to take the prey, but entreated that he might have those men restored to him whom Abram had saved from the Assyrians, because they belonged to him. But Abram would not do so; nor would make any other advantage of that prey than what his servants had eaten; but still insisted that he should afford a part to his friends that had assisted him in the battle. The first of them was called Eschol, and then Enner, and Mambre.

3. And God commended his virtue, and said, Thou shalt not however lose the rewards thou hast deserved to receive by such thy glorious actions. He answered, And what advantage will it be to me to have such rewards, when I have none to enjoy them after me?—for he was hitherto childless. And God promised that he should have a son, and that his posterity should be very numerous; insomuch that their number should be like the stars. When he heard that, he offered a sacrifice to God, as he commanded him. The manner of the sacrifice was this—He took an heifer of three years old, and a she-goat of three years old, and a ram in like manner of three years old, and a turtle-dove, and a pigeon[19] and as he was enjoined, he divided the three former, but the birds he did not divide. After which, before he built his altar, where the birds of prey flew about, as desirous of blood, a Divine voice came to him, declaring that their neighbors would be grievous to his posterity, when they should be in Egypt, for four hundred years;[20] during which time they should be afflicted, but afterwards should overcome their enemies, should conquer the Canaanites in war, and possess themselves of their land, and of their cities.

4. Now Abram dwelt near the oak called Ogyges,—the place belongs to Canaan, not far from the city of Hebron. But being uneasy at his wife's barrenness, he entreated God to grant that he might have male issue; and God required of him to be of good courage, and said that he would add to all the rest of the benefits that he had bestowed

---

19. It is worth noting here, that God required no other sacrifices under the law of Moses, than what were taken from these five kinds of animals which he here required of Abram. Nor did the Jews feed upon any other domestic animals than the three here named, as Reland observes on Antiq. B. IV. ch. 4. sect. 4.

20. As to this affliction of Abram's posterity for 400 years, see Antiq. B. II. ch. 9. sect. 1.

upon him, ever since he led him out of Mesopotamia, the gift of children. Accordingly Sarai, at God's command, brought to his bed one of her handmaidens, a woman of Egyptian descent, in order to obtain children by her; and when this handmaid was with child, she triumphed, and ventured to affront Sarai, as if the dominion were to come to a son to be born of her. But when Abram resigned her into the hand of Sarai, to punish her, she contrived to fly away, as not able to bear the instances of Sarai's severity to her; and she entreated God to have compassion on her. Now a Divine Angel met her, as she was going forward in the wilderness, and bid her return to her master and mistress, for if she would submit to that wise advice, she would live better hereafter; for that the reason of her being in such a miserable case was this, that she had been ungrateful and arrogant towards her mistress. He also told her, that if she disobeyed God, and went on still in her way, she should perish; but if she would return back, she should become the mother of a son who should reign over that country. These admonitions she obeyed, and returned to her master and mistress, and obtained forgiveness. A little while afterwards, she bare Ismael; which may be interpreted *Heard of God,* because God had heard his mother's prayer.

5. The forementioned son was born to Abram when he was eighty-six years old: but when he was ninety-nine, God appeared to him, and promised him that he Should have a son by Sarai, and commanded that his name should be Isaac; and showed him, that from this son should spring great nations and kings, and that they should obtain all the land of Canaan by war, from Sidon to Egypt. But he charged him, in order to keep his posterity unmixed with others, that they should be circumcised in the flesh of their foreskin, and that this should be done on the eighth day after they were born: the reason of which circumcision I will explain in another place. And Abram inquiring also concerning Ismael, whether he should live or not, God signified to him that he should live to be very old, and should be the father of great nations. Abram therefore gave thanks to God for these blessings; and then he, and all his family, and his son Ismael, were circumcised immediately; the son being that day thirteen years of age, and he ninety-nine.

11 *How God Overthrew the Nation of the Sodomites, Out of His Wrath Against Them for Their Sins*

1. ABOUT this time the Sodomites grew proud, on account of their riches and great wealth; they became unjust towards men, and impious towards God, insomuch that they did not call to mind the advantages they received from him: they hated strangers, and abused themselves with Sodomitical practices. God was therefore much displeased at them, and determined to punish them for their pride, and to overthrow their city, and to lay waste their country, until there should neither plant nor fruit grow out of it.

2. When God had thus resolved concerning the Sodomites, Abraham, as he sat by the oak of Mambre, at the door of his tent, saw three angels; and thinking them to be strangers, he rose up, and saluted them, and desired they would accept of an entertainment, and abide with him; to which, when they agreed, he ordered cakes of meal to be made presently; and when he had slain a calf, he roasted it, and brought it to them, as they sat under the oak. Now they made a show of eating; and besides, they asked him about his wife Sarah, where she was; and when he said she was within, they said they would come again hereafter, and find her become a mother. Upon which the woman laughed, and said that it was impossible she should bear children, since she was ninety years of age, and her husband was a hundred. Then they concealed themselves no longer, but declared that they were angels of God; and that one of them was sent to inform them about the child, and two of the overthrow of Sodom.

3. When Abraham heard this, he was grieved for the Sodomites; and he rose up, and besought God for them, and entreated him that he would not destroy the righteous with the wicked. And when God had replied that there was no good man among the Sodomites; for if there were but ten such man among them, he would not punish any of them for their sins, Abraham held his peace. And the angels came to the city of the Sodomites, and Lot entreated them to accept of a lodging with him; for he was a very generous and hospitable man, and one that had learned to imitate the goodness of Abraham. Now when the Sodomites saw the young men to be of beautiful countenances, and this to an extraordinary degree, and that they took up their lodgings with Lot, they resolved themselves to enjoy these beautiful boys by

force and violence; and when Lot exhorted them to sobriety, and not to offer any thing immodest to the strangers, but to have regard to their lodging in his house; and promised that if their inclinations could not be governed, he would expose his daughters to their lust, instead of these strangers; neither thus were they made ashamed.

4. But God was much displeased at their impudent behavior, so that he both smote those men with blindness, and condemned the Sodomites to universal destruction. But Lot, upon God's informing him of the future destruction of the Sodomites, went away, taking with him his wife and daughters, who were two, and still virgins; for those that were betrothed[21] to them were above the thoughts of going, and deemed that Lot's words were trifling. God then cast a thunderbolt upon the city, and set it on fire, with its inhabitants; and laid waste the country with the like burning, as I formerly said when I wrote the Jewish War.[22] But Lot's wife continually turning back to view the city as she went from it, and being too nicely inquisitive what would become of it, although God had forbidden her so to do, was changed into a pillar of salt;[23] for I have seen it, and it remains at this day. Now he and his daughters fled to a certain small place, encompassed with the fire, and settled in it: it is to this day called *Zoar*, for that is the word which the Hebrews use for a small thing. There it was that he lived a

---

21. These sons-in-law to Lot, as they are called, Genesis 19:12–14, might be so styled, because they were betrothed to Lot's daughters, though not yet married to them. See the note on Antiq. B. XIV. ch. 13. sect. 1.

22. Of the War, B. IV. ch. 8. sect. 4.

23. This pillar of salt was, we see here, standing in the days of Josephus, and he had seen it. That it was standing then is also attested by Clement of Rome, contemporary with Josephus; as also that it was so in the next century, is attested by Irenaeus, with the addition of an hypothesis, how it came to last so long, with all its members entire.—Whether the account that some modern travelers give be true, that it is still standing, I do not know. Its remote situation, at the most southern point of the Sea of Sodom, in the wild and dangerous deserts of Arabia, makes it exceeding difficult for inquisitive travelers to examine the place; and for common reports of country people, at a distance, they are not very satisfactory. In the mean time, I have no opinion of Le Clerc's dissertation or hypothesis about this question, which can only be determined by eye-witnesses. When Christian princes, so called, lay aside their foolish and unchristian wars and quarrels, and send a body of fit persons to travel over the east, and bring us faithful accounts of all ancient monuments, and procure us copies of all ancient records, at present lost among us, we may hope for full satisfaction in such inquiries; but hardly before.

miserable life, on account of his having no company, and his want of provisions.

5. But his daughters, thinking that all mankind were destroyed, approached to their father,[24] though taking care not to be perceived. This they did, that human kind might not utterly fail: and they bare sons; the son of the elder was named Moab, Which denotes one derived from his father; the younger bare Ammon, which name denotes one derived from a kinsman. The former of whom was the father of the Moabites, which is even still a great nation; the latter was the father of the Ammonites; and both of them are inhabitants of Celesyria. And such was the departure of Lot from among the Sodomites.

12 Concerning Abimelech; and Concerning Ismael the Son of Abraham; and Concerning the Arabians, Who Were His Posterity

1. ABRAHAM now removed to Gerar of Palestine, leading Sarah along with him, under the notion of his sister, using the like dissimulation that he had used before, and this out of fear: for he was afraid of Abimelech, the king of that country, who did also himself fall in love with Sarah, and was disposed to corrupt her; but he was restrained from satisfying his lust by a dangerous distemper which befell him from God. Now when his physicians despaired of curing him, he fell asleep, and saw a dream, warning him not to abuse the stranger's wife; and when he recovered, he told his friends that God had inflicted that disease upon him, by way of punishment, for his injury to the stranger; and in order to preserve the chastity of his wife, for that she did not accompany him as his sister, but as his legitimate wife; and that God had promised to be gracious to him for the time to come, if this person be once secure of his wife's chastity. When he had said this,

---

24. I see no proper wicked intention in these daughters of Lot, when in a case which appeared to them of unavoidable necessity, they procured themselves to be with child by their father. Without such an unavoidable necessity, incest is a horrid crime; but whether in such a case of necessity, as they apprehended this to be, according to Josephus, it was any such crime, I am not satisfied. In the mean time, their making their father drunk, and their solicitous concealment of what they did from him, shows that they despaired of persuading him to an action which, at the best, could not but be very suspicious and shocking to so good a man.

by the advice of his friends, he sent for Abraham, and bid him not to be concerned about his wife, or fear the corruption of her chastity; for that God took care of him, and that it was by his providence that he received his wife again, without her suffering any abuse. And he appealed to God, and to his wife's conscience; and said that he had not any inclination at first to enjoy her, if he had known she was his wife; but since, said he, thou leddest her about as thy sister, I was guilty of no offense. He also entreated him to be at peace with him, and to make God propitious to him; and that if he thought fit to continue with him, he should have what he wanted in abundance; but that if he designed to go away, he should be honorably conducted, and have whatsoever supply he wanted when he came thither. Upon his saying this, Abraham told him that his pretense of kindred to his wife was no lie, because she was his brother's daughter; and that he did not think himself safe in his travels abroad, without this sort of dissimulation; and that he was not the cause of his distemper, but was only solicitous for his own safety: he said also, that he was ready to stay with him. Whereupon Abimelech assigned him land and money; and they coventanted to live together without guile, and took an oath at a certain well called Beersheba, which may be interpreted, *The Well of the Oath:* and so it is named by the people of the country unto this day.

2. Now in a little time Abraham had a son by Sarah, as God had foretold to him, whom he named Isaac, which signifies *Laughter.* And indeed they so called him, because Sarah laughed when God[25] said that she should bear a son, she not expecting such a thing, as being past the age of child-bearing, for she was ninety years old, and Abraham a hundred; so that this son was born to them both in the last year of each of those decimal numbers. And they circumcised him upon the eighth day and from that time the Jews continue the custom of circumcising their sons within that number of days. But as for the

---

25. It is well worth observation, that Josephus here calls that principal Angel, who appeared to Abraham and foretold the birth of Isaac, directly God; which language of Josephus here, prepares us to believe those other expressions of his, that Jesus was a wise man, if it be lawful to call him a man, Antiq. B. XVIII. ch. 3. sect. 3, and of God the Word, in his homily concerning Hades, may be both genuine. Nor is the other expression of Divine Angel, used presently, and before, also of any other signification.

Arabians, they circumcise after the thirteenth year, because Ismael, the founder of their nation, who was born to Abraham of the concubine, was circumcised at that age; concerning whom I will presently give a particular account, with great exactness.

3. As for Sarah, she at first loved Ismael, who was born of her own handmaid Hagar, with an affection not inferior to that of her own son, for he was brought up in order to succeed in the government; but when she herself had borne Isaac, she was not willing that Ismael should be brought up with him, as being too old for him, and able to do him injuries when their father should be dead; she therefore persuaded Abraham to send him and his mother to some distant country. Now, at the first, he did not agree to what Sarah was so zealous for, and thought it an instance of the greatest barbarity, to send away a young child[26] and a woman unprovided of necessaries; but at length he agreed to it, because God was pleased with what Sarah had determined: so he delivered Ismael to his mother, as not yet able to go by himself; and commanded her to take a bottle of water, and a loaf of bread, and so to depart, and to take Necessity for her guide. But as soon as her necessary provisions failed, she found herself in an evil case; and when the water was almost spent, she laid the young child, who was ready to expire, under a fig-tree, and went on further, that so he might die while she was absent. But a Divine Angel came to her, and told her of a fountain hard by, and bid her take care, and bring up the child, because she should be very happy by the preservation of Ismael. She then took courage, upon the prospect of what was promised her, and, meeting with some shepherds, by their care she got clear of the distresses she had been in.

4. When the lad was grown up, he married a wife, by birth an Egyptian, from whence the mother was herself derived originally. Of

---

26. Josephus here calls Ismael a young child or infant, though he was about 13 years of age; as Judas calls himself and his brethren young men, when he was 47, and had two children, Antiq. B. II. ch. 6. sect. 8, and they were of much the same age; as is a damsel of 12 years old called a little child, Mark 5:39–42, five several times. Herod is also said by Josephus to be a very young man at 25. See the note on Antiq. B. XIV. ch. 9. sect 2, and of the War, B. I. ch. 10. And Aristobulus is styled a very little child at 16 years of age, Antiq. B. XV. ch. 2. sect. 6, 7. Domitian also is called by him a very young child, when he went on his German expedition at about 18 years of age, of the War, B. VII. ch. 4. sect. 2. Samson's wife, and Ruth, when they were widows, are called children, Antiq. B. V. ch. 8. sect. 6, and ch. 9. sect. 2 3.

this wife were born to Ismael twelve sons; Nabaioth, Kedar, Abdeel, Mabsam, Idumas, Masmaos, Masaos, Chodad, Theman, Jetur, Naphesus, Cadmas. These inhabited all the country from Euphrates to the Red Sea, and called it Nabatene. They are an Arabian nation, and name their tribes from these, both because of their own virtue, and because of the dignity of Abraham their father.

13   Concerning Isaac the Legitimate Son of Abraham

1. Now Abraham greatly loved Isaac, as being his only begotten[27] and given to him at the borders of old age, by the favor of God. The child also endeared himself to his parents still more, by the exercise of every virtue, and adhering to his duty to his parents, and being zealous in the worship of God. Abraham also placed his own happiness in this prospect, that, when he should die, he should leave this his son in a safe and secure condition; which accordingly he obtained by the will of God: who being desirous to make an experiment of Abraham's religious disposition towards himself, appeared to him, and enumerated all the blessings he had bestowed on him; how he had made him superior to his enemies; and that his son Isaac, who was the principal part of his present happiness, was derived from him; and he said that he required this son of his as a sacrifice and holy oblation. Accordingly he commanded him to carry him to the mountain Moriah, and to build an altar, and offer him for a burnt-offering upon it for that this would best manifest his religious disposition towards him, if he preferred what was pleasing to God, before the preservation of his own son.

2. Now Abraham thought that it was not right to disobey God in any thing, but that he was obliged to serve him in every circumstance of life, since all creatures that live enjoy their life by his providence, and the kindness he bestows on them. Accordingly he concealed this command of God, and his own intentions about the slaughter of his son, from his wife, as also from every one of his servants, otherwise he should have been hindered from his obedience to God; and he took

---

27. Note, that both here and Hebrews 11:17, Isaac is called Abraham's only begotten son, though he at the same time had another son, Ismael. The Septuagint expresses the true meaning, by rendering the text the beloved son.

Isaac, together with two of his servants, and laying what things were necessary for a sacrifice upon an ass, he went away to the mountain. Now the two servants went along with him two days; but on the third day, as soon as he saw the mountain, he left those servants that were with him till then in the plain, and, having his son alone with him, he came to the mountain. It was that mountain upon which king David afterwards built the temple.[28] Now they had brought with them every thing necessary for a sacrifice, excepting the animal that was to be offered only. Now Isaac was twenty-five years old. And as he was building the altar, he asked his father what he was about to offer, since there was no animal there for an oblation—to which it was answered, "That God would provide himself an oblation, he being able to make a plentiful provision for men out of what they have not, and to deprive others of what they already have, when they put too much trust therein; that therefore, if God pleased to be present and propitious at this sacrifice, he would provide himself an oblation."

3. As soon as the altar was prepared, and Abraham had laid on the wood, and all things were entirely ready, he said to his son, "O son, I poured out a vast number of prayers that I might have thee for my son; when thou wast come into the world, there was nothing that could contribute to thy support for which I was not greatly solicitous, nor any thing wherein I thought myself happier than to see thee grown up to man's estate, and that I might leave thee at my death the successor to my dominion; but since it was by God's will that I became thy father, and it is now his will that I relinquish thee, bear this consecration to God with a generous mind; for I resign thee up to God who has thought fit now to require this testimony of honor to himself, on account of the favors he hath conferred on me, in being to me a supporter and defender. Accordingly thou, my son, wilt now die, not in any common way of going out of the world, but sent to God, the Father of all men, beforehand, by thy own father, in the nature of a sacrifice. I suppose he thinks thee worthy to get clear of this world

---

28. Here is a plain error in the copies which say that king David afterwards built the temple on this Mount Moriah, while it was certainly no other than king Solomon who built that temple, as indeed Procopius cites it from Josephus. For it was for certain David, and not Solomon, who built the first altar there, as we learn, 2 Samuel 24:18, etc.; 1 Chronicles 21:22, etc.; and Antiq. B. VII. ch. 13. sect. 4.

neither by disease, neither by war, nor by any other severe way, by which death usually comes upon men, but so that he will receive thy soul with prayers and holy offices of religion, and will place thee near to himself, and thou wilt there be to me a succorer and supporter in my old age; on which account I principally brought thee up, and thou wilt thereby procure me God for my Comforter instead of thyself."

4. Now Isaac was of such a generous disposition as became the son of such a father, and was pleased with this discourse; and said, "That he was not worthy to be born at first, if he should reject the determination of God and of his father, and should not resign himself up readily to both their pleasures; since it would have been unjust if he had not obeyed, even if his father alone had so resolved." So he went immediately to the altar to be sacrificed. And the deed had been done if God had not opposed it; for he called loudly to Abraham by his name, and forbade him to slay his son; and said, "It was not out of a desire of human blood that he was commanded to slay his son, nor was he willing that he should be taken away from him whom he had made his father, but to try the temper of his mind, whether he would be obedient to such a command. Since therefore he now was satisfied as to that his alacrity, and the surprising readiness he showed in this his piety, he was delighted in having bestowed such blessings upon him; and that he would not be wanting in all sort of concern about him, and in bestowing other children upon him; and that his son should live to a very great age; that he should live a happy life, and bequeath a large principality to his children, who should be good and legitimate." He foretold also, that his family should increase into many nations[29] and that those patriarchs should leave behind them an everlasting

---

29. It seems both here, and in God's parallel blessing to Jacob, ch. 19. sect. 1, that Josephus had yet no notion of the hidden meaning of that most important and most eminent promise, "In thy seed shall all the families of the earth be blessed. He saith not, and of seeds, as of many, but as of one; and to thy seed, which is Christ," Galatians 3:16. Nor is it any wonder, he being, I think, as yet not a Christian. And had he been a Christian, yet since he was, to be sure, till the latter part of his life, no more than an Ebionite Christian, who, above all the apostles, rejected and despised St. Paul, it would be no great wonder if he did not now follow his interpretation. In the mean time, we have in effect St. Paul's exposition in the Testament of Reuben, sect. 6, in Authent. Rec. Part I. p. 302, who charges his sons "to worship the seed of Judah, who should die for them in visible and invisible wars; and should be among them an eternal king." Nor is that observation of a learned foreigner of my acquaintance to

name; that they should obtain the possession of the land of Canaan, and be envied by all men. When God had said this, he produced to them a ram, which did not appear before, for the sacrifice. So Abraham and Isaac receiving each other unexpectedly, and having obtained the promises of such great blessings, embraced one another; and when they had sacrificed, they returned to Sarah, and lived happily together, God affording them his assistance in all things they desired.

14 Concerning Sarah Abraham's Wife; and How She Ended Her Days

NOW Sarah died a little while after, having lived one hundred and twenty-seven years. They buried her in Hebron; the Canaanites publicly allowing them a burying-place; which piece of ground Abraham bought for four hundred shekels, of Ephron, an inhabitant of Hebron. And both Abraham and his descendants built themselves sepulchers in that place.

15 How the Nation of the Troglodytes Were Derived from Abraham by Keturah

ABRAHAM after this married Keturah, by whom six sons were born to him, men of courage, and of sagacious minds: Zambran, and Jazar, and Madan, and Madian, and Josabak, and Sous. Now the sons of Sous were Sabathan and Dadan. The sons of Dadan were Latusim, and Assur, and Luom. The sons of Madiau were Ephas, and Ophren, and Anoch, and Ebidas, and Eldas. Now, for all these sons and grandsons, Abraham contrived to settle them in colonies; and they took possession of Troglodytis, and the country of Arabia the Happy, as far as it reaches to the Red Sea. It is related of this Ophren, that he made war against Libya, and took it, and that his grandchildren, when they

---

be despised, who takes notice, that as seeds in the plural, must signify posterity, so seed in the singular may signify either posterity, or a single person; and that in this promise of all nations being happy in the seed of Abraham, or Isaac, or Jacob, etc. it is always used in the singular. To which I shall add, that it is sometimes, as it were, paraphrased by the son of Abraham, the son of David, etc., which is capable of no such ambiguity.

inhabited it, called it (from his name) Africa. And indeed Alexander Polyhistor gives his attestation to what I here say; who speaks thus: "Cleodemus the prophet, who was also called Malchus, who wrote a History of the Jews, in agreement with the History of Moses, their legislator, relates, that there were many sons born to Abraham by Keturah: nay, he names three of them, Apher, and Surim, and Japhran. That from Surim was the land of Assyria denominated; and that from the other two (Apher and Japbran) the country of Africa took its name, because these men were auxiliaries to Hercules, when he fought against Libya and Antaeus; and that Hercules married Aphra's daughter, and of her he begat a son, Diodorus; and that Sophon was his son, from whom that barbarous people called Sophacians were denominated."

16   *How Isaac Took Rebeka to Wife*

1. NOW when Abraham, the father of Isaac, had resolved to take Rebeka, who was grand-daughter to his brother Nahor, for a wife to his son Isaac, who was then about forty years old, he sent the ancientest of his servants to betroth her, after he had obliged him to give him the strongest assurances of his fidelity; which assurances were given after the manner following—They put each other's hands under each other's thighs; then they called upon God as the witness of what was to be done. He also sent such presents to those that were there as were in esteem, on account that that they either rarely or never were seen in that country, The servant got thither not under a considerable time; for it requires much time to pass through Meopotamia, in which it is tedious traveling, both in the winter for the depth of the clay, and in summer for want of water; and, besides this, for the robberies there committed, which are not to be avoided by travelers but by caution beforehand. However, the servant came to Haran; and when he was in the suburbs, he met a considerable number of maidens going to the water; he therefore prayed to God that Rebeka might be found among them, or her whom Abraham sent him as his servant to espouse to his son, in case his will were that this marriage should be consummated, and that she might be made known to him by the sign, That while others denied him water to drink, she might give it him.

2. With this intention he went to the well, and desired the maidens to give him some water to drink: but while the others refused, on pretense that they wanted it all at home, and could spare none for him, one only of the company rebuked them for their peevish behavior towards the stranger; and said, What is there that you will ever communicate to anybody, who have not so much as given the man some water? She then offered him water in an obliging manner. And now he began to hope that his grand affair would succeed; but desiring still to know the truth, he commended her for her generosity and good nature, that she did not scruple to afford a sufficiency of water to those that wanted it, though it cost her some pains to draw it; and asked who were her parents, and wished them joy of such a daughter. "And mayst thou be espoused," said he, "to their satisfaction, into the family of an agreeable husband, and bring him legitimate children." Nor did she disdain to satisfy his inquiries, but told him her family. "They," says she, "call me Rebeka; my father was Bethuel, but he is dead; and Laban is my brother; and, together with my mother, takes care of all our family affairs, and is the guardian of my virginity." When the servant heard this, he was very glad at what had happened, and at what was told him, as perceiving that God had thus plainly directed his journey; and producing his bracelets, and some other ornaments which it was esteemed decent for virgins to wear, he gave them to the damsel, by way of acknowledgment, and as a reward for her kindness in giving him water to drink; saying, it was but just that she should have them, because she was so much more obliging than any of the rest. She desired also that he would come and lodge with them, since the approach of the night gave him not time to proceed farther. And producing his precious ornaments for women, he said he desired to trust them to none more safely than to such as she had shown herself to be; and that he believed he might guess at the humanity of her mother and brother, that they would not be displeased, from the virtue he found in her; for he would not be burdensome, but would pay the hire for his entertainment, and spend his own money. To which she replied, that he guessed right as to the humanity of her parents; but complained that he should think them so parsimonious as to take money, for that he should have all on free cost. But she said she would first inform her brother Laban, and, if he gave her leave, she would conduct him in.

3. As soon then as this was over, she introduced the stranger; and for the camels, the servants of Laban brought them in, and took care of them; and he was himself brought in to supper by Laban. And, after supper, he says to him, and to the mother of the damsel, addressing himself to her, "Abraham is the son of Terah, and a kinsman of yours; for Nahor, the grandfather of these children, was the brother of Abraham, by both father and mother; upon which account he hath sent me to you, being desirous to take this damsel for his son to wife. He is his legitimate son, and is brought up as his only heir. He could indeed have had the most happy of all the women in that country for him, but he would not have his son marry any of them; but, out of regard to his own relations, he desired him to match here, whose affection and inclination I would not have you despise; for it was by the good pleasure of God that other accidents fell out in my journey, and that thereby I lighted upon your daughter and your house; for when I was near to the city, I saw a great many maidens coming to a well, and I prayed that I might meet with this damsel, which has come to pass accordingly. Do you therefore confirm that marriage, whose espousals have been already made by a Divine appearance; and show the respect you have for Abraham, who hath sent me with so much solicitude, in giving your consent to the marriage of this damsel." Upon this they understood it to be the will of God, and greatly approved of the offer, and sent their daughter, as was desired. Accordingly Isaac married her, the inheritance being now come to him; for the children by Keturah were gone to their own remote habitations.

17   Concerning the Death of Abraham

A LITTLE while after this Abraham died. He was a man of incomparable virtue, and honored by God in a manner agreeable to his piety towards him. The whole time of his life was one hundred seventy and five years, and he was buried in Hebron, with his wife Sarah, by their sons Isaac and Ismael.

18   Concerning the Sons of Isaac, Esau and Jacob; of Their Nativity and Education

1. NOW Isaac's wife proved with child, after the death of Abraham;[30] and when her belly was greatly burdened, Isaac was very anxious, and inquired of God; who answered, that Rebeka should bear twins; and that two nations should take the names of those sons; and that he who appeared the second should excel the elder. Accordingly she, in a little time, as God had foretold, bare twins; the elder of whom, from his head to his feet, was very rough and hairy; but the younger took hold of his heel as they were in the birth. Now the father loved the elder, who was called Esau, a name agreeable to his roughness, for the Hebrews call such a hairy roughness [Esau,[31] or] Seir; but Jacob the younger was best beloved by his mother.

2. When there was a famine in the land, Isaac resolved to go into Egypt, the land there being good; but he went to Gerar, as God commanded him. Here Abimelech the king received him, because Abraham had formerly lived with him, and had been his friend. And as in the beginning he treated him exceeding kindly, so he was hindered from continuing in the same disposition to the end, by his envy at him; for when he saw that God was with Isaac, and took such great care of him, he drove him away from him. But Isaac, when he saw how envy had changed the temper of Abimelech retired to a place called the Valley, not far from Gerar: and as he was digging a well, the shepherds fell upon him, and began to fight, in order to hinder the work; and because he did not desire to contend, the shepherds seemed to get the him, so he still retired, and dug another and when certain other shepherds of Abimelech began to offer him violence, he left that also, still retired, thus purchasing security to himself a rational and prudent conduct. At length the gave him leave to dig a well without disturbance. He named this well Rehoboth, which denotes *a large space;*

---

30. The birth of Jacob and Esau is here said to be after Abraham's death: it should have been after Sarah's death. The order of the narration in Genesis, not always exactly according to the order of time, seems to have led Josephus into this error, as Dr. Bernard observes here.

31. For Seir in Josephus, the coherence requires that we read Esau or Seir, which signify the same thing.

but of the former wells, one was called Escon, which denotes *strife,* the other Sitenna, name signifies *enmity.*

3. It was now that Isaac's affairs increased, and in a flourishing condition; and this his great riches. But Abimelech, thinking in opposition to him, while their living made them suspicious of each other, and retiring showing a secret enmity also, he

afraid that his former friendship with Isaac would not secure him, if Isaac should endeavor the injuries he had formerly offered him; he therefore renewed his friendship with him, Philoc, one of his generals. And when he had obtained every thing he desired, by reason of Isaac's good nature, who preferred the earlier friendship Abimelech had shown to himself and his father to his later wrath against him, he returned home.

4. Now when Esau, one of the sons of Isaac, whom the father principally loved, was now come to the age of forty years, he married Adah, the daughter of Helon, and Aholibamah, the daughter of Esebeon; which Helon and Esebeon were great lords among the Canaanites: thereby taking upon himself the authority, and pretending to have dominion over his own marriages, without so much as asking the advice of his father; for had Isaac been the arbitrator, he had not given him leave to marry thus, for he was not pleased with contracting any alliance with the people of that country; but not caring to be uneasy to his son by commanding him to put away these wives, he resolved to be silent.

5. But when he was old, and could not see at all, he called Esau to him, and told him, that besides his blindness, and the disorder of his eyes, his very old age hindered him from his worship of God [by sacrifice]; he bid him therefore to go out a hunting, and when he had caught as much venison as he could, to prepare him a supper[32] that

---

32. The supper of savory meat, as we call it, Genesis 27:4, to be caught by hunting, was intended plainly for a festival or a sacrifice; and upon the prayers that were frequent at sacrifices, Isaac expected, as was then usual in such eminent cases, that a divine impulse would come upon him, in order to the blessing of his son there present, and his foretelling his future behavior and fortune. Whence it must be, that when Isaac had unwittingly blessed Jacob, and was afterwards made sensible of his mistake, yet did he not attempt to alter it, how earnestly soever his affection for Esau might incline him to wish it might be altered, because he knew that this blessing came not from himself, but from God, and that an alteration was out of his power. A second

after this he might make supplication to God, to be to him a supporter and an assister during the whole time of his life; saying, that it was uncertain when he should die, and that he was desirous, by prayers for him, to procure, beforehand, God to be merciful to him.

6. Accordingly, Esau went out a hunting. But Rebeka[33] thinking it proper to have the supplication made for obtaining the favor of God to Jacob, and that without the consent of Isaac, bid him kill kids of the goats, and prepare a supper. So Jacob obeyed his mother, according to all her instructions. Now when the supper was got ready, he took a goat's skin, and put it about his arm, that by reason of its hairy roughness, he might by his father be believed to be Esau; for they being twins, and in all things else alike, differed only in this thing. This was done out of his fear, that before his father had made his supplications, he should be caught in his evil practice, and lest he should, on the contrary, provoke his father to curse him. So he brought in the supper to his father. Isaac perceivest to be Esau." So suspecting no deceit, he ate the supper, and betook himself to his prayers and intercessions with God; and said, "O Lord of all ages, and Creator of all substance; for it was thou that didst propose to my father great plenty of good things, and hast vouchsafed to bestow on me what I have;

---

afflatus then came upon him, and enabled him to foretell Esau's future behavior and foretell Esau's future behavior and fortune also.

33. Whether Jacob or his mother Rebeka were most blameable in this imposition upon Isaac in his old age, I cannot determine. However the blessing being delivered as a prediction of future events, by a Divine impulse, and foretelling things to befall to the posterity of Jacob and Esau in future ages, was for certain providential; and according to what Rebeka knew to be the purpose of God, when he answered her inquiry, "before the children were born," Genesis 25:23, "that one people should be stronger than the other people; and the elder, Esau, should serve the younger, Jacob." Whether Isaac knew or remembered this old oracle, delivered in our copies only to Rebeka; or whether, if he knew and remembered it, he did not endeavor to alter the Divine determination, out of his fondness for his elder and worser son Esau, to the damage of his younger and better son Jacob, as Josephus elsewhere supposes, Antiq. B. II. ch. 7. sect. 3; I cannot certainly say. if so, this might tempt Rebeka to contrive, and Jacob to put this imposition upon him. However, Josephus says here, that it was Isaac, and not Rebeka, who inquired of God at first, and received the forementioned oracle, sect. 1; which, if it be the true reading, renders Isaac's procedure more inexcusable. Nor was it probably any thing else that so much encouraged Esau formerly to marry two Canaanitish wives, without his parents' consent, as Isaac's unhappy fondness for him.

and hast promised to my posterity to be their kind supporter, and to bestow on them still greater blessings; do thou therefore confirm these thy promises, and do not overlook me, because of my present weak condition, on account of which I most earnestly pray to thee. Be gracious to this my son; and preserve him and keep him from every thing that is evil. Give him a happy life, and the possession of as many good things as thy power is able to bestow. Make him terrible to his enemies, and honorable and beloved among his friends."

7. Thus did Isaac pray to God, thinking his prayers had been made for Esau. He had but just finished them, when Esau came in from hunting. And when Isaac perceived his mistake, he was silent: but Esau required that he might be made partaker of the like blessing from his father that his brother had partook of; but his father refused it, because all his prayers had been spent upon Jacob: so Esau lamented the mistake. However, his father being grieved at his weeping, said, that "he should excel in hunting and strength of body, in arms, and all such sorts of work; and should obtain glory for ever on those accounts, he and his posterity after him; but still should serve his brother."

8. Now the mother delivered Jacob, when she was afraid that his brother would inflict some punishment upon him because of the mistake about the prayers of Isaac; for she persuaded her husband to take a wife for Jacob out of Mesopotamia, of her own kindred, Esau having married already Basemmath, the daughter of Ismael, without his father's consent; for Isaac did not like the Canaanites, so that he disapproved of Esau's former marriages, which made him take Basemmath to wife, in order to please him; and indeed he had a great affection for her.

19   *Concerning Jacob's Flight into Mesopotamia, by Reason of the Fear He Was in of His Brother*

1. Now Jacob was sent by his mother to Mesopotamia, in order to marry Laban her brother's daughter (which marriage was permitted by Isaac, on account of his obsequiousness to the desires of his wife); and he accordingly journeyed through the land of Canaan; and because he hated the people of that country, he would not lodge with any of them, but took up his lodging in the open air, and laid his

head on a heap of stones that he had gathered together. At which time he saw in his sleep such a vision standing by him:—he seemed to see a ladder that reached from the earth unto heaven, and persons descending upon the ladder that seemed more excellent than human; and at last God himself stood above it, and was plainly visible to him, who, calling him by his name, spake to him in these words:—

2. "O Jacob, it is not fit for thee, who art the son of a good father, and grandson of one who had obtained a great reputation for his eminent virtue, to be dejected at thy present circumstances, but to hope for better times, for thou shalt have great abundance of all good things, by my assistance: for I brought Abraham hither, out of Mesopotamia, when he was driven away by his kinsmen, and I made thy father a happy man, nor will I bestow a lesser degree of happiness on thyself: be of good courage, therefore, and under my conduct proceed on this thy journey, for the marriage thou goest so zealously about shall be consummated. And thou shalt have children of good characters, but their multitude shall be innumerable; and they shall leave what they have to a still more numerous posterity, to whom, and to whose posterity, I give the dominion of all the land, and their posterity shall fill the entire earth and sea, so far as the sun beholds them: but do not thou fear any danger, nor be afraid of the many labors thou must undergo, for by my providence I will direct thee what thou art to do in the time present, and still much more in the time to come."

3. Such were the predictions which God made to Jacob; whereupon he became very joyful at what he had seen and heard; and he poured oil on the stones, because on them the prediction of such great benefits was made. He also vowed a vow, that he would offer sacrifices upon them, if he lived and returned safe; and if he came again in such a condition, he would give the tithe of what he had gotten to God. He also judged the place to be honorable and gave it the name of Bethel, which, in the Greek, is interpreted, *The House of God*.

4. So he proceeded on his journey to Mesopotamia, and at length came to Haran; and meeting with shepherds in the suburbs, with boys grown up, and maidens sitting about a certain well, he staid with them, as wanting water to drink; and beginning to discourse with them, he asked them whether they knew such a one as Laban, and whether he was still alive. Now they all said they knew him, for he was not so inconsiderable a person as to be unknown to any of them; and that his

daughter fed her father's flock together with them; and that indeed they wondered that she was not yet come, for by her means thou mightest learn more exactly whatever thou desirest to know about that family. While they were saying this the damsel came, and the other shepherds that came down along with her. Then they showed her Jacob, and told her that he was a stranger, who came to inquire about her father's affairs. But she, as pleased, after the custom of children, with Jacob's coming, asked him who he was, and whence he came to them, and what it was he lacked that he came thither. She also wished it might be in their power to supply the wants he came about.

5. But Jacob was quite overcome, not so much by their kindred, nor by that affection which might arise thence, as by his love to the damsel, and his surprise at her beauty, which was so flourishing, as few of the women of that age could vie with. He said then, "There is a relation between thee and me, elder than either thy or my birth, if thou be the daughter of Laban; for Abraham was the son of Terah, as well as Haran and Nahor. Of the last of whom (Nahor) Bethuel thy grandfather was the son. Isaac my father was the son of Abraham and of Sarah, who was the daughter of Haran. But there is a nearer and later cement of mutual kindred which we bear to one another, for my mother Rebeka was sister to Laban thy father, both by the same father and mother; I therefore and thou are cousin-germans. And I am now come to salute you, and to renew that affinity which is proper between us." Upon this the damsel, at the mention of Rebeka, as usually happens to young persons, wept, and that out of the kindness she had for her father, and embraced Jacob, she having learned an account of Rebeka from her father, and knew that her parents loved to hear her named; and when she had saluted him, she said that "he brought the most desirable and greatest pleasures to her father, with all their family, who was always mentioning his mother, and always thinking of her, and her alone; and that this will make thee equal in his eyes to any advantageous circumstances whatsoever." Then she bid him go to her father, and follow her while she conducted him to him; and not to deprive him of such a pleasure, by staying any longer away from him.

6. When she had said thus, she brought him to Laban; and being owned by his uncle, he was secure himself, as being among his friends; and he brought a great deal of pleasure to them by his unexpected coning. But a little while afterward, Laban told him that he could not

express in words the joy he had at his coming; but still he inquired of him the occasion of his coming, and why he left his aged mother and father, when they wanted to be taken care of by him; and that he would afford him all the assistance he wanted. Then Jacob gave him an account of the whole occasion of his journey, and told him, "that Isaac had two sons that were twins, himself and Esau; who, because he failed of his father's prayers, which by his mother's wisdom were put up for him, sought to kill him, as deprived of the kingdom[34] which was to be given him of God, and of the blessings for which their father prayed; and that this was the occasion of his coming hither, as his mother had commanded him to do: for we are all (says he) brethren one to another; but our mother esteems an alliance with your family more than she does one with the families of the country; so I look upon yourself and God to be the supporters of my travels, and think myself safe in my present circumstances."

7. Now Laban promised to treat him with great humanity, both on account of his ancestors, and particularly for the sake of his mother, towards whom, he said, he would show his kindness, even though she were absent, by taking care of him; for he assured him he would make him the head shepherd of his flock, and give him authority sufficient for that purpose; and when he should have a mind to return to his parents, he would send him back with presents, and this in as honorable a manner as the nearness of their relation should require. This Jacob heard gladly; and said he would willingly, and with pleasure, undergo any sort of pains while he tarried with him, but desired Rachel to wife, as the reward of those pains, who was not only on other accounts esteemed by him, but also because she was the means of his coming to him; for he said he was forced by the love of the damsel to make this proposal. Laban was well pleased with this agreement, and consented to give the damsel to him, as not desirous to meet with any better son-in-law; and said he would do this, if he

---

34. By this "deprivation of the kingdom that was to be given Esau of God," as the first-born, it appears that Josephus thought that a "kingdom to be derived from God" was due to him whom Isaac should bless as his first-born, which I take to be that kingdom which was expected under the Messiah, who therefore was to be born of his posterity whom Isaac should so bless. Jacob therefore by obtaining this blessing of the first-born, became the genuine heir of that kingdom, in opposition to Esau.

would stay with him some time, for he was not willing to send his daughter to be among the Canaanites, for he repented of the alliance he had made already by marrying his sister there. And when Jacob had given his consent to this, he agreed to stay seven years; for so many years he had resolved to serve his father-in-law, that, having given a specimen of his virtue, it might be better known what sort of a man he was. And Jacob, accepting of his terms, after the time was over, he made the wedding-feast; and when it was night, without Jacob's perceiving it, he put his other daughter into bed to him, who was both elder than Rachel, and of no comely countenance: Jacob lay with her that night, as being both in drink and in the dark. However, when it was day, he knew what had been done to him; and he reproached Laban for his unfair proceeding with him; who asked pardon for that necessity which forced him to do what he did; for he did not give him Lea out of any ill design, but as overcome by another greater necessity: that, notwithstanding this, nothing should hinder him from marrying Rachel; but that when he had served another seven years, he would give him her whom he loved. Jacob submitted to this condition, for his love to the damsel did not permit him to do otherwise; and when another seven years were gone, he took Rachel to wife.

8. Now each of these had handmaids, by their father's donation. Zilpha was handmaid to Lea, and Bilha to Rachel; by no means slaves,[35] but however subject to their mistresses. Now Lea was sorely troubled at her husband's love to her sister; and she expected she should be better esteemed if she bare him children: so she entreated God perpetually; and when she had borne a son, and her husband was on that account better reconciled to her, she named her son Reubel,

---

35. Here we have the difference between slaves for life and servants, such as we now hire for a time agreed upon on both sides, and dismiss again after he time contracted for is over, which are no slaves, but free men and free women. Accordingly, when the Apostolical Constitutions forbid a clergyman to marry perpetual servants or slaves, B. VI. ch. 17., it is meant only of the former sort; as we learn elsewhere from the same Constitutions, ch. 47. Can. LXXXII. But concerning these twelve sons of Jacob, the reasons of their several names, and the times of their several births in the intervals here assigned, their several excellent characters, their several faults and repentance, the several accidents of their lives, with their several prophecies at their deaths, see the Testaments of these twelve patriarchs, still preserved at large in the Authent. Rec. Part I. p. 294–443.

because *God had had mercy upon her, in giving her a son,* for that is the signification of this name. After some time she bare three more sons; Simeon, which

name signifies *that God had hearkened to her prayer.* Then she bare Levi, *the confirmer of their friendship.* After him was born Judah, which denotes *thanksgiving.* But Rachel, fearing lest the fruitfulness of her sister should make herself enjoy a lesser share of Jacob's affections, put to bed to him her handmaid Bilha; by whom Jacob had Dan: one may interpret that name into the Greek tongue, *a divine judgment.* And after him Nephthalim, as it were, *unconquerable in stratagems,* since Rachel tried to conquer the fruitfulness of her sister by this stratagem. Accordingly, Lea took the same method, and used a counter-stratagem to that of her sister; for she put to bed to him her own handmaid. Jacob therefore had by Zilpha a son, whose name was Gad, which may be interpreted *fortune;* and after him Asher, which may be called *a happy man,* because he added glory to Lea. Now Reubel, the eldest son of Lea, brought apples of mandrakes[36] to his mother. When Rachel saw them, she desired that she would give her the apples, for she longed to eat them; but when she refused, and bid her be content that she had deprived her of the benevolence she ought to have had from her husband, Rachel, in order to mitigate her sister's anger, said she would yield her husband to her; and he should lie with her that evening. She accepted of the favor, and Jacob slept with Lea, by the favor of Rachel. She bare then these sons: Issachar, denoting *one born by hire:* and Zabulon, *one born as a pledge of benevolence towards her;* and a daughter, Dina. After some time Rachel had a son, named Joseph, which signified *there should be another added to him.*

9. Now Jacob fed the flocks of Laban his father-in-law all this time, being twenty years, after which he desired leave of his father-in-law to take his wives and go home; but when his father-in-law would not give him leave, he contrived to do it secretly. He made trial therefore

---

36. I formerly explained these mandrakes, as we, with the Septuagint, and Josephus, render the Hebrew word Dudaim, of the Syrian Maux, with Ludolphus, Antbent. Rec. Part I. p. 420; but have since seen such a very probable account in M. S. of my learned friend Mr. Samuel Barker, of what we still call mandrakes, and their description by the ancient naturalists and physicians, as inclines me to think these here mentioned were really mandrakes, and no other.

of the disposition of his wives what they thought of this journey;—when they appeared glad, and approved of it. Rachel took along with her the images of the gods, which, according to their laws, they used to worship in their own country, and ran away together with her sister. The children also of them both, and the handmaids, and what possessions they had, went along with them. Jacob also drove away half the cattle, without letting Laban know of it beforehand But the reason why Rachel took the images of the gods, although Jacob had taught her to despise such worship of those gods, was this, That in case they were pursued, and taken by her father, she might have recourse to these images, in order obtain his pardon.

10. But Laban, after one day's time, being acquainted with Jacob's and his daughters' departure, was much troubled, and pursued after them, leading a band of men with him; and on the seventh day overtook them, and found them resting on a certain hill; and then indeed he did not meddle with them, for it was even-tide; but God stood by him in a dream, and warned him to receive his son-in-law and his daughters in a peaceable manner; and not to venture upon any thing rashly, or in wrath to but to make a league with Jacob. And he him, that if he despised their small number, attacked them in a hostile manner, he would assist them. When Laban had been thus forewarned by God, he called Jacob to him the next day, in order to treat with him, and showed him what dream he had; in dependence whereupon he came confidently to him, and began to accuse him, alleging that he had entertained him when he was poor, and in want of all things, and had given him plenty of all things which he had. "For," said he, "I have joined my daughters to thee in marriage, and supposed that thy kindness to me be greater than before; but thou hast had no regard to either thy mother's relations to me, nor to the affinity now newly contracted between us; nor to those wives whom thou hast married; nor to those children, of whom I am the grandfather. Thou hast treated me as an enemy, driving away my cattle, and by persuading my daughters to run away from their father; and by carrying home those sacred paternal images which were worshipped by my forefathers, and have been honored with the like worship which they paid them by myself. In short, thou hast done this whilst thou art my kinsman, and my sister's son, and the husband of my daughters, and was hospiably treated by me, and didst eat at my table." When Laban had said this,

Jacob made his defense—That he was not the only person in whom God had implanted the love of his native country, but that he had made it natural to all men; and that therefore it was but reasonable that, after so long time, he should go back to it. "But as to the prey, of whose driving away thou accusest me, if any other person were the arbitrator, thou wouldst be found in the wrong; for instead of those thanks I ought to have had from thee, for both keeping thy cattle, and increasing them, how is it that thou art unjustly angry at me because I have taken, and have with me, a small portion of them? But then, as to thy daughters, take notice, that it is not through any evil practices of mine that they follow me in my return home, but from that just affection which wives naturally have to their husbands. They follow therefore not so properly myself as their own children." And thus far of his apology was made, in order to clear himself of having acted unjustly. To which he added his own complaint and accusation of Laban; saying, "While I was thy sister's son, and thou hadst given me thy daughters in marriage, thou hast worn me out with thy harsh commands, and detained me twenty years under them. That indeed which was required in order to my marrying thy daughters, hard as it was, I own to have been tolerable; but as to those that were put upon me after those marriages, they were worse, and such indeed as an enemy would have avoided." For certainly Laban had used Jacob very ill; for when he saw that God was assisting to Jacob in all that he desired, he promised him, that of the young cattle which should be born, he should have sometimes what was of a white color, and sometimes what should be of a black color; but when those that came to Jacob's share proved numerous, he did not keep his faith with him, but said he would give them to him the next year, because of his envying him the multitude of his possessions. He promised him as before, because he thought such an increase was not to be expected; but when it appeared to be fact, he deceived him.

11. But then, as to the sacred images, he bid him search for them; and when Laban accepted of the offer, Rachel, being informed of it, put those images into that camel's saddle on which she rode, and sat upon it; and said, that her natural purgation hindered her rising up: so Laban left off searching any further, not supposing that his daughter in such circumstances would approach to those images. So he made a league with Jacob, and bound it by oaths, that he would not bear

him any malice on account of what had happened; and Jacob made the like league, and promised to love Laban's daughters. And these leagues they confirmed with oaths also, which the made upon certain as whereon they erected a pillar, in the form of an altar: whence that hill is called Gilead; and from thence they call that land the Land of Gilead at this day. Now when they had feasted, after the making of the league, Laban returned home.

20   Concerning the Meeting of Jacob and Esau

1. NOW as Jacob was proceeding on his journey to the land of Canaan, angels appeared to him, and suggested to him good hope of his future condition; and that place he named the Camp of God. And being desirous of knowing what his brother's intentions were to him, he sent messengers, to give him an exact account of every thing, as being afraid, on account of the enmities between them. He charged those that were sent, to say to Esau, "Jacob had thought it wrong to live together with him while he was in anger against him, and so had gone out of the country; and that he now, thinking the length of time of his absence must have made up their differences, was returning; that he brought with him his wives, and his children, with what possessions he had gotten; and delivered himself, with what was most dear to him, into his hands; and should think it his greatest happiness to partake together with his brother of what God had bestowed upon him." So these messengers told him this message. Upon which Esau was very glad, and met his brother with four hundred men. And Jacob, when he heard that he was coming to meet him with such a number of men, was greatly afraid: however, he committed his hope of deliverance to God; and considered how, in his present circumstances, he might preserve himself and those that were with him, and overcome his enemies if they attacked him injuriously. He therefore distributed his company into parts; some he sent before the rest, and the others he ordered to come close behind, that so, if the first were overpowered when his brother attacked them, they might have those that followed as a refuge to fly unto. And when he had put his company in this order, he sent some of them to carry presents to his brother. The presents were made up of cattle, and a great number of four-footed beasts, of many kinds, such as would be very acceptable to those that received

them, on account of their rarity. Those who were sent went at certain intervals of space asunder, that, by following thick, one after another, they might appear to be more numerous, that Esau might remit of his anger on account of these presents, if he were still in a passion. Instructions were also given to those that were sent to speak gently to him.

2. When Jacob had made these appointments all the day, and night came on, he moved on with his company; and, as they were gone over a certain river called Jabboc, Jacob was left behind; and meeting with an angel, he wrestled with him, the angel beginning the struggle: but he prevailed over the angel, who used a voice, and spake to him in words, exhorting him to be pleased with what had happened to him, and not to suppose that his victory was a small one, but that he had overcome a divine angel, and to esteem the victory as a sign of great blessings that should come to him, and that his offspring should never fall, and that no man should be too hard for his power. He also commanded him to be called Israel, which in the Hebrew tongue signifies *one that struggled with the divine angel.*[37] These promises were made at the prayer of Jacob; for when he perceived him to be the angel of God, he desired he would signify to him what should befall him hereafter. And when the angel had said what is before related, he disappeared; but Jacob was pleased with these things, and named the place Phanuel, which signifies, *the face of God.* Now when he felt pain, by this struggling, upon his broad sinew, he abstained from eating that sinew himself afterward; and for his sake it is still not eaten by us.

3. When Jacob understood that his brother was near, he ordered his wives to go before, each by herself, with the handmaids, that they might see the actions of the men as they were fighting, if Esau were so disposed. He then went up to his brother Esau, and bowed down to him, who had no evil design upon him, but saluted him; and asked him about the company of the children and of the women; and desired, when he had understood all he wanted to know about them, that he would go along with him to their father; but Jacob pretending that

---

37. Perhaps this may be the proper meaning of the word Israel, by the present and the old Jerusalem analogy of the Hebrew tongue. In the mean time, it is certain that the Hellenists of the first century, in Egypt and elsewhere, interpreted Israel to be a man seeing God, as is evident from the argument fore-cited.

the cattle were weary, Esau returned to Seir, for there was his place of habitation, he having named the place Roughness, from his own hairy roughness.

21 Concerning the Violation of Dina's Chastity

1. HEREUPON Jacob came to the place, till this day called Tents (Succoth); from whence he went to Shechem, which is a city of the Canaanites. Now as the Shechemites were keeping a festival Dina, who was the only daughter of Jacob, went into the city to see the finery of the women of that country. But when Shechem, the son of Hamor the king, saw her, he defiled her by violence; and being greatly in love with her, desired of his father that he would procure the damsel to him for a wife. To which desire he condescended, and came to Jacob, desiring him to give leave that his son Shechem might, according to law, marry Dina. But Jacob, not knowing how to deny the desire of one of such great dignity, and yet not thinking it lawful to marry his daughter to a stranger, entreated him to give him leave to have a consultation about what he desired him to do. So the king went away, in hopes that Jacob would grant him this marriage. But Jacob informed his sons of the defilement of their sister, and of the address of Hamor; and desired them to give their advice what they should do. Upon fills, the greatest part said nothing, not knowing what advice to give. But Simeon and Levi, the brethren of the damsel by the same mother, agreed between themselves upon the action following: It being now the time of a festival, when the Shechemites were employed in ease and feasting, they fell upon the watch when they were asleep, and, coming into the city, slew all the males[38] as also the king, and his son, with them; but spared the women. And when they had done this without their father's consent, they brought away their sister.

2. Now while Jacob was astonished at the greatness of this act, and was severely blaming his sons for it, God stood by him, and bid him be of good courage; but to purify his tents, and to offer those sacrifices

---

38. Of this slaughter of the Shechemites by Simeon and Levi, see Authent. Rec. Part I. p. 309, 418, 432–439. But why Josephus has omitted the circumcision of these Shechemites, as the occasion of their death; and of Jacob's great grief, as in the Testament of Levi, sect. 5; I cannot tell.

which he had vowed to offer when he went first into Mesopotamia, and saw his vision. As he was therefore purifying his followers, he lighted upon the gods of Laban; (for he did not before know they were stolen by Rachel;) and he hid them in the earth, under an oak, in Shechem. And departing thence, he offered sacrifice at Bethel, the place where he saw his dream, when he went first into Mesopotamia.

3. And when he was gone thence, and was come over against Ephrata, he there buried Rachel, who died in child-bed: she was the only one of Jacob's kindred that had not the honor of burial at Hebron. And when he had mourned for her a great while, he called the son that was born of her Benjamin,[39] because of the sorrow the mother had with him. These are all the children of Jacob, twelve males and one female.—Of them eight were legitimate,—viz. six of Lea, and two of Rachel; and four were of the handmaids, two of each; all whose names have been set down already.

22   How Isaac Died, and Was Buried in Hebron

FROM thence Jacob came to Hebron, a city situate among the Canaanites; and there it was that Isaac lived: and so they lived together for a little while; for as to Rebeka, Jacob did not find her alive. Isaac also died not long after the coming of his son; and was buried by his sons, with his wife, in Hebron, where they had a monument belonging to them from their forefathers. Now Isaac was a man who was beloved of God, and was vouchsafed great instances of providence by God, after Abraham his father, and lived to be exceeding old; for when he had lived virtuously one hundred and eighty-five years, he then died.

---

39. Since Benoni signifies the son of my sorrow, and Benjamin the son of days, or one born in the father's old age, Genesis 44:20, I suspect Josephus's present copies to be here imperfect, and suppose that, in correspondence to other copies, he wrote that Rachel called her son's name Benoni, but his father called him Benjamin, Genesis 35:18. As for Benjamin, as commonly explained, the son of the right hand, it makes no sense at all, and seems to be a gross modern error only. The Samaritan always writes this name truly Benjamin, which probably is here of the same signification, only with the Chaldee termination in, instead of im in the Hebrew; as we pronounce cherubin or cherubim indifferently. Accordingly, both the Testament of Benjamin, sect. 2, p. 401, and Philo de Nominum Mutatione, p. 1059, write the name Benjamin, but explain it not the son of the right hand, but the son of days.

Book 2

Containing the Interval of Two Hundred and Twenty Years, from the Death of Isaac to the Exodus Out of Egypt

1 How Esau and Jacob, Isaac's Sons Divided Their Habitation; and Esau Possessed Idumea and Jacob Canaan

1. AFTER the death of Isaac, his sons divided their habitations respectively; nor did they retain what they had before; but Esau departed from the city of Hebron, and left it to his brother, and dwelt in Seir, and ruled over Idumea. He called the country by that name from himself, for he was named Adom; which appellation he got on the following occasion—One day returning from the toil of hunting very hungry, (it was when he was a child in age,) he lighted on his brother when he was getting ready lentile-pottage for his dinner, which was of a very red color; on which account he the more earnestly longed for it, and desired him to give him some of it to eat: but he made advantage of his brother's hunger, and forced him to resign up to him his birthright; and he, being pinched with famine, resigned it up to him, under an oath. Whence it came, that, on account of the redness of this pottage, he was, in way of jest, by his contemporaries, called *Adom*, for the Hebrews call what is red *Adom*; and this was the name given to the country; but the Greeks gave it a more agreeable pronunciation, and named it *Idumea*.

2. He became the father of five sons; of whom Jaus, and Jalomus, and Coreus, were by one wife, whose name was Alibama; but of the rest, Aliphaz was born to him by Ada, and Raguel by Basemmath: and

these were the sons of Esau. Aliphaz had five legitimate sons; Theman, Omer, Saphus, Gotham, and Kanaz; for Amalek was not legitimate, but by a concubine, whose name was Thamna. These dwelt in that part of Idumea which is called Gebalitis, and that denominated from Amalek, Amalekitis; for Idumea was a large country, and did then preserve the name of the whole, while in its several parts it kept the names of its peculiar inhabitants.

2 How Joseph, the Youngest of Jacob's Sons, Was Envied by His Brethren, When Certain Dreams Had Foreshown His Future Happiness

1. IT happened that Jacob came to so great happiness as rarely any other person had arrived at. He was richer than the rest of the inhabitants of that country; and was at once envied and admired for such virtuous sons, for they were deficient in nothing, but were of great souls, both for laboring with their hands and enduring of toil; and shrewd also in understanding. And God exercised such a providence over him, and such a care of his happiness, as to bring him the greatest blessings, even out of what appeared to be the most sorrowful condition; and to make him the cause of our forefathers' departure out of Egypt, him and his posterity. The occasion was this—When Jacob had his son Joseph born to him by Rachel, his father loved him above the rest of his sons, both because of the beauty of his body, and the virtues of his mind, for he excelled the rest in prudence. This affection of his father excited the envy and the hatred of his brethren; as did also his dreams which he saw, and related to his father, and to them, which foretold his future happiness, it being usual with mankind to envy their very nearest relations such their prosperity. Now the visions which Joseph saw in his sleep were these—

2. When they were in the middle of harvest, and Joseph was sent by his father, with his brethren, to gather the fruits of the earth, he saw a vision in a dream, but greatly exceeding the customary appearances that come when we are asleep; which, when he was got up, he told his brethren, that they might judge what it portended. He said, he saw the last night, that his wheat-sheaf stood still in the place where he set it, but that their sheaves ran to bow down to it, as servants bow down to

their masters. But as soon as they perceived the vision foretold that he should obtain power and great wealth, and that his power should be in opposition to them, they gave no interpretation of it to Joseph, as if the dream were not by them undestood: but they prayed that no part of what they suspected to be its meaning might come to pass; and they bare a still greater hatred to him on that account.

3. But God, in opposition to their envy, sent a second vision to Joseph, which was much more wonderful than the former; for it seemed to him that the sun took with him the moon, and the rest of the stars, and came down to the earth, and bowed down to him. He told the vision to his father, and that, as suspecting nothing of ill-will from his brethren, when they were there also, and desired him to interpret what it should signify. Now Jacob was pleased with the dream: for, considering the prediction in his mind, and shrewdly and wisely guessing at its meaning, he rejoiced at the great things thereby signified, because it declared the future happiness of his son; and that, by the blessing of God, the time would come when he should be honored, and thought worthy of worship by his parents and brethren, as guessing that the moon and sun were like his mother and father; the former, as she that gave increase and nourishment to all things; and the latter, he that gave form and other powers to them; and that the stars were like his brethren, since they were eleven in number, as were the stars that receive their power from the sun and moon.

4. And thus did Jacob make a judgment of this vision, and that a shrewd one also. But these interpretations caused very great grief to Joseph's brethren; and they were affected to him hereupon as if he were a certain stranger, that was to those good things which were signified by the dreams and not as one that was a brother, with whom it was probable they should be joint-partakers; and as they had been partners in the same parentage, so should they be of the same happiness. They also resolved to kill the lad; and having fully ratified that intention of theirs, as soon as their collection of the fruits was over, they went to Shechem, which is a country good for feeding of cattle, and for pasturage; there they fed their flocks, without acquainting their father with their removal thither; whereupon he had melancholy suspicions about them, as being ignorant of his sons' condition, and receiving no messenger from the flocks that could inform him of the true state they were in; so, because he was in great fear about them, he

sent Joseph to the flocks, to learn the circumstances his brethren were in, and to bring him word how they did.

3 How Joseph Was Thus Sold by His Brethren into Egypt, by Reason of Their Hatred to Him; and How He There Grew Famous and Illustrious and Had His Brethren under His Power

1. NOW these brethren rejoiced as soon as they saw their brother coming to them, not indeed as at the presence of a near relation, or as at the presence of one sent by their father, but as at the presence of an enemy, and one that by Divine Providence was delivered into their hands; and they already resolved to kill him, and not let slip the opportunity that lay before them. But when Reubel, the eldest of them, saw them thus disposed, and that they had agreed together to execute their purpose, he tried to restrain them, showing them the heinous enterprise they were going about, and the horrid nature of it; that this action would appear wicked in the sight of God, and impious before men, even though they should kill one not related to them; but much more flagitious and detestable to appear to have slain their own brother, by which act the father must be treated unjustly in the son's slaughter, and the mother[1] also be in perplexity while she laments that her son is taken away from her, and this not in a natural way neither. So he entreated them to have a regard to their own consciences, and wisely to consider what mischief would betide them upon the death of so good a child, and their youngest brother; that they would also fear God, who was already both a spectator and a witness of the designs they had against their brother; that he would love them if they abstained from this act, and yielded to repentance and amendment; but in case they proceeded to do the fact, all sorts of punishments would overtake them from God for this murder of their brother, since they polluted his providence, which was every where present, and which did not overlook what was done, either in deserts or in cities;

---

1. We may here observe, that in correspondence to Joseph's second dream, which implied that his mother, who was then alive, as well as his father, should come and bow down to him, Josephus represents her here as still alive after she was dead, for the decorum of the dream that foretold it, as the interpretation of the dream does also in all our copies, Genesis 37:10.

for wheresoever a man is, there ought he to suppose that God is also. He told them further, that their consciences would be their enemies, if they attempted to go through so wicked an enterprise, which they can never avoid, whether it be a good conscience; or whether it be such a one as they will have within them when once they have killed their brother. He also added this besides to what he had before said, that it was not a righteous thing to kill a brother, though he had injured them; that it is a good thing to forget the actions of such near friends, even in things wherein they might seem to have offended; but that they were going to kill Joseph, who had been guilty of nothing that was ill towards them, in whose case the infirmity of his small age should rather procure him mercy, and move them to unite together in the care of his preservation. That the cause of killing him made the act itself much worse, while they determined to take him off out of envy at his future prosperity, an equal share of which they would naturally partake while he enjoyed it, since they were to him not strangers, but the nearest relations, for they might reckon upon what God bestowed upon Joseph as their own; and that it was fit for them to believe, that the anger of God would for this cause be more severe upon them, if they slew him who was judged by God to be worthy of that prosperity which was to be hoped for; and while, by murdering him, they made it impossible for God to bestow it upon him.

2. Reubel said these and many other things, and used entreaties to them, and thereby endeavored to divert them from the murder of their brother. But when he saw that his discourse had not mollified them at all, and that they made haste to do the fact, he advised them to alleviate the wickedness they were going about, in the manner of taking Joseph off; for as he had exhorted them first, when they were going to revenge themselves, to be dissuaded from doing it; so, since the sentence for killing their brother had prevailed, he said that they would not, however, be so grossly guilty, if they would be persuaded to follow his present advice, which would include what they were so eager about, but was not so very bad, but, in the distress they were in, of a lighter nature. He begged of them, therefore, not to kill their brother with their own hands, but to cast him into the pit that was hard by, and so to let him die; by which they would gain so much, that they would not defile their own hands with his blood. To this the young men readily agreed; so Reubel took the lad and tied him to a cord, and

let him down gently into the pit, for it had no water at all in it; who, when he had done this, went his way to seek for such pasturage as was fit for feeding his flocks.

3. But Judas, being one of Jacob's sons also, seeing some Arabians, of the posterity of Ismael, carrying spices and Syrian wares out of the land of Gilead to the Egyptians, after Rubel was gone, advised his brethren to draw Joseph out of the pit, and sell him to the Arabians; for if he should die among strangers a great way off, they should be freed from this barbarous action. This, therefore, was resolved on; so they drew Joseph up out of the pit, and sold him to the merchants for twenty pounds[2] He was now seventeen years old. But Reubel, coming in the night-time to the pit, resolved to save Joseph, without the privity of his brethren; and when, upon his calling to him, he made no answer, he was afraid that they had destroyed him after he was gone; of which he complained to his brethren; but when they had told him what they had done, Reubel left off his mourning.

4. When Joseph's brethren had done thus to him, they considered what they should do to escape the suspicions of their father. Now they had taken away from Joseph the coat which he had on when he came to them at the time they let him down into the pit; so they thought proper to tear that coat to pieces, and to dip it into goats' blood, and then to carry it and show it to their father, that he might believe he was destroyed by wild beasts. And when they had so done, they came to the old man, but this not till what had happened to his son had already come to his knowledge. Then they said that they had not seen Joseph, nor knew what mishap had befallen him; but that they had found his coat bloody and torn to pieces, whence they had a suspicion that he had fallen among wild beasts, and so perished, if that was the coat he had on when he came from home. Now Jacob had before some better hopes that his son was only made a captive; but now he laid aside that notion, and supposed that this coat was an evident argument that he was dead, for he well remembered that this was the coat he had on when he sent him to his brethren; so he hereafter lamented the lad as now dead, and as if he had been the father of no more than one,

---

2. The Septuagint have twenty pieces of gold; the Testament of Gad thirty; the Hebrew and Samaritan twenty of silver; and the vulgar Latin thirty. What was the true number and true sum cannot therefore now be known.

without taking any comfort in the rest; and so he was also affected with his misfortune before he met with Joseph's brethren, when he also conjectured that Joseph was destroyed by wild beasts. He sat down also clothed in sackcloth and in heavy affliction, insomuch that he found no ease when his sons comforted him, neither did his pains remit by length of time.

4   Concerning the Signal Chastity of Joseph

1. NOW Potiphar, an Egyptian, who was chief cook to king Pharaoh, bought Joseph of the merchants, who sold him to him. He had him in the greatest honor, and taught him the learning that became a free man, and gave him leave to make use of a diet better than was allotted to slaves. He intrusted also the care of his house to him. So he enjoyed these advantages, yet did not he leave that virtue which he had before, upon such a change of his condition; but he demonstrated that wisdom was able to govern the uneasy passions of life, in such as have it in reality, and do not only put it on for a show, under a present state of prosperity.

2. For when his master's wife was fallen in love with him, both on account of his beauty of body, and his dexterous management of affairs; and supposed, that if she should make it known to him, she could easily persuade him to come and lie with her, and that he would look upon it as a piece of happy fortune that his mistress should entreat him, as regarding that state of slavery he was in, and not his moral character, which continued after his condition was changed. So she made known her naughty inclinations, and spake to him about lying with her. However, he rejected her entreaties, not thinking it agreeable to religion to yield so far to her, as to do what would tend to the affront and injury of him that purchased him, and had vouchsafed him so great honors. He, on the contrary, exhorted her to govern that passion; and laid before her the impossibility of her obtaining her desires, which he thought might be conquered, if she had no hope of succeeding; and he said, that as to himself, he would endure any thing whatever before he would be persuaded to it; for although it was fit for a slave, as he was, to do nothing contrary to his mistress, he might well be excused in a case where the contradiction was to such sort of commands only. But this opposition of Joseph, when she did

not expect it, made her still more violent in her love to him; and as she was sorely beset with this naughty passion, so she resolved to compass her design by a second attempt.

3. When, therefore, there was a public festival coming on, in which it was the custom for women to come to the public solemnity; she pretended to her husband that she was sick, as contriving an opportunity for solitude and leisure, that she might entreat Joseph again. Which opportunity being obtained, she used more kind words to him than before; and said that it had been good for him to have yielded to her first solicitation, and to have given her no repulse, both because of the reverence he ought to bear to her dignity who solicited him, and because of the vehemence of her passion, by which she was forced though she were his mistress to condescend beneath her dignity; but that he may now, by taking more prudent advice, wipe off the imputation of his former folly; for whether it were that he expected the repetition of her solicitations she had now made, and that with greater earnestness than before, for that she had pretended sickness on this very account, and had preferred his conversation before the festival and its solemnity; or whether he opposed her former discourses, as not believing she could be in earnest; she now gave him sufficient security, by thus repeating her application, that she meant not in the least by fraud to impose upon him; and assured him, that if he complied with her affections, he might expect the enjoyment of the advantages he already had; and if he were submissive to her, he should have still greater advantages; but that he must look for revenge and hatred from her, in case he rejected her desires, and preferred the reputation of chastity before his mistress; for that he would gain nothing by such procedure, because she would then become his accuser, and would falsely pretend to her husband, that he had attempted her chastity; and that Potiphar would hearken to her words rather than to his, let his be ever so agreeable to the truth.

4. When the woman had said thus, and even with tears in her eyes, neither did pity dissuade Joseph from his chastity, nor did fear compel him to a compliance with her; but he opposed her solicitations, and did not yield to her threatenings, and was afraid to do an ill thing, and chose to undergo the sharpest punishment rather than to enjoy his present advantages, by doing what his own conscience knew would justly deserve that he should die for it. He also put her in mind that

she was a married woman, and that she ought to cohabit with her husband only; and desired her to suffer these considerations to have more weight with her than the short pleasure of lustful dalliance, which would bring her to repentance afterwards, would cause trouble to her, and yet would not amend what had been done amiss. He also suggested to her the fear she would be in lest they should be caught; and that the advantage of concealment was uncertain, and that only while the wickedness was not known [would there be any quiet for them]; but that she might have the enjoyment of her husband's company without any danger. And he told her, that in the company of her husband she might have great boldness from a good conscience, both before God and before men. Nay, that she would act better like his mistress, and make use of her authority over him better while she persisted in her chastity, than when they were both ashamed for what wickedness they had been guilty of; and that it is much better to a life, well and known to have been so, than upon the hopes of the concealment of evil practices.

5. Joseph, by saying this, and more, tried to restrain the violent passion of the woman, and to reduce her affections within the rules of reason; but she grew more ungovernable and earnest in the matter; and since she despaired of persuading him, she laid her hands upon him, and had a mind to force him. But as soon as Joseph had got away from her anger, leaving also his garment with her, for he left that to her, and leaped out of her chamber, she was greatly afraid lest he should discover her lewdness to her husband, and greatly troubled at the affront he had offered her; so she resolved to be beforehand with him, and to accuse Joseph falsely to Potiphar, and by that means to revenge herself on him for his pride and contempt of her; and she thought it a wise thing in itself, and also becoming a woman, thus to prevent his accusation. Accordingly she sat sorrowful and in confusion, framing herself so hypocritically and angrily, that the sorrow, which was really for her being disappointed of her lust, might appear to be for the attempt upon her chastity; so that when her husband came home, and was disturbed at the sight of her and inquired what was the cause of the disorder she was in, she began to accuse Joseph: and, "O husband," said she, "mayst thou not live a day longer if thou dost not punish the wicked slave who has desired to defile thy bed; who has neither minded who he was when he came to our house, so as to behave

himself with modesty; nor has he been mindful of what favors he had received from thy bounty (as he must be an ungrateful man indeed, unless he, in every respect, carry himself in a manner agreeable to us): this man, I say, laid a private design to abuse thy wife, and this at the time of a festival, observing when thou wouldst be absent. So that it now is clear that his modesty, as it appeared to be formerly, was only because of the restraint he was in out of fear of thee, but that he was not really of a good disposition. This has been occasioned by his being advanced to honor beyond what he deserved, and what he hoped for; insomuch that he concluded, that he who was deemed fit to be trusted with thy estate and the government of thy family, and was preferred above thy eldest servants, might be allowed to touch thy wife also." Thus when she had ended her discourse, she showed him his garment, as if he then left it with her when he attempted to force her. But Potiphar not being able to disbelieve what his wife's tears showed, and what his wife said, and what he saw himself, and being seduced by his love to his wife, did not set himself about the examination of the truth; but taking it for granted that his wife was a modest woman, and condemning Joseph as a wicked man, he threw him into the malefactors' prison; and had a still higher opinion of his wife, and bare her witness that she was a woman of a becoming modesty and chastity.

5   *What Things Befell Joseph in Prison*

1. NOW Joseph, commending all his affairs to God, did not betake himself to make his defense, nor to give an account of the exact circumstances of the fact, but silently underwent the bonds and the distress he was in, firmly believing that God, who knew the cause of his affliction, and the truth of the fact, would be more powerful than those that inflicted the punishments upon him—a proof of whose providence he quickly received; for the keeper of the prison taking notice of his care and fidelity in the affairs he had set him about, and the dignity of his countenance, relaxed his bonds, and thereby made his heavy calamity lighter, and more supportable to him. He also permitted him to make use of a diet better than that of the rest of the prisoners. Now, as his fellow prisoners, when their hard labors were over, fell to discoursing one among another, as is usual in such

as are equal sufferers, and to inquire one of another what were the occasions of their being condemned to a prison: among them the king's cupbearer, and one that had been respected by him, was put in bonds, upon the king's anger at him. This man was under the same bonds with Joseph, and grew more familiar with him; and upon his observing that Joseph had a better understanding than the rest had, he told him of a dream he had, and desired he would interpret its meaning, complaining that, besides the afflictions he underwent from the king, God did also add to him trouble from his dreams.

2. He therefore said, that in his sleep he saw three clusters of grapes hanging upon three branches of a vine, large already, and ripe for gathering; and that he squeezed them into a cup which the king held in his hand; and when he had strained the wine, he gave it to the king to drink, and that he received it from him with a pleasant countenance. This, he said, was what he saw; and he desired Joseph, that if he had any portion of understanding in such matters, he would tell him what this vision foretold. Who bid him be of good cheer, and expect to be loosed from his bonds in three days' time, because the king desired his service, and was about to restore him to it again; for he let him know that God bestows the fruit of the vine upon men for good; which wine is poured out to him, and is the pledge of fidelity and mutual confidence among men; and puts an end to their quarrels, takes away passion and grief out of the minds of them that use it, and makes them cheerful. "Thou sayest that thou didst squeeze this wine from three clusters of grapes with thine hands, and that the king received it: know, therefore, that this vision is for thy good, and foretells a release from thy present distress within the same number of days as the branches had whence thou gatheredst thy grapes in thy sleep. However, remember what prosperity I have foretold thee when thou hast found it true by experience; and when thou art in authority, do not overlook us in this prison, wherein thou wilt leave us when thou art gone to the place we have foretold; for we are not in prison for any crime; but for the sake of our virtue and sobriety are we condemned to suffer the penalty of malefactors, and because we are not willing to injure him that has thus distressed us, though it were for our own pleasure." The cupbearer, therefore, as was natural to do, rejoiced to hear such an interpretation of his dream, and waited the completion of what had been thus shown him beforehand.

3. But another servant there was of the king, who had been chief baker, and was now bound in prison with the cupbearer; he also was in good hope, upon Joseph's interpretation of the other's vision, for he had seen a dream also; so he desired that Joseph would tell him what the visions he had seen the night before might mean. They were these that follow:—"Methought," says he, "I carried three baskets upon my head; two were full of loaves, and the third full of sweetmeats and other eatables, such as are prepared for kings; but that the fowls came flying, and eat them all up, and had no regard to my attempt to drive them away." And he expected a prediction like to that of the cupbearer. But Joseph, considering and reasoning about the dream, said to him, that he would willingly be an interpreter of good events to him, and not of such as his dream denounced to him; but he told him that he had only three days in all to live, for that the [three] baskets signify, that on the third day he should be crucified, and devoured by fowls, while he was not able to help himself. Now both these dreams had the same several events that Joseph foretold they should have, and this to both the parties; for on the third day before mentioned, when the king solemnized his birth-day, he crucified the chief baker, but set the butler free from his bonds, and restored him to his former ministration.

4. But God freed Joseph from his confinement, after he had endured his bonds two years, and had received no assistance from the cup-bearer, who did not remember what he had said to him formerly; and God contrived this method of deliverance for him. Pharaoh the king had seen in his sleep the same evening two visions; and after them had the interpretations of them both given him. He had forgotten the latter, but retained the dreams themselves. Being therefore troubled at what he had seen, for it seemed to him to be all of a melancholy nature, the next day he called together the wisest men among the Egyptians, desiring to learn from them the interpretation of his dreams. But when they hesitated about them, the king was so much the more disturbed. And now it was that the memory of Joseph, and his skill in dreams, came into the mind of the king's cupbearer, when he saw the confusion that Pharaoh was in; so he came and mentioned Joseph to him, as also the vision he had seen in prison, and how the event proved as he had said; as also that the chief baker was crucified on the very same day; and that this also happened to him according to the interpretation of Joseph. That Joseph himself was laid in bonds

by Potiphar, who was his head cook, as a slave; but, he said, he was one of the noblest of the stock of the Hebrews; and said further, his father lived in great splendor. "If, therefore, thou wilt send for him, and not despise him on the score of his misfortunes, thou wilt learn what thy dreams signify." So the king commanded that they should bring Joseph into his presence; and those who received the command came and brought him with them, having taken care of his habit, that it might be decent, as the king had enjoined them to do.

5. But the king took him by the hand; and, "O young man," says he, "for my servant bears witness that thou art at present the best and most skillful person I can consult with; vouchsafe me the same favors which thou bestowedst on this servant of mine, and tell me what events they are which the visions of my dreams foreshow; and I desire thee to suppress nothing out of fear, nor to flatter me with lying words, or with what may please me, although the truth should be of a melancholy nature. For it seemed to me that, as I walked by the river, I saw kine fat and very large, seven in number, going from the river to the marshes; and other kine of the same number like them, met them out of the marshes, exceeding lean and ill-favored, which ate up the fat and the large kine, and yet were no better than before, and not less miserably pinched with famine. After I had seen this vision, I awaked out of my sleep; and being in disorder, and considering with myself what this appearance should be, I fell asleep again, and saw another dream, much more wonderful than the foregoing, which still did more affright and disturb me:—I saw seven ears of corn growing out of one root, having their heads borne down by the weight of the grains, and bending down with the fruit, which was now ripe and fit for reaping; and near these I saw seven other ears of corn, meager and weak, for want of rain, which fell to eating and consuming those that were fit for reaping, and put me into great astonishment."

6. To which Joseph replied:—"This dream," said he, "O king, although seen under two forms, signifies one and the same event of things; for when thou sawest the fat kine, which is an animal made for the plough and for labor, devoured by the worser kine, and the ears of corn eaten up by the smaller ears, they foretell a famine, and want of the fruits of the earth for the same number of years, and equal with those when Egypt was in a happy state; and this so far, that the plenty of these years will be spent in the same number of

years of scarcity, and that scarcity of necessary provisions will be very difficult to be corrected; as a sign whereof, the ill-favored kine, when they had devoured the better sort, could not be satisfied. But still God foreshows what is to come upon men, not to grieve them, but that, when they know it beforehand, they may by prudence make the actual experience of what is foretold the more tolerable. If thou, therefore, carefully dispose of the plentiful crops which will come in the former years, thou wilt procure that the future calamity will not be felt by the Egyptians."

7. Hereupon the king wondered at the discretion and wisdom of Joseph; and asked him by what means he might so dispense the foregoing plentiful crops in the happy years, as to make the miserable crops more tolerable. Joseph then added this his advice: To spare the good crops, and not permit the Egyptians to spend them luxuriously, but to reserve what they would have spent in luxury beyond their necessity against the time of want. He also exhorted him to take the corn of the husbandmen, and give them only so much as will be sufficient for their food. Accordingly Pharaoh being surprised at Joseph, not only for his interpretation of the dream, but for the counsel he had given him, intrusted him with dispensing the corn; with power to do what he thought would be for the benefit of the people of Egypt, and for the benefit of the king, as believing that he who first discovered this method of acting, would prove the best overseer of it. But Joseph having this power given him by the king, with leave to make use of his seal, and to wear purple, drove in his chariot through all the land of Egypt, and took the corn of the husbandmen,[3] allotting as much to every one as would be sufficient for seed, and for food, but without discovering to any one the reason why he did so.

6   How Joseph When He Was Become Famous in Egypt, Had His Brethren in Subjection

1. JOSEPH was now grown up to thirty years of age, and enjoyed great honors from the king, who called him Psothom Phanech, out of regard to his prodigious degree of wisdom; for that name denotes

---

3. That is, bought it for Pharaoh at a very low price.

the revealer of secrets. He also married a wife of very high quality; for he married the daughter of Petephres,[4] one of the priests of Heliopolis; she was a virgin, and her name was Asenath. By her he had children before the scarcity came on; Manasseh, the elder, which signifies *forgetful*, because his present happiness made him forget his former misfortunes; and Ephraim, the younger, which signifies *restored*, because he was restored to the freedom of his forefathers. Now after Egypt had happily passed over seven years, according to Joseph's interpretation of the dreams, the famine came upon them in the eighth year; and because this misfortune fell upon them when they had no sense of it beforehand,[5] they were all sorely afflicted by it, and came running to the king's gates; and he called upon Joseph, who sold the corn to them, being become confessedly a savior to the whole multitude of the Egyptians. Nor did he open this market of corn for the people of that country only, but strangers had liberty to buy also; Joseph being willing that all men, who are naturally akin to one another, should have assistance from those that lived in happiness.

2. Now Jacob also, when he understood that foreigners might come, sent all his sons into Egypt to buy corn, for the land of Canaan was grievously afflicted with the famine; and this great misery touched the whole continent. He only retained Benjamin, who was born to him by Rachel, and was of the same mother with Joseph. These sons of Jacob then came into Egypt, and applied themselves to Joseph, wanting to buy corn; for nothing of this kind was done without his approbation, since even then only was the honor that was paid the king himself advantageous to the persons that paid it, when they took care to honor Joseph also. Now when he well knew his brethren, they thought

4. This Potiphar, or, as Josephus, Petephres, who was now a priest of On, or Heliopolis, is the same name in Josephus, and perhaps in Moses also, with him who is before called head cook or captain of the guard, and to whom Joseph was sold. See Genesis 37:36; 39:1, with 41:50. They are also affirmed to be one and the same person in the Testament of Joseph, sect. 18, for he is there said to have married the daughter of his master and mistress. Nor is this a notion peculiar to that Testament, but, as Dr. Bernard confesses, note on Antiq. B. II. ch. 4. sect. 1, common to Josephus, to the Septuagint interpreters, and to other learned Jews of old time.

5. This entire ignorance of the Egyptians of these years of famine before they came, told us before, as well as here, ch. 5. sect. 7, by Josephus, seems to me almost incredible. It is in no other copy that I know of.

nothing of him; for he was but a youth when he left them, and was now come to an age so much greater, that the lineaments of his face were changed, and he was not known by them: besides this, the greatness of the dignity wherein he appeared, suffered them not so much as to suspect it was he. He now made trial what sentiments they had about affairs of the greatest consequence; for he refused to sell them corn, and said they were come as spies of the king's affairs; and that they came from several countries, and joined themselves together, and pretended that they were of kin, it not being possible that a private man should breed up so many sons, and those of so great beauty of countenance as they were, such an education of so many children being not easily obtained by kings themselves. Now this he did in order to discover what concerned his father, and what happened to him after his own departure from him, and as desiring to know what was become of Benjamin his brother; for he was afraid that they had ventured on the like wicked enterprise against him that they had done to himself, and had taken him off also.

3. Now these brethren of his were under distraction and terror, and thought that very great danger hung over them; yet not at all reflecting upon their brother Joseph, and standing firm under the accusations laid against them, they made their defense by Reubel, the eldest of them, who now became their spokesman: "We come not hither," said he, "with any unjust design, nor in order to bring any harm to the king's affairs; we only want to be preserved, as supposing your humanity might be a refuge for us from the miseries which our country labors under, we having heard that you proposed to sell corn, not only to your own countrymen, but to strangers also, and that you determined to allow that corn, in order to preserve all that want it; but that we are brethren, and of the same common blood, the peculiar lineaments of our faces, and those not so much different from one another, plainly show. Our father's name is Jacob, an Hebrew man, who had twelve of us for his sons by four wives; which twelve of us, while we were all alive, were a happy family; but when one of our brethren, whose name was Joseph, died, our affairs changed for the worse, for our father could not forbear to make a long lamentation for him; and we are in affliction, both by the calamity of the death of our brother, and the miserable state of our aged father. We are now, therefore, come to buy corn, having intrusted the care of our father,

and the provision for our family, to Benjamin, our youngest brother; and if thou sendest to our house, thou mayst learn whether we are guilty of the least falsehood in what we say."

4. And thus did Reubel endeavor to persuade Joseph to have a better opinion of them. But when he had learned from them that Jacob was alive, and that his brother was not destroyed by them, he for the present put them in prison, as intending to examine more into their affairs when he should be at leisure. But on the third day he brought them out, and said to them, "Since you constantly affirm that you are not come to do any harm to the king's affairs; that you are brethren, and the sons of the father whom you named; you will satisfy me of the truth of what you say, if you leave one of your company with me, who shall suffer no injury here; and if, when ye have carried corn to your father, you will come to me again, and bring your brother, whom you say you left there, along with you, for this shall be by me esteemed an assurance of the truth of what you have told me." Hereupon they were in greater grief than before; they wept, and perpetually deplored one among another the calamity of Joseph; and said, "They were fallen into this misery as a punishment inflicted by God for what evil contrivances they had against him." And Reubel was large in his reproaches of them for their too late repentance, whence no profit arose to Joseph; and earnestly exhorted them to bear with patience whatever they suffered, since it was done by God in way of punishment, on his account. Thus they spake to one another, not imagining that Joseph understood their language. A general sadness also seized on them at Reubel's words, and a repentance for what they had done; and they condemned the wickedness they had perpetrated, for which they judged they were justly punished by God. Now when Joseph saw that they were in this distress, he was so affected at it that he fell into tears, and not being willing that they should take notice of him, he retired; and after a while came to them again, and taking Symeon[6] in order to his being a pledge for his brethren's return, he bid them take the corn they had bought, and go their way. He also

---

6. The reason why Symeon might be selected out of the rest for Joseph's prisoner, is plain in the Testament of Symeon, viz. that he was one of the bitterest of all Joseph's brethren against him, sect. 2; which appears also in part by the Testament of Zabulon, sect. 3.

commanded his steward privily to put the money which they had brought with them for the purchase of corn into their sacks, and to dismiss them therewith; who did what he was commanded to do.

5. Now when Jacob's sons were come into the land of Canaan, they told their father what had happened to them in Egypt, and that they were taken to have come thither as spies upon the king; and how they said they were brethren, and had left their eleventh brother with their father, but were not believed; and how they had left Symeon with the governor, until Benjamin should go thither, and be a testimonial of the truth of what they had said: and they begged of their father to fear nothing, but to send the lad along with them. But Jacob was not pleased with any thing his sons had done; and he took the detention of Symeon heinously, and thence thought it a foolish thing to give up Benjamin also. Neither did he yield to Reubel's persuasion, though he begged it of him, and gave leave that the grandfather might, in way of requital, kill his own sons, in case any harm came to Benjamin in the journey. So they were distressed, and knew not what to do; nay, there was another accident that still disturbed them more,—the money that was found hidden in their sacks of corn. Yet when the corn they had brought failed them, and when the famine still afflicted them, and necessity forced them, Jacob did[7] [not] still resolve to send Benjamin with his brethren, although there was no returning into Egypt unless they came with what they had promised. Now the misery growing every day worse, and his sons begging it of him, he had no other course to take in his present circumstances. And Judas, who was of a bold temper on other occasions, spake his mind very freely to him: "That it did not become him to be afraid on account of his son, nor to suspect the worst, as he did; for nothing could be done to his son but by the appointment of God, which must also for certain come to pass, though he were at home with him; that he ought not to condemn them to such manifest destruction; nor deprive them of that plenty of food they might have from Pharaoh, by his unreasonable fear about his son Benjamin, but ought to take care of the preservation of Symeon, lest, by attempting to hinder Benjamin's journey, Symeon should perish.

---

7. The coherence seems to me to show that the negative particle is here wanting, which I have supplied in brackets, and I wonder none have hitherto suspected that it ought to be supplied.

72

He exhorted him to trust God for him; and said he would either bring his son back to him safe, or, together with his, lose his own life." So that Jacob was at length persuaded, and delivered Benjamin to them, with the price of the corn doubled; he also sent presents to Joseph of the fruits of the land of Canaan, balsam and rosin, as also turpentine and honey.[8] Now their father shed many tears at the departure of his sons, as well as themselves. His concern was, that he might receive them back again safe after their journey; and their concern was, that they might find their father well, and no way afflicted with grief for them. And this lamentation lasted a whole day; so that the old man was at last tired with grief, and staid behind; but they went on their way for Egypt, endeavoring to mitigate their grief for their present misfortunes, with the hopes of better success hereafter.

6. As soon as they came into Egypt, they were brought down to Joseph: but here no small fear disturbed them, lest they should be accused about the price of the corn, as if they had cheated Joseph. They then made a long apology to Joseph's steward; and told him, that when they came home they found the money in their sacks, and that they had now brought it along with them. He said he did not know what they meant: so they were delivered from that fear. And when he had loosed Symeon, and put him into a handsome habit, he suffered him to be with his brethren; at which time Joseph came from his attendance on the king. So they offered him their presents; and upon his putting the question to them about their father, they answered that they found him well. He also, upon his discovery that Benjamin was alive, asked whether this was their younger brother; for he had seen him. Whereupon they said he was: he replied, that the God over all was his protector. But when his affection to him made him shed tears, he retired, desiring he might not be seen in that plight by his brethren. Then Joseph took them to supper, and they were set down in the same order as they used to sit at their father's table. And although Joseph treated them all kindly, yet did he send a mess to Benjamin that was double to what the rest of the guests had for their shares.

---

8. Of the precious balsam of Judea, and the turpentine, see the note on Antiq. B. VIII. ch. 6. sect. 6.

7. Now when after supper they had composed themselves to sleep, Joseph commanded his steward both to give them their measures of corn, and to hide its price again in their sacks; and that withal they should put into Benjamin's sack the golden cup, out of which he loved himself to drink.—which things he did, in order to make trial of his brethren, whether they would stand by Benjamin when he should be accused of having stolen the cup, and should appear to be in danger; or whether they would leave him, and, depending on their own innocency, go to their father without him. When the servant had done as he was bidden, the sons of Jacob, knowing nothing of all this, went their way, and took Symeon along with them, and had a double cause of joy, both because they had received him again, and because they took back Benjamin to their father, as they had promised. But presently a troop of horsemen encompassed them, and brought with them Joseph's servant, who had put the cup into Benjamin's sack. Upon which unexpected attack of the horsemen they were much disturbed, and asked what the reason was that they came thus upon men, who a little before had been by their lord thought worthy of an honorable and hospitable reception? They replied, by calling them wicked wretches, who had forgot that very hospitable and kind treatment which Joseph had given them, and did not scruple to be injurious to him, and to carry off that cup out of which he had, in so friendly a manner, drank to them, and not regarding their friendship with Joseph, no more than the danger they should be in if they were taken, in comparison of the unjust gain. Hereupon he threatened that they should be punished; for though they had escaped the knowledge of him who was but a servant, yet had they not escaped the knowledge of God, nor had gone off with what they had stolen; and, after all, asked why we come upon them, as if they knew nothing of the matter: and he told them that they should immediately know it by their punishment. This, and more of the same nature, did the servant say, in way of reproach to them: but they being wholly ignorant of any thing here that concerned them, laughed at what he said, and wondered at the abusive language which the servant gave them, when he was so hardy as to accuse those who did not before so much as retain the price of their corn, which was found in their sacks, but brought it again, though nobody else knew of any such thing,—so far were they from offering any injury to Joseph voluntarily. But still, supposing that a search would be a

more sure justification of themselves than their own denial of the fact, they bid him search them, and that if any of them had been guilty of the theft, to punish them all; for being no way conscious to themselves of any crime, they spake with assurance, and, as they thought, without any danger to themselves also. The servants desired there might be a search made; but they said the punishment should extend to him alone who should be found guilty of the theft. So they made the search; and, having searched all the rest, they came last of all to Benjamin, as knowing it was Benjamin's sack in which they had hidden the cup, they having indeed searched the rest only for a show of accuracy: so the rest were out of fear for themselves, and were now only concerned about Benjamin, but still were well assured that he would also be found innocent; and they reproached those that came after them for their hindering them, while they might, in the mean while, have gotten a good way on their journey. But as soon as they had searched Benjamin's sack, they found the cup, and took it from him; and all was changed into mourning and lamentation. They rent their garments, and wept for the punishment which their brother was to undergo for his theft, and for the delusion they had put on their father, when they promised they would bring Benjamin safe to him. What added to their misery was, that this melancholy accident came unfortunately at a time when they thought they had been gotten off clear; but they confessed that this misfortune of their brother, as well as the grief of their father for him, was owing to themselves, since it was they that forced their father to send him with them, when he was averse to it.

8. The horsemen therefore took Benjamin and brought him to Joseph, his brethren also following him; who, when he saw him in custody, and them in the habit of mourners, said, "How came you, vile wretches as you are, to have such a strange notion of my kindness to you, and of God's providence, as impudently to do thus to your benefactor, who in such an hospitable manner had entertained you ?" Whereupon they gave up themselves to be punished, in order to save Benjamin; and called to mind what a wicked enterprise they had been guilty of against Joseph. They also pronounced him more happy than themselves, if he were dead, in being freed from the miseries of this life; and if he were alive, that he enjoyed the pleasure of seeing God's vengeance upon them. They said further; that they were the plague

of their father, since they should now add to his former affliction for Joseph, this other affliction for Benjamin. Reubel also was large in cutting them upon this occasion. But Joseph dismissed them; for he said they had been guilty of no offense, and that he would content himself with the lad's punishment; for he said it was not a fit thing to let him go free, for the sake of those who had not offended; nor was it a fit thing to punish them together with him who had been guilty of stealing. And when he promised to give them leave to go away in safety, the rest of them were under great consternation, and were able to say nothing on this sad occasion. But Judas, who had persuaded their father to send the lad from him, being otherwise also a very bold and active man, determined to hazard himself for the preservation of his brother. "It is true,"[9] said he, "O governor, that we have been very wicked with regard to thee, and on that account deserved punishment; even all of us may justly be punished, although the theft were not committed by all, but only by one of us, and he the youngest also; but yet there remains some hope for us, who otherwise must be under despair on his account, and this from thy goodness, which promises us a deliverance out of our present danger. And now I beg thou wilt not look at us, or at that great crime we have been guilty of, but at thy own excellent nature, and take advice of thine own virtue, instead of that wrath thou hast against us; which passion those that otherwise are of lower character indulge, as they do their strength, and that not only on great, but also on very trifling occasions. Overcome, sir, that passion, and be not subdued by it, nor suffer it to slay those that do not otherwise presume upon their own safety, but are desirous to accept of it from thee; for this is not the first time that thou wilt bestow it on us, but before, when we came to buy corn, thou affordedst us great plenty of food, and gavest us leave to carry so much home to our family as has preserved them from perishing by famine. Nor is there any difference between not overlooking men that were perishing for want of necessaries, and not punishing those that seem to be offenders,

---

9. This oration seems to me too large, and too unusual a digression, to have been composed by Judas on this occasion. It seems to me a speech or declamation composed formerly, in the person of Judas, and in the way of oratory, that lay by him. and which he thought fit to insert on this occasion. See two more such speeches or declamations, Antiq. B. VI. ch. 14. sect. 4

and have been so unfortunate as to lose the advantage of that glorious benefaction which they received from thee. This will be an instance of equal favor, though bestowed after a different manner; for thou wilt save those this way whom thou didst feed the other; and thou wilt hereby preserve alive, by thy own bounty, those souls which thou didst not suffer to be distressed by famine, it being indeed at once a wonderful and a great thing to sustain our lives by corn, and to bestow on us that pardon, whereby, now we are distressed, we may continue those lives. And I am ready to suppose that God is willing to afford thee this opportunity of showing thy virtuous disposition, by bringing us into this calamity, that it may appear thou canst forgive the injuries that are done to thyself, and mayst be esteemed kind to others, besides those who, on other accounts, stand in need of thy assistance; since it is indeed a right thing to do well to those who are in distress for want of food, but still a more glorious thing to save those who deserve to be punished, when it is on account of heinous offenses against thyself; for if it be a thing deserving commendation to forgive such as have been guilty of small offenses, that tend to a person's loss, and this be praiseworthy in him that overlooks such offenses, to restrain a man's passion as to crimes which are capital to the guilty, is to be like the most excellent nature of God himself. And truly, as for myself, had it not been that we had a father, who had discovered, on occasion of the death of Joseph, how miserably he is always afflicted at the loss of his sons, I had not made any words on account of the saving of our own lives; I mean, any further than as that would be an excellent character for thyself, to preserve even those that would have nobody to lament them when they were dead, but we would have yielded ourselves up to suffer whatsoever thou pleasedst; but now (for we do not plead for mercy to ourselves, though indeed, if we die, it will be while we are young, and before we have had the enjoyment of life) have regard to our father, and take pity of his old age, on whose account it is that we make these supplications to thee. We beg thou wilt give us those lives which this wickedness of ours has rendered obnoxious to thy punishment; and this for his sake who is not himself wicked, nor does his being our father make us wicked. He is a good man, and not worthy to have such trials of his patience; and now, we are absent, he is afflicted with care for us. But if he hear of our deaths, and what was the cause of it, he will on that account die an immature death; and the reproachful manner of our ruin will hasten his end, and will directly kill him; nay, will bring him to a miserable death, while he will make haste to rid himself out of the world, and bring himself to a state of insensibility, before the sad story of our end come abroad into the rest of the world. Consider these things in this manner, although our wickedness does now provoke thee with a just desire of punishing that wickedness, and forgive it for our father's sake; and let thy commiseration of him weigh more with thee than our wickedness. Have regard to the old age of our father, who, if we perish, will be very lonely while he lives, and will soon die himself also. Grant this boon to the name of fathers, for thereby thou wilt honor him that begat thee, and will grant it to thyself also, who enjoyest already that denomination; thou wilt then, by that denomination, be preserved of God, the Father of all,—by showing a pious regard to which, in the case of our father, thou wilt appear to honor him who is styled by the same name; I mean, if thou wilt have this pity on our father, upon this consideration, how miserable he will be if he be deprived of his sons! It is thy part therefore to bestow on us what God has given us, when it is in thy power to take it away, and so to resemble him entirely in charity; for it is good to use that power, which can either give or take away, on the merciful side; and when it is in thy power to destroy, to forget that thou ever hadst that power, and to look on thyself as only allowed power for preservation; and that the more any one extends this power, the greater reputation does he gain to himself. Now, by forgiving our brother what he has unhappily committed, thou wilt preserve us all; for we cannot think of living if he be put to death, since we dare not show ourselves alive to our father without our brother, but here must we partake of one and the same catastrophe of his life. And so far we beg of thee, O governor, that if thou condemnest our brother to die, thou wilt punish us together with him, as partners of his crime,—for we shall not think it reasonable to be reserved to kill ourselves for grief of our brother's death, but so to die rather as equally guilty with him of this crime. I will only leave with thee this one consideration, and then will say no more, viz. that our brother committed this fault when he was young, and not yet of confirmed wisdom in his conduct; and that men naturally forgive such young persons. I end here, without adding what more I have to say, that in case thou condemnest us, that omission may be supposed to have hurt us, and permitted thee to take the severer side. But in case thou settest us free, that this may be ascribed to thy own goodness, of which thou art inwardly conscious, that thou freest us from condemnation; and that not by barely preserving us, but by granting us such a favor as will make us appear more righteous than we really are, and by representing to thyself more motives for our deliverance than we are able to produce ourselves. If, therefore, thou resolvest to slay him, I desire thou wilt slay me in his stead, and send him back to his father; or if thou pleasest to retain him with thee as a slave, I am fitter to labor for thy advantage in that capacity, and, as thou seest, am better prepared for either of those sufferings.[10] So Judas, being very willing to undergo any thing whatever for the deliverance of his brother, cast himself down at Joseph's feet, and earnestly labored to assuage and pacify his anger. All his brethren also fell down before him, weeping and delivering themselves up to destruction for the preservation of the life of Benjamin.

10. But Joseph, as overcome now with his affections, and no longer able to personate an angry man, commanded all that were present to depart, that he might make himself known to his brethren when they were alone; and when the rest were gone out, he made himself known to his brethren; and said, "I commend you for your virtue, and your kindness to our brother: I find you better men than I could have expected from what you contrived about me. Indeed, I did all this to try your love to your brother; so I believe you were not wicked by nature in what you did in my case, but that all has happened according to God's will, who has hereby procured our enjoyment of what good things we have; and, if he continue in a favorable disposition, of what we hope for hereafter. Since, therefore, I know that our father is safe and well, beyond expectation, and I see you so well disposed to your brother, I will no longer remember what guilt you seem to have had about me, but will leave off to hate you for that your wickedness; and do rather return you my thanks, that you have concurred with the intentions of God to bring things to their present state. I would have you also rather to forget the same, since that imprudence of

---

10. In all this speech of Judas we may observe, that Josephus still supposed that death was the punishment of theft in Egypt, in the days of Joseph, though it never was so among the Jews, by the law of Moses.

yours is come to such a happy conclusion, than to be uneasy and blush at those your offenses. Do not, therefore, let your evil intentions, when you condemned me, and that bitter remorse which might follow, be a grief to you now, because those intentions were frustrated. Go, therefore, your way, rejoicing in what has happened by the Divine Providence, and inform your father of it, lest he should be spent with cares for you, and deprive me of the most agreeable part of my felicity; I mean, lest he should die before he comes into my sight, and enjoys the good things that we now have. Bring, therefore, with you our father, and your wives and children, and all your kindred, and remove your habitations hither; for it is not proper that the persons dearest to me should live remote from me, now my affairs are so prosperous, especially when they must endure five more years of famine." When Joseph had said this, he embraced his brethren, who were in tears and sorrow; but the generous kindness of their brother seemed to leave among them no room for fear, lest they should be punished on account of what they had consulted and acted against him; and they were then feasting. Now the king, as soon as he heard that Joseph's brethren were come to him, was exceeding glad of it, as if it had been a part of his own good fortune; and gave them wagons full of corn and gold and silver, to be conveyed to his father. Now when they had received more of their brother part to be carried to their father, and part as free gifts to every one of themselves, Benjamin having still more than the rest, they departed.

7 The Removal of Joseph's Father with All His Family, to Him, on Account of the Famine

1. As soon as Jacob came to know, by his sons returning home, in what state Joseph was, that he had not only escaped death, for which yet he lived all along in mourning, but that he lived in splendor and happiness, and ruled over Egypt, jointly with the king, and had intrusted to his care almost all his affairs, he did not think any thing he was told to be incredible, considering the greatness of the works of God, and his kindness to him, although that kindness had, for some late times, been intermitted; so he immediately and zealously set out upon his journey to him.

2. When he came to the Well of the Oath, (Beersheba,) he offered sacrifice to God; and being afraid that the happiness there was in Egypt might tempt his posterity to fall in love with it, and settle in it, and no more think of removing into the land of Canaan, and possessing it, as God had promised them; as also being afraid, lest, if this descent into Egypt were made without the will of God, his family might be destroyed there; out of fear, withal, lest he should depart this life before he came to the sight of Joseph; he fell asleep, revolving these doubts in his mind.

3. But God stood by him, and called him twice by his name; and when he asked who he was, God said, "No, sure; it is not just that thou, Jacob, shouldst be unacquainted with that God who has been ever a protector and a helper to thy forefathers, and after them to thyself: for when thy father would have deprived thee of the dominion, I gave it thee; and by my kindness it was that, when thou wast sent into Mesopotamia all alone, thou obtainedst good wives, and returnedst with many children, and much wealth. Thy whole family also has been preserved by my providence; and it was I who conducted Joseph, thy son, whom thou gavest up for lost, to the enjoyment of great prosperity. I also made him lord of Egypt, so that he differs but little from a king. Accordingly, I come now as a guide to thee in this journey; and foretell to thee, that thou shalt die in the arms of Joseph: and I inform thee, that thy posterity shall be many ages in authority and glory, and that I will settle them in the land which I have promised them."

4. Jacob, encouraged by this dream, went on more cheerfully for Egypt with his sons, and all belonging to them. Now they were in all seventy. I once, indeed, thought it best not to set down the names of this family, especially because of their difficult pronunciation [by the Greeks]; but, upon the whole, I think it necessary to mention those names, that I may disprove such as believe that we came not originally from Mesopotamia, but are Egyptians. Now Jacob had twelve sons; of these Joseph was come thither before. We will therefore set down the names of Jacob's children and grandchildren. Reuben had four sons—Anoch, Phallu, Assaron, Charmi. Simeon had six—Jamuel, Jamin, Avod, Jachin, Soar, Saul. Levi had three sons—Gersom, Caath, Merari. Judas had three sons—Sala, Phares, Zerah; and by Phares two grandchildren, Esrom and Amar. Issachar had four sons—Thola, Phua, Jasob, Samaron. Zabulon had with him three sons—Sarad, Helon, Jalel. So far is the posterity of Lea; with whom went

her daughter Dinah. These are thirty-three. Rachel had two sons, the one of whom, Joseph, had two sons also, Manasses and Ephraim. The other, Benjamin, had ten sons—Bolau, Bacchar, Asabel, Geras, Naaman, Jes, Ros, Momphis, Opphis, Arad. These fourteen added to the thirty-three before enumerated, amount to the number forty-seven. And this was the legitimate posterity of Jacob. He had besides by Bilhah, the handmaid of Rachel, Dan and Nephtliali; which last had four sons that followed him—Jesel, Guni, Issari, and Sellim. Dan had an only begotten son, Usi. If these be added to those before mentioned, they complete the number fifty-four. Gad and Aser were the sons of Zilpha, who was the handmaid of Lea. These had with them, Gad seven—Saphoniah, Augis, Sunis, Azabon, Aerin, Erocd, Ariel. Aser had a daughter, Sarah, and six male children, whose names were Jomne, Isus, Isoui, Baris, Abar and Melchiel. If we add these, which are sixteen, to the fifty-four, the forementioned number [70] is completed[11] Jacob not being himself included in that number.

5. When Joseph understood that his father was coming, for Judas his brother was come before him, and informed him of his approach, he went out to meet him; and they met together at Heroopolis. But Jacob almost fainted away at this unexpected and great joy; however, Joseph revived him, being yet not himself able to contain from being affected in the same manner, at the pleasure he now had; yet was he not wholly overcome with his passion, as his father was. After this, he desired Jacob to travel on slowly; but he himself took five of his brethren with him, and made haste to the king, to tell him that Jacob and his family were come; which was a joyful hearing to him. He also bid Joseph tell him what sort of life his brethren loved to lead, that he might give them leave to follow the same, who told him they were good shepherds, and had been used to follow no other employment but this alone. Whereby he provided for them, that they should not be separated, but live in the same place, and take care of

---

11. All the Greek copies of Josephus have the negative particle here, that Jacob himself was not reckoned one of the 70 souls that came into Egypt; but the old Latin copies want it, and directly assure us he was one of them. It is therefore hardly certain which of these was Josephus's true reading, since the number 70 is made up without him, if we reckon Leah for one; but if she be not reckoned, Jacob must himself be one, to complete the number.

their father; as also hereby he provided, that they might be acceptable to the Egyptians, by doing nothing that would be common to them with the Egyptians; for the Egyptians are prohibited to meddle with feeding of sheep.[12]

6. When Jacob was come to the king, and saluted him, and wished all prosperity to his government, Pharaoh asked him how old he now was; upon whose answer, that he was a hundred and thirty years old, he admired Jacob on account of the length of his life. And when he had added, that still he had not lived so long as his forefathers, he gave him leave to live with his children in Heliopolis; for in that city the king's shepherds had their pasturage.

7. However, the famine increased among the Egyptians, and this heavy judgment grew more oppressive to them, because neither did the river overflow the ground, for it did not rise to its former height, nor did God send rain upon it;[13] nor did they indeed make the least provision for themselves, so ignorant were they what was to be done; but Joseph sold them corn for their money. But when their money failed them, they bought corn with their cattle and their slaves; and if any of them had a small piece of land, they gave up that to purchase them food, by which means the king became the owner of all their substance; and they were removed, some to one place, and some to another, that so the possession of their country might be firmly assured to the king, excepting the lands of the priests, for their country continued still in their own possession. And indeed this sore famine made their minds, as well as their bodies, slaves; and at length compelled them to procure a sufficiency of food by such dishonorable means. But when this misery ceased, and the river overflowed the ground, and the ground brought forth its fruits plentifully, Joseph

---

12. Josephus thought that the Egyptians hated or despised the employment of a shepherd in the days of Joseph; whereas Bishop Cumberland has shown that they rather hated such Poehnician or Canaanite shepherds that had long enslaved the Egyptians of old time. See his Sanchoniatho, p. 361, 362.

13. Reland here puts the question, how Josephus could complain of its not raining in Egypt during this famine, while the ancients affirm that it never does naturally rain there. His answer is, that when the ancients deny that it rains in Egypt, they only mean the Upper Egypt above the Delta, which is called Egypt in the strictest sense; but that in the Delta [and by consequence in the Lower Egypt adjoining to it] it did of old, and still does, rain sometimes. See the note on Antiq. B. III. ch. 1. sect. 6.

came to every city, and gathered the people thereto belonging together, and gave them back entirely the land which, by their own consent, the king might have possessed alone, and alone enjoyed the fruits of it. He also exhorted them to look on it as every one's own possession, and to fall to their husbandry with cheerfulness, and to pay as a tribute to the king, the fifth part[14] of the fruits for the land which the king, when it was his own, restored to them. These men rejoiced upon their becoming unexpectedly owners of their lands, and diligently observed what was enjoined them; and by this means Joseph procured to himself a greater authority among the Egyptians, and greater love to the king from them. Now this law, that they should pay the fifth part of their fruits as tribute, continued until their later kings.

8 Of the Death of Jacob and Joseph

1. NOW when Jacob had lived seventeen years in Egypt, he fell into a disease, and died in the presence of his sons; but not till he made his prayers for their enjoying prosperity, and till he had foretold to them prophetically how every one of them was to dwell in the land of Canaan. But this happened many years afterward. He also enlarged upon the praises of Joseph[15] how he had not remembered the evil doings of his brethren to their disadvantage; nay, on the contrary, was kind to them, bestowing upon them so many benefits, as seldom are bestowed on men's own benefactors. He then commanded his own sons that they should admit Joseph's sons, Ephraim and Manasses, into their number, and divide the land of Canaan in common with them; concerning whom we shall treat hereafter. However, he made it his request that he might be buried at Hebron. So he died, when he had

---

14. Josephus supposes that Joseph now restored the Egyptians their lands again. upon the payment of a fifth part as tribute. It seems to me rather that the land was now considered as Pharaoh's land, and this fifth part as its rent, to be paid to him, as he was their landlord, and they his tenants; and that the lands were not properly restored, and this fifth part reserved as tribute only, till the days of Sesostris. See Essay on the Old Testament, Append. 148, 149.

15. As to this encomium upon Joseph, as preparatory to Jacob's adopting Ephraim and Manasses into his own family, and to be admitted for two tribes, which Josephus here mentions, all our copies of Genesis omit it, ch. 48.; nor do we know whence he took it, or whether it be not his own embellishment only.

lived full a hundred and fifty years, three only abated, having not been behind any of his ancestors in piety towards God, and having such a recompense for it, as it was fit those should have who were so good as these were. But Joseph, by the king's permission, carried his father's dead body to Hebron, and there buried it, at a great expense. Now his brethren were at first unwilling to return back with him, because they were afraid lest, now their father was dead, he should punish them for their secret practices against him; since he was now gone, for whose sake he had been so gracious to them. But he persuaded them to fear no harm, and to entertain no suspicions of him: so he brought them along with him, and gave them great possessions, and never left off his particular concern for them.

2. Joseph also died when he had lived a hundred and ten years; having been a man of admirable virtue, and conducting all his affairs by the rules of reason; and used his authority with moderation, which was the cause of his so great felicity among the Egyptians, even when he came from another country, and that in such ill circumstances also, as we have already described. At length his brethren died, after they had lived happily in Egypt. Now the posterity and sons of these men, after some time, carried their bodies, and buried them at Hebron: but as to the bones of Joseph, they carried them into the land of Canaan afterward, when the Hebrews went out of Egypt, for so had Joseph made them promise him upon oath. But what became of every one of these men, and by what toils they got the possession of the land of Canaan, shall be shown hereafter, when I have first explained upon what account it was that they left Egypt.

9 *Concerning the Afflictions That Befell the Hebrews in Egypt, During Four Hundred Years*

1. NOW[16] it happened that the Egyptians grew delicate and lazy, as to pains-taking, and gave themselves up to other pleasures, and in particular to the love of gain. They also became very ill-affected

---

16. As to the affliction of Abraham's posterity for 400 years, see Antiq. B. I. ch. 10. sect. 3; and as to what cities they built in Egypt, under Pharaoh Sesostris. and of Pharaoh Sesostris's drowning in the Red Sea, see Essay on the Old Testament, Append. p. 132–162.

towards the Hebrews, as touched with envy at their prosperity; for when they saw how the nation of the Israelites flourished, and were become eminent already in plenty of wealth, which they had acquired by their virtue and natural love of labor, they thought their increase was to their own detriment. And having, in length of time, forgotten the benefits they had received from Joseph, particularly the crown being now come into another family, they became very abusive to the Israelites, and contrived many ways of afflicting them; for they enjoined them to cut a great number of channels for the river, and to build walls for their cities and ramparts, that they might restrain the river, and hinder its waters from stagnating, upon its running over its own banks: they set them also to build pyramids,[17] and by all this wore them out; and forced them to learn all sorts of mechanical arts, and to accustom themselves to hard labor. And four hundred years did they spend under these afflictions; for they strove one against the other which should get the mastery, the Egyptians desiring to destroy the Israelites by these labors, and the Israelites desiring to hold out to the end under them.

2. While the affairs of the Hebrews were in this condition, there was this occasion offered itself to the Egyptians, which made them more solicitous for the extinction of our nation. One of those sacred scribes,[18] who are very sagacious in foretelling future events truly, told the king, that about this time there would a child be born to the Israelites, who, if he were reared, would bring the Egyptian dominion low, and would raise the Israelites; that he would excel all men in virtue, and obtain a glory that would be remembered through all ages. Which thing was so feared by the king, that, according to this man's opinion, he commanded that they should cast every male child, which

---

17. Of this building of the pyramids of Egypt by the Israelites, see Perizonius Orig. Aegyptiac, ch. 21. It is not impossible they might build one or more of the small ones; but the larger ones seem much later. Only, if they be all built of stone, this does not so well agree with the Israelites' labors, which are said to have been in brick, and not in stone, as Mr. Sandys observes in his Travels. p. 127, 128.

18. Dr. Bernard informs us here, that instead of this single priest or prophet of the Egyptians, without a name in Josephus, the Targum of Jonathan names the two famous antagonists of Moses, Jannes and Jambres. Nor is it at all unlikely that it might be one of these who foreboded so much misery to the Egyptians, and so much happiness to the Israelites, from the rearing of Moses.

was born to the Israelites, into the river, and destroy it; that besides this, the Egyptian midwives[19] should watch the labors of the Hebrew women, and observe what is born, for those were the women who were enjoined to do the office of midwives to them; and by reason of their relation to the king, would not transgress his commands. He enjoined also, that if any parents should disobey him, and venture to save their male children alive,[20] they and their families should be destroyed. This was a severe affliction indeed to those that suffered it, not only as they were deprived of their sons, and while they were the parents themselves, they were obliged to be subservient to the destruction of their own children, but as it was to be supposed to tend to the extirpation of their nation, while upon the destruction of their children, and their own gradual dissolution, the calamity would become very hard and inconsolable to them. And this was the ill state they were in. But no one can be too hard for the purpose of God, though he contrive ten thousand subtle devices for that end; for this child, whom the sacred scribe foretold, was brought up and concealed from the observers appointed by the king; and he that foretold him did not mistake in the consequences of his preservation, which were brought to pass after the manner following:—3. A man whose name was Amram, one of the nobler sort of the Hebrews, was afraid for his whole nation, lest it should fail, by the want of young men to be brought up hereafter, and was very uneasy at it, his wife being then with child, and he knew not what to do. Hereupon he betook himself to prayer to God; and entreated him to have compassion on those men who had nowise transgressed the laws of his worship, and to afford them deliverance from the miseries they at that time endured,

---

19. Josephus is clear that these midwives were Egyptians, and not Israelites, as in our other copies: which is very probable, it being not easily to be supposed that Pharaoh could trust the Israelite midwives to execute so barbarous a command against their own nation. (Consult, therefore, and correct hence our ordinary copies, Exodus 1:15, 22. And, indeed, Josephus seems to have had much completer copies of the Pentateuch, or other authentic records now lost, about the birth and actions of Moses, than either our Hebrew, Samaritan, or Greek Bibles afford us, which enabled him to be so large and particular about him.

20. Of this grandfather of Sesostris, Ramestes the Great, who slew the Israelite infants, and of the inscription on his obelisk, containing, in my opinion, one of the oldest records of mankind, see Essay on the Old Test. Append. p. 139, 145, 147, 217–220.

and to render abortive their enemies' hopes of the destruction of their nation. Accordingly God had mercy on him, and was moved by his supplication. He stood by him in his sleep, and exhorted him not to despair of his future favors. He said further, that he did not forget their piety towards him, and would always reward them for it, as he had formerly granted his favor to their forefathers, and made them increase from a few to so great a multitude. He put him in mind, that when Abraham was come alone out of Mesopotamia into Canaan, he had been made happy, not only in other respects, but that when his wife was at first barren, she was afterwards by him enabled to conceive seed, and bare him sons. That he left to Ismael and to his posterity the country of Arabia; as also to his sons by Ketura, Troglodytis; and to Isaac, Canaan. That by my assistance, said he, he did great exploits in war, which, unless you be yourselves impious, you must still remember. As for Jacob, he became well known to strangers also, by the greatness of that prosperity in which he lived, and left to his sons, who came into Egypt with no more than seventy souls, while you are now become above six hundred thousand. Know therefore that I shall provide for you all in common what is for your good, and particularly for thyself what shall make thee famous; for that child, out of dread of whose nativity the Egyptians have doomed the Israelite children to destruction, shall be this child of thine, and shall be concealed from those who watch to destroy him: and when he is brought up in a surprising way, he shall deliver the Hebrew nation from the distress they are under from the Egyptians. His memory shall be famous while the world lasts; and this not only among the Hebrews, but foreigners also:—all which shall be the effect of my favor to thee, and to thy posterity. He shall also have such a brother, that he shall himself obtain my priesthood, and his posterity shall have it after him to the end of the world.

4. When the vision had informed him of these things, Amram awaked and told it to Jochebed who was his wife. And now the fear increased upon them on account of the prediction in Amram's dream; for they were under concern, not only for the child, but on account of the great happiness that was to come to him also. However, the mother's labor was such as afforded a confirmation to what was foretold by God; for it was not known to those that watched her, by the easiness of her pains, and because the throes of her delivery did

not fall upon her with violence. And now they nourished the child at home privately for three months; but after that time Amram, fearing he should be discovered, and, by falling under the king's displeasure, both he and his child should perish, and so he should make the promise of God of none effect, he determined rather to trust the safety and care of the child to God, than to depend on his own concealment of him, which he looked upon as a thing uncertain, and whereby both the child, so privately to be nourished, and himself should be in imminent danger; but he believed that God would some way for certain procure the safety of the child, in order to secure the truth of his own predictions. When they had thus determined, they made an ark of bulrushes, after the manner of a cradle, and of a bigness sufficient for an infant to be laid in, without being too straitened: they then daubed it over with slime, which would naturally keep out the water from entering between the bulrushes, and put the infant into it, and setting it afloat upon the river, they left its preservation to God; so the river received the child, and carried him along. But Miriam, the child's sister, passed along upon the bank over against him, as her mother had bid her, to see whither the ark would be carried, where God demonstrated that human wisdom was nothing, but that the Supreme Being is able to do whatsoever he pleases: that those who, in order to their own security, condemn others to destruction, and use great endeavors about it, fail of their purpose; but that others are in a surprising manner preserved, and obtain a prosperous condition almost from the very midst of their calamities; those, I mean, whose dangers arise by the appointment of God. And, indeed, such a providence was exercised in the case of this child, as showed the power of God.

5. Thermuthis was the king's daughter. She was now diverting herself by the banks of the river; and seeing a cradle borne along by the current, she sent some that could swim, and bid them bring the cradle to her. When those that were sent on this errand came to her with the cradle, and she saw the little child, she was greatly in love with it, on account of its largeness and beauty; for God had taken such great care in the formation of Moses, that he caused him to be thought worthy of bringing up, and providing for, by all those that had taken the most fatal resolutions, on account of the dread of his nativity, for the destruction of the rest of the Hebrew nation. Thermuthis bid them

bring her a woman that might afford her breast to the child; yet would not the child admit of her breast, but turned away from it, and did the like to many other women. Now Miriam was by when this happened, not to appear to be there on purpose, but only as staying to see the child; and she said, "It is in vain that thou, O queen, callest for these women for the nourishing of the child, who are no way of kin to it; but still, if thou wilt order one of the Hebrew women to be brought, perhaps it may admit the breast of one of its own nation." Now since she seemed to speak well, Thermuthis bid her procure such a one, and to bring one of those Hebrew women that gave suck. So when she had such authority given her, she came back and brought the mother, who was known to nobody there. And now the child gladly admitted the breast, and seemed to stick close to it; and so it was, that, at the queen's desire, the nursing of the child was entirely intrusted to the mother.

6. Hereupon it was that Thermuthis imposed this name *Mouses* upon him, from what had happened when he was put into the river; for the Egyptians call water by the name of *Mo,* and such as are saved out of it, by the name of *Uses:* so by putting these two words together, they imposed this name upon him. And he was, by the confession of all, according to God's prediction, as well for his greatness of mind as for his contempt of difficulties, the best of all the Hebrews, for Abraham was his ancestor of the seventh generation. For Moses was the son of Amram, who was the son of Caath, whose father Levi was the son of Jacob, who was the son of Isaac, who was the son of Abraham. Now Moses's understanding became superior to his age, nay, far beyond that standard; and when he was taught, he discovered greater quickness of apprehension than was usual at his age, and his actions at that time promised greater, when he should come to the age of a man. God did also give him that tallness, when he was but three years old, as was wonderful. And as for his beauty, there was nobody so unpolite as, when they saw Moses, they were not greatly surprised at the beauty of his countenance; nay, it happened frequently, that those that met him as he was carried along the road, were obliged to turn again upon seeing the child; that they left what they were about, and stood still a great while to look on him; for the beauty of the child was so remarkable and natural to him on many accounts, that it detained the spectators, and made them stay longer to look upon him.

7. Thermuthis therefore perceiving him to be so remarkable a child, adopted him for her son, having no child of her own. And when one time had carried Moses to her father, she showed him to him, and said she thought to make him her successor, if it should please God she should have no legitimate child of her own; and to him, "I have brought up a child who is of a divine form,[21] and of a generous mind; and as I have received him from the bounty of the river, in, I thought proper to adopt him my son, and the heir of thy kingdom." And she had said this, she put the infant into her father's hands: so he took him, and hugged him to his breast; and on his daughter's account, in a pleasant way, put his diadem upon his head; but Moses threw it down to the ground, and, in a puerile mood, he wreathed it round, and trod upon his feet, which seemed to bring along with evil presage concerning the kingdom of Egypt. But when the sacred scribe saw this, (he was the person who foretold that his nativity would the dominion of that kingdom low,) he made a violent attempt to kill him; and crying out in a frightful manner, he said, "This, O king! this child is he of whom God foretold, that if we kill him we shall be in no danger; he himself affords an attestation to the prediction of the same thing, by his trampling upon thy government, and treading upon thy diadem. Take him, therefore, out of the way, and deliver the Egyptians from the fear they are in about him; and deprive the Hebrews of the hope they have of being encouraged by him." But Thermuthis prevented him, and snatched the child away. And the king was not hasty to slay him, God himself, whose providence protected Moses, inclining the king to spare him. He was, therefore, educated with great care. So the Hebrews depended on him, and were of good hopes great things would be done by him; but the Egyptians were suspicious of what would follow such his education. Yet because, if Moses had been slain, there was no one, either akin or adopted, that had any oracle on his side for pretending to the crown of Egypt, and likely to be of greater advantage to them, they abstained from killing him.

---

21. What Josephus here says of the beauty of Moses, that he was of a divine form, is very like what St. Stephen says of the same beauty; that Moses was beautiful in the sight of Acts 7:20.

10 How Moses Made War with the Ethiopians

1. MOSES, therefore, when he was born, and brought up in the foregoing manner, and came to the age of maturity, made his virtue manifest to the Egyptians; and showed that he was born for the bringing them down, and raising the Israelites. And the occasion he laid hold of was this:—The Ethiopians, who are next neighbors to the Egyptians, made an inroad into their country, which they seized upon, and carried off the effects of the Egyptians, who, in their rage, fought against them, and revenged the affronts they had received from them; but being overcome in battle, some of them were slain, and the rest ran away in a shameful manner, and by that means saved themselves; whereupon the Ethiopians followed after them in the pursuit, and thinking that it would be a mark of cowardice if they did not subdue all Egypt, they went on to subdue the rest with greater vehemence; and when they had tasted the sweets of the country, they never left off the prosecution of the war: and as the nearest parts had not courage enough at first to fight with them, they proceeded as far as Memphis, and the sea itself, while not one of the cities was able to oppose them. The Egyptians, under this sad oppression, betook themselves to their oracles and prophecies; and when God had given them this counsel, to make use of Moses the Hebrew, and take his assistance, the king commanded his daughter to produce him, that he might be the general[22] of their army. Upon which, when she had made him swear he would do him no harm, she delivered him to the king, and supposed his assistance would be of great advantage to them. She withal reproached the priest, who, when they had before admonished the Egyptians to kill him, was not ashamed now to own their want of his help.

---

22. This history of Moses, as general of the Egyptians against the Ethiopians, is wholly omitted in our Bibles; but is thus by Irenaeus, from Josephus, and that soon after his own age:—"Josephus says, that when Moses was nourished in the palace, he was appointed general of the army against the Ethiopians, and conquered them, when he married that king's daughter; because, out of her affection for him, she delivered the city up to him." See the Fragments of Irenaeus. ap. edit. Grab. p. 472. Nor perhaps did St. Stephen refer to any thing else when he said of Moses, before he was sent by God to the Israelites, that he was not only learned in all the wisdom of the Egyptians, but was also mighty in words and in deeds, Acts 7:22.

2. So Moses, at the persuasion both of Thermuthis and the king himself, cheerfully undertook the business: and the sacred scribes of both nations were glad; those of the Egyptians, that they should at once overcome their enemies by his valor, and that by the same piece of management Moses would be slain; but those of the Hebrews, that they should escape from the Egyptians, because Moses was to be their general. But Moses prevented the enemies, and took and led his army before those enemies were apprized of his attacking them; for he did not march by the river, but by land, where he gave a wonderful demonstration of his sagacity; for when the ground was difficult to be passed over, because of the multitude of serpents, (which it produces in vast numbers, and, indeed, is singular in some of those productions, which other countries do not breed, and yet such as are worse than others in power and mischief, and an unusual fierceness of sight, some of which ascend out of the ground unseen, and also fly in the air, and so come upon men at unawares, and do them a mischief,) Moses invented a wonderful stratagem to preserve the army safe, and without hurt; for he made baskets, like unto arks, of sedge, and filled them with ibes,[23] and carried them along with them; which animal is the greatest enemy to serpents imaginable, for they fly from them when they come near them; and as they fly they are caught and devoured by them, as if it were done by the harts; but the ibes are tame creatures, and only enemies to the serpentine kind: but about these ibes I say no more at present, since the Greeks themselves are not unacquainted with this sort of bird. As soon, therefore, as Moses was come to the land which was the breeder of these serpents, he let loose the ibes, and by their means repelled the serpentine kind, and used them for his assistants before the army came upon that ground. When he had therefore proceeded thus on his journey, he came upon the Ethiopians before they expected him; and, joining battle with them, he beat them, and deprived them of the hopes they had of success against the Egyptians, and went on in overthrowing their cities, and indeed made a great slaughter of these Ethiopians. Now when the Egyptian army had once tasted of this prosperous success, by the

---

23. Pliny speaks of these birds called ibes; and says, "The Egyptians invoked them against the serpents," Hist. Nat. B. X. ch. 28. Strabo speaks of this island Meroe, and these rivers Astapus and Astaboras, B. XVI. p. 771, 786; and B XVII. p. 82].

means of Moses, they did not slacken their diligence, insomuch that the Ethiopians were in danger of being reduced to slavery, and all sorts of destruction; and at length they retired to Saba, which was a royal city of Ethiopia, which Cambyses afterwards named Mero, after the name of his own sister. The place was to be besieged with very great difficulty, since it was both encompassed by the Nile quite round, and the other rivers, Astapus and Astaboras, made it a very difficult thing for such as attempted to pass over them; for the city was situate in a retired place, and was inhabited after the manner of an island, being encompassed with a strong wall, and having the rivers to guard them from their enemies, and having great ramparts between the wall and the rivers, insomuch, that when the waters come with the greatest violence, it can never be drowned; which ramparts make it next to impossible for even such as are gotten over the rivers to take the city. However, while Moses was uneasy at the army's lying idle, (for the enemies durst not come to a battle,) this accident happened:— Tharbis was the daughter of the king of the Ethiopians: she happened to see Moses as he led the army near the walls, and fought with great courage; and admiring the subtility of his undertakings, and believing him to be the author of the Egyptians' success, when they had before despaired of recovering their liberty, and to be the occasion of the great danger the Ethiopians were in, when they had before boasted of their great achievements, she fell deeply in love with him; and upon the prevalency of that passion, sent to him the most faithful of all her servants to discourse with him about their marriage. He thereupon accepted the offer, on condition she would procure the delivering up of the city; and gave her the assurance of an oath to take her to his wife; and that when he had once taken possession of the city, he would not break his oath to her. No sooner was the agreement made, but it took effect immediately; and when Moses had cut off the Ethiopians, he gave thanks to God, and consummated his marriage, and led the Egyptians back to their own land.

11 *How Moses Fled Out of Egypt into Midian*

1. Now the Egyptians, after they had been preserved by Moses, entertained a hatred to him, and were very eager in compassing their designs against him, as suspecting that he would take occasion,

from his good success, to raise a sedition, and bring innovations into Egypt; and told the king he ought to be slain. The king had also some intentions of himself to the same purpose, and this as well out of envy at his glorious expedition at the head of his army, as out of fear of being brought low by him and being instigated by the sacred scribes, he was ready to undertake to kill Moses: but when he had learned beforehand what plots there were against him, he went away privately; and because the public roads were watched, he took his flight through the deserts, and where his enemies could not suspect he would travel; and, though he was destitute of food, he went on, and despised that difficulty courageously; and when he came to the city Midian, which lay upon the Red Sea, and was so denominated from one of Abraham's sons by Keturah, he sat upon a certain well, and rested himself there after his laborious journey, and the affliction he had been in. It was not far from the city, and the time of the day was noon, where he had an occasion offered him by the custom of the country of doing what recommended his virtue, and afforded him an opportunity of bettering his circumstances.

2. For that country having but little water, the shepherds used to seize on the wells before others came, lest their flocks should want water, and lest it should be spent by others before they came. There were now come, therefore, to this well seven sisters that were virgins, the daughters of Raguel, a priest, and one thought worthy by the people of the country of great honor. These virgins, who took care of their father's flocks, which sort of work it was customary and very familiar for women to do in the country of the Troglodytes, they came first of all, and drew water out of the well in a quantity sufficient for their flocks, into troughs, which were made for the reception of that water; but when the shepherds came upon the maidens, and drove them away, that they might have the command of the water themselves, Moses, thinking it would be a terrible reproach upon him if he overlooked the young women under unjust oppression, and should suffer the violence of the men to prevail over the right of the maidens, he drove away the men, who had a mind to more than their share, and afforded a proper assistance to the women; who, when they had received such a benefit from him, came to their father, and told him how they had been affronted by the shepherds, and assisted by a stranger, and entreated that he would not let this generous action

be done in vain, nor go without a reward. Now the father took it well from his daughters that they were so desirous to reward their benefactor; and bid them bring Moses into his presence, that he might be rewarded as he deserved. And when Moses came, he told him what testimony his daughters bare to him, that he had assisted them; and that, as he admired him for his virtue, he said that Moses had bestowed such his assistance on persons not insensible of benefits, but where they were both able and willing to return the kindness, and even to exceed the measure of his generosity. So he made him his son, and gave him one of his daughters in marriage; and appointed him to be the guardian and superintendent over his cattle; for of old, all the wealth of the barbarians was in those cattle.

12   Concerning the Burning Bush and the Rod of Moses

1. NOW Moses, when he had obtained the favor of Jethro, for that was one of the names of Raguel, staid there and fed his flock; but some time afterward, taking his station at the mountain called Sinai, he drove his flocks thither to feed them. Now this is the highest of all the mountains thereabout, and the best for pasturage, the herbage being there good; and it had not been before fed upon, because of the opinion men had that God dwelt there, the shepherds not daring to ascend up to it; and here it was that a wonderful prodigy happened to Moses; for a fire fed upon a thorn bush, yet did the green leaves and the flowers continue untouched, and the fire did not at all consume the fruit branches, although the flame was great and fierce. Moses was aftrighted at this strange sight, as it was to him; but he was still more astonished when the fire uttered a voice, and called to him by name, and spake words to him, by which it signified how bold he had been in venturing to come into a place whither no man had ever come before, because the place was divine; and advised him to remove a great way off from the flame, and to be contented with what he had seen; and though he were himself a good man, and the offspring of great men, yet that he should not pry any further; and he foretold to him, that he should have glory and honor among men, by the blessing of God upon him. He also commanded him to go away thence with confidence to Egypt, in order to his being the commander and conductor of the body of the Hebrews, and to his delivering his own people from the injuries

they suffered there: "For," said God, "they shall inhabit this happy land which your forefather Abraham inhabited, and shall have the enjoyment of all good things." But still he enjoined them, when he brought the Hebrews out of the land of Egypt, to come to that place, and to offer sacrifices of thanksgiving there, Such were the divine oracles which were delivered out of the fire.

2. But Moses was astonished at what he saw, and much more at what he heard; and he said, "I think it would be an instance of too great madness, O Lord, for one of that regard I bear to thee, to distrust thy power, since I myself adore it, and know that it has been made manifest to my progenitors: but I am still in doubt how I, who am a private man, and one of no abilities, should either persuade my own countrymen to leave the country they now inhabit, and to follow me to a land whither I lead them; or, if they should be persuaded, how can I force Pharaoh to permit them to depart, since they augment their own wealth and prosperity by the labors and works they put upon them ?"

3. But God persuaded him to be courageous on all occasions, and promised to be with him, and to assist him in his words, when he was to persuade men; and in his deeds, when he was to perform wonders. He bid him also to take a signal of the truth of what he said, by throwing his rod upon the ground, which, when he had done, it crept along, and was become a serpent, and rolled itself round in its folds, and erected its head, as ready to revenge itself on such as should assault it; after which it become a rod again as it was before. After this God bid Moses to put his right hand into his bosom: he obeyed, and when he took it out it was white, and in color like to chalk, but afterward it returned to its wonted color again. He also, upon God's command, took some of the water that was near him, and poured it upon the ground, and saw the color was that of blood. Upon the wonder that Moses showed at these signs, God exhorted him to be of good courage, and to be assured that he would be the greatest support to him; and bid him make use of those signs, in order to obtain belief among all men, that "thou art sent by me, and dost all things according to my commands. Accordingly I enjoin thee to make no more delays, but to make haste to Egypt, and to travel night and day, and not to draw out the time, and so make the slavery of the Hebrews and their sufferings to last the longer."

4. Moses having now seen and heard these wonders that assured him of the truth of these promises of God, had no room left him to disbelieve them: he entreated him to grant him that power when he should be in Egypt; and besought him to vouchsafe him the knowledge of his own name; and since he had heard and seen him, that he would also tell him his name, that when he offered sacrifice he might invoke him by such his name in his oblations. Whereupon God declared to him his holy name, which had never been discovered to men before; concerning which it is not lawful for me to say any more[24] Now these signs accompanied Moses, not then only, but always when he prayed for them: of all which signs he attributed the firmest assent to the fire in the bush; and believing that God would be a gracious supporter to him, he hoped he should be able to deliver his own nation, and bring calamities on the Egyptians.

13 How Moses and Aaron Returned into Egypt to Pharaoh

1. SO Moses, when he understood that the Pharaoh, in whose reign he fled away, was dead, asked leave of Raguel to go to Egypt, for the benefit of his own people. And he took with him Zipporah, the daughter of Raguel, whom he had married, and the children he had by her, Gersom and Eleazer, and made haste into Egypt. Now the former of those names, Gersom, in the Hebrew tongue, signifies *that he was in a strange land*; and Eleazer, *that, by the assistance of the God of his fathers, he had escaped from the Egyptians*. Now when they were near the borders, Aaron his brother, by the command of God, met him, to whom he declared what had befallen him at the mountain, and the commands that God had given him. But as they were going forward, the chief men

24. This superstitious fear of discovering the name with four letters, which of late we have been used falsely to pronounce Jehovah, but seems to have been originally pronounced Jahoh, or Jao, is never, I think, heard of till this passage of Josephus; and this superstition, in not pronouncing that name, has continued among the Rabbinical Jews to this day (though whether the Samaritans and Caraites observed it so early, does not appear). Josephus also durst not set down the very words of the ten commandments, as we shall see hereafter, Antiq. B. III. ch. 5. sect. 4, which superstitious silence I think has yet not been continued even by the Rabbins. It is, however, no doubt but both these cautious concealments were taught Josephus by the Pharisees, a body of men at once very wicked and very superstitious.

among the Hebrews, having learned that they were coming, met them: to whom Moses declared the signs he had seen; and while they could not believe them, he made them see them, So they took courage at these surprising and unexpected sights, and hoped well of their entire deliverance, as believing now that God took care of their preservation.

2. Since then Moses found that the Hebrews would be obedient to whatsoever he should direct, as they promised to be, and were in love with liberty, he came to the king, who had indeed but lately received the government, and told him how much he had done for the good of the Egyptians, when they were despised by the Ethiopians, and their country laid waste by them; and how he had been the commander of their forces, and had labored for them, as if they had been his own people and he informed him in what danger he had been during that expedition, without having any proper returns made him as he had deserved. He also informed him distinctly what things happened to him at Mount Sinai; and what God said to him; and the signs that were done by God, in order to assure him of the authority of those commands which he had given him. He also exhorted him not to disbelieve what he told him, nor to oppose the will of God.

3. But when the king derided Moses; he made him in earnest see the signs that were done at Mount Sinai. Yet was the king very angry with him and called him an ill man, who had formerly run away from his Egyptian slavery, and came now back with deceitful tricks, and wonders, and magical arts, to astonish him. And when he had said this, he commanded the priests to let him see the same wonderful sights; as knowing that the Egyptians were skillful in this kind of learning, and that he was not the only person who knew them, and pretended them to be divine; as also he told him, that when he brought such wonderful sights before him, he would only be believed by the unlearned. Now when the priests threw down their rods, they became serpents. But Moses was not daunted at it; and said, "O king, I do not myself despise the wisdom of the Egyptians, but I say that what I do is so much superior to what these do by magic arts and tricks, as Divine power exceeds the power of man: but I will demonstrate that what I do is not done by craft, or counterfeiting what is not really true, but that they appear by the providence and power of God." And when he had said this, he cast his rod down upon the ground, and commanded it to turn itself into a serpent. It obeyed him, and went all round, and devoured

the rods of the Egyptians, which seemed to be dragons, until it had consumed them all. It then returned to its own form, and Moses took it into his hand again.

4. However, the king was no more moved when was done than before; and being very angry, he said that he should gain nothing by this his cunning and shrewdness against the Egyptians;—and he commanded him that was the chief taskmaster over the Hebrews, to give them no relaxation from their labors, but to compel them to submit to greater oppressions than before; and though he allowed them chaff before for making their bricks, he would allow it them no longer, but he made them to work hard at brick-making in the day-time, and to gather chaff in the night. Now when their labor was thus doubled upon them, they laid the blame upon Moses, because their labor and their misery were on his account become more severe to them. But Moses did not let his courage sink for the king's threatenings; nor did he abate of his zeal on account of the Hebrews' complaints; but he supported himself, and set his soul resolutely against them both, and used his own utmost diligence to procure liberty to his countrymen. So he went to the king, and persuaded him to let the Hebrews go to Mount Sinai, and there to sacrifice to God, because God had enjoined them so to do. He persuaded him also not to counterwork the designs of God, but to esteem his favor above all things, and to permit them to depart, lest, before he be aware, he lay an obstruction in the way of the Divine commands, and so occasion his own suffering such punishments as it was probable any one that counterworked the Divine commands should undergo, since the severest afflictions arise from every object to those that provoke the Divine wrath against them; for such as these have neither the earth nor the air for their friends; nor are the fruits of the womb according to nature, but every thing is unfriendly and adverse towards them. He said further, that the Egyptians should know this by sad experience; and that besides, the Hebrew people should go out of their country without their consent.

14 Concerning the Ten Plagues Which Came Upon the Egyptians

1. BUT when the king despised the words of Moses, and had no regard at all to them, grievous plagues seized the Egyptians; every

one of which I will describe, both because no such plagues did ever happen to any other nation as the Egyptians now felt, and because I would demonstrate that Moses did not fail in any one thing that he foretold them; and because it is for the good of mankind, that they may learn this caution—Not to do anything that may displease God, lest he be provoked to wrath, and avenge their iniquities upon them. For the Egyptian river ran with bloody water at the command of God, insomuch that it could not be drunk, and they had no other spring of water neither; for the water was not only of the color of blood, but it brought upon those that ventured to drink of it, great pains and bitter torment. Such was the river to the Egyptians; but it was sweet and fit for drinking to the Hebrews, and no way different from what it naturally used to be. As the king therefore knew not what to do in these surprising circumstances, and was in fear for the Egyptians, he gave the Hebrews leave to go away; but when the plague ceased, he changed his mind again, end would not suffer them to go.

2. But when God saw that he was ungrateful, and upon the ceasing of this calamity would not grow wiser, he sent another plague upon the Egyptians:—An innumerable multitude of frogs consumed the fruit of the ground; the river was also full of them, insomuch that those who drew water had it spoiled by the blood of these animals, as they died in, and were destroyed by, the water; and the country was full of filthy slime, as they were born, and as they died: they also spoiled their vessels in their houses which they used, and were found among what they eat and what they drank, and came in great numbers upon their beds. There was also an ungrateful smell, and a stink arose from them, as they were born, and as they died therein. Now, when the Egyptians were under the oppression of these miseries, the king ordered Moses to take the Hebrews with him, and be gone. Upon which the whole multitude of the frogs vanished away; and both the land and the river returned to their former natures. But as soon as Pharaoh saw the land freed from this plague, he forgot the cause of it, and retained the Hebrews; and, as though he had a mind to try the nature of more such judgments, he would not yet suffer Moses and his people to depart, having granted that liberty rather out of fear than out of any good consideration.[25]

---

25. Of this judicial hardening the hearts and blinding the eyes of wicked men,

3. Accordingly, God punished his falseness with another plague, added to the former; for there arose out of the bodies of the Egyptians an innumerable quantity of lice, by which, wicked as they were, they miserably perished, as not able to destroy this sort of vermin either with washes or with ointments. At which terrible judgment the king of Egypt was in disorder, upon the fear into which he reasoned himself, lest his people should be destroyed, and that the manner of this death was also reproachful, so that he was forced in part to recover himself from his wicked temper to a sounder mind, for he gave leave for the Hebrews themselves to depart. But when the plague thereupon ceased, he thought it proper to require that they should leave their children and wives behind them, as pledges of their return; whereby he provoked God to be more vehemently angry at him, as if he thought to impose on his providence, and as if it were only Moses, and not God, who punished the Egyptians for the sake of the Hebrews: for he filled that country full of various sorts of pestilential creatures, with their various properties, such indeed as had never come into the sight of men before, by whose means the men perished themselves, and the land was destitute of husbandmen for its cultivation; but if any thing escaped destruction from them, it was killed by a distemper which the men underwent also.

4. But when Pharaoh did not even then yield to the will of God, but, while he gave leave to the husbands to take their wives with them, yet insisted that the children should be left behind, God presently resolved to punish his wickedness with several sorts of calamities, and those worse than the foregoing, which yet had so generally afflicted them; for their bodies had terrible boils, breaking forth with blains, while they were already inwardly consumed; and a great part of the Egyptians perished in this manner. But when the king was not brought to reason by this plague, hail was sent down from heaven; and such hail it was, as the climate of Egypt had never suffered before, nor was it like to that which falls in other climates in winter time,[26] but was larger than that which falls in the middle of spring to those that dwell

---

or infatuating them, as a just punishment for their other willful sins, to their own destruction, see the note on Antiq. B. VII. ch. 9. sect. 6.

26. As to this winter or spring hail near Egypt and Judea, see the like on thunder and lightning there, in the note on Antiq. B. VI. ch. 5. sect. 6.

in the northern and north-western regions. This hail broke down their boughs laden with fruit. After this a tribe of locusts consumed the seed which was not hurt by the hail; so that to the Egyptians all hopes of the future fruits of the ground were entirely lost.

5. One would think the forementioned calamities might have been sufficient for one that was only foolish, without wickedness, to make him wise, and to make him Sensible what was for his advantage. But Pharaoh, led not so much by his folly as by his wickedness, even when he saw the cause of his miseries, he still contested with God, and willfully deserted the cause of virtue; so he bid Moses take the Hebrews away, with their wives and children, to leave their cattle behind, since their own cattle were destroyed. But when Moses said that what he desired was unjust, since they were obliged to offer sacrifices to God of those cattle, and the time being prolonged on this account, a thick darkness, without the least light, spread itself over the Egyptians, whereby their sight being obstructed, and their breathing hindered by the thickness of the air, they died miserably, and under a terror lest they should be swallowed up by the dark cloud. Besides this, when the darkness, after three days and as many nights, was dissipated, and when Pharaoh did not still repent and let the Hebrews go, Moses came to him and said, "How long wilt thou be disobedient to the command of God? for he enjoins thee to let the Hebrews go; nor is there any other way of being freed from the calamities are under, unless you do so." But the king angry at what he said, and threatened to cut off his head if he came any more to trouble him these matters. Hereupon Moses said he not speak to him any more about them, for he himself, together with the principal men among the Egyptians, should desire the Hebrews away. So when Moses had said this, he his way.

6. But when God had signified, that with one plague he would compel the Egyptians to let Hebrews go, he commanded Moses to tell the people that they should have a sacrifice ready, and they should prepare themselves on the tenth day of the month Xanthicus, against the fourteenth, (which month is called by the Egyptians Pharmuth, Nisan by the Hebrews; but the Macedonians call it Xanthicus,) and that he should carry the Hebrews with all they had. Accordingly, he having got the Hebrews ready for their departure, and having sorted the people into tribes, he kept them together in one place: but when the fourteenth day was come, and all were ready to depart they offered

the sacrifice, and purified their houses with the blood, using bunches of hyssop for that purpose; and when they had supped, they burnt the remainder of the flesh, as just ready to depart. Whence it is that we do still offer this sacrifice in like manner to this day, and call this festival *Pascha* which signifies *the feast of the passover;* because on that day God passed us over, and sent the plague upon the Egyptians; for the destruction of the first-born came upon the Egyptians that night, so that many of the Egyptians who lived near the king's palace, persuaded Pharaoh to let the Hebrews go. Accordingly he called for Moses, and bid them be gone; as supposing, that if once the Hebrews were gone out of the country, Egypt should be freed from its miseries. They also honored the Hebrews with gifts;[27] some, in order to get them to depart quickly, and others on account of their neighborhood, and the friendship they had with them.

15   How the Hebrews under the Conduct of Moses Left Egypt

1. So the Hebrews went out of Egypt, while the Egyptians wept, and repented that they had treated them so hardly.—Now they took their journey by Letopolis, a place at that time deserted, but where Babylon was built afterwards, when Cambyses laid Egypt waste: but as they went away hastily, on the third day they came to a place called Beelzephon, on the Red Sea; and when they had no food out of the land, because it was a desert, they eat of loaves kneaded of flour, only warmed by a gentle heat; and this food they made use of for thirty days; for what they brought with them out of Egypt would not suffice them any longer time; and this only while they dispensed it to each

---

27. These large presents made to the Israelites, of vessels of and vessels of gold, and raiment, were, as Josephus truly calls them, gifts really given them; not lent them, as our English falsely renders them. They were spoils required, not of them, Genesis 15:14; Exodus 3:22; 11:2; Psalm 105:37,) as the same version falsely renders the Hebrew word Exodus 12:35, 36. God had ordered the Jews to demand these as their pay and reward, during their long and bitter slavery in Egypt, as atonements for the lives of the Egyptians, and as the condition of the Jews' departure, and of the Egyptians' deliverance from these terrible judgments, which, had they not now ceased, they had soon been all dead men, as they themselves confess, ch. 12. 33. Nor was there any sense in borrowing or lending, when the Israelites were finally departing out of the land for ever.

person, to use so much only as would serve for necessity, but not for satiety. Whence it is that, in memory of the want we were then in, we keep a feast for eight days, which is called *the feast of unleavened bread*. Now the entire multitude of those that went out, including the women and children, was not easy to be numbered, but those that were of an age fit for war, were six hundred thousand.

2. They left Egypt in the month Xanthicus, on the fifteenth day of the lunar month; four hundred and thirty years after our forefather Abraham came into Canaan, but two hundred and fifteen years only after Jacob removed into Egypt.[28] It was the eightieth year of the age of Moses, and of that of Aaron three more. They also carried out the bones of Joesph with them, as he had charged his sons to do.

3. But the Egyptians soon repented that the Hebrews were gone; and the king also was mightily concerned that this had been procured by the magic arts of Moses; so they resolved to go after them. Accordingly they took their weapons, and other warlike furniture, and pursued after them, in order to bring them back, if once they overtook them, because they would now have no pretense to pray to God against them, since they had already been permitted to go out; and they thought they should easily overcome them, as they had no armor, and would be weary with their journey; so they made haste in their pursuit, and asked of every one they met which way they were gone. And indeed that land was difficult to be traveled over, not only by armies, but by single persons. Now Moses led the Hebrews this way, that in case the Egyptians should repent and be desirous to pursue after them, they might undergo the punishment of their wickedness, and of the breach of those promises they had made to them. As also he led them this way on account of the Philistines, who had quarreled with them, and hated them of old, that by all means they might not know of their departure, for their country is near to that of Egypt; and thence it was that Moses led them not

---

28. Why our Masorete copy so groundlessly abridges this account in Exodus 12:40, as to ascribe 430 years to the sole peregrination of the Israelites in Egypt, when it is clear even by that Masorete chronology elsewhere, as well as from the express text itself, in the Samaritan, Septuagint, and Josephus, that they sojourned in Egypt but half that time,—and that by consequence, the other half of their peregrination was in the land of Canaan, before they came into Egypt,—is hard to say. See Essay on the Old Testament, p. 62, 63.

along the road that tended to the land of the Philistines, but he was desirous that they should go through the desert, that so after a long journey, and after many afflictions, they might enter upon the land of Canaan. Another reason of this was, that God commanded him to bring the people to Mount Sinai, that there they might offer him sacrifices. Now when the Egyptians had overtaken the Hebrews, they prepared to fight them, and by their multitude they drove them into a narrow place; for the number that pursued after them was six hundred chariots, with fifty thousand horsemen, and two hundred thousand foot-men, all armed. They also seized on the passages by which they imagined the Hebrews might fly, shutting them up[29] between inaccessible precipices and the sea; for there was [on each side] a [ridge of] mountains that terminated at the sea, which were impassable by reason of their roughness, and obstructed their flight; wherefore they there pressed upon the Hebrews with their army, where [the ridges of] the mountains were closed with the sea; which army they placed at the chops of the mountains, that so they might deprive them of any passage into the plain.

4. When the Hebrews, therefore, were neither able to bear up, being thus, as it were, besieged, because they wanted provisions, nor saw any possible way of escaping; and if they should have thought of

---

29. Take the main part of Reland's excellent note here, which greatly illustrates Josephus, and the Scripture, in this history, as follows: "[A traveller, says Reland, whose name was] Eneman, when he returned out of Egypt, told me that he went the same way from Egypt to Mount Sinai, which he supposed the Israelites of old traveled; and that he found several mountainous tracts, that ran down towards the Red Sea. He thought the Israelites had proceeded as far as the desert of Etham, Exodus 13:20, when they were commanded by God to return back, Exodus 14:2, and to pitch their camp between Migdol and the sea; and that when they were not able to fly, unless by sea, they were shut in on each side by mountains. He also thought we might evidently learn hence, how it might be said that the Israelites were in Etham before they went over the sea, and yet might be said to have come into Etham after they had passed over the sea also. Besides, he gave me an account how he passed over a river in a boat near the city Suez, which he says must needs be the Heroopolia of the ancients, since that city could not be situate any where else in that neighborhood."

As to the famous passage produced here by Dr. Bernard, out of Herodotus, as the most ancient heathen testimony of the Israelites coming from the Red Sea into Palestine, Bishop Cumberland has shown that it belongs to the old Canaanite or Phoenician shepherds, and their retiring out of Egypt into Canaan or Phoenicia, long before the days of Moses. Sanchoniatho, p. 374, &c.

fighting, they had no weapons; they expected a universal destruction, unless they delivered themselves up to the Egyptians. So they laid the blame on Moses, and forgot all the signs that had been wrought by God for the recovery of their freedom; and this so far, that their incredulity prompted them to throw stones at the prophet, while he encouraged them and promised them deliverance; and they resolved that they would deliver themselves up to the Egyptians. So there was sorrow and lamentation among the women and children, who had nothing but destruction before their eyes, while they were encompassed with mountains, the sea, and their enemies, and discerned no way of flying from them.

5. But Moses, though the multitude looked fiercely at him, did not, however, give over the care of them, but despised all dangers, out of his trust in God, who, as he had afforded them the several steps already taken for the recovery of their liberty, which he had foretold them, would not now suffer them to be subdued by their enemies, to be either made slaves or be slain by them; and, standing in midst of them, he said, "It is not just of us to distrust even men, when they have hitherto well managed our affairs, as if they would not be the same hereafter; but it is no better than madness, at this time to despair of the providence of God, by whose power all those things have been performed he promised, when you expected no such things: I mean all that I have been concerned in for deliverance and escape from slavery. Nay, when we are in the utmost distress, as you see we ought rather to hope that God will succor us, by whose operation it is that we are now this narrow place, that he may out of such difficulties as are otherwise insurmountable and out of which neither you nor your enemies expect you can be delivered, and may at once demonstrate his own power and his providence over us. Nor does God use to give his help in small difficulties to those whom he favors, but in such cases where no one can see how any hope in man can better their condition. Depend, therefore, upon such a Protector as is able to make small things great, and to show that this mighty force against you is nothing but weakness, and be not affrighted at the Egyptian army, nor do you despair of being preserved, because the sea before, and the mountains behind, afford you no opportunity for flying, for even these mountains, if God so please, may be made plain ground for you, and the sea become dry land."

16 How the Sea Was Divided Asunder for the Hebrews, When They Were Pursued by the Egyptians, and So Gave Them an Opportunity of Escaping from Them

1. WHEN Moses had said this, he led them to the sea, while the Egyptians looked on; for they were within sight. Now these were so distressed by the toil of their pursuit, that they thought proper to put off fighting till the next day. But when Moses was come to the sea-shore, he took his rod, and made supplication to God, and called upon him to be their helper and assistant; and said "Thou art not ignorant, O Lord, that it is beyond human strength and human contrivance to avoid the difficulties we are now under; but it must be thy work altogether to procure deliverance to this army, which has left Egypt at thy appointment. We despair of any other assistance or contrivance, and have recourse only to that hope we have in thee; and if there be any method that can promise us an escape by thy providence, we look up to thee for it. And let it come quickly, and manifest thy power to us; and do thou raise up this people unto good courage and hope of deliverance, who are deeply sunk into a disconsolate state of mind. We are in a helpless place, but still it is a place that thou possessest; still the sea is thine, the mountains also that enclose us are thine; so that these mountains will open themselves if thou commandest them, and the sea also, if thou commandest it, will become dry land. Nay, we might escape by a flight through the air, if thou shouldst determine we should have that way of salvation."

2. When Moses had thus addressed himself to God, he smote the sea with his rod, which parted asunder at the stroke, and receiving those waters into itself, left the ground dry, as a road and a place of flight for the Hebrews. Now when Moses saw this appearance of God, and that the sea went out of its own place, and left dry land, he went first of all into it, and bid the Hebrews to follow him along that divine road, and to rejoice at the danger their enemies that followed them were in; and gave thanks to God for this so surprising a deliverance which appeared from him.

3. Now, while these Hebrews made no stay, but went on earnestly, as led by God's presence with them, the Egyptians supposed first that they were distracted, and were going rashly upon manifest destruction. But when they saw that they were going a great way

without any harm, and that no obstacle or difficulty fell in their journey, they made haste to pursue them, hoping that the sea would be calm for them also. They put their horse foremost, and went down themselves into the sea. Now the Hebrews, while these were putting on their armor, and therein spending their time, were beforehand with them, and escaped them, and got first over to the land on the other side without any hurt. Whence the others were encouraged, and more courageously pursued them, as hoping no harm would come to them neither: but the Egyptians were not aware that they went into a road made for the Hebrews, and not for others; that this road was made for the deliverance of those in danger, but not for those that were earnest to make use of it for the others' destruction. As soon, therefore, as ever the whole Egyptian army was within it, the sea flowed to its own place, and came down with a torrent raised by storms of wind,[30] and encompassed the Egyptians. Showers of rain also came down from the sky, and dreadful thunders and lightning, with flashes of fire. Thunderbolts also were darted upon them. Nor was there any thing which used to be sent by God upon men, as indications of his wrath, which did not happen at this time, for a dark and dismal night oppressed them. And thus did all these men perish, so that there was not one man left to be a messenger of this calamity to the rest of the Egyptians.

4. But the Hebrews were not able to contain themselves for joy at their wonderful deliverance, and destruction of their enemies; now indeed supposing themselves firmly delivered, when those that would have forced them into slavery were destroyed, and when they found they had God so evidently for their protector. And now these Hebrews having escaped the danger they were in, after this manner, and besides that, seeing their enemies punished in such a way as is never recorded of any other men whomsoever, were all the night employed in singing of hymns, and in mirth.[31] Moses also composed a song unto

---

30. Of these storms of wind, thunder, and lightning, at this drowning of Pharaoh's army, almost wanting in our copies of Exodus, but fully extant in that of David, Psalm 77:16–18, and in that of Josephus here, see Essay on the Old Test. Append. p. 15,1, 155.

31. What some have here objected against this passage of the Israelites over the Red Sea, in this one night, from the common maps, viz. that this sea being here about thirty miles broad, so great an army conld not pass over it in so short a time, is a

God, containing his praises, and a thanksgiving for his kindness, in hexameter verse.[32]

5. As for myself, I have delivered every part of this history as I found it in the sacred books; nor let any one wonder at the strangeness of the narration if a way were discovered to those men of old time, who were free from the wickedness of the modern ages, whether it happened by the will of God or whether it happened of its own accord;—while, for the sake of those that accompanied Alexander, king of Macedonia, who yet lived, comparatively but a little while ago, the Pamphylian Sea retired and afforded them a passage[33] through

---

great mistake. Mons. Thevenot, an authentic eye-witness, informs us, that this sea, for about five days' journey, is no where more than about eight or nine miles over-cross, and in one place but four or five miles, according to De Lisle's map, which is made from the best travelers themselves, and not copied from others. What has been further objected against this passage of the Israelites, and drowning of the Egyptians, being miraculous also, viz. that Moses might carry the Israelites over at a low tide without any miracle, while yet the Egyptians, not knowing the tide so well as he, might be drowned upon the return of the tide, is a strange story indeed ! That Moses, who never had lived here, should know the quantity and time of the flux and reflux of the Red Sea better than the Egyptians themselves in its neighborhood! Yet does Artapanus, an ancient heathen historian, inform us, that this was what the more ignorant Memphites, who lived at a great distance, pretended, though he confesses, that the more learned Heliopolitans, who lived much nearer, owned the destruction of the Egyptians, and the deliverance of the Israelites, to have been miraculous: and De Castro, a mathematician, who surveyed this sea with great exactness, informs us, that there is no great flux or reflux in this part of the Red Sea, to give a color to this hypothesis; nay, that at the elevation of the tide there is little above half the height of a man. See Essay on the Old Test. Append. p. 239, 240. So vain and groundless are these and the like evasions and subterfuges of our modern sceptics and unbelievers, and so certainly do thorough inquiries and authentic evidence disprove and confute such evasions and subterfuges upon all occasions.

32. What that hexameter verse, in which Moses's triumphant song is here said to be written, distinctly means, our present ignorance of the old Hebrew metre or measure will not let us determine. Nor does it appear to me certain that even Josephus himself had a distinct notion of it, though he speaks of several sort of that metre or measure, both here and elsewhere. Antiq. B. IV. ch. 8. sect. 44; and B. VII. ch. 12. sect. 3.

33. Take here the original passages of the four old authors that still remain, as to this transit of Alexander the Great over the Pamphylian Sea: I mean, of Callisthenes, Strabu, Arrian, and Appian. As to Callisthenes, who himself accompanied Alexander in this expedition, Eustathius, in his Notes on the third Iliad of Homer, (as Dr. Bernard here informs us,) says, That "this Callisthenes wrote how the Pamphylian Sea did not only open a passage for Alexander, but, by rising and did pay him homage as its king."

itself, had no other way to go; I mean, when it was the will of God to destroy the monarchy of the Persians: and this is confessed to be true by all that have written about the actions of Alexander. But as to these events, let every one determine as he pleases.

6. On the next day Moses gathered together the weapons of the Egyptians, which were brought to the camp of the Hebrews by the current of the sea, and the force of the winds resisting it; and he conjectured that this also happened by Divine Providence, that so they might not be destitute of weapons. So when he had ordered the

---

Strabo's is this (Geog. B. XIV. p. 666): "Now about Phaselis is that narrow passage, by the sea-side, through which his army. There is a mountain called Climax, adjoins to the Sea of Pamphylia, leaving a narrow passage on the shore, which, in calm weather, is bare, so as to be passable by travelers, but when the sea overflows, it is covered to a great degree by the waves. Now then, the ascent by the mountains being round about and steep, in still weather they make use of the road along the coast. But Alexander fell into the winter season, and committing himself chiefly to fortune, he marched on before the waves retired; and so it happened that were a whole day in journeying over it, and were under water up to the navel." Arrian's account is this (B. I. p. 72, 73): Alexander removed from Phaselis, he sent some part his army over the mountains to Perga; which road the Thracians showed him. A difficult way it was, but short. he himself conducted those that were with him by the sea-shore. This road is impassable at any other time than when the north wind blows; but if the south wind prevail, there is no passing by the shore. Now at this time, after strong south winds, a north wind blew, and that not without the Divine Providence, (as both he and they that were with him supposed,) and afforded him an easy and quick passage." Appian, when he compares Caesar and Alexander together, (De Bel. Civil. B. II. p. 522,) says, "That they both depended on their boldness and fortune, as much as on their skill in war. As an instance of which, Alexander journeyed over a country without water, in the heat of summer, to the oracle of [Jupiter] Hammon, and quickly passed over the Bay of Pamphylia, when, by Divine Providence, the sea was cut off—thus Providence restraining the sea on his account, as it had sent him rain when he traveled [over the desert]."

N. B.—Since, in the days of Josephus, as he assures us, all the more numerous original historians of Alexander gave the account he has here set down, as to the providential going back of the waters of the Pamphylian Sea, when he was going with his army to destroy the Persian monarchy, which the fore-named authors now remaining fully confirm, it is without all just foundation that Josephus is here blamed by some late writers for quoting those ancient authors upon the present occasion; nor can the reflections of Plutarch, or any other author later than Josephus, be in the least here alleged to contradict him. Josephus went by all the evidence he then had, and that evidence of the most authentic sort also. So that whatever the moderns may think of the thing itself, there is hence not the least color for finding fault with Josephus: he would rather have been much to blame had he omitted these quotations.

Hebrews to arm themselves with them, he led them to Mount Sinai, in order to offer sacrifice to God, and to render oblations for the salvation of the multitude, as he was charged to do beforehand.

Book 3

Containing the Interval of Two Years, from the Exodus Out of Egypt, to the Rejection of That Generation

1   How Moses When He Had Brought the People Out of Egypt Led Them to Mount Sinai; but Not Till They Had Suffered Much in Their Journey

1. WHEN the Hebrews had obtained such a wonderful deliverance, the country was a great trouble to them, for it was entirely a desert, and without sustenance for them; and also had exceeding little water, so that it not only was not at all sufficient for the men, but not enough to feed any of the cattle, for it was parched up, and had no moisture that might afford nutriment to the vegetables; so they were forced to travel over this country, as having no other country but this to travel in. They had indeed carried water along with them from the land over which they had traveled before, as their conductor had bidden them; but when that was spent, they were obliged to draw water out of wells, with pain, by reason of the hardness of the soil. Moreover, what water they found was bitter, and not fit for drinking, and this in small quantities also; and as they thus traveled, they came late in the evening to a place called Marah,[1] which had that name from the badness of its water, for *Mar* denotes *bitterness.* Thither they came

---

1. Dr. Bernard takes notice here, that this place Mar, where the waters were bitter, is called by the Syrians and Arabians Mariri, and by the Syrians sometimes Morath, all derived from the Hebrew Mar. He also takes notice, that it is called The Bitter

113

afflicted both by the tediousness of their journey, and by their want of food, for it entirely failed them at that time. Now here was a well, which made them choose to stay in the place, which, although it were not sufficient to satisfy so great an army, did yet afford them some comfort, as found in such desert places; for they heard from those who had been to search, that there was nothing to be found, if they traveled on farther. Yet was this water bitter, and not fit for men to drink; and not only so, but it was intolerable even to the cattle themselves.

2. When Moses saw how much the people were cast down, and that the occasion of it could not be contradicted, for the people were not in the nature of a complete army of men, who might oppose a manly fortitude to the necessity that distressed them; the multitude of the children, and of the women also, being of too weak capacities to be persuaded by reason, blunted the courage of the men themselves,—he was therefore in great difficulties, and made everybody's calamity his own; for they ran all of them to him, and begged of him; the women begged for their infants, and the men for the women, that he would not overlook them, but procure some way or other for their deliverance. He therefore betook himself to prayer to God, that he would change the water from its present badness, and make it fit for drinking. And when God had granted him that favor, he took the top of a stick that lay down at his feet, and divided it in the middle, and made the section lengthways. He then let it down into the well, and persuaded the Hebrews that God had hearkened to his prayers, and had promised to render the water such as they desired it to be, in case they would be subservient to him in what he should enjoin them to do, and this not after a remiss or negligent manner. And when they asked what they were to do in order to have the water changed for the better, he bid the strongest men among them that stood there, to draw up water[2] and

---

Fountain by Pliny himself; which waters remain there to this day, and are still bitter, as Thevenot assures us and that there are also abundance of palm-trees. See his Travels, Part I. ch. 26. p. 166.

2. The additions here to Moses's account of the sweetening of the waters at Marah, seem derived from some ancient profane author, and he such an author also as looks less authentic than are usually followed by Josephus. Philo has not a syllable of these additions, nor any other ancienter writer that we know of. Had Josephus written these his Antiquities for the use of Jews, he would hardly have given them these very improbable circumstances; but writing to Gentiles, that they might not complain of

told them, that when the greatest part was drawn up, the remainder would be fit to drink. So they labored at it till the water was so agitated and purged as to be fit to drink.

3. And now removing from thence they came to Elim; which place looked well at a distance, for there was a grove of palm-trees; but when they came near to it, it appeared to be a bad place, for the palm-trees were no more than seventy; and they were ill-grown and creeping trees, by the want of water, for the country about was all parched, and no moisture sufficient to water them, and make them hopeful and useful, was derived to them from the fountains, which were in number twelve: they were rather a few moist places than springs, which not breaking out of the ground, nor running over, could not sufficiently water the trees. And when they dug into the sand, they met with no water; and if they took a few drops of it into their hands, they found it to be useless, on account of its mud. The trees were too weak to bear fruit, for want of being sufficiently cherished and enlivened by the water. So they laid the blame on their conductor, and made heavy complaints against him; and said that this their miserable state, and the experience they had of adversity, were owing to him; for that they had then journeyed an entire thirty days, and had spent all the provisions they had brought with them; and meeting with no relief, they were in a very desponding condition. And by fixing their attention upon nothing but their present misfortunes, they were hindered from remembering what deliverances they had received from God, and those by the virtue and wisdom of Moses also; so they were very angry at their conductor, and were zealous in their attempt to stone him, as the direct occasion of their present miseries.

---

his omission of any accounts of such miracles derived from Gentiles, he did not think proper to conceal what he had met with there about this matter. Which procedure is perfectly agreeable to the character and usage of Josephus upon many occasions. This note is, I confess, barely conjectural; and since Josephus never tells us when his own copy, taken out of the temple, had such additions, or when any ancient notes supplied them; or indeed when they are derived from Jewish, and when from Gentile antiquity,—we can go no further than bare conjectures in such cases; only the notions of Jews were generally so different from those of Gentiles, that we may sometimes make no improbable conjectures to which sort such additions belong. See also somewhat like these additions in Josephus's account of Elisha's making sweet the bitter and barren spring near Jericho, War, B. IV. ch. 8. sect. 3.

4. But as for Moses himself, while the multitude were irritated and bitterly set against him, he cheerfully relied upon God, and upon his consciousness of the care he had taken of these his own people; and he came into the midst of them, even while they clamored against him, and had stones in their hands in order to despatch him. Now he was of an agreeable presence, and very able to persuade the people by his speeches; accordingly he began to mitigate their anger, and exhorted them not to be over-mindful of their present adversities, lest they should thereby suffer the benefits that had formerly been bestowed on them to slip out of their memories; and he desired them by no means, on account of their present uneasiness, to cast those great and wonderful favors and gifts, which they had obtained of God, out of their minds, but to expect deliverance out of those their present troubles which they could not free themselves from, and this by the means of that Divine Providence which watched over them. Seeing it is probable that God tries their virtue, and exercises their patience by these adversities, that it may appear what fortitude they have, and what memory they retain of his former wonderful works in their favor, and whether they will not think of them upon occasion of the miseries they now feel. He told them, it appeared they were not really good men, either in patience, or in remembering what had been successfully done for them, sometimes by contemning God and his commands, when by those commands they left the land of Egypt; and sometimes by behaving themselves ill towards him who was the servant of God, and this when he had never deceived them, either in what he said, or had ordered them to do by God's command. He also put them in mind of all that had passed; how the Egyptians were destroyed when they attempted to detain them, contrary to the command of God; and after what manner the very same river was to the others bloody, and not fit for drinking, but was to them sweet, and fit for drinking; and how they went a new road through the sea, which fled a long way from them, by which very means they were themselves preserved, but saw their enemies destroyed; and that when they were in want of weapons, God gave them plenty of them;—and so he recounted all the particular instances, how when they were, in appearance, just going to be destroyed, God had saved them in a surprising manner; and that he had still the same power; and that they ought not even now to despair of his providence over them; and accordingly he exhorted

them to continue quiet, and to consider that help would not come too late, though it come not immediately, if it be present with them before they suffer any great misfortune; that they ought to reason thus: that God delays to assist them, not because he has no regard to them, but because he will first try their fortitude, and the pleasure they take in their freedom, that he may learn whether you have souls great enough to bear want of food, and scarcity of water, on its account; or whether you rather love to be slaves, as cattle are slaves to such as own them, and feed them liberally, but only in order to make them more useful in their service. That as for himself, he shall not be so much concerned for his own preservation; for if he die unjustly, he shall not reckon it any affliction, but that he is concerned for them, lest, by casting stones at him, they should be thought to condemn God himself.

5. By this means Moses pacified the people, and restrained them from stoning him, and brought them to repent of what they were going to do. And because he thought the necessity they were under made their passion less unjustifiable, he thought he ought to apply himself to God by prayer and supplication; and going up to an eminence, he requested of God for some succor for the people, and some way of deliverance from the want they were in, because in him, and in him alone, was their hope of salvation; and he desired that he would forgive what necessity had forced the people to do, since such was the nature of mankind, hard to please, and very complaining under adversities. Accordingly God promised he would take care of them, and afford them the succor they were desirous of. Now when Moses had heard this from God, he came down to the multitude. But as soon as they saw him joyful at the promises he had received from God, they changed their sad countenances into gladness. So he placed himself in the midst of them, and told them he came to bring them from God a deliverance from their present distresses. Accordingly a little after came a vast number of quails, which is a bird more plentiful in this Arabian Gulf than any where else, flying over the sea, and hovered over them, till wearied with their laborious flight, and, indeed, as usual, flying very near to the earth, they fell down upon the Hebrews, who caught them, and satisfied their hunger with them, and supposed that this was the method whereby God meant to supply them with food. Upon which Moses returned thanks to God for affording them his assistance so suddenly, and sooner than he had promised them.

6. But presently after this first supply of food, he sent them a second; for as Moses was lifting up his hands in prayer, a dew fell down; and Moses, when he found it stick to his hands, supposed this was also come for food from God to them. He tasted it; and perceiving that the people knew not what it was, and thought it snowed, and that it was what usually fell at that time of the year, he informed them that this dew did not fall from heaven after the manner they imagined, but came for their preservation and sustenance. So he tasted it, and gave them some of it, that they might be satisfied about what he told them. They also imitated their conductor, and were pleased with the food, for it was like honey in sweetness and pleasant taste, but like in its body to bdellium, one of the sweet spices, and in bigness equal to coriander seed. And very earnest they were in gathering it; but they were enjoined to gather it equally[3]—the measure of an omer for each one every day, because this food should not come in too small a quantity, lest the weaker might not be able to get their share, by reason of the overbearing of the strong in collecting it. However, these strong men, when they had gathered more than the measure appointed for them, had no more than others, but only tired themselves more in gathering it, for they found no more than an omer apiece; and the advantage they got by what was superfluous was none at all, it corrupting, both by the worms breeding in it, and by its bitterness. So divine and wonderful a food was this! It also supplied the want of other sorts of food to those that fed on it. And even now, in all that place, this manna comes down in rain,[4] according to what Moses then obtained of God, to send it to the people for their sustenance. Now the Hebrews call this food *manna:*

---

3. It seems to me, from what Moses, Exodus 16:18, St. Paul, 2 Corinthians 8:15, and Josephus here say, compared together, that the quantity of manna that fell daily, and did not putrefy, was just so much as came to an omer apiece, through the whole host of Israel, and no more.

4. This supposal, that the sweet honey-dew or manna, so celebrated in ancient and modern authors, as falling usually in Arabia, was of the very same sort with this manna sent to the Israelites, savors more of Gentilism than of Judaism or Christianity. It is not improbable that some ancient Gentile author, read by Josephus, so thought; nor would he here contradict him; though just before, and Antiq. B. IV. ch. 3. sect. 2, he seems directly to allow that it had not been seen before. However, this food from heaven is here described to be like snow; and in Artapanus, a heathen writer, it is compared to meal, color like to snow, rained down by God," Essay on the Old Test. Append. p. 239. But as to the derivation of the word manna, whether from man, which

for the particle *man,* in our language, is the asking of a question. *What is this ?* So the Hebrews were very joyful at what was sent them from heaven. Now they made use of this food for forty years, or as long as they were in the wilderness.

7. As soon as they were removed thence, they came to Rephidim, being distressed to the last degree by thirst; and while in the foregoing days they had lit on a few small fountains, but now found the earth entirely destitute of water, they were in an evil case. They again turned their anger against Moses; but he at first avoided the fury of the multitude, and then betook himself to prayer to God, beseeching him, that as he had given them food when they were in the greatest want of it, so he would give them drink, since the favor of giving them food was of no value to them while they had nothing to drink. And God did not long delay to give it them, but promised Moses that he would procure them a fountain, and plenty of water, from a place they did not expect any. So he commanded him to smite the rock which they saw lying there,[5] with his rod, and out of it to receive plenty of what they wanted; for he had taken care that drink should come to them without any labor or pains-taking. When Moses had received this command from God, he came to the people, who waited for him, and looked upon him, for they saw already that he was coming apace from his eminence. As soon as he was come, he told them that God would deliver them from their present distress, and had granted them an unexpected favor; and informed them, that a river should run for their sakes out of the rock. But they were amazed at that hearing, supposing they were of necessity to cut the rock in pieces, now they were distressed by their thirst and by their journey; while Moses only smiting the rock with his rod, opened a passage, and out of it burst water, and that in great abundance, and very clear. But they were astonished at this wonderful effect; and, as it were, quenched their

---

Josephus says then signified What is it or from mannah, to divide, i.e. a dividend or portion allotted to every one, it is uncertain: I incline to the latter derivation. This manna is called angels' food, Psalm 78:26, and by our Sacior, John 6:31, etc., as well as by Josephus here and elsewhere, Antiq. B. III. ch. 5. sect. 3, said to be sent the Jews from heaven.

5. This rock is there at this day, as the travelers agree; and must be the same that was there in the days of Moses, as being too large to be brought thither by our modern carriages.

thirst by the very sight of it. So they drank this pleasant, this sweet water; and such it seemed to be, as might well be expected where God was the donor. They were also in admiration how Moses was honored by God; and they made grateful returns of sacrifices to God for his providence towards them. Now that Scripture, which is laid up in the temple,[6] informs us, how God foretold to Moses, that water timid in this manner be derived out of the rock.'

2   How the Amalekites and the Neighbouring Nations, Made War with the Hebrews and Were Beaten and Lost a Great Part of Their Army

1. THE name of the Hebrews began already to be every where renowned, and rumors about them ran abroad. This made the inhabitants of those countries to be in no small fear. Accordingly they sent ambassadors to one another, and exhorted one another to defend themselves, and to endeavor to destroy these men. Those that induced the rest to do so, were such as inhabited Gobolitis and Petra. They were called *Amalekites,* and were the most warlike of the nations that lived thereabout; and whose kings exhorted one another, and their neighbors, to go to this war against the Hebrews; telling them that an army of strangers, and such a one as had run away from slavery under the Egyptians, lay in wait to ruin them; which army they were not, in common prudence and regard to their own safety, to overlook, but to crush them before they gather strength, and come to be in prosperity: and perhaps attack them first in a hostile manner, as presuming upon our indolence in not attacking them before; and that we ought to avenge ourselves of them for what they have done in the wilderness, but that this cannot be so well done when they have once laid their hands on our cities and our goods: that those who endeavor to crush a power in its first rise, are wiser than those that endeavor to put a stop to its progress when it is become formidable; for these last seem to be angry only at the flourishing of others, but the former do not leave any room for their enemies to become troublesome to them. After they

6. Note here, that the small book of the principal laws of Moses is ever said to be laid up in the holy house itself; but the larger Pentateuch, as here, some where within the limits of the temple and its courts only. See Antiq. B. V. ch. 1. sect. 17.

had sent such embassages to the neighboring nations, and among one another, they resolved to attack the Hebrews in battle.

2. These proceedings of the people of those countries occasioned perplexity and trouble to Moses, who expected no such warlike preparations. And when these nations were ready to fight, and the multitude of the Hebrews were obliged to try the fortune of war, they were in a mighty disorder, and in want of all necessaries, and yet were to make war with men who were thoroughly well prepared for it. Then therefore it was that Moses began to encourage them, and to exhort them to have a good heart, and rely on God's assistance by which they had been state of freedom and to hope for victory over those who were ready to fight with them, in order to deprive them of that blessing: that they were to suppose their own army to be numerous, wanting nothing, neither weapons, nor money, nor provisions, nor such other conveniences as, when men are in possession of, they fight undauntedly; and that they are to judge themselves to have all these advantages in the Divine assistance. They are also to suppose the enemy's army to be small, unarmed, weak, and such as want those conveniences which they know must be wanted, when it is God's will that they shall be beaten; and how valuable God's assistance is, they had experienced in abundance of trials; and those such as were more terrible than war, for that is only against men; but these were against famine and thirst, things indeed that are in their own nature insuperable; as also against mountains, and that sea which afforded them no way for escaping; yet had all these difficulties been conquered by God's gracious kindness to them. So he exhorted them to be courageous at this time, and to look upon their entire prosperity to depend on the present conquest of their enemies.

3. And with these words did Moses encourage the multitude, who then called together the princes of their tribes, and their chief men, both separately and conjointly. The young men he charged to obey their elders, and the elders to hearken to their leader. So the people were elevated in their minds, and ready to try their fortune in battle, and hoped to be thereby at length delivered from all their miseries: nay, they desired that Moses would immediately lead them against their enemies without the least delay, that no backwardness might be a hindrance to their present resolution. So Moses sorted all that were fit for war into different troops, and set Joshua, the son of Nun,

of the tribe of Ephraim, over them; one that was of great courage, and patient to undergo labors; of great abilities to understand, and to speak what was proper; and very serious in the worship of God; and indeed made like another Moses, a teacher of piety towards God. He also appointed a small party of the armed men to be near the water, and to take care of the children, and the women, and of the entire camp. So that whole night they prepared themselves for the battle; they took their weapons, if any of them had such as were well made, and attended to their commanders as ready to rush forth to the battle as soon as Moses should give the word of command. Moses also kept awake, teaching Joshua after what manner he should order his camp. But when the day began, Moses called for Joshua again, and exhorted him to approve himself in deeds such a one as a his reputation made men expect from him; and to gain glory by the present expedition, in the opinion of those under him, for his exploits in this battle. He also gave a particular exhortation to the principal men of the Hebrews, and encouraged the whole army as it stood armed before him. And when he had thus animated the army, both by his words and works, and prepared every thing, he retired to a mountain, and committed the army to God and to Joshua.

4. So the armies joined battle; and it came to a close fight, hand to hand, both sides showing great alacrity, and encouraging one another. And indeed while Moses stretched out his hand towards heaven[7] the Hebrews were too hard for the Amalekites: but Moses not being able to sustain his hands thus stretched out, (for as often as he let down his hands, so often were his own people worsted,) he bade his brother Aaron, and Hur their sister Miriam's husband, to stand

---

7. This eminent circumstance, that while Moses's hands were lift up towards heaven, the Israelites prevailed, and while they were let down towards the earth, the Amalekites prevailed, seems to me the earliest intimation we have of the proper posture, used of old, in solemn prayer, which was the stretching out of the hands [and eyes] towards heaven, as other passages of the Old and New Testament inform us. Nay, by the way, this posture seemed to have continued in the Christian church, till the clergy, instead of learning their prayers by heart, read them out of a book, which is in a great measure inconsistent with such an elevated posture, and which seems to me to have been only a later practice, introduced under the corrupt state of the church; though the constant use of divine forms of prayer, praise, and thanksgiving, appears to me to have been the practice of God's people, patriarchs, Jews, and Christians, in all the past ages.

on each side of him, and take hold of his hands, and not permit his weariness to prevent it, but to assist him in the extension of his hands. When this was done, the Hebrews conquered the Amalekites by main force; and indeed they had all perished, unless the approach of the night had obliged the Hebrews to desist from killing any more. So our forefathers obtained a most signal and most seasonable victory; for they not only overcame those that fought against them, but terrified also the neighboring nations, and got great and splendid advantages, which they obtained of their enemies by their hard pains in this battle: for when they had taken the enemy's camp, they got ready booty for the public, and for their own private families, whereas till then they had not any sort of plenty, of even necessary food. The forementioned battle, when they had once got it, was also the occasion of their prosperity, not only for the present, but for the future ages also; for they not only made slaves of the bodies of their enemies, but subdued their minds also, and after this battle, became terrible to all that dwelt round about them. Moreover, they acquired a vast quantity of riches; for a great deal of silver and gold was left in the enemy's camp; as also brazen vessels, which they made common use of in their families; many utensils also that were embroidered there were of both sorts, that is, of what were weaved, and what were the ornaments of their armor, and other things that served for use in the family, and for the furniture of their rooms; they got also the prey of their cattle, and of whatsoever uses to follow camps, when they remove from one place to another. So the Hebrews now valued themselves upon their courage, and claimed great merit for their valor; and they perpetually inured themselves to take pains, by which they deemed every difficulty might be surmounted. Such were the consequences of this battle.

5. On the next day, Moses stripped the dead bodies of their enemies, and gathered together the armor of those that were fled, and gave rewards to such as had signalized themselves in the action; and highly commended Joshua, their general, who was attested to by all the army, on account of the great actions he had done. Nor was any one of the Hebrews slain; but the slain of the enemy's army were too many to be enumerated. So Moses offered sacrifices of thanksgiving to God, and built an altar, which he named *The Lord the Conqueror.* He also foretold that the Amalekites should utterly be destroyed; and that hereafter none of them should remain, because they fought against the Hebrews,

and this when they were in the wilderness, and in their distress also. Moreover, he refreshed the army with feasting. And thus did they fight this first battle with those that ventured to oppose them, after they were gone out of Egypt. But when Moses had celebrated this festival for the victory, he permitted the Hebrews to rest for a few days, and then he brought them out after the fight, in order of battle; for they had now many soldiers in light armor. And going gradually on, he came to Mount Sinai, in three months' time after they were removed out of Egypt; at which mountain, as we have before related, the vision of the bush, and the other wonderful appearances, had happened.

3 That Moses Kindly Received-His Father-in-Law, Jethro, When He Came to Him to Mount Sinai

NOW when Raguel, Moses's father-in-law, understood in what a prosperous condition his affairs were, he willingly came to meet him. And Moses and his children, and pleased himself with his coming. And when he had offered sacrifice, he made a feast for the multitude, near the Bush he had formerly seen; which multitude, every one according to their families, partook of the feast. But Aaron and his family took Raguel, and sung hymns to God, as to Him who had been the author procurer of their deliverance and their freedom. They also praised their conductor, as him by whose virtue it was that all things had succeeded with them. Raguel also, in his eucharistical oration to Moses, made great encomiums upon the whole multitude; and he could not but admire Moses for his fortitude, and that humanity he had shewn in the delivery of his friends.

4 How Raguel Suggested to Moses to Set His People in Order, under Their Rulers of Thousands, and Rulers of Hundreds, Who Lived Without Order Before; and How Moses Complied in All Things with His Father-in-Law's Admonition

1. THE next day, as Raguel saw Moses in the of a crowd of business for he determined the differences of those that referred them to him, every one still going to him, and supposing that they should then only obtain justice, if he were the arbitrator; and those that lost their causes

thought it no harm, while they thought they lost them justly, and not by partiality. Raguel however said nothing to him at that time, as not desirous to be any hinderance to such as had a mind to make use of the virtue of their conductor. But afterward he took him to himself, and when he had him alone, he instructed him in what he ought to do; and advised him to leave the trouble of lesser causes to others, but himself to take care of the greater, and of the people's safety, for that certain others of the Hebrews might be found that were fit to determine causes, but that nobody but a Moses could take of the safety of so many ten thousands. "Be therefore," says he, "insensible of thine own virtue, and what thou hast done by ministering under God to the people's preservation. Permit, therefore, the determination of common causes to be done by others, but do thou reserve thyself to the attendance on God only, and look out for methods of preserving the multitude from their present distress. Make use of the method I suggest to you, as to human affairs; and take a review of the army, and appoint chosen rulers over tens of thousands, and then over thousands; then divide them into five hundreds, and again into hundreds, and into fifties; and set rulers over each of them, who may distinguish them into thirties, and keep them in order; and at last number them by twenties and by tens: and let there be one commander over each number, to be denominated from the number of those over whom they are rulers, but such as the whole multitude have tried, and do approve of, as being good and righteous men;[8] and let those rulers decide the controversies they have one with another. But if any great cause arise, let them bring the cognizance of it before the rulers of a higher dignity; but if any great difficulty arise that is too hard for even their determination, let them send it to thee. By these means two advantages will be gained; the Hebrews will have justice done them, and thou wilt be able to attend constantly on God, and procure him to be more favorable to the people."

2. This was the admonition of Raguel; and Moses received his advice very kindly, and acted according to his suggestion. Nor did

---

8. This manner of electing the judges and officers of the Israelites by the testimonies and suffrages of the people, before they were ordained by God, or by Moses, deserves to be carefully noted, because it was the pattern of the like manner of the choice and ordination of bishops, presbyters, and deacons, in the Christian church.

he conceal the invention of this method, nor pretend to it himself, but informed the multitude who it was that invented it: nay, he has named Raguel in the books he wrote, as the person who invented this ordering of the people, as thinking it right to give a true testimony to worthy persons, although he might have gotten reputation by ascribing to himself the inventions of other men; whence we may learn the virtuous disposition of Moses: but of such his disposition, we shall have proper occasion to speak in other places of these books.

5   How Moses Ascended Up to Mount Sinai, and Received Laws from God, and Delivered Them to the Hebrews

1. NOW Moses called the multitude together, and told them that he was going from them unto mount Sinai to converse with God; to receive from him, and to bring back with him, a certain oracle; but he enjoined them to pitch their tents near the mountain, and prefer the habitation that was nearest to God, before one more remote. When he had said this, he ascended up to Mount Sinai, which is the highest of all the mountains that are in that country[9] and is not only very difficult to be ascended by men, on account of its vast altitude, but because of the sharpness of its precipices also; nay, indeed, it cannot be looked at without pain of the eyes: and besides this, it was terrible and inaccessible, on account of the rumor that passed about, that God dwelt there. But the Hebrews removed their tents as Moses had bidden them, and took possession of the lowest parts of the mountain; and were elevated in their minds, in expectation that Moses would return from God with promises of the good things he had proposed to them. So they feasted and waited for their conductor, and kept themselves

---

9. Since this mountain, Sinai, is here said to be the highest of all the mountains that are in that country, it must be that now called St. Katherine's, which is one-third higher than that within a mile of it, now called Sinai, as Mons. Thevenot informs us, Travels, Part I. ch. 23. p. 168. The other name of it, Horeb, is never used by Josephus, and perhaps was its name among the Egyptians only, whence the Israelites were lately come, as Sinai was its name among the Arabians, Canaanites, and other nations. Accordingly when (1 Kings 9:8) the Scripture says that Elijah came to Horeb, the mount of God, Josephus justly says, Antiq. B. VIII. ch. 13. sect. 7, that he came to the mountain called Sinai: and Jerome, here cited by Dr. Hudson, says, that he took this mountain to have two names, Sinai and Choreb. De Nomin. Heb. p. 427.

pure as in other respects, and not accompanying with their wives for three days, as he had before ordered them to do. And they prayed to God that he would favorably receive Moses in his conversing with him, and bestow some such gift upon them by which they might live well. They also lived more plentifully as to their diet; and put on their wives and children more ornamental and decent clothing than they usually wore.

2. So they passed two days in this way of feasting; but on the third day, before the sun was up, a cloud spread itself over the whole camp of the Hebrews, such a one as none had before seen, and encompassed the place where they had pitched their tents; and while all the rest of the air was clear, there came strong winds, that raised up large showers of rain, which became a mighty tempest. There was also such lightning, as was terrible to those that saw it; and thunder, with its thunderbolts, were sent down, and declared God to be there present in a gracious way to such as Moses desired he should be gracious. Now, as to these matters, every one of my readers may think as he pleases; but I am under a necessity of relating this history as it is described in the sacred books. This sight, and the amazing sound that came to their ears, disturbed the Hebrews to a prodigious degree, for they were not such as they were accustomed to; and then the rumor that was spread abroad, how God frequented that mountain, greatly astonished their minds, so they sorrowfully contained themselves within their tents, as both supposing Moses to be destroyed by the Divine wrath, and expecting the like destruction for themselves.

3. When they were under these apprehensions, Moses appeared as joyful and greatly exalted. When they saw him, they were freed from their fear, and admitted of more comfortable hopes as to what was to come. The air also was become clear and pure of its former disorders, upon the appearance of Moses; whereupon he called together the people to a congregation, in order to their hearing what God would say to them: and when they were gathered together, he stood on an eminence whence they might all hear him, and said, "God has received me graciously, O Hebrews, as he has formerly done; and has suggested a happy method of living for you, and an order of political government, and is now present in the camp: I therefore charge you, for his sake and the sake of his works, and what we have done by his means, that you do not put a low value on what I am going to

say, because the commands have been given by me that now deliver them to you, nor because it is the tongue of a man that delivers them to you; but if you have a due regard to the great importance of the things themselves, you will understand the greatness of Him whose institutions they are, and who has not disdained to communicate them to me for our common advantage; for it is not to be supposed that the author of these institutions is barely Moses, the son of Amram and Jochebed, but He who obliged the Nile to run bloody for your sakes, and tamed the haughtiness of the Egyptians by various sorts of judgments; he who provided a way through the sea for us; he who contrived a method of sending us food from heaven, when we were distressed for want of it; he who made the water to issue out of a rock, when we had very little of it before; he by whose means Adam was made to partake of the fruits both of the land and of the sea; he by whose means Noah escaped the deluge; he by whose means our forefather Abraham, of a wandering pilgrim, was made the heir of the land of Canaan; he by whose means Isaac was born of parents that were very old; he by whose means Jacob was adorned with twelve virtuous sons; he by whose means Joseph became a potent lord over the Egyptians; he it is who conveys these instructions to you by me as his interpreter. And let them be to you venerable, and contended for more earnestly by you than your own children and your own wives; for if you will follow them, you will lead a happy life you will enjoy the land fruitful, the sea calm, and the fruit of the womb born complete, as nature requires; you will be also terrible to your enemies for I have been admitted into the presence of God and been made a hearer of his incorruptible voice so great is his concern for your nation, and its duration."

4. When he had said this, he brought the people, with their wives and children, so near the mountain, that they might hear God himself speaking to them about the precepts which they were to practice; that the energy of what should be spoken might not be hurt by its utterance by that tongue of a man, which could but imperfectly deliver it to their understanding. And they all heard a voice that came to all of them from above, insomuch that no one of these words escaped them, which

Moses wrote on two tables; which it is not lawful for us to set down directly, but their import we will declare[10]

5. The first commandment teaches us that there is but one God, and that we ought to worship him only. The second commands us not to make the image of any living creature to worship it. The third, that we must not swear by God in a false matter. The fourth, that we must keep the seventh day, by resting from all sorts of work. The fifth, that we must honor our parents. The sixth that we must abstain from murder. The seventh that we must not commit adultery. The eighth, that we must not be guilty of theft. The ninth, that we must not bear false witness. The tenth, that we must not admit of the desire of any thing that is another's.

6. Now when the multitude had heard God himself giving those precepts which Moses had discoursed of, they rejoiced at what was said; and the congregation was dissolved: but on the following days they came to his tent, and desired him to bring them, besides, other laws from God. Accordingly he appointed such laws, and afterwards informed them in what manner they should act in all cases; which laws I shall make mention of in their proper time; but I shall reserve most of those laws for another work,[11] and make there a distinct explication of them.

7. When matters were brought to this state, Moses went up again to Mount Sinai, of which he had told them beforehand. He made his ascent in their sight; and while he staid there so long a time, (for he was absent from them forty days,) fear seized upon the Hebrews, lest Moses should have come to any harm; nor was there any thing else so sad, and that so much troubled them, as this supposal that Moses was perished. Now there was a variety in their sentiments about it; some saying that he was fallen among wild beasts; and those that were of this opinion were chiefly such as were ill-disposed to him; but others said that he was departed, and gone to God; but the wiser sort were led by their reason to embrace neither of those opinions

---

10. Of this and another like superstitious notion of the Pharisees, which Josephus complied with, see the note on Antiq. B. II. ch. 12. sect. 4.

11. This other work of Josephus, here referred to, seems to be that which does not appear to have been ever published, which yet he intended to publish, about the reasons of many of the laws of Moses; of which see the note on the Preface, sect. 4.

with any satisfaction, thinking, that as it was a thing that sometimes happens to men to fall among wild beasts and perish that way, so it was probable enough that he might depart and go to God, on account of his virtue; they therefore were quiet, and expected the event: yet were they exceeding sorry upon the supposal that they were deprived of a governor and a protector, such a one indeed as they could never recover again; nor would this suspicion give them leave to expect any comfortable event about this man, nor could they prevent their trouble and melancholy upon this occasion. However, the camp durst not remove all this while, because Moses had bidden them afore to stay there.

8. But when the forty days, and as many nights, were over, Moses came down, having tasted nothing of food usually appointed for the nourishment of men. His appearance filled the army with gladness, and he declared to them what care God had of them, and by what manner of conduct of their lives they might live happily; telling them, that during these days of his absence he had suggested to him also that he would have a tabernacle built for him, into which he would descend when he came to them, and how we should carry it about with us when we remove from this place; and that there would be no longer any occasion for going up to Mount Sinai, but that he would himself come and pitch his tabernacle amongst us, and be present at our prayers; as also, that the tabernacle should be of such measures and construction as he had shown him, and that you are to fall to the work, and prosecute it diligently. When he had said this, he showed them the two tables, with the ten commandments engraven upon them, five upon each table; and the writing was by the hand of God.

6   Concerning the Tabernacle Which Moses Built in the Wilderness for the Honor of God and Which Seemed to Be a Temple

1. HEREUPON the Israelites rejoiced at what they had seen and heard of their conductor, and were not wanting in diligence according to their ability; for they brought silver, and gold, and brass, and of the best sorts of wood, and such as would not at all decay by putrefaction; camels' hair also, and sheep-skins, some of them dyed of a blue color, and some of a scarlet; some brought the flower for the purple color,

and others for white, with wool dyed by the flowers aforementioned; and fine linen and precious stones, which those that use costly ornaments set in ouches of gold; they brought also a great quantity of spices; for of these materials did Moses build the tabernacle, which did not at all differ from a movable and ambulatory temple. Now when these things were brought together with great diligence, (for every one was ambitious to further the work even beyond their ability,) he set architects over the works, and this by the command of God; and indeed the very same which the people themselves would have chosen, had the election been allowed to them. Now their names are set down in writing in the sacred books; and they were these: Besaleel, the son of Uri, of the tribe of Judah, the grandson of Miriam, the sister of their conductor and Aholiab, file son of Ahisamach, of the tribe of Dan. Now the people went on with what they had undertaken with so great alacrity, that Moses was obliged to restrain them, by making proclamation, that what had been brought was sufficient, as the artificers had informed him; so they fell to work upon the building of the tabernacle. Moses also informed them, according to the direction of God, both what the measures were to be, and its largeness; and how many vessels it ought to contain for the use of the sacrifices. The women also were ambitious to do their parts, about the garments of the priests, and about other things that would be wanted in this work, both for ornament and for the divine service itself.

2. Now when all things were prepared, the gold, and the silver, and the brass, and what was woven, Moses, when he had appointed beforehand that there should be a festival, and that sacrifices should be offered according to every one's ability, reared up the tabernacle[12] and when he had measured the open court, fifty cubits broad and a hundred long, he set up brazen pillars, five cubits high, twenty on each of the longer sides, and ten pillars for the breadth behind; every one of the pillars also had a ring. Their chapiters were of silver, but their bases were of brass: they resembled the sharp ends of spears, and were of brass, fixed into the ground. Cords were also put through the rings, and were tied at their farther ends to brass nails of a cubit long, which, at every pillar, were driven into the floor, and would keep the

---

12. Of this tabernacle of Moses, with its several parts and furniture, see my description at large, chap. 6. 7. 8. 9. 10. 11. 12. hereto belonging.

tabernacle from being shaken by the violence of winds; but a curtain of fine soft linen went round all the pillars, and hung down in a flowing and loose manner from their chapiters, and enclosed the whole space, and seemed not at all unlike to a wall about it. And this was the structure of three of the sides of this enclosure; but as for the fourth side, which was fifty cubits in extent, and was the front of the whole, twenty cubits of it were for the opening of the gates, wherein stood two pillars on each side, after the resemblance of open gates. These were made wholly of silver, and polished, and that all over, excepting the bases, which were of brass. Now on each side of the gates there stood three pillars, which were inserted into the concave bases of the gates, and were suited to them; and round them was drawn a curtain of fine linen; but to the gates themselves, which were twenty cubits in extent, and five in height, the curtain was composed of purple, and scarlet, and blue, and fine linen, and embroidered with many and divers sorts of figures, excepting the figures of animals. Within these gates was the brazen laver for purification, having a basin beneath of the like matter, whence the priests might wash their hands and sprinkle their feet; and this was the ornamental construction of the enclosure about the court of the tabernacle, which was exposed to the open air.

3. As to the tabernacle itself, Moses placed it in the middle of that court, with its front to the east, that, when the sun arose, it might send its first rays upon it. Its length, when it was set up, was thirty cubits, and its breadth was twelve [ten] cubits. The one of its walls was on the south, and the other was exposed to the north, and on the back part of it remained the west. It was necessary that its height should be equal to its breadth [ten cubits]. There were also pillars made of wood, twenty on each side; they were wrought into a quadrangular figure, in breadth a cubit and a half, but the thickness was four fingers: they had thin plates of gold affixed to them on both sides, inwardly and outwardly: they had each of them two tenons belonging to them, inserted into their bases, and these were of silver, in each of which bases there was a socket to receive the tenon; but the pillars on the west wall were six. Now all these tenons and sockets accurately fitted one another, insomuch that the joints were invisible, and both seemed to be one entire and united wall. It was also covered with gold, both within and without. The number of pillars was equal on the opposite sides, and there were on each part twenty, and every one of them had

the third part of a span in thickness; so that the number of thirty cubits were fully made up between them; but as to the wall behind, where the six pillars made up together only nine cubits, they made two other pillars, and cut them out of one cubit, which they placed in the corners, and made them equally fine with the other. Now every one of the pillars had rings of gold affixed to their fronts outward, as if they had taken root in the pillars, and stood one row over against another round about, through which were inserted bars gilt over with gold, each of them five cubits long, and these bound together the pillars, the head of one bar running into another, after the nature of one tenon inserted into another; but for the wall behind, there was but one row of bars that went through all the pillars, into which row ran the ends of the bars on each side of the longer walls; the male with its female being so fastened in their joints, that they held the whole firmly together; and for this reason was all this joined so fast together, that the tabernacle might not be shaken, either by the winds, or by any other means, but that it might preserve itself quiet and immovable continually.

4. As for the inside, Moses parted its length into three partitions. At the distance of ten cubits from the most secret end, Moses placed four pillars, the workmanship of which was the very same with that of the rest; and they stood upon the like bases with them, each a small matter distant from his fellow. Now the room within those pillars was the most holy place; but the rest of the room was the tabernacle, which was open for the priests. However, this proportion of the measures of the tabernacle proved to be an imitation of the system of the world; for that third part thereof which was within the four pillars, to which the priests were not admitted, is, as it were, a heaven peculiar to God. But the space of the twenty cubits, is, as it were, sea and land, on which men live, and so this part is peculiar to the priests only. But at the front, where the entrance was made, they placed pillars of gold, that stood on bases of brass, in number seven; but then they spread over the tabernacle veils of fine linen and purple, and blue, and scarlet colors, embroidered. The first veil was ten cubits every way, and this they spread over the pillars which parted the temple, and kept the most holy place concealed within; and this veil was that which made this part not visible to any. Now the whole temple was called *The Holy Place:* but that part which was within the four pillars, and to which none were admitted, was called *The Holy of Holies.* This veil was very

ornamental, and embroidered with all sorts of flowers which the earth produces; and there were interwoven into it all sorts of variety that might be an ornament, excepting the forms of animals. Another veil there was which covered the five pillars that were at the entrance. It was like the former in its magnitude, and texture, and color; and at the corner of every pillar a ring retained it from the top downwards half the depth of the pillars, the other half affording an entrance for the priests, who crept under it. Over this there was a veil of linen, of the same largeness with the former: it was to be drawn this way or that way by cords, the rings of which, fixed to the texture of the veil, and to the cords also, were subservient to the drawing and undrawing of the veil, and to the fastening it at the corner, that then it might be no hinderance to the view of the sanctuary, especially on solemn days; but that on other days, and especially when the weather was inclined to snow, it might be expanded, and afford a covering to the veil of divers colors. Whence that custom of ours is derived, of having a fine linen veil, after the temple has been built, to be drawn over the entrances. But the ten other curtains were four cubits in breadth, and twenty-eight in length; and had golden clasps, in order to join the one curtain to the other, which was done so exactly that they seemed to be one entire curtain. These were spread over the temple, and covered all the top and parts of the walls, on the sides and behind, so far as within one cubit of the ground. There were other curtains of the same breadth with these, but one more in number, and longer, for they were thirty cubits long; but these were woven of hair, with the like subtilty as those of wool were made, and were extended loosely down to the ground, appearing like a triangular front and elevation at the gates, the eleventh curtain being used for this very purpose. There were also other curtains made of skins above these, which afforded covering and protection to those that were woven both in hot weather and when it rained. And great was the surprise of those who viewed these curtains at a distance, for they seemed not at all to differ from the color of the sky. But those that were made of hair and of skins, reached down in the same manner as did the veil at the gates, and kept off the heat of the sun, and what injury the rains might do. And after this manner was the tabernacle reared.

5. There was also an ark made, sacred to God, of wood that was naturally strong, and could not be corrupted. This was called *Eron*

in our own language. Its construction was thus: its length was five spans, but its breadth and height was each of them three spans. It was covered all over with gold, both within and without, so that the wooden part was not seen. It had also a cover united to it, by golden hinges, after a wonderful manner; which cover was every way evenly fitted to it, and had no eminences to hinder its exact conjunction. There were also two golden rings belonging to each of the longer boards, and passing through the entire wood, and through them gilt bars passed along each board, that it might thereby be moved and carried about, as occasion should require; for it was not drawn in a cart by beasts of burden, but borne on the shoulders of the priests. Upon this its cover were two images, which the Hebrews call *Cherubims*; they are flying creatures, but their form is not like to that of any of the creatures which men have seen, though Moses said he had seen such beings near the throne of God. In this ark he put the two tables whereon the ten commandments were written, five upon each table, and two and a half upon each side of them; and this ark he placed in the most holy place.

6. But in the holy place he placed a table, like those at Delphi. Its length was two cubits, and its breadth one cubit, and its height three spans. It had feet also, the lower half of which were complete feet, resembling those which the Dorians put to their bedsteads; but the upper parts towards the table were wrought into a square form. The table had a hollow towards every side, having a ledge of four fingers' depth, that went round about like a spiral, both on the upper and lower part of the body of the work. Upon every one of the feet was there also inserted a ring, not far from the cover, through which went bars of wood beneath, but gilded, to be taken out upon occasion, there being a cavity where it was joined to the rings; for they were not entire rings; but before they came quite round they ended in acute points, the one of which was inserted into the prominent part of the table, and the other into the foot; and by these it was carried when they journeyed: Upon this table, which was placed on the north side of the temple, not far from the most holy place, were laid twelve unleavened loaves of bread, six upon each heap, one above another: they were made of two tenth-deals of the purest flour, which tenth-deal [an omer] is a measure of the Hebrews, containing seven Athenian *cotyloe*; and above those loaves were put two vials full of frankincense. Now after seven days other loaves were brought in their stead, on the day which is by us

called the *Sabbath*; for we call the seventh day the *Sabbath*. But for the occasion of this intention of placing loaves here, we will speak to it in another place.

7. Over against this table, near the southern wall, was set a candlestick of cast gold, hollow within, being of the weight of one hundred pounds, which the Hebrews call *Chinchares*, if it be turned into the Greek language, it denotes a *talent*. It was' made with its knops, and lilies, and pomegranates, and bowls (which ornaments amounted to seventy in all); by which means the shaft elevated itself on high from a single base, and spread itself into as many branches as there are planets, including the sun among them. It terminated in seven heads, in one row, all standing parallel to one another; and these branches carried seven lamps, one by one, in imitation of the number of the planets. These lamps looked to the east and to the south, the candlestick being situate obliquely.

8. Now between this candlestick and the table, which, as we said, were within the sanctuary, was the altar of incense, made of wood indeed, but of the same wood of which the foregoing vessels were made, such as was not liable to corruption; it was entirely crusted over with a golden plate. Its breadth on each side was a cubit, but the altitude double. Upon it was a grate of gold, that was extant above the altar, which had a golden crown encompassing it round about, whereto belonged rings and bars, by which the priests carried it when they journeyed. Before this tabernacle there was reared a brazen altar, but it was within made of wood, five cubits by measure on each side, but its height was but three, in like manner adorned with brass plates as bright as gold. It had also a brazen hearth of network; for the ground underneath received the fire from the hearth, because it had no basis to receive it. Hard by this altar lay the basins, and the vials, and the censers, and the caldrons, made of gold; but the other vessels, made for the use of the sacrifices, were all of brass. And such was the construction of the tabernacle; and these were the vessels thereto belonging.

7 *Concerning the Garments of the Priests, and of the High Priest*

1. THERE were peculiar garments appointed for the priests, and for all the rest, which they call *Cohanoeoe* [-priestly] garments, as also for

the high priests, which they call *Cahanoeoe Rabbae,* and denote the high priest's garments. Such was therefore the habit of the rest. But when the priest approaches the sacrifices, he purifies himself with the purification which the law prescribes; and, in the first place, he puts on that which is called *Machanase,* which means somewhat that is fast tied. It is a girdle, composed of fine twined linen, and is put about the privy parts, the feet being to be inserted into them in the nature of breeches, but above half of it is cut off, and it ends at the thighs, and is there tied fast.

2. Over this he wore a linen vestment, made of fine flax doubled: it is called *Chethone,* and denotes *linen,* for we call linen by the name of *Chethone.* This vestment reaches down to the feet, and sits close to the body; and has sleeves that are tied fast to the arms: it is girded to the breast a little above the elbows, by a girdle often going round, four fingers broad, but so loosely woven, that you would think it were the skin of a serpent. It is embroidered with flowers of scarlet, and purple, and blue, and fine twined linen, but the warp was nothing but fine linen. The beginning of its circumvolution is at the breast; and when it has gone often round, it is there tied, and hangs loosely there down to the ankles: I mean this, all the time the priest is not about any laborious service, for in this position it appears in the most agreeable manner to the spectators; but when he is obliged to assist at the offering sacrifices, and to do the appointed service, that he may not be hindered in his operations by its motion, he throws it to the left, and bears it on his shoulder. Moses indeed calls this belt *Albaneth;* but we have learned from the Babylonians to call it *Emia,* for so it is by them called. This vestment has no loose or hollow parts any where in it, but only a narrow aperture about the neck; and it is tied with certain strings hanging down from the edge over the breast and back, and is fastened above each shoulder: it is called *Massabazanes.*

3. Upon his head he wears a cap, not brought to a conic form nor encircling the whole head, but still covering more than the half of it, which is called *Masnaemphthes;* and its make is such that it seems to be a crown, being made of thick swathes, but the contexture is of linen; and it is doubled round many times, and sewed together; besides which, a piece of fine linen covers the whole cap from the upper part, and reaches down to the forehead, and hides the seams of the swathes, which would otherwise appear indecently: this adheres closely upon

the solid part of the head, and is thereto so firmly fixed, that it may not fall off during the sacred service about the sacrifices. So we have now shown you what is the habit of the generality of the priests.

4. The high priest is indeed adorned with the same garments that we have described, without abating one; only over these he puts on a vestment of a blue color. This also is a long robe, reaching to his feet, [in our language it is called .Meeir,] and is tied round with a girdle, embroidered with the same colors and flowers as the former, with a mixture of gold interwoven. To the bottom of which garment are hung fringes, in color like pomegranates, with golden bells[13] by a curious and beautiful contrivance; so that between two bells hangs a pomegranate, and between two pomegranates a bell. Now this vesture was not composed of two pieces, nor was it sewed together upon the shoulders and the sides, but it was one long vestment so woven as to have an aperture for the neck; not an oblique one, but parted all along the breast and the back. A border also was sewed to it, lest the aperture should look too indecently: it was also parted where the hands were to come out.

5. Besides these, the high priest put on a third garment, which was called the *Ephod*, which resembles the Epomis of the Greeks. Its make was after this manner: it was woven to the depth of a cubit, of several colors, with gold intermixed, and embroidered, but it left the middle of the breast uncovered: it was made with sleeves also; nor did it appear to be at all differently made from a short coat. But in the void place of this garment there was inserted a piece of the bigness of a span, embroidered with gold, and the other colors of the ephod, and was called *Essen*, [the breastplate,] which in the Greek language signifies

---

13. The use of these golden bells at the bottom of the high priest's long garment, seems to me to have been this: That by shaking his garment at the time of his offering incense in the temple, on the great day of expiation, or at other proper periods of his sacred ministrations there, on the great festivals, the people might have notice of it, and might fall to their own prayers at the time of incense, or other proper periods; and so the whole congregation might at once offer those common prayers jointly with the high priest himself to the Almighty See Luke 1:10; Revelation 8:3, 4. Nor probably is the son of Sirach to be otherwise understood, when he says of Aaron, the first high priest, Ecelus. 45:9, "And God encompassed Aaron with pomegranates, and with many golden bells round about, that as he went there might be a sound, and a noise made that might be heard in the temple, for a memorial to the children of his people."

the *Oracle*. This piece exactly filled up the void space in the ephod. It was united to it by golden rings at every corner, the like rings being annexed to the ephod, and a blue riband was made use of to tie them together by those rings; and that the space between the rings might not appear empty, they contrived to fill it up with stitches of blue ribands. There were also two sardonyxes upon the ephod, at the shoulders, to fasten it in the nature of buttons, having each end running to the sardonyxes of gold, that they might be buttoned by them. On these were engraven the names of the sons of Jacob, in our own country letters, and in our own tongue, six on each of the stones, on either side; and the elder sons' names were on the right shoulder. Twelve stones also there were upon the breast-plate, extraordinary in largeness and beauty; and they were an ornament not to be purchased by men, because of their immense value. These stones, however, stood in three rows, by four in a row, and were inserted into the breastplate itself, and they were set in ouches of gold, that were themselves inserted in the breastplate, and were so made that they might not fall out low the first three stones were a sardonyx, a topaz, and an emerald. The second row contained a carbuncle, a jasper, and a sapphire. The first of the third row was a ligure, then an amethyst, and the third an agate, being the ninth of the whole number. The first of the fourth row was a chrysolite, the next was an onyx, and then a beryl, which was the last of all. Now the names of all those sons of Jacob were engraven in these stones, whom we esteem the heads of our tribes, each stone having the honor of a name, in the order according to which they were born. And whereas the rings were too weak of themselves to bear the weight of the stones, they made two other rings of a larger size, at the edge of that part of the breastplate which reached to the neck, and inserted into the very texture of the breastplate, to receive chains finely wrought, which connected them with golden bands to the tops of the shoulders, whose extremity turned backwards, and went into the ring, on the prominent back part of the ephod; and this was for the security of the breastplate, that it might not fall out of its place. There was also a girdle sewed to the breastplate, which was of the forementioned colors, with gold intermixed, which, when it had gone once round, was tied again upon the seam, and hung down. There were also golden loops that admitted its fringes at each extremity of the girdle, and included them entirely.

6. The high priest's mitre was the same that we described before, and was wrought like that of all the other priests; above which there was another, with swathes of blue embroidered, and round it was a golden crown polished, of three rows, one above another; out of which arose a cup of gold, which resembled the herb which we call *Saccharus;* but those Greeks that are skillful in botany call it *Hyoscyamus.* Now, lest any one that has seen this herb, but has not been taught its name, and is unacquainted with its nature, or, having known its name, knows not the herb when he sees it, I shall give such as these are a description of it. This herb is oftentimes in tallness above three spans, but its root is like that of a turnip (for he that should compare it thereto would not be mistaken); but its leaves are like the leaves of mint. Out of its branches it sends out a calyx, cleaving. to the branch; and a coat encompasses it, which it naturally puts off when it is changing, in order to produce its fruit. This calyx is of the bigness of the bone of the little finger, but in the compass of its aperture is like a cup. This I will further describe, for the use of those that are unacquainted with it. Suppose a sphere be divided into two parts, round at the bottom, but having another segment that grows up to a circumference from that bottom; suppose it become narrower by degrees, and that the cavity of that part grow decently smaller, and then gradually grow wider again at the brim, such as we see in the navel of a pomegranate, with its notches. And indeed such a coat grows over this plant as renders it a hemisphere, and that, as one may say, turned accurately in a lathe, and having its notches extant above it, which, as I said, grow like a pomegranate, only that they are sharp, and end in nothing but prickles. Now the fruit is preserved by this coat of the calyx, which fruit is like the seed of the herb Sideritis: it sends out a flower that may seem to resemble that of poppy. Of this was a crown made, as far from the hinder part of the head to each of the temples; but this *Ephielis,* for so this calyx may be called, did not cover the forehead, but it was covered with a golden plate,[14] which had inscribed upon it the name of God in sacred characters. And such were the ornaments of the high priest.

---

14. The reader ought to take notice here, that the very Mosaic Petalon, or golden plate, for the forehead of the Jewish high priest, was itself preserved, not only till the days of Josephus, but of Origen; and that its inscription, Holiness to the Lord, was in the Samaritan characters. See Antiq. B. VIII. ch. 3. sect. 8, Essay on the Old Test. p. 154, and Reland, De pol. Templi, p. 132.

7. Now here one may wonder at the ill-will which men bear to us, and which they profess to bear on account of our despising that Deity which they pretend to honor; for if any one do but consider the fabric of the tabernacle, and take a view of the garments of the high priest, and of those vessels which we make use of in our sacred ministration, he will find that our legislator was a divine man, and that we are unjustly reproached by others; for if any one do without prejudice, and with judgment, look upon these things, he will find they were every one made in way of imitation and representation of the universe. When Moses distinguished the tabernacle into three parts,[15] and allowed two of them to the priests, as a place accessible and common, he denoted the land and the sea, these being of general access to all; but he set apart the third division for God, because heaven is inaccessible to men. And when he ordered twelve loaves to be set on the table, he denoted the year, as distinguished into so many months. By branching out the candlestick into seventy parts, he secretly intimated the *Decani,* or seventy divisions of the planets; and as to the seven lamps upon the candlesticks, they referred to the course of the planets, of which that is the number. The veils, too, which were composed of four things, they declared the four elements; for the fine linen was proper to signify the earth, because the flax grows out of the earth; the purple signified the sea, because that color is dyed by the blood of a sea shell-fish; the blue is fit to signify the air; and the scarlet will naturally be an indication of fire. Now the vestment of the high priest being made of linen, signified the earth; the blue denoted the sky, being like lightning in its pomegranates, and in the noise of the bells resembling thunder. And for the ephod, it showed that God had made the universe of four elements; and as for the gold interwoven, I suppose it related to the splendor by which all things are enlightened. He also appointed the breastplate to be placed in the middle of the ephod, to resemble the earth, for that has the very

---

15. When Josephus, both here and ch. 6. sect. 4, supposes the tabernacle to have been parted into three parts, he seems to esteem the bare entrance to be a third division, distinct from the holy and the most holy places; and this the rather, because in the temple afterward there was a real distinct third part, which was called the Porch: otherwise Josephus would contradict his own description of the tabernacle, which gives as a particular account of no more than two parts.

middle place of the world. And the girdle which encompassed the high priest round, signified the ocean, for that goes round about and includes the universe. Each of the sardonyxes declares to us the sun and the moon; those, I mean, that were in the nature of buttons on the high priest's shoulders. And for the twelve stones, whether we understand by them the months, or whether we understand the like number of the signs of that circle which the Greeks call the *Zodiac*, we shall not be mistaken in their meaning. And for the mitre, which was of a blue color, it seems to me to mean heaven; for how otherwise could the name of God be inscribed upon it? That it was also illustrated with a crown, and that of gold also, is because of that splendor with which God is pleased. Let this explication[16] suffice at present, since the course of my narration will often, and on many occasions, afford me the opportunity of enlarging upon the virtue of our legislator.

8 Of the Priesthood of Aaron

1. WHEN what has been described was brought to a conclusion, gifts not being yet presented, God appeared to Moses, and enjoined him to bestow the high priesthood upon Aaron his brother, as upon him that best of them all deserved to obtain that honor, on account of his virtue. And when he had gathered the multitude together, he gave them an account of Aaron's virtue, and of his good-will to them, and of the dangers he had undergone for their sakes. Upon which, when

---

16. This explication of the mystical meaning of the Jewish tabernacle and its vessels, with the garments of the high priest, is taken out of Philo, and fitted to Gentile philosophical notions. This may possibly be forgiven in Jews, greatly versed in heathen learning and philosophy, as Philo had ever been, and as Josephus had long been when he wrote these Antiquities. In the mean time, it is not to be doubted, but in their education they must have both learned more Jewish interpretations, such as we meet with in the Epistle of Barnabas, in that to the Hebrews, and elsewhere among the old Jews. Accordingly when Josephus wrote his books of the Jewish War, for the use of the Jews, at which time he was comparatively young, and less used to Gentile books, we find one specimen of such a Jewish interpretation; for there (B. VII. ch. 5. sect. 5) he makes the seven branches of the temple-candlestick, with their seven lamps, an emblem of the seven days of creation and rest, which are here emblems of the seven planets. Nor certainly ought ancient Jewish emblems to be explained any other way than according to ancient Jewish, and not Gentile, notions. See of the War, B. I. ch. 33. sect. 2.

they had given testimony to him in all respects, and showed their readiness to receive him, Moses said to them, "O you Israelites, this work is already brought to a conclusion, in a manner most acceptable to God, and according to our abilities. And now since you see that he is received into this tabernacle, we shall first of all stand in need of one that may officiate for us, and may minister to the sacrifices, and to the prayers that are to be put up for us. And indeed had the inquiry after such a person been left to me, I should have thought myself worthy of this honor, both because all men are naturally fond of themselves, and because I am conscious to myself that I have taken a great deal of pains for your deliverance; but now God himself has determined that Aaron is worthy of this honor, and has chosen him for his priest, as knowing him to be the most righteous person among you. So that he is to put on the vestments which are consecrated to God; he is to have the care of the altars, and to make provision for the sacrifices; and he it is that must put up prayers for you to God, who will readily hear them, not only because he is himself solicitous for your nation, but also because he will receive them as offered by one that he hath himself chosen to this office.[17] The Hebrews were pleased with what was said, and they gave their approbation to him whom God had ordained; for Aaron was of them all the most deserving of this honor, on account of his own stock and gift of prophecy, and his brother's virtue. He had at that time four sons, Nadab, Abihu, Eleazar, and Ithamar.

2. Now Moses commanded them to make use of all the utensils which were more than were necessary to the structure of the tabernacle, for covering the tabernacle itself, the candlestick, and altar of incense, and the other vessels, that they might not be at all hurt when they journeyed, either by the rain, or by the rising of the dust. And when he had gathered the multitude together again, he ordained that they should offer half a shekel for every man, as an oblation to God; which shekel is a piece among the Hebrews, and is equal to four

---

17. It is well worth our observation, that the two principal qualifications required in this section for the constitution of the first high priest, (viz. that he should have an excellent character for virtuous and good actions; as also that he should have the approbation of the people,) are here noted by Josephus, even where the nomination belonged to God himself; which are the very same qualifications which the Christian religion requires in the choice of Christian bishops, priests, and deacons; as the Apostolical Constitutions inform us, B. II. ch. 3.

Athenian drachmae.[18] Whereupon they readily obeyed what Moses had commanded; and the number of the offerers was six hundred and five thousand five hundred and fifty. Now this money that was brought by the men that were free, was given by such as were about twenty years old, but under fifty; and what was collected was spent in the uses of the tabernacle.

3. Moses now purified the tabernacle and the priests; which purification was performed after the following manner:—He commanded them to take five hundred shekels of choice myrrh, an equal quantity of cassia, and half the foregoing weight of cinnamon and calamus (this last is a sort of sweet spice); to beat them small, and wet them with an bin of oil of olives (an *hin* is our own country measure, and contains two Athenian *choas*, or *congiuses*); then mix them together, and boil them, and prepare them after the art of the apothecary, and make them into a very sweet ointment; and afterward to take it to anoint and to purify the priests themselves, and all the tabernacle, as also the sacrifices. There were also many, and those of various kinds, of sweet spices, that belonged to the tabernacle, and such as were of very great price, and were brought to the golden altar of incense; the nature of which I do not now describe, lest it should be troublesome to my readers; but incense[19] was to be offered twice a-day, both before sun-rising and at sun-setting. They were also to keep oil already purified for the lamps; three of which were to give light all day long,[20] upon the sacred candlestick, before God, and the rest were to be lighted at the evening.

---

18. This weight and value of the Jewish shekel, in the days of Josephus, equal to about 2s. 10d. sterling, is, by the learned Jews, owned to be one-fifth larger than were their old shekels; which determination agrees perfectly with the remaining shekels that have Samaritan inscriptions, coined generally by Simon the Maccabee, about 230 years before Josephus published his Antiquities, which never weigh more than 2s. 4d., and commonly but 2s. 4d. See Reland De Nummis Samaritanorum, p. 138.

19. The incense was here offered, according to Josephus's opinion, before sun-rising, and at sun-setting; but in the days of Pompey, according to the same Josephus, the sacrifices were offered in the morning, and at the ninth hour. Antiq. B. XIV. ch. 4. sect. 3.

20. Hence we may correct the opinions of the modern Rabbins, who say that only one of the seven lamps burned in the day-time; whereas our Josephus, an eyewitness, says there were three.

4. Now all was finished. Besaleel and Aholiab appeared to be the most skillful of the workmen; for they invented finer works than what others had done before them, and were of great abilities to gain notions of what they were formerly ignorant of; and of these, Besaleel was judged to be the best. Now the whole time they were about this work was the interval of seven months; and after this it was that was ended the first year since their departure out of Egypt. But at the beginning of the second year, on the month *Xanthicus,* as the Macedonians call it, but on the month *Nisan,* as the Hebrews call it, on the new moon, they consecrated the tabernacle, and all its vessels, which I have already described.

5. Now God showed himself pleased with the work of the Hebrews, and did not permit their labors to be in vain; nor did he disdain to make use of what they had made, but he came and sojourned with them, and pitched his tabernacle in the holy house. And in the following manner did he come to it:—The sky was clear, but there was a mist over the tabernacle only, encompassing it, but not with such a very deep and thick cloud as is seen in the winter season, nor yet in so thin a one as men might be able to discern any thing through it, but from it there dropped a sweet dew, and such a one as showed the presence of God to those that desired and believed it.

6. Now when Moses had bestowed such honorary presents on the workmen, as it was fit they should receive, who had wrought so well, he offered sacrifices in the open court of the tabernacle, as God commanded him; a bull, a ram, and a kid of the goats, for a sin-offering. Now I shall speak of what we do in our sacred offices in my discourse about sacrifices; and therein shall inform men in what cases Moses bid us offer a whole burnt-offering, and in what cases the law permits us to partake of them as of food. And when Moses had sprinkled Aaron's vestments, himself, and his sons, with the blood of the beasts that were slain, and had purified them with spring waters and ointment, they became God's priests. After this manner did he consecrate them and their garments for seven days together. The same he did to the tabernacle, and the vessels thereto belonging, both with oil first incensed, as I said, and with the blood of bulls and of rams, slain day by day one, according to its kind. But on the eighth day he appointed a feast for the people, and commanded them to offer sacrifice according to their ability. Accordingly they contended one

with another, and were ambitious to exceed each other in the sacrifices which they brought, and so fulfilled Moses's injunctions. But as the sacrifices lay upon the altar, a sudden fire was kindled from among them of its own accord, and appeared to the sight like fire from a flash of lightning, and consumed whatsoever was upon the altar.

7. Hereupon an affliction befell Aaron, considered as a man and a father, but was undergone by him with true fortitude; for he had indeed a firmness of soul in such accidents, and he thought this calamity came upon him according to God's will: for whereas he had four sons, as I said before, the two elder of them, Nadab and Abihu, did not bring those sacrifices which Moses bade them bring, but which they used to offer formerly, and were burnt to death. Now when the fire rushed upon them, and began to burn them, nobody could quench it. Accordingly they died in this manner. And Moses bid their father and their brethren to take up their bodies, to carry them out of the camp, and to bury them magnificently. Now the multitude lamented them, and were deeply affected at this their death, which so unexpectedly befell them. But Moses entreated their brethren and their father not to be troubled for them, and to prefer the honor of God before their grief about them; for Aaron had already put on his sacred garments.

8. But Moses refused all that honor which he saw the multitude ready to bestow upon him, and attended to nothing else but the service of God. He went no more up to Mount Sinai; but he went into the tabernacle, and brought back answers from God for what he prayed for. His habit was also that of a private man, and in all other circumstances he behaved himself like one of the common people, and was desirous to appear without distinguishing himself from the multitude, but would have it known that he did nothing else but take care of them. He also set down in writing the form of their government, and those laws by obedience whereto they would lead their lives so as to please God, and so as to have no quarrels one among another. However, the laws he ordained were such as God suggested to him; so I shall now discourse concerning that form of government, and those laws.

9. I will now treat of what I before omitted, the garment of the high priest: for he [Moses] left no room for the evil practices of [false] prophets; but if some of that sort should attempt to abuse the Divine

authority, he left it to God to be present at his sacrifices when he pleased, and when he pleased to be absent.[21] And he was willing this should be known, not to the Hebrews only, but to those foreigners also who were there. For as to those stones,[22] which we told you before, the high priest bare on his shoulders, which were sardonyxes, (and I

---

21. Of this strange expression, that Moses "left it to God to be present at his sacrifices when he pleased, and when he pleased to be absent," see the note on B. II. against Apion, sect. 16.

22. These answers by the oracle of Urim and Thummim, which words signify, light and perfection, or, as the Septuagint render them, revelation and truth, and denote nothing further, that I see, but the shining stones themselves, which were used, in this method of illumination, in revealing the will of God, after a perfect and true manner, to his people Israel: I say, these answers were not made by the shining of the precious stones, after an awkward manner, in the high priest's breastplate, as the modern Rabbins vainly suppose; for certainly the shining of the stones might precede or accompany the oracle, without itself delivering that oracle, see Antiq. B. VI. ch. 6. sect. 4; but rather by an audible voice from the mercy-seat between the cherubims. See Prideaux's Connect. at the year 534. This oracle had been silent, as Josephus here informs us, two hundred years before he wrote his Antiquities, or ever since the days of the last good high priest of the family of the Maccabees, John Hyrcanus. Now it is here very well worth our observation, that the oracle before us was that by which God appeared to be present with, and gave directions to, his people Israel as their King, all the while they submitted to him in that capacity; and did not set over them such independent kings as governed according to their own wills and political maxims, instead of Divine directions. Accordingly we meet with this oracle (besides angelic and prophetic admonitions) all along from the days of Moses and Joshua to the anointing of Saul, the first of the succession of the kings, Numbers 27:21; Joshua 6:6, etc.; 19:50; Judges 1:1; 18:4–6, 30, 31; 20:18, 23, 26–28; 21:1, etc.; 1 Samuel 1:17, 18; 3. per tot.; 4. per tot.; nay, till Saul's rejection of the Divine commands in the war with Amalek, when he took upon him to act as he thought fit, 1 Samuel 14:3, 18, 19, 36, 37, then this oracle left Saul entirely, (which indeed he had seldom consulted before, 1 Samuel 14:35; 1 Chronicles 10:14; 13:3; Antiq. B. 7 ch. 4 sect 2.) and accompanied David, who was anointed to succeed him, and who consulted God by it frequently, and complied with its directions constantly (1 Samuel 14:37, 41; 15:26; 22:13, 15; 23:9, 10; 30:7, 8, 18; 2 Samuel 2:1; 5:19, 23; 21:1; 23:14; 1 Chronicles 14:10, 14; Antiq. B IV ch. 12 sect. 5). Saul, indeed, long after his rejection by God, and when God had given him up to destruction for his disobedience, did once afterwards endeavor to consult God when it was too late; but God would not then answer him, neither by dreams, nor by Urim, nor by prophets, 1 Samuel 28:6. Nor did any of David's successors, the kings of Judah, that we know of, consult God by this oracle, till the very Babylonish captivity itself, when those kings were at an end; they taking upon them, I suppose, too much of despotic power and royalty, and too little owning the God of Israel for the supreme King of Israel, though a few of them consulted the prophets sometimes, and were answered by them. At the return of the two tribes, without the return of

think it needless to describe their nature, they being known to every body,) the one of them shined out when God was present at their sacrifices; I mean that which was in the nature of a button on his right shoulder, bright rays darting out thence, and being seen even by those that were most remote; which splendor yet was not before natural to the stone. This has appeared a wonderful thing to such as have not so far indulged themselves in philosophy, as to despise Divine revelation. Yet will I mention what is still more wonderful than this:

---

the kingly government, the restoration of this oracle was expected, Nehemiah 7;63; 1 Esd. 5:40; 1 Macc. 4:46; 14:41. And indeed it may seem to have been restored for some time after the Babylonish captivity, at least in the days of that excellent high priest, John Hyrcanus, whom Josephus esteemed as a king, a priest, and a prophet; and who, he says, foretold several things that came to pass accordingly; but about the time of his death, he here implies, that this oracle quite ceased, and not before. The following high priests now putting diadems on their heads, and ruling according to their own will, and by their own authority, like the other kings of the pagan countries about them; so that while the God of Israel was allowed to be the supreme King of Israel, and his directions to be their authentic guides, God gave them such directions as their supreme King and Governor, and they were properly under a theocracy, by this oracle of Urim, but no longer (see Dr. Bernard's notes here); though I confess I cannot but esteem the high priest Jaddus's divine dream, Antiq. B. XI. ch. 8. sect. 4, and the high priest Caiaphas's most remarkable prophecy, John 11:47–52, as two small remains or specimens of this ancient oracle, which properly belonged to the Jewish high priests: nor perhaps ought we entirely to forget that eminent prophetic dream of our Josephus himself, (one next to a high priest, as of the family of the Asamoneans or Maccabees,) as to the succession of Vespasian and Titus to the Roman empire, and that in the days of Nero, and before either Galba, Otho, or Vitellius were thought of to succeed him. Of the War, B. III. ch. 8. sect. 9. This, I think, may well be looked on as the very last instance of any thing like the prophetic Urim among the Jewish nation, and just preceded their fatal desolation: but how it could possibly come to pass that such great men as Sir John Marsham and Dr. Spenser, should imagine that this oracle of Urim and Thummim with other practices as old or older than the law of Moses, should have been ordained in imitation of somewhat like them among the Egyptians, which we never hear of till the days of Diodorus Siculus, Aelian, and Maimonides, or little earlier than the Christian era at the highest, is almost unaccountable; while the main business of the law of Moses was evidently to preserve the Israelites from the idolatrous and superstitious practices of the neighboring pagan nations; and while it is so undeniable, that the evidence for the great antiquity of Moses's law is incomparably beyond that for the like or greater antiquity of such customs in Egypt or other nations, which indeed is generally none at all, it is most absurd to derive any of Moses's laws from the imitation of those heathen practices, Such hypotheses demonstrate to us how far inclination can prevail over evidence, in even some of the most learned part of mankind.

for God declared beforehand, by those twelve stones which the high priest bare on his breast, and which were inserted into his breastplate, when they should be victorious in battle; for so great a splendor shone forth from them before the army began to march, that all the people were sensible of God's being present for their assistance. Whence it came to pass that those Greeks, who had a veneration for our laws, because they could not possibly contradict this, called that breastplate *the Oracle*. Now this breastplate, and this sardonyx, left off shining two hundred years before I composed this book, God having been displeased at the transgressions of his laws. Of which things we shall further discourse on a fitter opportunity; but I will now go on with my proposed narration.

10. The tabernacle being now consecrated, and a regular order being settled for the priests, the multitude judged that God now dwelt among them, and betook themselves to sacrifices and praises to God as being now delivered from all expectation of evils and as entertaining a hopeful prospect of better times hereafter. They offered also gifts to God some as common to the whole nation, and others as peculiar to themselves, and these tribe by tribe; for the heads of the tribes combined together, two by two, and brought a waggon and a yoke of oxen. These amounted to six, and they carried the tabernacle when they journeyed. Besides which, each head of a tribe brought a bowl, and a charger, and a spoon, of ten darics, full of incense. Now the charger and the bowl were of silver, and together they weighed two hundred shekels, but the bowl cost no more than seventy shekels; and these were full of fine flour mingled with oil, such as they used on the altar about the sacrifices. They brought also a young bullock, and a ram, with a lamb of a year old, for a whole burnt-offering, as also a goat for the forgiveness of sins. Every one of the heads of the tribes brought also other sacrifices, called *peace-offerings*, for every day two bulls, and five rams, with lambs of a year old, and kids of the goats. These heads of tribes were twelve days in sacrificing, one sacrificing every day. Now Moses went no longer up to Mount Sinai, but went into the tabernacle, and learned of God what they were to do, and what laws should be made; which laws were preferable to what have been devised by human understanding, and proved to be firmly observed for all time to come, as being believed to be the gift of God, insomuch that the Hebrews did not transgress any of those laws,

either as tempted in times of peace by luxury, or in times of war by distress of affairs. But I say no more here concerning them, because I have resolved to compose another work concerning our laws.

9   The Manner of Our Offering Sacrifices

1. I WILL now, however, make mention of a few of our laws which belong to purifications, and the like sacred offices, since I am accidentally come to this matter of sacrifices. These sacrifices were of two sorts; of those sorts one was offered for private persons, and the other for the people in general; and they are done in two different ways. In the one case, what is slain is burnt, as a whole burnt-offering, whence that name is given to it; but the other is a thank-offering, and is designed for feasting those that sacrifice. I will speak of the former. Suppose a private man offer a burnt-offering, he must slay either a bull, a lamb, or a kid of the goats, and the two latter of the first year, though of bulls he is permitted to sacrifice those of a greater age; but all burnt-offerings are to be of males. When they are slain, the priests sprinkle the blood round about the altar; they then cleanse the bodies, and divide them into parts, and salt them with salt, and lay them upon the altar, while the pieces of wood are piled one upon another, and the fire is burning; they next cleanse the feet of the sacrifices, and the inwards, in an accurate manner and so lay them to the rest to be purged by the fire, while the priests receive the hides. This is the way of offering a burnt-offering.

2. But those that offer thank-offerings do indeed sacrifice the same creatures, but such as are unblemished, and above a year old; however, they may take either males or females. They also sprinkle the altar with their blood; but they lay upon the altar the kidneys and the caul, and all the fat, and the lobe of the liver, together with the rump of the lamb; then, giving the breast and the right shoulder to the priests, the offerers feast upon the remainder of the flesh for two days; and what remains they burn.

3. The sacrifices for sins are offered in the same manner as is the thank-offering. But those who are unable to purchase complete sacrifices, offer two pigeons, or turtle doves; the one of which is made a burnt-offering to God, the other they give as food to the priests. But we shall treat more accurately about the oblation of these creatures

in our discourse concerning sacrifices. But if a person fall into sin by ignorance, he offers an ewe lamb, or a female kid of the goats, of the same age; and the priests sprinkle the blood at the altar, not after the former manner, but at the corners of it. They also bring the kidneys and the rest of the fat, together with the lobe of the liver, to the altar, while the priests bear away the hides and the flesh, and spend it in the holy place, on the same day;[23] for the law does not permit them to leave of it until the morning. But if any one sin, and is conscious of it himself, but hath nobody that can prove it upon him, he offers a ram, the law enjoining him so to do; the flesh of which the priests eat, as before, in the holy place, on the same day. And if the rulers offer sacrifices for their sins, they bring the same oblations that private men do; only they so far differ, that they are to bring for sacrifices a bull or a kid of the goats, both males.

4. Now the law requires, both in private and public sacrifices, that the finest flour be also brought; for a lamb the measure of one tenth deal,—for a ram two,—and for a bull three. This they consecrate upon the altar, when it is mingled with oil; for oil is also brought by those that sacrifice; for a bull the half of an hin, and for a ram the third part of the same measure, and one quarter of it for a lamb. This hin is an ancient Hebrew measure, and is equivalent to two Athenian choas (or congiuses). They bring the same quantity of oil which they do of wine, and they pour the wine about the altar; but if any one does not offer a complete sacrifice of animals, but brings fine flour only for a vow, he throws a handful upon the altar as its first-fruits, while the priests take the rest for their food, either boiled or mingled with oil, but made into cakes of bread. But whatsoever it be that a priest himself offers, it must of necessity be all burnt. Now the law forbids us to sacrifice any animal at the same time with its dam; and, in other cases, not till the eighth day after its birth. Other sacrifices there are also appointed for

---

23. What Reland well observes here, out of Josephus, as compared with the law of Moses, Leviticus 7:15, (that the eating of the sacrifice the same day it was offered, seems to mean only before the morning of the next, although the latter part, i.e. the night, be in strictness part of the next day, according to the Jewish reckoning,) is greatly to be observed upon other occasions also. The Jewish maxim in such cases, it seems, is this: That the day goes before the night; and this appears to me to be the language both of the Old and New Testament. See also the note on Antiq. B. IV. ch. 4. sect. 4, and Reland's note on B. IV. ch. 8. sect. 28.

escaping distempers, or for other occasions, in which meat-offerings are consumed, together with the animals that are sacrificed; of which it is not lawful to leave any part till the next day, only the priests are to take their own share.

10 Concerning the Festivals; and How Each Day of Such Festival Is to Be Observed

1. THE law requires, that out of the public expenses a lamb of the first year be killed every day, at the beginning and at the ending of the day; but on the seventh day, which is called the *Sabbath*, they kill two, and sacrifice them in the same manner. At the new moon, they both perform the daily sacrifices, and slay two bulls, with seven lambs of the first year, and a kid of the goats also, for the expiation of sins; that is, if they have sinned through ignorance.

2. But on the seventh month, which the Macedonians call *Hyperbere-taeus*, they make an addition to those already mentioned, and sacrifice a bull, a ram, and seven lambs, and a kid of the goats, for sins.

3. On the tenth day of the same lunar month, they fast till the evening; and this day they sacrifice a bull, and two rams, and seven lambs, and a kid of the goats, for sins. And, besides these, they bring two kids of the goats; the one of which is sent alive out of the limits of the camp into the wilderness for the scapegoat, and to be an expiation for the sins of the whole multitude; but the other is brought into a place of great cleanness, within the limits of the camp, and is there burnt, with its skin, without any sort of cleansing. With this goat was burnt a bull, not brought by the people, but by the high priest, at his own charges; which, when it was slain, he brought of the blood into the holy place, together with the blood of the kid of the goats, and sprinkled the ceiling with his finger seven times, as also its pavement, and again as often toward the most holy place, and about the golden altar: he also at last brings it into the open court, and sprinkles it about the great altar. Besides this, they set the extremities, and the kidneys, and the fat, with the lobe of the liver, upon the altar. The high priest likewise presents a ram to God as a burnt-offering.

4. Upon the fifteenth day of the same month, when the season of the year is changing for winter, the law enjoins us to pitch tabernacles

in every one of our houses, so that we preserve ourselves from the cold of that time of the year; as also that when we should arrive at our own country, and come to that city which we should have then for our metropolis, because of the temple therein to be built, and keep a festival for eight days, and offer burnt-offerings, and sacrifice thank-offerings, that we should then carry in our hands a branch of myrtle, and willow, and a bough of the palm-tree, with the addition of the pome citron: That the burnt-offering on the first of those days was to be a sacrifice of thirteen bulls, and fourteen lambs, and fifteen rams, with the addition of a kid of the goats, as an expiation for sins; and on the following days the same number of lambs, and of rams, with the kids of the goats; but abating one of the bulls every day till they amounted to seven only. On the eighth day all work was laid aside, and then, as we said before, they sacrificed to God a bullock, a ram, and seven lambs, with a kid of the goats, for an expiation of sins. And this is the accustomed solemnity of the Hebrews, when they pitch their tabernacles.

5. In the month of Xanthicus, which is by us called *Nisan,* and is the beginning of our year, on the fourteenth day of the lunar month, when the sun is in Aries, (for in this month it was that we were delivered from bondage under the Egyptians,) the law ordained that we should every year slay that sacrifice which I before told you we slew when we came out of Egypt, and which was called the *Passover;* and so we do celebrate this passover in companies, leaving nothing of what we sacrifice till the day following. The feast of unleavened bread succeeds that of the passover, and falls on the fifteenth day of the month, and continues seven days, wherein they feed on unleavened bread; on every one of which days two bulls are killed, and one ram, and seven lambs. Now these lambs are entirely burnt, besides the kid of the goats which is added to all the rest, for sins; for it is intended as a feast for the priest on every one of those days. But on the second day of unleavened bread, which is the sixteenth day of the month, they first partake of the fruits of the earth, for before that day they do not touch them. And while they suppose it proper to honor God, from whom they obtain this plentiful provision, in the first place, they offer the first-fruits of their barley, and that in the manner following: They take a handful of the ears, and dry them, then beat them small, and purge the barley from the bran; they then bring one tenth deal to the altar, to God; and,

casting one handful of it upon the fire, they leave the rest for the use of the priest. And after this it is that they may publicly or privately reap their harvest. They also at this participation of the first-fruits of the earth, sacrifice a lamb, as a burnt-offering to God.

6. When a week of weeks has passed over after this sacrifice, (which weeks contain forty and nine days,) on the fiftieth day, which is Pentecost, but is called by the Hebrews *Asartha,* which signifies *Pentecost,* they bring to God a loaf, made of wheat flour, of two tenth deals, with leaven; and for sacrifices they bring two lambs; and when they have only presented them to God, they are made ready for supper for the priests; nor is it permitted to leave any thing of them till the day following. They also slay three bullocks for a burnt-offering, and two rams; and fourteen lambs, with two kids of the goats, for sins; nor is there anyone of the festivals but in it they offer burnt-offerings; they also allow themselves to rest on every one of them. Accordingly, the law prescribes in them all what kinds they are to sacrifice, and how they are to rest entirely, and must slay sacrifices, in order to feast upon them.

7. However, out of the common charges, baked bread [was set on the table of shew-bread], without leaven, of twenty-four tenth deals of flour, for so much is spent upon this bread; two heaps of these were baked, they were baked the day before the sabbath, but were brought into the holy place on the morning of the sabbath, and set upon the holy table, six on a heap, one loaf still standing over against another; where two golden cups full of frankincense were also set upon them, and there they remained till another sabbath, and then other loaves were brought in their stead, while the loaves were given to the priests for their food, and the frankincense was burnt in that sacred fire wherein all their offerings were burnt also; and so other frankincense was set upon the loaves instead of what was there before. The [high priest also, of his own charges, offered a sacrifice, and that twice every day. It was made of flour mingled with oil, and gently baked by the fire; the quantity was one tenth deal of flour; he brought the half of it to the fire in the morning, and the other half at night. The account of these sacrifices I shall give more accurately hereafter; but I think I have premised what for the present may be sufficient concerning them.

11 Of the Purifications

1. MOSES took out the tribe of Levi from communicating with the rest of the people, and set them apart to be a holy tribe; and purified them by water taken from perpetual springs, and with such sacrifices as were usually offered to God on the like occasions. He delivered to them also the tabernacle, and the sacred vessels, and the other curtains, which were made for covering the tabernacle, that they might minister under the conduct of the priests, who had been already consecrated to God.

2. He also determined concerning animals; which of them might be used for food, and which they were obliged to abstain from; which matters, when this work shall give me occasion, shall be further explained; and the causes shall be added by which he was moved to allot some of them to be our food, and enjoined us to abstain from others. However, he entirely forbade us the use of blood for food, and esteemed it to contain the soul and spirit. He also forbade us to eat the flesh of an animal that died of itself, as also the caul, and the fat of goats, and sheep, and bulls.

3. He also ordered that those whose bodies were afflicted with leprosy, and that had a gonorrhea, should not come into the city;[24] nay, he removed the women, when they had their natural purgations, till the seventh day; after which he looked on them as pure, and permitted them to come in again. The law permits those also who have taken care of funerals to come in after the same manner, when this number of days is over; but if any continued longer than that number of days in a state of pollution, the law appointed the offering two lambs for a sacrifice; the one of which they are to purge by fire, and for the other, the priests take it for themselves. In the same manner do those sacrifice who have had the gonorrhea. But he that sheds his seed in his sleep, if he go down into cold water, has the same privilege with those that have lawfully accompanied with their wives. And for the lepers, he suffered them not to come into the city at all, nor to live with any others, as if they were in effect dead persons; but if any one had

---

24. We may here note, that Josephus frequently calls the camp the city, and the court of the Mosaic tabernacle a temple, and the tabernacle itself a holy house, with allusion to the latter city, temple, and holy house, which he knew so well long afterwards.

obtained by prayer to God, the recovery from that distemper, and had gained a healthful complexion again, such a one returned thanks to God, with several sorts of sacrifices; concerning which we will speak hereafter.

4. Whence one cannot but smile at those who say that Moses was himself afflicted with the leprosy when he fled out of Egypt, and that he became the conductor of those who on that account left that country, and led them into the land of Canaan; for had this been true, Moses would not have made these laws to his own dishonor, which indeed it was more likely he would have opposed, if others had endeavored to introduce them; and this the rather, because there are lepers in many nations, who yet are in honor, and not only free from reproach and avoidance, but who have been great captains of armies, and been intrusted with high offices in the commonwealth, and have had the privilege of entering into holy places and temples; so that nothing hindered, but if either Moses himself, or the multitude that was with him, had been liable to such a misfortune in the color of his skin, he might have made laws about them for their credit and advantage, and have laid no manner of difficulty upon them. Accordingly, it is a plain case, that it is out of violent prejudice only that they report these things about us. But Moses was pure from any such distemper, and lived with countrymen who were pure of it also, and thence made the laws which concerned others that had the distemper. He did this for the honor of God. But as to these matters, let every one consider them after what manner he pleases.

5. As to the women, when they have born a child, Moses forbade them to come into the temple, or touch the sacrifices, before forty days were over, supposing it to be a boy; but if she hath born a girl, the law is that she cannot be admitted before twice that number of days be over. And when after the before-mentioned time appointed for them, they perform their sacrifices, the priests distribute them before God.

6. But if any one suspect that his wife has been guilty of adultery, he was to bring a tenth deal of barley flour; they then cast one handful to God and gave the rest of it to the priests for food. One of the priests set the woman at the gates that are turned towards the temple, and took the veil from her head, and wrote the name of God on parchment, and enjoined her to swear that she had not at all injured her husband; and to wish that, if she had violated her chastity, her right thigh might

be put out of joint; that her belly might swell; and that she might die thus: but that if her husband, by the violence of his affection, and of the jealousy which arose from it, had been rashly moved to this suspicion, that she might bear a male child in the tenth month. Now when these oaths were over, the priest wiped the name of God out of the parchment, and wrung the water into a vial. He also took some dust out of the temple, if any happened to be there, and put a little of it into the vial, and gave it her to drink; whereupon the woman, if she were unjustly accused, conceived with child, and brought it to perfection in her womb: but if she had broken her faith of wedlock to her husband, and had sworn falsely before God, she died in a reproachful manner; her thigh fell off from her, and her belly swelled with a dropsy. And these are the ceremonies about sacrifices, and about the purifications thereto belonging, which Moses provided for his countrymen. He also prescribed the following laws to them:

Several Laws

1. AS for adultery, Moses forbade it entirely, as esteeming it a happy thing that men should be wise in the affairs of wedlock; and that it was profitable both to cities and families that children should be known to be genuine. He also abhorred men's lying with their mothers, as one of the greatest crimes; and the like for lying with the father's wife, and with aunts, and sisters, and sons' wives, as all instances of abominable wickedness. He also forbade a man to lie with his wife when she was defiled by her natural purgation: and not to come near brute beasts; nor to approve of the lying with a male, which was to hunt after unlawful pleasures on account of beauty. To those who were guilty of such insolent behavior, he ordained death for their punishment.

2. As for the priests, he prescribed to them a double degree of purity[25] for he restrained them in the instances above, and moreover forbade them to marry harlots. He also forbade them to marry a slave, or a captive, and such as got their living by cheating trades, and

---

25. These words of Josephus are remarkable, that the lawgiver of the Jews required of the priests a double degree of parity, in comparison of that required of the people, of which he gives several instances immediately. It was for certain the case also among the first Christians, of the clergy, in comparison of the laity, as the Apostolical Constitutions and Canons every where inform us,

by keeping inns; as also a woman parted from her husband, on any account whatsoever. Nay, he did not think it proper for the high priest to marry even the widow of one that was dead, though he allowed that to the priests; but he permitted him only to marry a virgin, and to retain her. Whence it is that the high priest is not to come near to one that is dead, although the rest are not prohibited from coming near to their brethren, or parents, or children, when they are dead; but they are to be unblemished in all respects. He ordered that the priest who had any blemish, should have his portion indeed among the priests, but he forbade him to ascend the altar, or to enter into the holy house. He also enjoined them, not only to observe purity in their sacred ministrations, but in their daily conversation, that it might be unblamable also. And on this account it is that those who wear the sacerdotal garments are without spot, and eminent for their purity and sobriety: nor are they permitted to drink wine so long as they wear those garments.[26] Moreover, they offer sacrifices that are entire, and have no defect whatsoever.

3. And truly Moses gave them all these precepts, being such as were observed during his own lifetime; but though he lived now in the wilderness, yet did he make provision how they might observe the same laws when they should have taken the land of Canaan. He gave them rest to the land from ploughing and planting every seventh year, as he had prescribed to them to rest from working every seventh day; and ordered, that then what grew of its own accord out of the earth should in common belong to all that pleased to use it, making no distinction in that respect between their own countrymen and foreigners: and he ordained, that they should do the same after seven times seven years, which in all are fifty years; and that fiftieth year is called by the Hebrews *The Jubilee*, wherein debtors are freed from their debts, and slaves are set at liberty; which slaves became such, though they were of the same stock, by transgressing some of those laws the punishment of which was not capital, but they were punished

---

26. We must here note with Reland, that the precept given to the priests of not drinking wine while they wore the sacred garments, is equivalent; to their abstinence from it all the while they ministered in the temple; because they then always, and then only, wore those sacred garments, which were laid up there from one time of ministration to another.

by this method of slavery. This year also restores the land to its former possessors in the manner following:—When the Jubilee is come, which name denotes *liberty,* he that sold the land, and he that bought it, meet together, and make an estimate, on one hand, of the fruits gathered; and, on the other hand, of the expenses laid out upon it. If the fruits gathered come to more than the expenses laid out, he that sold it takes the land again; but if the expenses prove more than the fruits, the present possessor receives of the former owner the difference that was wanting, and leaves the land to him; and if the fruits received, and the expenses laid out, prove equal to one another, the present possessor relinquishes it to the former owners. Moses would have the same law obtain as to those houses also which were sold in villages; but he made a different law for such as were sold in a city; for if he that sold it tendered the purchaser his money again within a year, he was forced to restore it; but in case a whole year had intervened, the purchaser was to enjoy what he had bought. This was the constitution of the laws which Moses learned of God when the camp lay under Mount Sinai, and this he delivered in writing to the Hebrews.

4. Now when this settlement of laws seemed to be well over, Moses thought fit at length to take a review of the host, as thinking it proper to settle the affairs of war. So he charged the heads of the tribes, excepting the tribe of Levi, to take an exact account of the number of those that were able to go to war; for as to the Levites, they were holy, and free from all such burdens. Now when the people had been numbered, there were found six hundred thousand that were able to go to war, from twenty to fifty years of age, besides three thousand six hundred and fifty. Instead of Levi, Moses took Manasseh, the son of Joseph, among the heads of tribes; and Ephraim instead of Joseph. It was indeed the desire of Jacob himself to Joseph, that he would give him his sons to be his own by adoption, as I have before related.

5. When they set up the tabernacle, they received it into the midst of their camp, three of the tribes pitching their tents on each side of it; and roads were cut through the midst of these tents. It was like a well-appointed market; and every thing was there ready for sale in due order; and all sorts of artificers were in the shops; and it resembled nothing so much as a city that sometimes was movable, and sometimes fixed. The priests had the first places about the tabernacle; then the Levites, who, because their whole multitude was reckoned

from thirty days old, were twenty-three thousand eight hundred and eighty males; and during the time that the cloud stood over the tabernacle, they thought proper to stay in the same place, as supposing that God there inhabited among them; but when that removed, they journeyed also.

6. Moreover, Moses was the inventor of the form of their trumpet, which was made of silver. Its description is this:—In length it was little less than a cubit. It was composed of a narrow tube, somewhat thicker than a flute, but with so much breadth as was sufficient for admission of the breath of a man's mouth: it ended in the form of a bell, like common trumpets. Its sound was called in the Hebrew tongue *Asosra.* Two of these being made, one of them was sounded when they required the multitude to come together to congregations. When the first of them gave a signal, the heads of the tribes were to assemble, and consult about the affairs to them properly belonging; but when they gave the signal by both of them, they called the multitude together. Whenever the tabernacle was removed, it was done in this solemn order:—At the first alarm of the trumpet, those whose tents were on the east quarter prepared to remove; when the second signal was given, those that were on the south quarter did the like; in the next place, the tabernacle was taken to pieces, and was carried in the midst of six tribes that went before, and of six that followed, all the Levites assisting about the tabernacle; when the third signal was given, that part which had their tents towards the west put themselves in motion; and at the fourth signal those on the north did so likewise. They also made use of these trumpets in their sacred ministrations, when they were bringing their sacrifices to the altar as well on the Sabbaths as on the rest of the [festival] days; and now it was that Moses offered that sacrifice which was called the *Passover in the Wilderness,* as the first he had offered after the departure out of Egypt.

12 Moses Removed from Mount Sinai, and Conducted the People to the Borders of the Canaanites

A LITTLE while afterwards he rose up, and went from Mount Sinai; and, having passed through several mansions, of which we will speak he came to a place called *Hazeroth,* where the multitude began again to be mutinous, and to Moses for the misfortunes they had suffered their travels; and that when he had persuaded to leave a good land, they at once had lost land, and instead of that happy state he had them, they were still wandering in their miserable condition, being already in want water; and if the manna should happen to fail, must then utterly perish. Yet while they spake many and sore things against the there was one of them who exhorted them to be unmindful of Moses, and of what great pains he had been at about their common safety; not to despair of assistance from God. The multitude thereupon became still more unruly, and mutinous against Moses than before. Hereupon Moses, although he was so basely abused by them encouraged them in their despairing conditioned and promised that he would procure them a quantity of flesh-meat, and that not for a few days only, but for many days. This they were not to believe; and when one of them asked, whence he could obtain such vast plenty of what he promised, he replied, "Neither God nor I, we hear such opprobrious language from will leave off our labors for you; and this soon appear also." As soon as ever he had this, the whole camp was filled with quails, they stood round about them, and gathered great numbers. However, it was not long ere God punished the Hebrews for their insolence, those reproaches they had used towards him, no small number of them died; and still to this day the place retains the memory of this destruction and is named *Kibrothhattaavah*, which is, *Graves of Lust*.

13   *How Moses Sent Some Persons to Search Out the Land of the Canaanites, and the Largeness of Their Cities; and Further That When Those Who Were Sent Were Returned, After Forty Days and Reported That They Should Not Be a Match for Them, and Extolled the Strengh of the Canaanites the Multitude Were Disturbed and Fell into Despair; and Were Resolved to Stone Moses, and to Return Back Again into Egypt, and Serve the Egyptians*

1. WHEN Moses had led the Hebrews away from thence to a place called *Paran*, which was near to the borders of the Canaanites, and a place difficult to be continued in, he gathered the multitude together to a congregation; and standing in the midst of them, he said, "Of

the two things that God determined to bestow upon us, liberty, and the possession of a Happy Country, the one of them ye already are partakers of, by the gift of God, and the other you will quickly obtain; for we now have our abode near the borders of the Canaanites, and nothing can hinder the acquisition of it, when we now at last are fallen upon it: I say, not only no king nor city, but neither the whole race of mankind, if they were all gathered together, could do it. Let us therefore prepare ourselves for the work, for the Canaanites will not resign up their land to us without fighting, but it must be wrested from them by great struggles in war. Let us then send spies, who may take a view of the goodness of the land, and what strength it is of; but, above all things, let us be of one mind, and let us honor God, who above all is our helper and assister."

2. When Moses had said thus, the multitude requited him with marks of respect; and chose twelve spies, of the most eminent men, one out of each tribe, who, passing over all the land of Canaan, from the borders of Egypt, came to the city Hamath, and to Mount Lebanon; and having learned the nature of the land, and of its inhabitants, they came home, having spent forty days in the whole work. They also brought with them of the fruits which the land bare; they also showed them the excellency of those fruits, and gave an account of the great quantity of the good things that land afforded, which were motives to the multitude to go to war. But then they terrified them again with the great difficulty there was in obtaining it; that the rivers were so large and deep that they could not be passed over; and that the hills were so high that they could not travel along for them; that the cities were strong with walls, and their firm fortifications round about them. They told them also, that they found at Hebron the posterity of the giants. Accordingly these spies, who had seen the land of Canaan, when they perceived that all these difficulties were greater there than they had met with since they came out of Egypt, they were aftrighted at them themselves, and endeavored to affright the multitude also.

3. So they supposed, from what they had heard, that it was imposs-ible to get the possession of the country. And when the congregation was dissolved, they, their wives and children, continued their lamenta-tion, as if God would not indeed assist them, but only promised them fair. They also again blamed Moses, and made a clamor against him and his brother Aaron, the high priest. Accordingly they passed that

night very ill, and with contumelious language against them; but in the morning they ran to a congregation, intending to stone Moses and Aaron, and so to return back into Egypt.

4. But of the spies, there were Joshua the son of Nun, of the tribe of Ephraim, and Caleb of the tribe of Judah, that were afraid of the consequence, and came into the midst of them, and stilled the multitude, and desired them to be of good courage; and neither to condemn God, as having told them lies, nor to hearken to those who had aftrighted them, by telling them what was not true concerning the Canaanites, but to those that encouraged them to hope for good success; and that they should gain possession of the happiness promised them, because neither the. height of mountains, nor the depth of rivers, could hinder men of true courage from attempting them, especially while God would take care of them beforehand, and be assistant to them. "Let us then go," said they, "against our enemies, and have no suspicion of ill success, trusting in God to conduct us, and following those that are to be our leaders." Thus did these two exhort them, and endeavor to pacify the rage they were in. But Moses and Aaron fell on the ground, and besought God, not for their own deliverance, but that he would put a stop to what the people were unwarily doing, and would bring their minds to a quiet temper, which were now disordered by their present passion. The cloud also did now appear, and stood over the tabernacle, and declared to them the presence of God to be there.

14   *How Moses Was Displeased at This, and Foretold That God Was Angry and That They Should Continue in the Wilderness for Forty Years and Not, During That Time, Either Return into Egypt or Take Possession of Canaan*

1. MOSES came now boldly to the multitude, and informed them that God was moved at their abuse of him, and would inflict punishment upon them, not indeed such as they deserved for their sins, but such as parents inflict on their children, in order to their correction. For, he said, that when he was in the tabernacle, and was bewailing with ears that destruction which was coming upon them God put him in mind what things he had done for them, and what benefits they had received from him, and yet how ungrateful they had been to him that

just now they had been induced, through the timorousness of the spies, to think that their words were truer than his own promise to them; and that on this account, though he would not indeed destroy them all, nor utterly exterminate their nation, which he had honored more than any other part of mankind, yet he would not permit them to take possession of the land of Canaan, nor enjoy its happiness; but would make them wander in the wilderness, and live without a fixed habitation, and without a city, for forty years together, as a punishment for this their transgression; but that he had promised to give that land to our children, and that he would make them the possessors of those good things which, by your ungoverned passions, you have deprived yourselves of.

2. When Moses had discoursed thus to them according to the direction of God, the multitude, grieved, and were in affliction; and entreated Most to procure their reconciliation to God, and to permit them no longer to wander in the wilderness, but bestow cities upon them. But he replied, that God would not admit of any such trial, for that God was not moved to this determination from any human levity or anger, but that he had judicially condemned them to that punishment. Now we are not to disbelieve that Moses, who was but a single person, pacified so many ten thousands when they werre in anger, and converted them to a mildness temper; for God was with him, and prepared way to his persuasions of the multitude; and as they had often been disobedient, they were now sensible that such disobedience was disadvantageous to them and that they had still thereby fallen into calamities.

3. But this man was admirable for his virtue, and powerful in making men give credit to what he delivered, not only during the time of his natural life, but even there is still no one of the Hebrews who does not act even now as if Moses were present, and ready to punish him if he should do any thing that is indecent; nay, there is no one but is obedient to what laws he ordained, although they might be concealed in their transgressions. There are also many other demonstrations that his power was more than human, for still some there have been, who have come from the parts beyond Euphrates, a journey of four months, through many dangers, and at great expenses, in honor of our temple; and yet, when they had offered their oblations, could not partake of their own sacrifices, because Moses had forbidden

it, by somewhat in the law that did not permit them, or somewhat that had befallen them, which our ancient customs made inconsistent therewith; some of these did not sacrifice at all, and others left their sacrifices in an imperfect condition; many were not able, even at first, so much as to enter the temple, but went their ways in this as preferring a submission to the laws of Moses before the fulfilling of their own inclinations, they had no fear upon them that anybody could convict them, but only out of a reverence to their own conscience. Thus this legislation, which appeared to be divine, made this man to be esteemed as one superior to his own nature. Nay, further, a little before the beginning of this war, when Claudius was emperor of the Romans, and Ismael was our high priest, and when so great a famine[27] was come upon us, that one tenth deal [of wheat] was sold for four drachmae, and when no less than seventy cori of flour were brought into the temple, at the feast of unleavened bread, (these cori are thirty-one Sicilian, but forty-one Athenian medimni,) not one of the priests was so hardy as to eat one crumb of it, even while so great a distress was upon the land; and this out of a dread of the law, and of that wrath which God retains against acts of wickedness, even when no one can accuse the actors. Whence we are not to wonder at what was then done, while to this very day the writings left by Moses have so great a force, that even those that hate us do confess, that he who established this settlement was God, and that it was by the means of Moses, and of his virtue; but as to these matters, let every one take them as he thinks fit.

---

27. See Antiq, B. XX. ch. 2. sect, 6. and Acts 11:28.

Book 4

Containing the Interval of Thirty-Eight Years, from the Rejection of That Generation to the Death of Moses

1 Fight of the Hebrews with the Canaanites Without the Consent of Moses; and Their Defeat

1. NOW this life of the Hebrews in the wilderness was so disagreeable and troublesome to them, and they were so uneasy at it, that although God had forbidden them to meddle with the Canaanites, yet could they not be persuaded to be obedient to the words of Moses, and to be quiet; but supposing they should be able to beat their enemies, without his approbation, they accused him, and suspected that he made it his business to keep in a distressed condition, that they might always stand in need of his assistance. Accordingly they resolved to fight with the Canaanites, and said that God gave them his assistance, not out of regard to Moses's intercessions, but because he took care of their entire nation, on account of their forefathers, whose affairs he took under his own conduct; as also, that it was on account of their own virtue that he had formerly procured them their liberty, and would be assisting to them, now they were willing to take pains for it. They also said that they were possessed of abilities sufficient for the conquest of their enemies, although Moses should have a mind to alienate God from them; that, however, it was for their advantage to be their own masters, and not so far to rejoice in their deliverance from the indignities they endured under the Egyptians, as to bear the tyranny of Moses over them, and to suffer themselves to be deluded, and live according to

his pleasure, as though God did only foretell what concerns us out of his kindness to him, as if they were not all the posterity of Abraham; that God made him alone the author of all the knowledge we have, and we must still learn it from him; that it would be a piece of prudence to oppose his arrogant pretenses, and to put their confidence in God, and to resolve to take possession of that land which he had promised them, and not to give ear to him, who on this account, and under the pretense of Divine authority, forbade them so to do. Considering, therefore, the distressed state they were in at present, and that in those desert places they were still to expect things would be worse with them, they resolved to fight with the Canaanites, as submitting only to God, their supreme Commander, and not waiting for any assistance from their legislator.

2. When, therefore, they had come to this resolution, as being best for them, they went against their enemies; but those enemies were not dismayed either at the attack itself, or at the great multitude that made it, and received them with great courage. Many of the Hebrews were slain; and the remainder of the army, upon the disorder of their troops, were pursued, and fled, after a shameful manner, to their camp. Whereupon this unexpected misfortune made them quite despond; and they hoped for nothing that was good; as gathering from it, that this affliction came from the wrath of God, because they rashly went out to war without his approbation.

3. But when Moses saw how deeply they were affected with this defeat, and being afraid lest the enemies should grow insolent upon this victory, and should be desirous of gaining still greater glory, and should attack them, he resolved that it was proper to withdraw the army into the wilderness to a further distance from the Canaanites: so the multitude gave themselves up again to his conduct, for they were sensible that, without his care for them, their affairs could not be in a good condition; and he caused the host to remove, and he went further into the wilderness, as intending there to let them rest, and not to permit them to fight the Canaanites before God should afford them a more favorable opportunity.

Chapter 2

2 The Sedition of Corah and of the Multitude Against Moses, and Against His Brother, Concerning the Priesthood

1. THAT which is usually the case of great armies, and especially upon ill success, to be hard to be pleased, and governed with difficulty, did now befall the Jews; for they being in number six hundred thousand, and by reason of their great multitude not readily subject to their governors, even in prosperity, they at this time were more than usually angry, both against one another and against their leader, because of the distress they were in, and the calamities they then endured. Such a sedition overtook them, as we have not the like example either among the Greeks or the Barbarians, by which they were in danger of being all destroyed, but were notwithstanding saved by Moses, who would not remember that he had been almost stoned to death by them. Nor did God neglect to prevent their ruin; but, notwithstanding the indignities they had offered their legislator and the laws, and disobedience to the commandments which he had sent them by Moses, he delivered them from those terrible calamities which, without his providential care, had been brought upon them by this sedition. So I will first explain the cause whence this sedition arose, and then will give an account of the sedition itself; as also of what settlements made for their government after it was over.

2. Corah, a Hebrew of principal account, both by his family and by his wealth, one that was also able to speak well, and one that could easily persuade the people by his speeches, saw that Moses was in an exceeding great dignity, and was at it, and envied him on that account, (he of the same tribe with Moses, and of kin to him,) was particularly grieved, because he thought he better deserved that honorable post on account of great riches, and not inferior to him in his birth. So he raised a clamor against him among the Levites, who were of the same tribe, and among his kindred, saying, "That it was a very sad thing that they should overlook Moses, while hunted after and paved the way to glory for himself, and by ill arts should obtain it, under the pretense of God's command, while, contrary to laws, he had given the priesthood to Aaron, the common suffrage of the multitude, but by his own vote, as bestowing dignities in a way on whom he pleased." He added, "That this concealed way of imposing on them was harder to be borne than if it had been done by an open force upon

them, because he did now not only their power without their consent, but even they were unapprised of his contrivances against them; for whosoever is conscious to himself that he deserves any dignity, aims to get it by persuasion, and not by an arrogant method of violence; those that believe it impossible to obtain honors justly, make a show of goodness, and do not introduce force, but by cunning tricks grow wickedly powerful. That it was proper for the multitude to punish such men, even while they think themselves concealed in their designs, and not suffer them to gain strength till they have them for their open enemies. For what account," added he, "is Moses able to give, why he has bestowed the priesthood on Aaron and his sons? for if God had determined to bestow that honor on one of the tribe of Levi, I am more worthy of it than he is; I myself being equal to Moses by my family, and superior to him both in riches and in age: but if God had determined to bestow it on the eldest be, that of Reuben might have it most justly; and then Dathan, and Abiram, and [On, the son of] Peleth, would have it; for these are the oldest men of that tribe, and potent on account of their great wealth also."

3. Now Corah, when he said this, had a mind to appear to take care of the public welfare, but in reality he was endeavoring to procure to have that dignity transferred by the multitude to himself. Thus did he, out of a malignant design, but with discourse to those of his own tribe; when these words did gradually spread to more people, and when the hearers still added to what tended to the scandals that were cast upon the whole army was full of them. Now of those that conspired with Corah, there were two hundred and fifty, and those of the principal men also, who were eager to have the priesthood taken away from Moses's brother, and to bring him into disgrace: nay, the multitude themselves were provoked to be seditious, and attempted to stone Moses, wad gathered themselves together after an indecent manner, with confusion and disorder. And now all were, in a tumultuous manner, raising a before the tabernacle of God, to prosecute the tyrant, and to relieve the multitude from their slavery under him who, under color of the Divine laid violent injunctions upon them; for had it been God who chose one that was to the office of a priest, he would have raised person to that dignity, and would not produced such a one as was inferior to many others nor have given him that office; and that in he had judged it fit to bestow it on Aaron, he would have permitted

it to the multitude to bestow it, and not have left it to be bestowed by his own brother.

4. Now although Moses had a great while ago foreseen this calumny of Corah, and had seen the people were irritated, yet was he not affrighted at it; but being of good courage, because given them right advice about their affairs, and knowing that his brother had been made partaker of the priesthood at the command of God, and not by his own favor to him, he came to the assembly; and as for the multitude, he said not a word to them, but spake as loud to Corah as he could; and being very skillful in making speeches, and having this natural talent, among others, that he could greatly move the multitude with his discourses, he said, "O Corah, both thou and all these with thee (pointing to the two hundred and fifty men) seem to be worthy of this honor; nor do I pretend but that this whole company may be worthy of the like dignity, although they may not be so rich or so great as you are: nor have I taken and given this office to my brother because he excelled others in riches, for thou exceedest us both in the greatness of thy wealth;[1] nor indeed because he was of an eminent family, for God, by giving us the same common ancestor, has made our families equal: nay, nor was it out of brotherly affection, which another might yet have justly done; for certainly, unless I had bestowed this honor out of regard to God, and to his laws, I had not passed by myself, and given it to another, as being nearer of kin to myself than to my brother, and having a closer intimacy with myself than I have with him; for surely it would not be a wise thing for me to expose myself to the dangers of offending, and to bestow the happy employment on this account upon another. But I am above such base practices: nor would God have overlooked this matter, and seen himself thus despised; nor would he have suffered you to be ignorant of what you were to do, in order to please him; but he hath himself chosen one that is to perform that sacred office to him, and thereby freed us from that care. So that it was not a thing that I pretend to give, but only according to the determination of God; I therefore propose it still to be contended for by such as please to put in for it, only desiring that he who has been

---

1. Reland here takes notice, that although our Bibles say little or nothing of these riches of Corah, yet that both the Jews and Mahommedans, as well as Josephus, are full of it.

already preferred, and has already obtained it, may be allowed now also to offer himself for a candidate. He prefers your peace, and your living without sedition, to this honorable employment, although in truth it was with your approbation that he obtained it; for though God were the donor, yet do we not offend when we think fit to accept it with your good-will; yet would it have been an instance of impiety not to have taken that honorable employment when he offered it; nay, it had been exceedingly unreasonable, when God had thought fit any one should have it for all time to come, and had made it secure and firm to him, to have refused it. However, he himself will judge again who it shall be whom he would have to offer sacrifices to him, and to have the direction of matters of religion; for it is absurd that Corah, who is ambitious of this honor, should deprive God of the power of giving it to whom he pleases. Put an end, therefore, to your sedition and disturbance on this account; and tomorrow morning do every one of you that desire the priesthood bring a censer from home, and come hither with incense and fire: and do thou, O Corah, leave the judgment to God, and await to see on which side he will give his determination upon this occasion, but do not thou make thyself greater than God. Do thou also come, that this contest about this honorable employment may receive determination. And I suppose we may admit Aaron without offense, to offer himself to this scrutiny, since he is of the same lineage with thyself, and has done nothing in his priesthood that can be liable to exception. Come ye therefore together, and offer your incense in public before all the people; and when you offer it, he whose sacrifice God shall accept shall be ordained to the priesthood, and shall be clear of the present calumny on Aaron, as if I had granted him that favor because he was my brother."

3 *How Those That Stirred Up This Sedition Were Destroyed, According to the Will of God; and How Aaron, Moses's Brother Both He and His Posterity, Retained the Priesthood*

1. WHEN Moses had said this, the multitude left off the turbulent behavior they had indulged, and the suspicion they had of Moses, and commended what he had said; for those proposals were good, and were so esteemed of the people. At that time therefore they dissolved

the assembly. But on the next day they came to the congregation, in order to be present at the sacrifice, and at the determination that was to be made between the candidates for the priesthood. Now this congregation proved a turbulent one, and the multitude were in great suspense in expectation of what was to be done; for some of them would have been pleased if Moses had been convicted of evil practices, but the wiser sort desired that they might be delivered from the present disorder and disturbance; for they were afraid, that if this sedition went on, the good order of their settlement would rather be destroyed; but the whole body of the people do naturally delight in clamors against their governors, and, by changing their opinions upon the harangues of every speaker, disturb the public tranquillity. And now Moses sent messengers for Abiram and Dathan, and ordered them to come to the assembly, and wait there for the holy offices that were to be performed. But they answered the messenger, that they would not obey his summons; nay, would not overlook Moses's behavior, who was growing too great for them by evil practices. Now when Moses heard of this their answer, he desired the heads of the people to follow him, and he went to the faction of Dathan, not thinking it any frightful thing at all to go to these insolent people; so they made no opposition, but went along with him. But Dathan, and his associates, when they understood that Moses and the principal of the people were coming to them, came out, with their wives and children, and stood before their tents, and looked to see what Moses would do. They had also their servants about them to defend themselves, in case Moses should use force against them.

2. But he came near, and lifted up his hands to heaven, and cried out with a loud voice, in order to be heard by the whole multitude, and said, "O Lord of the creatures that are in the heaven, in the earth, and in the sea; for thou art the most authentic witness to what I have done, that it has all been done by thy appointment, and that it was thou that affordedst us assistance when we attempted any thing, and showedst mercy on the Hebrews in all their distresses; do thou come now, and hear all that I say, for no action or thought escapes thy knowledge; so that thou wilt not disdain to speak what is true, for my vindication, without any regard to the ungrateful imputations of these men. As for what was done before I was born, thou knowest best, as not learning them by report, but seeing them, and being present

with them when they were done; but for what has been done of late, and which these men, although they know them well enough, unjustly pretend to suspect, be thou my witness. When I lived a private quiet life, I left those good things which, by my own diligence, and by thy counsel, I enjoyed with Raguel my father-in-law; and I gave myself up to this people, and underwent many miseries on their account. I also bore great labors at first, in order to obtain liberty for them, and now in order to their preservation; and have always showed myself ready to assist them in every distress of theirs. Now, therefore, since I am suspected by those very men whose being is owing to my labors, come thou, as it is reasonable to hope thou wilt; thou, I say, who showedst me that fire at mount Sinai, and madest me to hear its voice, and to see the several wonders which that place afforded thou who commandedst me to go to Egypt, and declare thy will to this people; thou who disturbest the happy estate of the Egyptians, and gavest us the opportunity of flying away from our under them, and madest the dominion of Pharaoh inferior to my dominion; thou who didst make the sea dry land for us, when we knew not whither to go, and didst overwhelm the Egyptians with those destructive waves which had been divided for us; thou who didst bestow upon us the security of weapons when we were naked; thou who didst make the fountains that were corrupted to flow, so as to be fit for drinking, and didst furnish us with water that came out of the rocks, when we were in want of it; thou who didst preserve our lives with [quails, which was] food from the sea, when the fruits of the ground failed us; thou didst send us such food from heaven as had never been seen before; thou who didst suggest to us the knowledge of thy laws, and appoint to us a of government,—come thou, I say, O Lord of the whole world, and that as such a Judge and a Witness to me as cannot be bribed, and show how I never admitted of any gift against justice from any of the Hebrews; and have never condemned a man that ought to have been acquitted, on account of one that was rich; and have never attempted to hurt this commonwealth. I am now and am suspected of a thing the remotest from my intentions, as if I had given the preisthood to Aaron, not at thy command, but out own favor to him; do thou at this time demonstrate that all things are administered by thy providence and that nothing happens by chance, but is governed by thy will, and thereby attains its end: as also demonstrate that thou takest care that have done good to the Hebrews; demonstrate this, I say, by the punishment of Abiram and Dathan, who condemn thee as an insensible Being, and one overcome by my contrivances. This thou do by inflicting such an open punishment on these men who so madly fly in the face of thy glory, as will take them out of the world, not in an manner, but so that it may appear they do die after the manner of other men: let that ground which they tread upon open about them and consume them, with their families and goods. This will be a demonstration of thy power to all and this method of their sufferings will be an instruction of wisdom for those that entertain profane sentiments of thee. By this means I shall be a good servant, in the precepts thou hast given by me. But if the calumnies they have raised against me be true, mayst thou preserve these men from every evil accident, and bring all that destruction on me which I have imprecated upon them. And when thou hast inflicted punishment on those that have endeavored to deal unjustly with this people, bestow upon them concord and peace. Save this multitude that follow thy commandments, and preserve them free from harm, and let them not partake of the punishment of those that have sinned; for thou knowest thyself it is not just, that for the wickedness of those men the whole body of the Israelites should suffer punishment."

3. When Moses had said this, with tears in his eyes, the ground was moved on a sudden; and the agitation that set it in motion was like that which the wind produces in waves of the sea. The people were all aftrighted; and the ground that was about their tents sunk down at the great noise, with a terrible sound, and carried whatsoever was dear to the seditious into itself, who so entirely perished, that there was not the least appearance that any man had ever been seen there, the earth that had opened itself about them, closing again, and becoming entire as it was before, insomuch that such as saw it afterward did not perceive that any such accident had happened to it. Thus did these men perish, and become a demonstration of the power of God. And truly, any one would lament them, not only on account of this calamity that befell them, which yet deserves our commiseration, but also because their kindred were pleased with their sufferings; for they forgot the relation they bare to them, and at the sight of this sad accident approved of the judgment given against them; and because

they looked upon the people about Dathan as pestilent men, they thought they perished as such, and did not grieve for them.

4. And now Moses called for those that contended about the priesthood, that trial might be made who should be priest, and that he whose sacrifice God was best pleased with might be ordained to that function. There attended two hundred and fifty men, who indeed were honored by the people, not only on account of the power of their ancestors, but also on account of their own, in which they excelled the others: Aaron also and Corah came forth, and they all offered incense, in those censers of theirs which they brought with them, before the tabernacle. Hereupon so great a fire shone out as no one ever saw in any that is made by the hand of man, neither in those eruptions out of the earth that are caused by subterraneous burn-rags, nor in such fires as arise of their own accord in the woods, when the agitation is caused by the trees rubbing one against another: but this fire was very bright, and had a terrible flame, such as is kindled at the command of God; by whose irruption on them, all the company, and Corah himself, were destroyed,[2] and this so entirely, that their very bodies left no remains behind them. Aaron alone was preserved, and not at all hurt by the fire, because it was God that sent the fire to burn those only who ought to be burned. Hereupon Moses, after these men were destroyed, was desirous that the memory of this judgment might be delivered down to posterity, and that future ages might be acquainted with it; and so he commanded Eleazar, the son of Aaron, to put their censers near the brazen altar, that they might be a memorial to posterity of what these men suffered, for supposing that the power of God might be eluded. And thus Aaron was now no longer esteemed to have the priesthood by the favor of Moses, but by the public judgment of God; and thus he and his children peaceably enjoyed that honor afterward.

---

2. It appears here, and from the Samaritan Pentateuch, and, in effect, from the psalmist, as also from the Apostolical Constitutions, from Clement's First Epistle to the Corinthians, from Ignatius's Epistle to the Magnesians, and from Eusebius, that Corah was not swallowed up with the Reubenites, but burned with the Levites of his own tribe. See Essay on the Old Testament, p. 64, 65.

4 *What Happened to the Hebrews During Thirty-Eight Years in the Wilderness*

1. HOWEVER, this sedition was so far from ceasing upon this destruction, that it grew much stronger, and became more intolerable. And the occasion of its growing worse was of that nature, as made it likely the calamity would never cease, but last for a long time; for the men, believing already that nothing is done without the providence of God, would have it that these things came thus to pass not without God's favor to Moses; they therefore laid the blame upon him that God was so angry, and that this happened not so much because of the wickedness of those that were punished, as because Moses procured the punishment; and that these men had been destroyed without any sin of theirs, only because they were zealous about the Divine worship; as also, that he who had been the cause of this diminution of the people, by destroying so many men, and those the most excellent of them all, besides his escaping any punishment himself, had now given the priesthood to his brother so firmly, that nobody could any longer dispute it with him; for no one else, to be sure, could now put in for it, since he must have seen those that first did so to have miserably perished. Nay, besides this, the kindred of those that were destroyed made great entreaties to the multitude to abate the arrogance of Moses, because it would be safest for them so to do.

2. Now Moses, upon his hearing for a good while that the people were tumultuous, was afraid that they would attempt some other innovation, and that some great and sad calamity would be the consequence. He called the multitude to a congregation, and patiently heard what apology they had to make for themselves, without opposing them, and this lest he should imbitter the multitude: he only desired the heads of the tribes to bring their rods,[3] with the names of their tribes inscribed upon them, and that he should receive the priesthood in whose rod God should give a sign. This was agreed to. So the rest brought their rods, as did Aaron also, who had written the tribe of Levi on his rod. These rods Moses laid up in the tabernacle of God. On the

---

3. Concerning these twelve rods of the twelve tribes of Israel, see St. Clement's account, much larger than that in our Bibles, 1 Epist. sect. 45; as is Josephus's present account in measure larger also.

next day he brought out the rods, which were known from one another by those who brought them, they having distinctly noted them, as had the multitude also; and as to the rest, in the same form Moses had received them, in that they saw them still; but they also saw buds and branches grown out of Aaron's rod, with ripe fruits upon them; they were almonds, the rod having been cut out of that tree. The people were so amazed at this strange sight, that though Moses and Aaron were before under some degree of hatred, they now laid that hatred aside, and began to admire the judgment of God concerning them; so that hereafter they applauded what God had decreed, and permitted Aaron to enjoy the priesthood peaceably. And thus God ordained him priest three several times, and he retained that honor without further disturbance. And hereby this sedition of the Hebrews, which had been a great one, and had lasted a great while, was at last composed.

3. And now Moses, because the tribe of Levi was made free from war and warlike expeditions, and was set apart for the Divine worship, lest they should want and seek after the necessaries of life, and so neglect the temple, commanded the Hebrews, according to the will of God, that when they should gain the possession of the land of Canaan, they should assign forty-eight good and fair cities to the Levites; and permit them to enjoy their suburbs, as far as the limit of two thousand cubits would extend from the walls of the city. And besides this, he appointed that the people should pay the tithe of their annual fruits of the earth, both to the Levites and to the priests. And this is what that tribe receives of the multitude; but I think it necessary to set down what is paid by all, peculiarly to the priests.

4. Accordingly he commanded the Levites to yield up to the priests thirteen of their forty-eight cities, and to set apart for them the tenth part of the tithes which they every year receive of the people; as also, that it was but just to offer to God the first-fruits of the entire product of the ground; and that they should offer the first-born of those four-footed beasts that are appointed for sacrifices, if it be a male, to the priests, to be slain, that they and their entire families may eat them in the holy city; but that the owners of those first-born which are not appointed for sacrifices in the laws of our country, should bring a shekel and a half in their stead: but for the first-born of a man, five shekels: that they should also have the first-fruits out of the shearing of the sheep; and that when any baked bread corn, and made loaves

of it, they should give somewhat of what they had baked to them. Moreover, when any have made a sacred vow, I mean those that are called *Nazarites,* that suffer their hair to grow long, and use no wine, when they consecrate their hair,[4] and offer it for a sacrifice, they are to allot that hair for the priests [to be thrown into the fire]. Such also as dedicate themselves to God, as a corban, which denotes what the Greeks call a *gift,* when they are desirous of being freed from that ministration, are to lay down money for the priests; thirty shekels if it be a woman, and fifty if it be a man; but if any be too poor to pay the appointed sum, it shall be lawful for the priests to determine that sum as they think fit. And if any slay beasts at home for a private festival, but not for a religious one, they are obliged to bring the maw and the cheek, [or breast,] and the right shoulder of the sacrifice, to the priests. With these Moses contrived that the priests should be plentifully maintained, besides what they had out of those offerings for sins which the people gave them, as I have set it down in the foregoing book. He also ordered, that out of every thing allotted for the priests, their servants, [their sons,] their daughters, and their wives, should partake, as well as themselves, excepting what came to them out of the sacrifices that were offered for sins; for of those none but the males of the family of the priests might eat, and this in the temple also, and that the same day they were offered.

5. When Moses had made these constitutions, after the sedition was over, he removed, together with the whole army, and came to the borders of Idumea. He then sent ambassadors to the king of the Idumeans, and desired him to give him a passage through his country; and agreed to send him what hostages he should desire, to secure him from an injury. He desired him also, that he would allow his army liberty to buy provisions; and, if he insisted upon it, he would pay down a price for the very water they should drink. But the king was not pleased with this embassage from Moses: nor did he allow a passage for the army, but brought his people armed to meet Moses, and to hinder them, in case they should endeavor to force their passage. Upon which Moses consulted God by the oracle, who would

---

4. Grotius, on Numbers 6:18, takes notice that the Greeks also, aswell as the Jews, sometimes consecrated the hair of their heads to the gods.

not have him begin the war first; and so he withdrew his forces, and traveled round about through the wilderness.

6. Then it was that Miriam, the sister of Moses, came to her end, having completed her fortieth year[5] since she left Egypt, on the first[6] day of the lunar month Xanthicus. They then made a public funeral for her, at a great expense. She was buried upon a certain mountain, which they call *Sin:* and when they had mourned for her thirty days, Moses purified the people after this manner: He brought a heifer that had never been used to the plough or to husbandry, that was complete in all its parts, and entirely of a red color, at a little distance from the camp, into a place perfectly clean. This heifer was slain by the high priest, and her blood sprinkled with his finger seven times before the tabernacle of God; after this, the entire heifer was burnt in that state, together with its skin and entrails; and they threw cedar-wood, and hyssop, and scarlet wool, into the midst of the fire; then a clean man gathered all her ashes together, and laid them in a place perfectly clean. When therefore any persons were defiled by a dead body, they put a little of these ashes into spring water, with hyssop, and, dipping part of these ashes in it, they sprinkled them with it, both on the third day, and on the seventh, and after that they were clean. This he enjoined them to do also when the tribes should come into their own land.

7. Now when this purification, which their leader made upon the mourning for his sister, as it has been now described, was over, he caused the army to remove and to march through the wilderness and through Arabia; and when he came to a place which the Arabians esteem their metropolis, which was formerly called *Arce,* but has now the name of *Petra,* at this place, which was encompassed with high mountains, Aaron went up one of them in the sight of the whole army, Moses having before told him that he was to die, for this place was over against them. He put off his pontifical garments, and delivered

5. Josephus here uses this phrase, "when the fortieth year was completed," for when it was begun; as does St. Luke when the day of Pentecost was completed," Acts 2:1.

6. Whether Miriam died, as Josephus's. Greek copies imply, on the first day of the month, may be doubted, because the Latin copies say it was on the tenth, and so say the Jewish calendars also, as Dr. Bernard assures us. It is said her sepulcher is still extant near Petra, the old capital city of Arabia Petraea, at this day; as also that of Aaron, not far off.

them to Eleazar his son, to whom the high priesthood belonged, because he was the elder brother; and died while the multitude looked upon him. He died in the same year wherein he lost his sister, having lived in all a hundred twenty and three years. He died on the first day of that lunar month which is called by the Athenians *Hecatombaeon*, by the Macedonians *Lous*, but by the Hebrews *Abba*.

5   *How Moses Conquered Sihon and Og Kings of the Amorites, and Destroyed Their Whole Army and Then Divided Their Land by Lot to Two Tribes and a Half of the Hebrews*

1. THE people mourned for Aaron thirty days, and when this mourning was over, Moses removed the army from that place, and came to the river Arnon, which, issuing out of the mountains of Arabia, and running through all that wilderness, falls into the lake Asphaltitis, and becomes the limit between the land of the Moabites and the land of the Amorites. This land is fruitful, and sufficient to maintain a great number of men, with the good things it produces. Moses therefore sent messengers to Sihon, the king of this country, desiring that he would grant his army a passage, upon what security he should please to require; he promised that he should be no way injured, neither as to that country which Sihon governed, nor as to its inhabitants; and that he would buy his provisions at such a price as should be to their advantage, even though he should desire to sell them their very water. But Sihon refused his offer, and put his army into battle array, and was preparing every thing in order to hinder their passing over Arnon.

2. When Moses saw that the Amorite king was disposed to enter upon hostilities with them, he thought he ought not to bear that insult; and, determining to wean the Hebrews from their indolent temper, and prevent the disorders which arose thence, which had been the occasion of their former sedition, (nor indeed were they now thoroughly easy in their minds,) he inquired of God, whether he would give him leave to fight? which when he had done, and God also promised him the victory, he was himself very courageous, and ready to proceed to fighting. Accordingly he encouraged the soldiers; and he desired of them that they would take the pleasure of fighting, now God gave them leave so to do. They then, upon the receipt of this

permission, which they so much longed for, put on their whole armor, and set about the work without delay. But the Amorite king was not now like to himself when the Hebrews were ready to attack him; but both he himself was affrighted at the Hebrews, and his army, which before had showed themselves to be of good courage, were then found to be timorous: so they could not sustain the first onset, nor bear up against the Hebrews, but fled away, as thinking this would afford them a more likely way for their escape than fighting, for they depended upon their cities, which were strong, from which yet they reaped no advantage when they were forced to fly to them; for as soon as the Hebrews saw them giving ground, they immediately pursued them close; and when they had broken their ranks, they greatly terrified them, and some of them broke off from the rest, and ran away to the cities. Now the Hebrews pursued them briskly, and obstinately persevered in the labors they had already undergone; and being very skillful in slinging, and very dexterous in throwing of darts, or any thing else of that kind, and also having nothing but light armor, which made them quick in the pursuit, they overtook their enemies; and for those that were most remote, and could not be overtaken, they reached them by their slings and their bows, so that many were slain; and those that escaped the slaughter were sorely wounded, and these were more distressed with thirst than with any of those that fought against them, for it was the summer season; and when the greatest number of them were brought down to the river out of a desire to drink, as also when others fled away by troops, the Hebrews came round them, and shot at them; so that, what with darts and what with arrows, they made a slaughter of them all. Sihon their king was also slain. So the Hebrews spoiled the dead bodies, and took their prey. The land also which they took was full of abundance of fruits, and the army went all over it without fear, and fed their cattle upon it; and they took the enemies prisoners, for they could no way put a stop to them, since all the fighting men were destroyed. Such was the destruction which overtook the Amorites, who were neither sagacious in counsel, nor courageous in action. Hereupon the Hebrews took possession of their land, which is a country situate between three rivers, and naturally resembled an island: the river Arnon being its southern; the river Jabbok determining its northern side, which running into Jordan loses its own name, and takes the other; while Jordan itself runs along by it, on its western coast.

3. When matters were come to this state, Og, the king of Gilead and Gaulanitis, fell upon the Israelites. He brought an army with him, and in haste to the assistance of his friend Sihon: but though he found him already slain, yet did he resolve still to come and fight the Hebrews, supposing he should be too hard for them, and being desirous to try their valor; but failing of his hope, he was both himself slain in the battle, and all his army was destroyed. So Moses passed over the river Jabbok, and overran the kingdom of Og. He overthrew their cities, and slew all their inhabitants, who yet exceeded in riches all the men in that part of the continent, on account of the goodness of the soil, and the great quantity of their wealth. Now Og had very few equals, either in the largeness of his body, or handsomeness of his appearance. He was also a man of great activity in the use of his hands, so that his actions were not unequal to the vast largeness and handsome appearance of his body. And men could easily guess at his strength and magnitude when they took his bed at Rabbath, the royal city of the Ammonites; its structure was of iron, its breadth four cubits, and its length a cubit more than double thereto. However, his fall did not only improve the circumstances of the Hebrews for the present, but by his death he was the occasion of further good success to them; for they presently took those sixty cities, which were encompassed with excellent walls, and had been subject to him, and all got both in general and in particular a great prey.

6   *Concerning Balaam the Prophet and What Kind of Man He Was,*

1. NOW Moses, when he had brought his army to Jordan; pitched his camp in the great plain over against Jericho. This city is a very happy situation, and very fit for producing palm-trees and balsam. And now the Israelites began to be very proud of themselves, and were very eager for fighting. Moses then, after he had offered for a few days sacrifices of thanksgiving to God, and feasted the people, sent a party of armed men to lay waste the country of the Midianites, and to take their cities. Now the occasion which he took for making war upon them was this that follows—

2. When Balak, the king of the Moabites, who had from his ancestors a friendship and league with the Midianites, saw how great the Israelites were grown, he was much affrighted on account of his own and his kingdom's danger; for he was not acquainted with this, that the Hebrews would not meddle with any other country, but were to be contented with the possession of the land of Canaan, God having forbidden them to go any farther[7] So he, with more haste than wisdom, resolved to make an attempt upon them by words; but he did not judge it prudent to fight against them, after they had such prosperous successes, and even became out of ill successes more happy than before, but he thought to hinder them, if he could, from growing greater, and so he resolved to send ambassadors to the Midianites about them. Now these Midianites knowing there was one Balaam, who lived by Euphrates, and was the greatest of the prophets at that time, and one that was in friendship with them, sent some of their honorable princes along with the ambassadors of Balak, to entreat the prophet to come to them, that he might imprecate curses to the destruction of the Israelites. So Balsam received the ambassadors, and treated them very kindly; and when he had supped, he inquired what was God's will, and what this matter was for which the Midianites entreated him to come to them. But when God opposed his going, he came to the ambassadors, and told them that he was himself very willing and desirous to comply with their request, but informed them that God was opposite to his intentions, even that God who had raised him to great reputation on account of the truth of his predictions; for that this army, which they entreated him to come and curse, was in the favor of God; on which account he advised them to go home again, and not to persist in their enmity against the Israelites; and when he had given them that answer, he dismissed the ambassadors.

3. Now the Midianites, at the earnest request and fervent entreaties of Balak, sent other ambassadors to Balaam, who, desiring to gratify

---

7. What Josephus here remarks is well worth our remark in this place also; viz. that the Israelites were never to meddle with the Moabites, or Ammonites, or any other people, but those belonging to the land of Canaan, and the countries of Sihon and Og beyond Jordan, as far as the desert and Euphrates, and that therefore no other people had reason to fear the conquests of the Israelites; but that those countries given them by God were their proper and peculiar portion among the nations, and that all who endeavored to dispossess them might ever be justly destroyed by them.

the men, inquired again of God; but he was displeased at [second] trial[8] and bid him by no means to contradict the ambassadors. Now Balsam did not imagine that God gave this injunction in order to deceive him, so he went along with the ambassadors; but when the divine angel met him in the way, when he was in a narrow passage, and hedged in with a wall on both sides, the ass on which Balaam rode understood that it was a divine spirit that met him, and thrust Balaam to one of the walls, without regard to the stripes which Balaam, when he was hurt by the wall, gave her; but when the ass, upon the angel's continuing to distress her, and upon the stripes which were given her, fell down, by the will of God, she made use of the voice of a man, and complained of Balaam as acting unjustly to her; that whereas he had no fault find with her in her former service to him, he now inflicted stripes upon her, as not understanding that she was hindered from serving him in what he was now going about, by the providence of God. And when he was disturbed by reason of the voice of the ass, which was that of a man, the angel plainly appeared to him, and blamed him for the stripes he had given his ass; and informed him that the brute creature was not in fault, but that he was himself come to obstruct his journey, as being contrary to the will of God. Upon which Balaam was afraid, and was preparing to return back again: yet did God excite him to go on his intended journey, but added this injunction, that he should declare nothing but what he himself should suggest to his mind.

---

8. Note that Josephus never supposes Balaam to be an idolater, nor to seek idolatrous enchantments, or to prophesy falsely, but to be no other than an ill-disposed prophet of the true God; and intimates that God's answer the second time, permitting him to go, was ironical, and on design that he deceived (which sort of deception, by way of punishment for former crimes, Josephus never scruples to admit, as ever esteeming such wicked men justly and providentially deceived). But perhaps we had better keep here close to the text which says Numbers 23:20, 21, that God only permitted Balaam to go along with the ambassadors, in case they came and called him, or positively insisted on his going along with them, on any terms; whereas Balaam seems out of impatience to have risen up in the morning, and saddled his ass, and rather to have called them, than staid for their calling him, so zealous does he seem to have been for his reward of divination, his wages of unrighteousness, Numbers 23:7, 17, 18, 37; 2 Peter 2:15; Jude 5, 11; which reward or wages the truly religious prophets of God never required nor accepted, as our Josephus justly takes notice in the cases of Samuel, Antiq. B. V. ch. 4. sect. 1, and Daniel, Antiq. B. X. ch. 11. sect. 3. See also Genesis 14:22, 23; 2 Kings 5:15, 16, 26, 27; and Acts 8;17–24.

4. When God had given him this charge, he came to Balak; and when the king had entertained him in a magnificent manner, he desired him to go to one of the mountains to take a view of the state of the camp of the Hebrews. Balak himself also came to the mountain, and brought the prophet along with him, with a royal attendance. This mountain lay over their heads, and was distant sixty furlongs from the camp. Now when he saw them, he desired the king to build him seven altars, and to bring him as many bulls and rams; to which desire the king did presently conform. He then slew the sacrifices, and offered them as burnt-offerings, that he might observe some signal of the flight of the Hebrews. Then said he, "Happy is this people, on whom God bestows the possession of innumerable good things, and grants them his own providence to be their assistant and their guide; so that there is not any nation among mankind but you will be esteemed superior to them in virtue, and in the earnest prosecution of the best rules of life, and of such as are pure from wickedness, and will leave those rules to your excellent children; and this out of the regard that God bears to you, and the provision of such things for you as may render you happier than any other people under the sun. You shall retain that land to which he hath sent you, and it shall ever be under the command of your children; and both all the earth, as well as the seas, shall be filled with your glory: and you shall be sufficiently numerous to supply the world in general, and every region of it in particular, with inhabitants out of your stock. However, O blessed army! wonder that you are become so many from one father: and truly, the land of Canaan can now hold you, as being yet comparatively few; but know ye that the whole world is proposed to be your place of habitation for ever. The multitude of your posterity also shall live as well in the islands as on the continent, and that more in number than are the stars of heaven. And when you are become so many, God will not relinquish the care of you, but will afford you an abundance of all good things in times of peace, with victory and dominion in times of war. May the children of your enemies have an inclination to fight against you; and may they be so hardy as to come to arms, and to assault you in battle, for they will not return with victory, nor will their return be agreeable to their children and wives. To so great a degree of valor will you be raised by the providence of God, who is able to diminish the affluence of some, and to supply the wants of others."

5. Thus did Balaam speak by inspiration, as not being in his own power, but moved to say what he did by the Divine Spirit. But then Balak was displeased, and said he had broken the contract he had made, whereby he was to come, as he and his confederates had invited him, by the promise of great presents: for whereas he came to curse their enemies, he had made an encomium upon them, and had declared that they were the happiest of men. To which Balaam replied, "O Balak, if thou rightly considerest this whole matter, canst thou suppose that it is in our power to be silent, or to say any thing, when the Spirit of God seizes upon us?—for he puts such words as he pleases in our mouths, and such discourses as we are not ourselves conscious of. I well remember by what entreaties both you and the Midianites so joyfully brought me hither, and on that account I took this journey. It was my prayer, that I might not put any affront upon you, as to what you desired of me; but God is more powerful than the purposes I had made to serve you; for those that take upon them to foretell the affairs of mankind, as from their own abilities, are entirely unable to do it, or to forbear to utter what God suggests to them, or to offer violence to his will; for when he prevents us and enters into us, nothing that we say is our own. I then did not intend to praise this army, nor to go over the several good things which God intended to do to their race; but since he was so favorable to them, and so ready to bestow upon them a happy life and eternal glory, he suggested the declaration of those things to me: but now, because it is my desire to oblige thee thyself, as well as the Midianites, whose entreaties it is not decent for me to reject, go to, let us again rear other altars, and offer the like sacrifices that we did before, that I may see whether I can persuade God to permit me to bind these men with curses." Which, when Balak had agreed to, God would not, even upon second sacrifices, consent to his cursing the Israelites.[9] Then fell Balaam upon his face, and foretold what calamities would befall the several kings of the nations, and the most eminent cities, some of which of old were

---

9. Whether Josephus had in his copy but two attempts of Balaam in all to curse Israel; or whether by this his twice offering sacrifice, he meant twice besides that first time already mentioned, which yet is not very probable; cannot now be certainly determined. In the mean time, all other copies have three such attempts of Balaam to curse them in the present history.

not so much as inhabited; which events have come to pass among the several people concerned, both in the foregoing ages, and in this, till my own memory, both by sea and by land. From which completion of all these predictions that he made, one may easily guess that the rest will have their completion in time to come.

6. But Balak being very angry that the Israelites were not cursed, sent away Balaam without thinking him worthy of any honor. Whereupon, when he was just upon his journey, in order to pass the Euphrates, he sent for Balak, and for the princes of the Midianites, and spake thus to them:—"O Balak, and you Midianites that are here present, (for I am obliged even without the will of God to gratify you,) it is true no entire destruction can seize upon the nation of the Hebrews, neither by war, nor by plague, nor by scarcity of the fruits of the earth, nor can any other unexpected accident be their entire ruin; for the providence of God is concerned to preserve them from such a misfortune; nor will it permit any such calamity to come upon them whereby they may all perish; but some small misfortunes, and those for a short time, whereby they may appear to be brought low, may still befall them; but after that they will flourish again, to the terror of those that brought those mischiefs upon them. So that if you have a mind to gain a victory over them for a short space of time, you will obtain it by following my directions:—Do you therefore set out the handsomest of such of your daughters as are most eminent for beauty,[10] and proper to force and conquer the modesty of those that behold them, and these decked and trimmed to the highest degree able. Then do you send them to be near camp, and give them in charge, that the young men of the Hebrews desire their allow it them; and when they see they are enamored of them, let them take leaves; and if they entreat them to stay, let give their consent till they have persuaded leave off their obedience to their own laws, the worship of that God who established them to worship the gods of the Midianites and for

---

10. Such a large and distinct account of this perversion of the Israelites by the Midianite women, of which our other copies give us but short intimations, Numbers 31:16 2 Peter 2:15; Jude 11; Revelation 2:14, is preserved, as Reland informs us, in the Samaritan Chronicle, in Philo, and in other writings of the Jews, as well as here by Josephus.

by this means God will be angry at them[11]. Accordingly, when Balaam had suggested counsel to them, he went his way.

7. So when the Midianites had sent their daughters,as Balaam had exhorted them, the Hebrew men were allured by their beauty, and came with them, and besought them not to grudge them the enjoyment of their beauty, nor to deny them their conversation. These daughters of Midianites received their words gladly, and consented to it, and staid with them; but when they brought them to be enamored of them, and their inclinations to them were grown to ripeness, they began to think of departing from them: then it was that these men became greatly disconsolate at the women's departure, and they were urgent with them not to leave them, but begged they would continue there, and become their wives; and they promised them they should be owned as mistresses all they had. This they said with an oath, and called God for the arbitrator of what they promised; and this with tears in their eyes, and all such marks of concern, as might shew how miserable they thought themselves without them, and so might move their compassion for them. So the women, as soon as they perceived they had made their slaves, and had caught them with their conservation began to speak thus to them:—8. "O you illustrious young men! we have of our own at home, and great plenty of good things there, together with the natural, affectionate parents and friends; nor is it out of our want of any such things that we came to discourse with you; nor did we admit of your invitation with design to prostitute the beauty of our bodies for gain; but taking you for brave and worthy men, we agreed to your request, that we might treat you with such honors as hospitality required: and now seeing you say that you have a great affection for us, and are troubled when you think we are departing, we are not averse to your entreaties; and if we may receive such assurance of your good-will as we think can be alone sufficient, we will be glad to lead our lives with you as your wives; but we are afraid that you will in time be weary of our company,

---

11. This grand maxim, That God's people of Israel could never be hurt nor destroyed, but by drawing them to sin against God, appears to be true, by the entire history of that people, both in the Bible and in Josephus; and is often taken notice of in them both. See in particular a most remarkable Ammonite testimony to this purpose, Judith 5:5–21.

and will then abuse us, and send us back to our parents, after an ignominious manner." And they desired that they would excuse them in their guarding against that danger. But the young men professed they would give them any assurance they should desire; nor did they at all contradict what they requested, so great was the passion they had for them. "If then," said they, "this be your resolution, since you make use of such customs and conduct of life as are entirely different from all other men,[12] insomuch that your kinds of food are peculiar to yourselves, and your kinds of drink not common to others, it will be absolutely necessary, if you would have us for your wives, that you do withal worship our gods. Nor can there be any other demonstration of the kindness which you say you already have, and promise to have hereafter to us, than this, that you worship the same gods that we do. For has any one reason to complain, that now you are come into this country, you should worship the proper gods of the same country? especially while our gods are common to all men, and yours such as belong to nobody else but yourselves." So they said they must either come into such methods of divine worship as all others came into, or else they must look out for another world, wherein they may live by themselves, according to their own laws.

9. Now the young men were induced by the fondness they had for these women to think they spake very well; so they gave themselves up to what they persuaded them, and transgressed their own laws, and supposing there were many gods, and resolving that they would sacrifice to them according to the laws of that country which ordained them, they both were delighted with their strange food, and went on to do every thing that the women would have them do, though in contradiction to their own laws; so far indeed that this transgression

---

12. What Josephus here puts into the mouths of these Midianite women, who came to entice the Israelites to lewdness and idolatry, viz. that their worship of the God of Israel, in opposition to their idol gods, implied their living according to the holy laws which the true God had given them by Moses, in opposition to those impure laws which were observed under their false gods, well deserves our consideration; and gives us a substantial reason for the great concern that was ever shown under the law of Moses to preserve the Israelites from idolatry, and in the worship of the true God; it being of no less consequence than, Whether God's people should be governed by the holy laws of the true God, or by the impure laws derived from demons, under the pagan idolatry.

was already gone through the whole army of the young men, and they fell into a sedition that was much worse than the former, and into danger of the entire abolition of their own institutions; for when once the youth had tasted of these strange customs, they went with insatiable inclinations into them; and even where some of the principal men were illustrious on account of the virtues of their fathers, they also were corrupted together with the rest.

10. Even Zimri, the head of the tribe of Simeon accompanied with Cozbi, a Midianitish women, who was the daughter of Sur, a man of authority in that country; and being desired by his wife to disregard the laws of Moses, and to follow those she was used to, he complied with her, and this both by sacrificing after a manner different from his own, and by taking a stranger to wife. When things were thus, Moses was afraid that matters should grow worse, and called the people to a congregation, but then accused nobody by name, as unwilling to drive those into despair who, by lying concealed, might come to repentance; but he said that they did not do what was either worthy of themselves, or of their fathers, by preferring pleasure to God, and to the living according to his will; that it was fit they should change their courses while their affairs were still in a good state, and think that to be true fortitude which offers not violence to their laws, but that which resists their lusts. And besides that, he said it was not a reasonable thing, when they had lived soberly in the wilderness, to act madly now when they were in prosperity; and that they ought not to lose, now they have abundance, what they had gained when they had little:—and so did he endeavor, by saying this, to correct the young inert, and to bring them to repentance for what they had done.

11. But Zimri arose up after him, and said, "Yes, indeed, Moses, thou art at liberty to make use of such laws as thou art so fond of, and hast, by accustoming thyself to them, made them firm; otherwise, if things had not been thus, thou hadst often been punished before now, and hadst known that the Hebrews are not easily put upon; but thou shalt not have me one of thy followers in thy tyrannical commands, for thou dost nothing else hitherto, but, under pretense of laws, and of God, wickedly impose on us slavery, and gain dominion to thyself, while thou deprivest us of the sweetness of life, which consists in acting according to our own wills, and is the right of free-men, and of those that have no lord over them. Nay, indeed, this man

is harder upon the Hebrews then were the Egyptians themselves, as pretending to punish, according to his laws, every one's acting what is most agreeable to himself; but thou thyself better deservest to suffer punishment, who presumest to abolish what every one acknowledges to be what is good for him, and aimest to make thy single opinion to have more force than that of all the rest; and what I now do, and think to be right, I shall not hereafter deny to be according to my own sentiments. I have married, as thou sayest rightly, a strange woman, and thou hearest what I do from myself as from one that is free, for truly I did not intend to conceal myself. I also own that I sacrificed to those gods to whom you do not think it fit to sacrifice; and I think it right to come at truth by inquiring of many people, and not like one that lives under tyranny, to suffer the whole hope of my life to depend upon one man; nor shall any one find cause to rejoice who declares himself to have more authority over my actions than myself."

12. Now when Zimri had said these things, about what he and some others had wickedly done, the people held their peace, both out of fear of what might come upon them, and because they saw that their legislator was not willing to bring his insolence before the public any further, or openly to contend with him; for he avoided that, lest many should imitate the impudence of his language, and thereby disturb the multitude. Upon this the assembly was dissolved. However, the mischievous attempt had proceeded further, if Zimri had not been first slain, which came to pass on the following occasion:—Phineas, a man in other respects better than the rest of the young men, and also one that surpassed his contemporaries in the dignity of his father, (for he was the son of Eleazar the high priest, and the grandson of [Aaron] Moses's brother,) who was greatly troubled at what was done by Zimri, he resolved in earnest to inflict punishment on him, before his unworthy behavior should grow stronger by impunity, and in order to prevent this transgression from proceeding further, which would happen if the ringleaders were not punished. He was of so great magnanimity, both in strength of mind and body, that when he undertook any very dangerous attempt, he did not leave it off till he overcame it, and got an entire victory. So he came into Zimri's tent, and slew him with his javelin, and with it he slew Cozbi also, Upon which all those young men that had a regard to virtue, and aimed to do a glorious action, imitated Phineas's boldness, and slew

those that were found to be guilty of the same crime with Zimri. Accordingly many of those that had transgressed perished by the magnanimous valor of these young men; and the rest all perished by a plague, which distemper God himself inflicted upon them; so that all those their kindred, who, instead of hindering them from such wicked actions, as they ought to have done, had persuaded them to go on, were esteemed by God as partners in their wickedness, and died. Accordingly there perished out of the army no fewer than fourteen[13] [twenty-four] thousand at this time.

13. This was the cause why Moses was provoked to send an army to destroy the Midianites, concerning which expedition we shall speak presently, when we have first related what we have omitted; for it is but just not to pass over our legislator's due encomium, on account of his conduct here, because, although this Balaam, who was sent for by the Midianites to curse the Hebrews, and when he was hindered from doing it by Divine Providence, did still suggest that advice to them, by making use of which our enemies had well nigh corrupted the whole multitude of the Hebrews with their wiles, till some of them were deeply infected with their opinions; yet did he do him great honor, by setting down his prophecies in writing. And while it was in his power to claim this glory to himself, and make men believe they were his own predictions, there being no one that could be a witness against him, and accuse him for so doing, he still gave his attestation to him, and did him the honor to make mention of him on this account. But let every one think of these matters as he pleases.

7 How the Hebrews Fought with the Midianites, and Overcame Them

1. Now Moses sent an army against the land of Midian, for the causes forementioned, in all twelve thousand, taking an equal number out of every

---

13. The mistake in all Josephus's copies, Greek and Latin which have here fourteen thousand instead of twenty-four thousand, is so flagrant, that our very learned editors, Bernard and Hudson, have put the latter number directly into the text. I choose rather to put it in brackets.

tribe, and appointed Phineas for their commander; of which Phineas we made mention a little before, as he that had guarded the laws of the Hebrews, and had inflicted punishment on Zimri when he had transgressed them. Now the Midianites perceived beforehand how the Hebrews were coming, and would suddenly be upon them: so they assembled their army together, and fortified the entrances into their country, and there awaited the enemy's coming. When they were come, and they had joined battle with them, an immense multitude of the Midianites fell; nor could they be numbered, they were so very many: and among them fell all their kings, five in number, viz. Evi, Zur, Reba, Hur, and Rekem, who was of the same name with a city, the chief and capital of all Arabia, which is still now so called by the whole Arabian nation, *Arecem,* from the name of the king that built it; but is by the Greeks called *Petra.* Now when the enemies were discomfited, the Hebrews spoiled their country, and took a great prey, and destroyed the men that were its inhabitants, together with the women; only they let the virgins alone, as Moses had commanded Phineas to do, who indeed came back, bringing with him an army that had received no harm, and a great deal of prey; fifty-two thousand beeves, seventy-five thousand six hundred sheep, sixty thousand asses, with an immense quantity of gold and silver furniture, which the Midianites made use of in their houses; for they were so wealthy, that they were very luxurious. There were also led captive about thirty-two thousand virgins.[14] So Moses parted the prey into parts, and gave one fiftieth

---

14. The slaughter of all the Midianite women that had prostituted themselves to the lewd Israelites, and the preservation of those that had not been guilty therein; the last of which were no fewer than thirty-two thousand, both here and Numbers 31:15–17, 35, 40, 46, and both by the particular command of God; are highly remarkable, and show that, even in nations otherwise for their wickedness doomed to destruction, the innocent were sometimes particularly and providentially taken care of, and delivered from that destruction; which directly implies, that it was the wickedness of the nations of Canaan, and nothing else, that occasioned their excision. See Genesis 15;16; 1 Samuel 15:18, 33; Apost. Constit. B. VIII. ch. 12. p. 402. In the first of which places, the reason of the delay of the punishment of the Amorites is given, because "their iniquity was not yet full." In the secured, Saul is ordered to go and "destroy the sinners, the Amalekites;" plainly implying that they were therefore to be destroyed, because they were sinners, and not otherwise. In the third, the reason is given why king Agag was not to be spared, viz. because of his former cruelty: "As thy sword hath made the (Hebrew) women childless, so shall thy mother be made childless among

part to Eleazar and the two priests, and another fiftieth part to the Levites; and distributed the rest of the prey among the people. After which they lived happily, as having obtained an abundance of good things by their valor, and there being no misfortune that attended them, or hindered their enjoyment of that happiness.

2. But Moses was now grown old, and appointed Joshua for his successor, both to receive directions from God as a prophet, and for a commander of the army, if they should at any time stand in need of such a one; and this was done by the command of God, that to him the care of the public should be committed. Now Joshua had been instructed in all those kinds of learning which concerned the laws and God himself, and Moses had been his instructor.

3. At this time it was that the two tribes of Gad and Reuben, and the half tribe of Manasseh, abounded in a multitude of cattle, as well as in all other kinds of prosperity; whence they had a meeting, and in a body came and besought Moses to give them, as their peculiar portion, that land of the Amorites which they had taken by right of war, because it was fruitful, and good for feeding of cattle; but Moses, supposing that they were afraid of fighting with the Canaanites, and invented this provision for their cattle as a handsome excuse for avoiding that war, he called them *arrant cowards*, and said they had only contrived a decent excuse for that cowardice; and that they had a mind to live in luxury and ease, while all the rest were laboring with great pains to obtain the land they were desirous to have; and that they were not willing to march along, and undergo the remaining hard service, whereby they were, under the Divine promise, to pass over Jordan, and overcome those our enemies which God had shown them, and so obtain their land. But these tribes, when they saw that Moses was angry with them, and when they could not deny but he had a just cause to be displeased at their petition, made an apology for themselves; and said, that it was not on account of their fear of

---

women by the Hebrews." In the last place, the apostles, or their amanuensis Clement, gave this reason for the necessity of the coming of Christ, that "men had formerly perverted both the positive law, and that of nature; and had cast out of their mind the memory of the Flood, the burning of Sodom, the plagues of the Egyptians, and the slaughter of the inhabitants of Palestine," as signs of the most amazing impenitence and insensibility, under the punishments of horrid wickedness.

dangers, nor on account of their laziness, that they made this request to him, but that they might leave the prey they had gotten in places of safety, and thereby might be more expedite, and ready to undergo difficulties, and to fight battles. They added this also, that when they had built cities, wherein they might preserve their children, and wives, and possessions, if he would bestow them upon them, they would go along with the rest of the army. Hereupon Moses was pleased with what they said; so he called for Eleazar the high priest, and Joshua, and the chief of the tribes, and permitted these tribes to possess the land of the Amorites; but upon this condition, that they should join with their kinsmen in the war until all things were settled. Upon which condition they took possession of the country, and built them strong cities, and put into them their children and their wives, and whatsoever else they had that might be an impediment to the labors of their future marches.

4. Moses also now built those ten cities which were to be of the number of the forty-eight [for the Levites;]; three of which he allotted to those that slew any person involuntarily, and fled to them; and he assigned the same time for their banishment with that of the life of that high priest under whom the slaughter and flight happened; after which death of the high priest he permitted the slayer to return home. During the time of his exile, the relations of him that was slain may, by this law, kill the manslayer, if they caught him without the bounds of the city to which he fled, though this permission was not granted to any other person. Now the cities which were set apart for this flight were these: Bezer, at the borders of Arabia; Ramoth, of the land of Gilead; and Golan, in the land of Bashan. There were to be also, by Moses's command, three other cities allotted for the habitation of these fugitives out of the cities of the Levites, but not till after they should be in possession of the land of Canaan.

5. At this time the chief men of the tribe of Manasseh came to Moses, and informed him that there was an eminent man of their tribe dead, whose name was Zelophehad, who left no male children, but left daughters; and asked him whether these daughters might inherit his land or not. He made this answer, That if they shall marry into their own tribe, they shall carry their estate along with them; but if they dispose of themselves in marriage to men of another tribe, they shall leave their inheritance in their father's tribe. And then it was that Moses ordained, that every one's inheritance should continue in his own tribe.

8   *The Polity Settled by Moses; and How He Disappeared from Among Mankind*

1. WHEN forty years were completed, within thirty days, Moses gathered the congregation together near Jordan, where the city Abila now stands, a place full of palm-trees; and all the people being come together, he spake thus to them:—2. "O you Israelites and fellow soldiers, who have been partners with me in this long and uneasy journey; since it is now the will of God, and the course of old age, at a hundred and twenty, requires it that I should depart out of this life; and since God has forbidden me to be a patron or an assistant to you in what remains to be done beyond Jordan; I thought it reasonable not to leave off my endeavors even now for your happiness, but to do my utmost to procure for you the eternal enjoyment of good things, and a memorial for myself, when you shall be in the fruition of great plenty and prosperity. Come, therefore, let me suggest to you by what means you may be happy, and may leave an eternal prosperous possession thereof to your children after you, and then let me thus go out of the world; and I cannot but deserve to be believed by you, both on account of the great things I have already done for you, and because, when souls are about to leave the body, they speak with the sincerest freedom. O children of Israel! there is but one source of happiness for all mankind, the favor of God[15] for he alone is able to give good things to those that deserve them, and to deprive those of them that sin against him; towards whom, if you behave yourselves according to his will, and according to what I, who well understand his mind, do exhort you to, you will both be esteemed blessed, and will be admired by all men; and will never come into misfortunes, nor cease to be happy: you will then preserve the possession of the good things you already have, and will quickly obtain those that you are at present in want of,—only do you be obedient to those whom God would have you to follow. Nor do you prefer any other constitution of government before the laws now given you; neither do you disregard that way of Divine worship which you now have, nor change it for any other

---

15. Josephus here, in this one sentence, sums up his notion of Moses's very long and very serious exhortations in the book of Deuteronomy; and his words are so true, and of such importance, that they deserve to be had in constant remembrance.

form: and if you do this, you will be the most courageous of all men, in undergoing the fatigues of war, and will not be easily conquered by any of your enemies; for while God is present with you to assist you, it is to be expected that you will be able to despise the opposition of all mankind; and great rewards of virtue are proposed for you, if you preserve that virtue through your whole lives. Virtue itself is indeed the principal and the first reward, and after that it bestows abundance of others; so that your exercise of virtue towards other men will make your own lives happy, and render you more glorious than foreigners can be, and procure you an undisputed reputation with posterity. These blessings you will be able to obtain, in case you hearken to and observe those laws which, by Divine revelation, I have ordained for you; that is, in case you withal meditate upon the wisdom that is in them. I am going from you myself, rejoicing in the good things you enjoy; and I recommend you to the wise conduct of your law, to the becoming order of your polity, and to the virtues of your commanders, who will take care of what is for your advantage. And that God, who has been till now your Leader, and by whose goodwill I have myself been useful to you, will not put a period now to his providence over you, but as long as you desire to have him your Protector in your pursuits after virtue, so long will you enjoy his care over you. Your high priest also Eleazar, as well as Joshua, with the senate, and chief of your tribes, will go before you, and suggest the best advices to you; by following which advices you will continue to be happy: to whom do you give ear without reluctance, as sensible that all such as know well how to be governed, will also know how to govern, if they be promoted to that authority themselves. And do not you esteem liberty to consist in opposing such directions as your governors think fit to give you for your practice,—as at present indeed you place your liberty in nothing else but abusing your benefactors; which error if you can avoid for the time to come, your affairs will be in a better condition than they have hitherto been. Nor do you ever indulge such a degree of passion in these matters, as you have oftentimes done when you have been very angry at me; for you know that I have been oftener in danger of death from you than from our enemies. What I now put you in mind of, is not done in order to reproach you; for I do not think it proper, now I am going out of the world, to bring this to your remembrance, in order to leave you offended at me, since, at the time when I underwent those hardships from you, I was not angry at you; but I do it in order to make you wiser hereafter, and to teach you that this will be for your security; I mean, that you never be injurious to those that preside over you, even when you are become rich, as you will be to a great degree when you have passed over Jordan, and are in possession of the land of Canaan. Since, when you shall have once proceeded so far by your wealth, as to a contempt and disregard of virtue, you will also forfeit the favor of God; and when you have made him your enemy, you will be beaten in war, and will have the land which you possess taken away again from you by your enemies, and this with great reproaches upon your conduct. You will be scattered over the whole world, and will, as slaves, entirely fill both sea and land; and when once you have had the experience of what I now say, you will repent, and remember the laws you have broken, when it is too late. Whence I would advise you, if you intend to preserve these laws, to leave none of your enemies alive when you have conquered them, but to look upon it as for your advantage to destroy them all, lest, if you permit them to live, you taste of their manners, and thereby corrupt your own proper institutions. I also do further exhort you, to overthrow their altars, and their groves, and whatsoever temples they have among them, and to burn all such, their nation, and their very memory with fire; for by this means alone the safety of your own happy constitution can be firmly secured to you. And in order to prevent your ignorance of virtue, and the degeneracy of your nature into vice, I have also ordained you laws, by Divine suggestion, and a form of government, which are so good, that if you regularly observe them, you will be esteemed of all men the most happy."

3. When he had spoken thus, he gave them the laws and the constitution of government written in a book. Upon which the people fell into tears, and appeared already touched with the sense that they should have a great want of their conductor, because they remembered what a number of dangers he had passed through, and what care he had taken of their preservation: they desponded about what would come upon them after he was dead, and thought they should never have another governor like him; and feared that God would then take less care of them when Moses was gone, who used to intercede for them. They also repented of what they had said to him in the wilderness when they were angry, and were in grief on those accounts,

insomuch that the whole body of the people fell into tears with such bitterness, that it was past the power of words to comfort them in their affliction. However, Moses gave them some consolation; and by calling them off the thought how worthy he was of their weeping for him, he exhorted them to keep to that form of government he had given them; and then the congregation was dissolved at that time.

4. Accordingly, I shall now first describe this form of government which was agreeable to the dignity and virtue of Moses; and shall thereby inform those that read these Antiquities, what our original settlements were, and shall then proceed to the remaining histories. Now those settlements are all still in writing, as he left them; and we shall add nothing by way of ornament, nor any thing besides what Moses left us; only we shall so far innovate, as to digest the several kinds of laws into a regular system; for they were by him left in writing as they were accidentally scattered in their delivery, and as he upon inquiry had learned them of God. On which account I have thought it necessary to premise this observation beforehand, lest any of my own countrymen should blame me, as having been guilty of an offense herein. Now part of our constitution will include the laws that belong to our political state. As for those laws which Moses left concerning our common conversation and intercourse one with another, I have reserved that for a discourse concerning our manner of life, and the occasions of those laws; which I propose to myself, with God's assistance, to write, after I have finished the work I am now upon.

5. When you have possessed yourselves of the land of Canaan, and have leisure to enjoy the good things of it, and when you have afterward determined to build cities, if you will do what is pleasing to God, you will have a secure state of happiness. Let there be then one city of the land of Canaan, and this situate in the most agreeable place for its goodness, and very eminent in itself, and let it be that which God shall choose for himself by prophetic revelation. Let there also be one temple therein, and one altar, not reared of hewn stones, but of such as you gather together at random; which stones, when they are whited over with mortar, will have a handsome appearance, and be

beautiful to the sight. Let the ascent to it be not by steps[16] but by an acclivity of raised earth. And let there be neither an altar nor a temple in any other city; for God is but one, and the nation of the Hebrews is but one.

6. He that blasphemeth God, let him be stoned; and let him hang upon a tree all that day, and then let him be buried in an ignominious and obscure manner.

7. Let those that live as remote as the bounds of the land which the Hebrews shall possess, come to that city where the temple shall be, and this three times in a year, that they may give thanks to God for his former benefits, and may entreat him for those they shall want hereafter; and let them, by this means, maintain a friendly correspondence with one another by such meetings and feastings together, for it is a good thing for those that are of the same stock, and under the same institution of laws, not to be unacquainted with each other; which acquaintance will be maintained by thus conversing together, and by seeing and talking with one another, and so renewing the memorials of this union; for if they do not thus converse together continually, they will appear like mere strangers to one another.

8. Let there be taken out of your fruits a tenth, besides that which you have allotted to give to the priests and Levites. This you may indeed sell in the country, but it is to be used in those feasts and sacrifices that are to be celebrated in the holy city; for it is fit that you should enjoy those fruits of the earth which God gives you to possess, so as may be to the honor of the donor.

---

16. This law, both here and Exodus 20:25, 26, of not going up to God's altar by ladder-steps, but on an acclivity, seems not to have belonged to the altar of the tabernacle, which was in all but three cubits high, Exodus 27:4; nor to that of Ezekiel, which was expressly to be gone up to by steps, ch. 43:17; but rather to occasional altars of any considerable altitude and largeness; as also probably to Solomon's altar, to which it is here applied by Josephus, as well as to that in Zorobabel's and Herod's temple, which were, I think, all ten cubits high. See 2 Chronicles 4:1, and Antiq. B. VIII. ch. 3. sect. 7. The reason why these temples, and these only, were to have this ascent on an acclivity, and not by steps, is obvious, that before the invention of stairs, such as we now use, decency could not be otherwise provided for in the loose garments which the priests wore, as the law required. See Lamy of the Tabernacle and Temple, p. 444.

9. You are not to offer sacrifices out of the hire of a woman who is a harlot[17] for the Deity is not pleased with any thing that arises from such abuses of nature; of which sort none can be worse than this prostitution of the body. In like manner no one may take the price of the covering of a bitch, either of one that is used in hunting, or in keeping of sheep, and thence sacrifice to God.

10. Let no one blaspheme those gods which other cities esteem such;[18] nor may any one steal what belongs to strange temples, nor take away the gifts that are dedicated to any god.

11. Let not any one of you wear a garment made of woolen and linen, for that is appointed to be for the priests alone.

12. When the multitude are assembled together unto the holy city for sacrificing every seventh year, at the feast of tabernacles, let the high priest stand upon a high desk, whence he may be heard, and let him read the laws to all the people; and let neither the women nor the children be hindered from hearing, no, nor the servants neither; for it is a good thing that those laws should be engraven in their souls, and preserved in their memories, that so it may not be possible to blot them out; for by this means they will not be guilty of sin, when they cannot plead ignorance of what the laws have enjoined them. The laws also will have a greater authority among them, as foretelling what they will suffer if they break them; and imprinting in their souls by this hearing what they command them to do, that so there may always be within their minds that intention of the laws which they have despised and broken, and have thereby been the causes of their own mischief. Let the children also learn the laws, as the first thing they are taught, which will be the best thing they can be taught, and will be the cause of their future felicity.

13. Let every one commemorate before God the benefits which he bestowed upon them at their deliverance out of the land of Egypt,

---

17. The hire of public or secret harlots was given to Venus in Syria, as Lucian informs us, p. 878; and against some such vile practice of the old idolaters this law seems to have been made.

18. The Apostolical Constitutions, B. II. ch. 26. sect. 31, expound this law of Moses, Exodus 22. 28, "Thou shalt not revile or blaspheme the gods," or magistrates, which is a much more probable exposition than this of Josephus, of heathen gillis, as here, and against Apion, B. II. ch. 3. sect. 31. What book of the law was thus publicly read, see the note on Antiq. B. X. ch. 5. sect. 5, and 1 Esd. 9:8–55.

and this twice every day, both when the day begins and when the hour of sleep comes on, gratitude being in its own nature a just thing, and serving not only by way of return for past, but also by way of invitation of future favors. They are also to inscribe the principal blessings they have received from God upon their doors, and show the same remembrance of them upon their arms; as also they are to bear on their forehead and their arm those wonders which declare the power of God, and his good-will towards them, that God's readiness to bless them may appear every where conspicuous about them.[19]

14. Let there be seven men to judge in every city,[20] and these such as have been before most zealous in the exercise of virtue and righteousness. Let every judge have two officers allotted him out of the tribe of Levi. Let those that are chosen to judge in the several cities be had in great honor; and let none be permitted to revile any others when these are present, nor to carry themselves in an insolent manner to them; it being natural that reverence towards those in high offices among men should procure men's fear and reverence towards God. Let those that judge be permitted to determine according as they think to be right, unless any one can show that they have taken bribes, to the perversion of justice, or can allege any other accusation against them, whereby it may appear that they have passed an unjust sentence; for it is not fit that causes should be openly determined out of regard to gain, or to the dignity of the suitors, but that the judges should esteem what is right before all other things, otherwise God will by that means be

---

19. Whether these phylacteries, and other Jewish memorials of the law here mentioned by Josephus, and by Muses, (besides the fringes on the borders of their garments, Numbers 15:37,) were literally meant by God, I much question. That they have been long observed by the Pharisees and Rabbinical Jews is certain; however, the Karaites, who receive not the unwritten traditions of the elders, but keep close to the written law, with Jerome and Grotius, think they were not literally to be understood; as Bernard and Reland here take notice. Nor indeed do I remember that, either in the ancienter books of the Old Testament, or in the books we call Apocrypha, there are any signs of such literal observations appearing among the Jews, though their real or mystical signification, i.e. the constant remembrance and observation of the laws of God by Moses, be frequently inculcated in all the sacred writings.

20. Here, as well as elsewhere, sect. 38, of his Life, sect. 14, and of the War, B. II. ch. 20. sect. 5, are but seven judges appointed for small cities, instead of twenty-three in the modern Rabidns; which modern Rabbis are always but of very little authority in comparison of our Josephus.

despised, and esteemed inferior to those, the dread of whose power has occasioned the unjust sentence; for justice is the power of God. He therefore that gratifies those in great dignity, supposes them more potent than God himself. But if these judges be unable to give a just sentence about the causes that come before them, (which case is not unfrequent in human affairs,) let them send the cause undetermined to the holy city, and there let the high priest, the prophet, and the sanhedrim, determine as it shall seem good to them.

15. But let not a single witness be credited, but three, or two at the least, and those such whose testimony is confirmed by their good lives. But let not the testimony of women be admitted, on account of the levity and boldness of their sex[21] Nor let servants be admitted to give testimony, on account of the ignobility of their soul; since it is probable that they may not speak truth, either out of hope of gain, or fear of punishment. But if any one be believed to have borne false witness, let him, when he is convicted, suffer all the very same punishments which he against whom he bore witness was to have suffered.

16. If a murder be committed in any place, and he that did it be not found, nor is there any suspicion upon one as if he had hated the man, and so had killed him, let there be a very diligent inquiry made after the man, and rewards proposed to any one who will discover him; but if still no information can be procured, let the magistrates and senate of those cities that lie near the place in which the murder was committed, assemble together, and measure the distance from the place where the dead body lies; then let the magistrates of the nearest city thereto purchase a heifer, and bring it to a valley, and to a place therein where there is no land ploughed or trees planted, and let them cut the sinews of the heifer; then the priests and Levites, and the senate of that city, shall take water and wash their hands over the head of the heifer; and they shall openly declare that their hands are innocent of this murder, and that they have neither done it themselves, nor been assisting to any that did it. They shall also beseech God to be merciful to them, that no such horrid act may any more be done in that land.

---

21. I have never observed elsewhere, that in the Jewish government women were not admitted as legal witnesses in courts of justice. None of our copies of the Pentateuch say a word of it. It is very probable, however, that this was the exposition of the scribes and Pharisees, and the practice of the Jews in the days of Josephus.

17. Aristocracy, and the way of living under it, is the best constitution: and may you never have any inclination to any other form of government; and may you always love that form, and have the laws for your governors, and govern all your actions according to them; for you need no supreme governor but God. But if you shall desire a king, let him be one of your own nation; let him be always careful of justice and other virtues perpetually; let him submit to the laws, and esteem God's commands to be his highest wisdom; but let him do nothing without the high priest and the votes of the senators: let him not have a great number of wives, nor pursue after abundance of riches, nor a multitude of horses, whereby he may grow too proud to submit to the laws. And if he affect any such things, let him be restrained, lest he become so potent that his state be inconsistent with your welfare.

18. Let it not be esteemed lawful to remove boundaries, neither our own, nor of those with whom we are at peace. Have a care you do not take those landmarks away which are, as it were, a divine and unshaken limitation of rights made by God himself, to last for ever; since this going beyond limits, and gaining ground upon others, is the occasion of wars and seditions; for those that remove boundaries are not far off an attempt to subvert the laws.

19. He that plants a piece of land, the trees of which produce fruits before the fourth year, is not to bring thence any first-fruits to God, nor is he to make use of that fruit himself, for it is not produced in its proper season; for when nature has a force put upon her at an unseasonable time, the fruit is not proper for God, nor for the master's use; but let the owner gather all that is grown on the fourth car, for then it is in its proper season. And let him that has gathered it carry it to the holy city, and spend that, together with the tithe of his other fruits, in feasting with his friends, with the orphans, and the widows. But on the fifth year the fruit is his own, and he may use it as he pleases.

20. You are not to sow with seed a piece of land which is planted with vines, for it is enough that it supply nourishment to that plant, and be not harassed by ploughing also. You are to plough your land with oxen, and not to oblige other animals to come under the same yoke with them; but to till your land with those beasts that are of the same kind with each other. The seeds are also to be pure, and without mixture, and not to be compounded of two or three sorts, since nature does not rejoice in the union of things that are not in their own nature

alike; nor are you to permit beasts of different kinds to gender together, for there is reason to fear that this unnatural abuse may extend from beasts of different kinds to men, though it takes its first rise from evil practices about such smaller things. Nor is any thing to be allowed, by imitation whereof any degree of subversion may creep into the constitution. Nor do the laws neglect small matters, but provide that even those may be managed after an unblamable manner.

21. Let not those that reap, and gather in the corn that is reaped, gather in the gleanings also; but let them rather leave some handfuls for those that are in want of the necessaries of life, that it may be a support and a supply to them, in order to their subsistence. In like manner when they gather their grapes, let them leave some smaller bunches for the poor, and let them pass over some of the fruits of the olive-trees, when they gather them, and leave them to be partaken of by those that have none of their own; for the advantage arising from the exact collection of all, will not be so considerable to the owners as will arise from the gratitude of the poor. And God will provide that the land shall more willingly produce what shall be for the nourishment of its fruits, in case you do not merely take care of your own advantage, but have regard to the support of others also. Nor are you to muzzle the mouths of the oxen when they tread the ears of corn in the thrashing-floor; for it is not just to restrain our fellow-laboring animals, and those that work in order to its production, of this fruit of their labors. Nor are you to prohibit those that pass by at the time when your fruits are ripe to touch them, but to give them leave to fill themselves full of what you have; and this whether they be of your own country or strangers,—as being glad of the opportunity of giving them some part of your fruits when they are ripe; but let it not be esteemed lawful for them to carry any away. Nor let those that gather the grapes, and carry them to the wine-presses, restrain those whom they meet from eating of them; for it is unjust, out of envy, to hinder those that desire it, to partake of the good things that come into the world according to God's will, and this while the season is at the height, and is hastening away as it pleases God. Nay, if some, out of bashfulness, are unwilling to touch these fruits, let them be encouraged to take of them (I mean, those that are Israelites) as if they were themselves the owners and lords, on account of the kindred there is between them. Nay, let them desire men that come from other

countries, to partake of these tokens of friendship which God has given in their proper season; for that is not to be deemed as idly spent, which any one out of kindness communicates to another, since God bestows plenty of good things on men, not only for themselves to reap the advantage, but also to give to others in a way of generosity; and he is desirous, by this means, to make known to others his peculiar kindness to the people of Israel, and how freely he communicates happiness to them, while they abundantly communicate out of their great superfluities to even these foreigners also. But for him that acts contrary to this law, let him be beaten with forty stripes save one[22] by the public executioner; let him undergo this punishment, which is a most ignominious one for a free-man, and this because he was such a slave to gain as to lay a blot upon his dignity; for it is proper for you who have had the experience of the afflictions in Egypt, and of those in the wilderness, to make provision for those that are in the like circumstances; and while you have now obtained plenty yourselves, through the mercy and providence of God, to distribute of the same plenty, by the like sympathy, to such as stand in need of it.

22. Besides those two tithes, which I have already said you are to pay every year, the one for the Levites, the other for the festivals, you are to bring every third year a third tithe to be distributed to those that want;[23] to women also that are widows, and to children that are orphans. But as to the ripe fruits, let them carry that which is ripe first of all into the temple; and when they have blessed God for that land which bare them, and which he had given them for a possession, when they have also offered those sacrifices which the law has commanded them to bring, let them give the first-fruits to the priests. But when any one hath done this, and hath brought the tithe of all that he hath, together with those first-fruits that are for the Levites, and for the festivals, and when he is about to go home, let him stand before the holy house, and return thanks to God, that he hath delivered them

---

22. This penalty of "forty stripes save one," here mentioned, and sect. 23, was five times inflicted on St. Paul himself by the Jews, 2 Corinthians 11:24

23. Josephus's plain and express interpretation of this law of Moses, Deuteronomy 14:28, 29; 26:12, etc., that the Jews were bound every third year to pay three tithes, that to the Levites, that for sacrifices at Jerusalem, and this for the indigent, the widow, and the orphans, is fully confirmed by the practice of good old Tobit, even when he was a captive in Assyria, against the opinions of the Rabbins, Tobit 1:6–8.

from the injurious treatment they had in Egypt, and hath given them a good land, and a large, and lets them enjoy the fruits thereof; and when he hath openly testified that he hath fully paid the tithes [and other dues] according to the laws of Moses, let him entreat God that he will be ever merciful and gracious to him, and continue so to be to all the Hebrews, both by preserving the good things which he hath already given them, and by adding what it is still in his power to bestow upon them.

23. Let the Hebrews marry, at the age fit for it, virgins that are free, and born of good parents. And he that does not marry a virgin, let him not corrupt another man's wife, and marry her, nor grieve her former husband. Nor let free men marry slaves, although their affections should strongly bias any of them so to do; for it is decent, and for the dignity of the persons themselves, to govern those their affections. And further, no one ought to marry a harlot, whose matrimonial oblations, arising from the prostitution of her body, God will not receive; for by these means the dispositions of the children will be liberal and virtuous; I mean, when they are not born of base parents, and of the lustful conjunction of such as marry women that are not free. If any one has been espoused to a woman as to a virgin, and does not afterward find her so to be, let him bring his action, and accuse her, and let him make use of such indications[24] to prove his accusation as he is furnished withal; and let the father or the brother of the damsel, or some one that is after them nearest of kin to her, defend her If the damsel obtain a sentence in her favor, that she had not been guilty, let her live with her husband that accused her; and let him not have any further power at all to put her away, unless she give him very great occasions of suspicion, and such as can be no way contradicted.

---

24. These tokens of virginity, as the Hebrew and Septuagint style them, Deuteronomy 22:15, 17, 20, seem to me very different from what our later interpreters suppose. They appear rather to have been such close linen garments as were never put off virgins, after, a certain age, till they were married, but before witnesses, and which, while they were entire, were certain evidences of such virginity. See these, Antiq. B. VII. ch. 8. sect. 1; 2 Samuel 13:18; Isaiah 6:1 Josephus here determines nothing what were these particular tokens of virginity or of corruption: perhaps he thought he could not easily describe them to the heathens, without saying what they might have thought a breach of modesty; which seeming breach of modesty laws cannot always wholly avoid.

Chapter 8

But for him that brings an accusation and calumny against his wife in an impudent and rash manner, let him be punished by receiving forty stripes save one, and let him pay fifty shekels to her father: but if the damsel be convicted, as having been corrupted, and is one of the common people, let her be stoned, because she did not preserve her virginity till she were lawfully married; but if she were the daughter of a priest, let her be burnt alive. If any one has two wives, and if he greatly respect and be kind to one of them, either out of his affection to her, or for her beauty, or for some other reason, while the other is of less esteem with him; and if the son of her that is beloved be the younger by birth than another born of the other wife, but endeavors to obtain the right of primogeniture from his father's kindness to his mother, and would thereby obtain a double portion of his father's substance, for that double portion is what I have allotted him in the laws,—let not this be permitted; for it is unjust that he who is the elder by birth should be deprived of what is due to him, on the father's disposition of his estate, because his mother was not equally regarded by him. He that hath corrupted a damsel espoused to another man, in case he had her consent, let both him and her be put to death, for they are both equally guilty; the man, because he persuaded the woman willingly to submit to a most impure action, and to prefer it to lawful wedlock; the woman, because she was persuaded to yield herself to be corrupted, either for pleasure or for gain. However, if a man light on a woman when she is alone, and forces her, where nobody was present to come to her assistance, let him only be put to death. Let him that hath corrupted a virgin not yet espoused marry her; but if the father of the damsel be not willing that she should be his wife, let him pay fifty shekels as the price of her prostitution. He that desires to be divorced from his wife for any cause[25] whatsoever, (and many such causes happen among men,) let him in writing give assurance that he will never use her as his wife any more; for by this means she may be at liberty to marry another husband, although before this bill of divorce be given, she is not to be permitted so to do: but if she be misused by him also, or if, when he is dead, her first husband would marry

---

25. These words of Josephus are very like those of the Pharisees to our Savior upon this very subject, Matthew 19:3, "Is it lawful for a man to put away his wife for every cause?"

her again, it shall not be lawful for her to return to him. If a woman's husband die, and leave her without children, let his brother marry her, and let him call the son that is born to him by his brother's name, and educate him as the heir of his inheritance, for this procedure will be for the benefit of the public, because thereby families will not fail, and the estate will continue among the kindred; and this will be for the solace of wives under their affliction, that they are to be married to the next relation of their former husbands. But if the brother will not marry her, let the woman come before the senate, and protest openly that this brother will not admit her for his wife, but will injure the memory of his deceased brother, while she is willing to continue in the family, and to hear him children. And when the senate have inquired of him for what reason it is that he is averse to this marriage, whether he gives a bad or a good reason, the matter must come to this issue, That the woman shall loose the sandals of the brother, and shall spit in his face, and say, He deserves this reproachful treatment from her, as having injured the memory of the deceased. And then let him go away out of the senate, and bear this reproach upon him all his life long; and let her marry to whom she pleases, of such as seek her in marriage. But now, if any man take captive, either a virgin, or one that hath been married,[26] and has a mind to marry her, let him not be allowed to bring her to bed to him, or to live with her as his wife, before she hath her head shaven, and hath put on her mourning habit, and lamented her relations and friends that were slain in the battle, that by this means she may give vent to her sorrow for them, and after that may betake herself to feasting and matrimony; for it is good for him that takes a woman, in order to have children by her, to be complaisant to her inclinations, and not merely to pursue his own pleasure, while he hath no regard to what is agreeable to her. But when thirty days are past, as the time of mourning, for so many are sufficient to prudent persons for lamenting the dearest friends, then let them proceed to the marriage; but in case when he hath satisfied his lust, he be too proud to retain her for his wife, let him not have it in his power to make her a slave,

---

26. Here it is supposed that this captive's husband, if she were before a married woman, was dead before, or rather was slain in this very battle, otherwise it would have been adultery in him that married her.

but let her go away whither she pleases, and have that privilege of a free woman.

24. As to those young men that despise their parents, and do not pay them honor, but offer them affronts, either because they are ashamed of them or think themselves wiser than they,—in the first place, let their parents admonish them in words, (for they are by nature of authority sufficient for becoming their judges,) and let them say thus to them:—That they cohabited together, not for the sake of pleasure, nor for the augmentation of their riches, by joining both their stocks together, but that they might have children to take care of them in their old age, and might by them have what they then should want. And say further to him, "That when thou wast born, we took thee up with gladness, and gave God the greatest thanks for thee, and brought time up with great care, and spared for nothing that appeared useful for thy preservation, and for thy instruction in what was most excellent. And now, since it is reasonable to forgive the sins of those that are young, let it suffice thee to have given so many indications Of thy contempt of us; reform thyself, and act more wisely for the time to come; considering that God is displeased with those that are insolent towards their parents, because he is himself the Father of the whole race of mankind, and seems to bear part of that dishonor which falls upon those that have the same name, when they do not meet with dire returns from their children. And on such the law inflicts inexorable punishment; of which punishment mayst thou never have the experience." Now if the insolence of young men be thus cured, let them escape the reproach which their former errors deserved; for by this means the lawgiver will appear to be good, and parents happy, while they never behold either a son or a daughter brought to punishment. But if it happen that these words and instructions, conveyed by them in order to reclaim the man, appear to be useless, then the offender renders the laws implacable enemies to the insolence he has offered his parents; let him therefore be brought forth[27] by these very parents out of the city, with a multitude following him, and there let him be stoned; and when he has continued there for one whole day, that all the people may see him, let him be buried in the night. And thus it is that we bury all whom the

---

27. See Herod the Great insisting on the execution of this law, with relation to two of his own sons, before the judges at Berytus, Antiq. B. XVI. ch. 11. sect. 2.

laws condemn to die, upon any account whatsoever. Let our enemies that fall in battle be also buried; nor let any one dead body lie above the ground, or suffer a punishment beyond what justice requires.

25. Let no one lend to any one of the Hebrews upon usury, neither usury of what is eaten or what is drunken, for it is not just to make advantage of the misfortunes of one of thy own countrymen; but when thou hast been assistant to his necessities, think it thy gain if thou obtainest their gratitude to thee; and withal that reward which will come to thee from God, for thy humanity towards him.

26. Those who have borrowed either silver or any sort of fruits, whether dry or wet, (I mean this, when the Jewish affairs shall, by the blessing of God, be to their own mind,) let the borrowers bring them again, and restore them with pleasure to those who lent them, laying them up, as it were, in their own treasuries, and justly expecting to receive them thence, if they shall want them again. But if they be without shame, and do not restore it, let not the lender go to the borrower's house, and take a pledge himself, before judgment be given concerning it; but let him require the pledge, and let the debtor bring it of himself, without the least opposition to him that comes upon him under the protection of the law. And if he that gave the pledge be rich, let the creditor retain it till what he lent be paid him again; but if he be poor, let him that takes it return it before the going down of the sun, especially if the pledge be a garment, that the debtor may have it for a covering in his sleep, God himself naturally showing mercy to the poor. It is also not lawful to take a millstone, nor any utensil thereto belonging, for a pledge, that the debtor, may not be deprived of instruments to get their food withal, and lest they be undone by their necessity.

27. Let death be the punishment for stealing a man; but he that hath purloined gold or silver, let him pay double. If any one kill a man that is stealing something out of his house, let him be esteemed guiltless, although the man were only breaking in at the wall. Let him that hath stolen cattle pay fourfold what is lost, excepting the case of an ox, for which let the thief pay fivefold. Let him that is so poor that he cannot pay what mulet is laid upon him, be his servant to whom he was adjudged to pay it.

28. If any one be sold to one of his own nation, let him serve him six years, and on the seventh let him go free. But if he have a son

by a woman servant in his purchaser's house, and if, on account of his good-will to his master, and his natural affection to his wife and children, he will be his servant still, let him be set free only at the coming of the year of jubilee, which is the fiftieth year, and let him then take away with him his children and wife, and let them be free also.

29. If any one find gold or silver on the road, let him inquire after him that lost it, and make proclamation of the place where he found it, and then restore it to him again, as not thinking it right to make his own profit by the loss of another. And the same rule is to be observed in cattle found to have wandered away into a lonely place. If the owner be not presently discovered, let him that is the finder keep it with himself, and appeal to God that he has not purloined what belongs to another.

30. It is not lawful to pass by any beast that is in distress, when in a storm it is fallen down in the mire, but to endeavor to preserve it, as having a sympathy with it in its pain.

31. It is also a duty to show the roads to those who do not know them, and not to esteem it a matter for sport, when we hinder others' advantages, by setting them in a wrong way.

32. In like manner, let no one revile a person blind or dumb.

33. If men strive together, and there be no instrument of iron, let him that is smitten be avenged immediately, by inflicting the same punishment on him that smote him: but if when he is carried home he lie sick many days, and then die, let him that smote him not escape punishment; but if he that is smitten escape death, and yet be at great expense for his cure, the smiter shall pay for all that has been expended during the time of his sickness, and for all that he has paid the physician. He that kicks a woman with child, so that the woman miscarry,[28] let him pay a fine in money, as the judges shall determine,

---

28. Philo and others appear to have understood this law, Exodus 21:22, 23, better than Josephus, who seems to allow, that though the infant in the mother's womb, even after the mother were quick, and so the infant had a rational soul, were killed by the stroke upon the mother, yet if the mother escaped, the offender should only be fined, and not put to death; while the law seems rather to mean, that if the infant in that case be killed, though the mother escape, the offender must be put to death, and not only when the mother is killed, as Josehus understood it. It seems this was the exposition of the Pharisees in the days of Josephus.

as having diminished the multitude by the destruction of what was in her womb; and let money also be given the woman's husband by him that kicked her; but if she die of the stroke, let him also be put to death, the law judging it equitable that life should go for life.

34. Let no one of the Israelites keep any poison[29] that may cause death, or any other harm; but if he be caught with it, let him be put to death, and suffer the very same mischief that he would have brought upon them for whom the poison was prepared.

35. He that maimeth any one, let him undergo the like himself, and be deprived of the same member of which he hath deprived the other, unless he that is maimed will accept of money instead of it[30] for the law makes the sufferer the judge of the value of what he hath suffered, and permits him to estimate it, unless he will be more severe.

36. Let him that is the owner of an ox which pusheth with his horn, kill him: but if he pushes and gores any one in the thrashing-floor, let him be put to death by stoning, and let him not be thought fit for food: but if his owner be convicted as having known what his nature was, and hath not kept him up, let him also be put to death, as being the occasion of the ox's having killed a man. But if the ox have killed a man-servant, or a maid-servant, let him be stoned; and let the owner of the ox pay thirty shekels[31] to the master of him that was slain; but if it be an ox that is thus smitten and killed, let both the oxen, that which smote the other and that which was killed, be sold, and let the owners of them divide their price between them.

37. Let those that dig a well or a pit be careful to lay planks over them, and so keep them shut up, not in order to hinder any persons from drawing water, but that there may be no danger of falling into them. But if any one's beast fall into such a well or pit thus digged, and not shut up, and perish, let the owner pay its price to the owner of the beast. Let there be a battlement round the tops of your houses

---

29. What we render a witch, according to our modern notions of witchcraft, Exodus 22:15, Philo and Josephus understood of a poisoner, or one who attempted by secret and unlawful drugs or philtra, to take away the senses or the lives of men.

30. This permission of redeeming this penalty with money is not in our copies, Exodus 21:24, 25; Leviticus 24:20; Deuteronomy 19:21.

31. We may here note, that thirty shekels, the price our Savior was sold for by Judas to the Jews, Matthew 26:15, and 27;3, was the old value of a bought servant or slave among that people.

instead of a wall, that may prevent any persons from rolling down and perishing.

38. Let him that has received any thing in trust for another, take care to keep it as a sacred and divine thing; and let no one invent any contrivance whereby to deprive him that hath intrusted it with him of the same, and this whether he be a man or a woman; no, not although he or she were to gain an immense sum of gold, and this where he cannot be convicted of it by any body; for it is fit that a man's own conscience, which knows what he hath, should in all cases oblige him to do well. Let this conscience be his witness, and make him always act so as may procure him commendation from others; but let him chiefly have regard to God, from whom no wicked man can lie concealed: but if he in whom the trust was reposed, without any deceit of his own, lose what he was intrusted withal, let him come before the seven judges, and swear by God that nothing hath been lost willingly, or with a wicked intention, and that he hath not made use of any part thereof, and so let him depart without blame; but if he hath made use of the least part of what was committed to him, and it be lost, let him be condemned to repay all that he had received. After the same manner as in these trusts it is to be, if any one defraud those that undergo bodily labor for him. And let it be always remembered, that we are not to defraud a poor man of his wages, as being sensible that God has allotted these wages to him instead of land and other possessions; nay, this payment is not at all to be delayed, but to be made that very day, since God is not willing to deprive the laborer of the immediate use of what he hath labored for.

39. You are not to punish children for the faults of their parents, but on account of their own virtue rather to vouchsafe them commiseration, because they were born of wicked parents, than hatred, because they were born of bad ones. Nor indeed ought we to impute the sin of children to their fathers, while young persons indulge themselves in many practices different from what they have been instructed in, and this by their proud refusal of such instruction.

40. Let those that have made themselves eunuchs be had in detestation; and do you avoid any conversation with them who have deprived themselves of their manhood, and of that fruit of generation which God has given to men for the increase of their kind: let such be driven away, as if they had killed their children, since they beforehand

have lost what should procure them; for evident it is, that while their soul is become effeminate, they have withal transfused that effeminacy to their body also. In like manner do you treat all that is of a monstrous nature when it is looked on; nor is it lawful to geld men or any other animals.[32]

41. Let this be the constitution of your political laws in time of peace, and God will be so merciful as to preserve this excellent settlement free from disturbance: and may that time never come which may innovate any thing, and change it for the contrary. But since it must needs happen that mankind fall into troubles and dangers, either undesignedly or intentionally, come let us make a few constitutions concerning them, that so being apprised beforehand what ought to be done, you may have salutary counsels ready when you want them, and may not then be obliged to go to seek what is to be done, and so be unprovided, and fall into dangerous circumstances. May you be a laborious people, and exercise your souls in virtuous actions, and thereby possess and inherit the land without wars; while neither any foreigners make war upon it, and so afflict you, nor any internal sedition seize upon it, whereby you may do things that are contrary to your fathers, and so lose the laws which they have established. And may you continue in the observation of those laws which God hath approved of, and hath delivered to you. Let all sort of warlike operations, whether they befall you now in your own time, or hereafter in the times of your posterity, be done out of your own borders: but when you are about to go to war, send embassages and heralds to those who are your voluntary enemies, for it is a right thing to make use of words to them before you come to your weapons of war; and assure them thereby, that although you have a numerous army, with horses and weapons, and, above these, a God merciful to you, and ready to assist you, you do however desire them not to compel you to fight against them, nor to take from them what they have, which will indeed be our gain, but what they will have no reason to wish we should take to ourselves. And if they

---

32. This law against castration, even of brutes, is said to be so rigorous elsewhere, as to inflict death on him that does it. which seems only a Pharisaical interpretation in the days of Josephus of that law, Leviticus 21:20, and 22:24: only we may hence observe, that the Jews could then have no oxen which are gelded, but only bulls and cows, in Judea.

hearken to you, it will be proper for you to keep peace with them; but if they trust in their own strength, as superior to yours, and will not do you justice, lead your army against them, making use of God as your supreme Commander, but ordaining for a lieutenant under him one that is of the greatest courage among you; for these different commanders, besides their being an obstacle to actions that are to be done on the sudden, are a disadvantage to those that make use of them. Lead an army pure, and of chosen men, composed of all such as have extraordinary strength of body and hardiness of soul; but do you send away the timorous part, lest they run away in the time of action, and so afford an advantage to your enemies. Do you also give leave to those that have lately built them houses, and have not yet lived in them a year's time; and to those that have planted them vineyards, and have not yet been partakers of their fruits,—to continue in their own country; as well as those also who have betrothed, or lately married them wives, lest they have such an affection for these things that they he too sparing of their lives, and, by reserving themselves for these enjoyments, they become voluntary cowards, on account of their wives.

42. When you have pitched your camp, take care that you do nothing that is cruel. And when you are engaged in a siege; and want timber for the making of warlike engines, do not you render the land naked by cutting down trees that bear fruit, but spare them, as considering that they were made for the benefit of men; and that if they could speak, they would have a just plea against you, because, though they are not occasions of the war, they are unjustly treated, and suffer in it, and would, if they were able, remove themselves into another land. When you have beaten your enemies in battle, slay those that have fought against you; but preserve the others alive, that they may pay you tribute, excepting the nation of the Canaanites; for as to that people, you must entirely destroy them.

43, Take care, especially in your battles, that no woman use the habit of a man, nor man the garment of a woman.

44. This was the form of political government which was left us by Moses. Moreover, he had already delivered laws in writing[33] in the fortieth year [after they came out of Egypt], concerning which

---

33. These laws seem to be those above-mentioned, sect, 4, of this chapter.

we will discourse in another book. But now on the following days
(for he called them to assemble continually) he delivered blessings
to them, and curses upon those that should not live according to
the laws, but should transgress the duties that were determined for
them to observe. After this, he read to them a poetic song, which
was composed in hexameter verse, and left it to them in the holy
book: it contained a prediction of what was to come to pass afterward;
agreeably whereto all things have happened all along, and do still
happen to us; and wherein he has not at all deviated from the truth.
Accordingly, he delivered these books to the priest,[34] with the ark;
into which he also put the ten commandments, written on two tables.
He delivered to them the tabernacle also, and exhorted the people,
that when they had conquered the land, and were settled in it, they
should not forget the injuries of the Amalekites, but make war against
them, and inflict punishment upon them for what mischief they did
them when they were in the wilderness; and that when they had
got possession of the land of the Canaanites, and when they had
destroyed the whole multitude of its inhabitants, as they ought to
do, they should erect an altar that should face the rising sun, not
far from the city of Shechem, between the two mountains, that of
Gerizzim, situate on the right hand, and that called Ebal, on the left;
and that the army should be so divided, that six tribes should stand
upon each of the two mountains, and with them the Levites and the
priests. And that first, those that were upon Mount Gerizzim should
pray for the best blessings upon those who were diligent about the
worship of God, and the observation of his laws, and who did not
reject what Moses had said to them; while the other wished them all
manner of happiness also; and when these last put up the like prayers,
the former praised them. After this, curses were denounced upon
those that should transgress those laws, they, answering one another
alternately, by way of confirmation of what had been said. Moses also
wrote their blessings and their curses, that they might learn them so
thoroughly, that they might never be forgotten by length of time. And
when he was ready to die, he wrote these blessings and curses upon
the altar, on each side of it; where he says also the people stood, and

---

34. What laws were now delivered to the priests, see the note on Antiq. B. III. ch. 1.
sect. 7,

then sacrificed and offered burnt-offerings, though after that day they never offered upon it any other sacrifice, for it was not lawful so to do. These are the constitutions of Moses; and the Hebrew nation still live according to them.

45. On the next day, Moses called the people together, with the women and children, to a congregation, so as the very slaves were present also, that they might engage themselves to the observation of these laws by oath; and that, duly considering the meaning of God in them, they might not, either for favor of their kindred, or out of fear of any one, or indeed for any motive whatsoever, think any thing ought to be preferred to these laws, and so might transgress them. That in case any one of their own blood, or any city, should attempt to confound or dissolve their constitution of government, they should take vengeance upon them, both all in general, and each person in particular; and when they had conquered them, should overturn their city to the very foundations, and, if possible, should not leave the least footsteps of such madness: but that if they were not able to take such vengeance, they should still demonstrate that what was done was contrary to their wills. So the multitude bound themselves by oath so to do.

46. Moses taught them also by what means their sacrifices might be the most acceptable to God; and how they should go forth to war, making use of the stones (in the high priest's breastplate) for their direction,[35] as I have before signified. Joshua also prophesied while Moses was present. And when Moses had recapitulated whatsoever he had done for the preservation of the people, both in their wars and in peace, and had composed them a body of laws, and procured them an excellent form of government, he foretold, as God had declared to

---

35. Of the exact place where this altar was to be built, whether nearer Mount Gerizzim or Mount Ebal, according to Josephus, see Essay on the Old Testament, p. 168—171.

Dr. Bernard well observes here, how unfortunate this neglect of consulting the Urim was to Joshua himself, in the case of the Gibeonites, who put a trick upon him, and ensnared him, together with the rest of the Jewish rulers, with a solemn oath to preserve them, contrary to his commission to extirpate all the Canaanites, root and branch; which oath he and the other rulers never durst break. See Scripture Politics, p. 55, 56; and this snare they were brought into because they "did not ask counsel at the mouth of the Lord," Joshua 9:14.

him "That if they transgressed that institution for the worship of God, they should experience the following miseries:—Their land should be full of weapons of war from their enemies, and their cities should be overthrown, and their temple should be burnt that they should be sold for slaves, to such men as would have no pity on them in their afflictions; that they would then repent, when that repentance would no way profit them under their sufferings. "Yet," said he, "will that God who founded your nation, restore your cities to your citizens, with their temple also; and you shall lose these advantages not once only, but often."

47. NOW when Moses had encouraged Joshua to lead out the army against the Canaanites, by telling him that God would assist him in all his undertakings, and had blessed the whole multitude, he said, "Since I am going to my forefathers, and God has determined that this should be the day of my departure to them, I return him thanks while I am still alive and present with you, for that providence he hath exercised over you, which hath not only delivered us from the miseries we lay under, but hath bestowed a state of prosperity upon us; as also, that he hath assisted me in the pains I took, and in all the contrivances I had in my care about you, in order to better your condition, and hath on all occasions showed himself favorable to us; or rather he it was who first conducted our affairs, and brought them to a happy conclusion, by making use of me as a vicarious general under him, and as a minister in those matters wherein he was willing to do you good: on which account I think it proper to bless that Divine Power which will take care of you for the time to come, and this in order to repay that debt which I owe him, and to leave behind me a memorial that we are obliged to worship and honor him, and to keep those laws which are the most excellent gift of all those he hath already bestowed upon us, or which, if he continue favorable to us, he will bestow upon us hereafter. Certainly a human legislator is a terrible enemy when his laws are affronted, and are made to no purpose. And may you never experience that displeasure of God which will be the consequence of the neglect of these his laws, which he, who is your Creator, hath given you."

48. When Moses had spoken thus at the end of his life, and had foretold what would befall to every one of their tribes[36] afterward, with the addition of a blessing to them, the multitude fell into tears, insomuch that even the women, by beating their breasts, made manifest the deep concern they had when he was about to die. The children also lamented still more, as not able to contain their grief; and thereby declared, that even at their age they were sensible of his virtue and mighty deeds; and truly there seemed to be a strife betwixt the young and the old who should most grieve for him. The old grieved because they knew what a careful protector they were to be deprived of, and so lamented their future state; but the young grieved, not only for that, but also because it so happened that they were to be left by him before they had well tasted of his virtue. Now one may make a guess at the excess of this sorrow and lamentation of the multitude, from what happened to the legislator himself; for although he was always persuaded that he ought not to be cast down at the approach of death, since the undergoing it was agreeable to the will of God and the law of nature, yet what the people did so overbore him, that he wept himself. Now as he went thence to the place where he was to vanish out of their sight, they all followed after him weeping; but Moses beckoned with his hand to those that were remote from him, and bade them stay behind in quiet, while he exhorted those that were near to him that they would not render his departure so lamentable. Whereupon they thought they ought to grant him that favor, to let him depart according as he himself desired; so they restrained themselves, though weeping still towards one another. All those who accompanied him were the senate, and Eleazar the high priest, and Joshua their commander. Now as soon as they were come to the mountain called *Abarim,* (which is a very high mountain, situate over against Jericho, and one that affords, to such as are upon it, a prospect of the greatest part of the excellent land of Canaan,) he dismissed the senate; and as he was going to embrace Eleazar and Joshua, and was still discoursing with them, a cloud stood over him on the sudden, and he disappeared in a certain

---

36. Since Josephus assures us here, as is most naturally to be supposed, and as the Septuagint gives the text, Deuteronomy 33:6, that Moses blessed every one of the tribes of Israel, it is evident that Simeon was not omitted in his copy, as it unhappily now is, both in our Hebrew and Samaritan copies.

valley, although he wrote in the holy books that he died, which was done out of fear, lest they should venture to say that, because of his extraordinary virtue, he went to God.

49. Now Moses lived in all one hundred and twenty years; a third part of which time, abating one month, he was the people's ruler; and he died on the last month of the year, which is called by the Macedonians *Dystrus,* but by us *Adar,* on the first day of the month. He was one that exceeded all men that ever were in understanding, and made the best use of what that understanding suggested to him. He had a very graceful way of speaking and addressing himself to the multitude; and as to his other qualifications, he had such a full command of his passions, as if he hardly had any such in his soul, and only knew them by their names, as rather perceiving them in other men than in himself. He was also such a general of an army as is seldom seen, as well as such a prophet as was never known, and this to such a degree, that whatsoever he pronounced, you would think you heard the voice of God himself. So the people mourned for him thirty days: nor did ever any grief so deeply affect the Hebrews as did this upon the death of Moses: nor were those that had experienced his conduct the only persons that desired him, but those also that perused the laws he left behind him had a strong desire after him, and by them gathered the extraordinary virtue he was master of. And this shall suffice for the declaration of the manner of the death of Moses.

Book 5

Containing the Interval of Four Hundred and Seventy-Six Years, from the Death of Moses to the Death of Eli

1 *How Joshua, the Commander of the Hebrews, Made War with the Canaanites, and Overcame Them, and Destroyed Them, and Divided Their Land by Lot to the Tribes of Israel*

1. WHEN Moses was taken away from among men, in the manner already described, and when all the solemnities belonging to the mourning for him were finished, and the sorrow for him was over, Joshua commanded the multitude to get themselves ready for an expedition. He also sent spies to Jericho to discover what forces they had, and what were their intentions; but he put his camp in order, as intending soon to pass over Jordan at a proper season. And calling to him the rulers of the tribe of Reuben, and the governors of the tribe of Gad, and [the half tribe of] Manasseh, for half of this tribe had been permitted to have their habitation in the country of the Amorites, which was the seventh part of the land of Canaan,[1] he put them in mind what they had promised Moses; and he exhorted them that, for

---

1. The Amorites were one of the seven nations of Canaan. Hence Reland is willing to suppose that Josephus did not here mean that their land beyond Jordan was a seventh part of the whole land of Canaan, but meant the Arnorites as a seventh nation. His reason is, that Josephus, as well as our Bible, generally distinguish the land beyond Jordan from the land of Canaan; nor can it be denied, that in strictness they were all fercot: yet after two tribes and a half of the twelve tribes came to inherit it, it might in a general way altogether be well included under the land of Canaan,

223

the sake of the care that Moses had taken of them who had never been weary of taking pains for them no, not when he was dying, and for the sake of the public welfare, they would prepare themselves, and readily perform what they had promised; so he took fifty thousand of them who followed him, and he marched from Abila to Jordan, sixty furlongs.

2. Now when he had pitched his camp, the spies came to him immediately, well acquainted with the whole state of the Canaanites; for at first, before they were at all discovered, they took a full view of the city of Jericho without disturbance, and saw which parts of the walls were strong, and which parts were otherwise, and indeed insecure, and which of the gates were so weak as might afford an entrance to their army. Now those that met them took no notice of them when they saw them, and supposed they were only strangers, who used to be very curious in observing everything in the city, and did not take them for enemies; but at even they retired to a certain inn that was near to the wall, whither they went to eat their supper; which supper when they had done, and were considering how to get away, information was given to the king as he was at supper, that there were some persons come from the Hebrews' camp to view the city as spies, and that they were in the inn kept by Rahab, and were very solicitous that they might not be discovered. So he sent immediately some to them, and commanded to catch them, and bring them to him, that he might examine them by torture, and learn what their business was there. As soon as Rahab understood that these messengers were coming, she hid the spies under stalks of flax, which were laid to dry on the top of her house; and said to the messengers that were sent by the king, that certain unknown strangers had supped with her a little before sun-setting, and were gone away, who might easily be taken, if they were any terror to the city, or likely to bring any danger to

---

or Palestine, or Judea, of which we have a clear example here before us in Josephus, whose words evidently imply, that taking the whole land of Canaan, or that inhabited by all the twelve tribes together, and parting it into seven parts, the part beyond Jordan was in quantity of ground one seventh part of the whole. And this well enough agrees to Reland's own map of that country, although this land beyond Jordan was so peculiarly fruitful, and good for pasturage, as the two tribes and a half took notice, Numbers 32:1, 4, 16, that it maintained about a fifth part of the whole people.

the king. So these messengers being thus deluded by the woman,[2] and suspecting no impositiq, went their ways, without so much as searching the inn; but they immediately pursued them along those roads which they most probably supposed them to have gone, and those particularly which led to the river, but could hear no tidings of them; so they left off the pains of any further pursuit. But when the tumult was over, Rahab brought the men down, and desired them as soon as they should have obtained possession of the land of Canaan, when it would be in their power to make her amends for her preservation of them, to remember what danger she had undergone for their sakes; for that if she had been caught concealing them, she could not have escaped a terrible destruction, she and all her family with her, and so bid them go home; and desired them to swear to her to preserve her and her family when they should take the city, and destroy all its inhabitants, as they had decreed to do; for so far she said she had been assured by those Divine miracles of which she had been informed. So these spies acknowledged that they owed her thanks for what she had done already, and withal swore to requite her kindness, not only in words, but in deeds. But they gave her this advice, That when she should perceive that the city was about to be taken, she should put her goods, and all her family, by way of security, in her inn, and to hang out scarlet threads before her doors, [or windows,] that the commander of the Hebrews might know her house, and take

---

2. It plainly appears by the history of these spies, and the innkeeper Rahab's deception of the king of Jericho's messengers, by telling them what was false in order to save the lives of the spies, and yet the great commendation of her faith and good works in the New Testament, Hebrews 11:31; James 2:25, as well as by many other parallel examples, both in the Old Testament and in Josephus, that the best men did not then scruple to deceive those public enemies who might justly be destroyed; as also might deceive ill men in order to save life, and deliver themselves from the tyranny of their unjust oppressors, and this by telling direct falsehoods; I mean, all this where no oath was demanded of them, otherwise they never durst venture on such a procedure. Nor was Josephus himself of any other opinion or practice, as I shall remark in the note on Antiq. B. IX. ch. 4. sect. 3. And observe, that I still call this woman Rahab, an innkeeper, not a harlot, the whole history, both in our copies, and especially in Josephus, implying no more. It was indeed so frequent a thing, that women who were innkeepers were also harlots, or maintainers of harlots, that the word commonly used for real harlots was usually given them. See Dr. Bernard's note here, and Judges 11:1, and Antiq. B. V. ch. 7. sect. 8.

care to do her no harm; for, said they, we will inform him of this matter, because of the concern thou hast had to preserve us: but if any one of thy family fall in the battle, do not thou blame us; and we beseech that God, by whom we have sworn, not then to be displeased with us, as though we had broken our oaths. So these men, when they had made this agreement, went away, letting themselves down by a rope from the wall, and escaped, and came and told their own people whatsoever they had done in their journey to this city. Joshua also told Eleazar the high priest, and the senate, what the spies had sworn to Rahab, who continued what had been sworn.

3. Now while Joshua, the commander, was in fear about their passing over Jordan, for the river ran with a strong current, and could not be passed over with bridges, for there never had been bridges laid over it hitherto; and while he suspected, that if he should attempt to make a bridge, that their enemies would not afford him thee to perfect it, and for ferry-boats they had none,—God promised so to dispose of the river, that they might pass over it, and that by taking away the main part of its waters. So Joshua, after two days, caused the army and the whole multitude to pass over in the manner following:—The priests went first of all, having the ark with them; then went the Levites bearing the tabernacle and the vessels which belonged to the sacrifices; after which the entire multitude followed, according to their tribes, having their children and their wives in the midst of them, as being afraid for them, lest they should be borne away by the stream. But as soon as the priests had entered the river first, it appeared fordable, the depth of the water being restrained and the sand appearing at the bottom, because the current was neither so strong nor so swift as to carry it away by its force; so they all passed over the river without fear, finding it to be in the very same state as God had foretold he would put it in; but the priests stood still in the midst of the river till the multitude should be passed over, and should get to the shore in safety; and when all were gone over, the priests came out also, and permitted the current to run freely as it used to do before. Accordingly the river, as soon as the Hebrews were come out of it, arose again presently, and carne to its own proper magnitude as before.

4. So the Hebrews went on farther fifty furlongs, and pitched their camp at the distance of ten furlongs from Jericho; but Joshua built an altar of those stones which all the heads of the tribes, at the command

of the prophets, had taken out of the deep, to be afterwards a memorial of the division of the stream of this river, and upon it offered sacrifice to God; and in that place celebrated the passover, and had great plenty of all the things which they wanted hitherto; for they reaped the corn of the Canaanites, which was now ripe, and took other things as prey; for then it was that their former food, which was manna, and of which they had eaten forty years, failed them.

5. Now while the Israelites did this, and the Canaanites did not attack them, but kept themselves quiet within their own walls, Joshua resolved to besiege them; so on the first day of the feast [of the passover], the priests carried the ark round about, with some part of the armed men to be a guard to it. These priests went forward, blowing with their seven trumpets; and exhorted the army to be of good courage, and went round about the city, with the senate following them; and when the priests had only blown with the trumpets, for they did nothing more at all, they returned to the camp. And when they had done this for six days, on the seventh Joshua gathered the armed men and all the people together, and told them these good tidings, That the city should now be taken, since God would on that day give it them, by the falling down of the walls, and this of their own accord, and without their labor. However, he charged them to kill every one they should take, and not to abstain from the slaughter of their enemies, either for weariness or for pity, and not to fall on the spoil, and be thereby diverted from pursuing their enemies as they ran away; but to destroy all the animals, and to take nothing for their own peculiar advantage. He commanded them also to bring together all the silver and gold, that it might be set apart as first-fruits unto God out of this glorious exploit, as having gotten them from the city they first took; only that they should save Rahab and her kindred alive, because of the oath which the spies had sworn to her.

6. When he had said this, and had set his army in order, be brought it against the city: so they went round the city again, the ark going before them, and the priests encouraging the people to be zealous in the work; and when they had gone round it seven times, and had stood still a little, the wall fell down, while no instruments of war, nor any other force, was applied to it by the Hebrews.

7. So they entered into Jericho, and slew all the men that were therein, while they were aftrighted at the surprising overthrow of the

walls, and their courage was become useless, and they were not able to defend themselves; so they were slain, and their throats cut, some in the ways, and others as caught in their houses; nothing afforded them assistance, but they all perished, even to the women and the children; and the city was filled with dead bodies, and not one person escaped. They also burnt the whole city, and the country about it; but they saved alive Rahab, with her family, who had fled to her inn. And when she was brought to him, Joshua owned to her that they owed her thanks for her preservation of the spies: so he said he would not appear to be behind her in his benefaction to her; whereupon he gave her certain lands immediately, and had her in great esteem ever afterwards.

8. And if any part of the city escaped the fire, he overthrew it from the foundation; and he denounced a curse[3] against its inhabitants, if any should desire to rebuild it; how, upon his laying the foundation of the walls, he should be deprived of his eldest son; and upon finishing it, he should lose his youngest son. But what happened hereupon we shall speak of hereafter.

9. Now there was an immense quantity of silver and gold, and besides those of brass also, that was heaped together out of the city when it was taken, no one transgressing the decree, nor purloining for their own peculiar advantage; which spoils Joshua delivered to the priests, to be laid up among their treasures. And thus did Jericho perish.

10. But there was one Achar,[4] the son [of Charmi, the son] of Zebedias, of the tribe of Judah, who finding a royal garment woven

---

3. Upon occasion of this devoting of Jericho to destruction, and the exemplary punishment of Achar, who broke that duerein or anathema, and of the punishment of the future breaker of it, Hiel, 1 Kings 16:34, as also of the punishment of Saul, for breaking the like chefera or anathema, against the Amalekites, 1 Samuel 15., we may observe what was the true meaning of that law, Leviticus 27:28: "None devoted which shall be devoted of shall be redeemed; but shall be put to death;" i.e. whenever any of the Jews' public enemies had been, for their wickedness, solemnly devoted to destruction, according to the Divine command, as were generally the seven wicked nations of Canaan, and those sinners the Amalekites, 1 Samuel 15:18, it was utterly unlawful to permit those enemies to be redeemed; but they were to be all utterly destroyed. See also Numbers 23:2, 3.

4. That the name of this chief was not Achan, as in the common copies, but Achar, as here in Josephus, and in the Apostolical Constit. B. VII. ch. 2., and elsewhere, is evident by the allusion to that name in the curse of Joshua, "Why hast thou troubled us?—the Lord shall trouble thee;" where the Hebrew word alludes only to the name

entirely of gold, and a piece of gold that weighed two hundred shekels;[5] and thinking it a very hard case, that what spoils he, by running some hazard, had found, he must give away, and offer it to God, who stood in no need of it, while he that wanted it must go without it,—made a deep ditch in his own tent, and laid them up therein, as supposing he should not only be concealed from his fellow soldiers, but from God himself also.

11. Now the place where Joshua pitched his camp was called Gilgal, which denotes *liberty*;[6] for since now they had passed over Jordan, they looked on themselves as freed from the miseries which they had undergone from the Egyptians, and in the wilderness.

12. Now, a few days after the calamity that befell Jericho, Joshua sent three thousand armed men to take Ai, a city situate above Jericho; but, upon the sight of the people of Ai, with them they were driven back, and lost thirty-six of their men. When this was told the Israelites, it made them very sad, and exceeding disconsolate, not so much because of the relation the men that were destroyed bare to them, though those that were destroyed were all good men, and deserved their esteem, as by the despair it occasioned; for while they believed that they were already, in effect, in possession of the land, and should bring back the army out of the battles without loss, as God had promised beforehand, they now saw unexpectedly their enemies bold with success; so they put sackcloth over their garments, and continued in tears and lamentation all the day, without the least inquiry after food, but laid what had happened greatly to heart.

13. When Joshua saw the army so much afflicted, and possessed with forebodings of evil as to their whole expedition, he used freedom with God, and said, "We are not come thus far out of any rashness of our own, as though we thought ourselves able to subdue this land

---

Achar, but not to Achan. Accordingly, this Valley of Achar, or Achor, was and is a known place, a little north of Gilgal, so called from the days of Joshua till this day. See Joshua 7:26; Isaiah 65:10; Hosea 2:15; and Dr. Bernard's notes here.

5. Here Dr. Bernard very justly observes, that a few words are dropped out of Josephus's copies, on account of the repetition of the word shekels, and that it ought to be read thus:—"A piece of gold that weighed fifty shekels, and one of silver that weighed two hundred shekels," as in our other copies, Joshua 7:21.

6. I agree here with Dr. Bernard, and approve of Josephus's interpretation of Gilgal for liberty. See Joshua 5:9.

with our own weapons, but at the instigation of Moses thy servant for this purpose, because thou hast promised us, by many signs, that thou wouldst give us this land for a possession, and that thou wouldst make our army always superior in war to our enemies, and accordingly some success has already attended upon us agreeably to thy promises; but because we have now unexpectedly been foiled, and have lost some men out of our army, we are grieved at it, as fearing what thou hast promised us, and what Moses foretold us, cannot be depended on by us; and our future expectation troubles us the more, because we have met with such a disaster in this our first attempt. But do thou, O Lord, free us from these suspicions, for thou art able to find a cure for these disorders, by giving us victory, which will both take away the grief we are in at present, and prevent our distrust as to what is to come."

14. These intercessions Joshua put up to God, as he lay prostrate on his face: whereupon God answered him, That he should rise up, and purify his host from the pollution that had got into it; that "things consecrated to me have been impudently stolen from me," and that "this has been the occasion why this defeat had happened to them;" and that when they should search out and punish the offender, he would ever take care they should have the victory over their enemies. This Joshua told the people; and calling for Eleazar the high priest, and the men in authority, he cast lots, tribe by tribe; and when the lot showed that this wicked action was done by one of the tribe of Judah, he then again proposed the lot to the several families thereto belonging; so the truth of this wicked action was found to belong to the family of Zachar; and when the inquiry was made man by man, they took Achar, who, upon God's reducing him to a terrible extremity, could not deny the fact: so he confessed the theft, and produced what he had taken in the midst of them, whereupon he was immediately put to death; and attained no more than to be buried in the night in a disgraceful manner, and such as was suitable to a condemned malefactor.

15. When Joshua had thus purified the host, he led them against Ai: and having by night laid an ambush round about the city, he attacked the enemies as soon as it was day; but as they advanced boldly against the Israelites, because of their former victory, he made them believe he retired, and by that means drew them a great way from the city, they

still supposing that they were pursuing their enemies, and despised them, as though the case had been the same with that in the former battle; after which Joshua ordered his forces to turn about, and placed them against their front. He then made the signals agreed upon to those that lay in ambush, and so excited them to fight; so they ran suddenly into the city, the inhabitants being upon the walls, nay, others of them being in perplexity, and coming to see those that were without the gates. Accordingly, these men took the city, and slew all that they met with; but Joshua forced those that came against him to come to a close fight, and discomfited them, and made them run away; and when they were driven towards the city, and thought it had not been touched, as soon as they saw it was taken, and perceived it was burnt, with their wives and children, they wandered about in the fields in a scattered condition, and were no way able to defend themselves, because they had none to support them. Now when this calamity was come upon the men of Ai, there were a great number of children, and women, and servants, and an immense quantity of other furniture. The Hebrews also took herds of cattle, and a great deal of money, for this was a rich country. So when Joshua came to Gilgal, he divided all these spoils among the soldiers.

16. But the Gibeonites, who inhabited very near to Jerusalem, when they saw what miseries had happened to the inhabitants of Jericho; and to those of Ai, and suspected that the like sore calamity would come as far as themselves, they did not think fit to ask for mercy of Joshua; for they supposed they should find little mercy from him, who made war that he might entirely destroy the nation of the Canaanites; but they invited the people of Cephirah and Kiriathjearim, who were their neighbors, to join in league with them; and told them that neither could they themselves avoid the danger they were all in, if the Israelites should prevent them, and seize upon them: so when they had persuaded them, they resolved to endeavor to escape the forces of the Israelites. Accordingly, upon their agreement to what they proposed, they sent ambassadors to Joshua to make a league of friendship with him, and those such of the citizens as were best approved of, and most capable of doing what was most advantageous to the multitude. Now these ambassadors thought it dangerous to confess themselves to be Canaanites, but thought they might by this contrivance avoid the danger, namely, by saying that they bare no

relation to the Canaanites at all, but dwelt at a very great distance from them: and they said further, that they came a long way, on account of the reputation he had gained for his virtue; and as a mark of the truth of what they said, they showed him the habit they were in, for that their clothes were new when they came out, but were greatly worn by the length of thee they had been on their journey; for indeed they took torn garments, on purpose that they might make him believe so. So they stood in the midst of the people, and said that they were sent by the people of Gibeon, and of the circumjacent cities, which were very remote from the land where they now were, to make such a league of friendship with them, and this on such conditions as were customary among their forefathers; for when they understood that, by the favor of God, and his gift to them, they were to have the possession of the land of Canaan bestowed upon them, they said that they were very glad to hear it, and desired to be admitted into the number of their citizens. Thus did these ambassadors speak; and showing them the marks of their long journey, they entreated the Hebrews to make a league of friendship with them. Accordingly Joshua, believing what they said, that they were not of the nation of the Canaanites, entered into friendship with them; and Eleazar the high priest, with the senate, sware to them that they would esteem them their friends and associates, and would attempt nothing that should be unfair against them, the multitude also assenting to the oaths that were made to them. So these men, having obtained what they desired, by deceiving the Israelites, went home: but when Joshua led his army to the country at the bottom of the mountains of this part of Canaan, he understood that the Gibeonites dwelt not far from Jerusalem, and that they were of the stock of the Canaanites; so he sent for their governors, and reproached them with the cheat they had put upon him; but they alleged, on their own behalf, that they had no other way to save themselves but that, and were therefore forced to have recourse to it. So he called for Eleazar the high priest, and for the senate, who thought it right to make them public servants, that they might not break the oath they had made to them; and they ordained them to be so. And this was the method by which these men found. safety and security under the calamity that was ready to overtake them.

17. But the king of Jerusalem took it to heart that the Gibeonites had gone over to Joshua; so he called upon the kings of the neighboring

nations to join together, and make war against them. Now when the Gibeonites saw these kings, which were four, besides the king of Jerusalem, and perceived that they had pitched their camp at a certain fountain not far from their city, and were getting ready for the siege of it, they called upon Joshua to assist them; for such was their case, as to expect to be destroyed by these Canaanites, but to suppose they should be saved by those that came for the destruction of the Canaanites, because of the league of friendship that was between them. Accordingly, Joshua made haste with his whole army to assist them, and marching day and night, in the morning he fell upon the enemies as they were going up to the siege; and when he had discomfited them, he followed them, and pursued them down the descent of the hills. The place is called Bethhoron; where he also understood that God assisted him, which he declared by thunder and thunderbolts, as also by the falling of hail larger than usual. Moreover, it happened that the day was lengthened[7] that the night might not come on too soon, and be an obstruction to the zeal of the Hebrews in pursuing their enemies; insomuch that Joshua took the kings, who were hidden in a certain cave at Makkedah, and put them to death. Now, that the day was lengthened at this thee, and was longer than ordinary, is expressed in the books laid up in the temple.[8]

18. These kings which made war with, and were ready to fight the Gibeonites, being thus overthrown, Joshua returned again to

---

7. Whether this lengthening of the day, by the standing still of the sun and moon, were physical and real, by the miraculous stoppage of the diurnal motion of the earth for about half a revolution, or whether only apparent, by aerial phosphori imitating the sun and moon as stationary so long, while clouds and the night hid the real ones, and this parhelion or mock sun affording sufficient light for Joshua's pursuit and complete victory, (which aerial phosphori in other shapes have been more than ordinarily common of late years,) cannot now be determined: philosophers and astronomers will naturally incline to this latter hypothesis. In the mean thee, the fact itself was mentioned in the book of Jasher, now lost, Joshua 10:13, and is confirmed by Isaiah, 28:21, Habakkuk, 3:11, and by the son of Sirach, Ecclus. 46:4. In the 18th Psalm of Solomon, yet. it is also said of the luminaries, with relation, no doubt, to this and the other miraculous standing still and going back, in the days of Joshua and Hezekiah, "They have not wandered, from the day that he created them; they have not forsaken their way, from ancient generations, unless it were when God enjoined them [so to do] by the command of his servants." See Authent. Rec. part i. p. 154.

8. Of the books laid up in the temple, see the note on Antiq. B. III. ch. 1. sect. 7.

the mountainous parts of Canaan; and when he had made a great slaughter of the people there, and took their prey, he came to the camp at Gilgal. And now there went a great fame abroad among the neighboring people of the courage of the Hebrews; and those that heard what a number of men were destroyed, were greatly aftrighted at it: so the kings that lived about Mount Libanus, who were Canaanites, and those Canaanites that dwelt in the plain country, with auxiliaries out of the land of the Philistines, pitched their camp at Beroth, a city of the Upper Galilee, not far from Cadesh, which is itself also a place in Galilee. Now the number of the whole army was three hundred thousand armed footmen, and ten thousand horsemen, and twenty thousand chariots; so that the multitude of the enemies aftrighted both Joshua himself and the Israelites; and they, instead of being full of hopes of good success, were superstitiously timorous, with the great terror with which they were stricken. Whereupon God upbraided them with the fear they were in, and asked them whether they desired a greater help than he could afford them; and promised them that they should overcome their enemies; and withal charged them to make their enemies' horses useless, and to burn their chariots. So Joshua became full of courage upon these promises of God, and went out suddenly against the enemies; and after five days' march he came upon them, and joined battle with them, and there was a terrible fight, and such a number were slain as could not be believed by those that heard it. He also went on in the pursuit a great way, and destroyed the entire army of the enemies, few only excepted, and all the kings fell in the battle; insomuch, that when there wanted men to be killed, Joshua slew their horses, and burnt their chariots and passed all over their country without opposition, no one daring to meet him in battle; but he still went on, taking their cities by siege, and again killing whatever he took.

19. The fifth year was now past, and there was not one of the Canaanites remained any longer, excepting some that had retired to places of great strength. So Joshua removed his camp to the mountainous country, and placed the tabernacle in the city of Shiloh, for that seemed a fit place for it, because of the beauty of its situation, until such thee as their affairs would permit them to build a temple; and from thence he went to Shechem, together with all the people, and raised an altar where Moses had beforehand directed; then did he

divide the army, and placed one half of them on Mount Gerizzim, and the other half on Mount Ebal, on which mountain the altar was; he also placed there the tribe of Levi, and the priests. And when they had sacrificed, and denounced the [blessings and the] curses, and had left them engraven upon the altar, they returned to Shiloh.

20. And now Joshua was old, and saw that the cities of the Canaanites were not easily to be taken, not only because they were situate in such strong places, but because of the strength of the walls themselves, which being built round about, the natural strength of the places on which the cities stood, seemed capable of repelling their enemies from besieging them, and of making those enemies despair of taking them; for when the Canaanites had learned that the Israelites came out of Egypt in order to destroy them, they were busy all that time in making their cities strong. So he gathered the people together to a congregation at Shiloh; and when they, with great zeal and haste, were come thither, he observed to them what prosperous successes they had already had, and what glorious things had been done, and those such as were worthy of that God who enabled them to do those things, and worthy of the virtue of those laws which they followed. He took notice also, that thirty-one of those kings that ventured to give them battle were overcome, and every army, how great soever it were, that confided in their own power, and fought with them, was utterly destroyed; so that not so much as any of their posterity remained. And as for the cities, since some of them were taken, but the others must be taken in length of thee, by long sieges, both on account of the strength of their walls, and of the confidence the inhabitants had in them thereby, he thought it reasonable that those tribes that came along with them from beyond Jordan, and had partaken of the dangers they had undergone, being their own kindred, should now be dismissed and sent home, and should have thanks for the pains they had taken together with them. As also, he thought it reasonable that they should send one man out of every tribe, and he such as had the testimony of extraordinary virtue, who should measure the land faithfully, and without any fallacy or deceit should inform them of its real magnitude.

21. Now Joshua, when he had thus spoken to them, found that the multitude approved of his proposal. So he sent men to measure their country, and sent with them some geometricians, who could not easily

fail of knowing the truth, on account of their skill in that art. He also gave them a charge to estimate the measure of that part of the land that was most fruitful, and what was not so good: for such is the nature of the land of Canaan, that one may see large plains, and such as are exceeding fit to produce fruit, which yet, if they were compared to other parts of the country, might be reckoned exceedingly fruitful; yet, if it be compared with the fields about Jericho, and to those that belong to Jerusalem, will appear to be of no account at all; and although it so falls out that these people have but a very little of this sort of land, and that it is, for the main, mountainous also, yet does it not come behind other parts, on account of its exceeding goodness and beauty; for which reason Joshua thought the land for the tribes should be divided by estimation of its goodness, rather than the largeness of its measure, it often happening that one acre of some sort of land was equivalent to a thousand other acres. Now the men that were sent, which were in number ten, traveled all about, and made an estimation of the land, and in the seventh month came to him to the city of Shiloh, where they had set up the tabernacle.

22. So Joshua took both Eleazar and the senate, and with them the heads of the tribes, and distributed the land to the nine tribes, and to the half-tribe of Manasseh, appointing the dimensions to be according to the largeness of each tribe. So when he had cast lots, Judah had assigned him by lot the upper part of Judea, reaching as far as Jerusalem, and its breadth extended to the Lake of Sodom. Now in the lot of this tribe there were the cities of Askelon and Gaza. The lot of Simeon, which was the second, included that part of Idumea which bordered upon Egypt and Arabia. As to the Benjamites, their lot fell so, that its length reached from the river Jordan to the sea, but in breadth it was bounded by Jerusalem and Bethel; and this lot was the narrowest of all, by reason of the goodness of the land, for it included Jericho and the city of Jerusalem. The tribe of Ephraim had by lot the land that extended in length from the river Jordan to Gezer; but in breadth as far as from Bethel, till it ended at the Great Plain. The half-tribe of Manasseh had the land from Jordan to the city of Dora; but its breadth was at Bethsham, which is now called Scythopolis. And after these was Issachar, which had its limits in length, Mount Carmel and the river, but its limit in breadth was Mount Tabor. The tribe of Zebulon's lot included the land which lay as far as the Lake of Genesareth, and that

which belonged to Carmel and the sea. The tribe of Aser had that part which was called the *Valley,* for such it was, and all that part which lay over-against Sidon. The city Arce belonged to their share, which is also named Actipus. The Naphthalites received the eastern parts, as far as the city of Damascus and the Upper Galilee, unto Mount Libanus, and the Fountains of Jordan, which rise out of that mountain; that is, out of that part of it whose limits belong to the neighboring city of Arce. The Danites' lot included all that part of the valley which respects the sun-setting, and were bounded by Azotus and Dora; as also they had all Jamnia and Gath, from Ekron to that mountain where the tribe of Judah begins.

23. After this manner did Joshua divide the six nations that bear the name of the sons of Canaan, with their land, to be possessed by the nine tribes and a half; for Moses had prevented him, and had already distributed the land of the Amorites, which itself was so called also from one of the sons of Canaan, to the two tribes and a half, as we have shown already. But the parts about Sidon, as also those that belonged to the Arkites, and the Amathites, and the Aradians, were not yet regularly disposed of.

24. But now was Joshua hindered by his age from executing what he intended to do (as did those that succeeded him in the government, take little care of what was for the advantage of the public); so he gave it in charge to every tribe to leave no remainder of the race of the Canaanites in the land that had been divided to them by lot; that Moses had assured them beforehand, and they might rest fully satisfied about it, that their own security and their observation of their own laws depended wholly upon it. Moreover, he enjoined them to give thirty-eight cities to the Levites, for they had already received ten in the country of the Amorites; and three of these he assigned to those that fled from the man-slayers, who were to inhabit there; for he was very solicitous that nothing should be neglected which Moses had ordained. These cities were, of the tribe of Judah, Hebron; of that of Ephraim, Shechem; and of that of Naphthali, Cadesh, which is a place of the Upper Galilee. He also distributed among them the rest of the prey not yet distributed, which was very great; whereby they had an affluence of great riches, both all in general, and every one in particular; and this of gold and of vestments, and of other furniture, besides a multitude of cattle, whose number could not be told.

25. After this was over, he gathered the army together to a congregation, and spake thus to those tribes that had their settlement in the land of the Amorites beyond Jordan,—for fifty thousand of them had armed themselves, and had gone to the war along with them:—"Since that God, who is the Father and Lord of the Hebrew nation, has now given us this land for a possession, and promised to preserve us in the enjoyment of it as our own for ever; and since you have with alacrity offered yourselves to assist us when we wanted that assistance on all occasions, according to his command; it is but just, now all our difficulties are over, that you should be permitted to enjoy rest, and that we should trespass on your alacrity to help us no longer; that so, if we should again stand in need of it, we may readily have it on any future emergency, and not tire you out so much now as may make you slower in assisting us another thee. We, therefore, return you our thanks for the dangers you have undergone with us, and we do it not at this thee only, but we shall always be thus disposed; and be so good as to remember our friends, and to preserve in mind what advantages we have had from them; and how you have put off the enjoyments of your own happiness for our sakes, and have labored for what we have now, by the goodwill of God, obtained, and resolved not to enjoy your own prosperity till you had afforded us that assistance. However, you have, by joining your labor with ours, gotten great plenty of riches, and will carry home with you much prey, with gold and silver, and, what is more than all these, our good-will towards you, and a mind willingly disposed to make a requital of your kindness to us, in what case soever you shall desire it, for you have not omitted any thing which Moses beforehand required of you, nor have you despised him because he was dead and gone from you, so that there is nothing to diminish that gratitude which we owe to you. We therefore dismiss you joyful to your own inheritances; and we entreat you to suppose, that there is no limit to be set to the intimate relation that is between us; and that you will not imagine, because this river is interposed between us, that you are of a different race from us, and not Hebrews; for we are all the posterity of Abraham, both we that inhabit here, and you that inhabit there; and it is the same God that brought our forefathers and yours into the world, whose worship and form of government we are to take care of, which he has ordained, and are most carefully to observe; because while you continue in those laws, God will also

show himself merciful and assisting to you; but if you imitate the other nations, and forsake those laws, he will reject your nation." When Joshua had spoken thus, and saluted them all, both those in authority one by one, and the whole multitude in common, he himself staid where he was; but the people conducted those tribes on their journey, and that not without tears in their eyes; and indeed they hardly knew how to part one from the other.

26. Now when the tribe of Reuben, and that of Gad, and as many of the Manassites as followed them, were passed over the river, they built an altar on the banks of Jordan, as a monument to posterity, and a sign of their relation to those that should inhabit on the other side. But when those on the other side heard that those who had been dismissed had built an altar, but did not hear with what intention they built it, but supposed it to be by way of innovation, and for the introduction of strange gods, they did not incline to disbelieve it; but thinking this defamatory report, as if it were built for divine worship, was credible, they appeared in arms, as though they would avenge themselves on those that built the altar; and they were about to pass over the river, and to punish them for their subversion of the laws of their country; for they did not think it fit to regard them on account of their kindred or the dignity of those that had given the occasion, but to regard the will of God, and the manner wherein he desired to be worshipped; so these men put themselves in array for war. But Joshua, and Eleazar the high priest, and the senate, restrained them; and persuaded them first to make trial by words of their intention, and afterwards, if they found that their intention was evil, then only to proceed to make war upon them. Accordingly, they sent as ambassadors to them Phineas the son of Eleazar, and ten more persons that were in esteem among the Hebrews, to learn of them what was in their mind, when, upon passing over the river, they had built an altar upon its banks. And as soon as these ambassadors were passed over, and were come to them, and a congregation was assembled, Phineas stood up and said, That the offense they had been guilty of was of too heinous a nature to be punished by words alone, or by them only to be amended for the future; yet that they did not so look at the heinousness of their transgression as to have recourse to arms, and to a battle for their punishment immediately, but that, on account of their kindred, and the probability there was that they might be reclaimed, they took

this method of sending an ambassage to them: "That when we have learned the true reasons by which you have been moved to build this altar, we may neither seem to have been too rash in assaulting you by our weapons of war, if it prove that you made the altar for justifiable reasons, and may then justly punish you if the accusation prove true; for we can hardly

hardly suppose that you, have been acquainted with the will of God and have been hearers of those laws which he himself hath given us, now you are separated from us, and gone to that patrimony of yours, which you, through the grace of God, and that providence which he exercises over you, have obtained by lot, can forget him, and can leave that ark and that altar which is peculiar to us, and can introduce strange gods, and imitate the wicked practices of the Canaanites. Now this will appear to have been a small crime if you repent now, and proceed no further in your madness, but pay a due reverence to, and keep in mind the laws of your country; but if you persist in your sins, we will not grudge our pains to preserve our laws; but we will pass over Jordan and defend them, and defend God also, and shall esteem of you as of men no way differing from the Canaanites, but shall destroy you in the like manner as we destroyed them; for do not you imagine that, because you are got over the river, you are got out of the reach of God's power; you are every where in places that belong to him, and impossible it is to overrun his power, and the punishment he will bring on men thereby: but if you think that your settlement here will be any obstruction to your conversion to what is good, nothing need hinder us from dividing the land anew, and leaving this old land to be for the feeding of sheep; but you will do well to return to your duty, and to leave off these new crimes; and we beseech you, by your children and wives, not to force us to punish you. Take therefore such measures in this assembly, as supposing that your own safety, and the safety of those that are dearest to you, is therein concerned, and believe that it is better for you to be conquered by words, than to continue in your purpose, and to experience deeds and war therefore."

27. When Phineas had discoursed thus, the governors of the assembly, and the whole multitude, began to make an apology for themselves, concerning what they were accused of; and they said, That they neither would depart from the relation they bare to them, nor had they built the altar by way of innovation; that they owned one and the

same common God with all the Hebrews, and that brazen altar which was before the tabernacle, on which they would offer their sacrifices; that as to the altar they had raised, on account of which they were thus suspected, it was not built for worship, "but that it might be a sign and a monument of our relation to you for ever, and a necessary caution to us to act wisely, and to continue in the laws of our country, but not a handle for transgressing them, as you suspect: and let God be our authentic witness, that this was the occasion of our building this altar: whence we beg you will have a better opinion of us, and do not impute such a thing to us as would render any of the posterity of Abraham well worthy of perdition, in case they attempt to bring in new rites, and such as are different from our usual practices."

28. When they had made this answer, and Phineas had commended them for it, he came to Joshua, and explained before the people what answer they had received. Now Joshua was glad that he was under no necessity of setting them in array, or of leading them to shed blood, and make war against men of their own kindred; and accordingly he offered sacrifices of thanksgiving to God for the same. So Joshua after that dissolved this great assembly of the people, and sent them to their own inheritances, while he himself lived in Shechem. But in the twentieth year after this, when he was very old, he sent for those of the greatest dignity in the several cities, with those in authority, and the senate, and as many of the common people as could be present; and when they were come, he put them in mind of all the benefits God had bestowed on them, which could not but be a great many, since from a low estate they were advanced to so great a degree of glory and plenty; and exhorted them to take notice of the intentions of God, which had been so gracious towards them; and told them that the Deity would continue their friend by nothing else but their piety; and that it was proper for him, now that he was about to depart out of this life, to leave such an admonition to them; and he desired that they would keep in memory this his exhortation to them.

29. So Joshua, when he had thus discoursed to them, died, having lived a hundred and ten years; forty of which he lived with Moses, in order to learn what might be for his advantage afterwards. He also became their commander after his death for twenty-five years. He was a man that wanted not wisdom nor eloquence to declare his intentions to the people, but very eminent on both accounts. He was

of great courage and magnanimity in action and in dangers, and very
sagacious in procuring the peace of the people, and of great virtue
at all proper seasons. He was buried in the city of Timnab, of the
tribe of Ephraim[9] About the same time died Eleazar the high priest,
leaving the high priesthood to his son Phineas. His monument also,
and sepulcher, are in the city of Gabatha.

2 How, After the Death of Joshua Their Commander, the Israelites Transgressed the Laws of Their Country, and Experienced Great Afflictions; and When There Was a Sedition Arisen, the Tribe of Benjamin Was Destroyed Excepting Only Six Hundred Men

1. AFTER the death of Joshua and Eleazar, Phineas prophesied,[10]
that according to God's will they should commit the government to
the tribe of Judah, and that this tribe should destroy the race of the
Canaanites; for then the people were concerned to learn what was the
will of God. They also took to their assistance the tribe of Simeon; but
upon this condition, that when those that had been tributary to the

---

9. Since not only Procopius and Suidas, but an earlier author, Moses Chorenensis,
p. 52, 53, and perhaps from his original author Mariba Carina, one as old as Alexander
the Great, sets down the famous inscription at Tangier concerning the old Canaanites
driven out of Palestine by Joshua, take it here in that author's own words: "We
are those exiles that were governors of the Canaanites, but have been driven away
by Joshua the robber, and are come to inhabit here." See the note there. Nor is it
unworthy of our notice what Moses Chorenensis adds, p. 53, and this upon a diligent
examination, viz. that "one of those eminent men among the Canaanites came at the
same thee into Armenia, and founded the Genthuniaa family, or tribe; and that this
was confirmed by the manners of the same family or tribe, as being like those of the
Canaanites."

10. By prophesying, when spoken of a high priest, Josephus, both here and
frequently elsewhere, means no more than consulting God by Urim, which the reader
is still to bear in mind upon all occasions. And if St. John, who was contemporary
with Josephus, and of the same country, made use of this style, when he says that
"Caiaphas being high priest that year, prophesied that Jesus should die for that nation,
and not for that nation only, but that also he should gather together in one the children
of God that were scattered abroad," chap. 11;51, 52, he may possibly mean, that this
was revealed to the high priest by an extraordinary voice from between the cherubims,
when he had his breastplate, or Urim and Thummim, on before; or the most holy
place of the temple, which was no other than the oracle of Urim and Thummim. Of
which above, in the note on Antiq. B. III. ch. 8. sect. 9.

tribe of Judah should be slain, they should do the like for the tribe of Simeon.

2. But the affairs of the Canaanites were at this thee in a flourishing condition, and they expected the Israelites with a great army at the city Bezek, having put the government into the hands of Adonibezek, which name denotes the *Lord of Bezek,* for *Adoni* in the Hebrew tongue signifies *Lord.* Now they hoped to have been too hard for the Israelites, because Joshua was dead; but when the Israelites had joined battle with them, I mean the two tribes before mentioned, they fought gloriously, and slew above ten thousand of them, and put the rest to flight; and in the pursuit they took Adonibezek, who, when his fingers and toes were cut off by them, said, "Nay, indeed, I was not always to lie concealed from God, as I find by what I now endure, while I have not been ashamed to do the same to seventy-two kings."[11] So they carried him alive as far as Jerusalem; and when he was dead, they buried him in the earth, and went on still in taking the cities: and when they had taken the greatest part of them, they besieged

---

11. This great number of seventy-two reguli, or small kings, over whom Adonibezek had tyrannized, and for which he was punished according to the lex talionis, as well as the thirty-one kings of Canaan subdued by Joshua, and named in one chapter, Joshua 12., and thirty-two kings, or royal auxiliaries to Benhadad king of Syria, 1 Kings 20:1; Antiq. B. VIII. ch. 14. sect. 1, intimate to us what was the ancient form of government among several nations before the monarchies began, viz. that every city or large town, with its neighboring villages, was a distinct government by itself; which is the more remarkable, because this was certainly the form of ecclesiastical government that was settled by the apostles, and preserved throughout the Christian church in the first ages of Christianity. Mr. Addison is of opinion, that "it would certainly be for the good of mankind to have all the mighty empires and monarchies of the world cantoned out into petty states and principalities, which, like so many large families, might lie under the observation of their proper governors, so that the care of the prince might extend itself to every individual person under his protection; though he despairs of such a scheme being brought about, and thinks that if it were, it would quickly be destroyed." Remarks on Italy, 4to, p. 151. Nor is it unfit to be observed here, that the Armenian records, though they give us the history of thirty-nine of their ancientest heroes or governors after the Flood, before the days of Sardanapalus, had no proper king till the fortieth, Parerus. See Moses Chorehensis, p. 55. And that Almighty God does not approve of such absolute and tyrannical monarchies, any one may learn that reads Deuteronomy 17:14–20, and 1 Samuel 8:1–22; although, if such kings are set up as own him for their supreme King, and aim to govern according to his laws, he hath admitted of them, and protected them and their subjects in all generations.

Jerusalem; and when they had taken the lower city, which was not under a considerable time, they slew all the inhabitants; but the upper city was not to be taken without great difficulty, through the strength of its walls, and the nature of the place.

3. For which reason they removed their camp to Hebron; and when they had taken it, they slew all the inhabitants. There were till then left the race of giants, who had bodies so large, and countenances so entirely different from other men, that they were surprising to the sight, and terrible to the hearing. The bones of these men are still shown to this very day, unlike to any credible relations of other men. Now they gave this city to the Levites as an extraordinary reward, with the suburbs of two thousand cities; but the land thereto belonging they gave as a free gift to Caleb, according to the injunctions of Moses. This Caleb was one of the spies which Moses sent into the land of Canaan. They also gave land for habitation to the posterity of Jethro, the Midianite, who was the father-in-law to Moses; for they had left their own country, and followed them, and accompanied them in the wilderness.

4. Now the tribes of Judah and Simeon took the cities which were in the mountainous part of Canaan, as also Askelon and Ashdod, of those that lay near the sea; but Gaza and Ekron escaped them, for they, lying in a flat country, and having a great number of chariots, sorely galled those that attacked them. So these tribes, when they were grown very rich by this war, retired to their own cities, and laid aside their weapons of war.

5. But the Benjamites, to whom belonged Jerusalem, permitted its inhabitants to pay tribute. So they all left off, the one to kill, and the other to expose themselves to danger, and had time to cultivate the ground. The rest of the tribes imitated that of Benjamin, and did the same; and, contenting themselves with the tributes that were paid them, permitted the Canaanites to live in peace.

6. However, the tribe of Ephraim, when they besieged Bethel, made no advance, nor performed any thing worthy of the time they spent, and of the pains they took about that siege; yet did they persist in it, still sitting down before the city, though they endured great trouble thereby: but, after some time, they caught one of the citizens that came to them to get necessaries, and they gave him some assurances that, if he would deliver up the city to them, they would preserve him and his

kindred; so he aware that, upon those terms, he would put the city into their hands. Accordingly, he that, thus betrayed the city was preserved with his family; and the Israelites slew all the inhabitants, and retained the city for themselves.

7. After this, the Israelites grew effeminate as to fighting any more against their enemies, but applied themselves to the cultivation of the land, which producing them great plenty and riches, they neglected the regular disposition of their settlement, and indulged themselves in luxury and pleasures; nor were they any longer careful to hear the laws that belonged to their political government: whereupon God was provoked to anger, and put them in mind, first, how, contrary to his directions, they had spared the Canaanites; and, after that, how those Canaanites, as opportunity served, used them very barbarously. But the Israelites, though they were in heaviness at these admonitions from God, yet were they still very unwilling to go to war; and since they got large tributes from the Canaanites, and were indisposed for taking pains by their luxury, they suffered their aristocracy to be corrupted also, and did not ordain themselves a senate, nor any other such magistrates as their laws had formerly required, but they were very much given to cultivating their fields, in order to get wealth; which great indolence of theirs brought a terrible sedition upon them, and they proceeded so far as to fight one against another, from the following occasion:—8. There was a Levite[12] a man of a vulgar family, that belonged to the tribe of Ephraim, and dwelt therein: this man married a wife from Bethlehem, which is a place belonging to the tribe of Judah. Now he was very fond of his wife, and overcome with her beauty; but he was unhappy in this, that he did not meet with the like return of affection from her, for she was averse to him, which did more inflame his passion for her, so that they quarreled one with another perpetually; and at last the woman was so disgusted at these quarrels, that she left her husband, and went to her parents in the fourth month.

---

12. Josephus's early date of this history before the beginning of the Judges, or when there was no king in Israel, Judges 19;1, is strongly confirmed by the large number of Benjamites, both in the days of Asa and Jehoshaphat, 2 Chronicles 14:8, and 16:17, who yet were here reduced to six hundred men; nor can those numbers be at all supposed genuine, if they were reduced so late as the end of the Judges, where our other copies place this reduction.

The husband being very uneasy at this her departure, and that out of his fondness for her, came to his father and mother-in-law, and made up their quarrels, and was reconciled to her, and lived with them there four days, as being kindly treated by her parents. On the fifth day he resolved to go home, and went away in the evening; for his wife's parents were loath to part with their daughter, and delayed the time till the day was gone. Now they had one servant that followed them, and an ass on which the woman rode; and when they were near Jerusalem, having gone already thirty furlongs, the servant advised them to take up their lodgings some where, lest some misfortune should befall them if they traveled in the night, especially since they were not far off enemies, that season often giving reason for suspicion of dangers from even such as are friends; but the husband was not pleased with this advice, nor was he willing to take up his lodging among strangers, for the city belonged to the Canaanites, but desired rather to go twenty furlongs farther, and so to take their lodgings in some Israelite city. Accordingly, he obtained his purpose, and came to Gibeah, a city of the tribe of Benjamin, when it was just dark; and while no one that lived in the market-place invited him to lodge with him, there came an old man out of the field, one that was indeed of the tribe of Ephraim, but resided in Gibeah, and met him, and asked him who he was, and for what reason he came thither so late, and why he was looking out for provisions for supper when it was dark? To which he replied, that he was a Levite, and was bringing his wife from her parents, and was going home; but he told him his habitation was in the tribe of Ephraim: so the old man, as well because of their kindred as because they lived in the same tribe, and also because they had thus accidentally met together, took him in to lodge with him. Now certain young men of the inhabitants of Gibeah, having seen the woman in the market-place, and admiring her beauty, when they understood that she lodged with the old man, came to the doors, as contemning the weakness and fewness of the old man's family; and when the old man desired them to go away, and not to offer any violence or abuse there, they desired him to yield them up the strange woman, and then he should have no harm done to him: and when the old man alleged that the Levite was of his kindred, and that they would be guilty of horrid wickedness if they suffered themselves to be overcome by their pleasures, and so offend against their laws, they despised his righteous admonition, and laughed him to scorn. They also threatened to kill him if he became an obstacle to their inclinations; whereupon, when he found himself in great distress, and yet was not willing to overlook his guests, and see them abused, he produced his own daughter to them; and told them that it was a smaller breach of the law to satisfy their lust upon her, than to abuse his guests, supposing that he himself should by this means prevent any injury to be done to those guests. When they no way abated of their earnestness for the strange woman, but insisted absolutely on their desires to have her, he entreated them not to perpetrate any such act of injustice; but they proceeded to take her away by force, and indulging still more the violence of their inclinations, they took the woman away to their house, and when they had satisfied their lust upon her the whole night, they let her go about daybreak. So she came to the place where she had been entertained, under great affliction at what had happened; and was very sorrowful upon occasion of what she had suffered, and durst not look her husband in the face for shame, for she concluded that he would never forgive her for what she had done; so she fell down, and gave up the ghost: but her husband supposed that his wife was only fast asleep, and, thinking nothing of a more melancholy nature had happened, endeavored to raise her up, resolving to speak comfortably to her, since she did not voluntarily expose herself to these men's lust, but was forced away to their house; but as soon as he perceived she was dead, he acted as prudently as the greatness of his misfortunes would admit, and laid his dead wife upon the beast, and carried her home; and cutting her, limb by limb, into twelve pieces, he sent them to every tribe, and gave it in charge to those that carried them, to inform the tribes of those that were the causes of his wife's death, and of the violence they had offered to her.

9. Upon this the people were greatly disturbed at what they saw, and at what they heard, as never having had the experience of such a thing before; so they gathered themselves to Shiloh, out of a prodigious and a just anger, and assembling in a great congregation before the tabernacle, they immediately resolved to take arms, and to treat the inhabitants of Gibeah as enemies; but the senate restrained them from doing so, and persuaded them, that they ought not so hastily to make war upon people of the same nation with them, before they discoursed them by words concerning the accusation laid against them; it being

part of their law, that they should not bring an army against foreigners themselves, when they appear to have been injurious, without sending an ambassage first, and trying thereby whether they will repent or not: and accordingly they exhorted them to do what they ought to do in obedience to their laws, that is, to send to the inhabitants of Gibeah, to know whether they would deliver up the offenders to them, and if they deliver them up, to rest satisfied with the punishment of those offenders; but if they despised the message that was sent them, to punish them by taking, up arms against them. Accordingly they sent to the inhabitants of Gibeah, and accused the young men of the crimes committed in the affair of the Levite's wife, and required of them those that had done what was contrary to the law, that they might be punished, as having justly deserved to die for what they had done; but the inhabitants of Gibeah would not deliver up the young men, and thought it too reproachful to them, out of fear of war, to submit to other men's demands upon them; vaunting themselves to be no way inferior to any in war, neither in their number nor in courage. The rest of their tribe were also making great preparation for war, for they were so insolently mad as also to resolve to repel force by force.

10. When it was related to the Israelites what the inhabitants of Gibeah had resolved upon, they took their oath that no one of them would give his daughter in marriage to a Benjamite, but make war with greater fury against them than we have learned our forefathers made war against the Canaanites; and sent out presently an army of four hundred thousand against them, while the Benjamites' army-was twenty-five thousand and six hundred; five hundred of whom were excellent at slinging stones with their left hands, insomuch that when the battle was joined at Gibeah the Benjamites beat the Israelites, and of them there fell two thousand men; and probably more had been destroyed had not the night came on and prevented it, and broken off the fight; so the Benjamites returned to the city with joy, and the Israelites returned to their camp in a great fright at what had happened. On the next day, when they fought again, the Benjamites beat them; and eighteen thousand of the Israelites were slain, and the rest deserted their camp out of fear of a greater slaughter. So they came

to Bethel,[13] a city that was near their camp, and fasted on the next day; and besought God, by Phineas the high priest, that his wrath against them might cease, and that he would be satisfied with these two defeats, and give them the victory and power over their enemies. Accordingly God promised them so to do, by the prophesying of Phineas.

11. When therefore they had divided the army into two parts, they laid the one half of them in ambush about the city Gibeah by night, while the other half attacked the Benjamites, who retiring upon the assault, the Benjamites pursued them, while the Hebrews retired by slow degrees, as very desirous to draw them entirely from the city; and the other followed them as they retired, till both the old men and the young men that were left in the city, as too weak to fight, came running out together with them, as willing to bring their enemies under. However, when they were a great way from the city the Hebrews ran away no longer, but turned back to fight them, and lifted up the signal they had agreed on to those that lay in ambush, who rose up, and with a great noise fell upon the enemy. Now, as soon as ever they perceived themselves to be deceived, they knew not what to do; and when they were driven into a certain hollow place which was in a valley, they were shot at by those that encompassed them, till they were all destroyed, excepting six hundred, which formed themselves into a close body of men, and forced their passage through the midst of their enemies, and fled to the neighboring mountains, and, seizing upon them, remained there; but the rest of them, being about twenty-five thousand, were slain. Then did the Israelites burn Gibeah, and slew the women, and the males that were under age; and did the same also to the other cities of the Benjamites; and, indeed, they were enraged to that degree, that they sent twelve thousand men out of the army, and gave them orders to destroy Jabesh Gilead, because it did not join with them in fighting against the Benjamites. Accordingly, those that were sent slew the men of war, with their children and

---

13. Josephus seems here to have made a small mistake, when he took the Hebrew word Bethel, which denotes the house of God, or the tabernacle, Judges 20:18, for the proper name of a place, Bethel, it no way appearing that the tabernacle was ever at Bethel; only so far it is true, that Shiloh, the place of the tabernacle in the days of the Judges, was not far from Bethel.

wives, excepting four hundred virgins. To such a degree had they proceeded in their anger, because they not only had the suffering of the Levite's wife to avenge, but the slaughter of their own soldiers.

12. However, they afterward were sorry for the calamity they had brought upon the Benjamites, and appointed a fast on that account, although they supposed those men had suffered justly for their offense against the laws; so they recalled by their ambassadors those six hundred which had escaped. These had seated themselves on a certain rock called *Rimmon*, which was in the wilderness. So the ambassadors lamented not only the disaster that had befallen the Benjamites, but themselves also, by this destruction of their kindred; and persuaded them to take it patiently; and to come and unite with them, and not, so far as in them lay, to give their suffrage to the utter destruction of the tribe of Benjamin; and said to them, "We give you leave to take the whole land of Benjamin to yourselves, and as much prey as you are able to carry away with you." So these men with sorrow confessed, that what had been done was according to the decree of God, and had happened for their own wickedness; and assented to those that invited them, and came down to their own tribe. The Israelites also gave them the four hundred virgins of Jabesh Gilead for wives; but as to the remaining two hundred, they deliberated about it how they might compass wives enough for them, and that they might have children by them; and whereas they had, before the war began, taken an oath, that no one would give his daughter to wife to a Benjamite, some advised them to have no regard to what they had sworn, because the oath had not been taken advisedly and judiciously, but in a passion, and thought that they should do nothing against God, if they were able to save a whole tribe which was in danger of perishing; and that perjury was then a sad and dangerous thing, not when it is done out of necessity, but when it is done with a wicked intention. But when the senate were affrighted at the very name of perjury, a certain person told them that he could show them a way whereby they might procure the Benjamites wives enough, and yet keep their oath. They asked him what his proposal was. He said, "That three times in a year, when we meet in Shiloh, our wives and our daughters accompany us: let then the Benjamites be allowed to steal away, and marry such women as they can catch, while we will neither incite them nor forbid them; and when their parents take it ill, and

desire us to inflict punishment upon them, we will tell them, that they were themselves the cause of what had happened, by neglecting to guard their daughters, and that they ought not to be over angry at the Benjamites, since that anger was permitted to rise too high already." So the Israelites were persuaded to follow this advice, and decreed, That the Benjamites should be allowed thus to steal themselves wives. So when the festival was coming on, these two hundred Benjamites lay in ambush before the city, by two and three together, and waited for the coming of the virgins, in the vineyards and other places where they could lie concealed. Accordingly the virgins came along playing, and suspected nothing of what was coming upon them, and walked after an unguarded manner, so those that laid scattered in the road, rose up, and caught hold of them: by this means these Benjamites got them wives, and fell to agriculture, and took good care to recover their former happy state. And thus was this tribe of the Benjamites, after they had been in danger of entirely perishing, saved in the manner forementioned, by the wisdom of the Israelites; and accordingly it presently flourished, and soon increased to be a multitude, and came to enjoy all other degrees of happiness. And such was the conclusion of this war.

3   *How the Israelites After This Misfortune Grew Wicked and Served the Assyrians; and How God Delivered Them by Othniel, Who Ruled over the Forty Years*

1. NOW it happened that the tribe of Dan suffered in like manner with the tribe of Benjamin; and it came to do so on the occasion following:—— When the Israelites had already left off the exercise of their arms for war, and were intent upon their husbandry, the Canaanites despised them, and brought together an army, not because they expected to suffer by them, but because they had a mind to have a sure prospect of treating the Hebrews ill when they pleased, and might thereby for the time to come dwell in their own cities the more securely; they prepared therefore their chariots, and gathered their soldiery together, their cities also combined together, and drew over to them Askelon and Ekron, which were within the tribe of Judah, and many more of those that lay in the plain. They also forced the Danites to fly into

the mountainous country, and left them not the least portion of the plain country to set their foot on. Since then these Danites were not able to fight them, and had not land enough to sustain them, they sent five of their men into the midland country, to seek for a land to which they might remove their habitation. So these men went as far as the neighborhood of Mount Libanus, and the fountains of the Lesser Jordan, at the great plain of Sidon, a day's journey from the city; and when they had taken a view of the land, and found it to be good and exceeding fruitful, they acquainted their tribe with it, whereupon they made an expedition with the army, and built there the city Dan, of the same name with the son of Jacob, and of the same name with their own tribe.

2. The Israelites grew so indolent, and unready of taking pains, that misfortunes came heavier upon them, which also proceeded in part from their contempt of the Divine worship; for when they had once fallen off from the regularity of their political government, they indulged themselves further in living according to their own pleasure, and according to their own will, till they were full of the evil doings that were common among the Canaanites. God therefore was angry with them, and they lost that their happy state which they had obtained by innumerable labors, by their luxury; for when Chushan, king of the Assyrians, had made war against them, they lost many of their soldiers in the battle, and when they were besieged, they were taken by force; nay, there were some who, out of fear, voluntarily submitted to him, and though the tribute laid upon them was more than they could bear, yet did they pay it, and underwent all sort of oppression for eight years; after which thee they were freed from them in the following manner:—3. There was one whose name was Othniel, the son of Kenaz, of the tribe of Judah, an active man and of great courage. He had an admonition from God not to overlook the Israelites in such a distress as they were now in, but to endeavor boldly to gain them their liberty; so when he had procured some to assist him in this dangerous undertaking, (and few they were, who, either out of shame at their present circumstances, or out of a desire of changing them, could be prevailed on to assist him,) he first of all destroyed that garrison which Chushan had set over them; but when it was perceived that he had not failed in his first attempt, more of the people came to his assistance; so they joined battle with the Assyrians,

and drove them entirely before them, and compelled them to pass over Euphrates. Hereupon Othniel, who had given such proofs of his valor, received from the multitude authority to judge the people; and when he had ruled over them forty years, he died.

4 *How Our People Served the Moabites Eighteen Years, and Were Then Delivered from Slavery by One Ehud Who Retained the Dominion Eighty Years*

1. WHEN Othniel was dead, the affairs of the Israelites fell again into disorder: and while they neither paid to God the honor due to him, nor were obedient to the laws, their afflictions increased, till Eglon, king of the Moabites, did so greatly despise them on account of the disorders of their political government, that he made war upon them, and overcame them in several battles, and made the most courageous to submit, and entirely subdued their army, and ordered them to pay him tribute. And when he had built him a royal palace at Jericho,[14] he omitted no method whereby he might distress them; and indeed he reduced them to poverty for eighteen years. But when God had once taken pity of the Israelites, on account of their afflictions, and was moved to compassion by their supplications put up to him, he freed them from the hard usage they had met with under the Moabites. This liberty he procured for them in the following manner;—2. There was a young man of the tribe of Benjamin, whose name was Ehud, the son of Gera, a man of very great courage in bold undertakings, and of a very strong body, fit for hard labor, but best skilled in using his left hand, in which was his whole strength; and he also dwelt at Jericho. Now this man became familiar with Eglon, and that by means of presents, with which he obtained his favor, and insinuated himself into his good opinion; whereby he was also beloved of those that were

---

14. It appears by the sacred history, Judges 1:16; 3:13, that Eglon's pavilion or palace was at the City of Palm-Trees, as the place where Jericho had stood is called after its destruction by Joshua, that is, at or near the demolished city. Accordingly, Josephus says it was at Jericho, or rather in that fine country of palm-trees, upon, or near to, the same spot of ground on which Jericho had formerly stood, and on which it was rebuilt by Hiel, 1 Kings 16:31. Our other copies that avoid its proper name Jericho, and call it the City of Palm-Trees only, speak here more accurately than Josephus.

about the king. Now, when on a time he was bringing presents to the king, and had two servants with him, he put a dagger on his right thigh secretly, and went in to him: it was then summer thee, and the middle of the day, when the guards were not strictly on their watch, both because of the heat, and because they were gone to dinner. So the young man, when he had offered his presents to the king, who then resided in a small parlor that stood conveniently to avoid the heat, fell into discourse with him, for they were now alone, the king having bid his servants that attended him to go their ways, because he had a mind to talk with Ehud. He was now sitting on his throne; and fear seized upon Ehud lest he should miss his stroke, and not give him a deadly wound; so he raised himself up, and said he had a dream to impart to him by the command of God; upon which the king leaped out of his throne for joy of the dream; so Ehud smote him to the heart, and leaving his dagger in his body, he went out and shut the door after him. Now the king's servants were very still, as supposing that the king had composed himself to sleep.

3. Hereupon Ehud informed the people of Jericho privately of what he had done, and exhorted them to recover their liberty; who heard him gladly, and went to their arms, and sent messengers over the country, that should sound trumpets of rams' horns; for it was our custom to call the people together by them. Now the attendants of Eglon were ignorant of what misfortune had befallen him for a great while; but, towards the evening, fearing some uncommon accident had happened, they entered into his parlor, and when they found him dead, they were in great disorder, and knew not what to do; and before the guards could be got together, the multitude of the Israelites came upon them, so that some of them were slain immediately, and some were put to flight, and ran away toward the country of Moab, in order to save themselves. Their number was above ten thousand. The Israelites seized upon the ford of Jordan, and pursued them, and slew them, and many of them they killed at the ford, nor did one of them escape out of their hands; and by this means it was that the Hebrews freed themselves from slavery under the Moabites. Ehud also was on this account dignified with the government over all the multitude,

and died after he had held the government eighty years[15] He was a man worthy of commendation, even besides what he deserved for the forementioned act of his. After him Shamgat, the son of Anath, was elected for their governor, but died in the first year of his government.

5   How the Canaanites Brought the Israelites under Slavery for Twenty Years; After Which They Were Delivered by Barak and Deborah, Who Ruled over Them for Forty Years

1. AND now it was that the Israelites, taking no warning by their former misfortunes to amend their manners, and neither worshipping God nor submitting to the laws, were brought under slavery by Jabin, the king of the Canaanites, and that before they had a short breathing time after the slavery under the Moabites; for this Jabin out of Hazor, a city that was situate over the Semechonitis, and had in pay three hundred footmen, and ten thousand horsemen, with fewer than three thousand chariots. Sisera was commander of all his army, and was the principal person in the king's favor. He so sorely beat the Israelites when they fought with him, that he ordered them to pay tribute.

2. So they continued to that hardship for twenty years, as not good enough of themselves to grow wise by their misfortunes. God was willing also hereby the more to subdue their obstinacy and ingratitude towards himself: so when at length they were become penitent, and were so wise as to learn that their calamities arose from their contempt of the laws, they besought Deborah, a certain prophetess among them, (which name in the Hebrew tongue signifies a *Bee,*) to pray to God to take pity on them, and not to overlook them, now they were ruined by the Canaanites. So God granted them deliverance, and chose them

---

15. These eighty years for the government of Ehud are necessary to Josephus's usual large numbers between the exodus and the building of the temple, of five hundred and ninety-two or six hundred and twelve years, but not to the smallest number of four hundred and eighty years, 1 Kings 6:1; which lesser number Josephus seems sometimes to have followed. And since in the beginning of the next chapter it is said by Josephus, that there was hardly a breathing time for the Israelites before Jabin came and enslaved them, it is highly probable that some of the copies in his time had here only eight years instead of eighty; as had that of Theophilus of Antioch, Ad Autolye. 1. iii., and this most probably from his copy of Josephus.

a general, Barak, one that was of the tribe of Naphtali. Now Barak, in the Hebrew tongue, signifies *Lightning*.

3. So Deborah sent for Barak, and bade him choose out ten thousand young men to go against the enemy, because God had said that that number was sufficient, and promised them victory. But when Barak said that he would not be the general unless she would also go as a general with him, she had indignation at what he said 'Thou, O Barak, deliverest up meanly that authority which God hath given thee into the hand of a woman, and I do not reject it!" So they collected ten thousand men, and pitched their camp at Mount Tabor, where, at the king's command, Sisera met them, and pitched his camp not far from the enemy; whereupon the Israelites, and Barak himself, were so affrighted at the multitude of those enemies, that they were resolved to march off, had not Deborah retained them, and commanded them to fight the enemy that very day, for that they should conquer them, and God would be their assistance.

4. So the battle began; and when they were come to a close fight, there came down from heaven a great storm, with a vast quantity of rain and hail, and the wind blew the rain in the face of the Canaanites, and so darkened their eyes, that their arrows and slings were of no advantage to them, nor would the coldness of the air permit the soldiers to make use of their swords; while this storm did not so much incommode the Israelites, because it came in their backs. They also took such courage, upon the apprehension that God was assisting them, that they fell upon the very midst of their enemies, and slew a great number of them; so that some of them fell by the Israelites, some fell by their own horses, which were put into disorder, and not a few were killed by their own chariots. At last Sisera, as soon as he saw himself beaten, fled away, and came to a woman whose name was Jael, a Kenite, who received him, when he desired to be concealed; and when he asked for somewhat to drink, she gave him sour milk, of which he drank so unmeasurably that he fell asleep; but when he was asleep, Jael took an iron nail, and with a hammer drove it through his temples into the floor; and when Barak came a little afterward, she showed Sisera nailed to the ground: and thus was this victory gained by a woman, as Deborah had foretold. Barak also fought with Jabin at Hazor; and when he met with him, he slew him: and when the general

was fallen, Barak overthrew the city to the foundation, and was the commander of the Israelites for forty years.

6 *How the Midianites and Other Nations Fought Against the Israelites and Beat Them, and Afflicted Their Country for Seven Years, How They Were Delivered by Gideon, Who Ruled over the Multitude for Forty Years*

1. NOW when Barak and Deborah were dead, whose deaths happened about the same time, afterwards the Midianites called the Amalekites and Arabians to their assistance, and made war against the Israelites, and were too hard for those that fought against them; and when they had burnt the fruits of the earth, they carried off the prey. Now when they had done this for three years, the multitude of the Israelites retired to the mountains, and forsook the plain country. They also made themselves hollows under ground, and caverns, and preserved therein whatsoever had escaped their enemies; for the Midianites made expeditions in harvest-time, but permitted them to plough the land in winter, that so, when the others had taken the pains, they might have fruits for them to carry away. Indeed, there ensued a famine and a scarcity of food; upon which they betook themselves to their supplications to God, and besought him to save them.

2. Gideon also, the son of Joash, one of the principal persons of the tribe of Manasseh, brought his sheaves of corn privately, and thrashed them at the wine-press; for he was too fearful of their enemies to thrash them openly in the thrashing-floor. At this time somewhat appeared to him in the shape of a young man, and told him that he was a happy man, and beloved of God. To which he immediately replied, "A mighty indication of God's favor to me, that I am forced to use this wine-press instead of a thrashing-floor!" But the appearance exhorted him to be of good courage, and to make an attempt for the recovery of their liberty. He answered, that it was impossible for him to recover it, because the tribe to which he belonged was by no means numerous; and because he was but young himself, and too inconsiderable to think of such great actions. But the other promised him, that God would supply what he was defective in, and would afford the Israelites victory under his conduct.

3. Now, therefore, as Gideon was relating this to some young men, they believed him, and immediately there was an army of ten thousand men got ready for fighting. But God stood by Gideon in his sleep, and told him that mankind were too fond of themselves, and were enemies to such as excelled in virtue. Now that they might not pass God over, but ascribe the victory to him, and might not fancy it obtained by their own power, because they were a great many, and able of themselves to fight their enemies, but might confess that it was owing to his assistance, he advised him to bring his army about noon, in the violence of the heat, to the river, and to esteem those that bent down on their knees, and so drank, to be men of courage; but for all those that drank tumultuously, that he should esteem them to do it out of fear, and as in dread of their enemies. And when Gideon had done as God had suggested to him, there were found three hundred men that took water with their hands tumultuously; so God bid him take these men, and attack the enemy. Accordingly they pitched their camp at the river Jordan, as ready the next day to pass over it.

4. But Gideon was in great fear, for God had told him beforehand that he should set upon his enemies in the night-time; but God, being willing to free him from his fear, bid him take one of his soldiers, and go near to the Midianites' tents, for that he should from that very place have his courage raised, and grow bold. So he obeyed, and went and took his servant Phurah with him; and as he came near to one of the tents, he discovered that those that were in it were awake, and that one of them was telling to his fellow soldier a dream of his own, and that so plainly that Gideon could hear him. The dream was this:—He thought he saw a barley-cake, such a one as could hardly be eaten by men, it was so vile, rolling through the camp, and overthrowing the royal tent, and the tents of all the soldiers. Now the other soldier explained this vision to mean the destruction of the army; and told them what his reason was which made him so conjecture, viz. That the seed called *barley* was all of it allowed to be of the vilest sort of seed, and that the Israelites were known to be the vilest of all the people of Asia, agreeably to the seed of barley, and that what seemed to look big among the Israelites was this Gideon and the army that was with him; "and since thou sayest thou didst see the cake overturning our tents, I am afraid lest God hath granted the victory over us to Gideon."

5. When Gideon had heard this dream, good hope and courage came upon him; and he commanded his soldiers to arm themselves, and told them of this vision of their enemies. They also took courage at what was told them, and were ready to perform what he should enjoin them. So Gideon divided his army into three parts, and brought it out about the fourth watch of the night, each part containing a hundred men: they all bare empty pitchers and lighted lamps in their hands, that their onset might not be discovered by their enemies. They had also each of them a ram's horn in his right hand, which he used instead of a trumpet. The enemy's camp took up a large space of ground, for it happened that they had a great many camels; and as they were divided into different nations, so they were all contained in one circle. Now when the Hebrews did as they were ordered beforehand, upon their approach to their enemies, and, on the signal given, sounded with their rams' horns, and brake their pitchers, and set upon their enemies with their lamps, and a great shout, and cried, "Victory to Gideon, by God's assistance," a disorder and a fright seized upon the other men while they were half asleep, for it was night-time, as God would have it; so that a few of them were slain by their enemies, but the greatest part by their own soldiers, on account of the diversity of their language; and when they were once put into disorder, they killed all that they met with, as thinking them to be enemies also. Thus there was a great slaughter made. And as the report of Gideon's victory came to the Israelites, they took their weapons and pursued their enemies, and overtook them in a certain valley encompassed with torrents, a place which these could not get over; so they encompassed them, and slew them all, with their kings, Oreb and Zeeb. But the remaining captains led those soldiers that were left, which were about eighteen thousand, and pitched their camp a great way off the Israelites. However, Gideon did not grudge his pains, but pursued them with all his army, and joining battle with them, cut off the whole enemies' army, and took the other leaders, Zeba and Zalmuna, and made them captives. Now there were slain in this battle of the Midianites, and of their auxiliaries the Arabians, about a hundred and twenty thousand; and the Hebrews took a great prey, gold, and silver, and garments, and camels, and asses. And when Gideon was come to his own country of Ophrah, he slew the kings of the Midianites.

6. However, the tribe of Ephraim was so displeased at the good success of Gideon, that they resolved to make war against him, accusing him because he did not tell them of his expedition against their enemies. But Gideon, as a man of temper, and that excelled in every virtue, pleaded, that it was not the result of his own authority or reasoning, that made him attack the enemy without them; but that it was the command of God, and still the victory belonged to them as well as those in the army. And by this method of cooling their passions, he brought more advantage to the Hebrews, than by the success he had against these enemies, for he thereby delivered them from a sedition which was arising among them; yet did this tribe afterwards suffer the punishment of this their injurious treatment of Gideon, of which we will give an account in due time.

7. Hereupon Gideon would have laid down the government, but was over-persuaded to take it, which he enjoyed forty years, and distributed justice to them, as the people came to him in their differences; and what he determined was esteemed valid by all. And when he died, he was buried in his own country of Ophrah.

7 That the Judges Who Succeeded Gideon Made War with the Adjoining Nations for a Long Time

1. NOW Gideon had seventy sons that were legitimate, for he had many wives; but he had also one that was spurious, by his concubine Drumah, whose name was Abimelech, who, after his father's death, retired to Shecbem to his mother's relations, for they were of that place: and when he had got money of such of them as were eminent for many instances of injustice, he came with them to his father's house, and slew all his brethren, except Jotham, for he had the good fortune to escape and be preserved; but Abimelech made the government tyrannical, and constituted himself a lord, to do what he pleased, instead of obeying the laws; and he acted most rigidly against those that were the patrons of justice.

2. Now when, on a certain time, there was a public festival at Shechem, and all the multitude was there gathered together, Jotham his brother, whose escape we before related, went up to Mount Gerizzim, which hangs over the city Shechem, and cried out so as to

be heard by the multitude, who were attentive to him. He desired they would consider what he was going to say to them: so when silence was made, he said, That when the trees had a human voice, and there was an assembly of them gathered together, they desired that the fig-tree would rule over them; but when that tree refused so to do, because it was contented to enjoy that honor which belonged peculiarly to the fruit it bare, and not that which should be derived to it from abroad, the trees did not leave off their intentions to have a ruler, so they thought proper to make the offer of that honor to the vine; but when the vine was chosen, it made use of the same words which the fig-tree had used before, and excused itself from accepting the government: and when the olive-tree had done the same, the brier, whom the trees had desired to take the kingdom, (it is a sort of wood good for firing,) it promised to take the government, and to be zealous in the exercise of it; but that then they must sit down under its shadow, and if they should plot against it to destroy it, the principle of fire that was in it should destroy them. He told them, that what he had said was no laughing matter; for that when they had experienced many blessings from Gideon, they overlooked Abimelech, when he overruled all, and had joined with him in slaying his brethren; and that he was no better than a fire himself. So when he had said this, he went away, and lived privately in the mountains for three years, out of fear of Abimelech.

3. A little while after this festival, the Shechemites, who had now repented themselves of having slain the sons of Gideon, drove Abimelech away, both from their city and their tribe; whereupon he contrived how he might distress their city. Now at the season of vintage, the people were afraid to go out and gather their fruits, for fear Abimelech should do them some mischief. Now it happened that there had come to them a man of authority, one Gaal, that sojourned with them, having his armed men and his kinsmen with him; so the Shechemites desired that he would allow them a guard during their vintage; whereupon he accepted of their desires, and so the people went out, and Gaal with them at the head of his soldiery. So they gathered their fruit with safety; and when they were at supper in several companies, they then ventured to curse Abimelech openly; and the magistrates laid ambushes in places about the city, and caught many of Abimelech's followers, and destroyed them.

4. Now there was one Zebul, a magistrate of the Shechemites, that had entertained Abimelech. He sent messengers, and informed him how much Gaal had irritated the people against him, and excited him to lay ambushes before the city, for that he would persuade Gaal to go out against him, which would leave it in his power to be revenged on him; and when that was once done, he would bring him to be reconciled to the city. So Abimelech laid ambushes, and himself lay with them. Now Gaal abode in the suburbs, taking little care of himself; and Zebul was with him. Now as Gaal saw the armed men coming on, he said to Zebul, That some armed men were coming; but the other replied, They were only shadows of huge stones: and when they were come nearer, Gaal perceived what was the reality, and said, They were not shadows, but men lying in ambush. Then said Zebul, "Didst not thou reproach Abimelech for cowardice? why dost thou not then show how very courageous thou art thyself, and go and fight him?" So Gaal, being in disorder, joined battle with Abimelech, and some of his men fell; whereupon he fled into the city, and took his men with him. But Zebul managed his matters so in the city, that he procured them to expel Gaal out of the city, and this by accusing him of cowardice in this action with the soldiers of Ahimelech. But Abimelech, when he had learned that the Shechemites were again coming out to gather their grapes, placed ambushes before the city, and when they were coming out, the third part of his army took possession of the gates, to hinder the citizens from returning in again, while the rest pursued those that were scattered abroad, and so there was slaughter every where; and when he had overthrown the city to the very foundations, for it was not able to bear a siege, and had sown its ruins with salt, he proceeded on with his army till all the Shechemites were slain. As for those that were scattered about the country, and so escaped the danger, they were gathered together unto a certain strong rock, and settled themselves upon it, and prepared to build a wall about it: and when Abimelech knew their intentions, he prevented them, and came upon them with his forces, and laid faggots of dry wood round the place, he himself bringing some of them, and by his example encouraging the soldiers to do the same. And when the rock was encompassed round about with these faggots, they set them on fire, and threw in whatsoever by nature caught fire the most easily: so a mighty flame was raised, and nobody could fly away from the rock, but every man perished, with

their wives and children, in all about fifteen hundred men, and the rest were a great number also. And such was the calamity which fell upon the Shechemites; and men's grief on their account had been greater than it was, had they not brought so much mischief on a person who had so well deserved of them, and had they not themselves esteemed this as a punishment for the same.

5. Now Abimelech, when he had aftrighted the Israelites with the miseries he had brought upon the Shechemites, seemed openly to affect greater authority than he now had, and appeared to set no bounds to his violence, unless it were with the destruction of all. Accordingly he marched to Thebes, and took the city on the sudden; and there being a great tower therein, whereunto the whole multitude fled, he made preparation to besiege it. Now as he was rushing with violence near the gates, a woman threw a piece of a millstone upon his head, upon which Abimelech fell down, and desired his armorbearer to kill him lest his death should be thought to be the work of a woman:—who did what he was bid to do. So he underwent this death as a punishment for the wickedness he had perpetrated against his brethren, and his insolent barbarity to the Shechemites. Now the calamity that happened to those Shechemites was according to the prediction of Jotham, However, the army that was with Abimelech, upon his fall, was scattered abroad, and went to their own homes.

6. Now it was that Jair the Gileadite,[16] of the tribe of Manasseh, took the government. He was a man happy in other respects also, but particularly in his children, who were of a good character. They were thirty in number, and very skillful in riding on horses, and were intrusted with the government of the cities of Gilead. He kept the government twenty-two years, and died an old man; and he was buried in Camon, a city of Gilead.

7. And now all the affairs of the Hebrews were managed uncertainly, and tended to disorder, and to the contempt of God and of the laws. So the Ammonites and Philistines had them in contempt, and

16. Our present copies of Josephus all omit Tola among the judges, though the other copies have him next after Abimelech, and allot twenty-three years to his administration, Judges 10:1, 2; yet do all Josephus's commentators conclude, that in Josephus's sum of the years of the judges, his twenty-three years are included; hence we are to confess, that somewhat has been here lost out of his copies.

laid waste the country with a great army; and when they had taken all Perea, they were so insolent as to attempt to gain the possession of all the rest. But the Hebrews, being now amended by the calamities they had undergone, betook themselves to supplications to God; and brought sacrifices to him, beseeching him not to be too severe upon them, but to be moved by their prayers to leave off his anger against them. So God became more merciful to them, and was ready to assist them.

8. When the Ammonites had made an expedition into the land of Gilead, the inhabitants of the country met them at a certain mountain, but wanted a commander. Now there was one whose name was Jephtha, who, both on account of his father's virtue, and on account of that army which he maintained at his own expenses, was a potent man: the Israelites therefore sent to him, and entreated him to come to their assistance, and promised him the dominion over them all his lifetime. But he did not admit of their entreaty; and accused them, that they did not come to his assistance when he was unjustly treated, and this in an open manner by his brethren; for they cast him off, as not having the same mother with the rest, but born of a strange mother, that was introduced among them by his father's fondness; and this they did out of a contempt of his inability [to vindicate himself]. So he dwelt in the country of Gilead, as it is called, and received all that came to him, let them come from what place soever, and paid them wages. However, when they pressed him to accept the dominion, and sware they would grant him the government over them all his life, he led them to the war.

9. And when Jephtha had taken immediate care of their affairs, he placed his army at the city Mizpeh, and sent a message to the Ammonite [king], complaining of his unjust possession of their land. But that king sent a contrary message; and complained of the exodus of the Israelites out of Egypt, and desired him to go out of the land of the Amorites, and yield it up to him, as at first his paternal inheritance. But Jephtha returned this answer: That he did not justly complain of his ancestors about the land of the Amorites, and ought rather to thank them that they left the land of the Ammonites to them, since Moses could have taken it also; and that neither would he recede from that land of their own, which God had obtained for them, and they

had now inhabited [above] three hundred years, but would fight with them about it.

10. And when he had given them this answer, he sent the ambassadors away. And when he had prayed for victory, and had vowed to perform sacred offices, and if he came home in safety, to offer in sacrifice what living creature soever should first meet him,[17] he joined battle with the enemy, and gained a great victory, and in his pursuit slew the enemies all along as far as the city of Minnith. He then passed over to the land of the Ammonites, and overthrew many of their cities, and took their prey, and freed his own people from that slavery which they had undergone for eighteen years. But as he came back, he fell into a calamity no way correspondent to the great actions he had done; for it was his daughter that came to meet him; she was also an only child and a virgin: upon this Jephtha heavily lamented the greatness of his affliction, and blamed his daughter for being so forward in meeting him, for he had vowed to sacrifice her to God. However, this action that was to befall her was not ungrateful to her, since she should die upon occasion of her father's victory, and the liberty of her fellow citizens: she only desired her father to give her leave, for two months, to bewail her youth with her fellow citizens; and then she agreed, that at the forementioned thee he might do with her according to his vow. Accordingly, when that time was over, he sacrificed his daughter as a burnt-offering, offering such an oblation as was neither conformable to the law nor acceptable to God, not weighing with himself what opinion the hearers would have of such a practice.

11. Now the tribe of Ephraim fought against him, because he did not take them along with him in his expedition against the Ammonites, but because he alone had the prey, and the glory of what was done to himself. As to which he said, first, that they were not ignorant how his kindred had fought against him, and that when they were invited, they did not come to his assistance, whereas they ought to have come

17. Josephus justly condemns Jephtha, as do the Apostolical Constitutions, B. VII. ch. 37., for his rash vow, whether it were for sacrificing his daughter, as Josephus thought, or for dedicating her, who was his only child, to perpetual virginity, at the tabernacle or elsewhere, which I rather suppose. If he had vowed her for a sacrifice, she ought to have been redeemed, Leviticus 27:1–8; but of the sense of ver. 28, 29, as relating not to things vowed to. God, but devoted to destruction, see the note on Antiq. B. V. ch. 1. sect. 8.

quickly, even before they were invited. And in the next place, that they were going to act unjustly; for while they had not courage enough to fight their enemies, they came hastily against their own kindred: and he threatened them that, with God's assistance, he would inflict a punishment upon them, unless they would grow wiser. But when he could not persuade them, he fought with them with those forces which he sent for out of Gilead, and he made a great slaughter among them; and when they were beaten, he pursued them, and seized on the passages of Jordan by a part of his army which he had sent before, and slew about forty-two thousand of them.

12. So when Jephtha had ruled six years, he died, and was buried in his own country, Sebee, which is a place in the land of Gilead.

13. Now when Jephtha was dead, Ibzan took the government, being of the tribe of Judah, and of the city of Bethlehem. He had sixty children, thirty of them sons, and the rest daughters; all whom he left alive behind him, giving the daughters in marriage to husbands, and taking wives for his sons. He did nothing in the seven years of his administration that was worth recording, or deserved a memorial. So he died an old man, and was buried in his own country.

14. When Ibzan was dead after this manner, neither did Helon, who succeeded him in the government, and kept it ten years, do any thing remarkable: he was of the tribe of Zebulon.

15. Abdon also, the son of Hilel, of the tribe of Ephraim, and born at the city Pyrathon, was ordained their supreme governor after Helon. He is only recorded to have been happy in his children; for the public affairs were then so peaceable, and in such security, that neither did he perform any glorious action. He had forty sons, and by them left thirty grandchildren; and he marched in state with these seventy, who were all very skillful in riding horses; and he left them all alive after him. He died an old man, and obtained a magnificent burial in Pyrathon.

8 Concerning the Fortitude of Samson, and What Mischiefs He Brought Upon the Philistines

1. AFTER Abdon was dead, the Philistines overcame the Israelites, and received tribute of them for forty years; from which distress they were delivered after this manner:—2. There was one Manoah, a person of

such great virtue, that he had few men his equals, and without dispute the principal person of his country. He had a wife celebrated for her beauty, and excelling her contemporaries. He had no children; and, being uneasy at his want of posterity, he entreated God to give them seed of their own bodies to succeed them; and with that intent he came constantly into the suburbs[18] together with his wife; which suburbs were in the Great Plain. Now he was fond of his wife to a degree of madness, and on that account was unmeasurably jealous of her. Now, when his wife was once alone, an apparition was seen by her: it was an angel of God, and resembled a young man beautiful and tall, and brought her the good news that she should have a son, born by God's providence, that should be a goodly child, of great strength; by whom, when he was grown up to man's estate, the Philistines should be afflicted. He exhorted her also not to poll his hair, and that he should avoid all other kinds of drink, (for so had God commanded,) and be entirely contented with water. So the angel, when he had delivered that message, went his way, his coming having been by the will of God.

3. Now the wife informed her husband when he came home of what the angel had said, who showed so great an admiration of the beauty and tallness of the young man that had appeared to her, that her husband was astonished, and out of himself for jealousy, and such suspicions as are excited by that passion: but she was desirous of having her husband's unreasonable sorrow taken away; accordingly she entreated God to send the angel again, that he might be seen by her husband. So the angel came again by the favor of God, while they were in the suburbs, and appeared to her when she was alone without her husband. She desired the angel to stay so long till she might bring her husband; and that request being granted, she goes to call Manoah. When he saw the angel he was not yet free from suspicion, and he desired him to inform him of all that he had told his wife; but when he said it was sufficient that she alone knew what he had said, he then requested of him to tell who he was, that when the child was born they might return him thanks, and give him a present. He replied that

---

18. I can discover no reason why Manoah and his wife came so constantly into these suburbs to pray for children, but because there was a synagogue or place of devotion in those suburbs.

he did not want any present, for that he did not bring them the good news of the birth of a son out of the want of any thing. And when Manoah had entreated him to stay, and partake of his hospitality, he did not give his consent. However he was persuaded, at the earnest request of Manoah to stay so long as while he brought him one mark of his hospitality; so he slew a kid of the goats, and bid his wife boil it. When all was ready, the angel enjoined him to set the loaves and the flesh, but without the vessels, upon the rock; which when they had done, he touched the flesh with the rod which he had in his hand, which, upon the breaking out of a flame, was consumed, together with the loaves; and the angel ascended openly, in their sight, up to heaven, by means of the smoke, as by a vehicle. Now Manoah was afraid that some danger would come to them from this sight of God; but his wife bade him be of good courage, for that God appeared to them for their benefit.

4. So the woman proved with child, and was careful to observe the injunctions that were given her; and they called the child, when he was born, Samson, which name signifies one that is *strong*. So the child grew apace; and it appeared evidently that he would be a prophet,[19] both by the moderation of his diet, and the permission of his hair to grow.

5. Now when he once came with his parents to Timhath, a city of the Philistines, when there was a great festival, he fell in love with a maid of that country, and he desired of his parents that they would procure him the damsel for his wife: but they refused so to do, because she was not of the stock of Israel; yet because this marriage was of God, who intended to convert it to the benefit of the Hebrews, he over-persuaded them to procure her to be espoused to him. And as he was continually coming to her parents, he met a lion, and though he was naked, he received his onset, and strangled him with his hands, and cast the wild beast into a woody piece of ground on the inside of the road.

6. And when he was going another time to the damsel, he lit upon a swarm of bees making their combs in the breast of that lion; and taking

---

19. Here, by a prophet, Josephus seems only to mean one that was born by a particular providence, lived after the manner of a Nazarite devoted to God, and was to have an extraordinary commission and strength from God for the judging and avenging his people Israel, without any proper prophetic revelations at all.

three honey-combs away, he gave them, together with the rest of his presents, to the damsel. Now the people of Timhath, out of a dread of the young man's strength, gave him during the time of the wedding-feast (for he then feasted them all) thirty of the most stout of their youth, in pretense to be his companions, but in reality to be a guard upon him, that he might not attempt to give them any disturbance. Now as they were drinking merrily and playing, Samson said, as was usual at such times, Come, if I propose you a riddle, and you can expound it in these seven days' thee, I will give you every one a linen shirt and a garment, as the reward of your wisdom." So they being very ambitious to obtain the glory of wisdom, together with the gains, desired him to propose his riddle. He, "That a devourer produced sweet food out of itself, though itself were very disagreeable." And when they were not able, in three days' time, to find out the meaning of the riddle, they desired the damsel to discover it by the means of her husband, and tell it them; and they threatened to burn her if she did not tell it them. So when the damsel entreated Samson to tell it her, he at first refused to do it; but when she lay hard at him, and fell into tears, and made his refusal to tell it a sign of his unkindness to her, he informed her of his slaughter of a lion, and how he found bees in his breast, and carried away three honey-combs, and brought them to her. Thus he, suspecting nothing of deceit, informed her of all, and she revealed it to those that desired to know it. Then on the seventh day, whereon they were to expound the riddle proposed to them, they met together before sun-setting, and said, "Nothing is more disagreeable than a lion to those that light on it, and nothing is sweeter than honey to those that make use of it." To which Samson made this rejoinder: "Nothing is more deceitful than a woman for such was the person that discovered my interpretation to you." Accordingly he gave them the presents he had promised them, making such Askelonites as met him upon the road his prey, who were themselves Philistines also. But he divorced this his wife; and the girl despised his anger, and was married to his companion, who made the former match between them.

7. At this injurious treatment Samson was so provoked, that he resolved to punish all the Philistines, as well as her: so it being then summer-time, and the fruits of the land being almost ripe enough for reaping, he caught three hundred foxes, and joining lighted torches to their tails, he sent them into the fields of the Philistines, by which

means the fruits of the fields perished. Now when the Philistines knew that this was Samson's doing, and knew also for what cause he did it, they sent their rulers to Timhath, and burnt his former wife, and her relations, who had been the occasion of their misfortunes.

8. Now when Samson had slain many of the Philistines in the plain country, he dwelt at Etam, which is a strong rock of the tribe of Judah; for the Philistines at that time made an expedition against that tribe: but the people of Judah said that they did not act justly with them, in inflicting punishments upon them while they paid their tribute, and this only on account of Samson's offenses. They answered, that in case they would not be blamed themselves, they must deliver up Samson, and put him into their power. So they being desirous not to be blamed themselves, came to the rock with three thousand armed men, and complained to Samson of the bold insults he had made upon the Philistines, who were men able to bring calamity upon the whole nation of the Hebrews; and they told him they were come to take him, and to deliver him up to them, and put him into their power; so they desired him to bear this willingly. Accordingly, when he had received assurance from them upon oath, that they would do him no other harm than only to deliver him into his enemies' hands, he came down from the rock, and put himself into the power of his countrymen. Then did they bind him with two cords, and lead him on, in order to deliver him to the Philistines; and when they came to a certain place, which is now called *the Jaw-bone,* on account of the great action there performed by Samson, though of old it had no particular name at all, the Philistines, who had pitched their camp not far off, came to meet them with joy and shouting, as having done a great thing, and gained what they desired; but Samson broke his bonds asunder, and catching up the jaw-bone of an ass that lay down at his feet, fell upon his enemies, and smiting them with his jaw-bone, slew a thousand of them, and put the rest to flight and into great disorder.

9. Upon this slaughter Samson was too proud of what he had performed, and said that this did not come to pass by the assistance of God, but that his success was to be ascribed to his own courage; and vaunted himself, that it was out of a dread of him that some of his enemies fell and the rest ran away upon his use of the jaw-bone; but when a great thirst came upon him, he considered that human courage is nothing, and bare his testimony that all is to be ascribed to God, and

besought him that he would not be angry at any thing he had said, nor give him up into the hands of his enemies, but afford him help under his affliction, and deliver him from the misfortune he was under. Accordingly God was moved with his entreaties, and raised him up a plentiful fountain of sweet water at a certain rock whence it was that Samson called the place the *Jaw-bone*,[20] and so it is called to this day.

10. After this fight Samson held the Philistines in contempt, and came to Gaza, and took up his lodgings in a certain inn. When the rulers of Gaza were informed of his coming thither, they seized upon the gates, and placed men in ambush about them, that he might not escape without being perceived; but Samson, who was acquainted with their contrivances against him, arose about midnight, and ran by force upon the gates, with their posts and beams, and the rest of their wooden furniture, and carried them away on his shoulders, and bare them to the mountain that is over Hebron, and there laid them down.

11. However, he at length[21] transgressed the laws of his country, and altered his own regular way of living, and imitated the strange customs of foreigners, which thing was the beginning of his miseries; for he fell in love with a woman that was a harlot among the Philistines: her name was Delilah, and he lived with her. So those that administered the public affairs of the Philistines came to her, and, with promises, induced her to get out of Samson what was the cause of that his strength, by which he became unconquerable to his enemies. Accordingly, when they were drinking, and had the like conversation together, she pretended to admire the actions he had done, and contrived to get out of him by subtlety, by what means he so much excelled others in strength. Samson, in order to delude Delilah, for he had not yet lost his senses, replied, that if he were bound with seven such green withs of a vine as might still be wreathed, he should be weaker than any other man. The woman said no more then, but told this to the rulers of the Philistines, and hid certain of the soldiers in ambush within the house; and when he was disordered in drink

---

20. This fountain, called Lehi, or the Jaw-bone, is still in being, as travelers assure us, and was known by this very name in the days of Josephus, and has been known by the same name in all those past ages. See Antiq. B. VII. ch. 12. sect. 4.

21. See this justly observed in the Apostolical Constitutions, B. VII. ch. 37., that Samson's prayer was heard, but that it was before this his transgression.

and asleep, she bound him as fast as possible with the withs; and then upon her awakening him, she told him some of the people were upon him; but he broke the withs, and endeavored to defend himself, as though some of the people were upon him. Now this woman, in the constant conversation Samson had with her, pretended that she took it very ill that he had such little confidence in her affections to him, that he would not tell her what she desired, as if she would not conceal what she knew it was for his interest to have concealed. However, he deluded her again, and told her, that if they bound him with seven cords, he should lose his strength. And when, upon doing this, she gained nothing, he told her the third thee, that his hair should be woven into a web; but when, upon doing this, the truth was not yet discovered, at length Samson, upon Delilah's prayer, (for he was doomed to fall into some affliction,) was desirous to please her, and told her that God took care of him, and that he was born by his providence, and that "thence it is that I suffer my hair to grow, God having charged me never to poll my head, and thence my strength is according to the increase and continuance of my hair." When she had learned thus much, and had deprived him of his hair, she delivered him up to his enemies, when he was not strong enough to defend himself from their attempts upon him; so they put out his eyes, and bound him, and had him led about among them.

12. But in process of time Samson's hair grew again. And there was a public festival among the Philistines, when the rulers, and those of the most eminent character, were feasting together; (now the room wherein they were had its roof supported by two pillars;) so they sent for Samson, and he was brought to their feast, that they might insult him in their cups. Hereupon he, thinking it one of the greatest misfortunes, if he should not be able to revenge himself when he was thus insulted, persuaded the boy that led him by the hand, that he was weary and wanted to rest himself, and desired he would bring him near the pillars; and as soon as he came to them, he rushed with force against them, and overthrew the house, by overthrowing its pillars, with three thousand men in it, who were all slain, and Samson with them. And such was the end of this man, when he had ruled over the Israelites twenty years. And indeed this man deserves to be admired for his courage and strength, and magnanimity at his death, and that his wrath against his enemies went so far as to die himself with them.

But as for his being ensnared by a woman, that is to be ascribed to human nature, which is too weak to resist the temptations to that sin; but we ought to bear him witness, that in all other respects he was one of extraordinary virtue. But his kindred took away his body, and buried it in Sarasat his own country, with the rest of his family.

9 How under Eli's Government of the Israelites Booz Married Ruth, from Whom Came Obed the Grandfather of David

1. NOW after the death of Samson, Eli the high priest was governor of the Israelites. Under him, when the country was afflicted with a famine, Elimelech of Bethlehem, which is a city of the tribe of Judah, being not able to support his family under so sore a distress, took with him Naomi his wife, and the children that were born to him by her, Chillon and Mahlon, and removed his habitation into the land of Moab; and upon the happy prosperity of his affairs there, he took for his sons wives of the Moabites, Orpah for Chillon, and Ruth for Mahlon. But in the compass of ten years, both Elimelech, and a little while after him, the sons, died; and Naomi being very uneasy at these accidents, and not being able to bear her lonesome condition, now those that were dearest to her were dead, on whose account it was that she had gone away from her own country, she returned to it again, for she had been informed it was now in a flourishing condition. However, her daughters-in-law were not able to think of parting with her; and when they had a mind to go out of the country with her, she could not dissuade them from it; but when they insisted upon it, she wished them a more happy wedlock than they had with her sons, and that they might have prosperity in other respects also; and seeing her own affairs were so low, she exhorted them to stay where they were, and not to think of leaving their own country, and partaking with her of that uncertainty under which she must return. Accordingly Orpah staid behind; but she took Ruth along with her, as not to be persuaded to stay behind her, but would take her fortune with her, whatsoever it should prove.

2. When Ruth was come with her mother-in-law to Bethlehem, Booz, who was near of kin to Elimelech, entertained her; and when Naomi was so called by her fellow citizens, according to her true name,

she said, "You might more truly call me *Mara.*" Now Naomi signifies in the Hebrew tongue *happiness,* and Mara, *sorrow.* It was now reaping thee; and Ruth, by the leave of her mother-in-law, went out to glean, that they might get a stock of corn for their food. Now it happened that she came into Booz's field; and after some thee Booz came thither, and when he saw the damsel, he inquired of his servant that was set over the reapers concerning the girl. The servant had a little before inquired about all her circumstances, and told them to his master, who kindly embraced her, both on account of her affection to her mother-in-law, and her remembrance of that son of hers to whom she had been married, and wished that she might experience a prosperous condition; so he desired her not to glean, but to reap what she was able, and gave her leave to carry it home. He also gave it in charge to that servant who was over the reapers, not to hinder her when she took it away, and bade him give her her dinner, and make her drink when he did the like to the reapers. Now what corn Ruth received of him she kept for her mother-in-law, and came to her in the evening, and brought the ears of corn with her; and Naomi had kept for her a part of such food as her neighbors had plentifully bestowed upon her. Ruth also told her mother-in-law what Booz had said to her; and when the other had informed her that he was near of kin to them, and perhaps was so pious a man as to make some provision for them, she went out again on the days following, to gather the gleanings with Booz's maidservants.

3. It was not many days before Booz, after the barley was winnowed, slept in his thrashing-floor. When Naomi was informed of this circumstance she contrived it so that Ruth should lie down by him, for she thought it might be for their advantage that he should discourse with the girl. Accordingly she sent the damsel to sleep at his feet; who went as she bade her, for she did not think it consistent with her duty to contradict any command of her mother-in-law. And at first she lay concealed from Booz, as he was fast asleep; but when he awaked about midnight, and perceived a woman lying by him, he asked who she was;—and when she told him her name, and desired that he whom she owned for her lord would excuse her, he then said no more; but in the morning, before the servants began to set about their work, he awaked her, and bid her take as much barley as she was able to carry, and go to her mother-in-law before any body there should see that

she had lain down by him, because it was but prudent to avoid any reproach that might arise on that account, especially when there had been nothing done that was ill. But as to the main point she aimed at, the matter should rest here,—"He that is nearer of kin than I am, shall be asked whether he wants to take thee to wife: if he says he does, thou shalt follow him; but if he refuse it, I will marry thee, according to the law."

4. When she had informed her mother-in-law of this, they were very glad of it, out of the hope they had that Booz would make provision for them. Now about noon Booz went down into the city, and gathered the senate together, and when he had sent for Ruth, he called for her kinsman also; and when he was come, he said, "Dost not thou retain the inheritance of Elimelech and his sons?" He confessed that he did retain it, and that he did as he was permitted to do by the laws, because he was their nearest kinsman. Then said Booz, "Thou must not remember the laws by halves, but do every thing according to them; for the wife of Mahlon is come hither, whom thou must marry, according to the law, in case thou wilt retain their fields." So the man yielded up both the field and the wife to Booz, who was himself of kin to those that were dead, as alleging that he had a wife already, and children also; so Booz called the senate to witness, and bid the woman to loose his shoe, and spit in his face, according to the law; and when this was done, Booz married Ruth, and they had a son within a year's time. Naomi was herself a nurse to this child; and by the advice of the women, called him *Obed,* as being to be brought up in order to be subservient to her in her old age, for Obed in the Hebrew dialect signifies a *servant.* The son of Obed was Jesse, and David was his son, who was king, and left his dominions to his sons for one and twenty generations. I was therefore obliged to relate this history of Ruth, because I had a mind to demonstrate the power of God, who, without difficulty, can raise those that are of ordinary parentage to dignity and splendor, to which he advanced David, though he were born of such mean parents.

10 *Concerning the Birth of Samuel; and How He Foretold the Calamity That Befell the Sons of Eli*

1. AND now upon the ill state of the affairs of the Hebrews, they made war again upon the Philistines. The occasion was this: Eli, the high priest, had two sons, Hophni and Phineas. These sons of Eli were guilty of injustice towards men, and of impiety towards God, and abstained from no sort of wickedness. Some of their gifts they carried off, as belonging to the honorable employment they had; others of them they took away by violence. They also were guilty of impurity with the women that came to worship God at the tabernacle, obliging some to submit to their lust by force, and enticing others by bribes; nay, the whole course of their lives was no better than tyranny. Their father therefore was angry at them for such their wickedness, and expected that God would suddenly inflict his punishments upon them for what they had done. The multitude took it heinously also. And as soon as God had foretold what calamity would befall Eli's sons, which he did both to Eli himself and to Samuel the prophet, who was yet but a child, he openly showed his sorrow for his sons' destruction.

2. I will first despatch what I have to say about the prophet Samuel, and after that will proceed to speak of the sons of Eli, and the miseries they brought on the whole people of the Hebrews. Elcanah, a Levite, one of a middle condition among his fellow citizens, and one that dwelt at Ramathaim, a city of the tribe of Ephraim, married two wives, Hannah and Peninnah. He had children by the latter; but he loved the other best, although she was barren. Now Elcanah came with his wives to the city Shiloh to sacrifice, for there it was that the tabernacle of God was fixed, as we have formerly said. Now when, after he had sacrificed, he distributed at that festival portions of the flesh to his wives and children, and when Hannah saw the other wife's children sitting round about their mother, she fell into tears, and lamented herself on account of her barrenness and lonesomeness; and suffering her grief to prevail over her husband's consolations to her, she went to the tabernacle to beseech God to give her seed, and to make her a mother; and to vow to consecrate the first son she should bear to the service of God, and this in such a way, that his manner of living should not be like that of ordinary men. And as she continued at her prayers a long time, Eli, the high priest, for he sat there before the tabernacle, bid

her go away, thinking she had been disordered with wine; but when she said she had drank water, but was in sorrow for want of children, and was beseeching God for them, he bid her be of good cheer, and told her that God would send her children.

3. So she came to her husband full of hope, and ate her meal with gladness. And when they had returned to their own country she found herself with child, and they had a son born to them, to whom they gave the name of Samuel, which may be styled one that was *asked of God*. They therefore came to the tabernacle to offer sacrifice for the birth of the child, and brought their tithes with them; but the woman remembered the vows she had made concerning her son, and delivered him to Eli, dedicating him to God, that he might become a prophet. Accordingly his hair was suffered to grow long, and his drink was water. So Samuel dwelt and was brought up in the temple. But Elcanah had other sons by Hannah, and three daughters.

4. Now when Samuel was twelve years old, he began to prophesy: and once when he was asleep, God called to him by his name; and he, supposing he had been called by the high priest, came to him: but when the high priest said he did not call him, God did so thrice. Eli was then so far illuminated, that he said to him, "Indeed, Samuel, I was silent now as well as before: it is God that calls thee; do thou therefore signify it to him, and say, I am here ready." So when he heard God speak again, he desired him to speak, and to deliver what oracles he pleased to him, for he would not fail to perform any ministration whatsoever he should make use of him in;—to which God replied, "Since thou art here ready, learn what miseries are coming upon the Israelites,—such indeed as words cannot declare, nor faith believe; for the sons of Eli shall die on one day, and the priesthood shall be transferred into the family of Eleazar; for Eli hath loved his sons more than he hath loved my worship, and to such a degree as is not for their advantage." Which message Eli obliged the prophet by oath to tell him, for otherwise he had no inclination to afflict him by telling it. And now Eli had a far more sure expectation of the perdition of his sons; but the glory of Samuel increased more and more, it being found by experience that whatsoever he prophesied came to pass accordingly.[22]

---

22. Although there had been a few occasional prophets before, yet was this Samuel

11   Herein Is Declared What Befell the Sons of Eli, the Ark, and the People and How Eli Himself Died Miserably

1. ABOUT this time it was that the Philistines made war against the Israelites, and pitched their camp at the city Aphek. Now when the Israelites had expected them a little while, the very next day they joined battle, and the Philistines were conquerors, and slew above four thousand of the Hebrews, and pursued the rest of their multitude to their camp.

2. So the Hebrews being afraid of the worst, sent to the senate, and to the high priest, and desired that they would bring the ark of God, that by putting themselves in array, when it was present with them, they might be too hard for their enemies, as not reflecting that he who had condemned them to endure these calamities was greater than the ark, and for whose sake it was that this ark came to be honored. So the ark came, and the sons of the high priest with it, having received a charge from their father, that if they pretended to survive the taking of the ark, they should come no more into his presence, for Phineas officiated already as high priest, his father having resigned his office to him, by reason of his great age. So the Hebrews were full of courage, as supposing that, by the coming of the ark, they should be too hard for their enemies: their enemies also were greatly concerned, and were afraid of the ark's coming to the Israelites: however, the upshot did not prove agreeable to the expectation of both sides, but when the battle was joined, that victory which the Hebrews expected was gained by the Philistines, and that defeat the Philistines were afraid of fell to the lot of the Israelites, and thereby they found that they had put their trust in the ark in vain, for they were presently beaten as soon as they came to a close fight with their enemies, and lost about thirty thousand men, among whom were the sons of the high priest; but the ark was carried away by the enemies.

---

the first of a constant succession of prophets in the Jewish nation, as is implied in St. Peter's words, Acts 3:24 "Yea, and all the prophets, from Samuel, and those that follow after, as many as have spoken, have likewise foretold of those days." See also Acts 13:20. The others were rather sometime called righteous men, Matthew 10:41; 13:17.

Bact To The Table Of Contents

3. When the news of this defeat came to Shiloh, with that of the captivity of the ark, (for a certain young man, a Benjamite, who was in the action, came as a messenger thither,) the whole city was full of lamentations. And Eli, the high priest, who sat upon a high throne at one of the gates, heard their mournful cries, and supposed that some strange thing had befallen his family. So he sent for the young man; and when he understood what had happened in the battle, he was not much uneasy as to his sons, or what was told him withal about the army, as having beforehand known by Divine revelation that those things would happen, and having himself declared them beforehand,—for what sad things come unexpectedly they distress men the most; but as soon as [he heard] the ark was carried captive by their enemies, he was very much grieved at it, because it fell out quite differently from what he expected; so he fell down from his throne and died, having in all lived ninety-eight years, and of them retained the government forty.

4. On the same day his son Phineas's wife died also, as not able to survive the misfortune of her husband; for they told her of her husband's death as she was in labor. However, she bare a son at seven months, who lived, and to whom they gave the name of Icabod, which name signifies *disgrace*,—and this because the army received a disgrace at this thee.

5. Now Eli was the first of the family of Ithamar, the other son of Aaron, that had the government; for the family of Eleazar officiated as high priest at first, the son still receiving that honor from the father which Eleazar bequeathed to his son Phineas; after whom Abiezer his son took the honor, and delivered it to his son, whose name was Bukki, from whom his son Ozi received it; after whom Eli, of whom we have been speaking, had the priesthood, and so he and his posterity until the thee of Solomon's reign; but then the posterity of Eleazar reassumed it.

Book 6

Containing the Interval of Thirty-Two Years, from the Death of Eli to the Death of Saul

1   The Destruction That Came Upon the Philistines, and Upon Their Land, by the Wrath of Go on Account of Their Having Carried the Ark Away Captive; and After What Manner They Sent It Back to the Hebrews

1. WHEN the Philistines had taken the ark of the Hebrews captive, as I said a little before, they carried it to the city of Ashdod, and put it by their own god, who was called Dagon,[1] as one of their spoils; but when they went into his temple the next morning to worship their god, they found him paying the same worship to the ark, for he lay along, as having fallen down from the basis whereon he had stood: so they took him up, and set him on his basis again, and were much troubled at what had happened; and as they frequently came to Dagon and found him still lying along, in a posture of adoration to the ark, they were in very great distress and confusion. At length God sent a very destructive disease upon the city and country of Ashdod, for they died of the dysentery or flux, a sore distemper, that brought death upon them very suddenly; for before the soul could, as usual in easy deaths, be well loosed from the body, they brought up their entrails,

---

1. Dagon, a famous maritime god or idol, is generally supposed to have been like a man above the navel, and like a fish beneath it.

and vomited up what they had eaten, and what was entirely corrupted by the disease. And as to the fruits of their country, a great multitude of mice arose out of the earth and hurt them, and spared neither the plants nor the fruits. Now while the people of Ashdod were under these misfortunes, and were not able to support themselves under their calamities, they perceived that they suffered thus because of the ark, and that the victory they had gotten, and their having taken the ark captive, had not happened for their good; they therefore sent to the people of Askelon, and desired that they would receive the ark among them. This desire of the people of Ashdod was not disagreeable to those of Askelon, so they granted them that favor. But when they had gotten the ark, they were in the same miserable condition; for the ark carried along with it the disasters that the people of Ashdod had suffered, to those who received it from them. Those of Askelon also sent it away from themselves to others: nor did it stay among those others neither; for since they were pursued by the same disasters, they still sent it to the neighboring cities; so that the ark went round, after this manner, to the five cities of the Philistines, as though it exacted these disasters as a tribute to be paid it for its coming among them.

2. When those that had experienced these miseries were tired out with them, and when those that heard of them were taught thereby not to admit the ark among them, since they paid so dear a tribute for it, at length they sought for some contrivance and method how they might get free from it: so the governors of the five cities, Gath, and Ekron, and Askelon, as also of Gaza, and Ashclod, met together, and considered what was fit to be done; and at first they thought proper to send the ark back to its own people, as allowing that God had avenged its cause; that the miseries they had undergone came along with it, and that these were sent on their cities upon its account, and together with it. However, there were those that said they should not do so, nor suffer themselves to be deluded, as ascribing the cause of their miseries to it, because it could not have such power and force upon them; for, had God had such a regard to it, it would not have been delivered into the hands of men. So they exhorted them to be quiet, and to take patiently what had befallen them, and to suppose there was no other cause of it but nature, which, at certain revolutions of time, produces such mutations in the bodies of men, in the earth, in plants, and in all things that grow out of the earth. But the counsel that prevailed over those

already described, was that of certain men, who were believed to have distinguished themselves in former times for their understanding and prudence, and who, in their present circumstances, seemed above all the rest to speak properly. These men said it was not right either to send the ark away, or to retain it, but to dedicate five golden images, one for every city, as a thank-offering to God, on account of his having taken care of their preservation, and having kept them alive when their lives were likely to be taken away by such distempers as they were not able to bear up against. They also would have them make five golden mice like to those that devoured and destroyed their country[2] to put them in a bag, and lay them upon the ark; to make them a new cart also for it, and to yoke milch kine to it[3] but to shut up their calves, and keep them from them, lest, by following after them, they should prove a hinderance to their dams, and that the dams might return the faster out of a desire of those calves; then to drive these milch kine that carried the ark, and leave it at a place where three ways met, and So leave it to the kine to go along which of those ways they pleased; that in case they went the way to the Hebrews, and ascended to their country, they should suppose that the ark was the cause of their misfortunes; but if they turned into another road, they said, "We will pursue after it, and conclude that it has no such force in it."

3. So they determined that these men spake well; and they immediately confirmed their opinion by doing accordingly. And when they had done as has been already described, they brought the cart to a place where three ways met, and left it there and went their ways; but the kine went the right way, and as if some persons had driven them, while the rulers of the Philistines followed after them, as desirous to

---

2. Spanheim informs us here, that upon the coins of Tenedos, and those of other cities, a field-mouse is engraven, together with Apollo Smintheus, or Apollo, the driver away of field-mice, on account of his being supposed to have freed certain tracts of ground from those mice; which coins show how great a judgment such mice have sometimes been, and how the deliverance from them was then esteemed the effect of a divine power; which observations are highly suitable to this history.

3. This device of the Philistines, of having a yoke of kine to draw this cart, into which they put the ark of the Hebrews, is greatly illustrated by Sanchoniatho's account, under his ninth generation, that Agrouerus, or Agrotes, the husbandman, had a much-worshipped statue and temple, carried about by one or more yoke of oxen, or kine, in Phoenicia, in the neighborhood of these Philistines. See Cumberland's Sanchoniatho, p. 27 and 247; and Essay on the Old Testament, Append. p. 172.

know where they would stand still, and to whom they would go. Now there was a certain village of the tribe of Judah, the name of which was Bethshemesh, and to that village did the kine go; and though there was a great and good plain before them to proceed in, they went no farther, but stopped the cart there. This was a sight to those of that village, and they were very glad; for it being then summer-time, and all the inhabitants being then in the fields gathering in their fruits, they left off the labors of their hands for joy, as soon as they saw the ark, and ran to the cart, and taking the ark down, and the vessel that had the images in it, and the mice, they set them upon a certain rock which was in the plain; and when they had offered a splendid sacrifice to God, and feasted, they offered the cart and the kine as a burnt-offering: and when the lords of the Philistines saw this, they returned back.

4. But now it was that the wrath of God overtook them, and struck seventy persons[4] of the village of Bethshemesh dead, who, not being priests, and so not worthy to touch the ark, had approached to it. Those of that village wept for these that had thus suffered, and made such a lamentation as was naturally to be expected on so great a misfortune that was sent from God; and every one mourned for his own relation. And since they acknowledged themselves unworthy of the ark's abode with them, they sent to the public senate of the Israelites, and informed them that the ark was restored by the Philistines; which when they knew, they brought it away to Kirjathjearim, a city in the neighborhood of Bethshemesh. In this city lived one Abinadab, by birth a Levite, and who was greatly commended for his righteous and religious course of life; so they brought the ark to his house, as to a place fit for God himself to abide in, since therein did inhabit a righteous man. His sons also ministered to the Divine service at the ark, and were the principal curators of it for twenty years; for so many years it continued in Kirjathjearim, having been but four months with the Philistines.

---

4. These seventy men, being not so much as Levites, touched the ark in a rash or profane manner, and were slain by the hand of God for such their rashness and profaneness, according to the Divine threatenings, Numbers 4:15, 20; but how other copies come to add such an incredible number as fifty thousand in this one town, or small city, I know not. See Dr. Wall's Critical Notes on 1 Samuel 6:19.

2 *The Expedition of the Philistines Against the Hebrews and the Hebrews' Victory under the Conduct of Samuel the Prophet, Who Was Their General*

1. Now while the city of Kirjathjearim had the ark with them, the whole body of the people betook themselves all that time to offer prayers and sacrifices to God, and appeared greatly concerned and zealous about his worship. So Samuel the prophet, seeing how ready they were to do their duty, thought this a proper time to speak to them, while they were in this good disposition, about the recovery of their liberty, and of the blessings that accompanied the same. Accordingly he used such words to them as he thought were most likely to excite that inclination, and to persuade them to attempt it: "O you Israelites," said he, "to whom the Philistines are still grievous enemies, but to whom God begins to be gracious, it behooves you not only to be desirous of liberty, but to take the proper methods to obtain it. Nor are you to be contented with an inclination to get clear of your lords and masters, while you still do what will procure your continuance under them. Be righteous then, and cast wickedness out of your souls, and by your worship supplicate the Divine Majesty with all your hearts, and persevere in the honor you pay to him; for if you act thus, you will enjoy prosperity; you will be freed from your slavery, and will get the victory over your enemies: which blessings it is not possible you should attain, either by weapons of war, or by the strength of your bodies, or by the multitude of your assistants; for God has not promised to grant these blessings by those means, but by being good and righteous men; and if you will be such, I will be security to you for the performance of God's promises." When Samuel had said thus, the multitude applauded his discourse, and were pleased with his exhortation to them, and gave their consent to resign themselves up to do what was pleasing to God. So Samuel gathered them together to a certain city called Mizpeh, which, in the Hebrew tongue, signifies a *watch-tower*; there they drew water, and poured it out to God, and fasted all day, and betook themselves to their prayers.

2. This their assembly did not escape the notice of the Philistines: so when they had learned that so large a company had met together, they fell upon the Hebrews with a great army and mighty forces, as hoping to assault them when they did not expect it, nor were prepared for

it. This thing affrighted the Hebrews, and put them into disorder and
terror; so they came running to Samuel, and said that their souls were
sunk by their fears, and by the former defeat they had received, and
"that thence it was that we lay still, lest we should excite the power
of our enemies against us. Now while thou hast brought us hither to
offer up our prayers and sacrifices, and take oaths [to be obedient], our
enemies are making an expedition against us, while we are naked and
unarmed; wherefore we have no other hope of deliverance but that by
thy means, and by the assistance God shall afford us upon thy prayers
to him, we shall obtain deliverance from the Philistines." Hereupon
Samuel bade them be of good cheer, and promised them that God
would assist them; and taking a sucking lamb, he sacrificed it for the
multitude, and besought God to hold his protecting hand over them
when they should fight with the Philistines, and not to overlook them,
nor suffer them to come under a second misfortune. Accordingly God
hearkened to his prayers, and accepting their sacrifice with a gracious
intention, and such as was disposed to assist them, he granted them
victory and power over their enemies. Now while the altar had the
sacrifice of God upon it, and had not yet consumed it wholly by its
sacred fire, the enemy's army marched out of their camp, and was put
in order of battle, and this in hope that they should be conquerors,
since the Jews[5] were caught in distressed circumstances, as neither
having their weapons with them, nor being assembled there in order
to fight. But things so fell out, that they would hardly have been
credited though they had been foretold by anybody: for, in the first
place, God disturbed their enemies with an earthquake, and moved
the ground under them to such a degree, that he caused it to tremble,
and made them to shake, insomuch that by its trembling, he made
some unable to keep their feet, and made them fall down, and by
opening its chasms, he caused that others should be hurried down into
them; after which he caused such a noise of thunder to come among
them, and made fiery lightning shine so terribly round about them,
that it was ready to burn their faces; and he so suddenly shook their
weapons out of their hands, that he made them fly and return home

---

5. This is the first place, so far as I remember, in these Antiquities, where Josephus
begins to call his nation Jews, he having hitherto usually, if not constantly, called them
either Hebrews or Israelites. The second place soon follows; see also ch. 3. sect. 5.

naked. So Samuel with the multitude pursued them to Bethcar, a place so called; and there he set up a stone as a boundary of their victory and their enemies' flight, and called it the *Stone of Power,* as a signal of that power God had given them against their enemies.

3. So the Philistines, after this stroke, made no more expeditions against the Israelites, but lay still out of fear, and out of remembrance of what had befallen them; and what courage the Philistines had formerly against the Hebrews, that, after this victory, was transferred to the Hebrews. Samuel also made an expedition against the Philistines, and slew many of them, and entirely humbled their proud hearts, and took from them that country, which, when they were formerly conquerors in battle, they had cut off from the Jews, which was the country that extended from the borders of Gath to the city of Ekron: but the remains of the Canaanites were at this time in friendship with the Israelites.

3 *How Samuel When He Was So Infirm with Old Age That He Could Not Take Care of the Public Affairs Intrusted Them to His Sons; and How Upon the Evil Administration of the Government by Them the Multitude Were So Angry, That They Required to Have a King to Govern Them, Although Samuel Was Much Displeased Thereat*

1. BUT Samuel the prophet, when he had ordered the affairs of the people after a convenient manner, and had appointed a city for every district of them, he commanded them to come to such cities, to have the controversies that they had one with another determined in them, he himself going over those cities twice in a year, and doing them justice; and by that means he kept them in very good order for a long time.

2. But afterwards he found himself oppressed with old age, and not able to do what he used to do, so he committed the government and the care of the multitude to his sons,—the elder of whom was called Joel, and the name of the younger was Abiah. He also enjoined them to reside and judge the people, the one at the city of Bethel, and the other at Beersheba, and divided the people into districts that should be under the jurisdiction of each of them. Now these men afford us an

evident example and demonstration how some children are not of the like dispositions with their parents; but sometimes perhaps good and moderate, though born of wicked parents; and sometimes showing themselves to be wicked, though born of good parents: for these men turning aside from their father's good courses, and taking a course that was contrary to them, perverted justice for the 'filthy lucre of gifts and bribes, and made their determinations not according to truth, but according to bribery, and turned aside to luxury, and a costly way of living; so that as, in the first place, they practiced what was contrary to the will of God, so did they, in the second place, what was contrary to the will of the prophet their father, who had taken a great deal of care, and made a very careful provision that the multitude should be righteous.

3. But the people, upon these injuries offered to their former constitution and government by the prophet's sons, were very uneasy at their actions, and came running to the prophet, who then lived at the city Ramah, and informed him of the transgressions of his sons; and said, That as he was himself old already, and too infirm by that age of his to oversee their affairs in the manner he used to do, so they begged of him, and entreated him, to appoint some person to be king over them, who might rule over the nation, and avenge them of the Philistines, who ought to be punished for their former oppressions. These words greatly afflicted Samuel, on account of his innate love of justice, and his hatred to kingly government, for he was very fond of an aristocracy, as what made the men that used it of a divine and happy disposition; nor could he either think of eating or sleeping, out of his concern and torment of mind at what they had said, but all the night long did he continue awake and revolved these notions in his mind.

4. While he was thus disposed, God appeared to him, and comforted him, saying, That he ought not to be uneasy at what the multitude desired, because it was not he, but Himself whom they so insolently despised, and would not have to be alone their king; that they had been contriving these things from the very day that they came out of Egypt; that however. in no long time they would sorely repent of what they did, which repentance yet could not undo what was thus done for futurity; that they would be sufficiently rebuked for their contempt, and the ungrateful conduct they have used towards

me, and towards thy prophetic office. "So I command thee to ordain them such a one as I shall name beforehand to be their king, when thou hast first described what mischiefs kingly government will bring upon them, and openly testified before them into what a great change of affairs they are hasting."

5. When Samuel had heard this, he called the Jews early in the morning, and confessed to them that he was to ordain them a king; but he said that he was first to describe to them what would follow, what treatment they would receive from their kings, and with how many mischiefs they must struggle. "For know ye," said he, "that, in the first place, they will take your sons away from you, and they will command some of them to be drivers of their chariots, and some to be their horsemen, and the guards of their body, and others of them to be runners before them, and captains of thousands, and captains of hundreds; they will also make them their artificers, makers of armor, and of chariots, and of instruments; they will make them their husbandmen also, and the curators of their own fields, and the diggers of their own vineyards; nor will there be any thing which they will not do at their commands, as if they were slaves bought with money. They will also appoint your daughters to be confectioners, and cooks, and bakers; and these will be obliged to do all sorts of work which women slaves, that are in fear of stripes and torments, submit to. They will, besides this, take away your possessions, and bestow them upon their eunuchs, and the guards of their bodies, and will give the herds of your cattle to their own servants: and to say briefly all at once, you, and all that is yours, will be servants to your king, and will become no way superior to his slaves; and when you suffer thus, you will thereby be put in mind of what I now say. And when you repent of what you have done, you will beseech God to have mercy upon you, and to grant you a quick deliverance from your kings; but he will not accept your prayers, but will neglect you, and permit you to suffer the punishment your evil conduct has deserved."

6. But the multitude was still so foolish as to be deaf to these predictions of what would befall them; and too peevish to suffer a determination which they had injudiciously once made, to be taken out of their mind; for they could not be turned from their purpose, nor did they regard the words of Samuel, but peremptorily insisted on their resolution, and desired him to ordain them a king immediately,

and not trouble himself with fears of what would happen hereafter, for that it was necessary they should have with them one to fight their battles, and to avenge them of their enemies, and that it was no way absurd, when their neighbors were under kingly government, that they should have the same form of government also. So when Samuel saw that what he had said had not diverted them from their purpose, but that they continued resolute, he said, "Go you every one home for the present; when it is fit I will send for you, as soon as I shall have learned from God who it is that he will give you for your king."

4 The Appointment of a King over the Israelites, Whose Name Was Saul; and This by the Command of God

1. THER was one of the tribe of Benjamin, a man of a good family, and of a virtuous disposition; his name was Kish. He had a son, a young man of a comely countenance, and of a tall body, but his understanding and his mind were preferable to what was visible in him: they called him Saul. Now this Kish had some fine she-asses that were wandered out of the pasture wherein they fed, for he was more delighted with these than with any other cattle he had; so he sent out his son, and one servant with him, to search for the beasts; but when he had gone over his own tribe in search after the asses, he went to other tribes, and when he found them not there neither, he determined to go his way home, lest he should occasion any concern to his father about himself. But when his servant that followed him told him as they were near the city of Ramah, that there was a true prophet in that city, and advised him to go to him, for that by him they should know the upshot of the affair of their asses, he replied, That if they should go to him, they had nothing to give him as a reward for his prophecy, for their subsistence money was spent. The servant answered, that he had still the fourth part of a shekel, and he would present him with that; for they were mistaken out of ignorance, as not knowing that the prophet received no such reward[6] So they went to him; and when they were before the gates, they lit upon certain maidens that were

---

6. Of this great mistake of Saul and his servant, as if true prophet of God would accept of a gift or present, for foretelling what was desired of him, see the note on B. IV. ch. 6. sect. 3.

going to fetch water, and they asked them which was the prophet's house. They showed them which it was; and bid them make haste before he sat down to supper, for he had invited many guests to a feast, and that he used to sit down before those that were invited. Now Samuel had then gathered many together to feast with him on this very account; for while he every day prayed to God to tell him beforehand whom he would make king, he had informed him of this man the day before, for that he would send him a certain young man out of the tribe of Benjamin about this hour of the day; and he sat on the top of the house in expectation of that time's being come. And when the time was completed, he came down and went to supper; so he met with Saul, and God discovered to him that this was he who should rule over them. Then Saul went up to Samuel and saluted him, and desired him to inform him which was the prophet's house; for he said he was a stranger and did not know it. When Samuel had told him that he himself was the person, he led him in to supper, and assured him that the asses were found which he had been to seek, and that the greatest of good things were assured to him: he replied, "I am too inconsiderable to hope for any such thing, and of a tribe to small to have kings made out of it, and of a family smaller than several other families; but thou tellest me this in jest, and makest me an object of laughter, when thou discoursest with me of greater matters than what I stand in need of." However, the prophet led him in to the feast, and made him sit down, him and his servant that followed him, above the other guests that were invited, which were seventy in number[7] and he gave orders to the servants to set the royal portion before Saul. And when the time of going to bed was come, the rest rose up, and every one of them went home; but Saul staid with the prophet, he and his servant, and slept with him.

2. Now as soon as it was day, Samuel raised up Saul out of his bed, and conducted him homeward; and when he was out of the city,

---

7. It seems to me not improbable that these seventy guests of Samuel, as here, with himself at the head of them, were a Jewish sanhedrim, and that hereby Samuel intimated to Saul that these seventy-one were to be his constant counselors, and that he was to act not like a sole monarch, but with the advice and direction of these seventy-one members of that Jewish sanhedrim upon all occasions, which yet we never read that he consulted afterward.

he desired him to cause his servant to go before, but to stay behind himself, for that he had somewhat to say to him when nobody else was present. Accordingly, Saul sent away his servant that followed him; then did the prophet take a vessel of oil, and poured it upon the head of the young man, and kissed him, and said, "Be thou a king, by the ordination of God, against the Philistines, and for avenging the Hebrews for what they have suffered by them; of this thou shalt have a sign, which I would have thee take notice of:—As soon as thou art departed hence, thou will find three men upon the road, going to worship God at Bethel; the first of whom thou wilt see carrying three loaves of bread, the second carrying a kid of the goats, and the third will follow them carrying a bottle of wine. These three men will salute thee, and speak kindly to thee, and will give thee two of their loaves, which thou shalt accept of. And thence thou shalt come to a place called *Rachel's Monument,* where thou shalt meet with those that will tell thee thy asses are found; after this, when thou comest to Gabatha, thou shalt overtake a company of prophets, and thou shalt be seized with the Divine Spirit,[8] and prophesy along with them, till every one that sees thee shall be astonished, and wonder, and say, Whence is it that the son of Kish has arrived at this degree of happiness? And when these signs have happened to thee, know that God is with thee; then do thou salute thy father and thy kindred. Thou shalt also come when I send for thee to Gilgal, that we may offer thank-offerings to God for these blessings." When Samuel had said this, and foretold these things, he sent the young man away. Now all things fell out to Saul according to the prophecy of Samuel.

3. But as soon as Saul came into the house of his kinsman Abner, whom indeed he loved better than the rest of his relations, he was asked by him concerning his journey, and what accidents happened to him therein; and he concealed none of the other things from him, no, not his coming to Samuel the prophet, nor how he told him the asses were found; but he said nothing to him about the kingdom, and what belonged thereto, which he thought would procure him envy, and when such things are heard, they are not easily believed; nor did he think it prudent to tell those things to him, although he appeared

---

8. An instance of this Divine fury we have after this in Saul, ch. 5. sect. 2, 3; 1 Samuel 11:6. See the like, Judges 3:10; 6:34; 11:29; 13:25; and 14:6.

very friendly to him, and one whom he loved above the rest of his relations, considering, I suppose, what human nature really is, that no one is a firm friend, neither among our intimates, nor of our kindred; nor do they preserve that kind disposition when God advances men to great prosperity, but they are still ill-natured and envious at those that are in eminent stations.

4. Then Samuel called the people together to the city Mizpeh, and spake to them in the words following, which he said he was to speak by the command of God:—That when he had granted them a state of liberty, and brought their enemies into subjection, they were become unmindful of his benefits, and rejected God that he should not be their King, as not considering that it would be most for their advantage to be presided over by the best of beings, for God is the best of beings, and they chose to have a man for their king; while kings will use their subjects as beasts, according to the violence of their own wills and inclinations, and other passions, as wholly carried away with the lust of power, but will not endeavor so to preserve the race of mankind as his own workmanship and creation, which, for that very reason, God would take cake of. "But since you have come to a fixed resolution, and this injurious treatment of God has quite prevailed over you, dispose yourselves by your tribes and scepters, and cast lots."

5. When the Hebrews had so done, the lot fell upon the tribe of Benjamin; and when the lot was cast for the families of this tribe, that which was called *Matri* was taken; and when the lot was cast for the single persons of that family, Saul, the son of Kish, was taken for their king. When the young man knew this, he prevented [their sending for him], and immediately went away and hid himself. I suppose that it was because he would not have it thought that he willingly took the government upon him; nay, he showed such a degree of command over himself, and of modesty, that while the greatest part are not able to contain their joy, even in the gaining of small advantages, but presently show themselves publicly to all men, this man did not only show nothing of that nature, when he was appointed to be the lord of so many and so great tribes, but crept away and concealed himself out of the sight of those he was to reign over, and made them seek him, and that with a good deal of trouble. So when the people were at a loss, and solicitous, because Saul disappeared, the prophet besought God to show where the young man was, and to produce him before them. So

when they had learned of God the place where Saul was hidden, they sent men to bring him; and when he was come, they set him in the midst of the multitude. Now he was taller than any of them, and his stature was very majestic.

6. Then said the prophet, God gives you this man to be your king: see how he is higher than any of the people, and worthy of this dominion." So as soon as the people had made acclamation, *God save the king,* the prophet wrote down what would come to pass in a book, and read it in the hearing of the king, and laid up the book in the tabernacle of God, to be a witness to future generations of what he had foretold. So when Samuel had finished this matter, he dismissed the multitude, and came himself to the city Rainah, for it was his own country. Saul also went away to Gibeah, where he was born; and many good men there were who paid him the respect that was due to him; but the greater part were ill men, who despised him and derided the others, who neither did bring him presents, nor did they in affection, or even in words, regard to please him.

5 Saul's Expedition Against the Nation of the Ammonites and Victory over Them and the Spoils He Took from Them

1. AFTER one month, the war which Saul had with Nahash, the king of the Ammonites, obtained him respect from all the people; for this Nahash had done a great deal of mischief to the Jews that lived beyond Jordan by the expedition he had made against them with a great and warlike army. He also reduced their cities into slavery, and that not only by subduing them for the present, which he did by force and violence, but by weakening them by subtlety and cunning, that they might not be able afterward to get clear of the slavery they were under to him; for he put out the right eyes[9] of those that either delivered themselves to him upon terms, or were taken by him in war; and this he did, that when their left eyes were covered by their shields, they might be wholly useless in war. Now when the king of the Ammonites had served those beyond Jordan in this manner, he led his

---

9. Take here Theodoret's note, cited by Dr. Hudson:—"He that exposes his shield to the enemy with his left hand, thereby hides his left eye, and looks at the enemy with his right eye: he therefore that plucks out that eye, makes men useless in war."

army against those that were called *Gileadites,* and having pitched his camp at the metropolis of his enemies, which was the city of Jabesh, he sent ambassadors to them, commanding them either to deliver themselves up, on condition to have their right eyes plucked out, or to undergo a siege, and to have their cities overthrown. He gave them their choice, whether they would cut off a small member of their body, or universally perish. However, the Gileadites were so affrighted at these offers, that they had not courage to say any thing to either of them, neither that they would deliver themselves up, nor that they would fight him. But they desired that he would give them seven days' respite, that they might send ambassadors to their countrymen, and entreat their assistance; and if they came to assist them, they would fight; but if that assistance were impossible to be obtained from them, they said they would deliver themselves up to suffer whatever he pleased to inflict upon them.

2. So Nabash, contemning the multitude of the Gileadites and the answer they gave, allowed them a respite, and gave them leave to send to whomsoever they pleased for assistance. So they immediately sent to the Israelites, city by city, and informed them what Nabash had threatened to do to them, and what great distress they were in. Now the people fell into tears and grief at the hearing of what the ambassadors from Jabesh said; and the terror they were in permitted them to do nothing more. But when the messengers were come to the city of king Saul, and declared the dangers in which the inhabitants of Jabesh were, the people were in the same affliction as those in the other cities, for they lamented the calamity of those related to them. And when Saul was returned from his husbandry into the city, he found his fellow citizens weeping; and when, upon inquiry, he had learned the cause of the confusion and sadness they were in, he was seized with a divine fury, and sent away the ambassadors from the inhabitants of Jabesh, and promised them to come to their assistance on the third day, and to beat their enemies before sun-rising, that the sun upon its rising might see that they had already conquered, and were freed from the fears they were under: but he bid some of them stay to conduct them the right way to Jabesh.

3. So being desirous to turn the people to this war against the Ammonites by fear of the losses they should otherwise undergo, and that they might the more suddenly be gathered together, he cut the

sinews of his oxen, and threatened to do the same to all such as did
not come with their armor to Jordan the next day, and follow him
and Samuel the prophet whithersoever they should lead them. So they
came together, out of fear of the losses they were threatened with,
at the appointed time. And the multitude were numbered at the city
Bezek. And he found the number of those that were gathered together,
besides that of the tribe of Judah, to be seven hundred thousand, while
those of that tribe were seventy thousand. So he passed over Jordan,
and proceeded in marching all that night, thirty furlongs, and came to
Jabesh before sun-rising. So he divided the army into three companies;
and fell upon their enemies on every side on the sudden, and when
they expected no such thing; and joining battle with them, they slew a
great many of the Ammonites, as also their king Nabash. This glorious
action was done by Saul, and was related with great commendation of
him to all the Hebrews; and he thence gained a wonderful reputation
for his valor: for although there were some of them that contemned
him before, they now changed their minds, and honored him, and
esteemed him as the best of men: for he did not content himself with
having saved the inhabitants of Jabesh only, but he made an expedition
into the country of the Ammonites, and laid it all waste, and took a
large prey, and so returned to his own country most gloriously. So the
people were greatly pleased at these excellent performances of Saul,
and rejoiced that they had constituted him their king. They also made
a clamor against those that pretended he would be of no advantage
to their affairs; and they said, Where now are these men?—let them be
brought to punishment, with all the like things that multitudes usually
say when they are elevated with prosperity, against those that lately
had despised the authors of it. But Saul, although he took the good-
will and the affection of these men very kindly, yet did he swear that
he would not see any of his countrymen slain that day, since it was
absurd to mix this victory, which God had given them, with the blood
and slaughter of those that were of the same lineage with themselves;
and that it was more agreeable to be men of a friendly disposition, and
so to betake themselves to feasting.

4. And when Samuel had told them that he ought to confirm the
kingdom to Saul by a second ordination of him, they all came together
to the city of Gilgal, for thither did he command them to come. So the
prophet anointed Saul with the holy oil in the sight of the multitude,

and declared him to be king the second time. And so the government of the Hebrews was changed into a regal government; for in the days of Moses, and his disciple Joshua, who was their general, they continued under an aristocracy; but after the death of Joshua, for eighteen years in all, the multitude had no settled form of government, but were in an anarchy; after which they returned to their former government, they then permitting themselves to be judged by him who appeared to be the best warrior and most courageous, whence it was that they called this interval of their government the *Judges*.

5. Then did Samuel the prophet call another assembly also, and said to them," I solemnly adjure you by God Almighty, who brought those excellent brethren, I mean Moses and Aaron, into the world, and delivered our fathers from the Egyptians, and from the slavery. they endured under them, that you will not speak what you say to gratify me, nor suppress any thing out of fear of me, nor be overborne by any other passion, but say, What have I ever done that was cruel or unjust? or what have I done out of lucre or covetousness, or to gratify others? Bear witness against me, if I have taken an ox or a sheep, or any such thing, which yet when they are taken to support men, it is esteemed blameless; or have I taken an ass for mine own use of any one to his grief?—lay some one such crime to my charge, now we are in your king's presence." But they cried out, that no such thing had been done by him, but that he had presided over the nation after a holy and righteous manner.

6. Hereupon Samuel, when such a testimony had been given him by them all, said, "Since you grant that you are not able to lay any ill thing to my charge hitherto, come on now, and do you hearken while I speak with great freedom to you. You have been guilty of great impiety against God, in asking you a king. It behoves you to remember that our grandfather Jacob came down into Egypt, by reason of a famine, with seventy souls only of our family, and that their posterity multiplied there to many ten thousands, whom the Egyptians brought into slavery and hard oppression; that God himself, upon the prayers of our fathers, sent Moses and Aaron, who were brethren, and gave them power to deliver the multitude out of their distress, and this without a king. These brought us into this very land which you now possess: and when you enjoyed these advantages from God, you betrayed his worship and religion; nay, moreover, when you

were brought under the hands of your enemies, he delivered you, first by rendering you superior to the Assyrians and their forces, he then made you to overcome the Ammonites and the Moabites, and last of all the Philistines; and these things have been achieved under the conduct of Jephtha and Gideon. What madness therefore possessed you to fly from God, and to desire to be under a king?—yet have I ordained him for king whom he chose for you. However, that I may make it plain to you that God is angry and displeased at your choice of kingly government, I will so dispose him that he shall declare this very plainly to you by strange signals; for what none of you ever saw here before, I mean a winter storm in the midst of harvest,[10] I will entreat of God, and will make it visible to you." Now, as soon as he had said this, God gave such great signals by thunder and lightning, and the descent of hail, as attested the truth of all that the prophet had said, insomuch that they were amazed and terrified, and confessed they had sinned, and had fallen into that sin through ignorance; and besought the prophet, as one that was a tender and gentle father to them, to render God so merciful as to forgive this their sin, which they had added to those other offenses whereby they had affronted him and transgressed against him. So he promised them that he would beseech God, and persuade him to forgive them these their sins. However, he advised them to be righteous, and to be good, and ever to remember the miseries that had befallen them on account of their departure from virtue: as also to remember the strange signs God had shown them, and the body of laws that Moses had given them, if they had any desire of being preserved and made happy with their king. But he said, that if they should grow careless of these things, great judgments would come from God upon them, and upon their king. And when Samuel had thus prophesied to the Hebrews, he dismissed them to their own homes, having confirmed the kingdom to Saul the second time.

---

10. Mr. Reland observes here, and proves elsewhere in his note on Antiq. B. III. ch. 1. sect. 6, that although thunder and lightning with us usually happen in summer, yet in Palestine and Syria they are chiefly confined to winter. Josephus takes notice of the same thing again, War, B. IV. ch. 4. sect. 5.

6 *How the Philistines Made Another Expedition Against the Hebrews and Were Beaten*

1. NOW Saul chose out of the multitude about three thousand men, and he took two thousand of them to be the guards of his own body, and abode in the city Bethel, but he gave the rest of them to Jonathan his son, to be the guards of his body; and sent him to Gibeah, where he besieged and took a certain garrison of the Philistines, not far from Gilgal; for the Philistines of Gibeah had beaten the Jews, and taken their weapons away, and had put garrisons into the strongest places of the country, and had forbidden them to carry any instrument of iron, or at all to make use of any iron in any case whatsoever. And on account of this prohibition it was that the husbandmen, if they had occasion to sharpen any of their tools, whether it were the coulter or the spade, or any instrument of husbandry, they came to the Philistines to do it. Now as soon as the Philistines heard of this slaughter of their garrison, they were in a rage about it, and, looking on this contempt as a terrible affront offered them, they made war against the Jews, with three hundred thousand footmen, and thirty thousand chariots, and six thousand horses; and they pitched their camp at the city Michmash. When Saul, the king of the Hebrews, was informed of this, he went down to the city Gilgal, and made proclamation over all the country, that they should try to regain their liberty; and called them to the war against the Philistines, diminishing their forces, and despising them as not very considerable, and as not so great but they might hazard a battle with them. But when the people about Saul observed how numerous the Philistines were, they were under a great consternation; and some of them hid themselves in caves and in dens under ground, but the greater part fled into the land beyond Jordan, which belonged to Gad and Reuben.

2. But Saul sent to the prophet, and called him to consult with him about the war and the public affairs; so he commanded him to stay there for him, and to prepare sacrifices, for he would come to him within seven days, that they might offer sacrifices on the seventh day, and might then join battle with their enemies. So he waited[11] as the prophet sent to him to do; yet did not he, however, observe

---

11. Saul seems to have staid till near the time of the evening sacrifice, on the seventh

the command that was given him, but when he saw that the prophet tarried longer than he expected, and that he was deserted by the soldiers, he took the sacrifices and offered them; and when he heard that Samuel was come, he went out to meet him. But the prophet said he had not done well in disobeying the injunctions he had sent to him, and had not staid till his coming, which being appointed according to the will of God, he had prevented him in offering up those prayers and those sacrifices that he should have made for the multitude, and that he therefore had performed Divine offices in an ill manner, and had been rash in performing them. Hereupon Saul made an apology for himself, and said that he had waited as many days as Samuel had appointed him; that he had been so quick in offering his sacrifices, upon account of the necessity he was in, and because his soldiers were departing from him, out of their fear of the enemy's camp at Michmash, the report being gone abroad that they were coming down upon him of Gilgal. To which Samuel replied, "Nay, certainly,

---

day, which Samuel the prophet of God had appointed him, but not till the end of that day, as he ought to have done; and Samuel appears, by delaying to come to the full time of the evening sacrifice on that seventh day, to have tried him (who seems to have been already for some time declining from his strict and bounden subordination to God and his prophet; to have taken life-guards for himself and his son, which was entirely a new thing in Israel, and savored of a distrust of God's providence; and to have affected more than he ought that independent authority which the pagan kings took to themselves); Samuel, I say, seems to have here tried Saul whether he would stay till the priest came, who alone could lawfully offer the sacrifices, nor would boldly and profanely usurp the priest's office, which he venturing upon, was justly rejected for his profaneness. See Apost. Constit. B. II. ch. 27. And, indeed, since Saul had accepted kingly power, which naturally becomes ungovernable and tyrannical, as God foretold, and the experience of all ages has shown, the Divine settlement by Moses had soon been laid aside under the kings, had not God, by keeping strictly to his laws, and severely executing the threatenings therein contained, restrained Saul and other kings in some degree of obedience to himself; nor was even this severity sufficient to restrain most of the future kings of Israel and Judah from the grossest idolatry and impiety. Of the advantage of which strictness, in the observing Divine laws, and inflicting their threatened penalties, see Antiq. B. VI. ch. 12. sect. 7; and Against Apion, B. II. sect. 30, where Josephus speaks of that matter; though it must be noted that it seems, at least in three instances, that good men did not always immediately approve of such Divine severity. There seems to be one instance, 1 Samuel 6:19, 20; another, 1 Samuel 15:11; and a third, 2 Samuel 6:8, 9; Antiq. B. VI. ch. 7. sect. 2; though they all at last acquiesced in the Divine conduct, as knowing that God is wiser than men.

if thou hadst been a righteous man,[12] and hadst not disobeyed me, nor slighted the commands which God suggested to me concerning the present state of affairs, and hadst not acted more hastily than the present circumstances required, thou wouldst have been permitted to reign a long time, and thy posterity after thee." So Samuel, being grieved at what happened, returned home; but Saul came to the city Gibeah, with his son Jonathan, having only six hundred men with him; and of these the greater part had no weapons, because of the scarcity of iron in that country, as well as of those that could make such weapons; for, as we showed a little before, the Philistines had not suffered them to have such iron or such workmen. Now the Philistines divided their army into three companies, and took as many roads, and laid waste the country of the Hebrews, while king Saul and his son Jonathan saw what was done, but were not able to defend the land, having no more than six hundred men with them. But as he, and his son, and Abiah the high priest, who was of the posterity of Eli the high priest, were sitting upon a pretty high hill, and seeing the land laid waste, they were mightily disturbed at it. Now Saul's son agreed with his armor-bearer, that they would go privately to the enemy's camp, and make a tumult and a disturbance among them. And when the armor-bearer had readily promised to follow him whithersoever he should lead him, though he should be obliged to die in the attempt, Jonathan made use of the young man's assistance, and descended from the hill, and went to their enemies. Now the enemy's camp was upon a precipice which had three tops, that ended in a small but sharp and

---

12. By this answer of Samuel, and that from a Divine commission, which is fuller in 1 Samuel 13:14, and by that parallel note in the Apostolical Constitutions just now quoted, concerning the great wickedness of Saul in venturing, even under a seeming necessity of affairs, to usurp the priest's office, and offer sacrifice without the priest, we are in some degree able to answer that question, which I have ever thought a very hard one, viz. Whether, if there were a city or country of lay Christians without any clergymen, it were lawful for the laity alone to baptize, or celebrate the eucharist, etc., or indeed whether they alone could ordain themselves either bishops, priests, or deacons, for the due performance of such sacerdotal ministrations; or whether they ought not rather, till they procure clergymen to come among them, to confine themselves within those bounds of piety and Christianity which belong alone to the laity; such particularly as are recommended in the first book of the Apostolical Constitutions, which peculiarly concern the laity, and are intimated in Clement's undoubted epistle, sect. 40. To which latter opinion I incline.

long extremity, while there was a rock that surrounded them, like lines made to prevent the attacks of an enemy. There it so happened, that the out-guards of the camp were neglected, because of the security that here arose from the situation of the place, and because they thought it altogether impossible, not only to ascend up to the camp on that quarter, but so much as to come near it. As soon, therefore, as they came to the camp, Jonathan encouraged his armor-bearer, and said to him, "Let us attack our enemies; and if, when they see us, they bid us come up to them, take that for a signal of victory; but if they say nothing, as not intending to invite us to come up, let us return back again." So when they were approaching to the enemy's camp, just after break of day, and the Philistines saw them, they said one to another, "The Hebrews come out of their dens and caves:" and they said to Jonathan and to his armor-bearer, "Come on, ascend up to us, that we may inflict a just punishment upon you, for your rash attempt upon us." So Saul's son accepted of that invitation, as what signified to him victory, and he immediately came out of the place whence they were seen by their enemies: so he changed his place, and came to the rock, which had none to guard it, because of its own strength; from thence they crept up with great labor and difficulty, and so far overcame by force the nature of the place, till they were able to fight with their enemies. So they fell upon them as they were asleep, and slew about twenty of them, and thereby filled them with disorder and surprise, insomuch that some of them threw away their entire armor and fled; but the greatest part, not knowing one another, because they were of different nations, suspected one another to be enemies, (for they did not imagine there were only two of the Hebrews that came up,) and so they fought one against another; and some of them died in the battle, and some, as they were flying away, were thrown down from the rock headlong.

3. Now Saul's watchmen told the king that the camp of the Philistines was in confusion; then he inquired whether any body was gone away from the army; and when he heard that his son, and with him his armor-bearer, were absent, he bade the high priest take the garments of his high priesthood, and prophesy to him what success they should have; who said that they should get the victory, and prevail against their enemies. So he went out after the Philistines, and set upon them as they were slaying one another. Those also who had fled to dens and

caves, upon hearing that Saul was gaining a victory, came running to him. When, therefore, the number of the Hebrews that came to Saul amounted to about ten thousand, he pursued the enemy, who were scattered all over the country; but then he fell into an action, which was a very unhappy one, and liable to be very much blamed; for, whether out of ignorance or whether out of joy for a victory gained so strangely, (for it frequently happens that persons so fortunate are not then able to use their reason consistently,) as he was desirous to avenge himself, and to exact a due punishment of the Philistines, he denounced a curse[13] upon the Hebrews: That if any one put a stop to his slaughter of the enemy, and fell on eating, and left off the slaughter or the pursuit before the night came on, and obliged them so to do, he should be accursed. Now after Saul had denounced this curse, since they were now in a wood belonging to the tribe of Ephraim, which was thick and full of bees, Saul's son, who did not hear his father denounce that curse, nor hear of the approbation the multitude gave to it, broke off a piece of a honey-comb, and ate part of it. But, in the mean time, he was informed with what a curse his father had forbidden them to taste any thing before sun-setting: so he left off eating, and said his father had not done well in this prohibition, because, had they taken some food, they had pursued the enemy with greater rigor and alacrity, and had both taken and slain many more of their enemies.

4. When, therefore, they had slain many ten thousands of the Philistines, they fell upon spoiling the camp of the Philistines, but not till late in the evening. They also took a great deal of prey and cattle, and killed them, and ate them with their blood. This was told to the king by the scribes, that the multitude were sinning against God as they sacrificed, and were eating before the blood was well washed away, and the flesh was made clean. Then did Saul give order that a great stone should be rolled into the midst of them, and he made

---

13. This rash vow or curse of Saul, which Josephus says was confirmed by the people, and yet not executed, I suppose principally because Jonathan did not know of it, is very remarkable; it being of the essence of the obligation of all laws, that they be sufficiently known and promulgated, otherwise the conduct of Providence, as to the sacredness of solemn oaths and vows, in God's refusing to answer by Urim till this breach of Saul's vow or curse was understood and set right, and God propitiated by public prayer, is here very remarkable, as indeed it is every where else in the Old Testament.

proclamation that they should kill their sacrifices upon it, and not feed upon the flesh with the blood, for that was not acceptable to God. And when all the people did as the king commanded them, Saul erected an altar there, and offered burnt-offerings upon it to God[14] This was the first altar that Saul built.

5. So when Saul was desirous of leading his men to the enemy's camp before it was day, in order to plunder it, and when the soldiers were not unwilling to follow him, but indeed showed great readiness to do as he commanded them, the king called Ahitub the high priest, and enjoined him to know of God whether he would grant them the favor and permission to go against the enemy's camp, in order to destroy those that were in it. And when the priest said that God did not give any answer, Saul replied, "And not without some cause does God refuse to answer what we inquire of him, while yet a little while ago he declared to us all that we desired beforehand, and even prevented us in his answer. To be sure there is some sin against him that is concealed from us, which is the occasion of his silence. Now I swear by him himself, that though he that hath committed this sin should prove to be my own son Jonathan, I will slay him, and by that means will appease the anger of God against us, and that in the very same manner as if I were to punish a stranger, and one not at all related to me, for the same offense." So when the multitude cried out to him so to do, he presently set all the rest on one side, and he and his son stood on the other side, and he sought to discover the offender by lot. Now the lot appeared to fall upon Jonathan himself. So when he was asked by his father what sin he had been guilty of, and what he was conscious of in the course of his life that might be esteemed instances of guilt or profaneness, his answer was this, "O father, I have done nothing more than that yesterday, without knowing of the curse and oath thou hadst denounced, while I was in pursuit of the enemy, I tasted of a honey-comb." But Saul sware that he would slay him, and

---

14. Here we have still more indications of Saul's affectation of despotic power, and of his entrenching upon the priesthood, and making and endeavoring to execute a rash vow or curse, without consulting Samuel or the sanhedrim. In this view it is also that I look upon this erection of a new altar by Saul, and his offering of burnt-offerings himself upon it, and not as any proper instance of devotion or religion, with other commentators.

prefer the observation of his oath before all the ties of birth and of nature. And Jonathan was not dismayed at this threatening of death, but, offering himself to it generously and undauntedly, he said, "Nor do I desire you, father, to spare me: death will be to me very acceptable, when it proceeds from thy piety, and after a glorious victory; for it is the greatest consolation to me that I leave the Hebrews victorious over the Philistines." Hereupon all the people were very sorry, and greatly afflicted for Jonathan; and they sware that they would not overlook Jonathan, and see him die, who was the author of their victory. By which means they snatched him out of the danger he was in from his father's curse, while they made their prayers to God also for the young man, that he would remit his sin.

6. So Saul, having slain about sixty thousand of the enemy, returned home to his own city, and reigned happily: and he also fought against the neighboring nations, and subdued the Ammonites, and Moabites, and Philistines, and Edomites, and Amalekites, as also the king of Zobah. He had three male children, Jonathan, and Isui, and Melchishua; with Merab and Michal his daughters. He had also Abner, his uncle's son, for the captain of his host: that uncle's name was Ner. Now Ner, and Kish the father of Saul, were brothers. Saul had also a great many chariots and horsemen, and against whomsoever he made war he returned conqueror, and advanced the affairs of the Hebrews to a great degree of success and prosperity, and made them superior to other nations; and he made such of the young men as were remarkable for tallness and comeliness the guards of his body.

7 Saul's War with the Amalekites, and Conquest of Them

1. NOW Samuel came unto Saul, and said to him, that he was sent by God to put him in mind that God had preferred him before all others, and ordained him king; that he therefore ought to be obedient to him, and to submit to his authority, as considering, that though he had the dominion over the other tribes, yet that God had the dominion over him, and over all things. That accordingly God said to him, that "because the Amalekites did the Hebrews a great deal of mischief while they were in the wilderness, and when, upon their coming out of Egypt, they were making their way to that country which is now their own, I enjoin thee to punish the Amalekites, by making war upon

them; and when thou hast subdued them, to leave none of them alive, but to pursue them through every age, and to slay them, beginning with the women and the infants, and to require this as a punishment to be inflicted upon them for the mischief they did to our forefathers; to spare nothing, neither asses nor other beasts, nor to reserve any of them for your own advantage and possession, but to devote them universally to God, and, in obedience to the commands of Moses, to blot out the name of Amalek entirely."[15]

2. So Saul promised to do what he was commanded; and supposing that his obedience to God would be shown, not only in making war against the Amalekites, but more fully in the readiness and quickness of his proceedings, he made no delay, but immediately gathered together all his forces; and when he had numbered them in Gilgal, he found them to be about four hundred thousand of the Israelites, besides the tribe of Judah, for that tribe contained by itself thirty thousand. Accordingly, Saul made an irruption into the country of the Amalekites, and set many men in several parties in ambush at the river, that so he might not only do them a mischief by open fighting, but might fall upon them unexpectedly in the ways, and might thereby compass them round about, and kill them. And when he had joined battle with the enemy, he beat them; and pursuing them as they fled, he destroyed them all. And when that undertaking had succeeded, according as God had foretold, he set upon the cities of the Amalekites; he besieged them, and took them by force, partly by warlike machines, partly by mines dug under ground, and partly by building walls on the outsides. Some they starved out with famine, and some they gained by other methods; and after all, he betook himself to slay the women and the children, and thought he did not act therein either barbarously or inhumanly; first, because they were enemies whom he thus treated, and, in the next place, because it was done by the command of God, whom it was dangerous not to obey. He also took

---

15. The reason of this severity is distinctly given, 1 Samuel 15:18, "Go and utterly destroy the sinners the Amalekites:" nor indeed do we ever meet with these Amalekites but as very cruel and bloody people, and particularly seeking to injure and utterly to destroy the nation of Israel. See Exodus 17:8–16; Numbers 14:45; Deuteronomy 25:17–19; Judges 6:3, 6; 1 Samuel 15:33; Psalms 83:7; and, above all, the most barbarous of all cruelties, that of Haman the Agagite, or one of the posterity of Agag, the old king of the Amalekites, Esther 3:1–15.

Agag, the enemies' king, captive,—the beauty and tallness of whose body he admired so much, that he thought him worthy of preservation. Yet was not this done however according to the will of God, but by giving way to human passions, and suffering himself to be moved with an unseasonable commiseration, in a point where it was not safe for him to indulge it; for God hated the nation of the Amalekites to such a degree, that he commanded Saul to have no pity on even those infants which we by nature chiefly compassionate; but Saul preserved their king and governor from the miseries which the Hebrews brought on the people, as if he preferred the fine appearance of the enemy to the memory of what God had sent him about. The multitude were also guilty, together with Saul; for they spared the herds and the flocks, and took them for a prey, when God had commanded they should not spare them. They also carried off with them the rest of their wealth and riches; but if there were any thing that was not worthy of regard, that they destroyed.

3. But when Saul had conquered all these Amalekites that reached from Pelusium of Egypt to the Red Sea, he laid waste all the rest of the enemy's country: but for the nation of the Shechemites, he did not touch them, although they dwelt in the very middle of the country of Midian; for before the battle, Saul had sent to them, and charged them to depart thence, lest they should be partakers of the miseries of the Amalekites; for he had a just occasion for saving them, since they were of the kindred of Raguel, Moses's father-in-law.

4. Hereupon Saul returned home with joy, for the glorious things he had done, and for the conquest of his enemies, as though he had not neglected any thing which the prophet had enjoined him to do when he was going to make war with the Amalekites, and as though he had exactly observed all that he ought to have done. But God was grieved that the king of the Amalekites was preserved alive, and that the multitude had seized on the cattle for a prey, because these things were done without his permission; for he thought it an intolerable thing that they should conquer and overcome their enemies by that power which he gave them, and then that he himself should be so grossly despised and disobeyed by them, that a mere man that was a king would not bear it. He therefore told Samuel the prophet, that he repented that he had made Saul king, while he did nothing that he had commanded him, but indulged his own inclinations. When Samuel heard that,

he was in confusion, and began to beseech God all that night to be reconciled to Saul, and not to be angry with him; but he did not grant that forgiveness to Saul which the prophet asked for, as not deeming it a fit thing to grant forgiveness of [such] sins at his entreaties, since injuries do not otherwise grow so great as by the easy tempers of those that are injured; or while they hunt after the glory of being thought gentle and good-natured, before they are aware they produce other sins. As soon therefore as God had rejected the intercession of the prophet, and it plainly appeared he would not change his mind, at break of day Samuel came to Saul at Gilgal. When the king saw him, he ran to him, and embraced him, and said, "I return thanks to God, who hath given me the victory, for I have performed every thing that he hath commanded me." To which Samuel replied, "How is it then that I hear the bleating of the sheep and the lowing of the greater cattle in the camp?" Saul made answer, That the people had reserved them for sacrifices; but that, as to the nation of the Amalekites, it was entirely destroyed, as he had received it in command to see done, and that no one man was left; but that he had saved alive the king alone, and brought him to him, concerning whom, he said, they would advise together what should be done with him." But the prophet said, "God is not delighted with sacrifices, but with good and with righteous men, who are such as follow his will and his laws, and never think that any thing is well done by them but when they do it as God had commanded them; that he then looks upon himself as affronted, not when any one does not sacrifice, but when any one appears to be disobedient to him. But that from those who do not obey him, nor pay him that duty which is the alone true and acceptable worship, he will not kindly accept their oblations, be those they offer ever so many and so fat, and be the presents they make him ever so ornamental, nay, though they were made of gold and silver themselves, but he will reject them, and esteem them instances of wickedness, and not of piety. And that he is delighted with those that still bear in mind this one thing, and this only, how to do that, whatsoever it be, which God pronounces or commands for them to do, and to choose rather to die than to transgress any of those commands; nor does he require so much as a sacrifice from them. And when these do sacrifice, though it be a mean oblation, he better accepts of it as the honor of poverty, than such oblations as come from the richest men that offer them to him. Wherefore take notice, that thou art under the wrath of God, for thou hast despised and neglected what he commanded thee. How dost thou then suppose that he will respect a sacrifice out of such things as he hath doomed to destruction? unless perhaps thou dost imagine that it is almost all one to offer it in sacrifice to God as to destroy it. Do thou therefore expect that thy kingdom will be taken from thee, and that authority which thou hast abused by such insolent behavior, as to neglect that God who bestowed it upon thee." Then did Saul confess that he had acted unjustly, and did not deny that he had sinned, because he had transgressed the injunctions of the prophet; but he said that it was out of a dread and fear of the soldiers, that he did not prohibit and restrain them when they seized on the prey. "But forgive me," said he, "and be merciful to me, for I will be cautious how I offend for the time to come." He also entreated the prophet to go back with him, that he might offer his thank-offerings to God; but Samuel went home, because he saw that God would not be reconciled to him.

5. But then Saul was so desirous to retain Samuel, that he took hold of his cloak, and because the vehemence of Samuel's departure made the motion to be violent, the cloak was rent. Upon which the prophet said, that after the same manner should the kingdom be rent from him, and that a good and a just man should take it; that God persevered in what he had decreed about him; that to be mutable and changeable in what is determined, is agreeable to human passions only, but is not agreeable to the Divine Power. Hereupon Saul said that he had been wicked, but that what was done could not be undone: he therefore desired him to honor him so far, that the multitude might see that he would accompany him in worshipping God. So Samuel granted him that favor, and went with him and worshipped God. Agag also, the king of the Amalekites, was brought to him; and when the king asked, How bitter death was? Samuel said, "As thou hast made many of the Hebrew mothers to lament and bewail the loss of their children, so shalt thou, by thy death, cause thy mother to lament thee also." Accordingly, he gave order to slay him immediately at Gilgal, and then went away to the city Ramah.

8 How, Upon Saul's Transgression of the Prophet's Commands, Samuel Ordained Another Person to Be King Privately, Whose Name Was David, as God Commanded Him

1. NOW Saul being sensible of the miserable condition he had brought himself into, and that he had made God to be his enemy, he went up to his royal palace at Gibeah, which name denotes a *hill*, and after that day he came no more into the presence of the prophet. And when Samuel mourned for him, God bid him leave off his concern for him, and to take the holy oil, and go to Bethlehem, to Jesse the son of Obed, and to anoint such of his sons as he should show him for their future king. But Samuel said, he was afraid lest Saul, when he came to know of it, should kill him, either by some private method or even openly. But upon God's suggesting to him a safe way of going thither, he came to the forementioned city; and when they all saluted him, and asked what was the occasion of his coming, he told them he came to sacrifice to God. When, therefore, he had gotten the sacrifice ready, he called Jesse and his sons to partake of those sacrifices; and when he saw his eldest son to be a tall and handsome man, he guessed by his comeliness that he was the person who was to be their future king. But he was mistaken in judging about God's providence; for when Samuel inquired of God whether he should anoint this youth, whom he so admired, and esteemed worthy of the kingdom, God said, "Men do not see as God seeth. Thou indeed hast respect to the fine appearance of this youth, and thence esteemest him worthy of the kingdom, while I propose the kingdom as a reward, not of the beauty of bodies, but of the virtue of souls, and I inquire after one that is perfectly comely in that respect; I mean one who is beautiful in piety, and righteousness, and fortitude, and obedience, for in them consists the comeliness of the soul." When God had said this, Samuel bade Jesse to show him all his sons. So he made five others of his sons to come to him; of all of whom Eliab was the eldest, Aminadab the second, Shammall the third, Nathaniel the fourth, Rael the fifth, and Asam the sixth. And when the prophet saw that these were no way inferior to the eldest in their countenances, he inquired of God which of them it was whom he chose for their king. And when God said it was none of them, he asked Jesse whether he had not some other sons besides these; and when he said that he had one more, named David, but that he was

a shepherd, and took care of the flocks, Samuel bade them call him immediately, for that till he was come they could not possibly sit down to the feast. Now, as soon as his father had sent for David, and he was come, he appeared to be of a yellow complexion, of a sharp sight, and a comely person in other respects also. This is he, said Samuel privately to himself, whom it pleases God to make our king. So he sat down to the feast, and placed the youth under him, and Jesse also, with his other sons; after which he took oil in the presence of David, and anointed him, and whispered him in the ear, and acquainted him that God chose him to be their king; and exhorted him to be righteous, and obedient to his commands, for that by this means his kingdom would continue for a long time, and that his house should be of great splendor, and celebrated in the world; that he should overthrow the Philistines; and that against what nations soever he should make war, he should be the conqueror, and survive the fight; and that while he lived he should enjoy a glorious name, and leave such a name to his posterity also.

2. So Samuel, when he had given him these admonitions, went away. But the Divine Power departed from Saul, and removed to David; who, upon this removal of the Divine Spirit to him, began to prophesy. But as for Saul, some strange and demoniacal disorders came upon him, and brought upon him such suffocations as were ready to choke him; for which the physicians could find no other remedy but this, That if any person could charm those passions by singing, and playing upon the harp, they advised them to inquire for such a one, and to observe when these demons came upon him and disturbed him, and to take care that such a person might stand over him, and play upon the harp, and recite hymns to him.[16] Accordingly Saul did not delay, but commanded them to seek out such a man. And when a certain stander-by said that he had seen in the city of Bethlehem a son of Jesse, who was yet no more than a child in age, but comely and beautiful, and in other respects one that was deserving of great regard, who was skillful in playing on the harp, and in singing

---

16. Spanheim takes notice here that the Greeks had such singers of hymns; and that usually children or youths were picked out for that service; as also, that those called singers to the harp, did the same that David did here, i.e. join their own vocal and instrumental music together.

of hymns, [and an excellent soldier in war,] he sent to Jesse, and desired him to take David away from the flocks, and send him to him, for he had a mind to see him, as having heard an advantageous character of his comeliness and his valor. So Jesse sent his son, and gave him presents to carry to Saul. And when he was come, Saul was pleased with him, and made him his armor-bearer, and had him in very great esteem; for he charmed his passion, and was the only physician against the trouble he had from the demons, whensoever it was that it came upon him, and this by reciting of hymns, and playing upon the harp, and bringing Saul to his right mind again. However, he sent to Jesse, the father of the child, and desired him to permit David to stay with him, for that he was delighted with his sight and company; which stay, that he might not contradict Saul, he granted.

9 *How the Philistines Made Another Expedition Against the Hebrews under the Reign of Saul; and How They Were Overcome by David's Slaying Goliath in Single Combat*

1. NOW the Philistines gathered themselves together again no very long time afterward; and having gotten together a great army, they made war against the Israelites; and having seized a place between Shochoh and Azekah, they there pitched their camp. Saul also drew out his army to oppose them; and by pitching his own camp on a certain hill, he forced the Philistines to leave their former camp, and to encamp themselves upon such another hill, over-against that on which Saul's army lay, so that a valley, which was between the two hills on which they lay, divided their camps asunder. Now there came down a man out of the camp of the Philistines, whose name was Goliath, of the city of Gath, a man of vast bulk, for he was of four cubits and a span in tallness, and had about him weapons suitable to the largeness of his body, for he had a breastplate on that weighed five thousand shekels: he had also a helmet and greaves of brass, as large as you would naturally suppose might cover the limbs of so vast a body. His spear was also such as was not carried like a light thing in his right hand, but he carried it as lying on his shoulders. He had also a lance of six hundred shekels; and many followed him to carry his armor. Wherefore this Goliath stood between the two armies, as they were

in battle array, and sent out aloud voice, and said to Saul and the Hebrews, "I will free you from fighting and from dangers; for what necessity is there that your army should fall and be afflicted? Give me a man of you that will fight with me, and he that conquers shall have the reward of the conqueror and determine the war; for these shall serve those others to whom the conqueror shall belong; and certainly it is much better, and more prudent, to gain what you desire by the hazard of one man than of all." When he had said this, he retired to his own camp; but the next day he came again, and used the same words, and did not leave off for forty days together, to challenge the enemy in the same words, till Saul and his army were therewith terrified, while they put themselves in array as if they would fight, but did not come to a close battle.

2. Now while this war between the Hebrews and the Philistines was going on, Saul sent away David to his father Jesse, and contented himself with those three sons of his whom he had sent to his assistance, and to be partners in the dangers of the war: and at first David returned to feed his sheep and his flocks; but after no long time he came to the camp of the Hebrews, as sent by his father, to carry provisions to his brethren, and to know what they were doing. While Goliath came again, and challenged them, and reproached them, that they had no man of valor among them that durst come down to fight him; and as David was talking with his brethren about the business for which his father had sent him, he heard the Philistine reproaching and abusing the army, and had indignation at it, and said to his brethren, "I am ready to fight a single combat with this adversary." Whereupon Eliab, his eldest brother, reproved him, and said that he spoke too rashly and improperly for one of his age, and bid him go to his flocks, and to his father. So he was abashed at his brother's words, and went away, but still he spake to some of the soldiers that he was willing to fight with him that challenged them. And when they had informed Saul what was the resolution of the young man, the king sent for him to come to him: and when the king asked what he had to say, he replied, "O king, be not cast down, nor afraid, for I will depress the insolence of this adversary, and will go down and fight with him, and will bring him under me, as tall and as great as he is, till he shall be sufficiently laughed at, and thy army shall get great glory, when he shall be slain by one that is not yet of man's estate, neither fit for

fighting, nor capable of being intrusted with the marshalling an army, or ordering a battle, but by one that looks like a child, and is really no elder in age than a child."

3. Now Saul wondered at the boldness and alacrity of David, but durst not presume on his ability, by reason of his age; but said he must on that account be too weak to fight with one that was skilled in the art of war. "I undertake this enterprise," said David, "in dependence on God's being with me, for I have had experience already of his assistance; for I once pursued after and caught a lion that assaulted my flocks, and took away a lamb from them; and I snatched the lamb out of the wild beast's mouth, and when he leaped upon me with violence, I took him by the tail, and dashed him against the ground. In the same manner did I avenge myself on a bear also; and let this adversary of ours be esteemed like one of these wild beasts, since he has a long while reproached our army, and blasphemed our God, who yet will reduce him under my power."

4. However, Saul prayed that the end might be, by God's assistance, not disagreeable to the alacrity and boldness of the child; and said, "Go thy way to the fight." So he put about him his breastplate, and girded on his sword, and fitted the helmet to his head, and sent him away. But David was burdened with his armor, for he had not been exercised to it, nor had he learned to walk with it; so he said, "Let this armor be thine, O king, who art able to bear it; but give me leave to fight as thy servant, and as I myself desire." Accordingly he laid by the armor, and taking his staff with him, and putting five stones out of the brook into a shepherd's bag, and having a sling in his right hand, he went towards Goliath. But the adversary seeing him come in such a manner, disdained him, and jested upon him, as if he had not such weapons with him as are usual when one man fights against another, but such as are used in driving away and avoiding of dogs; and said, "Dost thou take me not for a man, but a dog?" To which he replied, "No, not for a dog, but for a creature worse than a dog." This provoked Goliath to anger, who thereupon cursed him by the name of God, and threatened to give his flesh to the beasts of the earth, and to the fowls of the air, to be torn in pieces by them. To whom David answered, Thou comest to me with a sword, and with a spear, and with a breastplate; but I have God for my armor in coming against thee, who will destroy thee and all thy army by my hands for I will this day cut off thy head, and

cast the other parts of thy body to the dogs, and all men shall learn that God is the protector of the Hebrews, and that our armor and our strength is in his providence; and that without God's assistance, all other warlike preparations and power are useless." So the Philistine being retarded by the weight of his armor, when he attempted to meet David in haste, came on but slowly, as despising him, and depending upon it that he should slay him, who was both unarmed and a child also, without any trouble at all.

5. But the youth met his antagonist, being accompanied with an invisible assistant, who was no other than God himself. And taking one of the stones that he had out of the brook, and had put into his shepherd's bag, and fitting it to his sling, he slang it against the Philistine. This stone fell upon his forehead, and sank into his brain, insomuch that Goliath was stunned, and fell upon his face. So David ran, and stood upon his adversary as he lay down, and cut off his head with his own sword; for he had no sword himself. And upon the fall of Goliath the Philistines were beaten, and fled; for when they saw their champion prostrate on the ground, they were afraid of the entire issue of their affairs, and resolved not to stay any longer, but committed themselves to an ignominious and indecent flight, and thereby endeavored to save themselves from the dangers they were in. But Saul and the entire army of the Hebrews made a shout, and rushed upon them, and slew a great number of them, and pursued the rest to the borders of Garb, and to the gates of Ekron; so that there were slain of the Philistines thirty thousand, and twice as many wounded. But Saul returned to their camp, and pulled their fortification to pieces, and burnt it; but David carried the head of Goliath into his own tent, but dedicated his sword to God [at the tabernacle].

10 *Saul Envies David for His Glorious Success, and Takes an Occasion of Entrapping Him, from the Promise He Made Him of Giving Him His Daughter in Marriage; but This Upon Condition of His Bringing Him Six Hundred Heads of the Philistines*

1. NOW the women were an occasion of Saul's envy and hatred to David; for they came to meet their victorious army with cymbals, and drums, and all demonstrations of joy, and sang thus: The wives

said, that "Saul had slain his many thousands of the Philistines." The virgins replied, that "David had slain his ten thousands." Now, when the king heard them singing thus, and that he had himself the smallest share in their commendations, and the greater number, the ten thousands, were ascribed to the young man; and when he considered with himself that there was nothing more wanting to David, after such a mighty applause, but the kingdom; he began to be afraid and suspicious of David. Accordingly he removed him from the station he was in before, for he was his armor-bearer, which, out of fear, seemed to him much too near a station for him; and so he made him captain over a thousand, and bestowed on him a post better indeed in itself, but, as he thought, more for his own security; for he had a mind to send him against the enemy, and into battles, as hoping he would be slain in such dangerous conflicts.

2. But David had God going along with him whithersoever he went, and accordingly he greatly prospered in his undertakings, and it was visible that he had mighty success, insomuch that Saul's daughter, who was still a virgin, fell in love with him; and her affection so far prevailed over her, that it could not be concealed, and her father became acquainted with it. Now Saul heard this gladly, as intending to make use of it for a snare against David, and he hoped that it would prove the cause of destruction and of hazard to him; so he told those that informed him of his daughter's affection, that he would willingly give David the virgin in marriage, and said, "I engage myself to marry my daughter to him if he will bring me six hundred heads of my enemies[17] supposing that when a reward so ample was proposed to him, and when he should aim to get him great glory, by undertaking a thing so dangerous and incredible, he would immediately set about it, and so perish by the Philistines; and my designs about him will succeed finely to my mind, for I shall be freed from him, and get him slain, not by myself, but by another man." So he gave order to his

---

17. Josephus says thrice in this chapter, and twice afterwards, ch. 11. sect. 2, and B. VII. ch. 1. sect. 4, i.e. five times in all, that Saul required not a bare hundred of the foreskins of the Philistines, but six hundred of their heads. The Septuagint have 100 foreskins, but the Syriac and Arabic 200. Now that these were not foreskins, with our other copies, but heads, with Josephus's copy, seems somewhat probable, from 1 Samuel 29:4, where all copies say that it was with the heads of such Philistines that David might reconcile himself to his master, Saul.

servants to try how David would relish this proposal of marrying the damsel. Accordingly, they began to speak thus to him: That king Saul loved him, as well as did all the people, and that he was desirous of his affinity by the marriage of this damsel. To which he gave this answer:—"Seemeth it to you a light thing to be made the king's son-in-law? It does not seem so to me, especially when I am one of a family that is low, and without any glory or honor." Now when Saul was informed by his servants what answer David had made, he said,— "Tell him that I do not want any money nor dowry from him, which would be rather to set my daughter to sale than to give her in marriage; but I desire only such a son-in-law as hath in him fortitude, and all other kinds of virtue," of which he saw David was possessed, and that his desire was to receive of him, on account of his marrying his daughter, neither gold nor silver, nor that he should bring such wealth out of his father's house, but only some revenge on the Philistines, and indeed six hundred of their heads, than which a more desirable or a more glorious present could not be brought him, and that he had much rather obtain this, than any of the accustomed dowries for his daughter, viz. that she should be married to a man of that character, and to one who had a testimony as having conquered his enemies.

3. When these words of Saul were brought to David, he was pleased with them, and supposed that Saul was really desirous of this affinity with him; so that without bearing to deliberate any longer, or casting about in his mind whether what was proposed was possible, or was difficult or not, he and his companions immediately set upon the enemy, and went about doing what was proposed as the condition of the marriage. Accordingly, because it was God who made all things easy and possible to David, he slew many [of the Philistines], and cut off the heads of six hundred of them, and came to the king, and by showing him these heads of the Philistines, required that he might have his daughter in marriage. Accordingly, Saul having no way of getting off his engagements, as thinking it a base thing either to seem a liar when he promised him this marriage, or to appear to have acted treacherously by him, in putting him upon what was in a manner impossible, in order to have him slain, he gave him his daughter in marriage: her name was Michal.

BOOK 6

11 How David, Upon Saul's Laying Snares for Him, Did Yet Escape the Dangers He Was in by the Affection and Care of Jonathan and the Contrivances of His Wife Michal: And How He Came to Samuel the Prophet

1. HOWEVER, Saul was not disposed to persevere long in the state wherein he was, for when he saw that David was in great esteem, both with God and with the multitude, he was afraid; and being not able to conceal his fear as concerning great things, his kingdom and his life, to be deprived of either of which was a very great calamity, he resolved to have David slain, and commanded his son Jonathan and his most faithful servants to kill him: but Jonathan wondered at his father's change with relation to David, that it should be made to so great a degree, from showing him no small good-will, to contrive how to have him killed. Now, because he loved the young man, and reverenced him for his virtue, he informed him of the secret charge his father had given, and what his intentions were concerning him. However, he advised him to take care and be absent the next day, for that he would salute his father, and, if he met with a favorable opportunity, he would discourse with him about him, and learn the cause of his disgust, and show how little ground there was for it, and that for it he ought not to kill a man that had done so many good things to the multitude, and had been a benefactor to himself, on account of which he ought in reason to obtain pardon, had he been guilty of the greatest crimes; and "I will then inform thee of my father's resolution." Accordingly David complied with such an advantageous advice, and kept himself then out of the king's sight.

2. On the next day Jonathan came to Saul, as soon as he saw him in a cheerful and joyful disposition, and began to introduce a discourse about David: "What unjust action, O father, either little or great, hast thou found so exceptionable in David, as to induce thee to order us to slay a man who hath been of great advantage to thy own preservation, and of still greater to the punishment of the Philistines? A man who hath delivered the people of the Hebrews from reproach and derision, which they underwent for forty days together, when he alone had courage enough to sustain the challenge of the adversary, and after that brought as many heads of our enemies as he was appointed to bring, and had, as a reward for the same, my sister in marriage;

insomuch that his death would be very sorrowful to us, not only on account of his virtue, but on account of the nearness of our relation; for thy daughter must be injured at the same time that he is slain, and must be obliged to experience widowhood, before she can come to enjoy any advantage from their mutual conversation. Consider these things, and change your mind to a more merciful temper, and do no mischief to a man, who, in the first place, hath done us the greatest kindness of preserving thee; for when an evil spirit and demons had seized upon thee, he cast them out, and procured rest to thy soul from their incursions: and, in the second place, hath avenged us of our enemies; for it is a base thing to forget such benefits." So Saul was pacified with these words, and sware to his son that he would do David no harm, for a righteous discourse proved too hard for the king's anger and fear. So Jonathan sent for David, and brought him good news from his father, that he was to be preserved. He also brought him to his father; and David continued with the king as formerly.

3. About this time it was that, upon the Philistines making a new expedition against the Hebrews, Saul sent David with an army to fight with them; and joining battle with them he slew many of them, and after his victory he returned to the king. But his reception by Saul was not as he expected upon such success, for he was grieved at his prosperity, because he thought he would be more dangerous to him by having acted so gloriously: but when the demoniacal spirit came upon him, and put him into disorder, and disturbed him, he called for David into his bed-chamber wherein he lay, and having a spear in his hand, he ordered him to charm him with playing on his harp, and with singing hymns; which when David did at his command, he with great force threw the spear at him; but David was aware of it before it came, and avoided it, and fled to his own house, and abode there all that day.

4. But at night the king sent officers, and commanded that he should be watched till the morning, lest he should get quite away, that he might come into the judgment-hall, and so might be delivered up, and condemned and slain. But when Michal, David's wife, the king's daughter, understood what her father designed, she came to her husband, as having small hopes of his deliverance, and as greatly concerned about her own life also, for she could not bear to live in case she were deprived of him; and she said, "Let not the sun find thee here

when it rises, for if it do, that will be the last time it will see thee: fly away then while the night may afford thee opportunity, and may God lengthen it for thy sake; for know this, that if my father find thee, thou art a dead man." So she let him down by a cord out of the window, and saved him: and after she had done so, she fitted up a bed for him as if he were sick, and put under the bed-clothes a goat's liver[18] and when her father, as soon as it was day, sent to seize David, she said to those that were there, That he had not been well that night, and showed them the bed covered, and made them believe, by the leaping of the liver, which caused the bed-clothes to move also, that David breathed like one that was asthmatic. So when those that were sent told Saul that David had not been well in the night he ordered him to be brought in that condition, for he intended to kill him. Now when they came and uncovered the bed, and found out the woman's contrivance, they told it to the king; and when her father complained of her that she had saved his enemy, and had put a trick upon himself, she invented this plausible defense for herself, and said, That when he had threatened to kill her, she lent him her assistance for his preservation, out of fear; for which her assistance she ought to be forgiven, because it was not done of her own free choice, but out of necessity: "For," said she, "I do not suppose that thou wast so zealous to kill thy enemy, as thou wast that I should be saved." Accordingly Saul forgave the damsel; but David, when he had escaped this danger, came to the prophet Samuel to Ramah, and told him what snares the king had laid for him, and how he was very near to death by Saul's throwing a spear at him, although he had been no way guilty with relation to him, nor had he been cowardly in his battles with his enemies, but had succeeded well in them all, by God's assistance; which thing was indeed the cause of Saul's hatred to David.

5. When the prophet was made acquainted with the unjust proceedings of the king, he left the city Ramah, and took David with him, to a certain place called Naioth, and there he abode with him. But when

---

18. Since the modern Jews have lost the signification of the Hebrew word here used, cebr; and since the LXX., as well as Josephus, reader it the liver of the goat, and since this rendering, and Josephus's account, are here so much more clear and probable than those of others, it is almost unaccountable that our commentators should so much as hesitate about its true interpretation.

it was told Saul that David was with the prophet, he sent soldiers to him, and ordered them to take him, and bring him to him: and when they came to Samuel, and found there a congregation of prophets, they became partakers of the Divine Spirit, and began to prophesy; which when Saul heard of, he sent others to David, who prophesying in like manner as did the first, he again sent others; which third sort prophesying also, at last he was angry, and went thither in great haste himself; and when he was just by the place, Samuel, before he saw him, made him prophesy also. And when Saul came to him, he was disordered in mind[19] and under the vehement agitation of a spirit; and, putting off his garments,[20] he fell down, and lay on the ground all that day and night, in the presence of Samuel and David.

6. And David went thence, and came to Jonathan, the son of Saul, and lamented to him what snares were laid for him by his father; and said, that though he had been guilty of no evil, nor had offended against him, yet he was very zealous to get him killed. Hereupon Jonathan exhorted him not to give credit to such his own suspicions, nor to the calumnies of those that raised those reports, if there were any that did so, but to depend on him, and take courage; for that his father had no such intention, since he would have acquainted him with that matter, and have taken his advice, had it been so, as he used to consult with him in common when he acted in other affairs. But

---

19. These violent and wild agitations of Saul seem to me to have been no other than demoniacal; and that the same demon which used to seize him, since he was forsaken of God, and which the divine hymns and psalms which were sung to the harp by David used to expel, was now in a judicial way brought upon him, not only in order to disappoint his intentions against innocent David, but to expose him to the laughter and contempt of all that saw him, or heard of those agitations; such violent and wild agitations being never observed in true prophets, when they were under the inspiration of the Spirit of God. Our other copies, which say the Spirit of God came him, seem not so here copy, which mentions nothing of God at all. Nor does Josephus seem to ascribe this impulse and ecstasy of Saul to any other than to his old demoniacal spirit, which on all accounts appears the most probable. Nor does the former description of Saul's real inspiration by the Divine Spirit, 1 Samuel 10:9–12; Antiq. B. VI. ch. 4. sect. 2, which was before he was become wicked, well agree with the descriptions before us.

20. What is meant by Saul's lying down naked all that day, and all that night, 1 Samuel 19:4, and whether any more than laying aside his royal apparel, or upper garments, as Josephus seems to understand it, is by no means certain. See the note on Antiq. B. VIII. ch. 14. sect. 2.

David sware to him that so it was; and he desired him rather to believe him, and to provide for his safety, than to despise what he, with great sincerity, told him: that he would believe what he said, when he should either see him killed himself, or learn it upon inquiry from others: and that the reason why his father did not tell him of these things, was this, that he knew of the friendship and affection that he bore towards him.

7. Hereupon, when Jonathan found that this intention of Saul was so well attested, he asked him what he would have him do for him. To which David replied, "I am sensible that thou art willing to gratify me in every thing, and procure me what I desire. Now tomorrow is the new moon, and I was accustomed to sit down then with the king at supper: now, if it seem good to thee, I will go out of the city, and conceal myself privately there; and if Saul inquire why I am absent, tell him that I am gone to my own city Bethlehem, to keep a festival with my own tribe; and add this also, that thou gavest me leave so to do. And if he say, as is usually said in the case of friends that are gone abroad, It is well that he went, then assure thyself that no latent mischief or enmity may be feared at his hand; but if he answer otherwise, that will be a sure sign that he hath some designs against me, Accordingly thou shalt inform me of thy father's inclinations; and that out of pity to my case and out of thy friendship for me, as instances of which friendship thou hast vouchsafed to accept of the assurances of my love to thee, and to give the like assurances to me, that is, those of a master to his servant; but if thou discoverest any wickedness in me, do thou prevent thy father, and kill me thyself."

8. But Jonathan heard these last words with indignation, and promised to do what he desired of him, and to inform him if his father's answers implied any thing of a melancholy nature, and any enmity against him. And that he might the more firmly depend upon him, he took him out into the open field, into the pure air, and sware that he would neglect nothing that might tend to the preservation of David; and he said, "I appeal to that God, who, as thou seest, is diffused every where, and knoweth this intention of mine, before I explain it in words, as the witness of this my covenant with thee, that I will not leave off to make frequent trims of the purpose of my father till I learn whether there be any lurking distemper in the most secret parts of his soul; and when I have learnt it, I will not conceal it from thee, but will discover it to thee, whether he be gently or peevishly

disposed; for this God himself knows, that I pray he may always be with thee, for he is with thee now, and will not forsake thee, and will make thee superior to thine enemies, whether my father be one of them, or whether I myself be such. Do thou only remember what we now do; and if it fall out that I die, preserve my children alive, and requite what kindness thou hast now received to them." When he had thus sworn, he dismissed David, bidding him go to a certain place of that plain wherein he used to perform his exercises; for that, as soon as he knew the mind of his father, he would come thither to him, with one servant only; "and if," says he, "I shoot three darts at the mark, and then bid my servant to carry these three darts away, for they are before him, know thou that there is no mischief to be feared from my father; but if thou hearest me say the contrary, expect the contrary from the king. However, thou shalt gain security by my means, and shalt by no means suffer any harm; but see thou dost not forget what I have desired of thee in the time of thy prosperity, and be serviceable to my children." Now David, when he had received these assurances from Jonathan, went his way to the place appointed.

9. But on the next day, which was the new moon, the king, when he had purified himself, as the custom was, came to supper; and when there sat by him his son Jonathan on his right hand, and Abner, the captain of his host, on the other hand, he saw David's seat was empty, but said nothing, supposing that he had not purified himself since he had accompanied with his wife, and so could not be present; but when he saw that he was not there the second day of the month neither, he inquired of his son Jonathan why the son of Jesse did not come to the supper and the feast, neither the day before nor that day. So Jonathan said, That he was gone, according to the agreement between them, to his own city, where his tribe kept a festival, and that by his permission: that he also invited him to come to their sacrifice; "and," says Jonathan, "if thou wilt give me leave, I Will go thither, for thou knowest the good-will that I bear him." And then it was that Jonathan understood his father's hatred to David, and plainly saw his entire disposition; for Saul could not restrain his anger, but reproached Jonathan, and called him the son of a runagate, and an enemy; and said he was a partner with David, and his assistant, and that by his behavior he showed he had no regard to himself, or to his mother, and would not be persuaded of this,—that while David is alive, their kingdom

was not secure to them; yet did he bid him send for him, that he might be punished. And when Jonathan said, in answer, "What hath he done that thou wilt punish him?" Saul no longer contented himself to express his anger in bare words, but snatched up his spear, and leaped upon him, and was desirous to kill him. He did not indeed do what he intended, because he was hindered by his friends; but it appeared plainly to his son that he hated David, and greatly desired to despatch him, insomuch that he had almost slain his son with his own hands on his account.

10. And then it was that the king's son rose hastily from supper; and being unable to admit any thing into his mouth for grief, he wept all night, both because he had himself been near destruction, and because the death of David was determined: but as soon as it was day, he went out into the plain that was before the city, as going to perform his exercises, but in reality to inform his friend what disposition his father was in towards him, as he had agreed with him to do; and when Jonathan had done what had been thus agreed, he dismissed his servant that followed him, to return to the city; but he himself went into the desert, and came into his presence, and communed with him. So David appeared and fell at Jonathan's feet, and bowed down to him, and called him the preserver of his soul; but he lifted him up from the earth, and they mutually embraced one another, and made a long greeting, and that not without tears. They also lamented their age, and that familiarity which envy would deprive them of, and that separation which must now be expected, which seemed to them no better than death itself. So recollecting themselves at length from their lamentation, and exhorting one another to be mindful of the oaths they had sworn to each other, they parted asunder.

12 *How David Fled to Ahimelech and Afterwards to the Kings of the Philistines and of the Moabites, and How Saul Slew Ahimelech and His Family,*

1. BUT David fled from the king, and that death he was in danger of by him, and came to the city Nob, to Ahimelech the priest, who, when he saw him coming all alone, and neither a friend nor a servant with him, he wondered at it, and desired to learn of him the cause why

there was nobody with him. To which David answered, That the king had commanded him to do a certain thing that was to be kept secret, to which, if he had a mind to know so much, he had no occasion for any one to accompany him; "however, I have ordered my servants to meet me at such and such a place." So he desired him to let him have somewhat to eat; and that in case he would supply him, be would act the part of a friend, and be assisting to the business he was now about: and when he had obtained what he desired, he also asked him whether he had any weapons with him, either sword or spear. Now there was at Nob a servant of Saul, by birth a Syrian, whose name was Doeg, one that kept the king's mules. The high priest said that he had no such weapons; but, he added, "Here is the sword of Goliath, which, when thou hadst slain the Philistine, thou didst dedicate to God."

2. When David had received the sword, he fled out of the country of the Hebrews into that of the Philistines, over which Achish reigned; and when the king's servants knew him, and he was made known to the king himself, the servants informing him that he was that David who had killed many ten thousands of the Philistines, David was afraid lest the king should put him to death, and that he should experience that danger from him which he had escaped from Saul; so he pretended to be distracted and mad, so that his spittle ran out of his mouth; and he did other the like actions before the king of Gath, which might make him believe that they proceeded from such a distemper. Accordingly the king was very angry at his servants that they had brought him a madman, and he gave orders that they should eject David immediately [out of the city].

3. So when David had escaped in this manner out of Gath, he came to the tribe of Judah, and abode in a cave by the city of Adullam. Then it was that he sent to his brethren, and informed them where he was, who then came to him with all their kindred, and as many others as were either in want or in fear of king Saul, came and made a body together, and told him they were ready to obey his orders; they were in all about four hundred. Whereupon he took courage, now such a force and assistance was come to him; so he removed thence and came to the king of the Moabites, and desired him to entertain his parents in his country, while the issue of his affairs were in such an uncertain condition. The king granted him this favor, and paid great respect to David's parents all the time they were with him.

4. As for himself, upon the prophet's commanding him to leave the desert, and to go into the portion of the tribe of Judah, and abide there, he complied therewith; and coming to the city Hareth, which was in that tribe, he remained there. Now when Saul heard that David had been seen with a multitude about him, he fell into no small disturbance and trouble; but as he knew that David was a bold and courageous man, he suspected that somewhat extraordinary would appear from him, and that openly also, which would make him weep and put him into distress; so he called together to him his friends, and his commanders, and the tribe from which he was himself derived, to the hill where his palace was; and sitting upon a place called Aroura, his courtiers that were in dignities, and the guards of his body, being with him, he spake thus to them:—"You that are men of my own tribe, I conclude that you remember the benefits that I have bestowed upon you, and that I have made some of you owners of land, and made you commanders, and bestowed posts of honor upon you, and set some of you over the common people, and others over the soldiers; I ask you, therefore, whether you expect greater and more donations from the son of Jesse? for I know that you are all inclinable to him; (even my own son Jonathan himself is of that opinion, and persuades you to be of the same); for I am not unacquainted with the oaths and the covenants that are between him and David, and that Jonathan is a counselor and an assistant to those that conspire against me, and none of you are concerned about these things, but you keep silence and watch, to see what will be the upshot of these things." When the king had made this speech, not one of the rest of those that were present made any answer; but Doeg the Syrian, who fed his mules, said, that he saw David when he came to the city Nob to Ahimelech the high priest, and that he learned future events by his prophesying; that he received food from him, and the sword of Goliath, and was conducted by him with security to such as he desired to go to.

5. Saul therefore sent for the high priest, and for all his kindred; and said to them, "What terrible or ungrateful tiring hast thou suffered from me, that thou hast received the son of Jesse, and hast bestowed on him both food and weapons, when he was contriving to get the kingdom? And further, why didst thou deliver oracles to him concerning futurities? For thou couldst not be unacquainted that he was fled away from me, and that he hated my family." But the high

priest did not betake himself to deny what he had done, but confessed boldly that he had supplied him with these things, not to gratify David, but Saul himself: and he said, "I did not know that he was thy adversary, but a servant of thine, who was very faithful to thee, and a captain over a thousand of thy soldiers, and, what is more than these, thy son-in-law, and kinsman. Men do not choose to confer such favors on their adversaries, but on those who are esteemed to bear the highest good-will and respect to them. Nor is this the first time that I prophesied for him, but I have done it often, and at other times as well as now. And when he told me that he was sent by thee in great haste to do somewhat, if I had furnished him with nothing that he desired I should have thought that it was rather in contradiction to thee than to him; wherefore do not thou entertain any ill opinion of me, nor do thou have a suspicion of what I then thought an act of humanity, from what is now told thee of David's attempts against thee, for I did then to him as to thy friend and son-in-law, and captain of a thousand, and not as to thine adversary."

6. When the high priest had spoken thus, he did not persuade Saul, his fear was so prevalent, that he could not give credit to an apology that was very just. So he commanded his armed men that stood about him to kill him, and all his kindred; but as they durst not touch the high priest, but were more afraid of disobeying God than the king, he ordered Doeg the Syrian to kill them. Accordingly, he took to his assistance such wicked men as were like himself, and slew Ahimelech and all his family, who were in all three hundred and eighty-five. Saul also sent to Nob,[21] the city of the priests, and slew all that were there, without sparing either women or children, or any other age, and burnt it; only there was one son of Ahimelech, whose name was

---

21. This city Nob was not a city allotted to the priests, nor had the prophets, that we know of, any particular cities allotted them. It seems the tabernacle was now at Nob, and probably a school of the prophets was here also. It was full two days' journey on foot from Jerusalem, 1 Samuel 21:5. The number of priests here slain in Josephus is three hundred and eighty-five, and but eighty-five in our Hebrew copies; yet are they three hundred and five in the Septuagint. I prefer Josephus's number, the Hebrew having, I suppose, only dropped the hundreds, the other the tens. This city Nob seems to have been the chief, or perhaps the only seat of the family of Ithamar, which here perished, according to God's former terrible threatenings to Eli, 1 Samuel 2:27–36; 3:11–18. See ch. 14. sect. D, hereafter.

Abiathar, who escaped. However, these things came to pass as God had foretold to Eli the high priest, when he said that his posterity should be destroyed, on account of the transgression of his two sons.

7.[22] Now this king Saul, by perpetrating so barbarous a crime, and murdering the whole family of the high-priestly dignity, by having no pity of the infants, nor reverence for the aged, and by overthrowing the city which God had chosen for the property, and for the support of the priests and prophets which were there, and had ordained as the only city allotted for the education of such men, gives all to understand and consider the disposition of men, that while they are private persons, and in a low condition, because it is not in their power to indulge nature, nor to venture upon what they wish for, they are equitable and moderate, and pursue nothing but what is just, and bend their whole minds and labors that way; then it is that they have this belief about God, that he is present to all the actions of their lives, and that he does not only see the actions that are done, but clearly knows those their thoughts also, whence those actions do arise. But when once they are advanced into power and authority, then they put off all such notions, and, as if they were no other than actors upon a theater, they lay aside their disguised parts and manners, and take up boldness, insolence, and a contempt of both human and Divine laws, and this at a time when they especially stand in need of piety and righteousness, because they are then most of all exposed to envy, and all they think, and all they say, are in the view of all men; then it is that they become so insolent in their actions, as though God saw them no longer, or were afraid of them because of their power: and whatsoever it is that they either are afraid of by the rumors they hear, or they hate by inclination, or they love without reason, these seem

---

22. This section contains an admirable reflection of Josephus concerning the general wickedness of men in great authority, and the danger they are in of rejecting that regard to justice and humanity, to Divine Providence and the fear of God, which they either really had, or pretended to have, while they were in a lower condition. It can never be too often perused by kings and great men, nor by those who expect to obtain such elevated dignities among mankind. See the like reflections of our Josephus, Antiq. B. VII. ch. 1. sect. 5, at the end; and B. VIII. ch. 10. sect. 2, at the beginning. They are to the like purport with one branch of Agur's prayer: "One thing have I required of thee, deny it me not before I die: Give me not riches, lest I be full, and deny thee, and say, Who is the Lord ?" Proverbs 30:7–9.

to them to be authentic, and firm, and true, and pleasing both to men and to God; but as to what will come hereafter, they have not the least regard to it. They raise those to honor indeed who have been at a great deal of pains for them, and after that honor they envy them; and when they have brought them into high dignity, they do not only deprive them of what they had obtained, but also, on that very account, of their lives also, and that on wicked accusations, and such as on account of their extravagant nature, are incredible. They also punish men for their actions, not such as deserve condemnation, but from calumnies and accusations without examination; and this extends not only to such as deserve to be punished, but to as many as they are able to kill. This reflection is openly confirmed to us from the example of Saul, the son of Kish, who was the first king who reigned after our aristocracy and government under the judges were over; and that by his slaughter of three hundred priests and prophets, on occasion of his suspicion about Ahimelech, and by the additional wickedness of the overthrow of their city, and this is as he were endeavoring in some sort to render the temple [tabernacle] destitute both of priests and prophets, which endeavor he showed by slaying so many of them, and not suffering the very city belonging to them to remain, that so others might succeed them.

8. But Abiathar, the son of Ahimelech, who alone could be saved out of the family of priests slain by Saul, fled to David, and informed him of the calamity that had befallen their family, and of the slaughter of his father; who hereupon said, He was not unapprised of what would follow with relation to them when he saw Doeg there; for he had then a suspicion that the high priest would be falsely accused by him to the king, and he blamed himself as having been the cause of this misfortune. But he desired him to stay there, and abide with him, as in a place where he might be better concealed than any where else.

13   *How David, When He Had Twice the Opportunity of Killing Saul Did Not Kill Him. Also Concerning the Death of Samuel and Nabal*

1. ABOUT this time it was that David heard how the Philistines had made an inroad into the country of Keilah, and robbed it; so he offered

himself to fight against them, if God, when he should be consulted by the prophet, would grant him the victory. And when the prophet said that God gave a signal of victory, he made a sudden onset upon the Philistines with his companions, and he shed a great deal of their blood, and carried off their prey, and staid with the inhabitants of Keilah till they had securely gathered in their corn and their fruits. However, it was told Saul the king that David was with the men of Keilah; for what had been done and the great success that had attended him, were not confined among the people where the things were done, but the fame of it went all abroad, and came to the hearing of others, and both the fact as it stood, and the author of the fact, were carried to the king's ears. Then was Saul glad when he heard David was in Keilah; and he said, "God hath now put him into my hands, since he hath obliged him to come into a city that hath walls, and gates, and bars." So he commanded all the people suddenly, and when they had besieged and taken it to kill David. But when David perceived this, and learned of God that if he staid there the men of Keilah would deliver him up to Saul, he took his four hundred men and retired into a desert that was over against a city called Engedi. So that when the king heard he was fled away from the men of Keilah, he left off his expedition against him.

2. Then David removed thence, and came to a certain place called the New Place, belonging to Ziph; where Jonathan, the son of Saul, came to him, and saluted him, and exhorted him to be of good courage, and to hope well as to his condition hereafter, and not to despond at his present circumstances, for that he should be king, and have all the forces of the Hebrews under him: he told him that such happiness uses to come with great labor and pains: they also took oaths, that they would, all their lives long, continue in good-will and fidelity one to another; and he called God to witness, as to what execrations he had made upon himself if he should transgress his covenant, and should change to a contrary behavior. So Jonathan left him there, having rendered his cares and fears somewhat lighter, and returned home. Now the men of Ziph, to gratify Saul, informed him that David abode with them, and [assured him] that if he would come to them, they would deliver him up, for that if the king would seize on the Straits of Ziph, David would not escape to any other people. So the king commended them, and confessed that he had reason to thank

them, because they had given him information of his enemy; and he promised them, that it should not be long ere he would requite their kindness. He also sent men to seek for David, and to search the wilderness wherein he was; and he promised that he himself would follow them. Accordingly they went before the king, to hunt for and to catch David, and used endeavors, not only to show their good-will to Saul, by informing him where his enemy was, but to evidence the same more plainly by delivering him up into his power. But these men failed of those their unjust and wicked desires, who, while they underwent no hazard by not discovering such an ambition of revealing this to Saul, yet did they falsely accuse and promise to deliver up a man beloved of God, and one that was unjustly sought after to be put to death, and one that might otherwise have lain concealed, and this out of flattery, and expectation of gain from the king; for when David was apprized of the malignant intentions of the men of Ziph, and the approach of Saul, he left the Straits of that country, and fled to the great rock that was in the wilderness of Maon.

3. Hereupon Saul made haste to pursue him thither; for, as he was marching, he learned that David was gone away from the Straits of Ziph, and Saul removed to the other side of the rock. But the report that the Philistines had again made an incursion into the country of the Hebrews, called Saul another way from the pursuit of David, when he was ready to be caught; for he returned back again to oppose those Philistines, who were naturally their enemies, as judging it more necessary to avenge himself of them, than to take a great deal of pains to catch an enemy of his own, and to overlook the ravage that was made in the land.

4. And by this means David unexpectedly escaped out of the danger he was in, and came to the Straits of Engedi; and when Saul had driven the Philistines out of the land, there came some messengers, who told him that David abode within the bounds of Engedi: so he took three thousand chosen men that were armed, and made haste to him; and when he was not far from those places, he saw a deep and hollow cave by the way-side; it was open to a great length and breadth, and there it was that David with his four hundred men were concealed. When therefore he had occasion to ease nature, he entered into it by himself alone; and being seen by one of David's companions, and he that saw him saying to him, that he had now, by God's providence, an

opportunity of avenging himself of his adversary; and advising him to cut off his head, and so deliver himself out of that tedious, wandering condition, and the distress he was in; he rose up, and only cut off the skirt of that garment which Saul had on: but he soon repented of what he had done; and said it was not right to kill him that was his master, and one whom God had thought worthy of the kingdom; "for that although he were wickedly disposed towards us, yet does it not behoove me to be so disposed towards him." But when Saul had left the cave, David came near and cried out aloud, and desired Saul to hear him; whereupon the king turned his face back, and David, according to custom, fell down on his face before the king, and bowed to him; and said, "O king, thou oughtest not to hearken to wicked men, nor to such as forge calumnies, nor to gratify them so far as to believe what they say, nor to entertain suspicions of such as are your best friends, but to judge of the dispositions of all men by their actions; for calumny deludes men, but men's own actions are a clear demonstration of their kindness. Words indeed, in their own nature, may be either true or false, but men's actions expose their intentions nakedly to our view. By these, therefore it will be well for thee to believe me, as to my regard to thee and to thy house, and not to believe those that frame such accusations against me as never came into my mind, nor are possible to be executed, and do this further by pursuing after my life, and have no concern either day or night, but how to compass my life and to murder me, which thing I think thou dost unjustly prosecute; for how comes it about, that thou hast embraced this false opinion about me, as if I had a desire to kill thee? Or how canst thou escape the crime of impiety towards God, when thou wishest thou couldst kill, and deemest thine adversary, a man who had it in his power this day to avenge himself, and to punish thee, but would not do it? nor make use of such an opportunity, which, if it had fallen out to thee against me, thou hadst not let it slip, for when I cut off the skirt of thy garment, I could have done the same to thy head." So he showed him the piece of his garment, and thereby made him agree to what he said to be true; and added, "I, for certain, have abstained from taking a just revenge upon thee, yet art thou not ashamed to prosecute me with unjust hatred.[23] May God do justice, and determine about each of our dispositions."—But Saul was amazed at the strange delivery he had received; and being greatly affected with the moderation and the disposition of the young man, he groaned; and when David had done the same, the king answered that he had the justest occasion to groan, "for thou hast been the author of good to me, as I have been the author of calamity to thee; and thou hast demonstrated this day, that thou possessest the righteousness of the ancients, who determined that men ought to save their enemies, though they caught them in a desert place. I am now persuaded that God reserves the kingdom for thee, and that thou wilt obtain the dominion over all the Hebrews. Give me then assurances upon oath, That thou wilt not root out my family, nor, out of remembrance of what evil I have done thee, destroy my posterity, but save and preserve my house." So David sware as he desired, and sent back Saul to his own kingdom; but he, and those that were with him, went up the Straits of Mastheroth.

5. About this time Samuel the prophet died. He was a man whom the Hebrews honored in an extraordinary degree: for that lamentation which the people made for him, and this during a long time, manifested his virtue, and the affection which the people bore for him; as also did the solemnity and concern that appeared about his funeral, and about the complete observation of all his funeral rites. They buried him in his own city of Ramah; and wept for him a very great number of days, not looking on it as a sorrow for the death of another man, but as that in which they were every one themselves concerned. He was a righteous man, and gentle in his nature; and on that account he was very dear to God. Now he governed and presided over the people alone, after the death of Eli the high priest, twelve years, and eighteen years together with Saul the king. And thus we have finished the history of Samuel.

6. There was a man that was a Ziphite, of the city of Maon, who was rich, and had a vast number of cattle; for he fed a flock of

---

23. The phrase in David's speech to Saul, as set down in Josephus, that he had abstained from just revenge, puts me in mind of the like words in the Apostolical Constitutions, B. VII. ch. 2., "That revenge is not evil, but that patience is more honorable."

three thousand sheep, and another flock of a thousand goats. Now David had charged his associates to keep these flocks without hurt and without damage, and to do them no mischief, neither out of covetousness, nor because they were in want, nor because they were in the wilderness, and so could not easily be discovered, but to esteem freedom from injustice above all other motives, and to look upon the touching of what belonged to another man as a horrible crime, and contrary to the will of God. These were the instructions he gave, thinking that the favors he granted this man were granted to a good man, and one that deserved to have such care taken of his affairs. This man was Nabal, for that was his name,—a harsh man, and of a very wicked life, being like a cynic in the course of his behavior, but still had obtained for his wife a woman of a good character, wise and handsome. To this Nabal, therefore, David sent ten men of his attendants at the time when he sheared his sheep, and by them saluted him; and also wished he might do what he now did for many years to come, but desired him to make him a present of what he was able to give him, since he had, to be sure, learned from his shepherds that we had done them no injury, but had been their guardians a long time together, while we continued in the wilderness; and he assured him he should never repent of giving any thing to David. When the messengers had carried this message to Nabal, he accosted them after an inhuman and rough manner; for he asked them who David was? and when he heard that he was the son of Jesse, he said, "Now is the time that fugitives grow insolent, and make a figure, and leave their masters." When they told David this, he was wroth, and commanded four hundred armed men to follow him, and left two hundred to take care of the stuff, (for he had already six hundred,[24]) and went against Nabal: he also swore that he would that night utterly destroy the whole house and possessions of Nabal; for that he was grieved, not only that he had proved ungrateful to them, without making any

---

24. The number of men that came first to David, are distinctly in Josephus, and in our common copies, but four hundred. When he was at Keilah still but four hundred, both in Josephus and in the LXX.; but six hundred in our Hebrew copies, 1 Samuel 23:3; see 30:9, 10. Now the six hundred there mentioned are here estimated by Josephus to have been so many, only by an augmentation of two hundred afterward, which I suppose is the true solution of this seeming disagreement.

return for the humanity they had shown him, but that he had also reproached them, and used ill language to them, when he had received no cause of disgust from them.

7. Hereupon one of those that kept the flocks of Nabal, said to his mistress, Nabal's wife, that when David sent to her husband he had received no civil answer at all from him; but that her husband had moreover added very reproachful language, while yet David had taken extraordinary care to keep his flocks from harm, and that what had passed would prove very pernicious to his master. When the servant had said this, Abigail, for that was his wife's name, saddled her asses, and loaded them with all sorts of presents; and, without telling her husband any thing of what she was about, (for he was not sensible on account of his drunkenness,) she went to David. She was then met by David as she was descending a hill, who was coming against Nabal with four hundred men. When the woman saw David, she leaped down from her ass, and fell on her face, and bowed down to the ground; and entreated him not to bear in mind the words of Nabal, since he knew that he resembled his name. Now Nabal, in the Hebrew tongue, signifies *folly*. So she made her apology, that she did not see the messengers whom he sent. "Forgive me, therefore," said she, "and thank God, who hath hindered thee from shedding human blood; for so long as thou keepest thyself innocent, he will avenge thee of wicked men,[25] for what miseries await Nabal, they will fall upon the heads of thine enemies. Be thou gracious to me, and think me so far worthy as to accept of these presents from me; and, out of regard to me, remit that wrath and that anger which thou hast against my husband and his house, for mildness and humanity become thee, especially as thou art to be our king." Accordingly, David accepted her presents, and said, "Nay, but, O woman, it was no other than God's mercy which brought thee to us today, for, otherwise, thou hadst never seen another day, I

---

25. In this and the two next sections, we may perceive how Josephus, nay, how Abigail herself, would understand, the "not avenging ourselves, but heaping coals of fire on the head of the injurious," Proverbs 25:22; Romans 12:20, not as we do now, of them into but of leaving them to the judgment of God, "to whom vengeance belongeth," Deuteronomy 32:35; Psalms 94:1; Hebrews 10:30, and who will take vengeance on the wicked. And since all God's judgments are just, and all fit to be executed, and all at length for the good of the persons punished, I incline to think that to be the meaning of this phrase of "heaping coals of fire on their heads."

having sworn[26] to destroy Nabal's house this very night, and to leave alive not one of you who belonged to a man that was wicked and ungrateful to me and my companions; but now hast thou prevented me, and seasonably mollified my anger, as being thyself under the care of God's providence: but as for Nabal, although for thy sake he now escape punishment, he will not always avoid justice; for his evil conduct, on some other occasion, will be his ruin."

8. When David had said this, he dismissed the woman. But when she came home and found her husband feasting with a great company, and oppressed with wine, she said nothing to him then about what had happened; but on the next day, when he was sober, she told him all the particulars, and made his whole body to appear like that of a dead man by her words, and by that grief which arose from them; so Nabal survived ten days, and no more, and then died. And when David heard of his death, he said that God had justly avenged him of this man, for that Nabal had died by his own wickedness, and had suffered punishment on his account, while he had kept his own hands clean. At which time he understood that the wicked are prosecuted by God; that he does not overlook any man, but bestows on the good what is suitable to them, and inflicts a deserved punishment on the wicked. So he sent to Nabal's wife, and invited her to come to him, to live with him, and to be his wife. Whereupon she replied to those that came, that she was not worthy to touch his feet; however, she came, with all her servants, and became his wife, having received that honor on account of her wise and righteous course of life. She also obtained the same honor partly on account of her beauty. Now David had a wife before, whom he married from the city Abesar; for as to Michal, the daughter of king Saul, who had been David's wife, her father had given her in marriage to Phalti, the son of Laish, who was of the city of Gallim.

9. After this came certain of the Ziphites, and told Saul that David was come again into their country, and if he would afford them his

---

26. We may note here, that how sacred soever an oath was esteemed among the people of God in old times, they did not think it obligatory where the action was plainly unlawful. For so we see it was in this case of David, who, although he had sworn to destroy Nabal and his family, yet does he here, and 1 Samuel 25:32–41, bless God for preventing his keeping his oath, and shedding of blood, which he had swore to do.

assistance, they could catch him. So he came to them with three thousand armed men; and upon the approach of night, he pitched his camp at a certain place called Hachilah. But when David heard that Saul was coming against him, he sent spies, and bid them let him know to what place of the country Saul was already come; and when they told him that he was at Hachilah, he concealed his going away from his companions, and came to Saul's camp, having taken with him Abishai, his sister Zeruiah's son, and Ahimelech the Hittite. Now Saul was asleep, and the armed men, with Abner their commander, lay round about him in a circle. Hereupon David entered into the king's tent; but he did neither kill Saul, though he knew where he lay, by the spear that was stuck down by him, nor did he give leave to Abishai, who would have killed him, and was earnestly bent upon it so to do; for he said it was a horrid crime to kill one that was ordained king by God, although he was a wicked man; for that he who gave him the dominion would in time inflict punishment upon him. So he restrained his eagerness; but that it might appear to have been in his power to have killed him when he refrained from it, he took his spear, and the cruse of water which stood by Saul as he lay asleep, without being perceived by any in the camp, who were all asleep, and went securely away, having performed every thing among the king's attendants that the opportunity afforded, and his boldness encouraged him to do. So when he had passed over a brook, and was gotten up to the top of a hill, whence he might be sufficiently heard, he cried aloud to Saul's soldiers, and to Abner their commander, and awaked them out of their sleep, and called both to him and to the people. Hereupon the commander heard him, and asked who it was that called him. To whom David replied, "It is I, the son of Jesse, whom you make a vagabond. But what is the matter? Dost thou, that art a man of so great dignity, and of the first rank in the king's court, take so little care of thy master's body? and is sleep of more consequence to thee than his preservation, and thy care of him? This negligence of yours deserves death, and punishment to be inflicted on you, who never perceived when, a little while ago, some of us entered into your camp, nay, as far as to the king himself, and to all the rest of you. If thou look for the king's spear and his cruse of water, thou wilt learn what a mighty misfortune was ready to overtake you in your very camp without your knowing it." Now when Saul knew David's voice, and understood that when he had him in his power while he was asleep, and his guards took no care of him, yet did not he kill him, but spared him, when he might justly have cut him off, he said that he owed him thanks for his preservation; and exhorted him to be of good courage, and not be afraid of suffering any mischief from him any more, and to return to his own home, for he was now persuaded that he did not love himself so well as he was loved by him: that he had driven away him that could guard him, and had given many demonstrations of his good-will to him: that he had forced him to live so long in a state of banishment, and in great fears of his life, destitute of his friends and his kindred, while still he was often saved by him, and frequently received his life again when it was evidently in danger of perishing. So David bade them send for the spear and the cruse of water, and take them back; adding this withal, That God would be the judge of both their dispositions, and of the actions that flowed from the same, "who knows that then it was this day in my power to have killed thee I abstained from it."

10. Thus Saul having escaped the hands of David twice, he went his way to his royal palace, and his own city: but David was afraid, that if he staid there he should be caught by Saul; so he thought it better to go up into the land of the Philistines, and abide there. Accordingly, he came with the six hundred men that were with him to Achish, the king of Gath, which was one of their five cities. Now the king received both him and his men, and gave them a place to inhabit in. He had with him also his two wives, Ahinoam and Abigail, and he dwelt in Gath. But when Saul heard this, he took no further care about sending to him, or going after him, because he had been twice, in a manner, caught by him, while he was himself endeavoring to catch him. However, David had no mind to continue in the city of Gath, but desired the king, that since he had received him with such humanity, that he would grant him another favor, and bestow upon him some place of that country for his habitation, for he was ashamed, by living in the city, to be grievous and burdensome to him. So Achish gave him a certain village called Ziklag; which place David and his sons were fond of when he was king, and reckoned it to be their peculiar inheritance. But about those matters we shall give the reader further information elsewhere. Now the time that David dwelt in Ziklag, in the land of the Philistines, was four months and twenty days. And now he privately attacked those Geshurites and Amalekites that were neighbors to the

Philistines, and laid waste their country, and took much prey of their beasts and camels, and then returned home; but David abstained from the men, as fearing they should discover him to king Achish; yet did he send part of the prey to him as a free gift. And when the king inquired whom they had attacked when they brought away the prey, he said, those that lay to the south of the Jews, and inhabited in the plain; whereby he persuaded Achish to approve of what he had done, for he hoped that David had fought against his own nation, and that now he should have him for his servant all his life long, and that he would stay in his country.

14 *Now Saul Upon God's Not Answering Him Concerning the Fight with the Philistines Desired a Necromantic Woman to Raise Up the Soul of Samuel to Him; and How He Died, with His Sons Upon the Overthrow of the Hebrews in Battle,*

1. ABOUT the same time the Philistines resolved to make war against the Israelites, and sent to all their confederates that they would go along with them to the war to Reggan, [near the city Shunem,] whence they might gather themselves together, and suddenly attack the Hebrews. Then did Achish, the king of Gath, desire David to assist them with his armed men against the Hebrews. This he readily promised; and said that the time was now come wherein he might requite him for his kindness and hospitality. So the king promised to make him the keeper of his body, after the victory, supposing that the battle with the enemy succeeded to their mind; which promise of honor and confidence he made on purpose to increase his zeal for his service.

2. Now Saul, the king of the Hebrews, had cast out of the country the fortune-tellers, and the necromancers, and all such as exercised the like arts, excepting the prophets. But when he heard that the Philistines were already come, and had pitched their camp near the city Shunem, situate in the plain, he made haste to oppose them with his forces; and when he was come to a certain mountain called Gilboa, he pitched his camp over-against the enemy; but when he saw the enemy's army he was greatly troubled, because it appeared to him to be numerous, and superior to his own; and he inquired of God by

the prophets concerning the battle, that he might know beforehand what would be the event of it. And when God did not answer him, Saul was under a still greater dread, and his courage fell, foreseeing, as was but reasonable to suppose, that mischief would befall him, now God was not there to assist him; yet did he bid his servants to inquire out for him some woman that was a necromancer and called up the souls of the dead, that So he might know whether his affairs would succeed to his mind; for this sort of necromantic women that bring up the souls of the dead, do by them foretell future events to such as desire them. And one of his servants told him that there was such a woman in the city Endor, but was known to nobody in the camp; hereupon Saul put off his royal apparel, and took two of those his servants with him, whom he knew to be most faithful to him, and came to Endor to the woman, and entreated her to act the part of a fortune-teller, and to bring up such a soul to him as he should name to her. But when the woman opposed his motion, and said she did not despise the king, who had banished this sort of fortune-tellers, and that he did not do well himself, when she had done him no harm, to endeavor to lay a snare for her, and to discover that she exercised a forbidden art, in order to procure her to be punished, he sware that nobody should know what she did; and that he would not tell any one else what she foretold, but that she should incur no danger. As soon as he had induced her by this oath to fear no harm, he bid her bring up to him the soul of Samuel. She, not knowing who Samuel was, called him out of Hades. When he appeared, and the woman saw one that was venerable, and of a divine form, she was in disorder; and being astonished at the sight, she said, "Art not thou king Saul?" for Samuel had informed her who he was. When he had owned that to be true, and had asked her whence her disorder arose, she said that she saw a certain person ascend, who in his form was like to a god. And when he bid her tell him what he resembled, in what habit he appeared, and of what age he was, she told him he was an old man already, and of a glorious personage, and had on a sacerdotal mantle. So the king discovered by these signs that he was Samuel; and he fell down upon the ground, and saluted and worshipped him. And when the soul of Samuel asked him why he had disturbed him, and caused him to be brought up, he lamented the necessity he was under; for he said, that his enemies pressed heavily upon him; that he was in distress what to do in his present circumstances; that he was forsaken of God, and could obtain no prediction of what was coming, neither by prophets nor by dreams; and that "these were the reasons why I have recourse to time, who always took great care of me." But[27] Samuel, seeing that the end of Saul's life was come, said, "It is in vain for thee to desire to learn of me any thing future, when God hath forsaken thee: however, hear what I say, that David is to be king, and to finish this war with good success; and thou art to lose thy dominion and thy life, because thou didst not obey God in the war with the Amalekites, and hast not kept his commandments, as I foretold thee while I was alive. Know, therefore, that the people shall be made subject to their enemies, and that thou, with thy sons, shall fall in the battle tomorrow, and thou shalt then be with me [in Hades]."

3. When Saul heard this, he could not speak for grief, and fell down on the floor, whether it were from the sorrow that arose upon what Samuel had said, or from his emptiness, for he had taken no food the foregoing day nor night, he easily fell quite down: and when with difficulty he had recovered himself, the woman would force him to eat, begging this of him as a favor on account of her concern in that dangerous instance of fortune-telling, which it was not lawful for her to have done, because of the fear she was under of the king, while she knew not who he was, yet did she undertake it, and go through with it; on which account she entreated him to admit that a table and food might be set before him, that he might recover his strength, and so get safe to his own camp. And when he opposed her motion, and entirely rejected it, by reason of his anxiety, she forced him, and at last persuaded him to it. Now she had one calf that she was very fond of, and one that she took a great deal of care of, and fed it herself; for she

---

27. This history of Saul's consultation, not with a witch, as we render the Hebrew word here, but with a necromancer, as the whole history shows, is easily understood, especially if we consult the Recognitions of Clement, B. I. ch. 5. at large, and more briefly, and nearer the days of Samuel Ecclus. 46:20, "Samuel prophesied after his death, and showed the king his end, and lift up his voice from the earth in prophecy," to blot out "the wickedness of the people." Nor does the exactness of the accomplishment of this prediction, the very next day, permit us to suppose any imposition upon Saul in the present history; for as to all modern hypotheses against the natural sense of such ancient and authentic histories, I take them to be of very small value or consideration.

was a woman that got her living by the labor of her own hands, and had no other possession but that one calf; this she killed, and made ready its flesh, and set it before his servants and himself. So Saul came to the camp while it was yet night.

4. Now it is but just to recommend the generosity of this woman,[28] because when the king had forbidden her to use that art whence her circumstances were bettered and improved, and when she had never seen the king before, she still did not remember to his disadvantage that he had condemned her sort of learning, and did not refuse him as a stranger, and one that she had had no acquaintance with; but she had compassion upon him, and comforted him, and exhorted him to do what he was greatly averse to, and offered him the only creature she had, as a poor woman, and that earnestly, and with great humanity, while she had no requital made her for her kindness, nor hunted after any future favor from him, for she knew he was to die; whereas men are naturally either ambitious to please those that bestow benefits upon them, or are very ready to serve those from whom they may receive some advantage. It would be well therefore to imitate the example and to do kindnesses to all such as are in want and to think that nothing is better, nor more becoming mankind, than such a general beneficence, nor what will sooner render God favorable, and ready to bestow good things upon us. And so far may suffice to have spoken concerning this woman. But I shall speak further upon another subject, which will afford me all opportunity of discoursing on what is for the advantage of cities, and people, and nations, and suited to the taste of good men, and will encourage them all in the prosecution of virtue; and is capable of showing them the of acquiring glory, and an everlasting fame; and of imprinting in the kings of nations, and the rulers of cities, great inclination and diligence of doing well; as also of encouraging them to undergo dangers, and to die for their countries, and of instructing them how to despise all the most terrible adversities:

---

28. These great commendations of this necromantic woman of Endor, and of Saul's martial courage, when yet he knew he should die in the battle, are somewhat unusual digressions in Josephus. They seem to me extracted from some speeches or declamations of his composed formerly, in the way of oratory, that lay by him, and which he thought fit to insert upon this occasion. See before on Antiq. B. I. ch. 6 sect. 8.

and I have a fair occasion offered me to enter on such a discourse by Saul the king of the Hebrews; for although he knew what was coming upon him, and that he was to die immediately, by the prediction of the prophet, he did not resolve to fly from death, nor so far to indulge the love of life as to betray his own people to the enemy, or to bring a disgrace on his royal dignity; but exposing himself, as well as all his family and children, to dangers, he thought it a brave thing to fall together with them, as he was fighting for his subjects, and that it was better his sons should die thus, showing their courage, than to leave them to their uncertain conduct afterward, while, instead of succession and posterity, they gained commendation and a lasting name. Such a one alone seems to me to be a just, a courageous, and a prudent man; and when any one has arrived at these dispositions, or shall hereafter arrive at them, he is the man that ought to be by all honored with the testimony of a virtuous or courageous man: for as to those that go out to war with hopes of success, and that they shall return safe, supposing they should have performed some glorious action, I think those do not do well who call these valiant men, as so many historians and other writers who treat of them are wont to do, although I confess those do justly deserve some commendation also; but those only may be styled courageous and bold in great undertakings, and despisers of adversities, who imitate Saul: for as for those that do not know what the event of war will be as to themselves, and though they do not faint in it, but deliver themselves up to uncertain futurity, and are tossed this way and that way, this is not so very eminent an instance of a generous mind, although they happen to perform many great exploits; but when men's minds expect no good event, but they know beforehand they must die, and that they must undergo that death in the battle also, after this neither to be aftrighted, nor to be astonished at the terrible fate that is coming, but to go directly upon it, when they know it beforehand, this it is that I esteem the character of a man truly courageous. Accordingly this Saul did, and thereby demonstrated that all men who desire fame after they are dead are so to act as they may obtain the same: this especially concerns kings, who ought not to think it enough in their high stations that they are not wicked in the government of their subjects, but to be no more than moderately good to them. I could say more than this about Saul and his courage, the subject affording matter sufficient; but that I may not appear to run out improperly in his commendation, I return again to that history from which I made this digression.

5. Now when the Philistines, as I said before, had pitched their camp, and had taken an account of their forces, according to their nations, and kingdoms, and governments, king Achish came last of all with his own army; after whom came David with his six hundred armed men. And when the commanders of the Philistines saw him, they asked the king whence these Hebrews came, and at whose invitation. He answered that it was David, who was fled away from his master Saul, and that he had entertained him when he came to him, and that now he was willing to make him this requital for his favors, and to avenge himself upon Saul, and so was become his confederate. The commanders complained of this, that he had taken him for a confederate who was an enemy; and gave him counsel to send him away, lest he should unawares do his friends a great deal of mischief by entertaining him, for that he afforded him an opportunity of being reconciled to his master by doing a mischief to our army. They thereupon desired him, out of a prudent foresight of this, to send him away, with his six hundred armed men, to the place he had given him for his habitation; for that this was that David whom the virgins celebrated in their hymns, as having destroyed many ten thousands of the Philistines. When the king of Gath heard this, he thought they spake well; so he called David, and said to him, "As for myself, I can bear witness that thou hast shown great diligence and kindness about me, and on that account it was that I took thee for my confederate; however, what I have done does not please the commanders of the Philistines; go therefore within a day's time to the place I have given thee, without suspecting any harm, and there keep my country, lest any of our enemies should make an incursion upon it, which will be one part of that assistance which I expect from thee." So David came to Ziklag, as the king of Gath bade him; but it happened, that while he was gone to the assistance of the Philistines, the Amalekites had made an incursion, and taken Ziklag before, and had burnt it; and when they had taken a great deal of other prey out of that place, and out of the other parts of the Philistines' country, they departed.

6. Now when David found that Ziklag was laid waste, and that it was all spoiled, and that as well his own wives, who were two, as the wives of his companions, with their children, were made captives,

he presently rent his clothes, weeping and lamenting, together with his friends; and indeed he was so cast down with these misfortunes, that at length tears themselves failed him. He was also in danger of being stoned to death by his companions, who were greatly afflicted at the captivity of their wives and children, for they laid the blame upon him of what had happened. But when he had recovered himself out of his grief, and had raised up his mind to God, he desired the high priest Abiathar to put on his sacerdotal garments, and to inquire of God, and to prophesy to him, whether God would grant; that if he pursued after the Amalekites, he should overtake them, and save their wives and their children, and avenge himself on the enemies. And when the high priest bade him to pursue after them, he marched apace, with his four hundred men, after the enemy; and when he was come to a certain brook called Besor, and had lighted upon one that was wandering about, an Egyptian by birth, who was almost dead with want and famine, (for he had continued wandering about without food in the wilderness three days,) he first of all gave him sustenance, both meat and drink, and thereby refreshed him. He then asked him to whom he belonged, and whence he came. Whereupon the man told him he was an Egyptian by birth, and was left behind by his master, because he was so sick and weak that he could not follow him. He also informed him that he was one of those who had burnt and plundered, not only other parts of Judea, but Ziklag itself also. So David made use of him as a guide to find oat the Amalekites; and when he had overtaken them, as they lay scattered about on the ground, some at dinner, some disordered, and entirely drunk with wine, and in the fruition of their spoils and their prey, he fell upon them on the sudden, and made a great slaughter among them; for they were naked, and expected no such thing, but had betaken themselves to drinking and feasting; and so they were all easily destroyed. Now some of them that were overtaken as they lay at the table were slain in that posture, and their blood brought up with it their meat and their drink. They slew others of them as they were drinking to one another in their cups, and some of them when their full bellies had made them fall asleep; and for so many as had time to put on their armor, they slew them with the sword, with no less case than they did those that were naked; and for the partisans of David, they continued also the slaughter from the first hour of the day to the evening, so that there were, not above four hundred of the Amalekites left; and they only escaped by getting upon their dromedaries and camels. Accordingly David recovered not only all the other spoils which the enemy had carried away, but his wives also, and the wives of his companions. But when they were come to the place where they had left the two hundred men, which were not able to follow them, but were left to take care of the stuff, the four hundred men did not think fit to divide among them any other parts of what they had gotten, or of the prey, since they did not accompany them, but pretended to be feeble, and did not follow them in pursuit of the enemy, but said they should be contented to have safely recovered their wives; yet did David pronounce that this opinion of theirs was evil and unjust, and that when God had granted them such a favor, that they had avenged themselves on their enemies, and had recovered all that belonged to themselves, they should make an equal distribution of what they had gotten to all, because the rest had tarried behind to guard their stuff; and from that time this law obtained among them, that those who guarded the stuff, should receive an equal share with those that fought in the battle. Now when David was come to Ziklag, he sent portions of the spoils to all that had been familiar with him, and to his friends in the tribe of Judah. And thus ended the affairs of the plundering of Ziklag, and of the slaughter of the Amalekites.

7. Now upon the Philistines joining battle, there followed a sharp engagement, and the Philistine, became the conquerors, and slew a great number of their enemies; but Saul the king of Israel, and his sons, fought courageously, and with the utmost alacrity, as knowing that their entire glory lay in nothing else but dying honorably, and exposing themselves to the utmost danger from the enemy (for they had nothing else to hope for); so they brought upon themselves the whole power of the enemy, till they were encompassed round and slain, but not before they had killed many of the Philistines Now the sons of Saul were Jonathan, and Abinadab, and Malchisua; and when these were slain the multitude of the Hebrews were put to flight, and all was disorder, and confusion, and slaughter, upon the Philistines pressing in upon them. But Saul himself fled, having a strong body of soldiers about him; and upon the Philistines sending after them those that threw javelins and shot arrows, he lost all his company except a few. As for himself, he fought with great bravery; and when he

had received so many wounds, that he was not able to bear up nor to oppose any longer, and yet was not able to kill himself, he bade his armor-bearer draw his sword, and run him through, before the enemy should take him alive. But his armor-bearer not daring to kill his master, he drew his own sword, and placing himself over against its point, he threw himself upon it; and when he could neither run it through him, nor, by leaning against it, make the sword pass through him, he turned him round, and asked a certain young man that stood by who he was; and when he understood that he was an Amalekite, he desired him to force the sword through him, because he was not able to do it with his own hands, and thereby to procure him such a death as he desired. This the young man did accordingly; and he took the golden bracelet that was on Saul's arm, and his royal crown that was on his head, and ran away. And when Saul's armor-bearer saw that he was slain, he killed himself; nor did any of the king's guards escape, but they all fell upon the mountain called Gilboa. But when those Hebrews that dwelt in the valley beyond Jordan, and those who had their cities in the plain, heard that Saul and his sons were fallen, and that the multitude about them were destroyed, they left their own cities, and fled to such as were the best fortified and fenced; and the Philistines, finding those cities deserted, came and dwelt in them.

8. On the next day, when the Philistines came to strip their enemies that were slain, they got the bodies of Saul and of his sons, and stripped them, and cut off their heads; and they sent messengers all about their country, to acquaint them that their enemies were fallen; and they dedicated their armor in the temple of Astarte, but hung their bodies on crosses at the walls of the city Bethshun, which is now called Scythepolls. But when the inhabitants of Jabesh-Gilead heard that they had dismembered the dead bodies of Saul and of his sons, they deemed it so horrid a thing to overlook this barbarity, and to suffer them to be without funeral rites, that the most courageous and hardy among them (and indeed that city had in it men that were very stout both in body and mind) journeyed all night, and came to Bethshun, and approached to the enemy's wall, and taking down the bodies of Saul and of his sons, they carried them to Jabesh, while the enemy were not able enough nor bold enough to hinder them, because of their great courage. So the people of Jabesh wept all in general, and buried their bodies in the best place of their country, which was named

Areurn; and they observed a public mourning for them seven days, with their wives and children, beating their breasts, and lamenting the king and his sons, without either tasting meat or drink[29] [till the evening.]

9. To this his end did Saul come, according to the prophecy of Samuel, because he disobeyed the commands of God about the Amalekites, and on the account of his destroying the family of Ahimelech the high priest, with Ahimelech himself, and the city of the high priests. Now Saul, when he had reigned eighteen years while Samuel was alive, and after his death two [and twenty], ended his life in this manner.

---

29. This way of speaking in Josephus, of fasting "seven days without meat or drink," is almost like that of St. Paul, Acts 27:33, "This day is the fourteenth day that ye have tarried, and continued fasting, having taken nothing:" and as the nature of the thing, and the impossibility of strictly fasting so long, require us here to understand both Josephus and the sacred author of this history, 1 Samuel 30:13, from whom he took it, of only fasting fill the evening; so must we understand St. Paul, either that this was really the fourteenth day that they had taken nothing till the evening, or else that this was the fourteenth day of their tempestuous weather in the Adriatic Sea, as ver. 27, and that on this fourteenth day alone they had continued fasting, and had taken nothing before that evening. The mention of their long abstinence, ver. 21, inclines me to believe the former explication to be the truth, and that the case was then for a fortnight what it was here for a week, that they kept all those days entirely as lasts till the evening, but not longer. See Judges 20:26; 21:2; 1 Samuel 14:24; 2 Samuel 1:12; Antiq. B. VII. ch. 7. sect. 4.

Book 7

Containing the Interval of Forty Years, from the Death of Saul to the Death of David

1   *How David Reigned over One Tribe at Hebron While the Son of Saul Reigned over the Rest of the Multitude; and How, in the Civil War Which Then Arose Asahel and Abner Were Slain*

1. THIS fight proved to be on the same day whereon David was come back to Ziklag, after he had overcome the Amalekites. Now when he had been already two days at Ziklag, there came to him the man who slew Saul, which was the third day after the fight. He had escaped out of the battle which the Israelites had with the Philistines, and had his clothes rent, and ashes upon his head. And when he made his obeisance to David, he inquired of him whence he came. He replied, from the battle of the Israelites; and he informed him that the end of it was unfortunate, many ten thousands of the Israelites having been cut off, and Saul, together with his sons, slain. He also said that he could well give him this information, because he was present at the victory gained over the Hebrews, and was with the king when he fled. Nor did he deny that he had himself slain the king, when he was ready to be taken by the enemy, and he himself exhorted him to do it, because, when he was fallen on his sword, his great wounds had made him so weak that he was not able to kill himself. He also produced demonstrations that the king was slain, which were the golden bracelets that had been on the king's arms, and his crown, which he had taken away from Saul's dead body, and had brought them to him. So David having no longer any room to call in question

the truth of what he said, but seeing most evident marks that Saul was dead, he rent his garments, and continued all that day with his companions in weeping and lamentation. This grief was augmented by the consideration of Jonathan; the son of Saul, who had been his most faithful friend, and the occasion of his own deliverance. He also demonstrated himself to have such great virtue, and such great kindness for Saul, as not only to take his death to heart, though he had been frequently in danger of losing his life by his means, but to punish him that slew him; for when David had said to him that he was become his own accuser, as the very man who had slain the king, and when he had understood that he was the son of an Amalekite, he commanded him to be slain. He also committed to writing some lamentations and funeral commendations of Saul and Jonathan, which have continued to my own age.

2. Now when David had paid these honors to the king, he left off his mourning, and inquired of God by the prophet which of the cities of the tribe of Judah he would bestow upon him to dwell in; who answered that he bestowed upon him Hebron. So he left Ziklag, and came to Hebron, and took with him his wives, who were in number two, and his armed men; whereupon all the people of the forementioned tribe came to him, and ordained him their king. But when he heard that the inhabitants of Jabesh-gilead had buried Saul and his sons [honorably], he sent to them and commended them, and took what they had done kindly, and promised to make them amends for their care of those that were dead; and at the same time he informed them that the tribe of Judah had chosen him for their king.

3. But as soon as Abner, the son of Ner, who was general of Saul's army, and a very active man, and good-natured, knew that the king, and Jonathan, and his two other sons, were fallen in the battle, he made haste into the camp; and taking away with him the remaining son of Saul, whose name was Ishbosheth, he passed over to the land beyond Jordan, and ordained him the king of the whole multitude, excepting the tribe of Judah; and made his royal seat in a place called in our own language *Mahanaim*, but in the language of the Grecians, *The Camps;* from whence Abner made haste with a select body of soldiers, to fight with such of the tribe of Judah as were disposed to it, for he was angry that this tribe had set up David for their king. But Joab, whose father was Suri, and his mother Zeruiah, David's sister, who was general of

David's army, met him, according to David's appointment. He had with him his brethren, Abistiai and Asahel, as also all David's armed men. Now when he met Abner at a certain fountain, in the city of Gibeon, he prepared to fight. And when Abner said to him, that he had a mind to know which of them had the more valiant soldiers, it was agreed between them that twelve soldiers of each side should fight together. So those that were chosen out by both the generals for this fight came between the two armies, and throwing their lances one against the other, they drew their swords, and catching one another by the head, they held one another fast, and ran each other's swords into their sides and groins, until they all, as it were by mutual agreement, perished together. When these were fallen down dead, the rest of the army came to a sore battle, and Abner's men were beaten; and when they were beaten, Joab did not leave off pursuing them, but he pressed upon them, and excited the soldiers to follow them close, and not to grow weary of killing them. His brethren also pursued them with great alacrity, especially the younger, Asahel, who was the most eminent of them. He was very famous for his swiftness of foot, for he could not only be too hard for men, but is reported to have overrun a horse, when they had a race together. This Asahel ran violently after Abner, and would not turn in the least out of the straight way, either to the one side or to the other. Hereupon Abner turned back, and attempted artfully to avoid his violence. Sometimes he bade him leave off the pursuit, and take the armor of one of his soldiers; and sometimes, when he could not persuade him so to do, he exhorted him to restrain himself, and not to pursue him any longer, lest he should force him to kill him, and he should then not be able to look his brother in the face: but when Asahel would not admit of any persuasions, but still continued to pursue him, Abner smote him with his spear, as he held it in his flight, and that by a back-stroke, and gave him a deadly wound, so that he died immediately; but those that were with him pursuing Abner, when they came to the place where Asahel lay, they stood round about the dead body, and left off the pursuit of the enemy. However, both Joab[1] himself, and his brother Abishai, ran past the

---

1. It ought to be here noted, that Joab, Abishai, and Asahel were all three David's nephews, the sons of his sister Zeraiah, as 1 Chronicles 2:16; and that Amasa was also his nephew by his other sister Abigail, ver. 17.

dead corpse, and making their anger at the death of Asahel an occasion of greater zeal against Abner, they went on with incredible haste and alacrity, and pursued Abner to a certain place called Ammah: it was about sun-set. Then did Joab ascend a certain hill, as he stood at that place, having the tribe of Benjamin with him, whence he took a view of them, and of Abner also. Hereupon Abner cried aloud, and said that it was not fit that they should irritate men of the same nation to fight so bitterly one against another; that as for Asahel his brother, he was himself in the wrong, when he would not be advised by him not to pursue him any farther, which was the occasion of his wounding and death. So Joab consented to what he said, and accepted these his words as an excuse [about Asahel], and called the soldiers back with the sound of the trumpet, as a signal for their retreat, and thereby put a stop to any further pursuit. After which Joab pitched his camp there that night; but Abner marched all that night, and passed over the river Jordan, and came to Ishbosheth, Saul's son, to Mahanaim. On the next day Joab counted the dead men, and took care of all their funerals. Now there were slain of Abner's soldiers about three hundred and sixty; but of those of David nineteen, and Asahel, whose body Joab and Abishai carried to Bethlehem; and when they had buried him in the sepulcher of their fathers, they came to David to Hebron. From this time therefore there began an intestine war, which lasted a great while, in which the followers of David grew stronger in the dangers they underwent, and the servants and subjects of Saul's sons did almost every day become weaker.

4. About this time David was become the father of six sons, born of as many mothers. The eldest was by Ahinoam, and he was called Arenon; the second was Daniel, by his wife Abigail; the name of the third was Absalom, by Maacah, the daughter of Talmai, king of Geshur; the fourth he named Adonijah, by his wife Haggith; the fifth was Shephatiah, by Abital; the sixth he called Ithream, by Eglah. Now while this intestine war went on, and the subjects of the two kings came frequently to action and to fighting, it was Abner, the general of the host of Saul's son, who, by his prudence, and the great interest he had among the multitude, made them all continue with Ishbosheth; and indeed it was a considerable time that they continued of his party; but afterwards Abner was blamed, and an accusation was laid against him, that he went in unto Saul's concubine: her name

was Rispah, the daughter of Aiah. So when he was complained of by Ishbosheth, he was very uneasy and angry at it, because he had not justice done him by Ishbosheth, to whom he had shown the greatest kindness; whereupon he threatened to transfer the kingdom to David, and demonstrate that he did not rule over the people beyond Jordan by his own abilities and wisdom, but by his warlike conduct and fidelity in leading his army. So he sent ambassadors to Hebron to David, and desired that he would give him security upon oath that he would esteem him his companion and his friend, upon condition that he should persuade the people to leave Saul's son, and choose him king of the whole country; and when David had made that league with Abner, for he was pleased with his message to him, he desired that he would give this as the first mark of performance of the present league, that he might have his wife Michal restored to him, as her whom he had purchased with great hazards, and with those six hundred heads of the Philistines which he had brought to Saul her father. So Abner took Michal from Phaltiel, who was then her husband, and sent her to David, Ishbosheth himself affording him his assistance, for David had written to him that of right he ought to have this his wife restored to him. Abner also called together the elders of the multitude, the commanders and captains of thousands, and spake thus to them: That he had formerly dissuaded them from their own resolution, when they were ready to forsake Ishbosheth, and to join themselves to David; that, however, he now gave them leave so to do, if they had a mind to it, for they knew that God had appointed David to be king of all the Hebrews by Samuel the prophet; and had foretold that he should punish the Philistines, and overcome them, and bring them under. Now when the elders and rulers heard this, and understood that Abner was come over to those sentiments about the public affairs which they were of before, they changed their measures, and came in to David. When these men had agreed to Abner's proposal, he called together the tribe of Benjamin, for all of that tribe were the guards of Ishbosheth's body, and he spake to them to the same purpose. And when he saw that they did not in the least oppose what he said, but resigned themselves up to his opinion, he took about twenty of his friends and came to David, in order to receive himself security upon oath from him; for we may justly esteem those things to be firmer which every one of us do by ourselves, than those which we do by another. He also gave him an account of what he had said to the rulers, and to the whole tribe of Benjamin; and when David had received him in a courteous manner, and had treated him with great hospitality for many days, Abner, when he was dismissed, desired him to bring the multitude with him, that he might deliver up the government to him, when David himself was present, and a spectator of what was done.

5. When David had sent Abner away, Joab, the of his army, came immediately to Hebron; he had understood that Abner had been with David, and had parted with him a little before under leagues and agreements that the government should be delivered up to David, he feared lest David should place Abner, who had assisted him to gain the kingdom, in the first rank of dignity, especially since he was a shrewd man in other respects, in understanding affairs, and in managing them artfully, as proper seasons should require, and that he should himself be put lower, and be deprived of the command of the army; so he took a knavish and a wicked course. In the first place, he endeavored to calumniate Abner to the king, exhorting him to have a care of him, and not to give attention to what he had engaged to do for him, because all he did tended to confirm the government to Saul's son; that he came to him deceitfully and with guile, and was gone away in hopes of gaining his purpose by this management: but when he could not thus persuade David, nor saw him at all exasperated, he betook himself to a project bolder than the former:—he determined to kill Abner; and in order thereto, he sent some messengers after him, to whom he gave in charge, that when they should overtake him they should recall him in David's name, and tell him that he had somewhat to say to him about his affairs, which he had not remembered to speak of when he was with him. Now when Abner heard what the messengers said, (for they overtook him in a certain place called *Besira*, which was distant from Hebron twenty furlongs,) he suspected none of the mischief which was befalling him, and came back. Hereupon Joab met him in the gate, and received him in the kindest manner, as if he were Abner's most benevolent acquaintance and friend; for such as undertake the vilest actions, in order to prevent the suspicion of any private mischief intended, do frequently make the greatest pretenses to what really good men sincerely do. So he took him aside from his own followers, as if he would speak with him in private, and brought him into a void place of the gate, having himself nobody with him but his brother

Abishai; then he drew his sword, and smote him in the groin; upon which Abner died by this treachery of Joab, which, as he said himself, was in the way of punishment for his brother Asahel, whom Abner smote and slew as he was pursuing after him in the battle of Hebron, but as the truth was, out of his fear of losing his command of the army, and his dignity with the king, and lest he should be deprived of those advantages, and Abner should obtain the first rank in David's court. By these examples any one may learn how many and how great instances of wickedness men will venture upon for the sake of getting money and authority, and that they may not fail of either of them; for as when they are desirous of obtaining the same, they acquire them by ten thousand evil practices; so when they are afraid of losing them, they get them confirmed to them by practices much worse than the former, as if no other calamity so terrible could befall them as the failure of acquiring so exalted an authority; and when they have acquired it, and by long custom found the sweetness of it, the losing it again: and since this last would be the heaviest of all afflictions they all of them contrive and venture upon the most difficult actions, out of the fear of losing the same. But let it suffice that I have made these short reflections upon that subject.

6. When David heard that Abner was slain, it grieved his soul; and he called all men to witness, with stretching out his hands to God, and crying out that he was not a partaker in the murder of Abner, and that his death was not procured by his command or approbation. He also wished the heaviest curses might light upon him that slew him and upon his whole house; and he devoted those that had assisted him in this murder to the same penalties on its account; for he took care not to appear to have had any hand in this murder, contrary to the assurances he had given and the oaths he had taken to Abner. However, he commanded all the people to weep and lament this man, and to honor his dead body with the usual solemnities; that is, by rending their garments, and putting on sackcloth, and that things should be the habit in which they should go before the bier; after which he followed it himself, with the elders and those that were rulers, lamenting Abner, and by his tears demonstrating his good-will to him while he was alive, and his sorrow for him now he was dead, and that he was not taken off with his consent. So he buried him at Hebron in a magnificent manner, and indited funeral elegies for him;

he also stood first over the monument weeping, and caused others to do the same; nay, so deeply did the death of Abner disorder him, that his companions could by no means force him to take any food, but he affirmed with an oath that he would taste nothing till the sun was set. This procedure gained him the good-will of the multitude; for such as had an affection for Abner were mightily satisfied with the respect he paid him when he was dead, and the observation of that faith he had plighted to him, which was shown in his vouchsafing him all the usual ceremonies, as if he had been his kinsman and his friend, and not suffering him to be neglected and injured with a dishonorable burial, as if he had been his enemy; insomuch that the entire nation rejoiced at the king's gentleness and mildness of disposition, every one being ready to suppose that the king would have taken the same care of them in the like circumstances, which they saw be showed in the burial of the dead body of Abner. And indeed David principally intended to gain a good reputation, and therefore he took care to do what was proper in this case, whence none had any suspicion that he was the author of Abner's death. He also said this to the multitude, that he was greatly troubled at the death of so good a man; and that the affairs of the Hebrews had suffered great detriment by being deprived of him, who was of so great abilities to preserve them by his excellent advice, and by the strength of his hands in war. But he added, that "God, who hath a regard to all men's actions, will not suffer this man [Joab] to go off unrevenged; but know ye, that I am not able to do any thing to these sons of Zeruiah, Joab and Abishai, who have more power than I have; but God will requite their insolent attempts upon their own heads." And this was the fatal conclusion of the life of Abner.

2   That Upon the Slaughter of Ishbosheth by the Treachery of His Friends, David Received the Whole Kingdom

1. WHEN Ishbosheth, the son of Saul, had heard of the death of Abner, he took it to heart to be deprived of a man that was of his kindred, and had indeed given him the kingdom, but was greatly afflicted, and Abner's death very much troubled him; nor did he himself outlive any long time, but was treacherously set upon by the sons of Rimmon, (Baanah and Rechab were their names,) and was slain by them; for

these being of a family of the Benjamites, and of the first rank among them, thought that if they should slay Ishbosheth, they should obtain large presents from David, and be made commanders by him, or, however, should have some other trust committed to them. So when they once found him alone, and asleep at noon, in an upper room, when none of his guards were there, and when the woman that kept the door was not watching, but was fallen asleep also, partly on account of the labor she had undergone, and partly on account of the heat of the day, these men went into the room in which Ishbosheth, Saul's son, lay asleep, and slew him; they also cut off his head, and took their journey all that night, and the next day, as supposing themselves flying away from those they had injured, to one that would accept of this action as a favor, and would afford them security. So they came to Hebron, and showed David the head of Ishbosheth, and presented themselves to him as his well-wishers, and such as had killed one that was his enemy and antagonist. Yet David did not relish what they had done as they expected, but said to them, "You vile wretches, you shall immediately receive the punishment you deserve. Did not you know what vengeance I executed on him that murdered Saul, and brought me his crown of gold, and this while he who made this slaughter did it as a favor to him, that he might not be caught by his enemies? Or do you imagine that I am altered in my disposition, and suppose that I am not the same man I then was, but am pleased with men that are wicked doers, and esteem your vile actions, when you are become murderers of your master, as grateful to me, when you have slain a righteous man upon his bed, who never did evil to any body, and treated you with great good-will and respect? Wherefore you shall suffer the punishment due on his account, and the vengeance I ought to inflict upon you for killing Ishbosheth, and for supposing that I should take his death kindly at your hands; for you could not lay a greater blot on my honor, than by making such a supposal." When David had said this, he tormented them with all sorts of torments, and then put them to death; and he bestowed all accustomed rites on the burial of the head of Ishbosheth, and laid it in the grave of Abner.

2. When these things were brought to this conclusion, all the principal men of the Hebrew people came to David to Hebron, with the heads of thousands, and other rulers, and delivered themselves up to him, putting him in mind of the good-will they had borne to

him in Saul's lifetime, and the respect they then had not ceased to pay him when he was captain of a thousand, as also that he was chosen of God by Samuel the prophet, he and his sons;[2] and declaring besides, how God had given him power to save the land of the Hebrews, and to overcome the Philistines. Whereupon he received kindly this their alacrity on his account; and exhorted them to continue in it, for that they should have no reason to repent of being thus disposed to him. So when he had feasted them, and treated them kindly, he sent them out to bring all the people to him; upon which came to him about six thousand and eight hundred armed men of the tribe of Judah, who bare shields and spears for their weapons, for these had [till now] continued with Saul's son, when the rest of the tribe of Judah had ordained David for their king. There came also seven thousand and one hundred out of the tribe of Simeon. Out of the tribe of Levi came four thousand and seven hundred, having Jehoiada for their leader. After these came Zadok the high priest, with twenty-two captains of his kindred. Out of the tribe of Benjamin the armed men were four thousand; but the rest of the tribe continued, still expecting that some one of the house of Saul should reign over them. Those of the tribe of Ephraim were twenty thousand and eight hundred, and these mighty men of valor, and eminent for their strength. Out of the half tribe of Manasseh came eighteen thousand, of the most potent men. Out of the tribe of Issachar came two hundred, who foreknew what was to come hereafter,[3] but of armed men twenty thousand. Of the tribe of Zebulon fifty thousand chosen men. This was the only tribe that came universally in to David, and all these had the same weapons with the tribe of Gad. Out of the tribe of Naphtali the eminent men and rulers were one thousand, whose weapons were shields and spears,

---

2. This may be a true observation of Josephus's, that Samuel by command from God entailed the crown on David and his posteerity; for no further did that entail ever reach, Solomon himself having never had any promise made him that his posterity should always have the right to it.

3. These words of Josephus concerning the tribe of Issachar, who foreknew what was to come hereafter," are best paraphrased by the parallel text. 1 Chronicles 12:32, "Who had understanding of the times to know what Israel ought to do;" that is, who had so much knowledge in astronomy as to make calendars for the Israelites, that they might keep their festivals, and plough and sow, and gather in their harvests and vintage, in due season.

and the tribe itself followed after, being (in a manner) innumerable [thirty-seven thousand]. Out of the tribe of Dan there were of chosen men twenty-seven thousand and six hundred. Out of the tribe of Asher were forty thousand. Out of the two tribes that were beyond Jordan, and the rest of the tribe of Manasseh, such as used shields, and spears, and head-pieces, and swords, were a hundred and twenty thousand. The rest of the tribes also made use of swords. This multitude came together to Hebron to David, with a great quantity of corn, and wine, and all other sorts of food, and established David in his kingdom with one consent. And when the people had rejoiced for three days in Hebron, David and all the people removed and came to Jerusalem.

3 How David Laid Siege to Jerusalem; and When He Had Taken the City, He Cast the Canaanites Out of It, and Brought in the Jews to Inhabit Therein

1. NOW the Jebusites, who were the inhabitants of Jerusalem, and were by extraction Canaanites, shut their gates, and placed the blind, and the lame, and all their maimed persons, upon the wall, in way of derision of the king, and said that the very lame themselves would hinder his entrance into it. This they did out of contempt of his power, and as depending on the strength of their walls. David was hereby enraged, and began the siege of Jerusalem, and employed his utmost diligence and alacrity therein, as intending by the taking of this place to demonstrate his power, and to intimidate all others that might be of the like [evil] disposition towards him. So he took the lower city by force, but the citadel held out still;[4] whence it was that the king,

---

4. What our other copies say of Mount Sion, as alone properly called the city of David, 2 Samuel 5:6–9, and of this its siege and conquest now by David, Josephus applies to the whole city Jerusalem, though including the citadel also; by what authority we do not now know perhaps, after David had united them together, or joined the citadel to the lower city, as sect. 2, Josephus esteemed them as one city. However, this notion seems to be confirmed by what the same Josephus says concerning David's and many other kings of Judah's sepulchers, which as the authors of the books of Kings and Chronicles say were in the city of David, so does Josephus still say they were in Jerusalem. The sepulcher of David seems to have been also a known place in the several days of Hyrcanus, of Herod, and of St. Peter, Antiq. B. XIII. ch. 8. sect. 4 B. XVI. ch. 8. sect. 1; Acts 2:29. Now no such royal sepulchers have

knowing that the proposal of dignities and rewards would encourage the soldiers to greater actions, promised that he who should first go over the ditches that were beneath the citadel, and should ascend to the citadel itself and take it, should have the command of the entire people conferred upon him. So they all were ambitious to ascend, and thought no pains too great in order to ascend thither, out of their desire of the chief command. However, Joab, the son of Zeruiah, prevented the rest; and as soon as he was got up to the citadel, cried out to the king, and claimed the chief command.

2. When David had cast the Jebusites out of the citadel, he also rebuilt Jerusalem, and named it *The City of David*, and abode there all the time of his reign; but for the time that he reigned over the tribe of Judah only in Hebron, it was seven years and six months. Now when he had chosen Jerusalem to be his royal city, his affairs did more and more prosper, by the providence of God, who took care that they should improve and be augmented. Hiram also, the king of the Tyrians, sent ambassadors to him, and made a league of mutual friendship and assistance with him. He also sent him presents, cedar-trees, and mechanics, and men skillful in building and architecture, that they might build him a royal palace at Jerusalem. Now David made buildings round about the lower city: he also joined the citadel to it, and made it one body; and when he had encompassed all with walls, he appointed Joab to take care of them. It was David, therefore, who first cast the Jebusites out of Jerusalem, and called it by his own name, *The City of David:* for under our forefather Abraham it was called (Salem, or) Solyma;[5] but after that time, some say that Homer mentions it by that name of Solyma, [for he named the temple Solyma,

---

been found about Mount Sion, but are found close by the north wall of Jerusalem, which I suspect, therefore, to be these very sepulchers. See the note on ch. 15. sect. 3. In the meantime, Josephus's explication of the lame, and the blind, and the maimed, as set to keep this city or citadel, seems to be the truth, and gives the best light to that history in our Bible. Mr. Ottius truly observes, (up. Hayercamp, p. 305,) that Josephus never mentions Mount Sion by that name, as taking it for an appellative, as I suppose, and not for a proper name; he still either styles it The Citadel, or The Upper City; nor do I see any reason for Mr. Ottius's evil suspicions about this procedure of Josephus.

5. Some copies of Josephus have here Solyma, or Salem; and others Hierosolyma, or Jerusalem. The latter best agree to what Josephus says elsewhere, (Of the War, B. VI. ch. 10.,) that this city was called Solyma, or Salem, before the days of Melchisedec, but was by him called Hierosolyma, or Jerusalem. I rather suppose it to have been so

according to the Hebrew language, which denotes *security.]* Now the whole time from the warfare under Joshua our general against the Canaanites, and from that war in which he overcame them, and distributed the land among the Hebrews, (nor could the Israelites ever cast the Canaanites out of Jerusalem until this time, when David took it by siege,) this whole time was five hundred and fifteen years.

3. I shall now make mention of Araunah, who was a wealthy man among the Jebusites, but was not slain by David in the siege of Jerusalem, because of the good-will he bore to the Hebrews, and a particular benignity and affection which he had to the king himself; which I shall take a more seasonable opportunity to speak of a little afterwards. Now David married other wives over and above those which he had before: he had also concubines. The sons whom he had were in number eleven, whose names were Amnon, Emnos, Eban, Nathan, Solomon, Jeban, Elien, Phalna, Ennaphen, Jenae, Eliphale; and a daughter, Tamar. Nine of these were born of legitimate wives, but the two last-named of concubines; and Tamar had the same mother with Absalom.

4 That When David Had Conquered the Philistines Who Made War Against Him at Jerusalem, He Removed the Ark to Jerusalem and Had a Mind to Build a Temple

1. WHEN the Philistines understood that David was made king of the Hebrews, they made war against him at Jerusalem; and when they had seized upon that valley which is called *The Valley of the Giants,* and is a place not far from the city, they pitched their camp therein; but the king of the Jews, who never permitted himself to do any thing without

---

called after Abraham had received that oracle Jehovah Jireh, "The Lord will see, or provide," Genesis 22;14. The latter word, Jireh, with a little alteration, prefixed to the old name Salem, Peace, will be Jerusalem; and since that expression, "God will see," or rather, "God will provide himself a lamb for a burnt-offering," ver. 8, 14, is there said to have been proverbial till the days of Moses, this seems to me the most probable derivation of that name, which will then denote that God would provide peace by that "Lamb of God which was to take away the sins of the world." However, that which is put into brackets can hardly be supposed the genuine words of Josephus, as Dr. Hudson well judges.

prophecy,[6] and the command of God and without depending on him as a security for the time to come, bade the high priest to foretell to him what was the will of God, and what would be the event of this battle. And when he foretold that he should gain the victory and the dominion, he led out his army against the Philistines; and when the battle was joined, he came himself behind, and fell upon the enemy on the sudden, and slew some of them, and put the rest to flight. And let no one suppose that it was a small army of the Philistines that came against the Hebrews, as guessing so from the suddenness of their defeat, and from their having performed no great action, or that was worth recording, from the slowness of their march, and want of courage; but let him know that all Syria and Phoenicia, with many other nations besides them, and those warlike nations also, came to their assistance, and had a share in this war, which thing was the only cause why, when they had been so often conquered, and had lost so many ten thousands of their men, they still came upon the Hebrews with greater armies; nay, indeed, when they had so often failed of their purpose in these battles, they came upon David with an army three times as numerous as before, and pitched their camp on the same spot of ground as before. The king of Israel therefore inquired of God again concerning the event of the battle; and the high priest prophesied to him, that he should keep his army in the groves, called the *Groves of Weeping*, which were not far from the enemy's camp, and that he should not move, nor begin to fight, till the trees of the grove should be in motion without the wind's blowing; but as soon as these trees moved, and the time foretold to him by God was come, he should, without delay, go out to gain what was an already prepared and evident victory; for the several ranks of the enemy's army did not sustain him, but retreated at the first onset, whom he closely followed, and slew them as he went along, and pursued them to the city Gaza

---

6. It deserves here to be remarked, that Saul very rarely, and David very frequently, consulted God by Urim; and that David aimed always to depend, not on his own prudence or abilities but on the Divine direction, contrary to Saul's practice. See sect. 2, and the note on Antiq. B. III. ch. 8. sect. 9; and when Saul's daughter, (but David's wife,) Michal, laughed at David's dancing before the ark, 2 Samuel 6:16, &c., and here, sect. l, 2, 3, it is probable she did so, because her father Saul did not use to pay such a regard to the ark, to the Urim there inquired by, or to God's worship before it, and because she thought it beneath the dignity of a king to be so religious.

(which is the limit of their country): after this he spoiled their camp, in which he found great riches; and he destroyed their gods.

2. When this had proved the event of the battle, David thought it proper, upon a consultation with the elders, and rulers, and captains of thousands, to send for those that were in the flower of their age out of all his countrymen, and out of the whole land, and withal for the priests and the Levites, in order to their going to Kirjathjearim, to bring up the ark of God out of that city, and to carry it to Jerusalem, and there to keep it, and offer before it those sacrifices and those other honors with which God used to be well-pleased; for had they done thus in the reign of Saul, they had not undergone any great misfortunes at all. So when the whole body of the people were come together, as they had resolved to do, the king came to the ark, which the priest brought out of the house of Aminadab, and laid it upon a new cart, and permitted their brethren and their children to draw it, together with the oxen. Before it went the king, and the whole multitude of the people with him, singing hymns to God, and making use of all sorts of songs usual among them, with variety of the sounds of musical instruments, and with dancing and singing of psalms, as also with the sounds of trumpets and of cymbals, and so brought the ark to Jerusalem. But as they were come to the threshing-floor of Chidon, a place so called, Uzzah was slain by the anger of God; for as the oxen shook the ark, he stretched out his hand, and would needs take hold of it. Now, because he was not a priest[7] and yet touched the ark, God struck him dead. Hereupon both the king and the people were displeased at the death of Uzzah; and the place where he died is still called the *Breach of Uzzah* unto this day. So David was afraid; and supposing that if he received the ark to himself into the city, he might suffer in the like manner as Uzzah had suffered, who, upon his bare putting out his hand to the ark, died in the manner already mentioned, he did not receive

---

7. Josephus seems to be partly in the right, when he observes here that Uzzah was no priest, (though perhaps he might be a Levite,) and was therefore struck dead for touching the ark, contrary to the law, and for which profane rashness death was the penalty by that law, Numbers 4:15, 20. See the like before, Antiq. B. VI. ch. 1. sect. 4. It is not improbable that the putting this ark in a cart, when it ought to have been carried by the priests or Levites, as it was presently here in Josephus so carried from Obededom's house to David's, might be also an occasion of the anger of God on that breach of his law. See Numbers 4:15; 1 Chronicles 15:13.

it to himself into the city, but he took it aside unto a certain place belonging to a righteous man, whose name was Obededom, who was by his family a Levite, and deposited the ark with him; and it remained there three entire months. This augmented the house of Obededom, and conferred many blessings upon it. And when the king heard what had befallen Obededom, how he was become, of a poor man in a low estate, exceeding happy, and the object of envy to all those that saw or inquired after his house, he took courage, and, hoping that he should meet with no misfortune thereby, he transferred the ark to his own house; the priests carrying it, while seven companies of singers, who were set in that order by the king, went before it, and while he himself played upon the harp, and joined in the music, insomuch, that when his wife Michel, the daughter of Saul, who was our first king, saw him so doing, she laughed at him. But when they had brought in the ark, they placed it under the tabernacle which David had pitched for it, and he offered costly sacrifices and peace-offerings, and treated the whole multitude, and dealt both to the women, and the men, and the infants a loaf of bread and a cake, and another cake baked in a pan, with the portion of the sacrifice. So when he had thus feasted the people, he sent them away, and he himself returned to his own house.

3. But when Michal his wife, the daughter of Saul, came and stood by him, she wished him all other happiness, and entreated that whatsoever he should further desire, to the utmost possibility, might be given him by God, and that he might be favorable to him; yet did she blame him, that so great a king as he was should dance after an unseemly manner, and in his dancing, uncover himself among the servants and the handmaidens. But he replied, that he was not ashamed to do what was acceptable to God, who had preferred him before her father, and before all others; that he would play frequently, and dance, without any regard to what the handmaidens and she herself thought of it. So this Michal, who was David's wife, had no children; however, when she was afterward married to him to whom Saul her father had given her, (for at this time David had taken her away from him, and had her himself,) she bare five children. But concerning those matters I shall discourse in a proper place.

4. Now when the king saw that his affairs grew better almost every day, by the will of God, he thought he should offend him, if, while he himself continued in houses made of cedar, such as were of a great

height, and had the most curious works of architecture in them, he should overlook the ark while it was laid in a tabernacle, and was desirous to build a temple to God, as Moses had predicted such a temple should be built.[8] And when he had discoursed with Nathan the prophet about these things, and had been encouraged by him to do whatsoever he had a mind to do, as having God with him, and his helper in all things, he was thereupon the more ready to set about that building. But God appeared to Nathan that very night, and commanded him to say to David,[9] that he took his purpose and his desires kindly, since nobody had before now taken it into their head to build him a temple, although upon his having such a notion he would not permit him to build him that temple, because he had made many wars, and was defiled with the slaughter of his enemies; that, however, after his death, in his old age, and when he had lived a long life, there should be a temple built by a son of his, who should take the kingdom after him, and should be called Solomon, whom he promised to provide for, as a father provides for his son, by preserving the kingdom for his son's posterity, and delivering it to them; but that he would still punish him, if he sinned, with diseases and barrenness of land. When David understood this from the prophet, and was overjoyful at this knowledge of the sure continuance of the dominion to his posterity, and that his house should be splendid, and very famous, he came to the ark, and fell down on his face, and began to adore God, and to return thanks to him for all his benefits, as well for those that he had already bestowed upon him in raising him from a

---

8. Josephus here informs us, that, according to his understanding of the sense of his copy of the Pentateuch, Moses had himself foretold the building of the temple, which yet is no where, that I know of, in our present copies. And that this is not a mistake set down by him unwarily, appears by what he observed before, on Antiq. B. IV. ch. 8. sect. 46, how Moses foretold that, upon the Jews' future disobedience, their temple should be burnt and rebuilt, and that not once only, but several times afterward. See also Josephus's mention of God's former commands to build such a temple presently, ch. 14. sect. 2, contrary to our other copies, or at least to our translation of the Hebrew, 2 Samuel 7:6, 7; 1 Chronicles 17:5, 6.

9. Josephus seems, in this place, with our modern interpreters to confound the two distinct predictions which God made to David and to Nathan, concerning the building him a temple by one of David's posterity; the one belongeth to Solomon, the other to the Messiah; the distinction between which is of the greatest consequence to the Christian religion.

low state, and from the employment of a shepherd, to so great dignity of dominion and glory; as for those also which he had promised to his posterity; and besides, for that providence which he had exercised over the Hebrews in procuring them the liberty they enjoyed. And when he had said thus, and had sung a hymn of praise to God, he went his way.

5 *How David Brought under the Philistines, and the Moabites, and the Kings of Sophene and of Damascus, and of the Syrians as Also the Idumeans, in War; and How He Made a League with the King of Hamath; and Was Mindful of the Friendship That Jonathan, the Son of Saul, Had Borne Him*

1. A LITLLE while after this, he considered that he ought to make war against the Philistines, and not to see any idleness or laziness permitted in his management, that so it might prove, as God had foretold to him, that when he had overthrown his enemies, he should leave his posterity to reign in peace afterward: so he called together his army again, and when he had charged them to be ready and prepared for war, and when he thought that all things in his army were in a good state, he removed from Jerusalem, and came against the Philistines; and when he had overcome them in battle, and had cut off a great part of their country, and adjoined it to the country of the Hebrews, he transferred the war to the Moabites; and when he had overcome two parts of their army in battle, he took the remaining part captive, and imposed tribute upon them, to be paid annually. He then made war against Iadadezer, the son of Rehob, king of Sophene;[10] and when he had joined battle with him at 'the river Euphrates, he destroyed twenty thousand of his footmen, and about seven thousand of his horsemen. He also took a thousand of his chariots, and destroyed the greatest part of them, and ordered that no more than one hundred should be kept.[11]

---

10. Whether Syria Zobah, 2 Samuel 3:8; 1 Chronicles 18:3–8, be Sophene, as Josephus here supposes; which yet Ptolemy places beyond Euphrates, as Dr. Hudson observes here, whereas Zobah was on this side; or whether Josephus was not here guilty of a mistake in his geography; I cannot certainly determine.

11. David's reserving only one hundred chariots for himself out of one thousand he had taken from Hadadezer, was most probably in compliance with the law of

2. Now when Hadad, king of Damascus and of Syria, heard that David fought against Hadadezer, who was his friend, he came to his assistance with a powerful army, in hopes to rescue him; and when he had joined battle with David at the river Euphrates, he failed of his purpose, and lost in the battle a great number of his soldiers; for there were slain of the army of Hadad twenty thousand, and all the rest fled. Nicelens also [of Damascus] makes mention of this king in the fourth book of his histories; where he speaks thus: "A great while after these things had happened, there was one of that country whose name was Hadad, who was become very potent; he reigned over Damascus, and, the other parts of Syria, excepting Phoenicia. He made war against David, the king of Judea, and tried his fortune in many battles, and particularly in the last battle at Euphrates, wherein he was beaten. He seemed to have been the most excellent of all their kings in strength and manhood," Nay, besides this, he says of his posterity, that "they succeeded one another in his kingdom, and in his name;" where he thus speaks: "When Hadad was dead, his posterity reigned for ten generations, each of his successors receiving from his father *that* his dominion, and *this* his name; as did the Ptolemies in Egypt. But the third was the most powerful of them all, and was willing to avenge the defeat his forefather had received; so he made

---

Moses, which forbade a king of Israel "to multiply horses to himself," Deuteronomy 17:16; one of the principal uses of horses in Judea at that time being for drawing their chariots. See Joshua 12:6; and Antiq. B. V. ch. 1. sect. 18. It deserves here to be remarked, that this Hadad, being a very great king, was conquered by David, whose posterity yet for several generations were called Benhadad, or the son of Hadad, till the days of Hazael, whose son Adar or Ader is also in our Hebrew copy (2 Kings 13:24) written Benhadad, but in Josephus Adad or Adar. And strange it is, that the son of Hazael, said to be such in the same text, and in Josephus, Antiq. B. IX. ch. 8. sect. 7, should still be called the son of Hadad. I would, therefore, here correct our Hebrew copy from Josephus's, which seems to have the true reading. nor does the testimony of Nicolaus of Damascus, produced in this place by Josephus, seem to be faultless, when it says that he was the third of the Hadads, or second of the Benhadads, who besieged Samaria in the days of Ahab. He must rather have been the seventh or eighth, if there were ten in all of that name, as we are assured there were. For this testimony makes all the Hadads or Benhadads of the same line, and to have immediately succeeded one another; whereas Hazael was not of that line, nor is he called Hadad or Benhadad in any copy. And note, that from this Hadad, in the days of David, to the beginning of Hazael, were near two hundred years, according to the exactest chronology of Josephus.

an expedition against the Jews, and laid waste the city which is now called Samaria." Nor did he err from the truth; for this is that Hadad who made the expedition against Samaria, in the reign of Ahab, king of Israel, concerning whom we shall speak in due place hereafter.

3. Now when David had made an expedition against Damascus, and the other parts of Syria, and had brought it all into subjection, and had placed garrisons in the country, and appointed that they should pay tribute, he returned home. He also dedicated to God at Jerusalem the golden quivers, the entire armor which the guards of Hadad used to wear; which Shishak, the king of Egypt, took away when he fought with David's grandson, Rehoboam, with a great deal of other wealth which he carried out of Jerusalem. However, these things will come to be explained in their proper places hereafter. Now as for the king of the Hebrews, he was assisted by God, who gave him great success in his wars, and he made all expedition against the best cities of Hadadezer, Betah and Machen; so he took them by force, and laid them waste. Therein was found a very great quantity of gold and silver, besides that sort of brass which is said to be more valuable than gold; of which brass Solomon made that large vessel which was called *The [Brazen] Sea,* and those most curious lavers, when he built the temple for God.

4. But when the king of Hamath was informed of the ill success of Hadadezer, and had heard of the ruin of his army, he was afraid on his own account, and resolved to make a league of friendship and fidelity with David before he should come against him; so he sent to him his son Joram, and professed that he owed him thanks for fighting against Hadadezer, who was his enemy, and made a league with him of mutual assistance and friendship. He also sent him presents, vessels of ancient workmanship, both of gold, of silver, and of brass. So when David had made this league of mutual assistance with Toi, (for that was the name of the king of Hamath,) and had received the presents he sent him, he dismissed his son with that respect which was due on both sides; but then David brought those presents that were sent by him, as also the rest of the gold and silver which he had taken of the cities whom he had conquered, and dedicated them to God. Nor did God give victory and success to him only when he went to the battle himself, and led his own army, but he gave victory to Abishai, the

brother of Joab, general of his forces, over the Idumeans,[12] and by him to David, when he sent him with an army into Idumea: for Abishai destroyed eighteen thousand of them in the battle; whereupon the king [of Israel] placed garrisons through all Idumea, and received the tribute of the country, and of every head among them. Now David was in his nature just, and made his determination with regard to truth. He had for the general of his whole army Joab; and he made Jehoshaphat, the son of Ahilud, recorder. He also appointed Zadok, of the family of Phinehas, to be high priest, together with Abiathar, for he was his friend. He also made Seisan the scribe, and committed the command over the guards of his body to Benaiah; the son of Jehoiada. His elder sons were near his body, and had the care of it also.

5. He also called to mind the covenants and the oaths he had made with Jonathan, the son of Saul, and the friendship and affection Jonathan had for him; for besides all the rest of his excellent qualities with which he was endowed, he was also exceeding mindful of such as had at other times bestowed benefits upon him. He therefore gave order that inquiry should be made, whether any of Jonathan's lineage were living, to whom he might make return of that familiar acquaintance which Jonathan had had with him, and for which he was still debtor. And when one of Saul's freed men was brought to him, who was acquainted with those of his family that were still living, he asked him whether he could tell him of any one belonging to Jonathan that was now alive, and capable of a requital of the benefits which he had received from Jonathan. And he said, that a son of his was remaining, whose name was Mephibosheth, but that he was lame of his feet; for that when his nurse heard that the father and grandfather of the child were fallen in the battle, she snatched him up, and fled away, and let him fall from her shoulders, and his feet were lamed. So when he had learned where and by whom he was brought up, he sent messengers to Machir, to the city of Lodebar, for with him

---

12. By this great victory over the Idameans or Edomites, the posterity of Esau, and by the consequent tribute paid by that nation to the Jews, were the prophecies delivered to Rebecca before Jacob and Esau were born, and by old Isaac before his death, that the elder, Esau, (or the Edomites,) should serve and the younger, Jacob, (or the Israelites,) and Jacob (or the Israelites) should be Esau's (or the Edomites') lord, remarkably fulfilled. See Antiq. B. VIII. ch 7. sect. 6; Genesis 25;9,3; and the notes on Antiq. B. I. ch. 18. sect. 5, 6.

was the son of Jonathan brought up, and sent for him to come to him. So when Mephibosheth came to the king, he fell on his face and worshipped him; but David encouraged him, bade him be of good cheer, and expect better times. So he gave him his father's house, and all the estate which his grandfather Saul was in possession of, and bade him come and diet with him at his own table, and never to be absent one day from that table. And when the youth had worshipped him on account of his words and gifts given to him, he called for Ziba, and told him that he had given the youth his father's house, and all Saul's estate. He also ordered that Ziba should cultivate his land, and take care of it, and bring him the profits of all to Jerusalem. Accordingly, David brought him to his table every day, and bestowed upon the youth, Ziba and his sons, who were in number fifteen, and his servants, who were in number twenty. When the king had made these appointments, and Ziba had worshipped him, and promised to do all that he had bidden him, he went his way; so that this son of Jonathan dwelt at Jerusalem, and dieted at the king's table, and had the same care that a son could claim taken of him. He also had himself a son, whom he named Micha.

6   How the War Was Waged Against the Ammonites and Happily Concluded

1. THIS were the honors that such as were left of Saul's and Jonathan's lineage received from David. About this time died Nahash, the king of the Ammonites, who was a friend of David's; and when his son had succeeded his father in the kingdom, David sent ambassadors to him to comfort him; and exhorted him to take his father's death patiently, and to expect that he would continue the same kindness to himself which he had shown to his father. But the princes of the Ammonites took this message in evil part, and not as David's kind dispositions gave reason to take it; and they excited the king to resent it; and said that David had sent men to spy out the country, and what strength it had, under the pretense of humanity and kindness. They further advised him to have a care, and not to give heed to David's words, lest he should be deluded by him, and so fall into an inconsolable calamity. Accordingly Nahash's [son], the king of the

Ammonites, thought these princes spake what was more probable than the truth would admit, and so abused the ambassadors after a very harsh manner; for he shaved the one half of their beards, and cut off one half of their garments, and sent his answer, not in words, but in deeds. When the king of Israel saw this, he had indignation at it, and showed openly that he would not overlook this injurious and contumelious treatment, but would make war with the Ammonites, and would avenge this wicked treatment of his ambassadors on their king. So that king's intimate friends and commanders, understanding that they had violated their league, and were liable to be punished for the same, made preparations for war; they also sent a thousand talents to the Syrian king of Mesopotamia, and endeavored to prevail with him to assist them for that pay, and Shobach. Now these kings had twenty thousand footmen. They also hired the king of the country called Maacah, and a fourth king, by name Ishtob; which last had twelve thousand armed men.

2. But David was under no consternation at this confederacy, nor at the forces of the Ammonites; and putting his trust in God, because he was going to war in a just cause, on account of the injurious treatment he had met with, he immediately sent Joab, the captain of his host, against them, and gave him the flower of his army, who pitched his camp by Rabbah, the metropolis of the Ammonites; whereupon the enemy came out, and set themselves in array, not all of them together, but in two bodies; for the auxiliaries were set in array in the plain by themselves, but the army of the Ammonites at the gates over against the Hebrews. When Joab saw this, he opposed one stratagem against another, and chose out the most hardy part of his men, and set them in opposition to the king of Syria, and the kings that were with him, and gave the other part to his brother Abishai, and bid him set them in opposition to the Ammonites; and said to him, that in case he should see that the Syrians distressed him, and were too hard for him, he should order his troops to turn about and assist him; and he said that he himself would do the same to him, if he saw him in the like distress from the Ammonites. So he sent his brother before, and encouraged him to do every thing courageously and with alacrity, which would teach them to be afraid of disgrace, and to fight manfully; and so he dismissed him to fight with the Ammonites, while he fell upon the Syrians. And though they made a strong opposition for a while,

Joab slew many of them, but compelled the rest to betake themselves to flight; which, when the Ammonites saw, and were withal afraid of Abishai and his army, they staid no longer, but imitated their auxiliaries, and fled to the city. So Joab, when he had thus overcome the enemy, returned with great joy to Jerusalem to the king.

3. This defeat did not still induce the Ammonites to be quiet, nor to own those that were superior to them to be so, and be still, but they sent to Chalaman, the king of the Syrians, beyond Euphrates, and hired him for an auxiliary. He had Shobach for the captain of his host, with eighty thousand footmen, and ten thousand horsemen. Now when the king of the Hebrews understood that the Ammonites had again gathered so great an army together, he determined to make war with them no longer by his generals, but he passed over the river Jordan himself with all his army; and when he met them he joined battle with them, and overcame them, and slew forty thousand of their footmen, and seven thousand of their horsemen. He also wounded Shobach, the general of Chalaman's forces, who died of that stroke; but the people of Mesopotamia, upon such a conclusion of the battle, delivered themselves up to David, and sent him presents, who at winter time returned to Jerusalem. But at the beginning of the spring he sent Joab, the captain of his host, to fight against the Ammonites, who overran all their country, and laid it waste, and shut them up in their metropolis Rabbah, and besieged them therein.

7   *How David Fell in Love with Bathsheba, and Slew Her Husband Uriah, for Which He Is Reproved by Nathan*

1. BUT David fell now into a very grievous sin, though he were otherwise naturally a righteous and a religious man, and one that firmly observed the laws of our fathers; for when late in an evening he took a view round him from the roof of his royal palace, where he used to walk at that hour, he saw a woman washing herself in her own house: she was one of extraordinary beauty, and therein surpassed all other women; her name was Bathsheba. So he was overcome by that woman's beauty, and was not able to restrain his desires, but sent for her, and lay with her. Hereupon she conceived with child, and sent to the king, that he should contrive some way for concealing her sin

(for, according to the laws of their fathers, she who had been guilty of adultery ought to be put to death). So the king sent for Joab's armor-bearer from the siege, who was the woman's husband, and his name was Uriah. And when he was come, the king inquired of him about the army, and about the siege; and when he had made answer that all their affairs went according to their wishes, the king took some portions of meat from his supper, and gave them to him, and bade him go home to his wife, and take his rest with her. Uriah did not do so, but slept near the king with the rest of his armor-bearers. When the king was informed of this, he asked him why he did not go home to his house, and to his wife, after so long an absence; which is the natural custom of all men, when they come from a long journey. He replied, that it was not right, while his fellow soldiers, and the general of the army, slept upon the ground, in the camp, and in an enemy's country, that he should go and take his rest, and solace himself with his wife. So when he had thus replied, the king ordered him to stay there that night, that he might dismiss him the next day to the general. So the king invited Uriah to supper, and after a cunning and dexterous manlier plied him with drink at supper, till he was thereby disordered; yet did he nevertheless sleep at the king's gates without any inclination to go to his wife. Upon this the king was very angry at him; and wrote to Joab, and commanded him to punish Uriah, for he told him that he had offended him; and he suggested to him the manner in which he would have him punished, that it might not be discovered that he was himself the author of this his punishment; for he charged him to set him over against that part of the enemy's army where the attack would be most hazardous, and where he might be deserted, and be in the greatest jeopardy, for he bade him order his fellow soldiers to retire out of the fight. When he had written thus to him, and sealed the letter with his own seal, he gave it to Uriah to carry to Joab. When Joab had received it, and upon reading it understood the king's purpose, he set Uriah in that place where he knew the enemy would be most troublesome to them; and gave him for his partners some of the best soldiers in the army; and said that he would also come to their assistance with the whole army, that if possible they might break down some part of the wall, and enter the city. And he desired him to be glad of the opportunity of exposing himself to such great pains, and not to be displeased at it, since he was a valiant soldier, and had a great reputation for his valor, both with the king and with his countrymen. And when Uriah undertook the work he was set upon with alacrity, he gave private orders to those who were to be his companions, that when they saw the enemy make a sally, they should leave him. When, therefore, the Hebrews made an attack upon the city, the Ammonites were afraid that the enemy might prevent them, and get up into the city, and this at the very place whither Uriah was ordered; so they exposed their best soldiers to be in the forefront, and opened their gates suddenly, and fell upon the enemy with great vehemence, and ran violently upon them. When those that were with Uriah saw this, they all retreated backward, as Joab had directed them beforehand; but Uriah, as ashamed to run away and leave his post, sustained the enemy, and receiving the violence of their onset, he slew many of them; but being encompassed round, and caught in the midst of them, he was slain, and some other of his companions were slain with him.

2. When this was done, Joab sent messengers to the king, and ordered them to tell him that he did what he could to take the city soon; but that, as they made an assault on the wall, they had been forced to retire with great loss; and bade them, if they saw the king was angry at it, to add this, that Uriah was slain also. When the king had heard this of the messengers, he took it heinously, and said that they did wrong when they assaulted the wall, whereas they ought, by undermining and other stratagems of war, to endeavor the taking of rite city, especially when they had before their eyes the example of Abimelech, the son of Gideon, who would needs take the tower in Thebes by force, and was killed by a large stone thrown at him by an old woman; and although he was a man of great prowess, he died ignominiously by the dangerous manner of his assault: that they should remember this accident, and not come near the enemy's wall, for that the best method of making war with success was to call to mind the accidents of former wars, and what good or bad success had attended them in the like dangerous cases, that so they might imitate the one, and avoid the other. But when the king was in this disposition, the messenger told him that Uriah was slain also; whereupon he was pacified. So he bade the messenger go back to Joab and tell him that this misfortune is no other than what is common among mankind, and that such is the nature, and such the accidents of war, insomuch that sometimes the enemy will have success therein, and sometimes others;

but that he ordered him to go on still in his care about the siege, that no ill accident might befall him in it hereafter; that they should raise bulwarks and use machines in besieging the city; and when they have gotten it, to overturn its very foundations, and to destroy all those that are in it. Accordingly the messenger carried the king's message with which he was charged, and made haste to Joab. But Bathsheba, the wife of Uriah, when she was informed of the death of her husband, mourned for his death many days; and when her mourning was over, and the tears which she shed for Uriah were dried up, the king took her to wife presently; and a son was born to him by her.

3. With this marriage God was not well pleased, but was thereupon angry at David; and he appeared to Nathan the prophet in his sleep, and complained of the king. Now Nathan was a fair and prudent man; and considering that kings, when they fall into a passion, are guided more by that passion than they are by justice, he resolved to conceal the threatenings that proceeded from God, and made a good-natured discourse to him, and this after the. manner following:—He desired that the king would give him his opinion in the following case:—There were," said he, "two men inhabiting the same city, the one of them was rich, and [the other poor]. The rich man had a great many flocks of cattle, of sheep, and of kine; but the poor man had but one ewe lamb. This he brought up with his children, and let her eat her food with them; and he had the same natural affection for her which any one might have for a daughter. Now upon the coming of a stranger to the rich man, he would not vouchsafe to kill any of his own flocks, and thence feast his friend; but he sent for the poor man's lamb, and took her away from him, and made her ready for food, and thence feasted the stranger." This discourse troubled the king exceedingly; and he denounced to Nathan, that "this man was a wicked man who could dare to do such a thing; and that it was but just that he should restore the lamb fourfold, and be punished with death for it also." Upon this Nathan immediately said that he was himself the man who ought to suffer those punishments, and that by his own sentence; and that it was he who had perpetrated this 'great and horrid crime. He also revealed to him, and laid before him, the anger of God against him, who had made him king over the army of the Hebrews, and lord of all the nations, and those many and great nations round about him; who had formerly delivered him out of the hands of Saul, and had

given him such wives as he had justly and legally married; and now this God was despised by him, and affronted by his impiety, when he had married, and now had, another man's wife; and by exposing her husband to the enemy, had really slain him; 'that God would inflict punishments upon him on account of those instances of wickedness; that his own wives should be forced by one of his sons; and that he should be treacherously supplanted by the same son; and that although he had perpetrated his wickedness secretly, yet should that punishment which he was to undergo be inflicted publicly upon him; "that, moreover," said he, "the child which was born to thee of her shall soon die." When the king was troubled at these messages, and sufficiently confounded, and said with tears and sorrow that he had sinned, (for he was without controversy a pious man, and guilty of no sin at all in his whole life, excepting those in the matter of Uriah,) God had compassion on him, and was reconciled to him, and promised that he would preserve to him both his life and his kingdom; for he said that, seeing he repented of the things he had done, he was no longer displeased with him. So Nathan, when he had delivered this prophecy to the king, returned home.

4. However, God sent a dangerous distemper upon the child that was born to David of the wife of Uriah, at which the king was troubled, and did not take any food for seven days, although his servants almost forced him to take it; but he clothed himself in a black garment, and fell down, and lay upon the ground in sackcloth, entrusting God for the recovery of the child, for he vehemently loved the child's mother; but when, on the seventh day, the child was dead, the king's servants durst not tell him of it, as supposing that when he knew it, he would still less admit of food, and other care of himself, by reason of his grief at the death of his son, since when the child was only sick, he so greatly afflicted himself, and grieved for him: but when the king perceived that his servants were in disorder, and seemed to be affected, as those who are very desirous to conceal something, he understood that the child was dead; and when he had called one of his servants to him, and discovered that so it was, he arose up and washed himself, and took a white garment, and came into the tabernacle of God. He also commanded them to set supper before him, and thereby greatly surprised his kindred and servants, while he did nothing of this when the child was sick, but did it all when he was dead. Whereupon having

first begged leave to ask him a question, they besought him to tell them the reason of this his conduct; he then called them unskillful people, and instructed them how he had hopes of the recovery of the child while it was alive, and accordingly did all that was proper for him to do, as thinking by such means to render God propitious to him; but that when the child was dead, there was no longer any occasion for grief, which was then to no purpose. When he had said this, they commended the king's wisdom and understanding. He then went in unto Bathsheba his wife, and she conceived and bare a son; and by the command of Nathan the prophet called his name Solomon.

5. But Joab sorely distressed the Ammonites in the siege, by cutting off their waters, and depriving them of other means of subsistence, till they were in the greatest want of meat and drink, for they depended only on one small well of water, and this they durst not drink of too freely, lest the fountain should entirely fail them. So he wrote to the king, and informed him thereof; and persuaded him to come himself to take the city, that he might have the honor of the victory. Upon this letter of Joab's, the king accepted of his good-will and fidelity, and took with him his army, and came to the destruction of Rabbah; and when he had taken it by force, he gave it to his soldiers to plunder it; but he himself took the king of the Ammonites' crown, whose weight was a talent of gold;[13] and it had in its middle a precious stone called a sardonyx; which crown David ever after wore on his own head. He also found many other vessels in the city, and those both splendid and of great price; but as for the men, he tormented them,[14] and

---

13. That a talent of gold was about seven pounds weight, see the description of the temple ch. 13. Nor could Josephus well estimate it higher, since he here says that David wore it on his head perpetually.

14. Whether Josephus saw the words of our copies, 2 Samuel 12:31, and 1 Chronicles 20:3, that David put the inhabitants, or at least the garrison of Rabbah, and of the other Ammonite cities, which he besieged and took, under, or cut them with saws, and under, or with harrows of iron, and under, or with axes of iron, and made them pass through the brick-kiln, is not here directly expressed. If he saw them, as is most probable he did, he certainly expounded them of tormenting these Ammonites to death, who were none of those seven nations of Canaan whose wickedness had rendered them incapable of mercy; otherwise I should be inclinable to think that the meaning, at least as the words are in Samuel, might only be this: That they were made the lowest slaves, to work in sawing of timber or stone, in harrowing the fields,

then destroyed them; and when he had taken the other cities of the Ammonites by force, he treated them after the same manner.

8 How Absalom Murdered Amnon, Who Had Forced His Own Sister; and How He Was Banished and Afterwards Recalled by David

1. WHEN the king was returned to Jerusalem, a sad misfortune befell his house, on the occasion following: He had a daughter, who was yet a virgin, and very handsome, insomuch that she surpassed all the most beautiful women; her name was Tamar; she had the same mother with Absalom. Now Amnon, David's eldest son, fell in love with her, and being not able to obtain his desires, on account of her virginity, and the custody she was under, was so much out of order, nay, his grief so eat up his body, that he grew lean, and his color was changed. Now there was one Jenadab, a kinsman and friend of his, who discovered this his passion, for he was an extraordinary wise man, and of great sagacity of mind. When, therefore, he saw that every morning Amnon was not in body as he ought to be, he came to him, and desired him to tell him what was the cause of it: however, he said that he guessed that it arose from the passion of love. Amnon confessed his passion, that he was in love with a sister of his, who had the same father with himself. So Jenadab suggested to him by what method and contrivance he might obtain his desires; for he persuaded him to pretend sickness, and bade him, when his father should come to him, to beg of him that his sister might come and minister to him; for if that were done, he should be better, and should quickly recover from his distemper. So Amnon lay down on his bed, and pretended to be sick, as Jonadab had suggested. When his father came, and inquired how he did, he begged of him to send his sister to him. Accordingly, he presently ordered her to be brought to him; and when she was come, Amnon bade her make cakes for him, and fry them in a pan, and do it all with her own

---

in hewing timber, in making and burning bricks, and the like hard services, but without taking away their lives. We never elsewhere, that I remember, meet with such methods of cruelty in putting men to death in all the Bible, or in any other ancient history whatsoever; nor do the words in Samuel seem naturally to refer to any such thing.

hands, because he should take them better from her hand [than from any one's else]. So she kneaded the flour in the sight of her brother, and made him cakes, and baked them in a pan, and brought them to him; but at that time he would not taste them, but gave order to his servants to send all that were there out of his chamber, because he had a mind to repose himself, free from tumult and disturbance. As soon as what he had commanded was done, he desired his sister to bring his supper to him into the inner parlor; which, when the damsel had done, he took hold of her, and endeavored to persuade her to lie with him. Whereupon the damsel cried out, and said, "Nay, brother, do not force me, nor be so wicked as to transgress the laws, and bring upon thyself the utmost confusion. Curb this thy unrighteous and impure lust, from which our house will get nothing but reproach and disgrace." She also advised him to speak to his father about this affair; for he would permit him [to marry her]. This she said, as desirous to avoid her brother's violent passion at present. But he would not yield to her; but, inflamed with love and blinded with the vehemency of his passion, he forced his sister: but as soon as Amnon had satisfied his lust, he hated her immediately, and giving her reproachful words, bade her rise up and be gone. And when she said that this was a more injurious treatment than the former, if, now he had forced her, he would not let her stay with him till the evening, but bid her go away in the day-time, and while it was light, that she might meet with people that would be witnesses of her shame,—he commanded his servant to turn her out of his house. Whereupon she was sorely grieved at the injury and violence that had been offered to her, and rent her loose coat, (for the virgins of old time wore such loose coats tied at the hands, and let down to the ankles, that the inner coats might not be seen,) and sprinkled ashes on her head; and went up the middle of the city, crying out and lamenting for the violence that had been offered her. Now Absalom, her brother, happened to meet her, and asked her what sad thing had befallen her, that she was in that plight; and when she had told him what injury had been offered her, he comforted her, and desired her to be quiet, and take all patiently, and not to esteem her being corrupted by her brother as an injury. So she yielded to his advice, and left off her crying out, and discovering the force offered her to the multitude; and she continued as a widow with her brother Absalom a long time.

2. When David his father knew this, he was grieved at the actions of Amnon; but because he had an extraordinary affection for him, for he was his eldest son, he was compelled not to afflict him; but Absalom watched for a fit opportunity of revenging this crime upon him, for he thoroughly hated him. Now the second year after this wicked affair about his sister was over, and Absalom was about to go to shear his own sheep at Baalhazor, which is a city in the portion of Ephraim, he besought his father, as well as his brethren, to come and feast with him: but when David excused himself, as not being willing to be burdensome to him, Absalom desired he would however send his brethren; whom he did send accordingly. Then Absalom charged his own servants, that when they should see Amnon disordered and drowsy with wine, and he should give them a signal, they should fear nobody, but kill him.

3. When they had done as they were commanded, the rest of his brethren were astonished and disturbed, and were afraid for themselves, so they immediately got on horseback, and rode away to their father; but somebody there was who prevented them, and told their father they were all slain by Absalom; whereupon he was overcome with sorrow, as for so many of his sons that were destroyed at once, and that by their brother also; and by this consideration, that it was their brother that appeared to have slain them, he aggravated his sorrow for them. So he neither inquired what was the cause of this slaughter, nor staid to hear any thing else, which yet it was but reasonable to have done, when so very great, and by that greatness so incredible, a misfortune was related to him: he rent his clothes and threw himself upon the ground, and there lay lamenting the loss of all his sons, both those who, as he was informed, were slain, and of him who slew them. But Jonadab, the son of his brother Shemeah, entreated him not to indulge his sorrow so far, for as to the rest of his sons he did not believe that they were slain, for he found no cause for such a suspicion; but he said it might deserve inquiry as to Amnon, for it was not unlikely that Absalom might venture to kill him on account of the injury he had offered to Tamar. In the mean time, a great noise of horses, and a tumult of some people that were coming, turned their attention to them; they were the king's sons, who were fled away from the feast. So their father met them as they were in their grief, and he himself grieved with them; but it was more than he expected to

see those his sons again, whom he had a little before heard to have perished. However, their were tears on both sides; they lamenting their brother who was killed, and the king lamenting his son, who was killed also; but Absalom fled to Geshur, to his grandfather by his mother's side, who was king of that country, and he remained with him three whole years.

4. Now David had a design to send to Absalom, not that he should come to be punished, but that he might be with him, for the effects of his anger were abated by length of time. It was Joab, the captain of his host, that chiefly persuaded him so to do; for he suborned an ordinary woman, that was stricken in age, to go to the king in mourning apparel, who said thus to him:—That two of her sons, in a coarse way, had some difference between them, and that in the progress of that difference they came to an open quarrel, and that one was smitten by the other, and was dead; and she desired him to interpose in this case, and to do her the favor to save this her son from her kindred, who were very zealous to have him that had slain his brother put to death, that so she might not be further deprived of the hopes she had of being taken care of in her old age by him; and that if he would hinder this slaughter of her son by those that wished for it, he would do her a great favor, because the kindred would not be restrained from their purpose by any thing else than by the fear of him. And when the king had given his consent to what the woman had begged of him, she made this reply to him:—"I owe thee thanks for thy benignity to me in pitying my old age, and preventing the loss of my only remaining child; but in order to assure me of this thy kindness, be first reconciled to thine own son, and cease to be angry with him; for how shall I persuade myself that thou hast really bestowed this favor upon me, while thou thyself continuest after the like manner in thy wrath to thine own son? for it is a foolish thing to add willfully another to thy dead son, while the death of the other was brought about without thy consent." And now the king perceived that this pretended story was a subornation derived from Joab, and was of his contrivance; and when, upon inquiry of the old woman, he understood it to be so in reality, he called for Joab, and told him he had obtained what he requested according to his own mind; and he bid him bring Absalom back, for he was not now displeased, but had already ceased to be angry with him. So Joab bowed himself down to the king, and took his words

kindly, and went immediately to Geshur, and took Absalom with him, and came to Jerusalem.

5. However, the king sent a message to his son beforehand, as he was coming, and commanded him to retire to his own house, for he was not yet in such a disposition as to think fit at present to see him. Accordingly, upon the father's command, he avoided coming into his presence, and contented himself with the respects paid him by his own family only. Now his beauty was not impaired, either by the grief he had been under, or by the want of such care as was proper to be taken of a king's son, for he still surpassed and excelled all men in the tallness of his body, and was more eminent [in a fine appearance] than those that dieted the most luxuriously; and indeed such was the thickness of the hair of his head, that it was with difficulty that he was polled every eighth day; and his hair weighed two hundred shekels[15] which are five pounds. However, he dwelt in Jerusalem two years, and became the father of three sons, and one daughter; which daughter was of very great beauty, and which Rehoboam, the son of Solomon, took to wife afterward, and had by her a son named Abijah. But Absalom sent to Joab, and desired him to pacify his father entirely towards him; and to beseech him to give him leave to come to him to see him, and speak with him. But when Joab neglected so to do, he sent some of his own servants, and set fire to the field adjoining to him; which, when Joab understood, he came to Absalom, and accused him of what he had done; and asked him the reason why he did so. To which Absalom replied, that "I have found out this stratagem that might bring thee to us, while thou hast taken no care to perform the injunction I laid upon thee, which was this, to reconcile my father to me; and I really beg it of thee, now thou art here, to pacify my father as to me, since I esteem my coming hither to be more grievous than my banishment, while my father's wrath against me continues."

---

15. Of this weight of Absalom's hair, how in twenty or thirty years it might well amount to two hundred shekels, or to somewhat above six pounds avoirdupois, see the Literal Accomplishment of Prophecies, p. 77, 78. But a late very judicious author thinks that the LXXX. meant not its weight, but its value, Was twenty shekels.—Dr. Wall's Critical Notes on the Old Testament, upon 2 Samuel 14:26. It does not appear what was Josephus's opinion: he sets the text down honestly as he found it in his copies, only he thought that "at the end of days," when Absalom polled or weighed his hair, was once a week.

Hereby Joab was persuaded, and pitied the distress that Absalom was in, and became an intercessor with the king for him. And when he had discoursed with his father, he soon brought him to that amicable disposition towards Absalom, that he presently sent for him to come to him; and when he had cast himself down upon the ground, and had begged for the forgiveness of his offenses, the king raised him up, and promised him to forget what he had formerly done.

9 *Concerning the Insurrection of Absalom Against David and Concerning Ahithophel and Hushai; and Concerning Ziba and Shimei; and How Ahithophel Hanged Himself*

1. NOW Absalom, upon this his success with the king, procured to himself a great many horses, and many chariots, and that in a little time also. He had moreover fifty armor-bearers that were about him; and he came early every day to the king's palace, and spake what was agreeable to such as came for justice and lost their causes, as if that happened for want of good counselors about the king, or perhaps because the judges mistook in that unjust sentence they gave; whereby he gained the good-will of them all. He told them, that had he but such authority committed to him, he would distribute justice to them in a most equitable manner. When he had made himself so popular among the multitude, he thought he had already the good-will of the people secured to him; but when four years[16] had passed since his father's reconciliation to him, he came to him, and besought him to give him leave to go to Hebron, and pay a sacrifice to God, because he vowed it to him when he fled out of the country. So when David had granted his request, he went thither, and great multitudes came running together to him, for he had sent to a great number so to do.

2. Among them came Ahithophel the Gilonite, a counsellor of David's, and two hundred men out of Jerusalem itself, who knew not

---

16. This is one of the best corrections that Josephus's copy affords us of a text that in our ordinary copies is grossly corrupted. They say that this rebellion of Absalom was forty years after what went before, (of his reconciliation to his father,) whereas the series of the history shows it could not be more than four years after it, as here in Josephus; whose number is directly confirmed by that copy of the Septuagint version whence the Armenian translation was made, which gives us the small number of four years.

his intentions, but were sent for as to a sacrifice. So he was appointed king by all of them, which he obtained by this stratagem. As soon as this news was brought to David, and he was informed of what he did not expect from his son, he was aftrighted at this his impious and bold undertaking, and wondered that he was so far from remembering how his offense had been so lately forgiven him, that he undertook much worse and more wicked enterprises; first, to deprive him of that kingdom which was given him of God; and secondly, to take away his own father's life. He therefore resolved to fly to the parts beyond Jordan: so he called his most intimate friends together, and communicated to them all that he had heard of his son's madness. He committed himself to God, to judge between them about all their actions; and left the care of his royal palace to his ten concubines, and went away from Jerusalem, being willingly accompanied by the rest of the multitude, who went hastily away with him, and particularly by those six hundred armed men, who had been with him from his first flight in the days of Saul. But he persuaded Abiathar and Zadok, the high priests, who had determined to go away with him, as also all the Levites, who were with the ark, to stay behind, as hoping that God would deliver him without its removal; but he charged them to let him know privately how all things went on; and he had their sons, Ahimmaz the son of Zadok, and Jonathan the son of Abiathar, for faithful ministers in all things; but Ittai the Gitrite went out with him whether David would let him or not, for he would have persuaded him to stay, and on that account he appeared the more friendly to him. But as he was ascending the Mount of Olives barefooted, and all his company were in tears, it was told him that Ahithophel was with Absalom, and was of his side. This hearing augmented his grief; and he besought God earnestly to alienate the mind of Absalom from Ahithophel, for he was afraid that he should persuade him to follow his pernicious counsel, for he was a prudent man, and very sharp in seeing what was advantageous. When David was gotten upon the top of the mountain, he took a view of the city; and prayed to God with abundance of tears, as having already lost his kingdom; and here it was that a faithful friend of his, whose name was Hushai, met him. When David saw him with his clothes rent, and having ashes all over his head, and in lamentation for the great change of affairs, he comforted him, and exhorted him to leave off grieving; nay, at length he besought him to go back to Absalom, and appear as one of his party, and to fish out the secretest counsels of his mind, and to contradict the counsels of Ahithophel, for that he could not do him so much good by being with him as he might by being with Absalom. So he was prevailed on by David, and left him, and came to Jerusalem, whither Absalom himself came also a little while afterward.

3. When David was gone a little farther, there met him Ziba, the servant of Mephibosheth, (whom he had sent to take care of the possessions which had been given him, as the son of Jonathan, the son of Saul,) with a couple of asses, loaden with provisions, and desired him to take as much of them as he and his followers stood in need of. And when the king asked him where he had left Mephibosheth, he said he had left him in Jerusalem, expecting to be chosen king in the present confusions, in remembrance of the benefits Saul had conferred upon them. At this the king had great indignation, and gave to Ziba all that he had formerly bestowed on Mephibosheth; for he determined that it was much fitter that he should have them than the other; at which Ziba greatly rejoiced.

4. When David was at Bahurim, a place so called, there came out a kinsman of Saul's, whose name was Shimei, and threw stones at him, and gave him reproachful words; and as his friends stood about the king and protected him, he persevered still more in his reproaches, and called him a bloody man, and the author of all sorts of mischief. He bade him also go out of the land as an impure and accursed wretch; and he thanked God for depriving him of his kingdom, and causing him to be punished for what injuries he had done to his master [Saul], and this by the means of his own son. Now when they were all provoked against him, and angry at bin;, and particularly Abishai, who had a mind to kill Shimei, David restrained his anger. "Let us not," said he, "bring upon ourselves another fresh misfortune to those we have already, for truly I have not the least regard nor concern for this dog that raves at me: I submit myself to God, by whose permission this man treats me in such a wild manner; nor is it any wonder that I am obliged to undergo these abuses from him, while I experience the like from an impious son of my own; but perhaps God will have some commiseration upon us; if it be his will we shall overcome them." So he went on his way without troubling himself with Shimei, who ran along the other side of the mountain, and threw out his abusive

language plentifully. But when David was come to Jordan, he allowed those that were with him to refresh themselves; for they were weary.

5. But when Absalom, and Ahithophel his counselor, were come to Jerusalem, with all the people, David's friend, Hushai, came to them; and when he had worshipped Absalom, he withal wished that his kingdom might last a long time, and continue for all ages. But when Absalom said to him, "How comes this, that he who was so intimate a friend of my father's, and appeared faithful to him in all things, is not with him now, but hath left him, and is come over to me?" Hushai's answer was very pertinent and prudent; for he said, "We ought to follow God and the multitude of the people; while these, therefore, my lord and master, are with thee, it is fit that I should follow them, for thou hast received the kingdom from God. I will therefore, if thou believest me to be thy friend, show the same fidelity and kindness to thee, which thou knowest I have shown to thy father; nor is there any reason to be in the least dissatisfied with the present state of affairs, for the kingdom is not transferred into another, but remains still in the same family, by the son's receiving it after his father." This speech persuaded Absalom, who before suspected Hushai. And now he called Ahithophel, and consulted with him what he ought to do: he persuaded him to go in unto his father's concubines; for he said that "by this action the people would believe that thy difference with thy father is irreconcilable, and will thence fight with great alacrity against thy father, for hitherto they are afraid of taking up open enmity against him, out of an expectation that you will be reconciled again." Accordingly, Absalom was prevailed on by this advice, and commanded his servants to pitch him a tent upon the top of the royal palace, in the sight of the multitude; and he went in and lay with his father's concubines. Now this came to pass according to the prediction of Nathan, when he prophesied and signified to him that his son would rise up in rebellion against him.

6. And when Absalom had done what he was advised to by Ahithophel, he desired his advice, in the second place, about the war against his father. Now Ahithophel only asked him to let him have ten thousand chosen men, and he promised he would slay his father, and bring the soldiers back again in safety; and he said that then the kingdom would be firm to him when David was dead [but not otherwise]. Absalom was pleased with this advice, and called for

Hushai, David's friend (for so did he style him); and informing him of the opinion of Ahithophel, he asked, further, what was his opinion concerning that matter. Now he was sensible that if Ahithophel's counsel were followed, David would be in danger of being seized on, and slain; so he attempted to introduce a contrary opinion, and said, Thou art not unacquainted, O king, with the valor of thy father, and of those that are now with him; that he hath made many wars, and hath always come off with victory, though probably he now abides in the camp, for he is very skilful in stratagems, and in foreseeing the deceitful tricks of his enemies; yet will he leave his own soldiers in the evening, and will either hide himself in some valley, or will place an ambush at some rock; so that when our army joins battle with him, his soldiers will retire for a little while, but will come upon us again, as encouraged by the king's being near them; and in the mean time your father will show himself suddenly in the time of the battle, and will infuse courage into his own people when they are in danger, but bring consternation to thine. Consider, therefore, my advice, and reason upon it, and if thou canst not but acknowledge it to be the best, reject the opinion of Ahithophel. Send to the entire country of the Hebrews, and order them to come and fight with thy father; and do thou thyself take the army, and be thine own general in this war, and do not trust its management to another; then expect to conquer him with ease, when thou overtakest him openly with his few partisans, but hast thyself many ten thousands, who will be desirous to demonstrate to thee their diligence and alacrity. And if thy father shall shut himself up in some city, and bear a siege, we will overthrow that city with machines of war, and by undermining it." When Hushai had said this, he obtained his point against Ahithophel, for his opinion was preferred by Absalom before the other's: however, it was no other than God[17] who made the counsel of Hushai appear best to the mind of Absalom.

---

17. This reflection of Josephus's, that God brought to nought the dangerous counsel of Ahithophel, and directly infatuated wicked Absalom to reject it, (which infatuation is what the Scripture styles the judicial hardening the hearts and blinding the eyes of men, who, by their former voluntary wickedness, have justly deserved to be destroyed, and are thereby brought to destruction,) is a very just one, and in him not unfrequent. Nor does Josephus ever puzzle himself, or perplex his readers, with subtle hypotheses as to the manner of such judicial infatuations by God, while the justice of them is generally so obvious. That peculiar manner of the Divine operations, or permissions, or the means God makes use of in such cases, is often impenetrable

7. So Hushai made haste to the high priests, Zadok and Abiathar, and told them the opinion of Ahithophel, and his own, and that the resolution was taken to follow this latter advice. He therefore bade them send to David, and tell him of it, and to inform him of the counsels that had been taken; and to desire him further to pass quickly over Jordan, lest his son should change his mind, and make haste to pursue him, and so prevent him, and seize upon him before he be in safety. Now the high priests had their sons concealed in a proper place out of the city, that they might carry news to David of what was transacted. Accordingly, they sent a maid-servant, whom they could trust, to them, to carry the news of Absalom's counsels, and ordered them to signify the same to David with all speed. So they made no excuse nor delay, but taking along with them their fathers' injunctions, because pious and faithful ministers, and judging that quickness and suddenness was the best mark of faithful service, they made haste to meet with David. But certain horsemen saw them when they were two furlongs from the city, and informed Absalom of them, who immediately sent some to take them; but when the sons of the high priest perceived this, they went out of the road, and betook themselves to a certain village; that village was called Bahurim; there they desired a certain woman to hide them, and afford them security. Accordingly she let the young men down by a rope into a well, and laid fleeces of wool over them; and when those that pursued them came to her, and asked her whether she saw them, she did not deny that she had seen them, for that they staid with her some time, but she said they then went their ways; and she foretold that, however, if they would follow them directly, they would catch them; but when after a long pursuit they could not catch them, they came back again; and when the woman saw those men were returned, and that there was no longer any fear of the young men's being caught by them, she drew them up by the rope, and bade them go on their journey accordingly, they used

---

by us. "Secret things belong to the Lord our God; but those things that are revealed belong to us, and to our children for ever, that we may do all the words of this law," Deuteronomy 29:29. Nor have all the subtleties of the moderns, as far as I see, given any considerable light in this, and many other the like points of difficulty relating either to Divine or human operations.—See the notes on Antiq. B. V ch. 1. sect. 2; and Antiq. B. IX. ch. 4. sect. 3.

great diligence in the prosecution of that journey, and came to David, and informed him accurately of all the counsels of Absalom. So he commanded those that were with him to pass over Jordan while it was night, and not to delay at all on that account.

8. But Ahithophel, on rejection of his advice, got upon his ass, and rode away to his own country, Gilon; and, calling his family together, he told them distinctly what advice he had given Absalom; and since he had not been persuaded by it, he said he would evidently perish, and this in no long time, and that David would overcome him, and return to his kingdom again; so he said it was better that he should take his own life away with freedom and magnanimity, than expose himself to be punished by David, in opposition to whom he had acted entirely for Absalom. When he had discoursed thus to them, he went into the inmost room of his house, and hanged himself; and thus was the death of Ahithophel, who was self-condemned; and when his relations had taken him down from the halter, they took care of his funeral. Now, as for David, he passed over Jordan, as we have said already, and came to Mahanaim, every fine and very strong city; and all the chief men of the country received him with great pleasure, both out of the shame they had that he should be forced to flee away [from Jerusalem], and out of the respect they bare him while he was in his former prosperity. These were Barzillai the Gileadite, and Siphar the ruler among the Ammonites, and Machir the principal man of Gilead; and these furnished him with plentiful provisions for himself and his followers, insomuch that they wanted no beds nor blankets for them, nor loaves of bread, nor wine; nay, they brought them a great many cattle for slaughter, and afforded them what furniture they wanted for their refreshment when they were weary, and for food, with plenty of other necessaries.

10 How, When Absalom Was Beaten, He Was Caught in a Tree by His Hair and Was Slain

1. AND this was the state of David and his followers: but Absalom got together a vast army of the Hebrews to oppose his father, and passed therewith over the river Jordan, and sat down not far off Mahanaim, in the country of Gilead. He appointed Amasa to be captain of all his

host, instead of Joab his kinsman: his father was Ithra and his mother Abigail: now she and Zeruiah, the mother of Joab, were David's sisters. But when David had numbered his followers, and found them to be about four thousand, he resolved not to tarry till Absalom attacked him, but set over his men captains of thousands, and captains of hundreds, and divided his army into three parts; the one part he committed to Joab, the next to Abishai, Joab's brother, and the third to Ittai, David's companion and friend, but one that came from the city Gath; and when he was desirous of fighting himself among them, his friends would not let him: and this refusal of theirs was founded upon very wise reasons: "For," said they, "if we be conquered when he is with us, we have lost all good hopes of recovering ourselves; but if we should be beaten in one part of our army, the other parts may retire to him, and may thereby prepare a greater force, while the enemy will naturally suppose that he hath another army with him." So David was pleased with this their advice, and resolved himself to tarry at Mahanaim; and as he sent his friends and commanders to the battle, he desired them to show all possible alacrity and fidelity, and to bear in mind what advantages they had received from him, which, though they had not been very great, yet had they not been quite inconsiderable; and he begged of them to spare the young man Absalom, lest some mischief should befall himself, if he should be killed; and thus did he send out his army to the battle, and wished them victory therein.

2. Then did Joab put his army in battle-array over against the enemy in the Great Plain, where he had a wood behind him. Absalom also brought his army into the field to oppose him. Upon the joining of the battle, both sides showed great actions with their hands and their boldness; the one side exposing themselves to the greatest hazards, and using their utmost alacrity, that David might recover his kingdom; and the other being no way deficient, either in doing or suffering, that Absalom might not be deprived of that kingdom, and be brought to punishment by his father for his impudent attempt against him. Those also that were the most numerous were solicitous that they might not be conquered by those few that were with Joab, and with the other commanders, because that would be the greater disgrace to them; while David's soldiers strove greatly to overcome so many ten thousands as the enemy had with them. Now David's men were

conquerors, as superior in strength and skill in war; so they followed the others as they fled away through the forests and valleys; some they took prisoners, and many they slew, and more in the flight than in the battle for there fell about twenty thousand that day. But all David's men ran violently upon Absalom, for he was easily known by his beauty and tallness. He was himself also afraid lest his enemies should seize on him, so he got upon the king's mule, and fled; but as he was carried with violence, and noise, and a great motion, as being himself light, he entangled his hair greatly in the large boughs of a knotty tree that spread a great way, and there he hung, after a surprising manner; and as for the beast, it went on farther, and that swiftly, as if his master had been still upon his back; but he, hanging in the air upon the boughs, was taken by his enemies. Now when one of David's soldiers saw this, he informed Joab of it; and when the general said, that if he had shot at and killed Absalom, he would have given him fifty shekels,—he replied, "I would not have killed my master's son if thou wouldst have given me a thousand shekels, especially when he desired that the young man might be spared in the hearing of us all." But Joab bade him show him where it was that he saw Absalom hang; whereupon he shot him to the heart, and slew him, and Joab's armor-bearers stood round the tree, and pulled down his dead body, and cast it into a great chasm that was out of sight, and laid a heap of stones upon him, till the cavity was filled up, and had both the appearance and the bigness of a grave. Then Joab sounded a retreat, and recalled his own soldiers from pursuing the enemy's army, in order to spare their countrymen.

3. Now Absalom had erected for himself a marble pillar in the king's dale, two furlongs distant from Jerusalem, which he named Absalom's Hand, saying, that if his children were killed, his name would remain by that pillar; for he had three sons and one daughter, named Tamar, as we said before, who when she was married to David's grandson, Rehoboam, bare a son, Abijah by name, who succeeded his father in the kingdom; but of these we shall speak in a part of our history which will be more proper. After the death of Absalom, they returned every one to their own homes respectively.

4. But now Ahimaaz, the son of Zadok the high priest, went to Joab, and desired he would permit him to go and tell David of this victory, and to bring him the good news that God had afforded his assistance

and his providence to him. However, he did not grant his request, but said to him, "Wilt thou, who hast always been the messenger of good news, now go and acquaint the king that his son is dead?" So he desired him to desist. He then called Cushi, and committed the business to him, that he should tell the king what he had seen. But when Ahimaaz again desired him to let him go as a messenger, and assured him that he would only relate what concerned the victory, but not concerning the death of Absalom, he gave him leave to go to David. Now he took a nearer road than the former did, for nobody knew it but himself, and he came before Cushi. Now as David was sitting between the gates,[18] and waiting to see when somebody would come to him from the battle, and tell him how it went, one of the watchmen saw Ahimaaz running, and before be could discern who he was, be told David that he saw somebody coming to him, who said he was a good messenger. A little while after, he informed him that another messenger followed him; whereupon the king said that he also was a good messenger: but when the watchman saw Ahimaaz, and that he was already very near, he gave the king notice that it was the son of Zadok the high priest who came running. So David was very glad, and said he was a messenger of good tidings, and brought him some such news from the battle as be desired to hear.

5. While the king was saying thus, Ahimaaz appeared, and worshipped the king. And when the king inquired of him about the battle, he said he brought him the good news of victory and dominion. And when he inquired what he had to say concerning his son, he said that he came away on the sudden as soon as the enemy was defeated, but that he heard a great noise of those that pursued Absalom, and that he could learn no more, because of the haste be made when Joab sent him to inform him of the victory. But when Cushi was come, and had worshipped him, and informed him of the victory, he asked him about his son, who replied, "May the like misfortune befall thine enemies as

---

18. Those that take a view of my description of the gates of the temple, will not be surprised at this account of David's throne, both here and 2 Samuel 18:21, that it was between two gates or portals. Gates being in cities, as well as at the temple, large open places, with a portal at the entrance, and another at the exit, between which judicial causes were heard, and public consultations taken, as is well known from several places of Scripture, 2 Chronicles 31:2; Psalm 9:14; 137:5; Proverbs 1:21; 8:3, 31; 31:23, and often elsewhere.

hath befallen Absalom." That word did not permit either himself or his soldiers to rejoice for the victory, though it was a very great one; but David went up to the highest part of the city,[19] and wept for his son, and beat his breast, tearing [the hair of] his head, tormenting himself all manner of ways, and crying out, "O my son! I wish that I had died myself, and ended my days with thee!" for he was of a tender natural affection, and had extraordinary compassion for this son in particular. But when the army and Joab heard that the king mourned for his son, they were ashamed to enter the city in the habit of conquerors, but they all came in as cast down, and in tears, as if they had been beaten. Now while the king covered himself, and grievously lamented his son, Joab went in to him, and comforted him, and said, "O my lord the king, thou art not aware that thou layest a blot on thyself by what thou now doest; for thou seemest to hate those that love thee, and undergo dangers for thee nay, to hate thyself and thy family, and to love those that are thy bitter enemies, and to desire the company of those that are no more, and who have been justly slain; for had Absalom gotten the victory, and firmly settled himself in the kingdom, there had been none of us left alive, but all of us, beginning with thyself and thy children, had miserably perished, while our enemies had not wept for his, but rejoiced over us, and punished even those that pitied us in our misfortunes; and thou art not ashamed to do this in the case of one that has been thy bitter enemy, who, while he was thine own son hath proved so wicked to thee. Leave off, therefore, thy unreasonable grief, and come abroad and be seen of thy soldiers, and return them thanks for the alacrity they showed in the fight; for I myself will this day persuade the people to leave thee, and to give the kingdom to another, if thou continuest to do thus; and then I shall make thee to grieve bitterly and in earnest." Upon Joab's speaking thus to him, he made the king leave off his sorrow, and brought him to the consideration of his affairs. So David changed his habit, and exposed himself in a

---

19. Since David was now in Mahanairn, and in the open place of that city gate, which seems still to have been built the highest of any part of the wall, and since our other copies say he went up to the chamber over the gate, 2 Samuel 18:33, I think we ought to correct our present reading in Josephus, and for city, should read gate, i.e. instead of the highest part of the city, should say the highest part of the gate. Accordingly we find David presently, in Josephus, as well as in our other copies, 2 Samuel 19:8, sitting as before, in the gate of the city.

manner fit to be seen by the multitude, and sat at the gates; whereupon all the people heard of it, and ran together to him, and saluted him. And this was the present state of David's affairs.

11 *How David, When He Had Recovered His Kingdom, Was Reconciled to Shimei, and to Ziba; and Showed a Great Affection to Barzillai; and How, Upon the Rise of a Sedition, He Made Amasa Captain of His Host, in Order to Pursue Seba; Which Amasa Was Slain by Joab*

1. NOW those Hebrews that had been With Absalom, and had retired out of the battle, when they were all returned home, sent messengers to every city to put them in mind of what benefits David had bestowed upon them, and of that liberty which he had procured them, by delivering them from many and great wars. But they complained, that whereas they had ejected him out of his kingdom, and committed it to another governor, which other governor, whom they had set up, was already dead, they did not now beseech David to leave off his anger at them, and to become friends with them, and, as he used to do, to resume the care of their affairs, and take the kingdom again. This was often told to David. And, this notwithstanding, David sent to Zadok and Abiathar the high priests, that they should speak to the rulers of the tribe of Judah after the manner following: That it would be a reproach upon them to permit the other tribes to choose David for their king before their tribe, "and this," said he, "while you are akin to him, and of the same common blood." He commanded them also to say the same to Amasa the captain of their forces, That whereas he was his sister's son, he had not persuaded the multitude to restore the kingdom to David; that he might expect from him not only a reconciliation, for that was already granted, but that supreme command of the army also which Absalom had bestowed upon him. Accordingly the high priests, when they had discoursed with the rulers of the tribe, and said what the king had ordered them, persuaded Amasa to undertake the care of his affairs. So he persuaded that tribe to send immediately ambassadors to him, to beseech him to return to his own kingdom. The same did all the Israelites, at the like persuasion of Amasa.

2. When the ambassadors came to him, he came to Jerusalem; and the tribe of Judah was the first that came to meet the king at the river Jordan. And Shimei, the son of Gera, came with a thousand men, which he brought with him out of the tribe of Benjamin; and Ziba, the freed-man of Saul, with his sons, fifteen in number, and with his twenty servants. All these, as well as the tribe of Judah, laid a bridge [of boats] over the river, that the king, and those that were with him, might with ease pass over it. Now as soon as he was come to Jordan, the tribe of Judah saluted him. Shimei also came upon the bridge, and took hold of his feet, and prayed him to forgive him what he had offended, and not to be too bitter against him, nor to think fit to make him the first example of severity under his new authority; but to consider that he had repented of his failure of duty, and had taken care to come first of all to him. While he was thus entreating the king, and moving him to compassion, Abishai, Joab's brother, said, "And shall not this man die for this, that he hath cursed that king whom God hath appointed to reign over us?" But David turned himself to him, and said, "Will you never leave off, ye sons of Zeruiah? Do not you, I pray, raise new troubles and seditions among us, now the former are over; for I would not have you ignorant that I this day begin my reign, and therefore swear to remit to all offenders their punishments, and not to animadvert on any one that has sinned. Be thou, therefore," said he, "O Shimei, of good courage, and do not at all fear being put to death." So he worshipped him, and went on before him.

3. Mephibosheth also, Saul's grandson, met David, clothed in a sordid garment, and having his hair thick and neglected; for after David was fled away, he was in such grief that he had not polled his head, nor had he washed his clothes, as dooming himself to undergo such hardships upon occasion of the change-of the king's affairs. Now he had been unjustly calumniated to the king by Ziba, his steward. When he had saluted the king, and worshipped him, the king began to ask him why he did not go out of Jerusalem with him, and accompany him during his flight. He replied, that this piece of injustice was owing to Ziba; because, when he was ordered to get things ready for his going out with him, he took no care of it, but regarded him no more than if he had been a slave; "and, indeed, had I had my feet sound and strong, I had not deserted thee, for I could then have made use of them in my flight: but this is not all the injury that Ziba has done me, as to

my duty to thee, my lord and master, but he hath calumniated me besides, and told lies about me of his own invention; but I know thy mind will not admit of such calumnies, but is righteously disposed, and a lover of truth, which it is also the will of God should prevail. For when thou wast in the greatest danger of suffering by my grandfather, and when, on that account, our whole family might justly have been destroyed, thou wast moderate and merciful, and didst then especially forget all those injuries, when, if thou hadst remembered them, thou hadst the power of punishing us for them; but thou hast judged me to be thy friend, and hast set me every day at thine own table; nor have I wanted any thing which one of thine own kinsmen, of greatest esteem with thee, could have expected." When he had said this, David resolved neither to punish Mephibosheth, nor to condemn Ziba, as having belied his master; but said to him, that as he had [before] granted all his estate to Ziba, because he did not come along with him, so he [now] promised to forgive him, and ordered that the one half of his estate should be restored to him.[20] Whereupon Mephibosheth said, "Nay, let Ziba take all; it suffices me that thou hast recovered thy kingdom."

4. But David desired Barzillai the Gileadite, that great and good man, and one that had made a plentiful provision for him at Mahanaim, and had conducted him as far as Jordan, to accompany him to Jerusalem, for he promised to treat him in his old age with all manner of respect—to take care of him, and provide for him. But Barzillai was so desirous to live at home, that he entreated him to excuse him from attendance on him; and said that his age was too great to enjoy the pleasures [of a court,] since he was fourscore years old, and was therefore making provision for his death and burial: so he desired him to gratify him in this request, and dismiss him; for he had no relish of his meat, or his drink, by reason of his age; and that his ears were

---

20. By David's disposal of half Mephibosheth's estate to Ziba, one would imagine that he was a good deal dissatisfied, and doubtful whether Mephibosheth's story were entirely true or not; nor does David now invite him to diet with him, as he did before, but only forgives him, if he had been at all guilty. Nor is this odd way of mourning that Mephibosheth made use of here, and 2 Samuel 19:24, wholly free from suspicion by hypocrisy. If Ziba neglected or refused to bring Mephibosheh an ass of his own, on which he might ride to David, it is half to suppose that so great a man as he was should not be able to procure some other beast for the same purpose.

too much shut up to hear the sound of pipes, or the melody of other musical instruments, such as all those that live with kings delight in. When he entreated for this so earnestly, the king said, "I dismiss thee, but thou shalt grant me thy son Chimham, and upon him I will bestow all sorts of good things." So Barzillai left his son with him, and worshipped the king, and wished him a prosperous conclusion of all his affairs according to his own mind, and then returned home; but David came to Gilgal, having about him half the people [of Israel], and the [whole] tribe of Judah.

5. Now the principal men of the country came to Gilgal to him with a great multitude, and complained of the tribe of Judah, that they had come to him in a private manner; whereas they ought all conjointly, and with one and the same intention, to have given him the meeting. But the rulers of the tribe of Judah desired them not to be displeased, if they had been prevented by them; for, said they, "We are David's kinsmen, and on that account we the rather took care of him, and loved him, and. so came first to him;" yet had they not, by their early coming, received any gifts from him, which might give them who came last any uneasiness. When the rulers of the tribe of Judah had said this, the rulers of the other tribes were not quiet, but said further, "O brethren, we cannot but wonder at you when you call the king your kinsman alone, whereas he that hath received from God the power over all of us in common ought to be esteemed a kinsman to us all; for which reason the whole people have eleven parts in him, and you but one part[21] we are also elder than you; wherefore you have not done justly in coming to the king in this private and concealed manner."

6. While these rulers were thus disputing one with another,. a certain wicked man, who took a pleasure in seditious practices, (his name was Sheba, the son of Bichri, of the tribe of Benjamin,) stood up in the midst of the multitude, and cried aloud, and spake thus to them: "We have no part in David, nor inheritance in the son of Jesse." And

---

21. I clearly prefer Josephus's reading here, when it supposes eleven tribes, including Benjamin, to be on the one side, and the tribe of Judah alone on the other, since Benjamin, in general, had been still father of the house of Saul, and less firm to David hitherto, than any of the rest, and so cannot be supposed to be joined with Judah at this time, to make it double, especially when the following rebellion was headed by a Benjamite. See sect. 6, and 2 Samuel 20:2, 4.

when he had used those words, he blew with a trumpet, and declared war against the king; and they all left David, and followed him; the tribe of Judah alone staid with him, and settled him in his royal palace at Jerusalem. But as for his concubines, with whom Absalom his son had accompanied, truly he removed them to another house, and ordered those that had the care of them to make a plentiful provision for them, but he came not near them any more. He also appointed Amass for the captain of his forces, and gave him the same high office which Joab before had; and he commanded him to gather together, out of the tribe of Judah, as great an army as he could, and come to him within three days, that he might deliver to him his entire army, and might send him to fight against [Sheba] the son of Bichri. Now while Amass was gone out, and made some delay in gathering the army together, and so was not yet returned, on the third day the king said to Joab, "It is not fit we should make any delay in this affair of Sheba, lest he get a numerous army about him, and be the occasion of greater mischief, and hurt our affairs more than did Absalom himself; do not thou therefore wait any longer, but take such forces as thou hast at hand, and that [old] body of six hundred men, and thy brother Abishai, with thee, and pursue after our enemy, and endeavor to fight him wheresoever thou canst overtake him. Make haste to prevent him, lest he seize upon some fenced cities, and cause us great labor and pains before we take him."

7. So Joab resolved to make no delay, but taking with him his brother, and those six hundred men, and giving orders that the rest of the army which was at Jerusalem should follow him, he marched with great speed against Sheba; and when he was come to Gibeon, which is a village forty furlongs distant from Jerusalem, Amasa brought a great army with him, and met Joab. Now Joab was girded with a sword, and his breastplate on; and when Amasa came near him to salute him, he took particular care that his sword should fall out, as it were, of its own accord: so he took it up from the ground, and while he approached Amasa, who was then near him, as though he would kiss him, he took hold of Amasa's beard with his other hand, and he smote him in his belly when he did not foresee it, and slew him. This impious and altogether profane action Joab did to a good young man, and his kinsman, and one that had done him no injury, and this out of jealousy that he would obtain the chief command of the army, and be in equal

dignity with himself about the king; and for the same cause it was that he killed Abner. But as to that former wicked action, the death of his brother Asahel, which he seemed to revenge, afforded him a decent pretense, and made that crime a pardonable one; but in this murder of Amasa there was no such covering for it. Now when Joab had killed this general, he pursued after Sheba, having left a man with the dead body, who was ordered to proclaim aloud to the army, that Amasa was justly slain, and deservedly punished. "But," said he, "if you be for the king, follow Joab his general, and Abishai, Joab's brother:" but because the body lay on the road, and all the multitude came running to it, and, as is usual with the multitude, stood wondering a great while at it, he that guarded it removed it thence, and carried it to a certain place that was very remote from the road, and there laid it, and covered it with his garment. When this was done, all the people followed Joab. Now as he pursued Sheba through all the country of Israel, one told him that he was in a strong city, called Abelbeth-maachah. Hereupon Joab went thither, and set about it with his army, and cast up a bank round it, and ordered his soldiers to undermine the walls, and to overthrow them; and since the people in the city did not admit him, he was greatly displeased at them.

8. Now there was a woman of small account, and yet both wise and intelligent, who seeing her native city lying at the last extremity, ascended upon the wall, and, by means of the armed men, called for Joab; and when he came to her, she began to say, That "God ordained kings and generals of armies, that they might cut off the enemies of the Hebrews, and introduce a universal peace among them; but thou art endeavoring to overthrow and depopulate a metropolis of the Israelites, which hath been guilty of no offense." But he replied, "God continue to be merciful unto me: I am disposed to avoid killing any one of the people, much less would I destroy such a city as this; and if they will deliver me up Sheba, the son of Bichri, who hath rebelled against the king, I will leave off the siege, and withdraw the army from the place." Now as soon as the woman heard what Joab said, she desired him to intermit the siege for a little while, for that he should have the head of his enemy thrown out to him presently. So she went down to the citizens, and said to them, "Will you be so wicked as to perish miserably, with your children and wives, for the sake of a vile fellow, and one whom nobody knows who he is? And

will you have him for your king instead of David, who hath been so great a benefactor to you, and oppose your city alone to such a mighty and strong army?" So she prevailed with them, and they cut off the head of Sheba, and threw it into Joab's army. When this was done, the king's general sounded a retreat, and raised the siege. And when he was come to Jerusalem, he was again appointed to be general of all the people. The king also constituted Benaiah captain of the guards, and of the six hundred men. He also set Adoram over the tribute, and Sabathes and Achilaus over the records. He made Sheva the scribe, and appointed Zadok and Abiathar the high priests.

12   *How the Hebrews Were Delivered from a Famine When the Gibeonites Had Caused Punishment to Be Inflicted for Those of Them That Had Been Slain: As Also, What Great Actions Were Performed Against the Philistines by David, and the Men of Valor About Him*

1. AFTER this, when the country was greatly afflicted with a famine, David besought God to have mercy on the people, and to discover to him what was the cause of it, and how a remedy might be found for that distemper. And when the prophets answered, that God would have the Gibeonites avenged whom Saul the king was so wicked as to betray to slaughter, and had not observed the oath which Joshua the general and the senate had sworn to them: If, therefore, said God, the king would permit such vengeance to be taken for those that were slain as the Gibeonites should desire, he promised that he would be reconciled to them, and free the multitude from their miseries. As soon therefore as the king understood that this it was which God sought, he sent for the Gibeonites, and asked them what it was they should have; and when they desired to have seven sons of Saul delivered to them to be punished, he delivered them up, but spared Mephibosheth the son of Jonathan. So when the Gibeonites had received the men, they punished them as they pleased; upon which God began to send rain, and to recover the earth to bring forth its fruits as usual, and to free it from the foregoing drought, so that the country of the Hebrews flourished again. A little afterward the king made war against the Philistines; and when he had joined battle with them, and put them

to flight, he was left alone, as he was in pursuit of them; and when he was quite tired down, he was seen by one of the enemy, his name was Achmon, the son of Araph, he was one of the sons of the giants. He had a spear, the handle of which weighed three hundred shekels, and a breastplate of chain-work, and a sword. He turned back, and ran violently to slay [David] their enemy's king, for he was quite tired out with labor; but Abishai, Joab's brother, appeared on the sudden, and protected the king with his shield, as he lay down, and slew the enemy. Now the multitude were very uneasy at these dangers of the king, and that he was very near to be slain; and the rulers made him swear that he would no more go out with them to battle, lest he should come to some great misfortune by his courage and boldness, and thereby deprive the people of the benefits they now enjoyed by his means, and of those that they might hereafter enjoy by his living a long time among them.

2. When the king heard that the Philistines were gathered together at the city Gazara, he sent an army against them, when Sibbechai the Hittite, one of David's most courageous men, behaved himself so as to deserve great commendation, for he slew many of those that bragged they were the posterity of the giants, and vaunted themselves highly on that account, and thereby was the occasion of victory to the Hebrews. After which defeat, the Philistines made war again; and when David had sent an army against them, Nephan his kinsman fought in a single combat with the stoutest of all the Philistines, and slew him, and put the rest to flight. Many of them also were slain in the fight. Now a little while after this, the Philistines pitched their camp at a city which lay not far off the bounds of the country of the Hebrews. They had a man who was six cubits tall, and had on each of his feet and hands one more toe and finger than men naturally have. Now the person who was sent against them by David out of his army was Jonathan, the son of Shimea, who fought this man in a single combat, and slew him; and as he was the person who gave the turn to the battle, he gained the greatest reputation for courage therein. This man also vaunted himself to be of the sons of the giants. But after this fight the Philistines made war no more against the Israelites.

3. And now David being freed from wars and dangers, and enjoying for the future a profound peace,[22] composed songs and hymns to God of several sorts of metre; some of those which he made were *trimeters,* and some were *pentameters.* He also made instruments of music, and taught the Levites to sing hymns to God, both on that called the sabbath day, and on other festivals. Now the construction of the instruments was thus: The viol was an instrument of ten strings, it was played upon with a bow; the psaltery had twelve musical notes, and was played upon by the fingers; the cymbals were broad and large instruments, and were made of brass. And so much shall suffice to be spoken by us about these instruments, that the readers may not be wholly unacquainted with their nature.

4. Now all the men that were about David were men of courage. Those that were most illustrious and famous of them for their actions were thirty-eight; of five of whom I will only relate the performances, for these will suffice to make manifest the virtues of the others also; for these were powerful enough to subdue countries, and conquer great nations. First, therefore, was Jessai, the son of Achimaas, who frequently leaped upon the troops of the enemy, and did not leave off fighting till he overthrew nine hundred of them. After him was Eleazar, the son of Dodo, who was with the king at Arasam. This man, when once the Israelites were under a consternation at the multitude of the Philistines, and were running away, stood alone, and fell upon the enemy, and slew many of them, till his sword clung to his band by the blood he had shed, and till the Israelites, seeing the Philistines retire by his means, came down from the mountains and pursued them, and at that time won a surprising and a famous victory, while Eleazar slew the men, and the multitude followed and spoiled their dead bodies. The third was Sheba, the son of Ilus. Now this man, when, in the wars against the Philistines, they pitched their camp at a place

---

22. This section is a very remarkable one, and shows that, in the opinion of Josephus, David composed the Book of Psalms, not at several times before, as their present inscriptions frequently imply, but generally at the latter end of his life, or after his wars were over. Nor does Josephus, nor the authors of the known books of the Old and New Testament, nor the Apostolical Constitutions, seem to have ascribed any of them to any other author than to David himself. See Essay on the Old Testament, pages 174, 175. Of these metres of the Psalms, see the note on Antiq. B. II. ch. 16. sect. 4.

called Lehi, and when the Hebrews were again afraid of their army, and did not stay, he stood still alone, as an army and a body of men; and some of them he overthrew, and some who were not able to abide his strength and force he pursued. These are the works of the hands, and of fighting, which these three performed. Now at the time when the king was once at Jerusalem, and the army of the Philistines came upon him to fight him, David went up to the top of the citadel, as we have already said, to inquire of God concerning the battle, while the enemy's camp lay in the valley that extends to the city Bethlehem, which is twenty furlongs distant from Jerusalem. Now David said to his companions, "We have excellent water in my own city, especially that which is in the pit near the gate," wondering if any one would bring him some of it to drink; but he said that he would rather have it than a great deal of money. When these three men heard what he said, they ran away immediately, and burst through the midst of their enemy's camp, and came to Bethlehem; and when they had drawn the water, they returned again through the enemy's camp to the king, insomuch that the Philistines were so surprised at their boldness and alacrity, that they were quiet, and did nothing against them, as if they despised their small number. But when the water was brought to the king, he would not drink it, saying, that it was brought by the danger and the blood of men, and that it was not proper on that account to drink it. But he poured it out to God, and gave him thanks for the salvation of the men. Next to these was Abishai, Joab's brother; for he in one day slew six hundred. The fifth of these was Benaiah, by lineage a priest; for being challenged by [two] eminent men in the country of Moab, he overcame them by his valor, Moreover, there was a man, by nation an Egyptian, who was of a vast bulk, and challenged him, yet did he, when he was unarmed, kill him with his own spear, which he threw at him; for he caught him by force, and took away his weapons while he was alive and fighting, and slew him with his own weapons. One may also add this to the forementioned actions of the same man, either as the principal of them in alacrity, or as resembling the rest. When God sent a snow, there was a lion who slipped and fell into a certain pit, and because the pit's mouth was narrow it was evident he would perish, being enclosed with the snow; so when he saw no way to get out and save himself, he roared. When Benaiah heard the wild beast, he went towards him, and coming at the noise he made, he went down into the mouth of the pit and smote him, as he struggled, with a stake that lay there, and immediately slew him. The other thirty-three were like these in valor also.

13 That When David Had Numbered the People, They Were Punished; and How the Divine Compassion Restrained That Punishment

1. NOW king David was desirous to know how many ten thousands there were of the people, but forgot the commands of Moses,[23] who told them beforehand, that if the multitude were numbered, they should pay half a shekel to God for every head. Accordingly the king commanded Joab, the captain of his host, to go and number the whole multitude; but when he said there was no necessity for such a numeration, he was not persuaded [to countermand it], but he enjoined him to make no delay, but to go about the numbering of the Hebrews immediately. So Joab took with him the heads of the tribes,

---

23. The words of God by Moses, Exodus 30:12, sufficiently satisfy the reason here given by Josephus for the great plague mentioned in this chapter:—"When thou takest the sum of the children of Israel after their number, then shall they give a ransom for his soul unto the Lord, when thou numberest them; that there be no plague amongst them, when numberest them." Nor indeed could David's or the neglect of executing this law at this numeration of half a shekel apiece with them, when they came numbered. The great reason why nations are so committed by and with their wicked kings and governors that they almost constantly comply with them in their of or disobedience to the Divine laws, and suffer Divine laws to go into disuse or contempt, in order to kings and governors; and that they sub-political laws and commands of those governors, instead of the righteous laws of God, which all mankind ought ever to obey, let their kings and governors say what they please to the contrary; this preference of human before Divine laws seeming to me the principal character of idolatrous or antichristian nations. Accordingly, Josephus well observes, Antiq. B. IV. ch. 8. sect. 17, that it was the duty of the people of Israel to take care that their kings, when they should have them, did not exceed their proper limits of power, and prove ungovernable by the laws of God, which would certainly be a most pernicious thing to their Divine settlement. Nor do I think that negligence peculiar to the Jews: those nations which are called Christians, are sometimes indeed very solicitous to restrain their kings and governors from breaking the human laws of their several kingdoms, but without the like care for restraining them from breaking the laws of God. "Whether it be right in the sight of God to hearken unto men more than to God, judge ye," Acts 4:19. "We ought to obey God rather than men," ver. 29.

and the scribes, and went over the country of the Israelites, and took notice how numerous the multitude were, and returned to Jerusalem to the king, after nine months and twenty days; and he gave in to the king the number of the people, without the tribe of Benjamin, for he had not yet numbered that tribe, no more than the tribe of Levi, for the king repented of his having sinned against God. Now the number of the rest of the Israelites was nine hundred thousand men, who were able to bear arms and go to war; but the tribe of Judah, by itself, was four hundred thousand men.

2. Now when the prophets had signified to David that God was angry at him, he began to entreat him, and to desire he would be merciful to him, and forgive his sin. But God sent Nathan the prophet to him, to propose to him the election of three things, that he might choose which he liked best: Whether he would have famine come upon the country for seven years, or would have a war, and be subdued three months by his enemies? or, whether God should send a pestilence and a distemper upon the Hebrews for three days? But as he was fallen to a fatal choice of great miseries, he was in trouble, and sorely confounded; and when the prophet had said that he must of necessity make his choice, and had ordered him to answer quickly, that he might declare what he had chosen to God, the king reasoned with himself, that in case he should ask for famine, he would appear to do it for others, and without danger to himself, since he had a great deal of corn hoarded up, but to the harm of others; that in case he should choose to be overcome [by his enemies] for three months, he would appear to have chosen war, because he had valiant men about him, and strong holds, and that therefore he feared nothing therefrom: so he chose that affliction which is common to kings and to their subjects, and in which the fear was equal on all sides; and said this beforehand, that it was much better to fall into the hands of God, than into those of his enemies.

3. When the prophet had heard this, he declared it to God; who thereupon sent a pestilence and a mortality upon the Hebrews; nor did they die after one and the same manner, nor so that it was easy to know what the distemper was. Now the miserable disease was one indeed, but it carried them off by ten thousand causes and occasions, which those that were afflicted could not understand; for one died upon the neck of another, and the terrible malady seized them before they were

aware, and brought them to their end suddenly, some giving up the ghost immediately with very great pains and bitter grief, and some were worn away by their distempers, and had nothing remaining to be buried, but as soon as ever they fell were entirely macerated; some were choked, and greatly lamented their case, as being also stricken with a sudden darkness; some there were who, as they were burying a relation, fell down dead, without finishing the rites of the funeral. Now there perished of this disease, which began with the morning, and lasted till the hour of dinner, seventy thousand. Nay, the angel stretched out his hand over Jerusalem, as sending this terrible judgment upon it. But David had put on sackcloth, and lay upon the ground, entreating God, and begging that the distemper might now cease, and that he would be satisfied with those that had already perished. And when the king looked up into the air, and saw the angel carried along thereby into Jerusalem, with his sword drawn, he said to God, that he might justly be punished, who was their shepherd, but that the sheep ought to be preserved, as not having sinned at all; and he implored God that he would send his wrath upon him, and upon all his family, but spare the people.

4. When God heard his supplication, he caused the pestilence to cease, and sent Gad the prophet to him, and commanded him to go up immediately to the thrashing-floor of Araunah the Jebusite, and build an altar there to God, and offer sacrifices. When David heard that, he did not neglect his duty, but made haste to the place appointed him. Now Araunah was thrashing wheat; and when he saw the king and all his servants coming to him, he ran before, and came to him and worshipped him: he was by his lineage a Jebusite, but a particular friend of David's; and for that cause it was that, when he overthrew the city, he did him no harm, as we informed the reader a little before. Now Araunah inquired, "Wherefore is my lord come to his servant?" He answered, to buy of him the thrashing-floor, that he might therein build an altar to God, and offer a sacrifice. He replied, that he freely gave him both the thrashing-floor and the ploughs and the oxen for a burnt-offering; and he besought God graciously to accept his sacrifice. But the king made answer, that he took his generosity and magnanimity loudly, and accepted his good-will, but he desired him to take the price of them all, for that it was not just to offer a sacrifice that cost nothing. And when Araunah said he would do as he pleased,

he bought the thrashing-floor of him for fifty shekels. And when he had built an altar, he performed Divine service, and brought a burnt-offering, and offered peace-offerings also. With these God was pacified, and became gracious to them again. Now it happened that Abraham[24]came and offered his son Isaac for a burnt-offering at that very place; and when the youth was ready to have his throat cut, a ram appeared on a sudden, standing by the altar, which Abraham sacrificed in the stead of his son, as we have before related. Now when king David saw that God had heard his prayer, and had graciously accepted of his sacrifice, he resolved to call that entire place *The Altar of all the People*, and to build a temple to God there; which words he uttered very appositely to what was to be done afterward; for God sent the prophet to him, and told him that there should his son build him an altar, that son who was to take the kingdom after him.

14   *That David Made Great Preparations for the House of God; and That, Upon Adonijah's Attempt to Gain the Kingdom, He Appointed Solomon to Reign*

1. AFTER the delivery of this prophecy, the king commanded the strangers to be numbered; and they were found to be one hundred and eighty thousand; of these he appointed fourscore thousand to be hewers of stone, and the rest of the multitude to carry the stones, and of them he set over the workmen three thousand and five hundred. He also prepared a great quantity of iron and brass for the work, with many (and those exceeding large) cedar trees; the Tyrians and Sidonians sending them to him, for he had sent to them for a supply of those trees. And he told his friends that these things were now prepared, that he might leave materials ready for the building of the temple to his son, who was to reign after him, and that he might not have them to seek then, when he was very young, and by reason of his

---

24. What Josephus adds here is very remarkable, that this Mount Moriah was not only the very place where Abraham offered up Isaac long ago, but that God had foretold to David by a prophet, that here his son should build him a temple, which is not directly in any of our other copies, though very agreeable to what is in them, particularly in 1 Chronicles 21:25, 28; 22:1, to which places I refer the reader.

age unskillful in such matters, but might have them lying by him, and so might the more readily complete the work.

2. So David called his son Solomon, and charged him, when he had received the kingdom, to build a temple to God, and said, "!I was willing to build God a temple myself, but he prohibited me, because I was polluted with blood and wars; but he hath foretold that Solomon, my youngest son, should build him a temple, and should be called by that name; over whom he hath promised to take the like care as a father takes over his son; and that he would make the country of the Hebrews happy under him, and that, not only in other respects, but by giving it peace and freedom from wars, and from internal seditions, which are the greatest of all blessings. Since, therefore," says he, "thou wast ordained king by God himself before thou wast born, endeavor to render thyself worthy of this his providence, as in other instances, so particularly in being religious, and righteous, and courageous. Keep thou also his commands and his laws, which he hath given us by Moses, and do not permit others to break them. Be zealous also to dedicate to God a temple, which he hath chosen to be built under thy reign; nor be thou aftrighted by the vastness of the work, nor set about it timorously, for I will make all things ready before I die: and take notice, that there are already ten thousand talents of gold, and a hundred thousand talents of silver[25] collected together. I have also laid together brass and iron without number, and an immense quantity of timber and of stones. Moreover, thou hast many ten thousand stone-cutters and carpenters; and if thou shalt want any thing further, do thou add somewhat of thine own. Wherefore, if thou performest this work, thou wilt be acceptable to God, and have him for thy patron." David also further exhorted the rulers of the people to assist his son in this building, and to attend to the Divine service, when they should be free from all their misfortunes, for that they by this means should enjoy, instead of them, peace and a happy settlement, with which blessings God rewards such men as are religious and righteous. He also gave orders, that when the temple should be once built, they should put the ark therein, with the holy vessels; and he assured them that they ought to have had a temple long ago, if their fathers had not

---

25. Of the quantity of gold and silver expended in the building of Solomon's temple, and whence it arose, see the description of ch. 13.

been negligent of God's commands, who had given it in charge, that when they had got the possession of this land, they should build him a temple. Thus did David discourse to the governors, and to his son.

3. David was now in years, and his body, by length of time, was become cold, and benumbed, insomuch that he could get no heat by covering himself with many clothes; and when the physicians came together, they agreed to this advice, that a beautiful virgin, chosen out of the whole country, should sleep by the king's side, and that this damsel would communicate heat to him, and be a remedy against his numbness. Now there was found in the city one woman, of a superior beauty to all other women, (her name was Abishag,) who, sleeping with the king, did no more than communicate warmth to him, for he was so old that he could not know her as a husband knows his wife. But of this woman we shall speak more presently.

4. Now the fourth son of David was a beautiful young man, and tall, born to him of Haggith his wife. He was named Adonijah, and was in his disposition like to Absalom; and exalted himself as hoping to be king, and told his friends that he ought to take the government upon him. He also prepared many chariots and horses, and fifty men to run before him. When his father saw this, he did not reprove him, nor restrain him from his purpose, nor did he go so far as to ask wherefore he did so. Now Adonijah had for his assistants Joab the captain of the army, and Abiathar the high priest; and the only persons that opposed him were Zadok the high priest, and the prophet Nathan, and Benaiah, who was captain of the guards, and Shimei, David's friend, with all the other most mighty men. Now Adonijah had prepared a supper out of the city, near the fountain that was in the king's paradise, and had invited all his brethren except Solomon, and had taken with him Joab the captain of the army, and: Abiathar, and the rulers of the tribe of Judah, but had not invited to this feast either Zadok the high priest, or Nathan the prophet, or Benaiah the captain of the guards, nor any of those of the contrary party. This matter was told by Nathan the prophet to Bathsheba, Solomon's mother, that Adonijah was king, and that David knew nothing of it; and he advised her to save herself and her son Solomon, and to go by herself to David, and say to him, that he had indeed sworn that Solomon should reign after him, but that in the mean time Adonijah had already taken the kingdom. He said that he, the prophet himself, would come after her, and when

she had spoken thus to the king, would confirm what she had said. Accordingly Bathsheba agreed with Nathan, and went in to the king and worshipped him, and when she had desired leave to speak with him, she told him all things in the manner that Nathan had suggested to her; and related what a supper Adonijah had made, and who they were whom he had invited; Abiathar the and Joab the general, and David's sons, excepting Solomon and his intimate friends. She also said that all the people had their eyes upon him, to know whom he would choose for their king. She desired him also to consider how, after his departure, Adonijah, if he were king, would slay her and her son Solomon.

5. Now, as Bathsheba was speaking, the keeper of the king's chambers told him that Nathan desired to see him. And when the king had commanded that he should be admitted, he came in, and asked him whether he had ordained Adonijah to be king, and delivered the government to him, or not; for that he had made a splendid supper, and invited all his sons, except Solomon; as also that he had invited Joab, the captain of his host, [and Abiathar the high priest,] who are feasting with applauses, and many joyful sounds of instruments, and wish that his kingdom may last for ever; but he hath not invited me, nor Zadok the high priest, nor Benaiah the captain of the guards; and it is but fit that all should know whether this be done by thy approbation or not. When Nathan had said thus, the king commanded that they should call Bathsheba to him, for she had gone out of the room when the prophet came. And when Bathsheba was come, David said, "I swear by Almighty God, that thy son Solomon shall certainly he king, as I formerly swore; and that he shall sit upon my throne, and that this very day also." So Bathsheba worshipped him, and wished him a long life; and the king sent for Zadok the high priest, and Benaiah the captain of the guards; and when they were come, he ordered them to take with them Nathan the prophet, and all the armed men about the palace, and to set his son Solomon upon the king's mule, and to carry him out of the city to the fountain called Gihon, and to anoint him there with the holy oil, and to make him king. This he charged Zadok the high priest, and Nathan the prophet, to do, and commanded them to follow Solomon through the midst of the city, and to sound the trumpets, and wish aloud that Solomon the king may sit upon the royal throne for ever, that so all the people may know

that he is ordained king by his father. He also gave Solomon a charge concerning his government, to rule the whole nation of the Hebrews, and particularly the tribe of Judah, religiously and righteously. And when Benaiah had prayed to God to be favorable to Solomon, without any delay they set Solomon upon the mule, and brought him out of the city to the fountain, and anointed him with oil, and brought him into the city again, with acclamations and wishes that his kingdom might continue a long time: and when they had introduced him into the king's house, they set him upon the throne; whereupon all the people betook themselves to make merry, and to celebrate a festival, dancing and delighting themselves with musical pipes, till both the earth and the air echoed with the multitude of the instruments of music.

6. Now when Adonijah and his guests perceived this noise, they were in disorder; and Joab the captain of the host said he was not pleased with these echoes, and the sound of these trumpets. And when supper was set before them, nobody tasted of it, but they were all very thoughtful what would be the matter. Then Jonathan, the son of Abiathar the high priest, came running to them; and when Adonijah saw the young man gladly, and said to him that he was a good messenger, he declared to them the whole matter about Solomon, and the determination of king David: hereupon both Adonijah and all the guests rose hastily from the feast, and every one fled to their own homes. Adonijah also, as afraid of the king for what he had done, became a supplicant to God, and took hold of the horns of the altar, which were prominent. It was also told Solomon that he had so done; and that he desired to receive assurances from him that he would not remember the injury he had done, and not inflict any severe punishment for it. Solomon answered very mildly and prudently, that he forgave him this his offense; but said withal, that if he were found out in any attempt for new innovations, that he would be the author of his own punishment. So he sent to him, and raised him up from the place of his supplication. And when he was come to the king, and had worshipped him, the king bid him go away to his own house, and have no suspicion of any harm; and desired him to show himself a worthy man, as what would tend to his own advantage.

7. But David, being desirous of ordaining his son king of all the people, called together their rulers to Jerusalem, with the priests and the Levites; and having first numbered the Levites, he found them to

be thirty-eight thousand, from thirty years old to fifty; out of which he appointed twenty-three thousand to take care of the building of the temple, and out of the same, six thousand to be judges of the people and scribes, four thousand for porters to the house of God, and as many for singers, to sing to the instruments which David had prepared, as we have said already. He divided them also into courses: and when he had separated the priests from them, he found of these priests twenty-four courses, sixteen of the house of Eleazar, and eight of that of Ithamar; and he ordained that one course should minister to God eight days, from sabbath to sabbath. And thus were the courses distributed by lot, in the presence of David, and Zadok and Abiathar the high priests, and of all the rulers; and that course which came up first was written down as the first, and accordingly the second, and so on to the twenty-fourth; and this partition hath remained to this day. He also made twenty-four parts of the tribe of Levi; and when they cast lots, they came up in the same manner for their courses of eight days. He also honored the posterity of Moses, and made them the keepers of the treasures of God, and of the donations which the kings dedicated. He also ordained that all the tribe of Levi, as well as the priests, should serve God night and day, as Moses had enjoined them.

8. After this he parted the entire army into twelve parts, with their leaders [and captains of hundreds] and commanders. Now every part had twenty-four thousand, which were ordered to wait on Solomon, by thirty days at a time, from the first day till the last, with the captains of thousands and captains of hundreds. He also set rulers over every part, such as he knew to be good and righteous men. He set others also to take charge of the treasures, and of the villages, and of the fields, and of the beasts, whose names I do not think it necessary to mention. When David had ordered all these officers after the manner before mentioned, he called the rulers of the Hebrews, and their heads of tribes, and the officers over the several divisions, and those that were appointed over every work, and every possession; and standing upon a high pulpit, he said to the multitude as follows: "My brethren and my people, I would have you know that I intended to build a house for God, and prepared a large quantity of gold, and a hundred thousand talents of silver; but God prohibited me by the prophet Nathan, because of the wars I had on your account,

and because my right hand was polluted with the slaughter of our enemies; but he commanded that my son, who was to succeed me in the kingdom, should build a temple for him. Now therefore, since you know that of the twelve sons whom Jacob our forefather had Judah was appointed to be king, and that I was preferred before my six brethren, and received the government from God, and that none of them were uneasy at it, so do I also desire that my sons be not seditious one against another, now Solomon has received the kingdom, but to bear him cheerfully for their lord, as knowing that God hath chosen him; for it is not a grievous thing to obey even a foreigner as a ruler, if it be God's will, but it is fit to rejoice when a brother hath obtained that dignity, since the rest partake of it with him. And I pray that the promises of God may be fulfilled; and that this happiness which he hath promised to bestow upon king Solomon, over all the country, may continue therein for all time to come. And these promises O son, will be firm, and come to a happy end, if thou showest thyself to be a religious and a righteous man, and an observer of the laws of thy country; but if not, expect adversity upon thy disobedience to them."

9. Now when the king had said this, he left off; but gave the description and pattern of the building of the temple in the sight of them all to Solomon: of the foundations and of the chambers, inferior and superior; how many they were to be, and how large in height and in breadth; as also he determined the weight of the golden and silver vessels: moreover, he earnestly excited them with his words to use the utmost alacrity about the work; he exhorted the rulers also, and particularly the tribe of Levi, to assist him, both because of his youth, and because God had chosen him to take care of the building of the temple, and of the government of the kingdom. He also declared to them that the work would be easy, and not very laborious to them, because he had prepared for it many talents of gold, and more of silver, with timber, and a great many carpenters and stone-cutters, and a large quantity of emeralds, and all sorts of precious stones; and he said, that even now he would give of the proper goods of his own dominion two hundred talents, and three hundred other talents of pure gold, for the most holy place, and for the chariot of God, the cherubim, which are to stand over and cover the ark. Now when David had done speaking, there appeared great alacrity among the rulers, and the priests, and the Levites, who now contributed and made great

and splendid promises for a future Contribution; for they undertook to bring of gold five thousand talents, and ten thousand drams, and of silver ten thousand talents, and many ten thousand talents of iron; and if any one had a precious stone he brought it, and bequeathed it to be put among the treasures; of which Jachiel, one of the posterity of Moses, had the care.

10. Upon this occasion all the people rejoiced, as in particular did David, when he saw the zeal and forward ambition of the rulers, and the priests, and of all the rest; and he began to bless God with a loud voice, calling him the Father and Parent of the universe, and the Author of human and divine things, with which he had adorned Solomon, the patron and guardian of the Hebrew nation, and of its happiness, and of that kingdom which he hath given his son. Besides this, he prayed for happiness to all the people; and to Solomon his son, a sound and a righteous mind, and confirmed in all sorts of virtue; and then he commanded the multitude to bless God; upon which they all fell down upon the ground and worshipped him. They also gave thanks to David, on account of all the blessings which they had received ever since he had taken the kingdom. On the next day he presented sacrifices to God, a thousand bullocks, and as many lambs, which they offered for burnt-offerings. They also offered peace-offerings, and slew many ten thousand sacrifices; and the king feasted all day, together with all the people; and they anointed Solomon a second time with the oil, and appointed him to be king, and Zadok to be the high priest of the whole multitude. And when they had brought Solomon to the royal palace, and had set him upon his father's throne, they were obedient to him from that day.

15 What Charge David Gave to His Son Solomon at the Approach of His Death, and How Many Things He Left Him for the Building of the Temple

1. A LITTLE afterward David also fell into a distemper, by reason of his age; and perceiving that he was near to death, he called his son Solomon, and discoursed to him thus: "I am now, O my son, going to my grave, and to my fathers, which is the common way which all men that now are, or shall be hereafter, must go; from which way it is no

longer possible to return, and to know any thing that is done in this world. On which account I exhort thee, while I am still alive, though already very near to death, in the same manner as I have formerly said in my advice to thee, to be righteous towards thy subjects, and religious towards God, that hath given thee thy kingdom; to observe his commands and his laws, which he hath sent us by Moses; and neither do thou out of favor nor flattery allow any lust or other passion to weigh with thee to disregard them; for if thou transgressest his laws, thou wilt lose the favor of God, and thou wilt turn away his providence from thee in all things; but if thou behave thyself so as it behooves thee, and as I exhort thee, thou wilt preserve our kingdom to our family, and no other house will bear rule over the Hebrews but we ourselves for all ages. Be thou also mindful of the transgressions of Joab,[26] the captain of the host, who hath slain two generals out of envy, and those righteous and good men, Abner the son of Ner, and Amasa the son of Jether; whose death do thou avenge as shall seem good to thee, since Joab hath been too hard for me, and more potent than myself, and so hath escaped punishment hitherto. I also commit to thee the son of Barzillai the Gileadite, whom, in order to gratify me, thou shalt have in great honor, and take great care of; for we have not done good to him first, but we only repay that debt which we owe to his father for what he did to me in my flight. There is also Shimei

---

26. David is here greatly blamed by some for recommending Joab and Shimei to be punished by Solomon, if he could find a proper occasion, after he had borne with the first a long while, and seemed to have pardoned the other entirely, which Solomon executed accordingly; yet I cannot discern any fault either in David or Solomon in these cases. Joab's murder of Abner and Amasa were very barbarous, and could not properly be forgiven either by David or Solomon; for a dispensing power in kings for the crime of willful murder is warranted by no law of God, nay, is directly against it every where; nor is it, for certain, in the power of men to grant such a prerogative to any of their kings; though Joab was so nearly related to David, and so potent in the army under a warlike administration, that David durst not himself put him to death, 2 Samuel 3:39; 19:7. Shimei's cursing the Lord's anointed, and this without any just cause, was the highest act of treason against God and his anointed king, and justly deserved death; and though David could forgive treason against himself, yet had he done no more in the case of Shimei than promised him that he would not then, on the day of his return and reinauguration, or upon that occasion, himself put him to death, 2 Samuel 19:22; and he swore to him no further, ver. 23, as the words are in Josephus, than that he would not then put him to death, which he performed; nor was Solomon under any obligation to spare such a traitor.

the son of Gera, of the tribe of Benjamin, who, after he had cast many reproaches upon me, when, in my flight, I was going to Mahanaim, met me at Jordan, and received assurances that he should then suffer nothing. Do thou now seek out for some just occasion, and punish him."

2. When David had given these admonitions to his son about public affairs, and about his friends, and about those whom he knew to deserve punishment, he died, having lived seventy years, and reigned seven years and six months in Hebron over the tribe of Judah, and thirty-three years in Jerusalem over all the country. This man was of an excellent character, and was endowed with all virtues that were desirable in a king, and in one that had the preservation of so many tribes committed to him; for he was a man of valor in a very extraordinary degree, and went readily and first of all into dangers, when he was to fight for his subjects, as exciting the soldiers to action by his own labors, and fighting for them, and not by commanding them in a despotic way. He was also of very great abilities in understanding, and apprehension of present and future circumstances, when he was to manage any affairs. He was prudent and moderate, and kind to such as were under any calamities; he was righteous and humane, which are good qualities, peculiarly fit for kings; nor was he guilty of any offense in the exercise of so great an authority, but in the business of the wife of Uriah. He also left behind him greater wealth than any other king, either of the Hebrews or, of other nations, ever did.

3. He was buried by his son Solomon, in Jerusalem, with great magnificence, and with all the other funeral pomp which kings used to be buried with; moreover, he had great and immense wealth buried with him, the vastness of which may be easily conjectured at by what I shall now say; for a thousand and three hundred years afterward Hyrcanus the high priest, when he was besieged by Antiochus, that was called the Pious, the son of Demetrius, and was desirous of giving him money to get him to raise the siege and draw off his army, and having no other method of compassing the money, opened one room of David's sepulcher, and took out three thousand talents, and gave part of that sum to Antiochus; and by this means caused the siege to be raised, as we have informed the reader elsewhere. Nay, after him, and that many years, Herod the king opened another room, and took away a great deal of money, and yet neither of them came at the coffins

of the kings themselves, for their bodies were buried under the earth so artfully, that they did not appear to even those that entered into their monuments. But so much shall suffice us to have said concerning these matters.

Book 8

Containing the Interval of One Hundred and Sixty-Three Years, from the Death of David to the Death of Ahab

1   How Solomon, When He Had Received the Kingdom Took Off His Enemies

1. WE have already treated of David, and his virtue, and of the benefits he was the author of to his countrymen; of his wars also and battles, which he managed with success, and then died an old man, in the foregoing book. And when Solomon his son, who was but a youth in age, had taken the kingdom, and whom David had declared, while he was alive, the lord of that people, according to God's will; when he sat upon the throne, the whole body of the people made joyful acclamations to him, as is usual at the beginning of a reign; and wished that all his affairs might come to a blessed conclusion; and that he might arrive at a great age, and at the most happy state of affairs possible.

2. But Adonijah, who, while his father was living, attempted to gain possession of the government, came to the king's mother Bathsheba, and saluted her with great civility; and when she asked him, whether he came to her as desiring her assistance in any thing or not, and bade him tell her if that were the case, for that she would cheerfully afford it him; he began to say, that she knew herself that the kingdom was his, both on account of his elder age, and of the disposition of the multitude, and that yet it was transferred to Solomon her son, according to the will of God. He also said that he was contented to

be a servant under him, and was pleased with the present settlement; but he desired her to be a means of obtaining a favor from his brother to him, and to persuade him to bestow on him in marriage Abishag, who had indeed slept by his father, but, because his father was too old, he did not lie with her, and she was still a virgin. So Bathsheba promised him to afford him her assistance very earnestly, and to bring this marriage about, because the king would be willing to gratify him in such a thing, and because she would press it to him very earnestly. Accordingly he went away in hopes of succeeding in this match. So Solomon's mother went presently to her son, to speak to him about what she had promised, upon Adonijah's supplication to her. And when her son came forward to meet her, and embraced her, and when he had brought her into the house where his royal throne was set, he sat thereon, and bid them set another throne on the right hand for his mother. When Bathsheba was set down, she said, "O my son, grant me one request that I desire of thee, and do not any thing to me that is disagreeable or ungrateful, which thou wilt do if thou deniest me." And when Solomon bid her to lay her commands upon him, because it was agreeable to his duty to grant her every thing she should ask, and complained that she did not at first begin her discourse with a firm expectation of obtaining what she desired, but had some suspicion of a denial, she entreated him to grant that his brother Adonijah might marry Abishag.

3. But the king was greatly offended at these words, and sent away his mother, and said that Adonijah aimed at great things; and that he wondered that she did not desire him to yield up the kingdom to him, as to his elder brother, since she desired that he might marry Abishag; and that he had potent friends, Joab the captain of the host, and Abiathar the priest. So he called for Benaiah, the captain of the guards, and ordered him to slay his brother Adonijah. He also called for Abiathar the priest, and said to him, "I will not put thee to death because of those other hardships which thou hast endured with my father, and because of the ark which thou hast borne along with him; but I inflict this following punishment upon thee, because thou wast among Adonijah's followers, and wast of his party. Do not thou continue here, nor come any more into my sight, but go to thine own town, and live on thy own fields, and there abide all thy life; for thou hast offended so greatly, that it is not just that thou shouldst retain

thy dignity any longer." For the forementioned cause, therefore, it was that the house of Ithamar was deprived of the sacerdotal dignity, as God had foretold to Eli, the grandfather of Abiathar. So it was transferred to the family of Phineas, to Zadok. Now those that were of the family of Phineas, but lived privately during the time that the high priesthood was transferred to the house of Ithamar, (of which family Eli was the first that received it,)were these that follow: Bukki, the son of Abishua the high priest; his son was Joatham; Joatham's son was Meraioth; Meraioth's son was Arophseus; Aropheus's son was Ahitub; and Ahitub's son was Zadok, who was first made high priest in the reign of David.

4. Now when Joab the captain of the host heard of the slaughter of Adonijah, he was greatly afraid, for he was a greater friend to him than to Solomon; and suspecting, not without reason, that he was in danger, on account of his favor to Adonijah, he fled to the altar, and supposed he might procure safety thereby to himself, because of the king's piety towards God. But when some told the king what Joab's supposal was, he sent Benaiah, and commanded him to raise him up from the altar, and bring him to the judgment-seat, in order to make his defense. However, Joab said he would not leave the altar, but would die there rather than in another place. And when Benaiah had reported his answer to the king, Solomon commanded him to cut off his head there[1] and let him take that as a punishment for those two captains of the host whom he had wickedly slain, and to bury his body, that his sins might never leave his family, but that himself and his father, by Joab's death, might be guiltless. And when Benaiah had done what he was commanded to do, he was himself appointed to be captain of the whole army. The king also made Zadok to be alone the high priest, in the room of Abiathar, whom he had removed.

5. But as to Shimei, Solomon commanded that he should build him a house, and stay at Jerusalem, and attend upon him, and should not have authority to go over the brook Cedron; and that if he disobeyed that command, death should be his punishment. He also threatened

---

1. This execution upon Joab, as a murderer, by slaying him, even when he had taken sanctuary at God's altar, is perfectly agreeable to the law of Moses, which enjoins, that "if a man come presumptuously upon his neighbor to slay him with guile, thou shalt take him from mine altar that he die," Exodus 21:14.

him so terribly, that he compelled him to take all oath that he would obey. Accordingly Shimei said that he had reason to thank Solomon for giving him such an injunction; and added an oath, that he would do as he bade him; and leaving his own country, he made his abode in Jerusalem. But three years afterwards, when he heard that two of his servants were run away from him, and were in Gath, he went for his servants in haste; and when he was come back with them, the king perceived it, and was much displeased that he had contemned his commands, and, what was more, had no regard to the oaths he had sworn to God; so he called him, and said to him, "Didst not thou swear never to leave me, nor to go out of this city to another? Thou shalt not therefore escape punishment for thy perjury, but I will punish thee, thou wicked wretch, both for this crime, and for those wherewith thou didst abuse my father when he was in his flight, that thou mayst know that wicked men gain nothing at last, although they be not punished immediately upon their unjust practices; but that in all the time wherein they think themselves secure, because they have yet suffered nothing, their punishment increases, and is heavier upon them, and that to a greater degree than if they had been punished immediately upon the commission of their crimes." So Benaiah, on the king's command, slew Shimei.

2 Concerning the Wife of Solomon; Concerning His Wisdom and Riches; and Concerning What He Obtained of Hiram for the Building of the Temple

1. SOLOMON having already settled himself firmly in his kingdom, and having brought his enemies to punishment, he married the daughter of Pharaoh king of Egypt, and built the walls of Jerusalem much larger and stronger than those that had been before,[2] and thenceforward he managed public affairs very peaceably. Nor was his youth any hinderance in the exercise of justice, or in the observation of the laws, or in the remembrance of what charges his father had given

---

2. This building of the walls of Jerusalem, soon after David's death, illustrates the conclusion of the 51st Psalm, where David prays, "Build thou the walls of Jerusalem;" they being, it seems, unfinished or imperfect at that time. See ch. 6. sect. 1; and ch. 1. sect. 7; also 1 Kings 9:15.

him at his death; but he discharged every duty with great accuracy, that might have been expected from such as are aged, and of the greatest prudence. He now resolved to go to Hebron, and sacrifice to God upon the brazen altar that was built by Moses. Accordingly he offered there burnt-offerings, in number a thousand; and when he had done this, he thought he had paid great honor to God; for as he was asleep that very night God appeared to him, and commanded him to ask of him some gifts which he was ready to give him as a reward for his piety. So Solomon asked of God what was most excellent, and of the greatest worth in itself, what God would bestow with the greatest. joy, and what it was most profitable for man to receive; for he did not desire to have bestowed upon him either gold or silver, or any other riches, as a man and a youth might naturally have done, for these are the things that generally are esteemed by most men, as alone of the greatest worth, and the best gifts of God; but, said he, "Give me, O Lord, a sound mind, and a good understanding, whereby I may speak and judge the people according to truth and righteousness." With these petitions God was well pleased; and promised to give him all those things that he had not mentioned in his option, riches, glory, victory over his enemies; and, in the first place, understanding and wisdom, and this in such a degree as no other mortal man, neither kings nor ordinary persons, ever had. He also promised to preserve the kingdom to his posterity for a very long time, if he continued righteous and obedient to him, and imitated his father in those things wherein he excelled. When Solomon heard this from God, he presently leaped out of his bed; and when he had worshipped him, he returned to Jerusalem; and after he had offered great sacrifices before the tabernacle, he feasted all his own family.

2. In these days a hard cause came before him in judgment, which it was very difficult to find any end of; and I think it necessary to explain the fact about which the contest was, that such as light upon my writings may know what a difficult cause Solomon was to determine, and those that are concerned in such matters may take this sagacity of the king for a pattern, that they may the more easily give sentence about such questions. There were two women, who were harlots in the course of their lives, that came to him; of whom she that seemed to be injured began to speak first, and said, "O king, I and this other woman dwell together in one room. Now it came to pass that we both

bore a son at the same hour of the same day; and on the third day this woman overlaid her son, and killed it, and then took my son out of my bosom, and removed him to herself, and as I was asleep she laid her dead son in my arms. Now, when in the morning I was desirous to give the breast to the child, I did not find my own, but saw the woman's dead child lying by me; for I considered it exactly, and found it so to be. Hence it was that I demanded my son, and when I could not obtain him, I have recourse, my lord, to thy assistance; for since we were alone, and there was nobody there that could convict her, she cares for nothing, but perseveres in the stout denial of the fact." When this woman had told this her story, the king asked the other woman what she had to say in contradiction to that story. But when she denied that she had done what was charged upon her, and said that it was her child that was living, and that it was her antagonist's child that was dead, and when no one could devise what judgment could be given, and the whole court were blind in their understanding, and could not tell how to find out this riddle, the king alone invented the following way how to discover it. He bade them bring in both the dead child and the living child; and sent one of his guards, and commanded him to fetch a sword, and draw it, and to cut both the children into two pieces, that each of the women might have half the living and half the dead child. Hereupon all the people privately laughed at the king, as no more than a youth. But, in the mean time, she that was the real mother of the living child cried out that he should not do so, but deliver that child to the other woman as her own, for she would be satisfied with the life of the child, and with the sight of it, although it were esteemed the other's child; but the other woman was ready to see the child divided, and was desirous, moreover, that the first woman should be tormented. When the king understood that both their words proceeded from the truth of their passions, he adjudged the child to her that cried out to save it, for that she was the real mother of it; and he condemned the other as a wicked woman, who had not only killed her own child, but was endeavoring to see her friend's child destroyed also. Now the multitude looked on this determination as a great sign and demonstration of the king's sagacity and wisdom, and after that day attended to him as to one that had a divine mind.

3. Now the captains of his armies, and officers appointed over the whole country, were these: over the lot of Ephraim was Ures; over

the toparchy of Bethlehem was Dioclerus; Abinadab, who married Solomon's daughter, had the region of Dora and the sea-coast under him; the Great Plain was under Benaiah, the son of Achilus; he also governed all the country as far as Jordan; Gabaris ruled over Gilead and Gaulanitis, and had under him the sixty great and fenced cities [of Og]; Achinadab managed the affairs of all Galilee as far as Sidon, and had himself also married a daughter of Solomon's, whose name was Basima; Banacates had the seacoast about Arce; as had Shaphat Mount Tabor, and Carmel, and [the Lower] Galilee, as far as the river Jordan; one man was appointed over all this country; Shimei was intrusted with the lot of Benjamin; and Gabares had the country beyond Jordan, over whom there was again one governor appointed. Now the people of the Hebrews, and particularly the tribe of Judah, received a wonderful increase when they betook themselves to husbandry, and the cultivation of their grounds; for as they enjoyed peace, and were not distracted with wars and troubles, and having, besides, an abundant fruition of the most desirable liberty, every one was busy in augmenting the product of their own lands, and making them worth more than they had formerly been.

4. The king had also other rulers, who were over the land of Syria and of the Philistines, which reached from the river Euphrates to Egypt, and these collected his tributes of the nations. Now these contributed to the king's table, and to his supper every day[3] thirty cori of fine flour, and sixty of meal; as also ten fat oxen, and twenty oxen

---

3. It may not be amiss to compare the daily furniture of king Solomon's table, here set down, and 1 Kings 4;22, 23, with the like daily furniture of Nehemiah the governor's table, after the Jews were come back from Babylon; and to remember withal, that Nehemiah was now building the walls of Jerusalem, and maintained, more than usual, above a hundred and fifty considerable men every day, and that, because the nation was then very poor, at his own charges also, without laying any burden upon the people at all. "Now that which was prepared for me daily was one ox and six choice sheep; also fowls were prepared for me, and once in ten days store of all sorts of wine; and yet for all this required not the bread of the governor, because the bondage was heavy upon this people," Nehemiah 5:18: see the whole context, ver. 14–19. Nor did the governor's usual allowance of forty shekels of silver a-day, ver. 15, amount to 45 a day, nor to 1800 a-year. Nor does it indeed appear that, under the judges, or under Samuel the prophet, there was any such public allowance to those governors at all. Those great charges upon the public for maintaining courts came in with kings, as God foretold they would, 1 Samuel 8:11–18.

out of the pastures, and a hundred fat lambs; all these were besides what were taken by hunting harts and buffaloes, and birds and fishes, which were brought to the king by foreigners day by day. Solomon had also so great a number of chariots, that the stalls of his horses for those chariots were forty thousand; and besides these he had twelve thousand horsemen, the one half of which waited upon the king in Jerusalem, and the rest were dispersed abroad, and dwelt in the royal villages; but the same officer who provided for the king's expenses supplied also the fodder for the horses, and still carried it to the place where the king abode at that time.

5. Now the sagacity and wisdom which God had bestowed on Solomon was so great, that he exceeded the ancients; insomuch that he was no way inferior to the Egyptians, who are said to have been beyond all men in understanding; nay, indeed, it is evident that their sagacity was very much inferior to that of the king's. He also excelled and distinguished himself in wisdom above those who were most eminent among the Hebrews at that time for shrewdness; those I mean were Ethan, and Heman, and Chalcol, and Darda, the sons of Mahol. He also composed books of odes and songs a thousand and five, of parables and similitudes three thousand; for he spake a parable upon every sort of tree, from the hyssop to the cedar; and in like manner also about beasts, about all sorts of living creatures, whether upon the earth, or in the seas, or in the air; for he was not unacquainted with any of their natures, nor omitted inquiries about them, but described them all like a philosopher, and demonstrated his exquisite knowledge of their several properties. God also enabled him to learn that skill which expels demons,[4] which is a science useful and sanative to men. He

---

4. Some pretended fragments of these books of conjuration of Solomon are still extant in Fabricius's Cod. Pseudepigr. Vet. Test. page 1054, though I entirely differ from Josephus in this his supposal, that such books and arts of Solomon were parts of that wisdom which was imparted to him by God in his younger days; they must rather have belonged to such profane but curious arts as we find mentioned Acts 19:13–20, and had been derived from the idolatry and superstition of his heathen wives and concubines in his old age, when he had forsaken God, and God had forsaken him, and given him up to demoniacal delusions. Nor does Josephus's strange account of the root Baara (Of the War, B. VIII. ch. 6. sect. 3) seem to be other than that of its magical use in such conjurations. As for the following history, it confirms what Christ says, Matthew 12;27 "If I by Beelzebub cast out demons, by whom do your Sons cast them out?"

composed such incantations also by which distempers are alleviated. And he left behind him the manner of using exorcisms, by which they drive away demons, so that they never return; and this method of cure is of great force unto this day; for I have seen a certain man of my own country, whose name was Eleazar, releasing people that were demoniacal in the presence of Vespasian, and his sons, and his captains, and the whole multitude of his soldiers. The manner of the cure was this: He put a ring that had a Foot of one of those sorts mentioned by Solomon to the nostrils of the demoniac, after which he drew out the demon through his nostrils; and when the man fell down immediately, he abjured him to return into him no more, making still mention of Solomon, and reciting the incantations which he composed. And when Eleazar would persuade and demonstrate to the spectators that he had such a power, he set a little way off a cup or basin full of water, and commanded the demon, as he went out of the man, to overturn it, and thereby to let the spectators know that he had left the man; and when this was done, the skill and wisdom of Solomon was shown very manifestly: for which reason it is, that all men may know the vastness of Solomon's abilities, and how he was beloved of God, and that the extraordinary virtues of every kind with which this king was endowed may not be unknown to any people under the sun for this reason, I say, it is that we have proceeded to speak so largely of these matters.

6. Moreover Hiram, king of Tyre, when he had heard that Solonion succeeded to his father's kingdom, was very glad of it, for he was a friend of David's. So he sent ambassadors to him, and saluted him, and congratulated him on the present happy state of his affairs. Upon which Solomon sent him an epistle, the contents of which here follow:

Solomon to King Hiram

"[5]Know thou that my father would have built a temple to God, but was hindered by wars, and continual expeditions; for he did not leave off to overthrow his enemies till he made them all subject to tribute. But I give thanks to God for the peace I at present enjoy, and on that account

---

5. These epistles of Solomon and Hiram are those in 1 Kings 5:3–9, and, as enlarged, in 2 Chronicles 2:3–16, but here given us by Josephus in his own words.

I am at leisure, and design to build a house to God, for God foretold to my father that such a house should he built by me; wherefore I desire thee to send some of thy subjects with mine to Mount Lebanon to cut down timber, for the Sidonians are more skillful than our people in cutting of wood. As for wages to the hewers of wood, I will pay whatsoever price thou shalt determine."

7. When Hiram had read this epistle, he was pleased with it; and wrote back this answer to Solomon.

Hiram to King Solomon

"It is fit to bless God that he hath committed thy father's government to thee, who art a wise man, and endowed with all virtues. As for myself, I rejoice at the condition thou art in, and will be subservient to thee in all that thou sendest to me about; for when by my subjects I have cut down many and large trees of cedar and cypress wood, I will send them to sea, and will order my subjects to make floats of them, and to sail to what place soever of thy country thou shalt desire, and leave them there, after which thy subjects may carry them to Jerusalem. But do thou take care to procure us corn for this timber, which we stand in need of, because we inhabit in an island."[6]

---

6. What Josephus here puts into his copy of Hiram's epistle to Solomon, and repeats afterwards, ch. 5. sect. 3, that Tyre was now an island, is not in any of the three other copies, viz. that of the Kings, Chronicles, or Eusebius; nor is it any other, I suppose, than his own conjectural paraphrase; for when I, many years ago, inquired into this matter, I found the state of this famous city, and of the island whereupon it stood, to have been very different at different times. The result of my inquiries in this matter, with the addition of some later improvements, stands thus: That the best testimonies hereto relating, imply, that Paketyrus, or Oldest Tyre, was no other than that most ancient smaller fort or city Tyre, situated on the continent, and mentioned in Joshua 19:29, out of which the Canaanite or Phoenician inhabitants were driven into a large island, that lay not far off in the sea, by Joshua: that this island was then joined to the continent at the present remains of Paketyrus, by a neck of land over against Solomon's cisterns, still so called; and the city's fresh water, probably, was carried along in pipes by that neck of land; and that this island was therefore, in strictness, no other than a peninsula, having villages in its fields, Ezekiel 26:6, and a wall about it, Amos 1:10, and the city was not of so great reputation as Sitlon for some ages: that it was attacked both by sea and land by Salmanasser, as Josephus informs us, Antiq. B. IX. ch. 14. sect. 2, and afterwards came to be the metropolis of Phoenicia; and was afterwards taken and destroyed by Nebuchadnezzar, according to the numerous

8. The copies of these epistles remain at this day, and are preserved not only in our books, but among the Tyrians also; insomuch that if any one would know the certainty about them, he may desire of the keepers of the public records of Tyre to show him them, and he will find what is there set down to agree with what we have said. I have said so much out of a desire that my readers may know that we speak nothing but the truth, and do not compose a history out of some plausible relations, which deceive men and please them at the same time, nor attempt to avoid examination, nor desire men to believe us immediately; nor are we at liberty to depart from speaking truth, which is the proper commendation of an historian, and yet be blameless: but we insist upon no admission of what we say, unless we be able to manifest its truth by demonstration, and the strongest vouchers.

9. Now king Solomon, as soon as this epistle of the king of Tyre was brought him, commended the readiness and good-will he declared therein, and repaid him in what he desired, and sent him yearly twenty thousand cori of wheat, and as many baths of oil: now the bath is able to contain seventy-two sextaries. He also sent him the same measure of wine. So the friendship between Hiram and Solomon hereby increased more and more; and they swore to continue it for ever. And the king appointed a tribute to be laid on all the people, of thirty thousand laborers, whose work he rendered easy to them

---

Scripture prophecies thereto relating, Isaiah 23.; Jeremiah 25:22; 27:3; 47:4; Ezekiel 26., 27., 28.: that seventy years after that destruction by Nebuchadnezzar, this city was in some measure revived and rebuilt, Isaiah 23:17, 18, but that, as the prophet Ezekiel had foretold, chap. 26:3–5, 14; 27: 34, the sea arose higher than before, till at last it over flowed, not only the neck of land, but the main island or peninsula itself, and destroyed that old and famous city for ever: that, however, there still remained an adjoining smaller island, once connected to Old Tyre itself by Hiram, which was afterwards inhabited; to which Alexander the Great, with incredible pains, raised a new bank or causeway: and that it plainly appears from Ifaundreh, a most authentic eye-witness, that the old large and famous city, on the original large island, is now laid so generally under water, that scarce more than forty acres of it, or rather of that adjoining small island remain at this day; so that, perhaps, not above a hundredth part of the first island and city is now above water. This was foretold in the same prophecies of Ezekiel; and according to them, as Mr. Maundrell distinctly observes, these poor remains of Old Tyre are now "become like the top of a rock, a place for the spreading of nets in the midst of the sea."

by prudently dividing it among them; for he made ten thousand cut timber in Mount Lebanon for one month; and then to come home, and rest two months, until the time when the other twenty thousand had finished their task at the appointed time; and so afterward it came to pass that the first ten thousand returned to their work every fourth month: and it was Adoram who was over this tribute. There were also of the strangers who were left by David, who were to carry the stones and other materials, seventy thousand; and of those that cut the stones, eighty thousand. Of these three thousand and three hundred were rulers over the rest. He also enjoined them to cut out large stones for the foundations of the temple, and that they should fit them and unite them together in the mountain, and so bring them to the city. This was done not only by our own country workmen, but by those workmen whom Hiram sent also.

3   Of the Building of This Temple

1. SOLOMON began to build the temple in the fourth year of his reign, on the second month, which the Macedonians call *Artemisius,* and the Hebrews *Jur,* five hundred and ninety-two years after the Exodus out of Egypt; but one thousand and twenty years from Abraham's coming out of Mesopotamia into Canaan, and after the deluge one thousand four hundred and forty years; and from Adam, the first man who was created, until Solomon built the temple, there had passed in all three thousand one hundred and two years. Now that year on which the temple began to be built was already the eleventh year of the reign of Hiram; but from the building of Tyre to the building of the temple, there had passed two hundred and forty years.

2. Now, therefore, the king laid the foundations of the temple very deep in the ground, and the materials were strong stones, and such as would resist the force of time; these were to unite themselves with the earth, and become a basis and a sure foundation for that superstructure which was to be erected over it; they were to be so strong, in order to sustain with ease those vast superstructures and precious ornaments, whose own weight was to be not less than the weight of those other high and heavy buildings which the king designed to be very ornamental and magnificent. They erected its entire body, quite up to the roof, of white stone; its height was sixty

cubits, and its length was the same, and its breadth twenty. There was another building erected over it, equal to it in its measures; so that the entire altitude of the temple was a hundred and twenty cubits. Its front was to the east. As to the porch, they built it before the temple; its length was twenty cubits, and it was so ordered that it might agree with the breadth of the house; and it had twelve cubits in latitude, and its height was raised as high as a hundred and twenty cubits. He also built round about the temple thirty small rooms, which might include the whole temple, by their closeness one to another, and by their number and outward position round it. He also made passages through them, that they might come into on through another. Every one of these rooms had five cubits in breadth,[7] and the same in length, but in height twenty. Above these there were other rooms, and others above them, equal, both in their measures and number; so that these reached to a height equal to the lower part of the house; for the upper part had no buildings about it. The roof that was over the house was of cedar; and truly every one of these rooms had a roof of their own, that was not connected with the other rooms; but for the other parts, there was a covered roof common to them all, and built with very long beams, that passed through the rest, and rough the whole building, that so the middle walls, being strengthened by the same beams of timber, might be thereby made firmer: but as for that part of the roof that was under the beams, it was made of the same materials, and was all made smooth, and had ornaments proper for roofs, and plates of gold nailed upon them. And as he enclosed the walls with boards of cedar, so he fixed on them plates of gold, which had sculptures upon them; so that the whole temple shined, and dazzled the eyes of such as entered, by the splendor of the gold that was on every side of them, Now the whole structure of the temple was made with great skill of polished stones, and those laid together so very harmoniously and smoothly, that there appeared to the spectators no sign of any

---

7. Of the temple of Solomon here described by Josephus, in this and the following sections of this chapter, see my description of the temples belonging to this work, ch. 13, These small rooms, or side chambers, seem to have been, by Josephus's description, no less than twenty cubits high a piece, otherwise there must have been a large interval between one and the other that was over it; and this with double floors, the one of six cubits distance from the floor beneath it, as 1 Kings 6:5

hammer, or other instrument of architecture; but as if, without any use of them, the entire materials had naturally united themselves together, that the agreement of one part with another seemed rather to have been natural, than to have arisen from the force of tools upon them. The king also had a fine contrivance for an ascent to the upper room over the temple, and that was by steps in the thickness of its wall; for it had no large door on the east end, as the lower house had, but the entrances were by the sides, through very small doors. He also overlaid the temple, both within and without, with boards of cedar, that were kept close together by thick chains, so that this contrivance was in the nature of a support and a strength to the building.

3. Now when the king had divided the temple into two parts, he made the inner house of twenty cubits [every way], to be the most secret chamber, but he appointed that of forty cubits to be the sanctuary; and when he had cut a door-place out of the wall, he put therein doors of Cedar, and overlaid them with a great deal of gold, that had sculptures upon it. He also had veils of blue, and purple, and scarlet, and the brightest and softest linen, with the most curious flowers wrought upon them, which were to be drawn before those doors. He also dedicated for the most secret place, whose breadth was twenty cubits, and length the same, two cherubims of solid gold; the height of each of them was five cubits[8] they had each of them two wings stretched out as far as five cubits; wherefore Solomon set them up not far from each other, that with one wing they might touch the southern wall of the secret place, and with another the northern: their other wings, which joined to each other, were a covering to the ark, which was set between them; but nobody can tell, or even conjecture, what was the shape of these cherubims. He also laid the floor of the temple with plates of gold; and he added doors to the gate of the temple, agreeable to the measure of the height of the wall, but in breadth twenty cubits, and on them he glued gold plates. And, to say all in one word, he left no part of the temple, neither internal nor

---

8. Josephus says here that the cherubims were of solid gold, and only five cubits high, while our Hebrew copies (1 Kings 6;23, 28) say they were of the olive tree, and the LXXX. of the cypress tree, and only overlaid with gold; and both agree they were ten cubits high. I suppose the number here is falsely transcribed, and that Josephus wrote ten cubits also.

external, but what was covered with gold. He also had curtains drawn over these doors in like manner as they were drawn over the inner doors of the most holy place; but the porch of the temple had nothing of that sort.

4. Now Solomon sent for an artificer out of Tyre, whose name was Hiram; he was by birth of the tribe of Naphtali, on the mother's side, (for she was of that tribe,) but his father was Ur, of the stock of the Israelites. This man was skillful in all sorts of work; but his chief skill lay in working in gold, and silver, and brass; by whom were made all the mechanical works about the temple, according to the will of Solomon. Moreover, this Hiram made two [hollow] pillars, whose outsides were of brass, and the thickness of the brass was four fingers' breadth, and the height of the pillars was eighteen cubits and their circumference twelve cubits; but there was cast with each of their chapiters lily-work that stood upon the pillar, and it was elevated five cubits, round about which there was net-work interwoven with small palms, made of brass, and covered the lily-work. To this also were hung two hundred pomegranates, in two rows. The one of these pillars he set at the entrance of the porch on the right hand, and called it *Jachin*[9] and the other at the left hand, and called it *Booz*.

5. Solomon also cast a brazen sea, whose figure was that of a hemisphere. This brazen vessel was called *a sea* for its largeness, for the laver was ten feet in diameter, and cast of the thickness of a palm. Its middle part rested on a short pillar that had ten spirals round it, and that pillar was ten cubits in diameter. There stood round about it twelve oxen, that looked to the four winds of heaven, three to each wind, having their hinder parts depressed, that so the hemispherical vessel might rest upon them, which itself was also depressed round about inwardly. Now this sea contained three thousand baths.

6. He also made ten brazen bases for so many quadrangular lavers; the length of every one of these bases was five cubits, and the breadth four cubits, and the height six cubits. This vessel was partly turned, and was thus contrived: There were four small quadrangular pillars

---

9. As for these two famous pillars, Jachin and Booz, their height could be no more than eighteen cubits, as here, and 1 Kings 7:15; 2 Kings 25:17; Jeremiah 3:21; those thirty-five cubits in 2 Chronicles 3:15, being contrary to all the rules of architecture in the world.

that stood one at each corner; these had the sides of the base fitted to them on each quarter; they were parted into three parts; every interval had a border fitted to support [the laver]; upon which was engraven, in one place a lion, and in another place a bull, and an eagle. The small pillars had the same animals engraven that were engraven on the sides. The whole work was elevated, and stood upon four wheels, which were also cast, which had also naves and felloes, and were a foot and a half in diameter. Any one who saw the spokes of the wheels, how exactly they were turned, and united to the sides of the bases, and with what harmony they agreed to the felloes, would wonder at them. However, their structure was this: Certain shoulders of hands stretched out held the corners above, upon which rested a short spiral pillar, that lay under the hollow part of the laver, resting upon the fore part of the eagle and the lion, which were adapted to them, insomuch that those who viewed them would think they were of one piece: between these were engravings of palm trees. This was the construction of the ten bases. He also made ten large round brass vessels, which were the lavers themselves, each of which contained forty baths;[10] for it had its height four cubits, and its edges were as much distant from each other. He also placed these lavers upon the ten bases that were called Mechonoth; and he set five of the lavers on the left side of the temple[11] which was that side towards the north

10. The round or cylindrical lavers of four cubits in diameter, and four in height, both in our copies, 1 Kings 7:38, 39, and here in Josephus, must have contained a great deal more than these forty baths, which are always assigned them. Where the error lies is hard to say: perhaps Josephus honestly followed his copies here, though they had been corrupted, and he was not able to restore the true reading. In the mean time, the forty baths are probably the true quantity contained in each laver, since they went upon wheels, and were to be drawn by the Levites about the courts of the priests for the washings they were designed for; and had they held much more, they would have been too heavy to have been so drawn.

11. Here Josephus gives us a key to his own language, of right and left hand in the tabernacle and temple; that by the right hand he means what is against our left, when we suppose ourselves going up from the east gate of the courts towards the tabernacle or temple themselves, and so vice versa; whence it follows, that the pillar Jachin, on the right hand of the temple was on the south, against our left hand; and Booz on the north, against our right hand. Of the golden plate on the high priest's forehead that was in being in the days of Josephus, and a century or two at least later, seethe note on Antiq. B. III. ch. 7. sect. 6.

wind, and as many on the right side, towards the south, but looking towards the east; the same [eastern] way he also set the sea Now he appointed the sea to be for washing the hands and the feet of the priests, when they entered into the temple and were to ascend the altar, but the lavers to cleanse the entrails of the beasts that were to be burnt-offerings, with their feet also.

7. He also made a brazen altar, whose length was twenty cubits, and its breadth the same, and its height ten, for the burnt-offerings. He also made all its vessels of brass, the pots, and the shovels, and the basons; and besides these, the snuffers and the tongs, and all its other vessels, he made of brass, and such brass as was in splendor and beauty like gold. The king also dedicated a great number of tables, but one that was large and made of gold, upon which they set the loaves of God; and he made ten thousand more that resembled them, but were done after another manner, upon which lay the vials and the cups; those of gold were twenty thousand, those of silver were forty thousand. He also made ten thousand candlesticks, according to the command of Moses, one of which he dedicated for the temple, that it might burn in the day time, according to the law; and one table with loaves upon it, on the north side of the temple, over against the candlestick; for this he set on the south side, but the golden altar stood between them. All these vessels were contained in that part of the holy house, which was forty cubits long, and were before the veil of that most secret place wherein the ark was to be set.

8. The king also made pouring vessels, in number eighty thousand, and a hundred thousand golden vials, and twice as many silver vials: of golden dishes, in order therein to offer kneaded fine flour at the altar, there were eighty thousand, and twice as many of silver. Of large basons also, wherein they mixed fine flour with oil, sixty thousand of gold, and twice as many of silver. Of the measures like those which Moses called the *Hin* and the *Assaron*, (a tenth deal,) there were twenty thousand of gold, and twice as many of silver. The golden censers, in which they carried the incense to the altar, were twenty thousand; the other censers, in which they carried fire from the great altar to the little altar, within the temple, were fifty thousand. The sacerdotal garments which belonged to the high priest, with the long robes, and the oracle, and the precious stones, were a thousand. But the crown

upon which Moses wrote [the name of God],[12] was only one, and hath remained to this very day. He also made ten thousand sacerdotal garments of fine linen, with purple girdles for every priest; and two hundred thousand trumpets, according to the command of Moses; also two hundred thousand garments of fine linen for the singers, that were Levites. And he made musical instruments, and such as were invented for singing of hymns, called ,*Nablee* and *Cindree,* [psalteries and harps,] which were made of electrum, [the finest brass,] forty thousand.

9. Solomon made all these things for the honor of God, with great variety and magnificence, sparing no cost, but using all possible liberality in adorning the temple; and these things he dedicated to the treasures of God. He also placed a partition round about the temple, which in our tongue we call *Gison,* but it is called *Thrigcos* by the Greeks, and he raised it up to the height of three cubits; and it was for the exclusion of the multitude from coming into the temple, and showing that it was a place that was free and open only for the priests. He also built beyond this court a temple, whose figure was that of a quadrangle, and erected for it great and broad cloisters; this was entered into by very high gates, each of which had its front exposed to one of the [four] winds, and were shut by golden doors. Into this temple all the people entered that were distinguished from the rest by being pure and observant of the laws. But he made that temple which was beyond this a wonderful one indeed, and such as exceeds all description in words; nay, if I may so say, is hardly believed upon sight; for when he had filled up great valleys with earth, which, on account of their immense depth, could not be looked on, when you bended down to see them, without pain, and had elevated the ground four hundred cubits, he made it to be on a level with the top of the mountain, on which the temple was built, and by this means the outmost temple, which was exposed to the air, was even with the temple itself.[13] He encompassed this also with a building of a double row of cloisters, which stood on high upon pillars of native stone,

---

12. Of the golden plate on the High priests forehead that was in being in the days of Josephus, and a century or two at least later, see the note on Antiq. B. III. ch.vii. sect. 6.

13. When Josephus here says that the floor of the outmost temple or court of the Gentiles was with vast labor raised to be even, or of equal height, with the floor of the inner, or court of the priests, he must mean this in a gross estimation only; for he

while the roofs were of cedar, and were polished in a manner proper for such high roofs; but he made all the doors of this temple of silver.

4   *How Solomon Removed the Ark into the Temple How He Made Supplication to God, and Offered Public Sacrifices to Him*

1. WHEN king Solomon had finished these works, these large and beautiful buildings, and had laid up his donations in the temple, and all this in the interval of seven years, and had given a demonstration of his riches and alacrity therein, insomuch that any one who saw it would have thought it must have been an immense time ere it could have been finished; and would be surprised that so much should be finished in so short a time; short, I mean, if compared with the greatness of the work: he also wrote to the rulers and elders of the Hebrews, and ordered all the people to gather themselves together to Jerusalem, both to see the temple which he had built, and to remove the ark of God into it; and when this invitation of the whole body of the people to come to Jerusalem was every where carried abroad, it was the seventh month before they came together; which month is by our countrymen called *Thisri*, but by the Macedonians *Hyperberetoets*. The feast of tabernacles happened to fall at the same time, which was celebrated by the Hebrews as a most holy and most eminent feast. So they carried the ark and the tabernacle which Moses had pitched, and all the vessels that were for ministration, to the sacrifices of God, and removed them to the temple.[14] The king himself, and all the people and the Levites, went before, rendering the ground moist

---

and all others agree, that the inner temple, or court of the priests, was a few cubits more elevated than the middle court, the court of Israel, and that much more was the court of the priests elevated several cubits above that outmost court, since the court of Israel was lower than the one and higher than the other. The Septuagint say that "they prepared timber and stones to build the temple for three years," 1 Kings 5:18; and although neither our present Hebrew copy, nor Josephus, directly name that number of years, yet do they both say the building itself did not begin till Solomon's fourth year; and both speak of the preparation of materials beforehand, 1 Kings v. 18; Antiq. B. VIII. ch. 5. sect. 1. There is no reason, therefore, to alter the Septuagint's number; but we are to suppose three years to have been the just time of the preparation, as I have done in my computation of the expense in building that temple.

14. This solemn removal of the ark from Mount Sion to Mount Moriah, at the distance of almost three quarters of a mile, confutes that notion of the modern Jews,

with sacrifices, and drink-offerings, and the blood of a great number of oblations, and burning an immense quantity of incense, and this till the very air itself every where round about was so full of these odors, that it met, in a most agreeable manner, persons at a great distance, and was an indication of God's presence; and, as men's opinion was, of his habitation with them in this newly built and consecrated place, for they did not grow weary, either of singing hymns or of dancing, until they came to the temple; and in this manner did they carry the ark. But when they should transfer it into the most secret place, the rest of the multitude went away, and only those priests that carried it set it between the two cherubims, which embracing it with their wings, (for so were they framed by the artificer,) they covered it, as under a tent, or a cupola. Now the ark contained nothing else but those two tables of stone that preserved the ten commandments, which God spake to Moses in Mount Sinai, and which were engraved upon them; but they set the candlestick, and the table, and the golden altar in the temple, before the most secret place, in the very same places wherein they stood till that time in the tabernacle. So they offered up the daily sacrifices; but for the brazen altar, Solomon set it before the temple, over against the door, that when the door was opened, it might be exposed to sight, and the sacred solemnities, and the richness of the sacrifices, might be thence seen; and all the rest of the vessels they gathered together, and put them within the temple.

2. Now as soon as the priests had put all things in order about the ark, and were gone out, there cane down a thick cloud, and stood there, and spread itself, after a gentle manner, into the temple; such a cloud it was as was diffused and temperate, not such a rough one as we see full of rain in the winter season. This cloud so darkened the place, that one priest could not discern another, but it afforded to the minds of all a visible image and glorious appearance of God's having descended into this temple, and of his having gladly pitched his tabernacle therein. So these men were intent upon this thought. But Solomon rose up, (for he was sitting before,) and used such words to God as he thought agreeable to the Divine nature to receive, and fit for him to give; for he said, "Thou hast an eternal house, O Lord, and such a one as thou hast

---

and followed by many Christians also, as if those two were after a sort one and the same mountain, for which there is, I think, very little foundation.

created for thyself out of thine own works; we know it to be the heaven, and the air, and the earth, and the sea, which thou pervadest, nor art thou contained within their limits. I have indeed built this temple to thee, and thy name, that from thence, when we sacrifice, and perform sacred operations, we may send our prayers up into the air, and may constantly believe that thou art present, and art not remote from what is thine own; for neither when thou seest all things, and hearest all things, nor now, when it pleases thee to dwell here, dost thou leave the care of all men, but rather thou art very near to them all, but especially thou art present to those that address themselves to thee, whether by night or by day." When he had thus solemnly addressed himself to God, he converted his discourse to the multitude, and strongly represented the power and providence of God to them;—how he had shown all things that were come to pass to David his father, as many of those things had already come to pass, and the rest would certainly come to pass hereafter; and how he had given him his name, and told to David what he should be called before he was born; and foretold, that when he should be king after his father's death, he should build him a temple, which since they saw accomplished, according to his prediction, he required them to bless God, and by believing him, from the sight of what they had seen accomplished, never to despair of any thing that he had promised for the future, in order to their happiness, or suspect that it would not come to pass.

3. When the king had thus discoursed to the multitude, he looked again towards the temple, and lifting up his right hand to the multitude, he said," It is not possible by what men can do to return sufficient thanks to God for his benefits bestowed upon them, for the Deity stands in need of nothing, and is above any such requital; but so far as we have been made superior, O Lord, to other animals by thee, it becomes us to bless thy Majesty, and it is necessary for us to return thee thanks for what thou hast bestowed upon our house, and on the Hebrew people; for with what other instrument can we better appease thee when thou art angry at us, or more properly preserve thy favor, than with our voice? which, as we have it from the air, so do we know that by that air it ascends upwards [towards thee]. I therefore ought myself to return thee thanks thereby, in the first place, concerning my father, whom thou hast raised from obscurity unto so great joy; and, in the next place, concerning myself, since thou hast performed all

that thou hast promised unto this very day. And I beseech thee for the time to come to afford us whatsoever thou, O God, hast power to bestow on such as thou dost esteem; and to augment our house for all ages, as thou hast promised to David my father to do, both in his lifetime and at his death, that our kingdom shall continue, and that his posterity should successively receive it to ten thousand generations. Do not thou therefore fail to give us these blessings, and to bestow on my children that virtue in which thou delightest. And besides all this, I humbly beseech thee that thou wilt let some portion of thy Spirit come down and inhabit in this temple, that thou mayst appear to be with us upon earth. As to thyself, the entire heavens, and the immensity of the things that are therein, are but a small habitation for thee, much more is this poor temple so; but I entreat thee to keep it as thine own house, from being destroyed by our enemies for ever, and to take care of it as thine own possession: but if this people be found to have sinned, and be thereupon afflicted by thee with any plague, because of their sin, as with dearth or pestilence, or any other affliction which thou usest to inflict on those that transgress any of thy holy laws, and if they fly all of them to this temple, beseeching thee, and begging of time to deliver them, then do thou hear their prayers, as being within thine house, and have mercy upon them, and deliver them from their afflictions. Nay, moreover, this help is what I implore of thee, not for the Hebrews only, when they are in distress, but when any shall come hither from any ends of the world whatsoever, and shall return from their sins and implore thy pardon, do thou then pardon them, and hear their prayer. For hereby all shall learn that thou thyself wast pleased with the building of this house for thee; and that we are not ourselves of an unsociable nature, nor behave ourselves like enemies to such as are not of our own people; but are willing that thy assistance should be communicated by thee to all men in common, and that they may have the enjoyment of thy benefits bestowed upon them."

4. When Solomon had said this, and had cast himself upon the ground, and worshipped a long time, he rose up, and brought sacrifices to the altar; and when he had filled it with unblemished victims, he most evidently discovered that God had with pleasure accepted of all that he had sacrificed to him, for there came a fire running out of the air, and rushed with violence upon the altar, in the sight of all, and caught hold of and consumed the sacrifices. Now when this Divine

appearance was seen, the people supposed it to be a demonstration of God's abode in the temple, and were pleased with it, and fell down upon the ground and worshipped. Upon which the king began to bless God, and exhorted the multitude to do the same, as now having sufficient indications of God's favorable disposition to them; and to pray that they might always have the like indications from him, and that he would preserve in them a mind pure from all wickedness, in righteousness and religious worship, and that they might continue in the observation of those precepts which God had given them by Moses, because by that means the Hebrew nation would be happy, and indeed the most blessed of all nations among all mankind. He exhorted them also to be mindful, that by what methods they had attained their present good things, by the same they must preserve them sure to themselves, and make them greater and more than they were at present; for that it was not sufficient for them to suppose they had received them on account of their piety and righteousness, but that they had no other way of preserving them for the time to come; for that it is not so great a thing for men to acquire somewhat which they want, as to preserve what they have acquired, and to be guilty of no sin whereby it may be hurt.

5. So when the king had spoken thus to the multitude, he dissolved the congregation, but not till he had completed his oblations, both for himself and for the Hebrews, insomuch that he sacrificed twenty and two thousand oxen, and a hundred and twenty thousand sheep; for then it was that the temple did first of all taste of the victims, and all the Hebrews, with their wives and children, feasted therein: nay, besides this, the king then observed splendidly and magnificently the feast which is called the *Feast of Tabernacles*, before the temple, for twice seven days; and he then feasted together with all the people.

6. When all these solemnities were abundantly satisfied, and nothing was omitted that concerned the Divine worship, the king dismissed them; and they every one went to their own homes, giving thanks to the king for the care he had taken of them, and the works he had done for them; and praying to God to preserve Solomon to be their king for a long time. They also took their journey home with rejoicing, and making merry, and singing hymns to God. And indeed the pleasure they enjoyed took away the sense of the pains they all underwent in their journey home. So when they had brought the ark

into the temple, and had seen its greatness, and how fine it was, and had been partakers of the many sacrifices that had been offered, and of the festivals that had been solemnized, they every one returned to their own cities. But a dream that appeared to the king in his sleep informed him that God had heard his prayers; and that he would not only preserve the temple, but would always abide in it; that is, in case his posterity and the whole multitude would be righteous. And for himself, it said, that if he continued according to the admonitions of his father, he would advance him to an immense degree of dignity and happiness, and that then his posterity should be kings of that country, of the tribe of Judah, for ever; but that still, if he should be found a betrayer of the ordinances of the law, and forget them, and turn away to the worship of strange gods, he would cut him off by the roots, and would neither suffer any remainder of his family to continue, nor would overlook the people of Israel, or preserve them any longer from afflictions, but would utterly destroy them with ten thousand wars and misfortunes; would cast them out of the land which he had given their fathers, and make them sojourners in strange lands; and deliver that temple which was now built to be burnt and spoiled by their enemies, and that city to be utterly overthrown by the hands of their enemies; and make their miseries deserve to be a proverb, and such as should very hardly be credited for their stupendous magnitude, till their neighbors, when they should hear of them, should wonder at their calamities, and very earnestly inquire for the occasion, why the Hebrews, who had been so far advanced by God to such glory and wealth, should be then so hated by him? and that the answer that should be made by the remainder of the people should be, by confessing their sins, and their transgression of the laws of their country. Accordingly we have it transmitted to us in writing, that thus did God speak to Solomon in his sleep.

5 *How Solomon Built Himself a Royal Palace, Very Costly and Splendid; and How He Solved the Riddles Which Were Sent Him by Hiram*

1. AFTER the building of the temple, which, as we have before said, was finished in seven years, the king laid the foundation of his palace,

which be did not finish under thirteen years, for he was not equally zealous in the building of this palace as he had been about the temple; for as to that, though it was a great work, and required wonderful and surprising application, yet God, for whom it was made, so far co-operated therewith, that it was finished in the forementioned number of years: but the palace, which was a building much inferior in dignity to the temple, both on account that its materials had not been so long beforehand gotten ready, nor had been so zealously prepared, and on account that this was only a habitation for kings, and not for God, it was longer in finishing. However, this building was raised so magnificently, as suited the happy state of the Hebrews, and of the king thereof. But it is necessary that I describe the entire structure and disposition of the parts, that so those that light upon this book may thereby make a conjecture, and, as it were, have a prospect of its magnitude.

2. This house was a large and curious building, and was supported by many pillars, which Solomon built to contain a multitnde for hearing causes, and taking cognizance of suits. It was sufficiently capacious to contain a great body of men, who would come together to have their causes determined. It was a hundred cubits long, and fifty broad, and thirty high, supported by quadrangular pillars, which were all of cedar; but its roof was according to the Corinthian order,[15] with folding doors, and their adjoining pillars of equal magnitude, each fluted with three cavities; which building as at once firm, and very ornamental. There was also another house so ordered, that its

---

15. This mention of the Corinthian ornaments of architecture in Solomon's palace by Josephus seems to be here set down by way of prophecy although it appears to me that the Grecian and Roman most ancient orders of architecture were taken from Solomon's temple, as from their original patterns, yet it is not so clear that the last and most ornamental order of the Corinthian was so ancient, although what the same Josephus says, (Of the War, B. V. ch. 5. sect. 3,) that one of the gates of Herod's temple was built according to the rules of this Corinthian order, is no way improbable, that order being, without dispute, much older than the reign of Herod. However, upon some trial, I confess I have not hitherto been able fully to understand the structure of this palace of Solomon, either as described in our Bibles, or even with the additional help of this description here by Josephus; only the reader may easily observe with me, that the measures of this first building in Josephus, a hundred cubits long, and fifty cubits broad, are the very same with the area of the cart of the tabernacle of Moses. and just hall' an Egyptian orout, or acre.

entire breadth was placed in the middle; it was quadrangular, and its breadth was thirty cubits, having a temple over against it, raised upon massy pillars; in which temple there was a large and very glorious room, wherein the king sat in judgment. To this was joined another house that was built for his queen. There were other smaller edifices for diet, and for sleep, after public matters were over; and these were all floored with boards of cedar. Some of these Solomon built with stones of ten cubits, and wainscoted the walls with other stones that were sawed, and were of great value, such as are dug out of the earth for the ornaments of temples, and to make fine prospects in royal palaces, and which make the mines whence they are dug famous. Now the contexture of the curious workmanship of these stones was in three rows, but the fourth row would make one admire its sculptures, whereby were represented trees, and all sorts of plants; with the shades that arose from their branches, and leaves that hung down from them. Those trees anti plants covered the stone that was beneath them, and their leaves were wrought so prodigious thin and subtile, that you would think they were in motion; but the other part up to the roof, was plastered over, and, as it were, embroidered with colors and pictures. He, moreover, built other edifices for pleasure; as also very long cloisters, and those situate in an agreeable place of the palace; and among them a most glorious dining room, for feastings and compotations, and full of gold, and such other furniture as so fine a room ought to have for the conveniency of the guests, and where all the vessels were made of gold. Now it is very hard to reckon up the magnitude and the variety of the royal apartments; how many rooms there were of the largest sort, how many of a bigness inferior to those, and how many that were subterraneous and invisible; the curiosity of those that enjoyed the fresh air; and the groves for the most delightful prospect, for the avoiding the heat, and covering of their bodies. And, to say all in brief, Solomon made the whole building entirely of white stone, and cedar wood, and gold, and silver. He also adorned the roofs and walls with stones set in gold, and beautified them thereby in the same manner as he had beautified the temple of God with the like stones. He also made himself a throne of prodigious bigness, of ivory, constructed as a seat of justice, and having six steps to it; on every one of which stood, on each end of the step two lions, two other lions standing above also; but at the sitting place of the throne hands came out and received the king; and when he sat backward, he rested on half a bullock, that looked towards his back; but still all was fastened together with gold.

3. When Solomon had completed all this in twenty years' time, because Hiram king of Tyre had contributed a great deal of gold, and more silver to these buildings, as also cedar wood and pine wood, he also rewarded Hiram with rich presents; corn he sent him also year by year, and wine and oil, which were the principal things that he stood in need of, because he inhabited an island, as we have already said. And besides these, he granted him certain cities of Galilee, twenty in number, that lay not far from Tyre; which, when Hiram went to, and viewed, and did not like the gift, he sent word to Solomon that he did not want such cities as they were; and after that time these cities were called the land of Cabul; which name, if it be interpreted according to the language of the Phoenicians, denotes *what does not please.* Moreover, the king of Tyre sent sophisms and enigmatical sayings to Solomon, and desired he would solve them, and free them from the ambiguity that was in them. Now so sagacious and understanding was Solomon, that none of these problems were too hard for him; but he conquered them all by his reasonings, and discovered their hidden meaning, and brought it to light. Menander also, one who translated the Tyrian archives out of the dialect of the Phoenicians into the Greek language, makes mention of these two kings, where he says thus: "When Abibalus was dead,. his son Hiram received the kingdom from him, who, when he had lived fifty-three years, reigned thirty-four. He raised a bank in the large place, and dedicated the golden pillar which is in Jupiter's temple. He also went and cut down materials of timber out of the mountain called Libanus, for the roof of temples; and when he had pulled down the ancient temples, he both built the temple of Hercules and that of Astarte; and he first set up the temple of Hercules in the month Peritius; he also made an expedition against the Euchii, or Titii, who did not pay their tribute, and when he had subdued them to himself he returned. Under this king there was Abdemon, a very youth in age, who always conquered the difficult problems which Solomon, king of Jerusalem, commanded him to explain. Dius also makes mention of him, where he says thus: "When Abibalus was dead, his son Hiram reigned. He raised the eastern parts of the city higher, and made the city itself larger. He also joined the temple of Jupiter,

445

which before stood by itself, to the city, by raising a bank in the middle between them; and he adorned it with donations of gold. Moreover, he went up to Mount Libanus, and cut down materials of wood for the building of the temples." He says also, that Solomon, who was then king of Jerusalem, sent riddles to Hiram, and desired to receive the like from him, but that he who could not solve them should pay money to them that did solve them, and that Hiram accepted the conditions; and when he was not able to solve the riddles proposed by Solomon, he paid a great deal of money for his fine; but that he afterward did solve the proposed riddles by means of Abdemon, a man of Tyre; and that Hiram proposed other riddles, which, when Solomon could not solve, he paid back a great deal of money to Hiram." This it is which Dius wrote.

6 *How Solomon Fortified the City of Jerusalem, and Built Great Cities; and How He Brought Some of the Canaanites into Subjection, and Entertained the Queen of Egypt and of Ethiopia*

1. Now when the king saw that the walls of Jerusalem stood in need of being better secured, and made stronger, (for he thought the wails that encompassed Jerusalem ought to correspond to the dignity of the city,) he both repaired them, and made them higher, with great towers upon them; he also built cities which might be counted among the strongest, Hazor and Megiddo, and the third Gezer, which had indeed belonged to the Philistines; but Pharaoh, the king of Egypt, had made an expedition against it, and besieged it, and taken it by force; and when he had slain all its inhabitants, he utterly overthrew it, and gave it as a present to his daughter, who had been married to Solomon; for which reason the king rebuilt it, as a city that was naturally strong, and might be useful in wars, and the mutations of affairs that sometimes happen. Moreover, he built two other cities not far from it, Beth-horon was the name of one of them, and Baalath of the other. He also built other cities that lay conveniently for these, in order to the enjoyment of pleasures and delicacies in them, such as were naturally of a good temperature of the air, and agreeable for fruits ripe in their proper seasons, and well watered with springs. Nay, Solomon went as far as the desert above Syria, and possessed himself of it, and

built there a very great city, which was distant two days' journey from Upper Syria, and one day's journey from Euphrates, and six long days' journey from Babylon the Great. Now the reason why this city lay so remote from the parts of Syria that are inhabited is this, that below there is no water to be had, and that it is in that place only that there are springs and pits of water. When he had therefore built this city, and encompassed it with very strong walls, he gave it the name of Tadmor, and that is the name it is still called by at this day among the Syrians, but the Greeks name it Palmyra.

2. Now Solomon the king was at this time engaged in building these cities. But if any inquire why all the kings of Egypt from Menes, who built Memphis, and was many years earlier than our forefather Abraham, until Solomon, where the interval was more than one thousand three hundred years, were called Pharaohs, and took it from one Pharaoh that lived after the kings of that interval, I think it necessary to inform them of it, and this in order to cure their ignorance, and to make the occasion of that name manifest. Pharaoh, in the Egyptian tongue, signifies a *king*[16] but I suppose they made use of other names from their childhood; but when they were made kings, they changed them into the name which in their own tongue denoted their authority; for thus it was also that the kings of Alexandria, who were called formerly by other names, when they took the kingdom, were named Ptolemies, from their first king. The Roman emperors also were from their nativity called by other names, but are styled Caesars, their empire and their dignity imposing that name upon them, and not suffering them to continue in those names which their fathers gave them. I suppose also that Herodotus of Halicarnassus, when he said

---

16. This signification of the name Pharaoh appears to be true. But what Josephus adds presently, that no king of Egypt was called Pharaoh after Solomon's father-in-law, does hardly agree to our copies, which have long afterwards the names of Pharaoh Neehob, and Pharaoh Hophrah, 2 Kings 23:29; Jeremiah 44:30, besides the frequent mention of that name Pharaoh in the prophets. However, Josephus himself, in his own speech to the Jews, Of the War, B. V. ch. 9. sect. 4, speaks of Neehao, who was also called Pharaoh, as the name of that king of Egypt with whom Abraham was concerned; of which name Neehao yet we have elsewhere no mention till the days of Josiah, but only of Pharaoh. And, indeed, it must be conceded, that here, and sect. 5, we have more mistakes made by Josephus, and those relating to the kings of Egypt, and to that queen of Egypt and Ethiopia, whom he supposes to have come to see Solomon, than almost any where else in all his Antiquities.

there were three hundred and thirty kings of Egypt after Menes, who built Memphis, did therefore not tell us their names, because they were in common called Pharaohs; for when after their death there was a queen reigned, he calls her by her name Nicaule, as thereby declaring, that while the kings were of the male line, and so admitted of the same nature, while a woman did not admit the same, he did therefore set down that her name, which she could not naturally have. As for myself, I have discovered from our own books, that after Pharaoh, the father-in-law of Solomon, no other king of Egypt did any longer use that name; and that it was after that time when the forenamed queen of Egypt and Ethiopia came to Solomon, concerning whom we shall inform the reader presently; but I have now made mention of these things, that I may prove that our books and those of the Egyptians agree together in many things.

3. But king Solomon subdued to himself the remnant of the Canaanites that had not before submitted to him; those I mean that dwelt in Mount Lebanon, and as far as the city Hamath; and ordered them to pay tribute. He also chose out of them every year such as were to serve him in the meanest offices, and to do his domestic works, and to follow husbandry; for none of the Hebrews were servants [in such low employments]: nor was it reasonable, that when God had brought so many nations under their power, they should depress their own people to such mean offices of life, rather than those nations; while all the Israelites were concerned in warlike affairs, and were in armor; and were set over the chariots and the horses, rather than leading the life of slaves. He appointed also five hundred and fifty rulers over those Canaanites who were reduced to such domestic slavery, who received the entire care of them from the king, and instructed them in those labors and operations wherein he wanted their assistance.

4. Moreover, the king built many ships in the Egyptian Bay of the Red Sea, in a certain place called Ezion-geber: it is now called Berenice, and is not far from the city Eloth. This country belonged formerly to the Jews, and became useful for shipping from the donations of Hiram king of Tyre; for he sent a sufficient number of men thither for pilots, and such as were skillful in navigation, to whom Solomon gave this command: That they should go along with his own stewards to the land that was of old called Ophir, but now the Aurea Chersonesus, which belongs to India, to fetch him gold. And when they had

gathered four hundred talents together, they returned to the king again.

5. There was then a woman queen of Egypt and Ethiopia;[17] she was inquisitive into philosophy, and one that on other accounts also was to be admired. When this queen heard of the virtue and prudence of Solomon, she had a great mind to see him; and the reports that went every day abroad induced her to come to him, she being desirous to be satisfied by her own experience, and not by a bare hearing; (for reports thus heard are likely enough to comply with a false opinion, while they wholly depend on the credit of the relators;) so she resolved to come to him, and that especially in order to have a trial of his wisdom, while she proposed questions of very great difficulty, and entreated that he would solve their hidden meaning. Accordingly she came to Jerusalem with great splendor and rich furniture; for she brought with her camels laden with gold, with several sorts of sweet spices, and with precious stones. Now, upon the king's kind reception of her, he both showed a great desire to please her, and easily comprehending in his mind the meaning of the curious questions she propounded to him, he resolved them sooner than any body could have expected. So she was amazed at the wisdom of Solomon, and discovered that it was more excellent upon trial than what she had heard by report beforehand; and especially she was surprised at the fineness and largeness of his royal palace, and not less so at the good order of the apartments, for she observed that the king had therein shown great wisdom; but she was beyond measure astonished at the house which was called the *Forest of Lebanon,* as also at the magnificence of his daily table, and the circumstances of its preparation and ministration, with the apparel of his servants that waited, and the skillful and decent management of their attendance: nor was she less affected with those daily sacrifices which were offered to God, and the careful management which the priests and Levites used about them. When

---

17. That this queen of Sheba was a queen of Sabea in South Arabia, and not of Egypt and Ethiopia, as Josephus here asserts, is, I suppose, now generally agreed. And since Sabea is well known to be a country near the sea in the south of Arabia Felix, which lay south from Judea also; and since our Savior calls this queen, "the queen of the south," and says, "she came from the utmost parts of the earth," Matthew 12:42; Luke 11:31, which descriptions agree better to this Arabia than to Egypt and Ethiopia; there is little occasion for doubting in this matter.

she saw this done every day, she was in the greatest admiration imaginable, insomuch that she was not able to contain the surprise she was in, but openly confessed how wonderfully she was affected; for she proceeded to discourse with the king, and thereby owned that she was overcome with admiration at the things before related; and said, "All things indeed, O king, that came to our knowledge by report, came with uncertainty as to our belief of them; but as to those good things that to thee appertain, both such as thou thyself possessest, I mean wisdom and prudence, and the happiness thou hast from thy kingdom, certainly the same that came to us was no falsity; it was not only a true report, but it related thy happiness after a much lower manner than I now see it to be before my eyes. For as for the report, it only attempted to persuade our hearing, but did not so make known the dignity of the things themselves as does the sight of them, and being present among them. I indeed, who did not believe what was reported, by reason of the multitude and grandeur of the things I inquired about, do see them to be much more numerous than they were reported to be. Accordingly I esteem the Hebrew people, as well as thy servants and friends, to be happy, who enjoy thy presence and hear thy wisdom every day continually. One would therefore bless God, who hath so loved this country, and those that inhabit therein, as to make thee king over them."

6. Now when the queen had thus demonstrated in words how deeply the king had affected her, her disposition was known by certain presents, for she gave him twenty talents of gold, and an immense quantity of spices and precious stones. (They say also that we possess the root of that balsam which our country still bears by this woman's gift.)[18] Solomon also repaid her with many good things,

---

18. Some blame Josephus for supposing that the balsam tree might be first brought out of Arabia, or Egypt, or Ethiopia, into Judea, by this queen of Sheba, since several have said that of old no country bore this precious balsam but Judea; yet it is not only false that this balsam was peculiar to Judea but both Egypt and Arabia, and particularly Sabea; had it; which last was that very country whence Josephus, if understood not of Ethiopia, but of Arabia, intimates this queen might bring it first into Judea. Nor are we to suppose that the queen of Sabaea could well omit such a present as this balsam tree would be esteemed by Solomon, in case it were then almost peculiar to her own country. Nor is the mention of balm or balsam, as carried by merchants, and sent as a present out of Judea by Jacob, to the governor of Egypt,

and principally by bestowing upon her what she chose of her own inclination, for there was nothing that she desired which he denied her; and as he was very generous and liberal in his own temper, so did he show the greatness of his soul in bestowing on her what she herself desired of him. So when this queen of Ethiopia had obtained what we have already given an account of, and had again communicated to the king what she brought with her, she returned to her own kingdom.

7 How Solomon Grew Rich, and Fell Desperately in Love with Women and How God, Being Incensed at It, Raised Up Ader and Jeroboam Against Him. Concerning the Death of Solomon

1. ABOUT the same time there were brought to the king from the Aurea Chersonesus, a country so called, precious stones, and pine trees, and these trees he made use of for supporting the temple and the palace, as also for the materials of musical instruments, the harps and the psalteries, that the Levites might make use of them in their hymns to God. The wood which was brought to him at this time was larger and finer than any that had ever been brought before; but let no one imagine that these pine trees were like those which are now so named, and which take that their denomination from the merchants, who so call them, that they may procure them to be admired by those that purchase them; for those we speak of were to the sight like the wood of the fig tree, but were whiter, and more shining. Now we have said thus much, that nobody may be ignorant of the difference between these sorts of wood, nor unacquainted with the nature of the genuine pine tree; and we thought it both a seasonable and humane thing, when we mentioned it, and the uses the king made of it, to explain this difference so far as we have done.

2. Now the weight of gold that was brought him was six hundred and sixty-six talents, not including in that sum what was brought by the merchants, nor what the toparchs and kings of Arabia gave him

---

Genesis 37:25; 43:11, to be alleged to the contrary, since what we there render balm or balsam, denotes rather that turpentine which we now call turpentine of Chio, or Cyprus, the juice of the turpentine tree, than this precious balm. This last is also the same word that we elsewhere render by the same mistake balm of Gilead; it should be rendered, the turpentine of Gilead, Jeremiah 8:22.

in presents. He also cast two hundred targets of gold, each of them weighing six hundred shekels. He also made three hundred shields, every one weighing three pounds of gold, and he had them carried and put into that house which was called *The Forest of Lebanon*. He also made cups of gold, and of [precious] stones, for the entertainment of his guests, and had them adorned in the most artificial manner; and he contrived that all his other furniture of vessels should be of gold, for there was nothing then to be sold or bought for silver; for the king had many ships which lay upon the sea of Tarsus, these he commanded to carry out all sorts of merchandise unto the remotest nations, by the sale of which silver and gold were brought to the king, and a great quantity of ivory, and Ethiopians, and apes; and they finished their voyage, going and returning, in three years' time.

3. Accordingly there went a great fame all around the neighboring countries, which proclaimed the virtue and wisdom of Solomon, insomuch that all the kings every where were desirous to see him, as not giving credit to what was reported, on account of its being almost incredible: they also demonstrated the regard they had for him by the presents they made him; for they sent him vessels of gold, and silver, and purple garments, and many sorts of spices, and horses, and chariots, and as many mules for his carriages as they could find proper to please the king's eyes, by their strength and beauty. This addition that he made to those chariots and horses which he had before from those that were sent him, augmented the number of his chariots by above four hundred, for he had a thousand before, and augmented the number of his horses by two thousand, for he had twenty thousand before. These horses also were so much exercised, in order to their making a fine appearance, and running swiftly, that no others could, upon the comparison, appear either finer or swifter; but they were at once the most beautiful of all others, and their swiftness was incomparable also. Their riders also were a further ornament to them, being, in the first place, young men in the most delightful flower of their age, and being eminent for their largeness, and far taller than other men. They had also very long heads of hair hanging down, and were clothed in garments of Tyrian purple. They had also dust of gold every day sprinkled on their hair, so that their heads sparkled with the reflection of the sun-beams from the gold. The king himself rode upon a chariot in the midst of these men, who were still in armor,

and had their bows fitted to them. He had on a white garment, and used to take his progress out of the city in the morning. There was a certain place about fifty furlongs distant from Jerusalem, which is called Etham, very pleasant it is in fine gardens, and abounding in rivulets of water;[19] thither did he use to go out in the morning, sitting on high [in his chariot.]

4. Now Solomon had a divine sagacity in all things, and was very diligent and studious to have things done after an elegant manner; so he did not neglect the care of the ways, but he laid a causeway of black stone along the roads that led to Jerusalem, which was the royal city, both to render them easy for travelers, and to manifest the grandeur of his riches and government. He also parted his chariots, and set them in a regular order, that a certain number of them should be in every city, still keeping a few about him; and those cities he called the *cities of his chariots*. And the king made silver as plentiful in Jerusalem as stones in the street; and so multiplied cedar trees in the plains of Judea, which did not grow there before, that they were like the multitude of common sycamore trees. He also ordained the Egyptian merchants that brought him their merchandise to sell him a chariot, with a pair of horses, for six hundred drachmae of silver, and he sent them to the kings of Syria, and to those kings that were beyond Euphrates.

5. But although Solomon was become the most glorious of kings, and the best beloved by God, and had exceeded in wisdom and riches those that had been rulers of the Hebrews before him, yet did not he persevere in this happy state till he died. Nay, he forsook the observation of the laws of his fathers, and came to an end no way suitable to our foregoing history of him. He grew mad in his love of women, and

---

19. Whether these fine gardens and rivulets of Etham, about six miles from Jerusalem, whither Solomon rode so often in state, be not those alluded to, Ecclesiastes 2:5, 6, where he says, "He made him gardens and orchards, and planted trees in them of all kinds of fruits: he made him pools of water, to water the wood that bringeth forth trees;" and to the finest part whereof he seems to allude, when, in the Canticles, he compares his spouse to a garden "enclosed," to a "spring shut up," to a "fountain sealed," ch. 4. 12 (part of which from rains are still extant, as Mr. Matmdrell informs us, page 87, 88); cannot now be certainly determined, but may very probably be conjectured. But whether this Etham has any relation to those rivers of Etham, which Providence once dried up in a miraculous manner, Psalm 74:15, in the Septuagint, I cannot say.

laid no restraint on himself in his lusts; nor was he satisfied with the women of his country alone, but he married many wives out of foreign nations; Sidontans, and Tyrians, and Ammonites, and Edomites; and he transgressed the laws of Moses, which forbade Jews to marry any but those that were of their own people. He also began to worship their gods, which he did in order to the gratification of his wives, and out of his affection for them. This very thing our legislator suspected, and so admonished us beforehand, that we should not marry women of other countries, lest we should be entangled with foreign customs, and apostatize from our own; lest we should leave off to honor our own God, and should worship their gods. But Solomon was Gllen headlong into unreasonable pleasures, and regarded not those admonitions; for when he had married seven hundred wives,[20] the daughters of princes and of eminent persons, and three hundred concubines, and those besides the king of Egypt's daughter, he soon was governed by them, till he came to imitate their practices. He was forced to give them this demonstration of his kindness and affection to them, to live according to the laws of their countries. And as he grew into years, and his reason became weaker by length of time, it was not sufficient to recall to his mind the institutions of his own country; so he still more and more contemned his own God, and continued to regard the gods that his marriages had introduced nay, before this happened, he sinned, and fell into an error about the observation of the laws, when he made the images of brazen oxen that supported the brazen sea,[21] and the images

---

20. These seven hundred wives, or the daughters of great men, and the three hundred concubines, the daughters of the ignoble, make one thousand in all; and are, I suppose, those very one thousand women intimated elsewhere by Solomon himself, when he speaks of his not having found one [good] woman among that very number, Ecclesiastes 7:28.

21. Josephus is here certainly too severe upon Solomon, who, in making the cherubims, and these twelve brazen oxen, seems to have done no more than imitate the patterns left him by David, which were all given David by Divine inspiration. See my description of the temples, ch. 10. And although God gave no direction for the lions that adorned his throne, yet does not Solomon seem therein to have broken any law of Moses; for although the Pharisees and latter Rabbins have extended the second commandment, to forbid the very making of any image, though without any intention to have it worshipped, yet do not I suppose that Solomon so understood it, nor that it ought to be so understood. The making any other altar for worship but that at the tabernacle was equally forbidden by Moses, Antiq. B. IV. ch. 8. sect. 5; yet

of lions about his own throne; for these he made, although it was not agreeable to piety so to do; and this he did, notwithstanding that he had his father as a most excellent and domestic pattern of virtue, and knew what a glorious character he had left behind him, because of his piety towards God. Nor did he imitate David, although God had twice appeared to him in his sleep, and exhorted him to imitate his father. So he died ingloriously. There came therefore a prophet to him, who was sent by God, and told him that his wicked actions were not concealed from God; and threatened him that he should not long rejoice in what he had done; that, indeed, the kingdom should not be taken from him while he was alive, because God had promised to his father David that he would make him his successor, but that he would take care that this should befall his son when he was dead; not that he would withdraw all the people from him, but that he would give ten tribes to a servant of his, and leave only two tribes to David's grandson for his sake, because he loved God, and for the sake of the city of Jerusalem, wherein he should have a temple.

6. When Solomon heard this he was grieved, and greatly confounded, upon this change of almost all that happiness which had made him to be admired, into so bad a state; nor had there much time passed after the prophet had foretold what was coming before God raised up an enemy against him, whose name was Ader, who took the following occasion of his enmity to him. He was a child of the stock of the Edomites, and of the blood royal; and when Joab, the captain of David's host, laid waste the land of Edom, and destroyed all that were men grown, and able to bear arms, for six months' time, this Hadad fled away, and came to Pharaoh the king of Egypt, who received him kindly, and assigned him a house to dwell in, and a country to supply him with food; and when he was grown up he loved him exceedingly, insomuch that he gave him his wife's sister, whose name was Tahpenes, to wife, by whom he had a son; who was brought up with the king's children. When Hadad heard in Egypt that both David and Joab were dead, he came to Pharaoh, and desired that he would permit him to go to his own country; upon which the king asked what it was that he wanted, and what hardship he had met

---

did not the two tribes and a half offend when they made an altar for a memorial only, Joshua 22; Antiq. B. V. ch. 1. sect. 26, 27.

with, that he was so desirous to leave him. And when he was often troublesome to him, and entreated him to dismiss him, he did not then do it; but at the time when Solomon's affairs began to grow worse, on account of his forementioned transgressions[22] and God's anger against him for the same, Hadad, by Pharaoh's permission, came to Edom; and when he was not able to make the people forsake Solomon, for it was kept under by many garrisons, and an innovation was not to be made with safety, he removed thence, and came into Syria; there he lighted upon one Rezon, who had run away from Hadadezer, king of Zobah, his master, and was become a robber in that country, and joined friendship with him, who had already a band of robbers about him. So he went up, and seized upon that part of Syria, and was made king thereof. He also made incursions into the land of Israel, and did it no small mischief, and spoiled it, and that in the lifetime of Solomon. And this was the calamity which the Hebrews suffered by Hadad.

7. There was also one of Solomon's own nation that made an attempt against him, Jeroboam the son of Nebat, who had an expectation of rising, from a prophecy that had been made to him long before. He was left a child by his father, and brought up by his mother; and when Solomon saw that he was of an active and bold disposition, he made him the curator of the walls which he built round about Jerusalem; and he took such care of those works, that the king approved of his behavior, and gave him, as a reward for the same, the charge of the tribe of Joseph. And when about that time Jeroboam was once going out of Jerusalem, a prophet of the city Shilo, whose name was Ahijah, met him and saluted him; and when he had taken him a little aside to a place out of the way, where there was not one other person present, he rent the garment he had on into twelve pieces, and bid Jeroboam take ten of them; and told him beforehand, that "this is the will of God; he will part the dominion of Solomon, and give one tribe, with that which is next it, to his son, because of the promise made to David for his succession, and will have ten tribes to thee, because Solomon

---

22. Since the beginning of Solomon's evil life and adversity was the time when Hadad or Ader, who was born at least twenty or thirty years before Solomon came to the crown, in the days of David, began to give him disturbance, this implies that Solomon's evil life began early, and continued very long, which the multitude of his wives and concubines does imply also; I suppose when he was not fifty years of age.

hath sinned against him, and delivered up himself to women, and to their gods. Seeing therefore thou knowest the cause for which God hath changed his mind, and is alienated from Solomon, be thou

8. So Jeroboam was elevated by these words of the prophet; and being a young man,[23] of a warm temper, and ambitious of greatness, he could not be quiet; and when he had so great a charge in the government, and called to mind what had been revealed to him by Ahijah, he endeavored to persuade the people to forsake Solomon, to make a disturbance, and to bring the government over to himself. But when Solomon understood his intention and treachery, he sought to catch him and kill him; but Jeroboam was informed of it beforehand, and fled to Shishak, the king of Egypt, and there abode till the death of Solomon; by which means he gained these two advantages to suffer no harm from Solomon, and to be preserved for the kingdom. So Solomon died when he was already an old man, having reigned eighty years, and lived ninety-four. He was buried in Jerusalem, having been superior to all other kings in happiness, and riches, and wisdom, excepting that when he was growing into years he was deluded by women, and transgressed the law; concerning which transgressions, and the miseries which befell the Hebrews thereby, I think proper to discourse at another opportunity.

8 How, Upon the Death of Solomon the People Forsook His Son Rehoboam, and Ordained Jeroboam King over the Ten Tribes

1. NOW when Solomon was dead, and his son Rehoboam (who was born of an Amntonite wife; whose name was Naamah) had succeeded him in the kingdom, the rulers of the multitude sent immediately into Egypt, and called back Jeroboam; and when he was come to them, to the city Shethem, Rehoboam came to it also, for he had resolved to

---

23. This youth of Jeroboam, when Solomon built the walls of righteous and keep the laws, because he hath proposed to thee the greatest of all rewards for thy piety, and the honor thou shalt pay to God, namely, to be as greatly exalted as thou knowest David to have been." Jerusalem, not very long after he had finished his twenty years building of the temple and his own palace, or not very long after the twenty-fourth of his reign, 1 Kings 9:24; 2 Chronicles 8:11, and his youth here still mentioned, when Solomon's wickedness was become intolerable, fully confirm my former observation, that such his wickedness began early, and continued very long. See Ecclus. 47:14.

declare himself king to the Israelites while they were there gathered together. So the rulers of the people, as well as Jeroboam, came to him, and besought him, and said that he ought to relax, and to be gentler than his father, in the servitude he had imposed on them, because they had borne a heavy yoke, and that then they should be better affected to him, and be well contented to serve him under his moderate government, and should do it more out of love than fear. But Rehoboam told them they should come to him again in three days' time, when he would give an answer to their request. This delay gave occasion to a present suspicion, since he had not given them a favorable answer to their mind immediately; for they thought that he should have given them a humane answer off-hand, especially since he was but young. However, they thought that this consultation about it, and that he did not presently give them a denial, afforded them some good hope of success.

2. Rehoboam now called his father's friends, and advised with them what sort of answer he ought to give to the multitude; upon which they gave him the advice which became friends, and those that knew the temper of such a multitude. They advised him to speak in a way more popular than suited the grandeur of a king, because he would thereby oblige them to submit to him with goodwill, it being most agreeable to subjects that their kings should be almost upon the level with them. But Rehoboam rejected this so good, and in general so profitable, advice, (it was such, at least, at that time when he was to be made king,) God himself, I suppose, causing what was most advantageous to be condemned by him. So he called for the young men who were brought up with him, and told them what advice the elders had given him, and bade them speak what they thought he ought to do. They advised him to give the following answer to the people (for neither their youth nor God himself suffered them to discern what was best): That his little finger should be thicker than his father's loins; and if they had met with hard usage from his father, they should experience much rougher treatment from him; and if his father had chastised them with whips, they must expect that he would do it with scorpions.[24] The king was pleased with this advice, and

---

24. That by scorpions is not here meant that small animal so called, which was never used in corrections, but either a shrub, furze bush, or else some terrible sort of whip of the like nature see Hudson's and Spanheim's notes here.

thought it agreeable to the dignity of his government to give them such an answer. Accordingly, when the multitude was come together to hear his answer on the third day, all the people were in great expectation, and very intent to hear what the king would say to them, and supposed they should hear somewhat of a kind nature; but he passed by his friends, and answered as the young men had given him counsel. Now this was done according to the will of God, that what Ahijah had foretold might come to pass.

3. By these words the people were struck as it were by all iron hammer, and were so grieved at the words, as if they had already felt the effects of them; and they had great indignation at the king; and all cried out aloud, and said, "We will have no longer any relation to David or his posterity after this day." And they said further, "We only leave to Rehoboam the temple which his father built;" and they threatened to forsake him. Nay, they were so bitter, and retained their wrath so long, that when he sent Adoram, which was over the tribute, that he might pacify them, and render them milder, and persuade them to forgive him, if he had said any thing that was rash or grievous to them in his youth, they would not hear it, but threw stones at him, and killed him. When Rehoboam saw this, he thought himself aimed at by those stones with which they had killed his servant, and feared lest he should undergo the last of punishments in earnest; so he got immediately into his chariot, and fled to Jerusalem, where the tribe of Judah and that of Benjamin ordained him king; but the rest of the multitude forsook the sons of David from that day, and appointed Jeroboam to be the ruler of their public affairs. Upon this Rehoboam, Solomon's son, assembled a great congregation of those two tribes that submitted to him, and was ready to take a hundred and eighty thousand chosen men out of the army, to make an expedition against Jeroboam and his people, that he might force them by war to be his servants; but he was forbidden of God by the prophet [Shemaiah] to go to war, for that it was not just that brethren of the same contry should fight one against another. He also said that this defection of the multitude was according to the purpose of God. So he did not proceed in this expedition. And now I will relate first the actions of Jeroboam the king of Israel, after which we will relate what are therewith connected, the actions of Rehoboam, the king of the two

tribes; by this means we shall preserve the good order of the history entire.

4. When therefore Jeroboam had built him a palace in the city Shechem, he dwelt there. He also built him another at Penuel, a city so called. And now the feast of tabernacles was approaching in a little time, Jeroboam considered, that if he should permit the multitude to go to worship God at Jerusalem, and there to celebrate the festival, they would probably repent of what they had done, and be enticed by the temple, and by the worship of God there performed, and would leave him, and return to their first kings; and if so, he should run the risk of losing his own life; so he invented this contrivance; He made two golden heifers, and built two little temples for them, the one in the city Bethel, and the other in Dan, which last was at the fountains of the Lesser Jordan[25] and he put the heifers into both the little temples, in the forementioned cities. And when he had called those ten tribes together over whom he ruled, he made a speech to the people in these words: "I suppose, my countrymen, that you know this, that every place hath God in it; nor is there any one determinate place in which he is, but he every where hears and sees those that worship him; on which account I do not think it right for you to go so long a journey to Jerusalem, which is an enemy's city, to worship him. It was a man that built the temple: I have also made two golden heifers, dedicated to the same God; and the one of them I have consecrated in the city Bethel, and the other in Dan, to the end that those of you that dwell nearest those cities may go to them, and worship God there; and I will ordain for you certain priests and Levites from among yourselves, that you may have no want of the tribe of Levi, or of the sons of Aaron; but let him that is desirous among you of being a priest, bring to God a bullock and a ram, which they say Aaron the first priest brought also."

---

25. Whether these "fountains of the Lesser Jordan" were near a place called Dan, and the fountains of the Greater near a place called Jor, before their conjunction; or whether there was only one fountain, arising at the lake Phiala, at first sinking under ground, and then arising near the mountain Paneum, and thence running through the lake Scmochonitis to the Sea of Galilee, and so far called the Lesser Jordan; is hardly certain, even in Josephus himself, though the latter account be the most probable. However, the northern idolatrous calf, set up by Jeroboam, was where Little Jordan fell into Great Jordan, near a place called Daphnae, as Josephus elsewhere informs us, Of the War, B. IV. ch. 1. sect. 1: see the note there.

When Jeroboam had said this, he deluded the people, and made them to revolt from the worship of their forefathers, and to transgress their laws. This was the beginning of miseries to the Hebrews, and the cause why they were overcome in war by foreigners, and so fell into captivity. But we shall relate those things in their proper places hereafter.

5. When the feast [of tabernacles] was just approaching, Jeroboam was desirous to celebrate it himself in Bethel, as did the two tribes celebrate it in Jerusalem. Accordingly he built an altar before the heifer, and undertook to be high priest himself. So he went up to the altar, with his own priests about him; but when he was going to offer the sacrifices and the burnt-offerings, in the sight of all the people, a prophet, whose name was Jadon, was sent by God, and came to him from Jerusalem, who stood in the midst of the multitude, and in the 'hearing of' the king, and directing his discourse to the altar, said thus: God foretells that there shall be a certain man of the family of David, Josiah by name, who shall slay upon thee those false priests that shall live at that time, and upon thee shall burn the bones of those deceivers of the people, those impostors' and wicked wretches. However, that this people may believe that these things shall so come to pass, I foretell a sign to them that shall also come to pass. This altar shall be broken to pieces immediately, and all the fat of the sacrifices that is upon it shall be poured upon the ground." When the prophet had said this, Jeroboam fell into a passion, and stretched out his hand, and bid them lay hold of him; but that hand which he stretched out was enfeebled, and he was not able to pull it in again to him, for it was become withered, and hung down, as if it were a dead hand. The altar also was broken to pieces, and all that was upon it was poured out, as the prophet had foretold should come to pass. So the king understood that he was a man of veracity, and had a Divine foreknowledge; and entreated him to pray to God that he would restore his right hand. Accordingly the prophet did pray to God to grant him that request. So the king, having his hand recovered to its natural state, rejoiced at it, and invited the prophet to sup with him; but Jadon said that he could not endure to come into his house, nor to taste of bread or water in this city, for that was a thing God had forbidden him to do; as also to go back by the same way which he came, but he said he was to return by another way. So the king wondered at the abstinence of the man, but was himself in fear, as suspecting a change of his affairs for the worse, from what had been said to him.

9   *How Jadon the Prophet Was Persuaded by Another Lying Prophet and Returned [to Bethel,] and Was Afterwards Slain by a Lion. as Also What Words the Wicked Prophet Made Use of to Persuade the King, and Thereby Alienated His Mind from God*

1. NOW there was a certain wicked man in that city, who was a false prophet, whom Jeroboam had in great esteem, but was deceived by him and his flattering words. This man was bedrid, by reason or the infirmities of old age: however, he was informed by his sons concerning the prophet that was come from Jerusalem, and concerning the signs done by him; and how, when Jeroboam's right hand had been enfeebled, at the prophet's prayer he had it revived again. Whereupon he was afraid that this stranger and prophet should be in better esteem with the king than himself, and obtain greater honor from him: and he gave orders to his sons to saddle his ass presently, and make all ready that he might go out. Accordingly they made haste to do what they were commanded, and he got upon the ass and followed after the prophet.; and when he had overtaken him, as he was resting himself under a very large oak tree that was thick and shady, he at first saluted him, but presently he complained of him, because he had not come into his house, and partaken of his hospitality. And when the other said that God had forbidden him to taste of any one's provision in that city, he replied, that "for certain God had not forbidden that I should set food before thee, for I am a prophet as thou art, and worship God in the same manner that thou dost; and I am now come as sent by him, in order to bring thee into my house, and make thee my guest." Now Jadon gave credit to this lying prophet, and returned back with him. But when they were at dinner, and merry together, God appeared to Jadon, and said that he should suffer punishment for transgressing his commands,—and he told him what that punishment should be for he said that he should meet with a lion as he was going on his way, by which lion he should be torn in pieces, and be deprived of burial in the sepulchers of his fathers; which things came to pass, as I suppose, according to the will of God, that so Jeroboam might not give heed to the words of Jadon as of one that had been convicted of lying. However, as Jadon was again going to Jerusalem, a lion assaulted him, and pulled him off the beast he rode on, and slew him; yet did he not at all hurt the ass, but sat by him, and kept him, as also the

prophet's body. This continued till some travelers that saw it came and told it in the city to the false prophet, who sent his sons, and brought the body unto the city, and made a funeral for him at great expense. He also charged his sons to bury himself with him and said that all which he had foretold against that city, and the altar, and priests, and false prophets, would prove true; and that if he were buried with him, he should receive no injurious treatment after his death, the bones not being then to be distinguished asunder. But now, when he had performed those funeral rites to the prophet, and had given that charge to his sons, as he was a wicked and an impious man, he goes to Jeroboam, and says to him, "And wherefore is it now that thou art disturbed at the words of this silly fellow?" And when the king had related to him what had happened about the altar, and about his own hand, and gave him the names *of divine man,* and *an excellent prophet,* he endeavored by a wicked trick to weaken that his opinion; and by using plausible words concerning what had happened, he aimed to injure the truth that was in them; for he attempted to persuade him that his hand was enfeebled by the labor it had undergone in supporting the sacrifices, and that upon its resting awhile it returned to its former nature again; and that as to the altar, it was but new, and had borne abundance of sacrifices, and those large ones too, and was accordingly broken to pieces, and fallen down by the weight of what had been laid upon it. He also informed him of the death of him that had foretold those things, and how he perished; [whence he concluded that] he had not any thing in him of a prophet, nor spake any thing like one. When he had thus spoken, he persuaded the king, and entirely alienated his mind from God, and from doing works that were righteous and holy, and encouraged him to go on in his impious practices[26] and

---

26. How much a larger and better copy Josephus had in this remarkable history of the true prophet of Judea, and his concern with Jeroboam, and with the false prophet of Bethel, than our other copies have, is evident at first sight. The prophet's very name, Jadon, or, as the Constitutions call him, Adonias, is wanting in our other copies; and it is there, with no little absurdity, said that God revealed Jadon the true prophet's death, not to himself as here, hut to the false prophet. Whether the particular account of the arguments made use of, after all, by the false prophet against his own belief and his own conscience, in order to persuade Jeroboam to persevere in his idolatry and wickedness, than which more plausible could not be invented, was intimated in Josephus's copy, or in some other ancient book, cannot now be determined; our other copies say not one word of it.

accordingly he was to that degree injurious to God, and so great a transgressor, that he sought for nothing else every day but how he might be guilty of some new instances of wickedness, and such as should be more detestable than what he had been so insolent as to do before. And so much shall at present suffice to have said concerning Jeroboam.

10 Concerning Rehoboam, and How God Inflicted Punishment Upon Him for His Impiety by Shishak [King of Egypt]

1. Now Rehoboam, the son of Solomon, who, as we said before, was king of the two tribes, built strong and large cities, Bethlehem, and Etare, and Tekoa, and Bethzur, and Shoco, and Adullam, and Ipan, and Maresha, and Ziph, and Adorlam, and Lachlsh, and Azekah, and Zorah, and Aijalon, and Hebron; these he built first of all in the tribe of Judah. He also built other large cities in the tribe of Benjamin, and walled them about, and put garrisons in them all, and captains, and a great deal of corn, and wine, and oil, and he furnished every one of them plentifully with other provisions that were necessary for sustenance; moreover, he put therein shields and spears for many ten thousand men. The priests also that were in all Israel, and the Levites, and if there were any of the multitude that were good and righteous men, they gathered themselves together to him, having left their own cities, that they might worship God in Jerusalem; for they were not willing to be forced to worship the heifers which Jeroboam had made; and they augmented the kingdom of Rehoboam for three years. And after he had married a woman of his own kindred, and had by her three children born to him, he married also another of his own kindred, who was daughter of Absalom by Tamar, whose name was Maachah, and by her he had a son, whom he named Abijah. He had moreover many other children by other wives, but he loved Maachah above them all. Now he had eighteen legitimate wives, and thirty concubines; and he had born to him twenty-eight sons and threescore daughters; but he appointed Abijah, whom he had by Maachah, to be his successor in the kingdom, and intrusted him already with the treasures and the strongest cities.

2. Now I cannot but think that the greatness of a kingdom, and its change into prosperity, often become the occasion of mischief and of

transgression to men; for when Rehoboam saw that his kingdom was so much increased, he went out of the right way unto unrighteous and irreligious practices, and he despised the worship of God, till the people themselves imitated his wicked actions: for so it usually happens, that the manners of subjects are corrupted at the same time with those of their governors, which subjects then lay aside their own sober way of living, as a reproof of their governors' intemperate courses, and follow their wickedness as if it were virtue; for it is not possible to show that men approve of the actions of their kings, unless they do the same actions with them. Agreeable whereto it now happened to the subjects of Rehoboam; for when he was grown impious, and a transgressor himself, they endeavored not to offend him by resolving still to be righteous. But God sent Shishak, king of Egypt, to punish them for their unjust behavior towards him, concerning whom Herodotus was mistaken, and applied his actions to Sesostris; for this Shishak,[27] in the fifth year of the reign of Rehoboam, made an expedition [into Judea] with many ten thousand men; for he had one thousand two hundred chariots in number that followed him, and threescore thousand horsemen, and four hundred thousand footmen. These he brought with him, and they were the greatest part of them Libyans and Ethiopians. Now therefore when he fell upon the country of the Hebrews, he took the strongest cities of Rehoboam's kingdom without fighting; and when he had put garrisons in them, he came last of all to Jerusalem.

3. Now when Rehoboam, and the multitude with him, were shut up in Jerusalem by the means of the army of Shishak, and when they besought God to give them victory and deliverance, they could not persuade God to be on their side. But Shemaiah the prophet told them, that God threatened to forsake them, as they had themselves forsaken his worship. When they heard this, they were immediately in a consternation of mind; and seeing no way of deliverance, they all earnestly set themselves to confess that God might justly overlook them, since they had been guilty of impiety towards him, and had let

---

27. That this Shishak was not the same person with the famous Sesostris, as some have very lately, in contradiction to all antiquity, supposed, and that our Josephus did not take him to be the same, as they pretend, but that Sesostris was many centuries earlier than Shishak, see Authent. Records, part II. page 1024.

his laws lie in confusion. So when God saw them in that disposition, and that they acknowledge their sins, he told the prophet that he would not destroy them, but that he would, however, make them servants to the Egyptians, that they may learn whether they will suffer less by serving men or God. So when Shishak had taken the city without fighting, because Rehoboam was afraid, and received him into it, yet did not Shishak stand to the covenants he had made, but he spoiled the temple, and emptied the treasures of God, and those of the king, and carried off innumerable ten thousands of gold and silver, and left nothing at all behind him. He also took away the bucklers of gold, and the shields, which Solomon the king had made; nay, he did not leave the golden quivers which David had taken from the king of Zobah, and had dedicated to God; and when he had thus done, he returned to his own kingdom. Now Herodotus of Halicarnassus mentions this expedition, having only mistaken the king's name; and [in saying that] he made war upon many other nations also, and brought Syria of Palestine into subjection, and took the men that were therein prisoners without fighting. Now it is manifest that he intended to declare that our nation was subdued by him; for he saith that he left behind him pillars in the land of those that delivered themselves up to him without fighting, and engraved upon them the secret parts of women. Now our king Rehoboam delivered up our city without fighting. He says withal[28] that the Ethiopians learned to circumcise their privy parts from the Egyptians, with this addition, that the

---

28. Herodotus, as here quoted by Josephus, and as this passage still stands in his present copies, B. II. ch. 14., affirms, that "the Phoenicians and Syrians in Palestine [which last are generally supposed to denote the Jews] owned their receiving circumcision from the Egyptians;" whereas it is abnudantly evident that the Jews received their circumcision from the patriarch Abraham, Genesis 17:9–14; John 7:22, 23, as I conclude the Egyptian priests themselves did also. It is not therefore very unlikely that Herodotus, because the Jews had lived long in Egypt, and came out of it circumcised, did thereupon think they had learned that circumcision in Egypt, and had it not broke. Manetho, the famous Egyptian chronologer and historian, who knew the history of his own country much better than Herodotus, complains frequently of his mistakes about their affairs, as does Josephus more than once in this chapter. Nor indeed does Herodotus seem at all acquainted with the affairs of the Jews; for as he never names them, so little or nothing of what he says about them, their country, or maritime cities, two of which he alone mentions, Cadytus and Jenysus, proves true; nor indeed do there appear to have ever been any such cities on their coast.

Phoenicians and Syrians that live in Palestine confess that they learned it of the Egyptians. Yet it is evident that no other of the Syrians that live in Palestine, besides us alone, are circumcised. But as to such matters, let every one speak what is agreeable to his own opinion.

4. When Shishak was gone away, king Rehoboam made bucklers and shields of brass, instead of those of gold, and delivered the same number of them to the keepers of the king's palace. So, instead of warlike expeditions, and that glory which results from those public actions, he reigned in great quietness, though not without fear, as being always an enemy to Jeroboam, and he died when he had lived fifty-seven years, and reigned seventeen. He was in his disposition a proud and a foolish man, and lost [part of his] dominions by not hearkening to his father's friends. He was buried in Jerusalem, in the sepulchers of the kings; and his son Abijah succeeded him in the kingdom, and this in the eighteenth year of Jeroboam's reign over the ten tribes; and this was the conclusion of these affairs. It must be now our business to relate the affairs of Jeroboam, and how he ended his life; for he ceased not nor rested to be injurious to God, but every day raised up altars upon high mountains, and went on making priests out of the multitude.

11 *Concerning the Death of a Son of Jeroboam. How Jeroboam Was Beaten by Abijah Who Died a Little Afterward and Was Succeeded in His Kingdom by Asa. and Also How, After the Death of Jeroboam Baasha Destroyed His Son Nadab and All the House of Jeroboam*

1. HOWEVER, God was in no long time ready to return Jeroboam's wicked actions, and the punishment they deserved, upon his own head, and upon the heads of all his house. And whereas a soil of his lay sick at that time, who was called Abijah, he enjoined his wife to lay aside her robes, and to take the garments belonging to a private person, and to go to Ahijah the prophet, for that he was a wonderful man in foretelling futurities, it having been he who told me that I should be king. He also enjoined her, when she came to him, to inquire concerning the child, as if she were a stranger, whether he should escape this distemper. So she did as her husband bade her, and

changed her habit, and came to the city Shiloh, for there did Ahijah live. And as she was going into his house, his eyes being then dim with age, God appeared to him, and informed him of two things; that the wife of Jeroboam was come to him, and what answer he should make to her inquiry. Accordingly, as the woman was coming into the house like a private person and a stranger, he cried out, "Come in, O thou wife of Jeroboam! Why concealest thou thyself? Thou art not concealed from God, who hath appeared to me, and informed me that thou wast coming, and hath given me in command what I shall say to thee." So he said that she should go away to her husband, and speak to him thus: "Since I made thee a great man when thou wast little, or rather wast nothing, and rent the kingdom from the house of David, and gave it to thee, and thou hast been unmindful of these benefits, hast left off my worship, hast made thee molten gods and honored them, I will in like manner cast thee down again, and will destroy all thy house, and make them food for the dogs and the fowls; for a certain king is rising up, by appointment, over all this people, who shall leave none of the family of Jeroboam remaining. The multitude also shall themselves partake of the same punishment, and shall be cast out of this good land, and shall be scattered into the places beyond Euphrates, because they have followed the wicked practices of their king, and have worshipped the gods that he made, and forsaken my sacrifices. But do thou, O woman, make haste back to thy husband, and tell him this message; but thou shalt then find thy son dead, for as thou enterest the city he shall depart this life; yet shall he be buried with the lamentation of all the multitude, and honored with a general mourning, for he was the only person of goodness of Jeroboam's family." When the prophet had foretold these events, the woman went hastily away with a disordered mind, and greatly grieved at the death of the forenamed child. So she was in lamentation as she went along the road, and mourned for the death of her son, that was just at hand. She was indeed in a miserable condition at the unavoidable misery of his death, and went apace, but in circumstances very unfortunate, because of her son: for the greater haste she made, she would the sooner see her son dead, yet was she forced to make such haste on account of her husband. Accordingly, when she was come back, she found that the child had given up the ghost, as the prophet had said; and she related all the circumstances to the king.

2. Yet did not Jeroboam lay any of these things to heart, but he brought together a very numerous army, and made a warlike expedition against Abijah, the son of Rehoboam, who had succeeded his father in the kingdom of the two tribes; for he despised him because of his age. But when he heard of the expedition of Jeroboam, he was not affrighted at it, but proved of a courageous temper of mind, superior both to his youth and to the hopes of his enemy; so he chose him an army out of the two tribes, and met Jeroboam at a place called Mount Zemaraim, and pitched his camp near the other, and prepared everything necessary for the fight. His army consisted of four hundred thousand, but the army of Jeroboam was double to it. Now as the armies stood in array, ready for action and dangers, and were just going to fight, Abijah stood upon an elevated place, and beckoning with his hand, he desired the multitude and Jeroboam himself to hear first with silence what he had to say. And when silence was made, he began to speak, and told them,—"God had consented that David and his posterity should be their rulers for all time to come, and this you yourselves are not unacquainted with; but I cannot but wonder how you should forsake my father, and join yourselves to his servant Jeroboam, and are now here with him to fight against those who, by God's own determination, are to reign, and to deprive them of that dominion which they have still retained; for as to the greater part of it, Jeroboam is unjustly in possession of it. However, I do not suppose he will enjoy it any longer; but when he hath suffered that punishment which God thinks due to him for what is past, he will leave off the transgressions he hath been guilty of, and the injuries he hath offered to him, and which he hath still continued to offer and hath persuaded you to do the same: yet when you were not any further unjustly treated by my father, than that he did not speak to you so as to please you, and this only in compliance with the advice of wicked men, you in anger forsook him, as you pretended, but, in reality, you withdrew yourselves from God, and from his laws, although it had been right for you to have forgiven a man that was young in age, and not used to govern people, not only some disagreeable words, but if his youth and unskilfulness in affairs had led him into some unfortunate actions, and that for the sake of his father Solomon, and the benefits you received from him; for men ought to excuse the sins of posterity on account of the benefactions of parent; but you considered nothing of all this then,

neither do you consider it now, but come with so great an army against us. And what is it you depend upon for victory? Is it upon these golden heifers, and the altars that you have on high places, which are demonstrations of your impiety, and not of religious worship? Or is it the exceeding multitude of your army which gives you such good hopes? Yet certainly there is no strength at all in an army of many ten thousands, when the war is unjust; for we ought to place our surest hopes of success against our enemies in righteousness alone, and in piety towards God; which hope we justly have, since we have kept the laws from the beginning, and have worshipped our own God, who was not made by hands out of corruptible matter; nor was he formed by a wicked king, in order to deceive the multitude; but who is his own workmanship,[29] and the beginning and end of all things. I therefore give you counsel even now to repent, and to take better advice, and to leave off the prosecution of the war; to call to mind the laws of your country, and to reflect what it hath been that hath advanced you to so happy a state as you are now in."

3. This was the speech which Abijah made to the multitude. But while he was still speaking Jeroboam sent some of his soldiers privately to encompass Abijab round about, on certain parts of the camp that were not taken notice of; and when he was thus within the compass of the enemy, his army was affrighted, and their courage failed them; but Abijah encouraged them, and exhorted them to place their hopes on God, for that he was not encompassed by the enemy. So they all at once implored the Divine assistance, while the priests sounded with the trumpet, and they made a shout, and fell upon their enemies, and God brake the courage and cast down the force of their enemies, and made Ahijah's army superior to them; for God vouchsafed to grant them a wonderful and very famous victory; and such a slaughter was now made of Jeroboam's army[30] as is never recorded to have happened in any other war, whether it were of

---

29. This is a strange expression in Josephus, that God is his own workmanship, or that he made himself, contrary to common sense and to catholic Christianity; perhaps he only means that he was not made by one, but was unoriginated.

30. By this terrible and perfectly unparalleled slaughter of five hundred thousand men of the newly idolatrous and rebellious ten tribes, God's high displeasure and indignation against that idolatry and rebellion fully appeared; the remainder were thereby seriously cautioned not to persist in them, and a kind of balance or

the Greeks or of the Barbarians, for they overthrew [and slew] five hundred thousand of their enemies, and they took their strongest cities by force, and spoiled them; and besides those, they did the same to Bethel and her towns, and Jeshanah and her towns. And after this defeat Jeroboam never recovered himself during the life of Abijah, who yet did not long survive, for he reigned but three years, and was buried in Jerusalem in the sepulchers of his forefathers. He left behind him twenty-two sons, and sixteen daughters; and he had also those children by fourteen wives; and Asa his son succeeded in the kingdom; and the young man's mother was Michaiah. Under his reign the country of the Israelites enjoyed peace for ten years.

4. And so far concerning Abijah, the son of Rehoboam, the son of Solomon, as his history hath come down to us. But Jeroboam, the king of the ten tribes, died when he had governed them two and twenty years; whose son Nadab succeeded him, in the second year of the reign of Asa. Now Jeroboam's son governed two years, and resembled his father in impiety and wickedness. In these two years he made an expedition against Gibbethon, a city of the Philistines, and continued the siege in order to take it; but he was conspired against while he was there by a friend of his, whose name was Baasha, the son of Ahijah, and was slain; which Baasha took the kingdom after the other's death, and destroyed the whole house of Jeroboam. It also came to pass, according as God had foretold, that some of Jeroboam's kindred that died in the city were torn to pieces and devoured by dogs, and that others of them that died in the fields were torn and devoured by the fowls. So the house of Jeroboam suffered the just punishment of his impiety, and of his wicked actions.

---

equilibrium was made between the ten and the two tribes for the time to come; while otherwise the perpetually idolatrous and rebellious ten tribes would naturally have been too powerful for the two tribes, which were pretty frequently free both from such idolatry and rebellion; nor is there any reason to doubt of the truth of the prodigious number upmost: signal an occasion.

12 How Zerah, King of the Ethiopians, Was Beaten by Asa; and How Asa, Upon Baasha's Making War Against Him, Invited the King of the Damascens to Assist Him; and How, on the Destruction of the House of Baasha Zimri Got the Kingdom as Did His Son Ahab After Him

1. Now Asa, the king of Jerusalem, was of an excellent character, and had a regard to God, and neither did nor designed any thing but what had relation to the observation of the laws. He made a reformation of his kingdom, and cut off whatsoever was wicked therein, and purified it from every impurity. Now he had an army of chosen men that were armed with targets and spears; out of the tribe of Judah three hundred thousand; and out of the tribe of Benjamin, that bore shields and drew bows, two hundred and fifty thousand. But when he had already reigned ten years, Zerah, king of Ethiopia,[31] made an expedition against him, with a great army, of nine hundred thousand footmen, and one hundred thousand horsemen, and three hundred chariots, and came as far as Mareshah, a city that belonged to the tribe of Judah. Now when Zerah had passed so far with his own army, Asa met him, and put his army in array over against him, in a valley called Zephathah, not far from the city; and when he saw the multitude of the Ethiopians, he cried out, and besought God to give him the victory, and that he might kill many ten thousands of the enemy: "For," said he,[32] "I depend on nothing else but that assistance which I expect from thee, which is able to make the fewer superior to the more numerous, and the weaker to the stronger; and thence it is alone that I venture to meet Zerah, and fight him."

2. While Asa was saying this, God gave him a signal of victory, and joining battle cheerfully on account of what God had foretold about it, he slew a great many of the Ethiopians; and when he had put them to flight, he pursued them to the country of Gerar; and when they left off killing their enemies, they betook themselves to spoiling them, (for the

---

31. The reader is to remember that Cush is not Ethiopia, but Arabia. See Bochart, B. IV. ch. 2.

32. Here is a very great error in our Hebrew copy in this place, 2 Chronicles 15:3–6, as applying what follows to times past, and not to times future; whence that text is quite misapplied by Sir Isaac Newton.

city Gerar was already taken,) and to spoiling their camp, so that they carried off much gold, and much silver, and a great deal of [other] prey, and camels, and great cattle, and flocks of sheep. Accordingly, when Asa and his army had obtained such a victory, and such wealth from God, they returned to Jerusalem. Now as they were coming, a prophet, whose name was Azariah, met them on the road, and bade them stop their journey a little; and began to say to them thus: That the reason why they had obtained this victory from God was this, that they had showed themselves righteous and religious men, and had done every thing according to the will of God; that therefore, he said, if they persevered therein, God would grant that they should always overcome their enemies, and live happily; but that if they left off his worship, all things shall fall out on the contrary; and a time should come, wherein no true prophet shall be left in your whole multitude, nor a priest who shall deliver you a true answer from the oracle; but your cities shall be overthrown, and your nation scattered over the whole earth, and live the life of strangers and wanderers. So he advised them, while they had time, to be good, and not to deprive themselves of the favor of God. When the king and the people heard this, they rejoiced; and all in common, and every one in particular, took great care to behave themselves righteously. The king also sent some to take care that those in the country should observe the laws also.

3. And this was the state of Asa, king of the two tribes. I now return to Baasha, the king of the multitude of the Israelites, who slew Nadab, the son of Jeroboam, and retained the government. He dwelt in the city Tirzah, having made that his habitation, and reigned twenty-four years. He became more wicked and impious than Jeroboam or his son. He did a great deal of mischief to the multitude, and was injurious to God, who sent the prophet Jehu, and told him beforehand that his whole family should be destroyed, and that he would bring the same miseries on his house which had brought that of Jeroboam to ruin; because when he had been made king by him, he had not requited his kindness, by governing the multitude righteously and religiously; which things, in the first place, tended to their own happiness, and, in the next place, were pleasing to God: that he had imitated this very wicked king Jeroboam; and although that man's soul had perished, yet did he express to the life his wickedness; and he said that he should therefore justly experience the like calamity with him, since he

had been guilty of the like wickedness. But Baasha, though he heard beforehand what miseries would befall him and his whole family for their insolent behavior, yet did not he leave off his wicked practices for the time to come, nor did he care to appear other than worse and worse till he died; nor did he then repent of his past actions, nor endeavor to obtain pardon of God for them, but did as those do who have rewards proposed to them, when they have once in earnest set about their work, they do not leave off their labors; for thus did Baasha, when the prophet foretold to him what would come to pass, grow worse, as if what were threatened, the perdition of his family, and the destruction of his house, (which are really among the greatest of evils,) were good things; and, as if he were a combatant for wickedness, he every day took more and more pains for it: and at last he took his army and assaulted a certain considerable city called Ramah, which was forty furlongs distant from Jerusalem; and when he had taken it, he fortified it, having determined beforehand to leave a garrison in it, that they might thence make excursions, and do mischief to the kingdom of Asa.

4. Whereupon Asa was afraid of the attempts the enemy might make upon him; and considering with himself how many mischiefs this army that was left in Ramah might do to the country over which he reigned, he sent ambassadors to the king of the Damascenes, with gold and silver, desiring his assistance, and putting him in mind that we have had a friendship together from the times of our forefathers. So he gladly received that sum of money, and made a league with him, and broke the friendship he had with Baasha, and sent the commanders of his own forces unto the cities that were under Baasha's dominion, and ordered them to do them mischief. So they went and burnt some of them, and spoiled others; Ijon, and Dan, and Abelmain[33]

---

33. This Abelmain, or, in Josephus's copy, Abellane, that belonged to the land of Israel, and bordered on the country of Damascus, is supposed, both by Hudson and Spanheim, to be the same with Abel, or Ahila, whence came Abilene. This may be that city so denominated from Abel the righteous, there buried, concerning the shedding of whose blood within the compass of the land of Israel, I understand our Savior's words about the fatal war and overthrow of Judea by Titus and his Roman army; "That upon you may come all the righteous blood shed upon the land, from the blood of righteous Abel to the blood of Zacharias son of Barnchins, whom ye slew between the temple and the altar. Verily, I say unto you, all these things shall come upon this generation," Matthew 23;35, 36; Luke 11:51.

and many others. Now when the king of Israel heard this, he left off building and fortifying Ramah, and returned presently to assist his own people under the distresses they were in; but Asa made use of the materials that were prepared for building that city, for building in the same place two strong cities, the one of which was called Geba, and the other Mizpah; so that after this Baasha had no leisure to make expeditions against Asa, for he was prevented by death, and was buried in the city Tirzah; and Elah his son took the kingdom, who, when he had reigned two years, died, being treacherously slain by Zimri, the captain of half his army; for when he was at Arza, his steward's house, he persuaded some of the horsemen that were under him to assault Elah, and by that means he slew him when he was without his armed men and his captains, for they were all busied in the siege of Gibbethon, a city of the Philistines.

5. When Zimri, the captain of the army, had killed Elah, he took the kingdom himself, and, according to Jehu's prophecy, slew all the house of Baasha; for it came to pass that Baasha's house utterly perished, on account of his impiety, in the same manner as we have already described the destruction of the house of Jeroboam. But the army that was besieging. Gibbethon, when they heard what had befallen the king, and that when Zimri had killed him, he had gained the kingdom, they made Omri their general king, who drew off his army from Gibbethon, and came to Tirzah, where the royal palace was, and assaulted the city, and took it by force. But when Zimri saw that the city had none to defend it, he fled into the inmost part of the palace, and set it on fire, and burnt himself with it, when he had reigned only seven days. Upon which the people of Israel were presently divided, and part of them would have Tibni to be king, and part Omri; but when those that were for Omri's ruling had beaten Tibni, Omri reigned over all the multitude. Now it was in the thirtieth year of the reign of Asa that Omri reigned for twelve years; six of these years he reigned in the city Tirzah, and the rest in the city called Semareon, but named by the Greeks Samaria; but he himself called it Semareon, from Semer, who sold him the mountain whereon he built it. Now Omri was no way different from those kings that reigned before him, but that he grew worse than they, for they all sought how they might turn the people away from God by their daily wicked practices; and oil that account it was that God made one of them to be slain by another, and

that no one person of their families should remain. This Omri also died in Samaria and Ahab his son succeeded him.

6. Now by these events we may learn what concern God hath for the affairs of mankind, and how he loves good men, and hates the wicked, and destroys them root and branch; for many of these kings of Israel, they and their families, were miserably destroyed, and taken away one by another, in a short time, for their transgression and wickedness; but Asa, who was king of Jerusalem, and of the two tribes, attained, by God's blessing, a long and a blessed old age, for his piety and righteousness, and died happily, when he had reigned forty and one years; and when he was dead, his son Jehoshaphat succeeded him in the government. He was born of Asa's wife Azubah. And all men allowed that he followed the works of David his forefather, and this both in courage and piety; but we are not obliged now to speak any more of the affairs of this king.

13 How Ahab When He Had Taken Jezebel to Wife Became More Wicked Than All the Kings That Had Been Before Him; of the Actions of the Prophet Elijah, and What Befell Naboth

1. NOW Ahab the king of Israel dwelt in Samaria, and held the government for twenty-two years; and made no alteration in the conduct of the kings that were his predecessors, but only in such things as were of his own invention for the worse, and in his most gross wickedness. He imitated them in their wicked courses, and in their injurious behavior towards God, and more especially he imitated the transgression of Jeroboam; for he worshipped the heifers that he had made; and he contrived other absurd objects of worship besides those heifers: he also took to wife the daughter of Ethbaal, king of the Tyrians and Sidonians, whose name was Jezebel, of whom he learned to worship her own gods. This woman was active and bold, and fell into so great a degree of impurity and madness, that she built a temple to the god of the Tyrians, Which they call Belus, and planted a grove of all sorts of trees; she also appointed priests and false prophets to this god. The king also himself had many such about him, and so exceeded in madness and wickedness all [the kings] that went before him.

2. There was now a prophet of God Almighty, of Thesbon, a country in Gilead, that came to Ahab, and said to him, that God foretold he

would not send rain nor dew in those years upon the country but when he should appear. And when he had confirmed this by an oath, he departed into the southern parts, and made his abode by a brook, out of which he had water to drink; for as for his food, ravens brought it to him every day: but when that river was dried up for want of rain, he came to Zarephath, a city not far from Sidon and Tyre, for it lay between them, and this at the command of God, for [God told him] that he should there find a woman who was a widow that should give him sustenance. So when he was not far off the city, he saw a woman that labored with her own hands, gathering of sticks: so God informed him that this was the woman who was to give him sustenance. So he came and saluted her, and desired her to bring him some water to drink; but as she was going so to do, he called to her, and would have her to bring him a loaf of bread also; whereupon she affirmed upon oath that she had at home nothing more than one handful of meal, and a little oil, and that she was going to gather some sticks, that she might knead it, and make bread for herself and her son; after which, she said, they must perish, and be consumed by the famine, for they had nothing for themselves any longer. Hereupon he said, "Go on with good courage, and hope for better things; and first of all make me a little cake, and bring it to me, for I foretell to thee that this vessel of meal and this cruse of oil shall not fail until God send rain." When the prophet had said this, she came to him, and made him the before-named cake; of which she had part for herself, and gave the rest to her son, and to the prophet also; nor did any thing of this fall until the drought ceased. Now Menander mentions this drought in his account of the acts of Ethbaal, king of the Tyrians; where he says thus: "Under him there was a want of rain from the month Hyperberetmus till the month Hyperberetmus of the year following; but when he made supplications, there came great thunders. This Ethbaal built the city Botrys in Phoenicia, and the city Auza in Libya." By these words he designed the want of rain that was in the days of Ahab, for at that time it was that Ethbaal also reigned over the Tyrians, as Menander informs us.

3. Now this woman, of whom we spake before, that sustained the prophet, when her son was fallen into a distemper till he gave up the ghost, and appeared to be dead, came to the prophet weeping, and beating her breasts with her hands, and sending out such expressions

as her passions dictated to her, and complained to him that he had come to her to reproach her for her sins, and that on this account it was that her son was dead. But he bid her be of good cheer, and deliver her son to him, for that he would deliver him again to her alive. So when she had delivered her son up to him, he carried him into an upper room, where he himself lodged, and laid him down upon the bed, and cried unto God, and said, that God had not done well, in rewarding the woman who had entertained him and sustained him, by taking away her son; and he prayed that he would send again the soul of the child into him, and bring him to life again. Accordingly God took pity on the mother, and was willing to gratify the prophet, that he might not seem to have come to her to do her a mischief, and the child, beyond all expectation, came to life again. So the mother returned the prophet thanks, and said she was then clearly satisfied that God did converse with him.

4. After a little while Elijah came to king Ahab, according to God's will, to inform him that rain was coming. Now the famine had seized upon the whole country, and there was a great want of what was necessary for sustenance, insomuch that it was after the recovery of the widow's son of Sarepta, God sent not only men that wanted it, but the earth itself also, which did not produce enough for the horse and the other beasts of what was useful for them to feed on, by reason of the drought. So the king called for Obadiah, who was steward over his cattle, and said to him, that he would have him go to the fountains of water, and to the brooks, that if any herbs could be found for them, they might mow it down, and reserve it for the beasts. And when he had sent persons all over the habitable earth[34] to discover the prophet

---

34. Josephus, in his present copies, says, that a little while rain upon the earth; whereas, in our other copies, it is after many days, 1 Kings 18:1. Several years are also intimated there, and in Josephus, sect. 2, as belonging to this drought and famine; nay, we have the express mention of the third year, which I suppose was reckoned from the recovery of the widow's son, and the ceasing of this drought in Phmuiela (which, as Menander informs us here, lasted one whole year); and both our Savior and St. James affirm, that this drought lasted in all three years and six months. as their copies of the Old Testament then informed them, Luke 4:25; James 5:17. Josephus here seems to mean, that this drought affected all the habitable earth, and presently all the earth, as our Savior says it was upon all the earth, Luke 4:25. They who restrain these expressions to the land of Judea alone, go without sufficient authority or examples.

Elijah, and they could not find him, he bade Obadiah accompany him. So it was resolved they should make a progress, and divide the ways between them; and Obadiah took one road, and the king another. Now it happened that the same time when queen Jezebel slew the prophets, that this Obadiah had hidden a hundred prophets, and had fed them with nothing but bread and water. But when Obadiah was alone, and absent from the king, the prophet Elijah met him; and Obadiah asked him who he was; and when he had learned it from him, he worshipped him. Elijah then bid him go to the king, and tell him that I am here ready to wait on him. But Obadiah replied, "What evil have I done to thee, that thou sendest me to one who seeketh to kill thee, and hath sought over all the earth for thee? Or was he so ignorant as not to know that the king had left no place untouched unto which he had not sent persons to bring him back, in order, if they could take him, to have him put to death?" For he told him he was afraid lest God should appear to him again, and he should go away into another place; and that when the king should send him for Elijah, and he should miss of him, and not be able to find him any where upon earth, he should be put to death. He desired him therefore to take care of his preservation; and told him how diligently he had provided for those of his own profession, and had saved a hundred prophets, when Jezebel slew the rest of them, and had kept them concealed, and that they had been sustained by him. But Elijah bade him fear nothing, but go to the king; and he assured him upon oath that he would certainly show himself to Ahab that very day.

5. So when Obadiah had informed the king that Elijah was there, Ahab met him, and asked him, in anger, if he were the man that afflicted the people of the Hebrews, and was the occasion of the drought they lay under? But Elijah, without any flattery, said that he was himself the man, he and his house, which brought such sad afflictions upon them, and that by introducing strange gods into their country, and worshipping them, and by leaving their own, who was the only true God, and having no manner of regard to him. However, he bade him go his way, and gather together all the people to him to Mount Carmel, with his own prophets, and those of his wife, telling him how many there were of them, as also the prophets of the groves, about four hundred in number. And as all the men whom Ahab sent for ran away to the forenamed mountain, the prophet Elijah stood

in the midst of them, and said, "How long will you live thus in uncertainty of mind and opinion?" He also exhorted them, that in case they esteemed their own country God to be the true and the only God, they would follow him and his commandments; but in case they esteemed him to be nothing, but had an opinion of the strange gods, and that they ought to worship them, his counsel was, that they should follow them. And when the multitude made no answer to what he said, Elijah desired that, for a trial of the power of the strange gods, and of their own God, he, who was his only prophet, while they had four hundred, might take a heifer and kill it as a sacrifice, and lay it upon pieces of wood, and not kindle any fire, and that they should do the same things, and call upon their own gods to set the wood on fire; for if that were done, they would thence learn the nature of the true God. This proposal pleased the people. So Elijah bade the prophets to choose out a heifer first, and kill it, and to call on their gods. But when there appeared no effect of the prayer or invocation of the prophets upon their sacrifice, Elijah derided them, and bade them call upon their gods with a loud voice, for they might either be on a journey, or asleep; and when these prophets had done so from morning till noon, and cut themselves with swords and lances,[35] according to the customs of their country, and he was about to offer his sacrifice, he bade [the prophets] go away, but bade [the people] come near and observe what he did, lest he should privately hide fire among the pieces of wood. So, upon the approach of the multitude, he took twelve stones, one for each tribe of the people of the Hebrews, and built an altar with them, and dug a very deep trench; and when he had laid the pieces of wood upon the altar, and upon them had laid the pieces of the sacrifices, he ordered them to fill four barrels with the water of the fountain, and to pour it upon the altar, till it ran over it, and till the trench was filled with the water poured into it. When he had done this, he began to pray to God, and to invoke him to make manifest his power to a people that had already been in an error a long time; upon which words a fire came on a sudden from heaven in the sight

---

35. Mr. Spanheim takes notice here, that in the worship of Mithra (the god of the Persians) the priests cut themselves in the same manner as did these priests in their invocation of Baal (the god of the Phoenicians).

of the multitude, and fell upon the altar, and consumed the sacrifice, till the very water was set on fire, and the place was become dry.

6. Now when the Israelites saw this, they fell down upon the ground, and worshipped one God, and called him *The great and the only true God;* but they called the others mere names, framed by the evil and vile opinions of men. So they caught their prophets, and, at the command of Elijah, slew them. Elijah also said to the king, that he should go to dinner without any further concern, for that in a little time he would see God send them rain. Accordingly Ahab went his way. But Elijah went up to the highest top of Mount Carmel, and sat down upon the ground, and leaned his head upon his knees, and bade his servant go up to a certain elevated place, and look towards the sea, and when he should see a cloud rising any where, he should give him notice of it, for till that time the air had been clear. When the Servant had gone up, and had said many times that he saw nothing, at the seventh time of his going up, he said that he saw a small black thing in the sky, not larger than a man's foot. When Elijah heard that, he sent to Ahab, and desired him to go away to the city before the rain came down. So he came to the city Jezreel; and in a little time the air was all obscured, and covered with clouds, and a vehement storm of wind came upon the earth, and with it a great deal of rain; and the prophet was under a Divine fury, and ran along with the king's chariot unto Jezreel a city of Izar[36] [Issaachar].

7. When Jezebel, the wife of Ahab, understood what signs Elijah had wrought, and how he had slain her prophets, she was angry, and sent messengers to him, and by them threatened to kill him, as he had destroyed her prophets. At this Elijah was affrighted, and fled to the city called Beersheba, which is situate at the utmost limits of the country belonging to the tribe of Judah, towards the land of Edom; and there he left his servant, and went away into the desert. He prayed also that he might die, for that he was not better than his fathers, nor need he be very desirous to live, when they were dead; and he lay and slept under a certain tree; and when somebody awakened him,

---

36. For Izar we may here read (with Hudson and Cocceius) Isachar, i.e of the tribe of Isachar, for to that tribe did Jezreel belong; and presently at the beginning of sect. 8, as also ch. 15. sect. 4, we may read for Iar, with one MS. nearly, and the Scripture, Jezreel, for that was the city meant in the history of Naboth.

and he was risen up, he found food set by him and water: so when he had eaten, and recovered his strength by that his food, he came to that mountain which is called Sinai, where it is related that Moses received his laws from God; and finding there a certain hollow cave, he entered into it, and continued to make his abode in it. But when a certain voice came to him, but from whence he knew not, and asked him, why he was come thither, and had left the city? he said, that because he had slain the prophets of the foreign gods, and had persuaded the people that he alone whom they had worshipped from the beginning was God, he was sought for by the king's wife to be punished for so doing. And when he had heard another voice, telling him that he should come out the next day into the open air, and should thereby know what he was to do, he came out of the cave the next day accordingly, When he both heard an earthquake, and saw the bright splendor of a fire; and after a silence made, a Divine voice exhorted him not to be disturbed with the circumstances he was in, for that none of his enemies should have power over him. The voice also commanded him to return home, and to ordain Jehu, the son of Nimshi, to be king over their own multitude; and Hazael, of Damascus, to be over the Syrians; and Elisha, of the city Abel, to be a prophet in his stead; and that of the impious multitude, some should be slain by Hazael, and others by Jehu. So Elijah, upon hearing this charge, returned into the land of the Hebrews. And when he found Elisha, the son of Shaphat, ploughing, and certain others with him, driving twelve yoke of oxen, he came to him, and cast his own garment upon him; upon which Elisha began to prophesy presently, and leaving his oxen, he followed Elijah. And when he desired leave to salute his parents, Elijah gave him leave so to do; and when he had taken his leave of them, he followed him, and became the disciple and the servant of Elijah all the days of his life. And thus have I despatched the affairs in which this prophet was concerned.

8. Now there was one Naboth, of the city Izar, [Jezreel,] who had a field adjoining to that of the king: the king would have persuaded him to sell him that his field, which lay so near to his own lands, at what price he pleased, that he might join them together, and make them one farm; and if he would not accept of money for it, he gave him leave to choose any of his other fields in its stead. But Naboth said he would not do so, but would keep the possession of that land

of his own, which he had by inheritance from his father. Upon this the king was grieved, as if he had received an injury, when he could not get another man's possession, and he would neither wash himself, nor take any food: and when Jezebel asked him what it was that troubled him, and why he would neither wash himself, nor eat either dinner or supper, he related to her the perverseness of Naboth, and how, when he had made use of gentle words to him, and such as were beneath the royal authority, he had been affronted, and had not obtained what he desired. However, she persuaded him not to be cast down at this accident, but to leave off his grief, and return to the usual care of his body, for that she would take care to have Naboth punished; and she immediately sent letters to the rulers of the Israelites [Jezreelites] in Ahab's name, and commanded them to fast and to assemble a congregation, and to set Naboth at the head of them, because he was of an illustrious family, and to have three bold men ready to bear witness that he had blasphemed God and the king, and then to stone him, and slay him in that manner. Accordingly, when Naboth had been thus testified against, as the queen had written to them, that he had blasphemed against God and Ahab the king, she desired him to take possession of Naboth's vineyard on free cost. So Ahab was glad at what had been done, and rose up immediately from the bed whereon he lay to go to see Naboth's vineyard; but God had great indignation at it, and sent Elijah the prophet to the field of Naboth, to speak to Ahab, and to say to him, that he had slain the true owner of that field unjustly. And as soon as he came to him, and the king had said that he might do with him what he pleased, (for he thought it a reproach to him to be thus caught in his sin,) Elijah said, that in that very place in which the dead body of Naboth was eaten by dogs both his own blood and that of his wife's should be shed, and that all his family should perish, because he had been so insolently wicked, and had slain a citizen unjustly, and contrary to the laws of his country. Hereupon Ahab began to be sorry for the things he had done, and to repent of them; and he put on sackcloth, and went barefoot[37] and would not

---

37. "The Jews weep to this day," (says Jerome, here cited by Reland,) "and roll themselves upon sackcloth, in ashes, barefoot, upon such occasions." To which Spanheim adds, "that after the same manner Bernice, when his life was in danger, stood at the tribunal of Florus barefoot." Of the War, B. II. ch. 15. sect. 1. See the like of David, 2 Samuel 15:30; Antiq. B. VII. ch. 9. sect. 2.

touch any food; he also confessed his sins, and endeavored thus to appease God. But God said to the prophet, that while Ahab was living he would put off the punishment of his family, because he repented of those insolent crimes he had been guilty of, but that still he would fulfill his threatening under Ahab's son; which message the prophet delivered to the king.

14 How Hadad King of Damascus and of Syria, Made Two Expeditions Against Ahab and Was Beaten

1. WHEN the affairs of Ahab were thus, at that very time the son of Hadad, [Benhadad,] who was king of the Syrians and of Damascus, got together an army out of all his country, and procured thirty-two kings beyond Euphrates to be his auxiliaries: so he made an expedition against Ahab; but because Ahab's army was not like that of Benhadad, he did not set it in array to fight him, but having shut up every thing that was in the country in the strongest cities he had, he abode in Samaria himself, for the walls about it were very strong, and it appeared to be not easily to be taken in other respects also. So the king of Syria took his army with him, and came to Samaria, and placed his army round about the city, and besieged it. He also sent a herald to Ahab, and desired he would admit the ambassadors he would send him, by whom he would let him know his pleasure. So, upon the king of Israel's permission for him to send, those ambassador's came, and by their king's command spake thus: That Ahab's riches, and his children, and his wives were Benhadad's, and if he would make an agreement, and give him leave to take as much of what he had as he pleased, he would withdraw his army, and leave off the siege. Upon this Ahab bade the ambassadors to go back, and tell their king, that both he himself and all that he hath are his possessions. And when these ambassadors had told this to Berthadad, he sent to him again, and desired, since he confessed that all he had was his, that he would admit those servants of his which he should send the next day; and he commanded him to deliver to those whom he should send whatsoever, upon their searching his palace, and the houses of his friends and kindred, they should find to be excellent in its kind, but that what did not please them they should leave to him. At this second embassage

of the king of Syria, Ahab was surprised, and gathered together the multitude to a congregation, and told them that, for himself, he was ready, for their safety and peace, to give up his own wives and children to the enemy, and to yield to him all his own possessions, for that was what the Syrian king required at his first embassage; but that now he desires to send his servants to search all their houses, and in them to leave nothing that is excellent in its kind, seeking an occasion of fighting against him, "as knowing that I would not spare what is mine own for your sakes, but taking a handle from the disagreeable terms he offers concerning you to bring a war upon us; however, I will do what you shall resolve is fit to be done." But the multitude advised him to hearken to none of his proposals, but to despise him, and be in readiness to fight him. Accordingly, when he had given the ambassadors this answer to be reported, that he still continued in the mind to comply with what terms he at first desired, for the safety of the citizens; but as for his second desires, he cannot submit to them,—he dismissed them.

2. Now when Benhadad heard this, he had indignation, and sent ambassadors to Ahab the third time, and threatened that his army would raise a bank higher than those walls, in confidence of whose strength he despised him, and that by only each man of his army taking a handful of earth; hereby making a show of the great number of his army, and aiming to affright him. Ahab answered, that he ought not to vaunt himself when he had only put on his armor, but when he should have conquered his enemies in the battle. So the ambassadors came back, and found the king at supper with his thirty-two kings, and informed him of Ahab's answer; who then immediately gave order for proceeding thus: To make lines round the city, and raise a bulwark, and to prosecute the siege all manner of ways. Now, as this was doing, Ahab was in a great agony, and all his people with him; but he took courage, and was freed from his fears, upon a certain prophet coming to him, and saying to him, that God had promised to subdue so many ten thousands of his enemies under him. And when he inquired by whose means the victory was to be obtained, be said," By the sons of the princes; but under thy conduct as their leader, by reason of their unskilfulness [in war]." Upon which he called for the sons of the princes, and found them to be two hundred and thirty-two persons. So when he was informed that the king of Syria had

betaken himself to feasting and repose, he opened the gates, and sent out the princes' sons. Now when the sentinels told Benhadad of it, he sent some to meet them, and commanded them, that if these men were come out for fighting, they should bind them, and bring them to him; and that if they came out peaceably, they should do the same. Now Ahab had another army ready within the walls, but the sons of the princes fell upon the out-guard, and slew many of them, and pursued the rest of them to the camp; and when the king of Israel saw that these had the upper hand, he sent out all the rest of his army, which, falling suddenly upon the Syrians, beat them, for they did not think they would have come out; on which account it was that they assaulted them when they were naked[38] and drunk, insomuch that they left all their armor behind them when they fled out of the camp, and the king himself escaped with difficulty, by fleeing away on horseback. But Ahab went a great way in pursuit of the Syrians; and when he had spoiled their camp, which contained a great deal of wealth, and moreover a large quantity of gold and silver, he took Benhadad's chariots and horses, and returned to the city; but as the prophet told him he ought to have his army ready, because the Syrian king would make another expedition against him the next year, Ahab was busy in making provision for it accordingly.

---

38. Mr. Reland notes here very truly, that the word naked does not always signify entirely naked, but sometimes without men's usual armor, without heir usual robes or upper garments; as when Virgil bids the husbandman plough naked, and sow naked; when Josephus says (Antiq. B. IV. ch. 3. sect. 2) that God had given the Jews the security of armor when they were naked; and when he here says that Ahab fell on the Syrians when they were naked and drunk; when (Antiq. B. XI. ch. 5. sect. 8) he says that Nehemiah commanded those Jews that were building the walls of Jerusalem to take care to have their armor on upon occasion, that the enemy might not fall upon them naked. I may add, that the case seems to be the same in the Scripture, when it says that Saul lay down naked among the prophets, 1 Samuel 19:24; when it says that Isaiah walked naked and barefoot, Isaiah 20:2, 3; and when it says that Peter, before he girt his fisher's coat to him, was naked, John 21:7. What is said of David also gives light to this, who was reproached by Michal for "dancing before the ark, and uncovering himself in the eyes of his handmaids, as one of the vain fellows shamelessly uncovereth himself," 2 Samuel 6:14, 20; yet it is there expressly said (ver. 14) that "David was girded with a linen ephod," i.e. he had laid aside his robes of state, and put on the sacerdotal, Levitical, or sacred garments, proper for such a solemnity.

3. Now Benhadad, when he had saved himself, and as much of his army as he could, out of the battle, he consulted with his friends how he might make another expedition against the Israelites. Now those friends advised him not to fight with them on the hills, because their God was potent in such places, and thence it had come to pass that they had very lately been beaten; but they said, that if they joined battle with them in the plain, they should beat them. They also gave him this further advice, to send home those kings whom he had brought as his auxiliaries, but to retain their army, and to set captains over it instead of the kings, and to raise an army out of their country, and let them be in the place of the former who perished in the battle, together with horses and chariots. So he judged their counsel to be good, and acted according to it in the management of the army.

4. At the beginning of the spring, Benhadad took his army with him, and led it against the Hebrews; and when he was come to a certain city which was called Aphek, he pitched his camp in the great plain. Ahab also went to meet him with his army, and pitched his camp over against him, although his army was a very small one, if it were compared with the enemy's; but the prophet came again to him, and told him, that God would give him the victory, that he might demonstrate his own power to be, not only on the mountains, but on the plains also; which it seems was contrary to the opinion of the Syrians. So they lay quiet in their camp seven days; but on the last of those days, when the enemies came out of their camp, and put themselves in array in order to fight, Ahab also brought out his own army; and when the battle was joined, and they fought valiantly, he put the enemy to flight, and pursued them, and pressed upon them, and slew them; nay, they were destroyed by their own chariots, and by one another; nor could any more than a few of them escape to their own city Aphek, who were also killed by the walls falling upon them, being in number twenty-seven thousand.[39] Now there were slain in this battle a hundred thousand more; but Benhadad, the

---

39. Josephus's number, two myriads and seven thousand, agrees here with that in our other copies, as those that were slain by the falling down of the walls of Aphek; but I suspected at first that this number in Josephus's present copies could not be his original number, because he calls them "oligoi," a few, which could hardly be said of so many as twenty-seven thousand, and because of the improbability of the fall of a particular wall killing so many; yet when I consider Josephus's next words, how

king of the Syrians, fled away, with certain others of his most faithful servants, and hid himself in a cellar under ground; and when these told him that the kings of Israel were humane and merciful men, and that they might make use of the usual manner of supplication, and obtain deliverance from Ahab, in case he would give them leave to go to him, he gave them leave accordingly. So they came to Ahab, clothed in sackcloth, with ropes about their heads, (for this was the ancient manner of supplication among the Syrians,)[40] and said, that Benhadad desired he would save him, and that he would ever be a servant to him for that favor. Ahab replied he was glad that he was alive, and not hurt in the battle; and he further promised him the same honor and kindness that a man would show to his brother. So they received assurances upon oath from him, that when he came to him he should receive no harm from him, and then went and brought him out of the cellar wherein he was hid, and brought him to Ahab as he sat in his chariot. So Benhadad worshipped him; and Ahab gave him his hand, and made him come up to him into his chariot, and kissed him, and bid him be of good cheer, and not to expect that any mischief should be done to him. So Berthadad returned him thanks, and professed that he would remember his kindness to him all the days of his life; and promised he would restore those cities of the Israelites which the former kings had taken from them, and grant that he should have leave to come to Damascus, as his forefathers had to come to Samaria. So they confirmed their covenant by oaths, and Ahab made him many presents, and sent him back to his own kingdom. And this was the conclusion of the war that Benhadad made against Ahab and the Israelites.

---

the rest which were slain in the battle were "ten other myriads," that twenty-seven thousand are but a few in comparison of a hundred thousand, and that it was not "a wall," as in our English version, but "the walls" or "the entire walls" of the city that fell down, as in all the originals, I lay aside that suspicion, and firmly believe that Josephus himself hath, with the rest, given us the just number, twenty-seven thousand.

40. This manner of supplication for men's lives among the Syrians, with ropes or halters about their heads or necks, is, I suppose, no strange thing in later ages, even in our own country.

5. But a certain prophet, whose name was Micaiah,[41] came to one of the Israelites, and bid him smite him on the head, for by so doing he would please God; but when he would not do so, he foretold to him, that since he disobeyed the commands of God, he should meet with a lion, and be destroyed by him. When that sad accident had befallen the man, the prophet came again to another, and gave him the same injunction; so he smote him, and wounded his skull; upon which he bound up his head, and came to the king, and told him that he had been a soldier of his, and had the custody of one of the prisoners committed to him by an officer, and that the prisoner being run away, he was in danger of losing his own life by the means of that officer, who had threatened him, that if the prisoner escaped he would kill him. And when Ahab had said that he would justly die, he took off the binding about his head, and was known by the king to be Micaiah the prophet, who made use of this artifice as a prelude to his following words; for he said that God would punish him who had suffered Benhadad, a blasphemer against him, to escape punishment; and that he would so bring it about, that he should die by the other's means[42] and his people by the other's army. Upon which Ahab was very angry at the prophet, and gave commandment that he should be put in prison, and there kept; but for himself, he was in confusion at the words of Micaiah, and returned to his own house.

---

41. It is here remarkable, that in Josephus's copy this prophet, whose severe denunciation of a disobedient person's slaughter by a lion had lately come to pass, was no other than Micaiah, the son of Imlah, who, as he now denounced God's judgment on disobedient Ahab, seems directly to have been that very prophet whom the same Ahab, in 1 Kings 22:8, 18, complains of, "as one whom he hated, because he did not prophesy good concerning him, but evil," and who in that chapter openly repeats his denunciations against him; all which came to pass accordingly; nor is there any reason to doubt but this and the former were the very same prophet.

42. What is most remarkable in this history, and in many histories on other occasions in the Old Testament, is this, that during the Jewish theocracy God acted entirely as the supreme King of Israel, and the supreme General of their armies, and always expected that the Israelites should be in such absolute subjection to him, their supreme and heavenly King, and General of their armies, as subjects and soldiers are to their earthly kings and generals, and that usually without knowing the particular reasons of their injunctions.

15 *Concerning Jehoshaphat the King of Jerusalem and How Ahab Made an Expedition Against the Syrians and Was Assisted Therein by Jehoshaphat, but Was Himself Overcome in Battle and Perished Therein*

1. AND these were the circumstances in which Ahab was. But I now return to Jehoshaphat, the king of Jerusalem, who, when he had augmented his kingdom, had set garrisons in the cities of the countries belonging to his subjects, and had put such garrisons no less into those cities which were taken out of the tribe of Ephraim by his grandfather Abijah, when Jeroboam reigned over the ten tribes [than he did into the other]. But then he had God favorable and assisting to him, as being both righteous and religious, and seeking to do somewhat every day that should be agreeable and acceptable to God. The kings also that were round about him honored him with the presents they made him, till the riches that he had acquired were immensely great, and the glory he had gained was of a most exalted nature.

2. Now, in the third year of this reign, he called together the rulers of the country, and the priests, and commanded them to go round the land, and teach all the people that were under him, city by city, the laws of Moses, and to keep them, and to be diligent in the worship of God. With this the whole multitude was so pleased, that they were not so eagerly set upon or affected with any thing so much as the observation of the laws. The neighboring nations also continued to love Jehoshaphat, and to be at peace with him. The Philistines paid their appointed tribute, and the Arabians supplied him every year with three hundred and sixty lambs, and as many kids of the goats. He also fortified the great cities, which were many in number, and of great consequence. He prepared also a mighty army of soldiers and weapons against their enemies. Now the army of men that wore their armor, was three hundred thousand of the tribe of Judah, of whom Adnah was the chief; but John was chief of two hundred thousand. The same man was chief of the tribe of Benjamin, and had two hundred thousand archers under him. There was another chief, whose name was Jehozabad, who had a hundred and fourscore thousand armed men. This multitude was distributed to be ready for the king's service, besides those whom he sent to the best fortified cities.

490

3. Jehoshaphat took for his son Jehoram to wife the daughter of Ahab, the king of the ten tribes, whose name was Athaliah. And when, after some time, he went to Samaria, Ahab received him courteously, and treated the army that followed him in a splendid manner, with great plenty of corn and wine, and of slain beasts; and desired that he would join with him in his war against the king of Syria, that he might recover from him the city Ramoth, in Gilead; for though it had belonged to his father, yet had the king of Syria's father taken it away from him; and upon Jehoshaphat's promise to afford him his assistance, (for indeed his army was not inferior to the other,) and his sending for his army from Jerusalem to Samaria, the two kings went out of the city, and each of them sat on his own throne, and each gave their orders to their several armies. Now Jehoshaphat bid them call some of the prophets, if there were any there, and inquire of them concerning this expedition against the king of Syria, whether they would give them counsel to make that expedition at this time, for there was peace at that time between Ahab and the king of Syria, which had lasted three years, from the time he had taken him captive till that day.

4. So Ahab called his own prophets, being in number about four hundred, and bid them inquire of God whether he would grant him the victory, if he made an expedition against Benhadad, and enable him to overthrow that city, for whose sake it was that he was going to war. Now these prophets gave their counsel for making this expedition, and said that he would beat the king of Syria, and, as formerly, would reduce him under his power. But Jehoshaphat, understanding by their words that they were false prophets, asked Ahab whether there were not some other prophet, and he belonging to the true God, that we may have surer information concerning futurities. Hereupon Ahab said there was indeed such a one, but that he hated him, as having prophesied evil to him, and having foretold that he should be overcome and slain by the king of Syria, and that for this cause he had him now in prison, and that his name was Micaiah, the son of Imlah. But upon Jehoshaphat's desire that he might be produced, Ahab sent a eunuch, who brought Micaiah to him. Now the eunuch had informed him by the way, that all the other prophets had foretold that the king should gain the victory; but he said, that it was not lawful for him to lie against God, but that he must speak what he should say to him

about the king, whatsoever it were. When he came to Ahab, and he had adjured him upon oath to speak the truth to him, he said that God had shown to him the Israelites running away, and pursued by the Syrians, and dispersed upon the mountains by them, as flocks of sheep are dispersed when their shepherd is slain. He said further, that God signified to him, that those Israelites should return :in peace to their own home, and that he only should fall in the battle. When Micalab had thus spoken, Ahab said to Jehoshaphat, "I told thee a little while ago the disposition of the man with regard to me, and that he uses to prophesy evil to me." Upon which Micaiah replied, that he ought to hear all, whatsoever it be, that God foretells; and that in particular, they were false prophets that encouraged him to make this war in hope of victory, whereas he must fight and be killed. Whereupon the king was in suspense with himself: but Zedekiah, one of those false prophets, came near, and exhorted him not to hearken to Micaiah, for he did not at all speak truth; as a demonstration of which he instanced in what Elijah had said, who was a better prophet in foretelling futurities than Micaiah[43] for he foretold that the dogs should lick his blood in the city of Jezreel, in the field of Naboth, as they licked the blood of Naboth, who by his means was there stoned to death by the multitude; that therefore it was plain that this Micalab was a liar, as contradicting a greater prophet than himself, and saying that he should be slain at three days' journey distance: "and [said he] you shall soon know whether he be a true prophet, and hath the power of the Divine Spirit; for I will smite him, and let him then hurt my hand, as Jadon caused the hand of Jeroboam the king to wither when he would have caught him; for I suppose thou hast certainly heard of that accident." So when, upon his smiting Micaiah, no harm happened to him, Ahab took courage, and readily led his army against the king of Syria; for, as I suppose, fate was too hard for him, and made him believe that the false prophets spake truer than the true one, that it might take an occasion

---

43. These reasonings of Zedekiah the false prophet, in order to persuade Ahab not to believe Micaiah the true prophet, are plausible; but being omitted in our other copies, we cannot now tell whence Josephus had them, whether from his own temple copy, from some other original author, or from certain ancient notes. That some such plausible objection was now raised against Micaiah is very likely, otherwise Jehoshaphat, who used to disbelieve all such false prophets, could never have been induced to accompany Ahab in these desperate circumstances.

of bringing him to his end. However, Zedekiah made horns of iron, and said to Ahab, that God made those horns signals, that by them he should overthrow all Syria. But Micaiah replied, that Zedekiah, in a few days, should go from one secret chamber to another to hide himself, that he might escape the punishment of his lying. Then did the king give orders that they should take Micaiah away, and guard him to Amon, the governor of the city, and to give him nothing but bread and water.

5. Then did Ahab, and Jehoshaphat the king of Jerusalem, take their forces, and marched to Ramoth a city of Gilead; and when the king of Syria heard of this expedition, he brought out his army to oppose them, and pitched his camp not far from Ramoth. Now Ahalx and Jehoshaphat had agreed that Ahab should lay aside his royal robes, but that the king of Jerusalem should put on his [Ahab's] proper habit, and stand before the army, in order to disprove, by this artifice, what Micaiah had foretold.[44] But Ahab's fate found him out without his robes; for Benhadad, the king of Assyria, had charged his army, by the means of their commanders, to kill nobody else but only the king of Israel. So when the Syrians, upon their joining battle with the Israelites, saw Jehoshaphat stand before the army, and conjectured that he was Ahab, they fell violently upon him, and encompassed him round; but when they were near, and knew that it was not he, they all returned back; and while the fight lasted from the morning till late in the evening, and the Syrians were conquerors, they killed nobody, as their king had commanded them. And when they sought to kill Ahab alone, but could not find him, there was a young nobleman belonging to king Benhadad, whose name was Naaman; he drew his bow against the enemy, and wounded the king through his breastplate, in his lungs. Upon this Ahab resolved not to make his mischance known to his army, lest they should run away; but he bid the driver of his chariot

---

44. This reading of Josephus, that Jehoshaphat put on not his own, but Ahab's robes, in order to appear to be Ahab, while Ahab was without any robes at all, and hoped thereby to escape his own evil fate, and disprove Micaiah's prophecy against him, is exceeding probable. It gives great light also to this whole history; and shows, that although Ahab hoped Jehoshaphat would be mistaken for him, and run the only risk of being slain in the battle, yet he was entirely disappointed, while still the escape of the good man Jehoshaphat, and the slaughter of the bad man Ahab, demonstrated the great distinction that Divine providence made betwixt them.

to turn it back, and carry him out of the battle, because he was sorely and mortally wounded. However, he sat in his chariot and endured the pain till sunset, and then he fainted away and died.

6. And now the Syrian army, upon the coming on of the night, retired to their camp; and when the herald belonging to the camp gave notice that Ahab was dead, they returned home; and they took the dead body of Ahab to Samaria, and buried it there; but when they had washed his chariot in the fountain of Jezreel, which was bloody with the dead body of the king, they acknowledged that the prophecy of Elijah was true, for the dogs licked his blood, and the harlots continued afterwards to wash themselves in that fountain; but still he died at Ramoth, as Micaiah had foretold. And as what things were foretold should happen to Ahab by the two prophets came to pass, we ought thence to have high notions of God, and every where to honor and worship him, and never to suppose that what is pleasant and agreeable is worthy of belief before what is true, and to esteem nothing more advantageous than the gift of prophecy[45] and that foreknowledge of future events which is derived from it, since God shows men thereby what we ought to avoid. We may also guess, from what happened to this king, and have reason to consider the power of fate; that there is no way of avoiding it, even when we know it. It creeps upon human souls, and flatters them with pleasing hopes, till it leads them about to the place where it will be too hard for them. Accordingly Ahab appears to have been deceived thereby, till he disbelieved those that foretold his defeat; but, by giving credit to such as foretold what was grateful to him, was slain; and his son Ahaziah succeeded him.

---

45. We have here a very wise reflection of Josephus about Divine Providence, and what is derived from it, prophecy, and the inevitable certainty of its accomplishment; and that when wicked men think they take proper methods to elude what is denounced against them, and to escape the Divine judgments thereby threatened them, without repentance, they are ever by Providence infatuated to bring about their own destruction, and thereby withal to demonstrate the perfect veracity of that God whose predictions they in vain endeavored to elude.

Book 9

Containing the Interval of One Hundred and Fifty-Seven Years, from the Death of Ahab to the Captivity of the Ten Tribes

1 Concerning Jehoshaphat Again; How He Constituted Judges and, by God's Assistance Overcame His Enemies

1. WHEN Jehoshaphat the king was come to Jerusalem, from the assistance he had afforded Ahab, the king of Israel, when he fought with Benhadad, king of Syria, the prophet Jehu met him, and accused him for assisting Ahab, a man both impious and wicked; and said to him, that God was displeased with him for so doing, but that he delivered him from the enemy, notwithstanding he had sinned, because of his own proper disposition, which was good. Whereupon the king betook himself to thanksgivings and sacrifices to God; after which he presently went over all that country which he ruled round about, and taught the people, as well the laws which God gave them by Moses, as that religious worship that was due to him. He also constituted judges in every one of the cities of his kingdom; and charged them to have regard to nothing so much in judging the multitude as to do justice, and not to be moved by bribes, nor by the dignity of men eminent for either their riches or their high birth, but to distribute justice equally to all, as knowing that God is conscious of every secret action of theirs. When he had himself instructed them thus, and gone over every city of the two tribes, he returned to Jerusalem. He there also constituted judges out of the priests and the Levites, and principal persons of the multitude, and admonished them

to pass all their sentences with care and justice[1] And that if any of the people of his country had differences of great consequence, they should send them out of the other cities to these judges, who would be obliged to give righteous sentences concerning such causes; and this with the greater care, because it is proper that the sentences which are given in that city wherein the temple of God is, and wherein the king dwells, be given with great care and the utmost justice. Now he set over them Amariah the priest, and Zebadiah, [both] of the tribe of Judah; and after this manner it was that the king ordered these affairs.

2. About the same time the Moabites and Ammonites made an expedition against Jehoshaphat, and took with them a great body of Arabians, and pitched their camp at Engedi, a city that is situate at the lake Asphaltiris, and distant three hundred furlongs from Jerusalem. In that place grows the best kind of palm trees, and the opobalsamum.[2] Now Jehoshaphat heard that the enemies had passed over the lake, and had made an irruption into that country which belonged to his kingdom; at which news he was aftrighted, and called the people of Jerusalem to a congregation in the temple, and standing over against the temple itself, he called upon God to afford him power and strength, so as to inflict punishment on those that made this expedition against them (for that those who built this his temple had prayed, that he would protect that city, and take vengeance on those that were so bold as to come against it); for they are come to take from us that land which thou hast given us for a possession. When he had prayed thus, he fell into tears; and the whole multitude, together with their wives and children, made their supplications also: upon which a certain prophet, Jahaziel by name, came into the midst of the assembly, and cried out, and spake both to the multitude and to the king, that God heard their prayers, and promised to fight against their enemies. He also gave order that the king should draw his forces out the next day, for that he should find them between Jerusalem and the ascent of Engedi, at a place called The Eminence, and that he should not fight against them,

---

1. These judges constituted by Jehoshaphat were a kind of Jerusalem Sanhedrim, out of the priests, the Levites, and the principal of the people, both here and 2 Chronicles 19:8; much like the old Christian judicatures of the bishop, the presbyters, the deacons, and the people.

2. Concerning this precious balsam, see the note on Atiq. B. VIII. ch. 6. sect. 6.

but only stand still, and see how God would fight against them. When the prophet had said this, both the king and the multitude fell upon their faces, and gave thanks to God, and worshipped him; and the Levites continued singing hymns to God with their instruments of music.

3. As soon as it was day, and the king was come into that wilderness which is under the city of Tekoa, he said to the multitude, "that they ought to give credit to what the prophet had said, and not to set themselves in array for fighting; but to set the priests with their trumpets, and the Levites with the singers of hymns, to give thanks to God, as having already delivered our country from our enemies." This opinion of the king pleased [the people], and they did what he advised them to do. So God caused a terror and a commotion to arise among the Ammonites, who thought one another to be enemies, and slew one another, insomuch that not one man out of so great an army escaped; and when Jehoshaphat looked upon that valley wherein their enemies had been encamped, and saw it full of dead men, he rejoiced at so surprising an event, as was this assistance of God, while he himself by his own power, and without their labor, had given them the victory. He also gave his army leave to take the prey of the enemy's camp, and to spoil their dead bodies; and indeed so they did for three days together, till they were weary, so great was the number of the slain; and on the fourth day, all the people were gathered together unto a certain hollow place or valley, and blessed God for his power and assistance, from which the place had this name given it, the Valley of [Berachah, or] Blessing.

4. And when the king had brought his army back to Jerusalem, he betook himself to celebrate festivals, and offer sacrifices, and this for many days. And indeed, after this destruction of their enemies, and when it came to the ears of the foreign nations, they were all greatly aftrighted, as supposing that God would openly fight for him hereafter. So Jehoshaphat from that time lived in great glory and splendor, on account of his righteousness and his piety towards God. He was also in friendship with Ahab's son, who was king of Israel; and he joined with him in the building of ships that were to sail to Pontus, and the traffic

cities of Thrace[3] but he failed of his gains, for the ships were destroyed by being so great [and unwieldy]; on which account he was no longer concerned about shipping. And this is the history of Jehoshaphat, the king of Jerusalem.

2 Concerning Ahaziah; the King of Israel; and Again Concerning the Prophet Elijah

1. AND now Ahaziah, the son of Ahab, reigned over Israel, and made his abode in Samaria. He was a wicked man, and in all respects like to both his parents and to Jeroboam, who first of all transgressed, and began to deceive the people. In the second year of his reign, the king of Moab fell off from his obedience, and left off paying those tributes which he before paid to his father Ahab. Now it happened that Ahaziah, as he was coming down from the top of his house, fell down from it, and in his sickness sent to the Fly, which was the god of Ekron, for that was this god's name, to inquire about his recovery[4] but the God of the Hebrews appeared to Elijah the prophet, and commanded him to go and meet the messengers that were sent, and to ask them, whether the people of Israel had pot a God of their own, that the king sent to a foreign god to inquire about his recovery? and to bid them return and tell the king that he would not escape this disease. And when Elijah had performed what God had commanded him, and the messengers had heard what he said, they returned to the king immediately; and when the king wondered how they could return so soon, and asked them the reason of it, they said that a certain man

3. What are here Pontus and Thrace, as the places whither Jehoshaphat's fleet sailed, are in our other copies Ophir and Tarshish, and the place whence it sailed is in them Eziongeber, which lay on the Red Sea, whence it was impossible for any ships to sail to Pontus or Thrace; so that Josephus's copy differed from our other copies, as is further plain from his own words, which render what we read, that "the ships were broken at Eziongeber, from their unwieldy greatness." But so far we may conclude, that Josephus thought one Ophir to be some where in the Mediterranean, and not in the South Sea, though perhaps there might be another Ophir in that South Sea also, and that fleets might then sail both from Phoenicia and from the Red Sea to fetch the gold of Ophir.

4. This god of flies seems to have been so called, as was the like god among the Greeks, from his supposed power over flies, in driving them away from the flesh of their sacrifices, which otherwise would have been very troublesome to them.

met them, and forbade them to go on any farther; but to return and tell thee, from the command of the God of Israel, that this disease will have a bad end. And when the king bid them describe the man that said this to them, they replied that he was a hairy man, and was girt about with a girdle of leather. So the king understood by this that the man who was described by the messengers was Elijah; whereupon he sent a captain to him, with fifty soldiers, and commanded them to bring Elijah to him; and when the captain that was sent found Elijah sitting upon the top of a hill, he commanded him to come down, and to come to the king, for so had he enjoined; but that in case he refused, they would carry him by force. Elijah said to him, "That you may have a trial whether I be a true prophet, I will pray that fire may fall from heaven, and destroy both the soldiers and yourself."[5] So he prayed, and a whirlwind of fire fell [from heaven], and destroyed the captain, and those that were with him. And when the king was informed of the destruction of these men, he was very angry, and sent another captain with the like number of armed men that were sent before. And when this captain also threatened the prophet, that unless he came down of his own accord, he would take him and carry him away, upon his prayer against him, the fire [from heaven] slew this captain as well the other. And when, upon inquiry, the king was informed of what happened to him, he sent out a third captain. But

---

5. It is commonly esteemed a very cruel action of Elijah, when he called for fire from heaven, and consumed no fewer than two captains and a hundred soldiers, and this for no other crime than obeying the orders of their king, in attempting to seize him; and it is owned by our Savior, that it was an instance of greater severity than the spirit of the New Testament allows, Luke 9:54. But then we must consider that it is not unlikely that these captains and soldiers believed that they were sent to fetch the prophet, that he might be put to death for foretelling the death of the king, and this while they knew him to be the prophet of the true God, the supreme King of Israel, (for they were still under the theocracy,) which was no less than impiety, rebellion, and treason, in the highest degree: nor would the command of a subaltern, or inferior captain, contradicting the commands of the general, when the captain and the soldiers both knew it to be so, as I suppose, justify or excuse such gross rebellion and disobedience in soldiers at this day. Accordingly, when Saul commanded his guards to slay Ahimelech and the priests at Nob, they knew it to be an unlawful command, and would not obey it, 1 Samuel 22:17. From which cases both officers and soldiers may learn, that the commands of their leaders or kings cannot justify or excuse them in doing what is wicked in the sight of God, or in fighting in an unjust cause, when they know it so to be.

when this captain, who was a wise man, and of a mild disposition, came to the place where Elijah happened to be, and spake civilly to him; and said that he knew that it was without his own consent, and only in submission to the king's command that he came to him; and that those that came before did not come willingly, but on the same account;—he therefore desired him to have pity on those armed men that were with him, and that he would come down and follow him to the king. So Elijah accepted of his discreet words and courteous behavior, and came down and followed him. And when he came to the king, he prophesied to him and told him that God said, "Since thou hast despised him as not being God, and so unable to foretell the truth about thy distemper, but hast sent to the god of Ekron to inquire of him what will be the end of this thy distemper, know this, that thou shalt die."

2. Accordingly the king in a very little time died, as Elijah had foretold; but Jehoram his brother succeeded him in the kingdom, for he died without children: but for this Jehoram, he was like his father Ahab in wickedness, and reigned twelve years, indulging himself in all sorts of wickedness and impiety towards God, for, leaving off his worship, he worshipped foreign gods; but in other respects he was an active man. Now at this time it was that Elijah disappeared from among men, and no one knows of his death to this very day; but he left behind him his disciple Elisha, as we have formerly declared. And indeed, as to Elijah, and as to Enoch, who was before the deluge, it is written in the sacred books that they disappeared, but so that nobody knew that they died.

3　How Joram and Jehoshaphat Made an Expedition Against the Moabites; as Also Concerning the Wonders of Elisha; and the Death of Jehoshaphat

1. WHEN Joram had taken upon him the kingdom, he determined to make an expedition against the king of Moab, whose name was Mesha; for, as we told you before, he was departed from his obedience to his brother [Ahaziah], while he paid to his father Ahab two hundred thousand sheep, with their fleeces of wool. When therefore he had gathered his own army together, he sent also to Jehoshaphat, and

entreated him, that since he had from the beginning been a friend to his father, he would assist him in the war that he was entering into against the Moabites, who had departed from their obedience, who not only himself promised to assist him, but would also oblige the king of Edom, who was under his authority, to make the same expedition also. When Joram had received these assurances of assistance from Jehoshaphat, he took his army with him, and came to Jerusalem; and when he had been sumptuously entertained by the king of Jerusalem, it was resolved upon by them to take their march against their enemies through the wilderness of Edom. And when they had taken a compass of seven days' journey, they were in distress for want of water for the cattle, and for the army, from the mistake of their roads by the guides that conducted them, insomuch that they were all in an agony, especially Joram; and cried to God, by reason of their sorrow, and [desired to know] what wickedness had been committed by them that induced him to deliver three kings together, without fighting, unto the king of Moab. But Jehoshaphat, who was a righteous man, encouraged him, and bade him send to the camp, and know whether any prophet of God was come along with them, that we might by him learn from God what we should do. And when one of the servants of Joram said that he had seen there Elisha, the son of Shaphat, the disciple of Elijah, the three kings went to him, at the entreaty of Jehoshaphat; and when they were come at the prophet's tent, which tent was pitched out of the camp, they asked him what would become of the army? and Joram was particularly very pressing with him about it. And when he replied to him, that he should not trouble him, but go to his father's and mother's prophets, for they [to be sure] were true prophets, he still desired him to prophesy, and to save them. So he swore by God that he would not answer him, unless it were on account of Jehoshaphat, who was a holy and righteous man; and when, at his desire, they brought him a man that could play on the psaltery, the Divine Spirit came upon him as the music played, and he commanded them to dig many trenches in the valley; for, said he, "though there appear neither cloud, nor wind, nor storm of rain, ye shall see this river full of water, till the army and the cattle be saved for you by drinking of it. Nor will this be all the favor that you shall receive from God, but you shall also overcome your enemies, and take the best and strongest cities of the

Moabites, and you shall cut down their fruit trees,[6] and lay waste their country, and stop up their fountains and rivers."

2. When the prophet had said this, the next day, before the sunrising, a great torrent ran strongly; for God had caused it to rain very plentifully at the distance of three days' journey into Edom, so that the army and the cattle found water to drink in abundance. But when the Moabites heard that the three kings were coming upon them, and made their approach through the wilderness, the king of Moab gathered his army together presently, and commanded them to pitch their camp upon the mountains, that when the enemies should attempt to enter their country, they might not be concealed from them. But when at the rising of the sun they saw the water in the torrent, for it was not far from the land of Moab, and that it was of the color of blood, for at such a time the water especially looks red, by the shining of the sun upon it, they formed a false notion of the state of their enemies, as if they had slain one another for thirst; and that the river ran with their blood. However, supposing that this was the case, they desired their king would send them out to spoil their enemies; whereupon they all went in haste, as to an advantage already gained, and came to the enemy's camp, as supposing them destroyed already. But their hope deceived them; for as their enemies stood round about them, some of them were cut to pieces, and others of them were dispersed, and fled to their own country. And when the kings fell into the land of Moab, they overthrew the cities that were in it, and spoiled their fields, and marred them, filling them with stones out of the brooks, and cut down the best of their trees, and stopped up their fountains of water, and overthrew their walls to their foundations. But the king of Moab, when he was pursued, endured a siege; and seeing his city in danger of being overthrown by force, made a sally, and went out with seven hundred men, in order to break through the enemy's camp

---

6. This practice of cutting down, or plucking up by the roots, the fruit trees was forbidden, even in ordinary wars, by the law of Moses, Deuteronomy 20:19, 20, and only allowed by God in this particular case, when the Moabites were to be punished and cut off in an extraordinary manner for their wickedness See Jeremiah 48:11–13, and many the like prophecies against them. Nothing could therefore justify this practice but a particular commission from God by his prophet, as in the present case, which was ever a sufficient warrant for breaking any such ritual or ceremonial law whatsoever.

with his horsemen, on that side where the watch seemed to be kept most negligently; and when, upon trial, he could not get away, for he lighted upon a place that was carefully watched, he returned into the city, and did a thing that showed despair and the utmost distress; for he took his eldest son, who was to reign after him, and lifting him up upon the wall, that he might be visible to all the enemies, he offered him as a whole burnt-offering to God, whom, when the kings saw, they commiserated the distress that was the occasion of it, and were so affected, in way of humanity and pity, that they raised the siege, and every one returned to his own house. So Jehoshaphat came to Jerusalem, and continued in peace there, and outlived this expedition but a little time, and then died, having lived in all sixty years, and of them reigned twenty-five. He was buried in a magnificent manner in Jerusalem, for he had imitated the actions of David.

4   Jehoram Succeeds Jehoshaphat; How Joram, His Namesake, King of Israel, Fought with the Syrians;and What Wonders Were Done by the Prophet Elisha

1. JEHOSHAPAT had a good number of children; but he appointed his eldest son Jehoram to be his successor, who had the same name with his mother's brother, that was king of Israel, and the son of Ahab. Now when the king of Israel was come out of the land of Moab to Samaria, he had with him Elisha the prophet, whose acts I have a mind to go over particularly, for they were illustrious, and worthy to be related, as we have them set down in the sacred books.

2. For they say that the widow of Obadiah[7] Ahab's steward, came to him, and said, that he was not ignorant how her husband had

---

7. That this woman who cried to Elisha, and who in our Bible is styled "the wife of one of the sons of the prophets," 2 Kings 4:1, was no other than the widow of Obadiah, the good steward of Ahab, is confirmed by the Chaldee paraphrast, and by the Rabbins and others. Nor is that unlikely which Josephus here adds, that these debts were contracted by her husband for the support of those "hundred of the Lord's prophets, whom he maintained by fifty in a cave," in the days of Ahab and Jezebel, 1 Kings 18:4; which circumstance rendered it highly fit that the prophet Elisha should provide her a remedy, and enable her to redeem herself and her sons from the fear of that slavery which insolvent debtors were liable to by the law of Moses, Leviticus 25:39; Matthew 18:25; which he did accordingly, with God's help, at the expense of a miracle.

preserved the prophets that were to be slain by Jezebel, the wife of Ahab; for she said that he hid a hundred of them, and had borrowed money for their maintenance, and that, after her husband's death, she and her children were carried away to be made slaves by the creditors; and she desired of him to have mercy upon her on account of what her husband did, and afford her some assistance. And when he asked her what she had in the house, she said, "Nothing but a very small quantity of oil in a cruse." So the prophet bid her go away, and borrow a great many empty vessels of her neighbors, and when she had shut her chamber door, to pour the oil into them all; for that God would fill them full. And when the woman had done what she was commanded to do, and bade her children bring every one of the vessels, and all were filled, and not one left empty, she came to the prophet, and told him that they were all full; upon which he advised her to go away, and sell the oil, and pay the creditors what was owing them, for that there would be some surplus of the price of the oil, which she might make use of for the maintenance of her children. And thus did Elisha discharge the woman's debts, and free her from the vexation of her creditors.

3. Elisha also sent a hasty message to Joram,[8] and exhorted him to take care of that place, for that therein were some Syrians lying

---

8. Dr. Hudson, with very good reason, suspects that there is no small defect in our present copies of Josephus, just before the beginning of this section, and that chiefly as to that distinct account which he had given us reason to expect in the first section, and to which he seems to refer, ch. 8. sect. 6. concerning the glorious miracles which Elisha wrought, which indeed in our Bibles are not a few, 2 Kings 6–9., but of which we have several omitted in Josephus's present copies. One of those histories, omitted at present, was evidently in his Bible, I mean that of the curing of Nanman's leprosy, 2 Kings 5.; for he plainly alludes to it, B. III. ch. 11. sect. 4, where he observes, that "there were lepers in many nations who yet have been in honor, and not only free from reproach and avoidance, but who have been great captains of armies, and been intrusted with high offices in the commonwealth, and have had the privilege of entering into holy places and temples." But what makes me most regret the want of that history in our present copies of Josephus is this, that we have here, as it is commonly understood, one of the greatest difficulties in all the Bible, that in 2 Kings 5:18, 19, where Naaman, after he had been miraculously cured by a prophet of the true God, and had thereupon promised (ver. 17) that "he would henceforth offer neither burnt-offering nor sacrifice unto other gods, but unto the Lord," adds, "In this thing the Lord pardon thy servant, that when my master goeth into the house of Rimnu to worship there, and he leaneth on my hands, and I bow myself in the house of Rimmort; when I bow down myself in the house of Rimmort, the Lord pardon

in ambush to kill him. So the king did as the prophet exhorted him, and avoided his going a hunting. And when Benhadad missed of the success of his lying in ambush, he was wroth with his own servants, as if they had betrayed his ambushment to Joram; and he sent for them, and said they were the betrayers of his secret counsels; and he threatened that he would put them to death, since such their practice was evident, because he had intrusted this secret to none but them, and yet it was made known to his enemy. And one that was present said that he should not mistake himself, nor suspect that they had discovered to his enemy his sending men to kill him, but that he ought to know that it was Elisha the prophet who discovered all to him, and laid open all his counsels. So he gave order that they should send some to learn in what city Elisha dwelt. Accordingly those that were sent brought word that he was in Dothan; wherefore Benhadad sent to that city a great army, with horses and chariots, to take Elisha: so they encompassed the city round about by night, and kept him therein confined; but when the prophet's servant in the morning perceived this, and that his enemies sought to take Elisha, he came running, and crying out after a disordered manner to him, and told him of it; but he encouraged him, and bid him not be afraid, and to despise the enemy, and trust in the assistance of God, and was himself without fear; and he besought God to make manifest to his servant his power and presence, so far as was possible, in order to the inspiring him with hope and courage. Accordingly God heard the prayer of the prophet, and made the servant see a multitude of chariots and horses encompassing Elisha, till he laid aside his fear, and his courage revived at the sight of what he supposed was come to their assistance. After this Elisha did further entreat God, that he would dim the eyes of their enemies, and cast a mist before them, whereby they might not discern him. When this was done, he went into the midst of his enemies, and asked them who it was that they came to seek; and when they replied, "The prophet Elisha," he promised he would deliver him to them, if they would follow him to the city where he was. So these men were so darkened by God in their sight and in their mind, that they

---

thy servant in this thing. And Elisha said, Go in peace." This looks like a prophet's permission for being partaker in idolatry itself, out of compliance with an idolatrous court.

followed him very diligently; and when Elisha had brought them to Samaria, he ordered Joram the king to shut the gates, and to place his own army round about them; and prayed to God to clear the eyes of these their enemies, and take the mist from before them. Accordingly, when they were freed from the obscurity they had been in, they saw themselves in the midst of their enemies; and as the Syrians were strangely amazed and distressed, as was but reasonable, at an action so Divine and surprising, and as king Joram asked the prophet if he would give him leave to shoot at them, Elisha forbade him so to do; and said, that "it is just to kill those that are taken in battle, but that these men had done the country no harm, but, without knowing it, were come thither by the Divine Power:"—so that his counsel was to treat them in a hospitable manner at his table, and then send them away without hurting them.[9] Wherefore Joram obeyed the prophet; and when he had feasted the Syrians in a splendid and magnificent manner, he let them go to Benhadad their king.

4. Now when these men were come back, and had showed Benhadad how strange an accident had befallen them, and what an appearance and power they had experienced of the God of Israel, he wondered at it, as also at that prophet with whom God was so evidently present; so he determined to make no more secret attempts upon the king of Israel, out of fear of Elisha, but resolved to make open war with them, as supposing he could be too hard for his enemies by the multitude of his army and power. So he made an expedition with a great army against Joram, who, not thinking himself a match for him, shut himself up in Samaria, and depended on the strength of its walls; but Benhadad supposed he should take the city, if not by his engines of war, yet that he should overcome the Samaritans by famine, and the want of necessaries, and brought his army upon them, and besieged the city; and the plenty of necessaries was brought so low with Joram, that from the extremity of want an ass's head was sold in Samaria

---

9. Upon occasion of this stratagem of Elisha, in Josephus, we may take notice, that although Josephus was one of the greatest lovers of truth in the world, yet in a just war he seems to have had no manner of scruple upon him by all such stratagems possible to deceive public enemies. See this Josephus's account of Jeremiah's imposition on the great men of the Jews in somewhat like case, Antiq. B. X. ch. 7. sect. 6; 2 Samuel 16:16, &c.

for fourscore pieces of silver, and the Hebrews bought a sextary of dore's dung, instead of salt, for five pieces of silver. Now Joram was in fear lest somebody should betray the city to the enemy, by reason of the famine, and went every day round the walls and the guards to see whether any such were concealed among them; and by being thus seen, and taking such care, he deprived them of the opportunity of contriving any such thing; and if they had a mind to do it, he, by this means, prevented them: but upon a certain woman's crying out, "Have pity on me, my lord," while he thought that she was about to ask for somewhat to eat, he imprecated God's curse upon her, and said he had neither thrashing-floor nor wine-press, whence he might give her any thing at her petition. Upon which she said she did not desire his aid in any such thing, nor trouble him about food, but desired that he would do her justice as to another woman. And when be bade her say on, and let him know what she desired, she said she had made an agreement with the other woman who was her neighbor and her friend, that because the famine and want was intolerable, they should kill their children, each of them having a son of their own, and we will live upon them ourselves for two days, the one day upon one son, and the other day upon the other; and," said she, I have killed my son the first day, and we lived upon my son yesterday; but this other woman will not do the same thing, but hath broken her agreement, and hath hid her son." This story mightily grieved Joram when he heard it; so he rent his garment, and cried out with a loud voice, and conceived great wrath against Elisha the prophet, and set himself eagerly to have him slain, because he did not pray to God to provide them some exit and way of escape out of the miseries with which they were surrounded; and sent one away immediately to cut off his head, who made haste to kill the prophet. But Elisha was not unacquainted with the wrath of the king against him; for as he sat in his house by himself, with none but his disciples about him, he told them that Joram,[10] who was the

---

10. This son of a murderer was Joram, the son of Ahab, which Ahab slew, or permitted his wife Jezebel to slay, the Lord's prophets, and Naboth, 1 Kings 18:4; 21:19; and he is here called by this name, I suppose, because he had now also himself sent an officer to murder him; yet is Josephus's account of Joram's coming himself at last. as repenting of his intended cruelty, much more probable than that in our copies, 2 Kings 6:33, which rather implies the contrary.

son of a murderer, had sent one to take away his head; "but," said he, "when he that is commanded to do this comes, take care that you do not let him come in, but press the door against him, and hold him fast there, for the king himself will follow him, and come to me, having altered his mind." Accordingly, they did as they were bidden, when he that was sent by the king to kill Elisha came. But Joram repented of his wrath against the prophet; and for fear he that was commanded to kill him should have done it before he came, he made haste to hinder his slaughter, and to save the prophet: and when he came to him, he accused him that he did not pray to God for their deliverance from the miseries they now lay under, but saw them so sadly destroyed by them. Hereupon Elisha promised, that the very next day, at the very same hour in which the king came to him, they should have great plenty of food, and that two seahs of barley should be sold in the market for a shekel, and a seah of fine flour should be sold for a shekel. This prediction made Joram, and those that were present, very joyful, for they did not scruple believing what the prophet said, on account of the experience they had of the truth of his former predictions; and the expectation of plenty made the want they were in that day, with the uneasiness that accompanied it, appear a light thing to them: but the captain of the third band, who was a friend of the king, and on whose hand the king leaned, said, "Thou talkest of incredible things, O prophet! for as it is impossible for God to pour down torrents of barley, or fine flour, out of heaven, so is it impossible that what thou sayest should come to pass." To which the prophet made this reply," Thou shalt see these things come to pass, but thou shalt not be in the least a partaker of them."

5. Now what Elisha had thus foretold came to pass in the manner following: There was a law at Samaria[11] that those that had the leprosy, and whose bodies were not cleansed from it, should abide without the city: and there were four men that on this account abode before the gates, while nobody gave them any food, by reason of the extremity of the famine; and as they were prohibited from entering into the city by the law, and they considered that if they were permitted to enter, they should miserably perish by the famine; as also, that if they staid where

---

11. This law of the Jews, for the exclusion of lepers out of the camp in the wilderness, and out of the cities in Judea, is a known one, Leviticus 13:46; Numbers 5:14.

they were, they should suffer in the same manner,—they resolved to deliver themselves up to the enemy, that in case they should spare them, they should live; but if they should be killed, that would be an easy death. So when they had confirmed this their resolution, they came by night to the enemy's camp. Now God had begun to affright and disturb the Syrians, and to bring the noise of chariots and armor to their ears, as though an army were coming upon them, and had made them suspect that it was coming nearer and nearer to them In short, they were in such a dread of this army, that they left their tents, and ran together to Benhadad, and said that Joram the king of Israel had hired for auxiliaries both the king of Egypt and the king of the Islands, and led them against them for they heard the noise of them as they were coming. And Benhadad believed what they said (for there came the same noise to his ears as well as it did to theirs); so they fell into a mighty disorder and tumult, and left their horses and beasts in their camp, with immense riches also, and betook themselves to flight. And those lepers who had departed from Samaria, and were gone to the camp of the Syrians, of whom we made mention a little before, when they were in the camp, saw nothing but great quietness and silence: accordingly they entered into it, and went hastily into one of their tents; and when they saw nobody there, they eat and drank, and carried garments, and a great quantity of gold, and hid it out of the camp; after which they went into another tent, and carried off what was in it, as they did at the former, and this did they for several times, without the least interruption from any body. So they gathered thereby that the enemies were departed; whereupon they reproached themselves that they did not inform Joram and the citizens of it. So they came to the walls of Samaria, and called aloud to the watchmen, and told them in what state the enemies were, as did these tell the king's guards, by whose means Joram came to know of it; who then sent for his friends, and the captains of his host, and said to them, that he suspected that this departure of the king of Syria was by way of ambush and treachery, and that out of despair of ruining you by famine, when you imagine them to be fled away, you may come out of the city to spoil their camp, and he may then fall upon you on a sudden, and may both kill you, and take the city without fighting; whence it is that I exhort you to guard the city carefully, and by no means to go out of it, or proudly to despise your enemies, as though they were really gone away." And when a certain person said that he did very well and wisely to admit such a suspicion, but that he still advised him to send a couple of horsemen to search all the country as far as Jordan, that "if they were seized by an ambush of the enemy, they might be a security to your army, that they may not go out as if they suspected nothing, nor undergo the like misfortune; and," said he, "those horsemen may be numbered among those that have died by the famine, supposing they be caught and destroyed by the enemy." So the king was pleased with this opinion, and sent such as might search out the truth, who performed their journey over a road that was without any enemies, but found it full of provisions, and of weapons, that they had therefore thrown away, and left behind them, in order to their being light and expeditious in their flight. When the king heard this, he sent out the multitude to take the spoils of the camp; which gains of theirs were not of things of small value, but they took a great quantity of gold, and a great quantity of silver, and flocks of all kinds of cattle. They also possessed themselves of [so many] ten thousand measures of wheat and barley, as they never in the least dreamed of; and were not only freed from their former miseries, but had such plenty, that two seahs of barley were bought for a shekel, and a seah of fine flour for a shekel, according to the prophecy of Elisha. Now a seah is equal to an Italian modius and a half. The captain of the third band was the only man that received no benefit by this plenty; for as he was appointed by the king to oversee the gate, that lm might prevent the too great crowd of the multitude, and they might not endanger one another to perish, by treading on one another in the press, he suffered himself in that very way, and died in that very manner, as Elisha had foretold such his death, when he alone of them all disbelieved what he said concerning that plenty of provisions which they should soon have.

6. Hereupon, when Benhadad, the king of Syria, had escaped to Damascus, and understood that it was God himself that cast all his army into this fear and disorder, and that it did not arise from the invasion of enemies, he was mightily cast down at his having God so greatly for his enemy, and fell into a distemper. Now it happened that Elisha the prophet, at that time, was gone out of his own country to Damascus, of which Berthadad was informed: he sent Hazael, the most faithful of all his servants, to meet him, and to carry him presents,

and bade him inquire of him about his distemper, and whether he should escape the danger that it threatened. So Hazael came to Elisha with forty camels, that carried the best and most precious fruits that the country of Damascus afforded, as well as those which the king's palace supplied. He saluted him kindly, and said that he was sent to him by king Berthadad, and brought presents with him, in order to inquire concerning his distemper, whether he should recover from it or not. Whereupon the prophet bid him tell the king no melancholy news; but still he said he would die. So the king's servant was troubled to hear it; and Elisha wept also, and his tears ran down plenteously at his foresight of what miseries his people would undergo after the death of Berthadad. And when Hazael asked him what was the occasion of this confusion he was in, he said that he wept out of his commiseration for the multitude of the Israelites, and what terrible miseries they will suffer by thee; "for thou wilt slay the strongest of them, and wilt burn their strongest cities, and wilt destroy their children, and dash them against the stones, and wilt rip up their women with child." And when Hazael said, "How can it be that I should have power enough to do such things?" the prophet replied, that God had informed him that he should be king of Syria. So when Hazael was come to Benhadad, he told him good news concerning his distemper[12] but on the next day he spread a wet cloth, in the nature of a net, over him, and strangled him, and took his dominion. He was an active man, and had the good-will of the Syrians, and of the people of Damascus, to a great degree; by whom both Benhadad himself, and Hazael, who ruled after him, are honored to this day as gods, by reason of their benefactions, and their building them temples by which they adorned the city of the Damascenes. They also every day do with great pomp pay their

---

12. Since Elijah did not live to anoint Hazael king of Syria himself, as he was empowered to do, 1 Kings 19:15, it was most probably now done, in his name, by his servant and successor Elisha. Nor does it seem to me otherwise but that Benhadad immediately recovered of his disease, as the prophet foretold; and that Hazael, upon his being anointed to succeed him though he ought to have staid till he died by the course of nature, or some other way of Divine punishment, as did David for many years in the like case, was too impatient, and the very next day smothered or strangled him, in order to come directly to the succession.

worship to these kings,[13] and value themselves upon their antiquity; nor do they know that these kings are much later than they imagine, and that they are not yet eleven hundred years old. Now when Joram, the king of Israel, heard that Berthadad was dead, he recovered out of the terror and dread he had been in on his account, and was very glad to live in peace.

5 Concerning the Wickedness of Jehoram King O Jerusalem; His Defeat and Death

1. Now Jehoram the king of Jerusalem, for we have said before that he had the same name with the king of Israel, as soon as he had taken the government upon him, betook himself to the slaughter of his brethren, and his father's friends, who were governors under him, and thence made a beginning and a demonstration of his wickedness; nor was he at all better than those kings of Israel who at first transgressed against the laws of their country, and of the Hebrews, and against God's worship. And it was Athaliah, the daughter of Ahab, whom he had married, who taught him to be a bad man in other respects, and also to worship foreign gods. Now God would not quite root out this family, because of the promise he had made to David. However, Jehoram did not leave off the introduction of new sorts of customs to the propagation of impiety, and to the ruin of the customs of his own country. And when the Edomites about that time had revolted from him, and slain their former king, who was in subjection to his father, and had set up one of their own choosing, Jehoram fell upon the land of Edom, with the horsemen that were about him, and the chariots,

---

13. What Mr. Le Clerc pretends here, that it is more probable that Hazael and his son were worshipped by the Syrians and people of Damascus till the days of Josephus, than Benhadad and Hazael, because under Benhadad they had greatly suffered, and because it is almost incredible that both a king and that king's murderer should be worshipped by the same Syrians, is of little force against those records, out of which Josephus drew this history, especially when it is likely that they thought Benhadad died of the distemper he labored under, and not by Hazael's treachery. Besides, the reason that Josephus gives for this adoration, that these two kings had been great benefactors to the inhabitants of Damascus, and had built them temples, is too remote from the political suspicions of Le Clerc; nor ought such weak suspicions to be deemed of any force against authentic testimonies of antiquity.

by night, and destroyed those that lay near to his own kingdom, but did not proceed further. However, this expedition did him no service, for they all revolted from him, with those that dwelt in the country of Libnah. He was indeed so mad as to compel the people to go up to the high places of the mountains, and worship foreign gods.

2. As he was doing this, and had entirely cast his own country laws out of his mind, there was brought him an epistle from Elijah the prophet[14] which declared that God would execute great judgments upon him, because he had not imitated his own fathers, but had followed the wicked courses of the kings of Israel; and had compelled the tribe of Judah, and the citizens of Jerusalem, to leave the holy worship of their own God, and to worship idols, as Ahab had compelled the Israelites to do, and because he had slain his brethren, and the men that were good and righteous. And the prophet gave him notice in this epistle what punishment he should undergo for these crimes, namely, the destruction of his people, with the corruption of the king's own wives and children; and that he should himself die of a distemper in his bowels, with long torments, those his bowels falling out by the violence of the inward rottenness of the parts, insomuch that, though he see his own misery, he shall not be able at all to help himself, but shall die in that manner. This it was which Elijah denounced to him in that epistle.

3. It was not long after this that an army of those Arabians that lived near to Ethiopia, and of the Philistines, fell upon the kingdom of Jehoram, and spoiled the country and the king's house. Moreover, they slew his sons and his wives: one only of his sons was left him, who escaped the enemy; his name was Ahaziah; after which calamity, he himself fell into that disease which was foretold by the prophet, and lasted a great while, (for God inflicted this punishment upon him in his belly, out of his wrath against him,) and so he died miserably, and saw his own bowels fall out. The people also abused his dead body; I

---

14. This epistle, in some copies of Josephus, is said to come to Jotare from Elijah, with this addition," for he was yet upon earth," which could not be true of Elijah, who, as all agree, was gone from the earth about four years before, and could only be true of Elisha; nor perhaps is there any more mystery here, than that the name of Elijah has very anciently crept into the text instead of Elisha, by the copiers, there being nothing in any copy of that epistle peculiar to Elijah.

suppose it was because they thought that such his death came upon him by the wrath of God, and that therefore he was not worthy to partake of such a funeral as became kings. Accordingly, they neither buried him in the sepulchers of his fathers, nor vouchsafed him any honors, but buried him like a private man, and this when he had lived forty years, and reigned eight. And the people of Jerusalem delivered the government to his son Ahaziah.

6   How Jehu Was Anointed King, and Slew Both Joram and Ahaziah; as Also What He Did for the Punishment of the Wicked

1. NOW Joram, the king of Israel, after the death of Benhadad, hoped that he might now take Ramoth, a city of Gilead, from the Syrians. Accordingly he made an expedition against it, with a great army; but as he was besieging it, an arrow was shot at him by one of the Syrians, but the wound was not mortal. So he returned to have his wound healed in Jezreel, but left his whole army in Ramorb, and Jehu, the son of Nimshi, for their general; for he had already taken the city by force; and he proposed, after he was healed,: to make war with the Syrians; but Elisha the prophet sent one of his disciples to Ramoth, and gave him holy oil to anoint Jehu, and to tell him that God had chosen him to be their king. He also sent him to say other things to him, and bid him to take his journey as if he fled, that when he came away he might escape the knowledge of all men. So when he was come to the city, he found Jehu sitting in the midst of the captains of the army, as Elisha had foretold he should find him. So he came up to him, and said that he desired to speak with him about certain matters; and when he was arisen, and had followed him into an inward chamber, the young man took the oil, and poured it on his head, and said that God ordained him to be king, in order to his destroying the house of Ahab, and that he might revenge the blood of the prophets that were unjustly slain by Jezebel, that so their house might utterly perish, as those of Jeroboam the son of Nebat, and of Baasha, had perished for their wickedness, and no seed might remain of Ahab's family. So when he had said this, he went away hastily out of the chamber, and endeavored not to be seen by any of the army.

2. But Jehu came out, and went to the place where he before sat with the captains; and when they asked him, and desired him to tell

them, wherefore it was that this young man came to him, and added withal that he was mad, he replied,—"You guess right, for the words he spake were the words of a madman;" and when they were eager about the matter, and desired he would tell them, he answered, that God had said he had chosen him to be king over the multitude. When he had said this, every one of them put off his garment,[15] and strewed it under him, and blew with trumpets, and gave notice that Jehu was king. So when he had gotten the army together, he was preparing to set out immediately against Joram, at the city Jezreel, in which city, as we said before, he was healing of the wound which he had received in the siege of Ramoth. It happened also that Ahaziah, king of Jerusalem, was now come to Joram, for he was his sister's son, as we have said already, to see how he did after his wound, and this upon account of their kindred; but as Jehu was desirous to fall upon Joram, and those with him, on the sudden, he desired that none of the soldiers might run away and tell to Joram what had happened, for that this would be an evident demonstration of their kindness to him, and would show that their real inclinations were to make him king.

3. So they were pleased with what he did, and guarded the roads, lest somebody should privately tell the thing to those that were at Jezreel. Now Jehu took his choice horsemen, and sat upon his chariot, and went on for Jezreel; and when he was come near, the watchman whom Joram had set there to spy out such as came to the city, saw Jehu marching on, and told Joram that he saw a troop of horsemen marching on. Upon which he immediately gave orders, that one of his horsemen should be sent out to meet them, and to know who it was that was coming. So when the horseman came up to Jehu, he asked him in what condition the army was, for that the king wanted to know it; but Jehu bid him not at all to meddle with such matters, but to follow him. When the watchman saw this, he told Joram that the horseman had mingled himself among the company, and came along with them. And when the king had sent a second messenger, Jehu commanded him to do as the former did; and as soon as the watchman told this also to Joram, he at last got upon his chariot himself, together with Ahaziah, the king of Jerusalem; for, as we said before, he was

---

15. Spanheim here notes, that this putting off men's garments, and strewing them under a king, was an Eastern custom, which he had elsewhere explained.

there to see how Joram did, after he had been wounded, as being his relation. So he went out to meet Jehu, who marched slowly,[16] and in good order; and when Joram met him in the field of Naboth, he asked him if all things were well in the camp; but Jehu reproached him bitterly, and ventured to call his mother a witch and a harlot. Upon this the king, fearing what he intended, and suspecting he had no good meaning, turned his chariot about as soon as he could, and said to Ahaziah, "We are fought against by deceit and treachery." But Jehu drew his bow, and smote him, the arrow going through his heart: so Joram fell down immediately on his knee, and gave up the ghost. Jehu also gave orders to Bidkar, the captain of the third part of his army, to cast the dead body of Joram into the field of Naboth, putting him in mind of the prophecy which Elijah prophesied to Ahab his father, when he had slain Naboth, that both he and his family should perish in that place; for that as they sat behind Ahab's chariot, they heard the prophet say so, and that it was now come to pass according to his prophecy. Upon the fall of Joram, Ahaziah was afraid of his own life, and turned his chariot into another road, supposing he should not be seen by Jehu; but he followed after him, and overtook him at a certain acclivity, and drew his bow, and wounded him; so he left his chariot, and got upon his horse, and fled from Jehu to Megiddo; and though he was under cure, in a little time he died of that wound, and was carried to Jerusalem, and buried there, after he had reigned one year, and had proved a wicked man, and worse than his father.

4. Now when Jehu was come to Jezreel, Jezebel adorned herself and stood upon a tower, and said, he was a fine servant that had killed his master! And when he looked up to her, he asked who she was, and commanded her to come down to him. At last he ordered the eunuchs to throw her down from the tower; and being thrown down, she be-sprinkled the wall with her blood, and was trodden upon by

---

16. Our copies say that this "driving of the chariots was like the driving of Jehu the son of Nimshi; for he driveth furiously," 2 Kings 9:20; whereas Josephus's copy, as he understood it, was this, that, on the contrary, Jehu marched slowly, and in good order. Nor can it be denied, that since there was interval enough for king Joram to send out two horsemen, one after another, to Jehu, and at length to go out with king Ahaziah to meet him, and all this after he was come within sight of the watchman, and before he was come to Jezreel, the probability is greatly on the side of Josephus's copy or interpretation.

the horses, and so died. When this was done, Jehu came to the palace with his friends, and took some refreshment after his journey, both with other things, and by eating a meal. He also bid his servants to take up Jezebel and bury her, because of the nobility of her blood, for she was descended from kings; but those that were appointed to bury her found nothing else remaining but the extreme parts of her body, for all the rest were eaten by dogs. When Jehu heard this, he admired the prophecy of Elijah, for he foretold that she should perish in this manner at Jezreel.

5. Now Ahab had seventy sons brought up in Samaria. So Jehu sent two epistles, the one to them that brought up the children, the other to the rulers of Samaria, which said, that they should set up the most valiant of Ahab's sons for king, for that they had abundance of chariots, and horses, and armor, and a great army, and fenced cities, and that by so doing they might avenge the murder of Ahab. This he wrote to try the intentions of those of Samaria. Now when the rulers, and those that had brought up the children, had read the letter, they were afraid; and considering that they were not at all able to oppose him, who had already subdued two very great kings, they returned him this answer: That they owned him for their lord, and would do whatsoever he bade them. So he wrote back to them such a reply as enjoined them to obey what he gave order for, and to cut off the heads of Ahab's sons, and send them to him. Accordingly the rulers sent for those that brought up the sons of Ahab, and commanded them to slay them, to cut off their heads, and send them to Jehu. So they did whatsoever they were commanded, without omitting any thing at all, and put them up in wicker baskets, and sent them to Jezreel. And when Jehu, as he was at supper with his friends, was informed that the heads of Ahab's' sons were brought, he ordered them to make two heaps of them, one before each of the gates; and in the morning he went out to take a view of them, and when he saw them, he began to say to the people that were present, that he did himself make an expedition against his master [Joram], and slew him, but that it was not he that slew all these; and he desired them to take notice, that as to Ahab's family, all things had come to pass according to God's prophecy, and his house was perished, according as Elijah had foretold. And when he had further destroyed all the kindred of Ahab that were found in Jezreel, he went to Samaria; and as he was upon the road,

he met the relations of Ahaziah king of Jerusalem, and asked them whither they were going? they replied, that they came to salute Joram, and their own king Ahaziah, for they knew not that he had slain them both. So Jehu gave orders that they should catch these, and kill them, being in number forty-two persons.

6. After these, there met him a good and a righteous man, whose name was Jehonadab, and who had been his friend of old. He saluted Jehu, and began to commend him, because he had done every thing according to the will of God, in extirpating the house of Ahab. So Jehu desired him to come up into his chariot, and make his entry with him into Samaria; and told him that he would not spare one wicked man, but would punish the false prophets, and false priests, and those that deceived the multitude, and persuaded them to leave the worship of God Almighty, and to worship foreign gods; and that it was a most excellent and most pleasing sight to a good and a righteous man to see the wicked punished. So Jehonadab was persuaded by these arguments, and came up into Jehu's chariot, and came to Samaria. And Jehu sought out for all Ahab's kindred, and slew them. And being desirous that none of the false prophets, nor the priests of Ahab's god, might escape punishment, he caught them deceitfully by this wile; for he gathered all the people together, and said that he would worship twice as many gods as Ahab worshipped, and desired that his priests, and prophets, and servants might be present, because he would offer costly and great sacrifices to Ahab's god; and that if any of his priests were wanting, they should be punished with death. Now Ahab's god was called Baal; and when he had appointed a day on which he would offer those sacrifices, he sent messengers through all the country of the Israelites, that they might bring the priests of Baal to him. So Jehu commanded to give all the priests vestments; and when they had received them, he went into the house [of Baal], with his friend Jehonadab, and gave orders to make search whether there were not any foreigner or stranger among them, for he would have no one of a different religion to mix among their sacred offices. And when they said that there was no stranger there, and they were beginning their sacrifices, he set fourscore men without, they being such of his soldiers as he knew to be most faithful to him, and bid them slay the prophets, and now vindicate the laws of their country, which had been a long time in disesteem. He also threatened, that if any one of them

---

escaped, their own lives should go for them. So they slew them all with the sword, and burnt the house of Baal, and by that means purged Samaria of foreign customs [idolatrous worship]. Now this Baal was the god of the Tyrians; and Ahab, in order to gratify his father-in-law, Ethbaal, who was the king of Tyre and Sidon, built a temple for him in Samaria, and appointed him prophets, and worshipped him with all sorts of worship, although, when this god was demolished, Jehu permitted the Israelites to worship the golden heifers. However, because he had done thus, and taken care to punish the wicked, God foretold by his prophet that his sons should reign over Israel for four generations. And in this condition was Jehu at this time.

7 *How Athaliah Reigned over Jerusalem for Five [Six] Years When Jehoiada the High Priest Slew Her and Made Jehoash, the Son of Ahaziah, King*

1. Now when Athaliah, the daughter of Ahab, heard of the death of her brother Joram, and of her son Ahaziah, and of the royal family, she endeavored that none of the house of David might be left alive, but that the whole family might be exterminated, that no king might arise out of it afterward; and, as she thought, she had actually done it; but one of Ahaziah's sons was preserved, who escaped death after the manner following: Ahaziah had a sister by the same father, whose name was Jehosheba, and she was married to the high priest Jehoiada. She went into the king's palace, and found Jehoash, for that was the little child's name, who was not above a year old, among those that were slain, but concealed with his nurse; so she took him with her into a secret bed-chamber, and shut him up there, and she and her husband Jehoiada brought him up privately in the temple six years, during which time Athaliah reigned over Jerusalem and the two tribes.

2. Now, on the Seventh year, Jehoiada communicated the matter to certain of the captains of hundreds, five in number, and persuaded them to be assisting to what attempts he was making against Athaliah, and to join with him in asserting the kingdom to the child. He also received such oaths from them as are proper to secure those that assist one another from the fear of discovery; and he was then of good hope that they should depose Athaliah. Now those men whom Jehoiada

the priest had taken to be his partners went into all the country, and gathered together the priests and the Levites, and the heads of the tribes out of it, and came and brought them to Jerusalem to the high priest. So he demanded the security of an oath of them, to keep private whatsoever he should discover to them, which required both their silence and their assistance. So when they had taken the oath, and had thereby made it safe for him to speak, he produced the child that he had brought up of the family of David, and said to them, "This is your king, of that house which you know God hath foretold should reign over you for all time to come. I exhort you therefore that one-third part of you guard him in the temple, and that a fourth part keep watch at all the gates of the temple, and that the next part of you keep guard at the gate which opens and leads to the king's palace, and let the rest of the multitude be unarmed in the temple, and let no armed person go into the temple, but the priest only." He also gave them this order besides, "That a part of the priests and the Levites should be about the king himself, and be a guard to him, with their drawn swords, and to kill that man immediately, whoever he be, that should be so bold as to enter armed into the temple; and bid them be afraid of nobody, but persevere in guarding the king." So these men obeyed what the high priest advised them to, and declared the reality of their resolution by their actions. Jehoiada also opened that armory which David had made in the temple, and distributed to the captains of hundreds, as also to the priests and Levites, all the spears and quivers, and what kind of weapons soever it contained, and set them armed in a circle round about the temple, so as to touch one another's hands, and by that means excluding those from entering that ought not to enter. So they brought the child into the midst of them, and put on him the royal crown, and Jehoiada anointed him with the oil, and made him king; and the multitude rejoiced, and made a noise, and cried, "God save the king!"

3. When Athaliah unexpectedly heard the tumult and the acclamations, she was greatly disturbed in her mind, and suddenly issued out of the royal palace with her own army; and when she was come to the temple, the priests received her; but as for those that stood round about the temple, as they were ordered by the high priest to do, they hindered the armed inert that followed her from going in. But when Athaliah saw the child standing upon a pillar, with the royal crown

upon his head, she rent her clothes, and cried out vehemently, and commanded [her guards] to kill him that had laid snares for her, and endeavored to deprive her of the government. But Jehoiada called for the captains of hundreds, and commanded them to bring Athaliah to the valley of Cedron, and slay her there, for he would not have the temple defiled with the punishments of this pernicious woman; and he gave order, that if any one came near to help her, he should be slain also; wherefore those that had the charge of her slaughter took hold of her, and led her to the gate of the king's mules, arid slew her there.

4. Now as soon as what concerned Athaliah was by this stratagem, after this manner, despatched, Jehoiada called together the people and the armed men into the temple, and made them take an oath that they would be obedient to the king, and take care of his safety, and of the safety of his government; after which he obliged the king to give security [upon oath] that he would worship God, and not transgress the laws of Moses. They then ran to the house of Baal, which Athaliah and her husband Jehoram had built, to the dishonor of the God of their fathers, and to the honor of Ahab, and demolished it, and slew Mattan, that had his priesthood. But Jehoiada intrusted the care and custody of the temple to the priests and Levites, according to the appointment of king David, and enjoined them to bring their regular burnt-offerings twice a day, and to offer incense according to the law. He also ordained some of the Levites, with the porters, to be a guard to the temple, that no one that was defiled might come there.

5. And when Jehoiada had set these things in order, he, with the captains of hundreds, and the rulers, and all the people, took Jehoash out of the temple into the king's palace; and when he had set him upon the king's throne, the people shouted for joy, and betook themselves to feasting, and kept a festival for many days; but the city was quiet upon the death of Athaliah. Now Jehoash was seven years old when he took the kingdom. His mother's name was Zibiah, of the city Beersheba. And all the time that Jehoiada lived Jehoash was careful that the laws should be kept, and very zealous in the worship of God; and when he was of age, he married two wives, who were given to him by the high priest, by whom were born to him both sons and daughters. And thus much shall suffice to have related concerning king Jehoash, how he escaped the treachery of Athaliah, and how he received the kingdom.

8   *Hazael Makes an Expedition Against the People of Israel and the*
     Inhabitants of Jerusalem. Jehu Dies, and Jehoahaz Succeeds in the
     Government. Jehoash the King of Jerusalem at First Is Careful
     About the Worship of God but Afterwards Becomes Impious and
     Commands Zechariah to Be Stoned. When Jehoash [King of Judah]
     Was Dead, Amaziah Succeeds Him in the Kingdom

1. NOW Hazael, king of Syria, fought against the Israelites and their
king Jehu, and spoiled the eastern parts of the country beyond Jordan,
which belonged to the Reubenites and Gadites, and to [the half tribe
of] Manassites; as also Gilead and Bashan, burning, and spoiling, and
offering violence to all that he laid his hands on, and this without
impeachment from Jehu, who made no haste to defend the country
when it was under this distress; nay, he was become a contemner of
religion, and a despiser of holiness, and of the laws, and died when he
had reigned over the Israelites twenty-seven years. He was buried in
Samaria, and left Jehoahaz his son his successor in the government.

2. Now Jehoash, king of Jerusalem, had an inclination to repair the
temple of God; so he called Jehoiada, and bid him send the Levites
and priests through all the country, to require half a shekel of silver
for every head, towards the rebuilding and repairing of the temple,
which was brought to decay by Jehoram, and Athaliah and her sons.
But the high priest did not do this, as concluding that no one would
willingly pay that money; but in the twenty-third year of Jehoash's
reign, when the king sent for him and the Levites, and complained
that they had not obeyed what he enjoined them, and still commanded
them to take care of the rebuilding the temple, he used this stratagem
for collecting the money, with which the multitude was pleased. He
made a wooden chest, and closed it up fast on all sides, but opened one
hole in it; he then set it in the temple beside the altar, and desired every
one to cast into it, through the hole, what he pleased, for the repair of
the temple. This contrivance was acceptable to the people, and they
strove one with another, and brought in jointly large quantities of
silver and gold; and when the scribe and the priest that were over
the treasuries had emptied the chest, and counted the money in the
king's presence, they then set it in its former place, and thus did they
every day. But when the multitude appeared to have cast in as much

as was wanted, the high priest Jehoiada, and king Joash, sent to hire masons and carpenters, and to buy large pieces of timber, and of the most curious sort; and when they had repaired the temple, they made use of the remaining gold and silver, which was not a little, for bowls, and basons, and cups, and other vessels, and they went on to make the altar every day fat with sacrifices of great value. And these things were taken suitable care of as long as Jehoiada lived.

3. But as soon as he was dead (which was when he had lived one hundred and thirty years, having been a righteous, and in every respect a very good man, and was buried in the king's sepulchers at Jerusalem, because he had recovered the kingdom to the family of David) king Jehoash betrayed his [want of] care about God. The principal men of the people were corrupted also together with him, and offended against their duty, and what their constitution determined to be most for their good. Hereupon God was displeased with the change that was made on the king, and on the rest of the people, and sent prophets to testify to them what their actions were, and to bring them to leave off their wickedness; but they had gotten such a strong affection and so violent an inclination to it, that neither could the examples of those that had offered affronts to the laws, and had been so severely punished, they and their entire families, nor could the fear of what the prophets now foretold, bring them to repentance, and turn them back from their course of transgression to their former duty. But the king commanded that Zechariah, the son of the high priest Jehoiada, should be stoned to death in the temple, and forgot the kindnesses he had received from his father; for when God had appointed him to prophesy, he stood in the midst of the multitude, and gave this counsel to them and to the king: That they should act righteously; and foretold to them, that if they would not hearken to his admonitions, they should suffer a heavy punishment. But as Zechariah was ready to die, he appealed to God as a witness of what he suffered for the good counsel he had given them, and how he perished after a most severe and violent manner for the good deeds his father had done to Jehoash.

4. However, it was not long before the king suffered punishment for his transgression; for when Hazael, king of Syria, made an irruption into his country, and when he had overthrown Gath, and spoiled it, he made an expedition against Jerusalem; upon which Jehoash was

afraid, and emptied all the treasures of God and of the kings [before him], and took down the gifts that had been dedicated [in the temple], and sent them to the king of Syria, and procured so much by them, that he was not besieged, nor his kingdom quite endangered; but Hazael was induced by the greatness of the sum of money not to bring his army against Jerusalem; yet Jehoash fell into a severe distemper, and was set upon by his friends, in order to revenge the death of Zechariah, the son of Jehoiada. These laid snares for the king, and slew him. He was indeed buried in Jerusalem, but not in the royal sepulchers of his forefathers, because of his impiety. He lived forty-seven years, and Amaziah his son succeeded him in the kingdom.

5. In the one and twentieth year of the reign of Jehoash, Jehoahaz, the son of Jehu, took the government of the Israelites in Samaria, and held it seventeen years. He did not [properly] imitate his father, but was guilty of as wicked practices as hose that first had God in contempt: but the king of Syria brought him low, and by an expedition against him did so greatly reduce his forces, that there remained no more of so great an army than ten thousand armed men, and fifty horsemen. He also took away from him his great cities, and many of them also, and destroyed his army. And these were the things that the people of Israel suffered, according to the prophecy of Elisha, when he foretold that Hazael should kill his master, and reign over the Syrians and Damcenes. But when Jehoahaz was under such unavoidable miseries, he had recourse to prayer and supplication to God, and besought him to deliver him out of the hands of Hazael, and not overlook him, and give him up into his hands. Accordingly God accepted of his repentance instead of virtue; and being desirous rather to admonish those that might repent, and not to determine that they should be utterly destroyed, he granted him deliverance from war and dangers. So the country having obtained peace, returned again to its former condition, and flourished as before.

6. Now after the death of Jehoahaz, his son Joash took the kingdom, in the thirty-seventh year of Jehoash, the king of the tribe of Judah. This Joash then took the kingdom of Israel in Samaria, for he had the same name with the king of Jerusalem, and he retained the kingdom

sixteen years. He was a good man,[17] and in his disposition was not at all like his father. Now at this time it was that when Elisha the prophet, who was already very old, and was now fallen into a disease, the king of Israel came to visit him; and when he found him very near death, he began to weep in his sight, and lament, to call him his father, and his weapons, because it was by his means that he never made use of his weapons against his enemies, but that he overcame his own adversaries by his prophecies, without fighting; and that he was now departing this life, and leaving him to the Syrians, that were already armed, and to other enemies of his that were under their power; so he said it was not safe for him to live any longer, but that it would be well for him to hasten to his end, and depart out of this life with him. As the king was thus bemoaning himself, Elisha comforted him, and bid the king bend a bow that was brought him; and when the king had fitted the bow for shooting, Elisha took hold of his hands and bid him shoot; and when he had shot three arrows, and then left off, Elisha said, "If thou hadst shot more arrows, thou hadst cut the kingdom of Syria up by the roots; but since thou hast been satisfied with shooting three times only, thou shalt fight and beat the Syrians no more times than three, that thou mayst recover that country which they cut off from thy kingdom in the reign of thy father." So when the king had heard that, he departed; and a little while after the prophet died. He was

---

17. This character of Joash, the son of Jehoahaz, that "he was a good man, and in his disposition not at all like to his father," seems a direct contradiction to our ordinary copies, which say (2 Kings 13:11) that "he did evil in the sight of the Lord; and that he departed not from all the sins of Jeroboam, the son of Nebat, who made Israel to sin: he walked therein." Which copies are here the truest it is hard positively to determine. If Josephus's be true, this Joash is the single instance of a good king over the ten tribes; if the other be true, we have not one such example. The account that follows, in all copies, of Elisha the prophet's concern for him, and his concern for Elisha, greatly favors Josephus's copies, and supposes this king to have been then a good man, and no idolater, with whom God's prophets used not to be so familiar. Upon the whole, since it appears, even by Josephus's own account, that Amaziah, the good king of Judah, while he was a good king, was forbidden to make use of the hundred thousand auxiliaries he had hired of this Joash, the king of Israel, as if he and they were then idolaters, 2 Chronicles 25:6–9, it is most likely that these different characters of Joash suited the different parts of his reign, and that, according to our common copies, he was at first a wicked king, and afterwards was reclaimed, and became a good one, according to Josephus.

a man celebrated for righteousness, and in eminent favor with God. He also performed wonderful and surprising works by prophecy, and such as were gloriously preserved in memory by the Hebrews. He also obtained a magnificent funeral, such a one indeed as it was fit a person so beloved of God should have. It also happened, that at that time certain robbers cast a man whom they had slain into Elisha's grave, and upon his dead body coming close to Elisha's body, it revived again. And thus far have we enlarged about the actions of Elisha the prophet, both such as he did while he was alive, and how he had a Divine power after his death also.

7. Now, upon the death of Hazael, the king of Syria, that kingdom came to Adad his son, with whom Joash, king of Israel, made war; and when he had beaten him in three battles, he took from him all that country, and all those cities and villages, which his father Hazael had taken from the kingdom of Israel, which came to pass, however, according to the prophecy of Elisha. But when Joash happened to die, he was buried in Samaria, and the government devolved on his son Jeroboam.

9 *How Amaziah Made an Expedition Against the Edomites and Amalekites and Conquered Them; but When He Afterwards Made War Against Joash, He Was Beaten and Not Long After Was Slain, and Uzziah Succeeded in the Government*

1. Now, in the second year of the reign of Joash over Israel, Amaziah reigned over the tribe of Judah in Jerusalem. His mother's name was Jehoaddan, who was born at Jerusalem. He was exceeding careful of doing what was right, and this when he was very young; but when he came to the management of affairs, and to the government, he resolved that he ought first of all to avenge his father Je-hoash, and to punish those his friends that had laid violent hands upon him: so he seized upon them all, and put them to death; yet did he execute no severity on their children, but acted therein according to the laws of Moses, who did not think it just to punish children for the sins of their fathers. After this he chose him an army out of the tribe of Judah and Benjamin, of such as were in the flower of their age, and about twenty years old; and when he had collected about three hundred thousand

of them together, he set captains of hundreds over them. He also sent
to the king of Israel, and hired a hundred thousand of his soldiers for
a hundred talents of silver, for he had resolved to make an expedition
against the nations of the Amatekites, and Edomites, and Gebalites:
but as he was preparing for his expedition, and ready to go out to the
war, a prophet gave him counsel to dismiss the army of the Israelites,
because they were bad men, and because God foretold that he should
be beaten, if he made use of them as auxiliaries; but that he should
overcome his enemies, though he had but a few soldiers, when it so
pleased God. And when the king grudged at his having already paid
the hire of the Israelites, the prophet exhorted him to do what God
would have him, because he should thereby obtain much wealth from
God. So he dismissed them, and said that he still freely gave them
their pay, and went himself with his own army, and made war with the
nations before mentioned; and when he had beaten them in battle, he
slew of them ten thousand, and took as many prisoners alive, whom
he brought to the great rock which is in Arabia, and threw them down
from it headlong. He also brought away a great deal of prey and vast
riches from those nations. But while Amaziah was engaged in this
expedition, those Israelites whom he had hired, and then dismissed,
were very uneasy at it, and taking their dismission for an affront, (as
supposing that this would not have been done to them but out of
contempt,) they fell upon his kingdom, and proceeded to spoil the
country as far as Beth-horon, and took much cattle, and slew three
thousand men.

2. Now upon the victory which Amaziah had gotten, and the great
acts he had done, he was puffed up, and began to overlook God, who
had given him the victory, and proceeded to worship the gods he had
brought out of the country of the Amalekites. So a prophet came to
him, and said, that he wondered how he could esteem these to be gods,
who had been of no advantage to their own people who paid them
honors, nor had delivered them from his hands, but had overlooked
the destruction of many of them, and had suffered themselves to
be carried captive, for that they had been carried to Jerusalem in
the same manner as any one might have taken some of the enemy
alive, and led them thither. This reproof provoked the king to anger,
and he commanded the prophet to hold his peace, and threatened to
punish him if he meddled with his conduct. So he replied, that he

should indeed hold his peace; but foretold withal, that God would not overlook his attempts for innovation. But Amaziah was not able to contain himself under that prosperity which God had given him, although he had affronted God thereupon; but in a vein of insolence he wrote to Joash, the king of Israel, and commanded that he and all his people should be obedient to him, as they had formerly been obedient to his progenitors, David and Solomon; and he let him know, that if he would not be so wise as to do what he commanded him, he must fight for his dominion. To which message Joash returned this answer in writing: "King Joash to king Amaziah. There was a vastly tall cypress tree in Mount Lebanon, as also a thistle; this thistle sent to the cypress tree to give the cypress tree's daughter in marriage to the thistle's son; but as the thistle was saying this, there came a wild beast, and trod down the thistle: and this may be a lesson to thee, not to be so ambitious, and to have a care, lest upon thy good success in the fight against the Amalekites thou growest so proud, as to bring dangers upon thyself and upon thy kingdom."

3. When Amaziah had read this letter, he was more eager upon this expedition, which, I suppose, was by the impulse of God, that he might be punished for his offense against him. But as soon as he led out his army against Joash, and they were going to join battle with him, there came such a fear and consternation upon the army of Amaziah, as God, when he is displeased, sends upon men, and discomfited them, even before they came to a close fight. Now it happened, that as they were scattered about by the terror that was upon them, Amaziah was left alone, and was taken prisoner by the enemy; whereupon Joash threatened to kill him, unless he would persuade the people of Jerusalem to open their gates to him, and receive him and his army into the city. Accordingly Amaziah was so distressed, and in such fear of his life, that he made his enemy to be received into the city. So Joash over threw a part of the wall, of the length of four hundred cubits, and drove his chariot through the breach into Jerusalem, and led Amaziah captive along with him; by which means he became master of Jerusalem, and took away the treasures of God, and carried off all the gold and silver that was in the king's palace, and then freed the king from captivity, and returned to Samaria. Now these things happened to the people of Jerusalem in the fourteenth year of the reign of Amaziah, who after this had a conspiracy made against him

by his friends, and fled to the city Lachish, and was there slain by the conspirators, who sent men thither to kill him. So they took up his dead body, and carried it to Jerusalem, and made a royal funeral for him. This was the end of the life of Amaziah, because of his innovations in religion, and his contempt of God, when he had lived fifty-four years, and had reigned twenty-nine. He was succeeded by his son, whose name was Uzziah.

10 Concerning Jeroboam King of Israel and Jonah the Prophet; and How After the Death of Jeroboam His Son Zachariah Took the Government. How Uzziah, King of Jerusalem, Subdued the Nations That Were Round About Him; and What Befell Him When He Attempted to Offer Incense to God

1. IN the fifteenth year of the reign of Amaziah, Jeroboam the son of Joash reigned over Israel in Samaria forty years. This king was guilty of contumely against God,[18] and became very wicked in worshipping of idols, and in many undertakings that were absurd and foreign. He was also the cause of ten thousand misfortunes to the people of Israel. Now one Jonah, a prophet, foretold to him that he should make war with the Syrians, and conquer their army, and enlarge the bounds of his kingdom on the northern parts to the city Hamath, and on the southern to the lake Asphaltitis; for the bounds of the Canaanites originally were these, as Joshua their general had determined them. So Jeroboam made an expedition against the Syrians, and overran all their country, as Jonah had foretold.

2. Now I cannot but think it necessary for me, who have promised to give an accurate account of our affairs, to describe the actions of

---

18. What I have above noted concerning Jehoash, seems to me to have been true also concerning his son Jeroboam II., viz. that although he began wickedly, as Josephus agrees with our other copies, and, as he adds, "was the cause of a vast number of misfortunes to the Israelites" in those his first years, (the particulars of which are unhappily wanting both in Josephus and in all our copies,) so does it seem to me that he was afterwards reclaimed, and became a good king, and so was encouraged by the prophet Jonah, and had great successes afterward, when "God had saved the Israelites by the hand of Jeroboam, the son of Joash," 2 Kings 14:27; which encouragement by Jonah, and great successes, are equally observable in Josephus, and in the other copies.

this prophet, so far as I have found them written down in the Hebrew books. Jonah had been commanded by God to go to the kingdom of Nineveh; and when he was there, to publish it in that city, how it should lose the dominion it had over the nations. But he went not, out of fear; nay, he ran away from God to the city of Joppa, and finding a ship there, he went into it, and sailed to Tarsus, in Cilicia[19] and upon the rise of a most terrible storm, which was so great that the ship was in danger of sinking, the mariners, the master, and the pilot himself, made prayers and vows, in case they escaped the sea: but Jonah lay still and covered [in the ship,] without imitating any thing that the others did; but as the waves grew greater, and the sea became more violent by the winds, they suspected, as is usual in such cases, that some one of the persons that sailed with them was the occasion of this storm, and agreed to discover by lot which of them it was. When they had cast lots,[20] the lot fell upon the prophet; and when they asked him whence he came, and what he had done? he replied, that he was a Hebrew by nation, and a prophet of Almighty God; and he persuaded them to cast him into the sea, if they would escape the danger they were in, for that he was the occasion of the storm which was upon them. Now at the first they durst not do so, as esteeming it a wicked thing to cast a man who was a stranger, and who had committed his life to them, into such manifest perdition; but at last, when their

---

19. When Jonah is said in our Bibles to have gone to Tarshish, Jonah 1:3, Josephus understood it that he went to Tarsus in Cilicia, or to the Mediterranean Sea, upon which Tarsus lay; so that he does not appear to have read the text, 1 Kings 22:48, as our copies do, that ships of Tarshish could lie at Ezion-geber, upon the Red Sea. But as to Josephus's assertion, that Jonah's fish was carried by the strength of the current, upon a nean, it is by no means an improbable determination in Josephus.

20. This ancient piece of religion, of supposing there was great sin where there was great misery, and of casting lots to discover great sinners, not only among the Israelites, but among these heathen mariners, seems a remarkable remains of the ancient tradition which prevailed of old over all mankind, that I Providence used to interpose visibly in all human affairs, and storm, as far as the Euxine Sea, it is no way impossible; and since the storm might have driven the ship, while Jonah was in it never to bring, or at least not long to continue, notorious judge, near to that Euxine Sea, and since in three more days, while but for notorious sins, which the most ancient Book of he was in the fish's belly, that current might bring him to the Job shows to have been the state of mankind for about the Assyrian coast, and since withal that coast could bring him former three thousand years of the world, till the days of Job nearer to Nineveh than could any coast of the Mediterranian and Moses.

misfortune overbore them, and the ship was just going to be drowned, and when they were animated to do it by the prophet himself, and by the fear concerning their own safety, they cast him into the sea; upon which the sea became calm. It is also reported that Jonah was swallowed down by a whale, and that when he had been there three days, and as many nights, he was vomited out upon the Euxine Sea, and this alive, and without any hurt upon his body; and there, on his prayer to God, he obtained pardon for his sins, and went to the city Nineveh, where he stood so as to be heard, and preached, that in a very little time they should lose the dominion of Asia. And when he had published this, he returned. Now I have given this account about him as I found it written [in our books.]

3. When Jeroboam the king had passed his life in great happiness, and had ruled forty years, he died, and was buried in Samaria, and his son Zachariah took the kingdom. After the same manner did Uzziah, the son of Amaziah, begin to reign over the two tribes in Jerusalem, in the fourteenth year of the reign of Jeroboam. He was born of Jecoliah, his mother, who was a citizen of Jerusalem. He was a good man, and by nature righteous and magnanimous, and very laborious in taking care of the affairs of his kingdom. He made an expedition also against the Philistines, and overcame them in battle, and took the cities of Gath and Jabneh, and brake down their walls; after which expedition he assaulted those Arabs that adjoined to Egypt. He also built a city upon the Red Sea, and put a garrison into it. He, after this, overthrew the Ammonites, and appointed that they should pay tribute. He also overcame all the countries as far as the bounds of Egypt, and then began to take care of Jerusalem itself for the rest of his life; for he rebuilt and repaired all those parts of the wall which had either fallen down by length of time, or by the carelessness of the kings, his predecessors, as well as all that part which had been thrown down by the king of Israel, when he took his father Amaziah prisoner, and entered with him into the city. Moreover, he built a great many towers, of one hundred and fifty cubits high, and built walled towns in desert places, and put garrisons into them, and dug many channels for conveyance of water. He had also many beasts for labor, and an immense number of cattle; for his country was fit for pasturage. He was also given to husbandry, and took care to cultivate the ground, and planted it with all sorts of plants, and sowed it with all sorts of

seeds. He had also about him an army composed of chosen men, in number three hundred and seventy thousand, who were governed by general officers and captains of thousands, who were men of valor, and of unconquerable strength, in number two thousand. He also divided his whole army into bands, and armed them, giving every one a sword, with brazen bucklers and breastplates, with bows and slings; and besides these, he made for them many engines of war for besieging of cities, such as cast stones and darts, with grapplers, and other instruments of that sort.

4. While Uzziah was in this state, and making preparation [for futurity], he was corrupted in his mind by pride, and became insolent, and this on account of that abundance which he had of things that will soon perish, and despised that power which is of eternal duration (which consisted in piety towards God, and in the observation of the laws); so he fell by occasion of the good success of his affairs, and was carried headlong into those sins of his father, which the splendor of that prosperity he enjoyed, and the glorious actions he had done, led him into, while he was not able to govern himself well about them. Accordingly, when a remarkable day was come, and a general festival was to be celebrated, he put on the holy garment, and went into the temple to offer incense to God upon the golden altar, which he was prohibited to do by Azariah the high priest, who had fourscore priests with him, and who told him that it was not lawful for him to offer sacrifice, and that "none besides the posterity of Aaron were permitted so to do." And when they cried out that he must go out of the temple, and not transgress against God, he was wroth at them, and threatened to kill them, unless they would hold their peace. In the mean time a great earthquake shook the ground[21] and a rent was made in the temple, and the bright rays of the sun shone through it, and fell upon the king's face, insomuch that the leprosy seized upon him immediately. And before the city, at a place called Eroge, half

---

21. This account of an earthquake at Jerusalem at the very same time when Uzziah usurped the priest's office, and went into the sanctuary to burn incense, and of the consequences of the earthquake, is entirely wanting in our other copies, though it be exceeding like to a prophecy of Jeremiah, now in Zechariah 14:4, 5; in which prophecy mention is made of "fleeing from that earthquake, as they fled from this earthquake in the days of Uzziah king of Judah;" so that there seems to have been some considerable resemblance between these historical and prophetical earthquakes.

the mountain broke off from the rest on the west, and rolled itself four furlongs, and stood still at the east mountain, till the roads, as well as the king's gardens, were spoiled by the obstruction. Now, as soon as the priests saw that the king's face was infected with the leprosy, they told him of the calamity he was under, and commanded that he should go out of the city as a polluted person. Hereupon he was so confounded at the sad distemper, and sensible that he was not at liberty to contradict, that he did as he was commanded, and underwent this miserable and terrible punishment for an intention beyond what befitted a man to have, and for that impiety against God which was implied therein. So he abode out of the city for some time, and lived a private life, while his son Jotham took the government; after which he died with grief and anxiety at what had happened to him, when he had lived sixty-eight years, and reigned of them fifty-two; and was buried by himself in his own gardens.

11 *How Zachariah Shallum, Menahem Pekahiah and Pekah Took the Government over the Israelites; and How Pul and Tiglath-Pileser Made an Expedition Against the Israelites. How Jotham, the Son of Uzziah Reigned over the Tribe of Judah; and What Things Nahum Prophesied Against the Assyrians*

1. Now when Zachariah, the son of Jeroboam, had reigned six months over Israel, he was slain by the treachery of a certain friend of his, whose name was Shallum, the son of Jabesh, who took the kingdom afterward, but kept it no longer than thirty days; for Menahem, the general of his army, who was at that time in the city Tirzah, and heard of what had befallen Zachariah, removed thereupon with all his forces to Samaria, and joining battle with Shallum, slew him; and when he had made himself king, he went thence, and came to the city Tiphsah; but the citizens that were in it shut their gates, and barred them against the king, and would not admit him: but in order to be avenged on them, he burnt the country round about it, and took the city by force, upon a siege; and being very much displeased at what the inhabitants of Tiphsah had done, he slew them all, and spared not so much as the infants, without omitting the utmost instances of cruelty and barbarity; for he used such severity upon his own countrymen, as would not

be pardonable with regard to strangers who had been conquered by him. And after this manner it was that this Menahem continued to reign with cruelty and barbarity for ten years. But when Pul, king of Assyria, had made an expedition against him, he did not think meet to fight or engage in battle with the Assyrians, but he persuaded him to accept of a thousand talents of silver, and to go away, and so put an end to the war. This sum the multitude collected for Menahem, by exacting fifty drachme as poll-money for every head;[22] after which he died, and was buried in Samaria, and left his son Pekahiah his successor in the kingdom, who followed the barbarity of his father, and so ruled but two years only, after which he was slain with his friends at a feast, by the treachery of one Pekah, the general of his horse, and the son of Remaliah, who laid snares for him. Now this Pekah held the government twenty years, and proved a wicked man and a transgressor. But the king of Assyria, whose name was Tiglath-Pileser, when he had made an expedition against the Israelites, and had overrun all the land of Gilead, and the region beyond Jordan, and the adjoining country, which is called Galilee, and Kadesh, and Hazor, he made the inhabitants prisoners, and transplanted them into his own kingdom. And so much shall suffice to have related here concerning the king of Assyria.

2. Now Jotham the son of Uzziah reigned over the tribe of Judah in Jerusalem, being a citizen thereof by his mother, whose name was Jerusha. This king was not defective in any virtue, but was religious towards God, and righteous towards men, and careful of the good of the city (for what part soever wanted to be repaired or adorned he magnificently repaired and adorned them). He also took care of the foundations of the cloisters in the temple, and repaired the walls that were fallen down, and built very great towers, and such as were

---

22. Dr. Wall, in his critical notes on 2 Kings 15:20, observes, "that when this Menahem is said to have exacted the money of Israel of all the mighty men of wealth, of each man fifty shekels of silver, to give Pul, the king of Assyria, a thousand talents, this is the first public money raised by any [Israelite] king by tax on the people; that they used before to raise it out of the treasures of the house of the Lord, or of their own house; that it was a poll-money on the rich men, [and them only,] to raise £353,000, or, as others count a talent, £400,000, at the rate of £6 or £7 per head; and that God commanded, by Ezekiel, ch. 45:8; 46:18, that no such thing should be done [at the Jews' restoration], but the king should have land of his own."

almost impregnable; and if any thing else in his kingdom had been neglected, he took great care of it. He also made an expedition against the Ammonites, and overcame them in battle, and ordered them to pay tribute, a hundred talents, and ten thousand cori of wheat, and as many of barley, every year, and so augmented his kingdom, that his enemies could not despise it, and his own people lived happily.

3. Now there was at that time a prophet, whose name was Nahum, who spake after this manner concerning the overthrow of the Assyrians and of Nineveh: "Nineveh shall be a pool of water in motion[23] so shall all her people be troubled, and tossed, and go away by flight, while they say one to another, Stand, stand still, seize their gold and silver, for there shall be no one to wish them well, for they will rather save their lives than their money; for a terrible contention shall possess them one with another, and lamentation, and loosing of the members, and their countenances shall be perfectly black with fear. And there will be the den of the lions, and the mother of the young lions! God says to thee, Nineveh, that they shall deface thee, and the lion shall no longer go out from thee to give laws to the world." And indeed this prophet prophesied many other things besides these concerning Nineveh, which I do not think necessary to repeat, and I here omit them, that I may not appear troublesome to my readers; all which thing happened about Nineveh a hundred and fifteen years afterward: so this may suffice to have spoken of these matters.

---

23. This passage is taken out of the prophet Nahum, ch. 2:8–13, and is the principal, or rather the only, one that is given us almost verbatim, but a little abridged, in all Josephus's known writings: by which quotation we learn what he himself always asserts, viz. that he made use of the Hebrew original and not of the Greek version]; as also we learn, that his Hebrew copy considerably differed from ours. See all three texts particularly set down and compared together in the Essay on the Old Testament, page 187.

*12 How Upon the Death of Jotham, Ahaz Reigned in His Stead;
Against Whom Rezin, King of Syria and Pekah King of Israel,
Made War; and How Tiglath-Pileser, King of Assyria Came to
the Assistance of Ahaz, and Laid Syria Waste and Removing the
Damascenes into Media Placed Other Nations in Their Room*

1. NOW Jotham died when he had lived forty-one years, and of them
reigned sixteen, and was buried in the sepulchers of the kings; and the
kingdom came to his son Ahaz, who proved most impious towards
God, and a transgressor of the laws of his country. He imitated the
kings of Israel, and reared altars in Jerusalem, and offered sacrifices
upon them to idols; to which also he offered his own son as a burnt-
offering, according to the practices of the Canaanites. His other actions
were also of the same sort. Now as he was going on in this mad course,
Rezin, the king of Syria and Damascus, and Pekah, the king of Israel,
who were now at amity one with another, made war with him; and
when they had driven him into Jerusalem, they besieged that city a
long while, making but a small progress, on account of the strength of
its walls; and when the king of Syria had taken the city Elath, upon the
Red Sea, and had slain the inhabitants, he peopled it with Syrians; and
when he had slain those in the [other] garrisons, and the Jews in their
neighborhood, and had driven away much prey, he returned with his
army back to Damascus. Now when the king of Jerusalem knew that
the Syrians were returned home, he, supposing himself a match for the
king of Israel, drew out his army against him, and joining battle with
him was beaten; and this happened because God was angry with him,
on account of his many and great enormities. Accordingly there were
slain by the Israelites one hundred and twenty thousand of his men
that day, whose general, Amaziah by name, slew Zechariah the king's
son, in his conflict with Ahaz, as well as the governor of the kingdom,
whose name was Azricam. He also carried Elkanah, the general of the
troops of the tribe of Judah, into captivity. They also carried the women
and children of the tribe of Benjamin captives; and when they had
gotten a great deal of prey, they returned to Samaria.

2. Now there was one Obed, who was a prophet at that time in
Samaria; he met the army before the city walls, and with a loud
voice told them that they had gotten the victory not by their own
strength, but by reason of the anger God had against king Ahaz. And

he complained that they were not satisfied with the good success they had had against him, but were so bold as to make captives out of their kinsmen the tribes of Judah and Benjamin. He also gave them counsel to let them go home without doing them any harm, for that if they did not obey God herein, they should be punished. So the people of Israel came together to their assembly, and considered of these matters, when a man whose name was Berechiah, and who was one of chief reputation in the government, stood up, and the others with him, and said, "We will not suffer the citizens to bring these prisoners into the city, lest we be all destroyed by God; we have sins enough of our own that we have committed against him, as the prophets assure us; nor ought we therefore to introduce the practice of new crimes." When the soldiers heard that, they permitted them to do what they thought best. So the forenamed men took the captives, and let them go, and took care of them, and gave them provisions, and sent them to their own country, without doing them any harm. However, these four went along with them, and conducted them as far as Jericho, which is not far from Jerusalem, and returned to Samaria.

3. Hereupon king Ahaz, having been so thoroughly beaten by the Israelites, sent to Tiglath-Pileser, king of the Assyrians, and sued for assistance from him in his war against the Israelites, and Syrians, and Damascenes, with a promise to send him much money; he sent him also great presents at the same time. Now this king, upon the reception of those ambassadors, came to assist Ahaz, and made war upon the Syrians, and laid their country waste, and took Damascus by force, and slew Rezin their king, and transplanted the people of Damascus into the Upper Media, and brought a colony of Assyrians, and planted them in Damascus. He also afflicted the land of Israel, and took many captives out of it. While he was doing thus with the Syrians, king Ahaz took all the gold that was in the king's treasures, and the silver, and what was in the temple of God, and what precious gifts were there, and he carried them with him, and came to Damascus, and gave it to the king of Assyria, according to his agreement. So he confessed that he owed him thanks for all he had done for him, and returned to Jerusalem. Now this king was so sottish and thoughtless of what was for his own good, that he would not leave off worshipping the Syrian gods when he was beaten by them, but he went on in worshipping them, as though they would procure him the victory;

and when he was beaten again, he began to honor the gods of the Assyrians; and he seemed more desirous to honor any other gods than his own paternal and true God, whose anger was the cause of his defeat; nay, he proceeded to such a degree of despite and contempt [of God's worship], that he shut up the temple entirely, and forbade them to bring in the appointed sacrifices, and took away the gifts that had been given to it. And when he had offered these indignities to God, he died, having lived thirty-six years, and of them reigned sixteen; and he left his son Hezekiah for his successor.

13 How Pekah Died by the Treachery of Hoshea Who Was a Little After Subdued by Shalmaneser; and How Hezekiah Reigned Instead of Ahaz; and What Actions of Piety and Justice He Did

1. ABOUT the same time Pekah, the king of Israel, died by the treachery of a friend of his, whose name was Hoshea, who retained the kingdom nine years' time, but was a wicked man, and a despiser of the Divine worship; and Shalmaneser, the king of Assyria, made an expedition against him, and overcame him, (which must have been because he had not God favorable nor assistant to him,) and brought him to submission, and ordered him to pay an appointed tribute. Now, in the fourth year of the reign of Hoshea, Hezekiah, the son of Ahaz, began to reign in Jerusalem; and his mother's name was Abijah, a citizen of Jerusalem. His nature was good, and righteous, and religious; for when he came to the kingdom, he thought that nothing was prior, or more necessary, or more advantageous to himself, and to his subjects, than to worship God. Accordingly, he called the people together, and the priests, and the Levites, and made a speech to them, and said, "You are not ignorant how, by the sins of my father, who transgressed that sacred honor which was due to God, you have had experience of many and great miseries, while you were corrupted in your mind by him, and were induced to worship those which he supposed to be gods; I exhort you, therefore, who have learned by sad experience how dangerous a thing impiety is, to put that immediately out of your memory, and to purify yourselves from your former pollutions, and to open the temple to these priests and Levites who are here convened, and to cleanse it with the accustomed sacrifices,

and to recover all to the ancient honor which our fathers paid to it; for by this means we may render God favorable, and he will remit the anger he hath had to us."

2. When the king had said this, the priests opened the temple; and when they had set in order the vessels of God, and east out what was impure, they laid the accustomed sacrifices upon the altar. The king also sent to the country that was under him, and called the people to Jerusalem to celebrate the feast of unleavened bread, for it had been intermitted a long time, on account of the wickedness of the forementioned kings. He also sent to the Israelites, and exhorted them to leave off their present way of living, and return to their ancient practices, and to worship God, for that he gave them leave to come to Jerusalem, and to celebrate, all in one body, the feast of unleavened bread; and this he said was by way of invitation only, and to be done of their own good-will, and for their own advantage, and not out of obedience to him, because it would make them happy. But the Israelites, upon the coming of the ambassadors, and upon their laying before them what they had in charge from their own king, were so far from complying therewith, that they laughed the ambassadors to scorn, and mocked them as fools: as also they affronted the prophets, which gave them the same exhortations, and foretold what they would suffer if they did not return to the worship of God, insomuch that at length they caught them, and slew them; nor did this degree of transgressing suffice them, but they had more wicked contrivances than what have been described: nor did they leave off, before God, as a punishment for their impiety, brought them under their enemies: but of that more hereafter. However, many there were of the tribe of Manasseh, and of Zebulon, and of Issachar, who were obedient to what the prophets exhorted them to do, and returned to the worship of God. Now all these came running to Jerusalem, to Hezekiah, that they might worship God [there].

3. When these men were come, king Hezekiah went up into the temple, with the rulers and all the people, and offered for himself seven bulls, and as many rams, with seven lambs, and as many kids of the goats. The king also himself, and the rulers, laid their hands on the heads of the sacrifices, and permitted the priests to complete the sacred offices about them. So they both slew the sacrifices, and burnt the burnt-offerings, while the Levites stood round about them,

with their musical instruments, and sang hymns to God, and played on their psalteries, as they were instructed by David to do, and this while the rest of the priests returned the music, and sounded the trumpets which they had in their hands; and when this was done, the king and the multitude threw themselves down upon their face, and worshipped God. He also sacrificed seventy bulls, one hundred rams, and two hundred lambs. He also granted the multitude sacrifices to feast upon, six hundred oxen, and three thousand other cattle; and the priests performed all things according to the law. Now the king was so pleased herewith, that he feasted with the people, and returned thanks to God; but as the feast of unleavened bread was now come, when they had offered that sacrifice which is called the passover, they after that offered other sacrifices for seven days. When the king had bestowed on the multitude, besides what they sanctified of themselves, two thousand bulls, and seven thousand other cattle, the same thing was done by the rulers; for they gave them a thousand bulls, and a thousand and forty other cattle. Nor had this festival been so well observed from the days of king Solomon, as it was now first observed with great splendor and magnificence; and when the festival was ended, they went out into the country and purged it, and cleansed the city of all the pollution of the idols. The king also gave order that the daily sacrifices should be offered, at his own charges, and according to the law; and appointed that the tithes and the first-fruits should be given by the multitude to the priests and Levites, that they might constantly attend upon Divine service, and never be taken off from the worship of God. Accordingly, the multitude brought together all sorts of their fruits to the priests and the Levites. The king also made garners and receptacles for these fruits, and distributed them to every one of the priests and Levites, and to their children and wives; and thus did they return to their old form of Divine worship. Now when the king had settled these matters after the manner already described, he made war upon the Philistines, and beat them, and possessed himself of all the enemy's cities, from Gaza to Gath; but the king of Assyria sent to him, and threatened to overturn all his dominions, unless he would pay him the tribute which his father paid him formerly; but king Hezekiah was not concerned at his threatenings, but depended on his piety towards God, and upon Isaiah the prophet, by whom he inquired and accurately knew all future events. And thus much shall suffice for the present concerning this king Hezekiah.

14 *How Shalmaneser Took Samaria by Force and How He Transplanted the Ten Tribes into Media, and Brought the Nation of the Cutheans into Their Country [in Their Room]*

1. WHEN Shalmaneser, the king of Assyria, had it told him, that [Hoshea] the king of Israel had sent privately to So, the king of Egypt, desiring his assistance against him, he was very angry, and made an expedition against Samaria, in the seventh year of the reign of Hoshea; but when he was not admitted [into the city] by the king,[24] he besieged Samaria three years, and took it by force in the ninth year of the reign of Hoshea, and in the seventh year of Hezekiah, king of Jerusalem, and quite demolished the government of the Israelites, and transplanted all the people into Media and Persia among whom he took king Hoshea alive; and when he had removed these people out of this their land he transplanted other nations out of Cuthah, a place so called, (for there is [still] a river of that name in Persia,) into Samaria, and into the country of the Israelites. So the ten tribes of the Israelites were removed out of Judea nine hundred and forty-seven years after their forefathers were come out of the land of Egypt, and possessed themselves of the country, but eight hundred years after Joshua had been their leader, and, as I have already observed, two hundred and forty years, seven months, and seven days after they had revolted from Rehoboam, the grandson of David, and had given the kingdom to Jeroboam. And such a conclusion overtook the Israelites, when they had transgressed the laws, and would not hearken to the prophets, who foretold that this calamity would come upon them, if they would not leave off their evil doings. What gave birth to these evil doings, was that sedition

---

24. This siege of Samaria, though not given a particular account of, either in our Hebrew or Greek Bibles, or in Josephus, was so very long, no less than three years, that it was no way improbable but that parents, and particularly mothers, might therein be reduced to eat their own children, as the law of Moses had threatened upon their disobedience, Leviticus 26;29; Deuteronomy 28:53–57; and as was accomplished in the other shorter sieges of both the capital cities, Jerusalem and Samaria; the former mentioned Jeremiah 19:9; Antiq. B. IX. ch. 4. sect. 4, and the latter, 2 Kings 6:26–29.

which they raised against Rehoboam, the grandson of David, when they set up Jeroboam his servant to be their king, when, by sinning against God, and bringing them to imitate his bad example, made God to be their enemy, while Jeroboam underwent that punishment which he justly deserved.

2. And now the king of Assyria invaded all Syria and Phoenicia in a hostile manner. The name of this king is also set down in the archives of Tyre, for he made an expedition against Tyre in the reign of Eluleus; and Menander attests to it, who, when he wrote his Chronology, and translated the archives of Tyre into the Greek language, gives us the following history: "One whose name was Eluleus reigned thirty-six years; this king, upon the revolt of the Citteans, sailed to them, and reduced them again to a submission. Against these did the king of Assyria send an army, and in a hostile manner overrun all Phoenicia, but soon made peace with them all, and returned back; but Sidon, and Ace, and Palsetyrus revolted; and many other cities there were which delivered themselves up to the king of Assyria. Accordingly, when the Tyrians would not submit to him, the king returned, and fell upon them again, while the Phoenicians had furnished him with threescore ships, and eight hundred men to row them; and when the Tyrians had come upon them in twelve ships, and the enemy's ships were dispersed, they took five hundred men prisoners, and the reputation of all the citizens of Tyre was thereby increased; but the king of Assyria returned, and placed guards at their rivers and aqueducts, who should hinder the Tyrians from drawing water. This continued for five years; and still the Tyrians bore the siege, and drank of the water they had out of the wells they dug." And this is what is written in the Tyrian archives concerning Shalmaneser, the king of Assyria.

3. But now the Cutheans, who removed into Samaria, (for that is the name they have been called by to this time, because they were brought out of the country called Cuthah, which is a country of Persia, and there is a river of the same name in it,) each of them, according to their nations, which were in number five, brought their own gods into Samaria, and by worshipping them, as was the custom of their own countries, they provoked Almighty God to be angry and displeased at them, for a plague seized upon them, by which they were destroyed; and when they found no cure for their miseries, they learned by the oracle that they ought to worship Almighty God, as the method for

their deliverance. So they sent ambassadors to the king of Assyria, and desired him to send them some of those priests of the Israelites whom he had taken captive. And when he thereupon sent them, and the people were by them taught the laws, and the holy worship of God, they worshipped him in a respectful manner, and the plague ceased immediately; and indeed they continue to make use of the very same customs to this very time, and are called in the Hebrew tongue Cutlans, but in the Greek tongue Samaritans. And when they see the Jews in prosperity, they pretend that they are changed, and allied to them, and call them kinsmen, as though they were derived from Joseph, and had by that means an original alliance with them; but when they see them falling into a low condition, they say they are no way related to them, and that the Jews have no right to expect any kindness or marks of kindred from them, but they declare that they are sojourners, that come from other countries. But of these we shall have a more seasonable opportunity to discourse hereafter.

Book 10

Containing the Interval of One Hundred and Eighty-Two Years and a Half, from the Captivity of the Ten Tribes to the First Year of Cyrus

1 *How Sennacherib Made an Expedition Against Hezekiah; What Threatenings Rabshakeh Made to Hezekiah When Sennacherib Was Gone Against the Egyptians; How Isaiah the Prophet Encouraged Him; How Sennacherib Having Failed of Success in Egypt, Returned Thence to Jerusalem; and How Upon His Finding His Army Destroyed, He Returned Home; and What Befell Him a Little Afterward*

1. IT was now the fourteenth year of the government of Hezekiah, king of the two tribes, when the king of Assyria, whose name was Sennacherib, made an expedition against him with a great army, and took all the cities of the tribes of Judah and Benjamin by force; and when he was ready to bring his army against Jerusalem, Hezekiah sent ambassadors to him beforehand, and promised to submit, and pay what tribute he should appoint. Hereupon Sennacherib, when he heard of what offers the ambassadors made, resolved not to proceed in the war, but to accept of the proposals that were made him; and if he might receive three hundred talents of silver, and thirty talents of gold, he promised that he would depart in a friendly manner; and he gave security upon oath to the ambassadors that he would then do him no harm, but go away as he came. So Hezekiah submitted, and emptied

his treasures, and sent the money, as supposing he should be freed from his enemy, and from any further distress about his kingdom. Accordingly, the Assyrian king took it, and yet had no regard to what he had promised; but while he himself went to the war against the Egyptians and Ethiopians, he left his general Rabshakeh, and two other of his principal commanders, with great forces, to destroy Jerusalem. The names of the two other commanders were Tartan and Rabsaris.

2. Now as soon as they were come before the walls, they pitched their camp, and sent messengers to Hezekiah, and desired that they might speak with him; but he did not himself come out to them for fear, but he sent three of his most intimate friends; the name of one was Eliakim, who was over the kingdom, and Shebna, and Joah the recorder. So these men came out, and stood over against the commanders of the Assyrian army; and when Rabshakeh saw them, he bid them go and speak to Hezekiah in the manner following: That Sennacherib, the great king,[1] desires to know of him, on whom it is that he relies and depends, in flying from his lord, and will not hear him, nor admit his army into the city? Is it on account of the Egyptians, and in hopes that his army would be beaten by them? Whereupon he lets him know, that if this be what he expects, he is a foolish man, and like one who leans on a broken reed; while such a one will not only fall down, but will have his hand pierced and hurt by it. That he ought to know he makes this expedition against him by the will of God, who hath granted this favor to him, that he shall overthrow the kingdom of Israel, and that in the very same manner he shall destroy those that are his subjects also. When Rabshakeh had made this speech in the Hebrew tongue, for he was skillful in that language, Eliakim was afraid lest the multitude that heard him should be disturbed; so he desired him to speak in the Syrian tongue. But the general, understanding what he meant, and perceiving the fear that he was in, he made his answer with a greater and a louder voice, but in the Hebrew tongue; and said, that "since they all heard what were the king's commands, they would consult their own advantage

---

1. This title of great king, both in our Bibles, 2 Kings 18:19; Isaiah 36:4, and here in Josephus, is the very same that Herodotus gives this Sennacherib, as Spanheim takes notice on this place.

in delivering up themselves to us; for it is plain the both you and your king dissuade the people from submitting by vain hopes, and so induce them to resist; but if you be courageous, and think to drive our forces away, I am ready to deliver to you two thousand of these horses that are with me for your use, if you can set as many horsemen on their backs, and show your strength; but what you have not you cannot produce. Why therefore do you delay to deliver up yourselves to a superior force, who can take you without your consent? although it will be safer for you to deliver yourselves up voluntarily, while a forcible capture, when you are beaten, must appear more dangerous, and will bring further calamities upon you."

3. When the people, as well as the ambassadors, heard what the Assyrian commander said, they related it to Hezekiah, who thereupon put off his royal apparel, and clothed himself with sackcloth, and took the habit of a mourner, and, after the manner of his country, he fell upon his face, and besought God, and entreated him to assist them, now they had no other hope of relief. He also sent some of his friends, and some of the priests, to the prophet Isaiah, and desired that he would pray to God, and offer sacrifices for their common deliverance, and so put up supplications to him, that he would have indignation at the expectations of their enemies, and have mercy upon his people. And when the prophet had done accordingly, an oracle came from God to him, and encouraged the king and his friends that were about him; and foretold that their enemies should be beaten without fighting, and should go away in an ignominious manner, and not with that insolence which they now show, for that God would take care that they should be destroyed. He also foretold that Sennacherib, the king of Assyria, should fail of his purpose against Egypt, and that when he came home he should perish by the sword.

4. About the same time also the king of Assyria wrote an epistle to Hezekiah, in which he said he was a foolish man, in supposing that he should escape from being his servant, since he had already brought under many and great nations; and he threatened, that when he took him, he would utterly destroy him, unless he now opened the gates, and willingly received his army into Jerusalem. When he read this epistle, he despised it, on account of the trust that be had in God; but he rolled up the epistle, and laid it up within the temple. And as he made his further prayers to God for the city, and for the

preservation of all the people, the prophet Isaiah said that God had heard his prayer, and that he should not be besieged at this time by the king of Assyria[2] that for the future he might be secure of not being at all disturbed by him; and that the people might go on peaceably, and without fear, with their husbandry and other affairs. But after a little while the king of Assyria, when he had failed of his treacherous designs against the Egyptians, returned home without success, on the following occasion: He spent a long time in the siege of Pelusium; and when the banks that he had raised over against the walls were of a great height, and when he was ready to make an immediate assault upon them, but heard that Tirhaka, king of the Ethiopians, was coming and bringing great forces to aid the Egyptians, and was resolved to march through the desert, and so to fall directly upon the Assyrians, this king Sennacherib was disturbed at the news, and, as I said before, left Pelusium, and returned back without success. Now concerning this Sennacherib, Herodotus also says, in the second book of his histories, how "this king came against the Egyptian king, who was the priest of Vulcan; and that as he was besieging Pelusium, he broke up the siege on the following occasion: This Egyptian priest prayed to God, and God heard his prayer, and sent a judgment upon the Arabian king." But in this Herodotus was mistaken, when he called this king not king of the Assyrians, but of the Arabians; for he saith that "a multitude of mice gnawed to pieces in one night both the bows and the rest of the armor of the Assyrians, and that it was on that account that the king, when he had no bows left, drew off his army from Pelusium." And Herodotus does indeed give us this history; nay, and Berosus, who wrote of the affairs of Chaldea, makes mention of

---

2. What Josephus says here, how Isaiah the prophet assured Hezekiah that "at this time he should not be besieged by the king of Assyria; that for the future he might be secure of being not at all disturbed by him; and that [afterward] the people might go on peaceably, and without fear, with their husbandry and other affairs," is more distinct in our other copies, both of the Kings and of Isaiah, and deserves very great consideration. The words are these: "This shall be a sign unto thee, Ye shall eat this year such as groweth of itself, and the second year that which springeth of the same; and in the third year sow ye, and reap, and plant vineyards, and eat the fruit thereof," 2 Kings 19:29; Isaiah 37:30; which seem to me plainly to design a Sabbatic year, a year of jubilee next after it, and the succeeding usual labors and fruits of them on the third and following years.

this king Sennacherib, and that he ruled over the Assyrians, and that he made an expedition against all Asia and Egypt; and says thus:[3]

5. "Now when Sennacherib was returning from his Egyptian war to Jerusalem, he found his army under Rabshakeh his general in danger [by a plague], for God had sent a pestilential distemper upon his army; and on the very first night of the siege, a hundred fourscore and five thousand, with their captains and generals, were destroyed. So the king was in a great dread and in a terrible agony at this calamity; and being in great fear for his whole army, he fled with the rest of his forces to his own kingdom, and to his city Nineveh; and when he had abode there a little while, he was treacherously assaulted, and died by the hands of his elder sons,[4] Adrammelech and Seraser, and was slain in his own temple, which was called Araske. Now these sons of his were driven away on account of the murder of their father by the citizens, and went into Armenia, while Assarachoddas took the kingdom of Sennacherib." And this proved to be the conclusion of this Assyrian expedition against the people of Jerusalem.

2   *How Hezekiah Was Sick, and Ready to Die; and How God Bestowed Upon Him Fifteen Years Longer Life, [and Secured That Promise] by the Going Back of the Shadow Ten Degrees*

1. NOW king Hezekiah being thus delivered, after a surprising manner, from the dread he was in, offered thank-offerings to God, with all his people, because nothing else had destroyed some of their enemies, and made the rest so fearful of undergoing the same fate that they departed from Jerusalem, but that Divine assistance. Yet, while he was very zealous and diligent about the worship of God, did he soon afterwards fall into a severe distemper, insomuch that the physicians despaired of him, and expected no good issue of his sickness, as

---

3. That this terrible calamity of the slaughter of the 185,000 Assyrians is here delivered in the words of Berosus the Chaldean, and that it was certainly and frequently foretold by the Jewish prophets, and that it was certainly and undeniably accomplished, see Authent. Rec. part II. p. 858.

4. We are here to take notice, that these two sons of Sennacherib, that ran away into Armenia, became the heads of two famous families there, the Arzerunii and the Genunii; of which see the particular histories in Moses Chorenensis, p. 60.

neither did his friends: and besides the distemper[5] itself, there was a very melancholy circumstance that disordered the king, which was the consideration that he was childless, and was going to die, and leave his house and his government without a successor of his own body; so he was troubled at the thoughts of this his condition, and lamented himself, and entreated of God that he would prolong his life for a little while till he had some children, and not suffer him to depart this life before he was become a father. Hereupon God had mercy upon him, and accepted of his supplication, because the trouble he was under at his supposed death was not because he was soon to leave the advantages he enjoyed in the kingdom, nor did he on that account pray that he might have a longer life afforded him, but in order to have sons, that might receive the government after him. And God sent Isaiah the prophet, and commanded him to inform Hezekiah, that within three days' time he should get clear of his distemper, and should survive it fifteen years, and that he should have children also. Now, upon the prophet's saying this, as God had commanded him, he could hardly believe it, both on account of the distemper he was under, which was very sore, and by reason of the surprising nature of what was told him; so he desired that Isaiah would give him some sign or wonder, that he might believe him in what he had said, and be sensible that he came from God; for things that are beyond expectation, and greater than our hopes, are made credible by actions of the like nature. And when Isaiah had asked him what sign he desired to be exhibited, he desired that he would make the shadow of the sun, which he had already made to go down ten steps [or degrees] in his house, to return

---

5. Josephus, and all our copies, place the sickness of Hezekiah after the destruction of Sennacherib's army, because it appears to have been after his first assault, as he was going into Arabia and Egypt, where he pushed his conquests as far as they would go, and in order to despatch his story altogether; yet does no copy but this of Josephus say it was after that destruction, but only that it happened in those days, or about that time of Hezekiah's life. Nor will the fifteen years' prolongation of his life after his sickness, allow that sickness to have been later than the former part of the fifteenth year of his reign, since chronology does not allow him in all above twenty-nine years and a few months; whereas the first assault of Sennacherib was on the fourteenth year of Hezekiah, but the destruction of Sennacherib's army was not till his eighteenth year.

again to the same place,[6] and to make it as it was before. And when the prophet prayed to God to exhibit this sign to the king, he saw what he desired to see, and was freed from his distemper, and went up to the temple, where he worshipped God, and made vows to him.

2. At this time it was that the dominion of the Assyrians was overthrown by the Medes;[7] but of these things I shall treat elsewhere. But the king of Babylon, whose name was Baladan, sent ambassadors to Hezekiah, with presents, and desired he would be his ally and his friend. So he received the ambassadors gladly, and made them a feast, and showed them his treasures, and his armory, and the other wealth he was possessed of, in precious stones and in gold, and gave them presents to be carried to Baladan, and sent them back to him. Upon which the prophet Isaiah came to him, and inquired of him whence those ambassadors came; to which he replied, that they came from Babylon, from the king; and that he had showed them all he had, that by the sight of his riches and forces he might thereby guess at [the plenty he was in], and be able to inform the king of it. But the prophet rejoined, and said, "Know thou, that, after a little while, these riches

---

6. As to this regress of the shadow, either upon a sun-dial, or the steps of the royal palace built by Ahaz, whether it were physically done by the real miraculous revolution of the earth in its diurnal motion backward from east to west for a while, and its return again to its old natural revolution from west to east; or whether it were not apparent only, and performed by an aerial phosphorus, which imitated the sun's motion backward, while a cloud hid the real sun; cannot now be determined. Philosophers and astronomers will naturally incline to the latter hypothesis. However, it must be noted, that Josephus seems to have understood it otherwise than we generally do, that the shadow was accelerated as much at first forward as it was made to go backward afterward, and so the day was neither longer nor shorter than usual; which, it must be confessed agrees best of all to astronomy, whose eclipses, older than the time were observed at the same times of the day as if this miracle had never happened. After all, this wonderful signal was not, it seems, peculiar to Judea, but either seen, or at least heard of, at Babylon also, as appears by 2 Chronicles 32:31, where we learn that the Babylonian ambassadors were sent to Hezekiah, among other things, to inquire of the wonder that was done in the land.

7. This expression of Josephus, that the Medes, upon this destruction of the Assyrian army, "overthrew" the Assyrian empire, seems to be too strong; for although they immediately cast off the Assrian yoke, and set up Deioces, a king of their own, yet it was some time before the Medes and Babylonians overthrew Nineveh, and some generations ere the Medes and Persians under Cyaxares and Cyrus overthrew the Assyrian or Babylonian empire, and took Babylon.

of thine shall be carried away to Babylon, and thy posterity shall be made eunuchs there, and lose their manhood, and be servants to the king of Babylon; for that God foretold such things would come to pass." Upon which words Hezekiah was troubled, and said that he was himself unwilling that his nation should fall into such calamities; yet since it is not possible to alter what God had determined, he prayed that there might be peace while he lived. Berosus also makes mention of this Baladan, king of Babylon. Now as to this prophet [Isaiah], he was by the confession of all, a divine and wonderful man in speaking truth; and out of the assurance that he had never written what was false, he wrote down all his prophecies, and left them behind him in books, that their accomplishment might be judged of from the events by posterity: nor did this prophet do so alone, but the others, which were twelve in number, did the same. And whatsoever is done among us, Whether it be good, or whether it be bad, comes to pass according to their prophecies; but of every one of these we shall speak hereafter.

3   *How Manasseh Reigned After Hezekiah; and How When He Was in Captivity He Returned to God and Was Restored to His Kingdom and Left It to [His Son] Amon*

1. WHEN king Hezekiah had survived the interval of time already mentioned, and had dwelt all that time in peace, he died, having completed fifty-four years of his life, and reigned twenty-nine. But when his son Manasseh, whose mother's name was Hephzibah, of Jerusalem, had taken the kingdom, he departed from the conduct of his father, and fell into a course of life quite contrary thereto, and showed himself in his manners most wicked in all respects, and omitted no sort of impiety, but imitated those transgressions of the Israelites, by the commission of which against God they had been destroyed; for he was so hardy as to defile the temple of God, and the city, and the whole country; for, by setting out from a contempt of God, he barbarously slew all the righteous men that were among the Hebrews; nor would he spare the prophets, for he every day slew some of them, till Jerusalem was overflown with blood. So God was angry at these proceedings, and sent prophets to the king, and to the multitude, by whom he threatened the very same calamities to them which their

brethren the Israelites, upon the like affronts offered to God, were now under. But these men would not believe their words, by which belief they might have reaped the advantage of escaping all those miseries; yet did they in earnest learn that what the prophets had told them was true.

2. And when they persevered in the same course of life, God raised up war against them from the king of Babylon and Chaldea, who sent an army against Judea, and laid waste the country; and caught king Manasseh by treachery, and ordered him to be brought to him, and had him under his power to inflict what punishment he pleased upon him. But then it was that Manasseh perceived what a miserable condition he was in, and esteeming himself the cause of all, he besought God to render his enemy humane and merciful to him. Accordingly, God heard his prayer, and granted him what he prayed for. So Manasseh was released by the king of Babylon, and escaped the danger he was in; and when he was come to Jerusalem, he endeavored, if it were possible, to cast out of his memory those his former sins against God, of which he now repented, and to apply himself to a very religious life. He sanctified the temple, and purged the city, and for the remainder of his days he was intent on nothing but to return his thanks to God for his deliverance, and to preserve him propitious to him all his life long. He also instructed the multitude to do the same, as having very nearly experienced what a calamity he was fallen into by a contrary conduct. He also rebuilt the altar, and offered the legal sacrifices, as Moses commanded. And when he had re-established what concerned the Divine worship, as it ought to be, he took care of the security of Jerusalem: he did not only repair the old walls with great diligence, but added another wall to the former. He also built very lofty towers, and the garrisoned places before the city he strengthened, not only in other respects, but with provisions of all sorts that they wanted. And indeed, when he had changed his former course, he so led his life for the time to come, that from the time of his return to piety towards God he was deemed a happy man, and a pattern for imitation. When therefore he had lived sixty-seven years, he departed this life, having reigned fifty-five years, and was buried in his own garden; and the kingdom came to his son Amon, whose mother's name was Meshulemeth, of the city of Jotbath.

4 *How Amon Reigned Instead of Manasseh; and After Amon Reigned Josiah; He Was Both Righteous and Religious. as Also Concerning Huldah the Prophetess*

1. THIS Amon imitated those works of his father which he insolently did when he was young: so he had a conspiracy made against him by his own servants, and was slain in his own house, when he had lived twenty-four years, and of them had reigned two. But the multitude punished those that slew Amon, and buried him with his father, and gave the kingdom to his son Josiah, who was eight years old. His mother was of the city of Boscath, and her name was Jedidah. He was of a most excellent disposition, and naturally virtuous, and followed the actions of king David, as a pattern and a rule to him in the whole conduct of his life. And when he was twelve years old, he gave demonstrations of his religious and righteous behavior; for he brought the people to a sober way of living, and exhorted them to leave off the opinion they had of their idols, because they were not gods, but to worship their own God. And by repeating on the actions of his progenitors, he prudently corrected what they did wrong, like a very elderly man, and like one abundantly able to understand what was fit to be done; and what he found they had well done, he observed all the country over, and imitated the same. And thus he acted in following the wisdom and sagacity of his own nature, and in compliance with the advice and instruction of the elders; for by following the laws it was that he succeeded so well in the order of his government, and in piety with regard to the Divine worship. And this happened because the transgressions of the former kings were seen no more, but quite vanished away; for the king went about the city, and the whole country, and cut down the groves which were devoted to strange gods, and overthrew their altars; and if there were any gifts dedicated to them by his forefathers, he made them ignominious, and plucked them down; and by this means he brought the people back from their opinion about them to the worship of God. He also offered his accustomed sacrifices and burnt-offerings upon the altar. Moreover, he ordained certain judges and overseers, that they might order the matters to them severally belonging, and have regard to justice above all things, and distribute it with the same concern they would have about their own soul. He also sent over all the country, and desired such as pleased to

bring gold and silver for the repairs of the temple, according to every one's inclinations and abilities. And when the money was brought in, he made one Maaseiah the governor of the city, and Shaphan the scribe, and Joab the recorder, and Eliakim the high priest, curators of the temple, and of the charges contributed thereto; who made no delay, nor put the work off at all, but prepared architects, and whatsoever was proper for those repairs, and set closely about the work. So the temple was repaired by this means, and became a public demonstration of the king's piety.

2. But when he was now in the eighteenth year of his reign, he sent to Eliakim the high priest, and gave order, that out of what money was overplus, he should cast cups, and dishes, and vials, for ministration [in the temple]; and besides, that they should bring all the gold or silver which was among the treasures, and expend that also in making cups and the like vessels. But as the high priest was bringing out the gold, he lighted upon the holy books of Moses that were laid up in the temple; and when he had brought them out, he gave them to Shaphan the scribe, who, when he had read them, came to the king, and informed him that all was finished which he had ordered to be done. He also read over the books to him, who, when he had heard them read, rent his garment, and called for Eliakim the high priest, and for [Shaphan] the scribe, and for certain [other] of his most particular friends, and sent them to Huldah the prophetess, the wife of Shallum, (which Shallum was a man of dignity, and of an eminent family,) and bid them go to her, and say that [he desired] she would appease God, and endeavor to render him propitious to them, for that there was cause to fear, lest, upon the transgression of the laws of Moses by their forefathers, they should be in peril of going into captivity, and of being cast out of their own country; lest they should be in want of all things, and so end their days miserably. When the prophetess had heard this from the messengers that were sent to her by the king, she bid them go back to the king, and say that "God had already given sentence against them, to destroy the people, and cast them out of their country, and deprive them of all the happiness they enjoyed; which sentence none could set aside by any prayers of theirs, since it was passed on account of their transgressions of the laws, and of their not having repented in so long a time, while the prophets had exhorted them to amend, and had foretold the punishment that would ensue on their impious

practices; which threatening God would certainly execute upon them, that they might be persuaded that he is God, and had not deceived them in any respect as to what he had denounced by his prophets; that yet, because Josiah was a righteous man, he would at present delay those calamities, but that after his death he would send on the multitude what miseries he had determined for them.

3. So these messengers, upon this prophecy of the woman, came and told it to the king; whereupon he sent to the people every where, and ordered that the priests and the Levites should come together to Jerusalem; and commanded that those of every age should be present also. And when they had gathered together, he first read to them the holy books; after which he stood upon a pulpit, in the midst of the multitude, and obliged them to make a covenant, with an oath, that they would worship God, and keep the laws of Moses. Accordingly, they gave their assent willingly, and undertook to do what the king had recommended to them. So they immediately offered sacrifices, and that after an acceptable manner, and besought God to be gracious and merciful to them. He also enjoined the high priest, that if there remained in the temple any vessel that was dedicated to idols, or to foreign gods, they should cast it out. So when a great number of such vessels were got together, he burnt them, and scattered their ashes abroad, and slew the priests of the idols that were not of the family of Aaron.

4. And when he had done thus in Jerusalem, he came into the country, and utterly destroyed what buildings had been made therein by king Jeroboam, in honor of strange gods; and he burnt the bones of the false prophets upon that altar which Jeroboam first built; and, as the prophet [Jadon], who came to Jeroboam when he was offering sacrifice, and when all the people heard him, foretold what would come to pass, viz. that a certain man of the house of David, Josiah by name, should do what is here mentioned. And it happened that those predictions took effect after three hundred and sixty-one years.

5. After these things, Josiah went also to such other Israelites as had escaped captivity and slavery under the Assyrians, and persuaded them to desist from their impious practices, and to leave off the honors they paid to strange gods, but to worship rightly their own Almighty God, and adhere to him. He also searched the houses, and the villages, and the cities, out of a suspicion that somebody might

have one idol or other in private; nay, indeed, he took away the chariots [of the sun] that were set up in his royal palace,[8] which his predecessors had framed, and what thing soever there was besides which they worshipped as a god. And when he had thus purged all the country, he called the people to Jerusalem, and there celebrated the feast of unleavened bread, and that called the passover. He also gave the people for paschal sacrifices, young kids of the goats, and lambs, thirty thousand, and three thousand oxen for burnt-offerings. The principal of the priests also gave to the priests against the passover two thousand and six hundred lambs; the principal of the Levites also gave to the Levites five thousand lambs, and five hundred oxen, by which means there was great plenty of sacrifices; and they offered those sacrifices according to the laws of Moses, while every priest explained the matter, and ministered to the multitude. And indeed there had been no other festival thus celebrated by the Hebrews from the times of Samuel the prophet; and the plenty of sacrifices now was the occasion that all things were performed according to the laws, and according to the custom of their forefathers. So when Josiah had after this lived in peace, nay, in riches and reputation also, among all men, he ended his life in the manner following.

5   *How Josiah Fought with Neco [King of Egypt.] and Was Wounded and Died in a Little Time Afterward; as Also How Neco Carried Jehoahaz, Who Had Been Made King into Egypt and Delivered the Kingdom to Jehoiakim; and [Lastly] Concerning Jeremiah and Ezekiel*

1. NOW Neco, king of Egypt, raised an army, and marched to the river Euphrates, in order to fight with the Medes and Babylonians, who

---

8. It is hard to reconcile the account in the Second Book of Kings (ch. 23:11) with this account in Josephus, and to translate this passage truly in Josephus, whose copies are supposed to be here imperfect. However, the general sense of both seems to be this: That there were certain chariots, with their horses, dedicated to the idol of the sun, or to Moloch; which idol might be carried about in procession, and worshipped by the people; which chariots were now "taken away," as Josephus says, or, as the Book of Kings says, "burnt with fire, by Josiah."

had overthrown the dominion of the Assyrians,[9] for he had a desire to reign over Asia. Now when he was come to the city Mendes, which belonged to the kingdom of Josiah, he brought an army to hinder him from passing through his own country, in his expedition against the Medes. Now Neco sent a herald to Josiah, and told him that he did not make this expedition against him, but was making haste to Euphrates; and desired that he would not provoke him to fight against him, because he obstructed his march to the place whither he had resolved to go. But Josiah did not admit of this advice of Neco, but put himself into a posture to hinder him from his intended march. I suppose it was fate that pushed him on this conduct, that it might take an occasion against him; for as he was setting his army in array,[10] and rode about in his chariot, from one wing of his army to another, one of the Egyptians shot an arrow at him, and put an end to his eagerness of fighting; for being sorely wounded, he command a retreat to be sounded for his army, and returned to Jerusalem, and died of that wound; and was magnificently buried in the sepulcher of his fathers, when he had lived thirty-nine years, and of them had reigned thirty-one. But all the people mourned greatly for him, lamenting and grieving on his account many days; and Jeremiah the prophet composed an elegy to lament him,[11] which is extant till tills time also. Moreover, this prophet denounced beforehand the sad calamities that were coming upon the city. He also left behind him in writing a description of that destruction of our nation which has lately happened in our days, and the taking of Babylon; nor was he the only prophet who delivered such predictions beforehand to the multitude, but so did Ezekiel also,

---

9. This is a remarkable passage of chronology in Josephus, that about the latter end of the reign of Josiah, the Medes and Babylonians overthrew the empire of the Assyrians; or, in the words of Tobit's continuator, that "before Tobias died, he heard of the destruction of Nineveh, which was taken by Nebuchodonosor the Babylonian, and Assuerus the Mede," Tob. 14:15. See Dean Prideaux's Connexion, at the year 612.

10. This battle is justly esteemed the very same that Herodotus (B. II. sect. 156) mentions, when he says, that "Necao joined battle with the Syrians [or Jews] at Magdolum, [Megiddo,] and beat them," as Dr. Hudson here observes.

11. Whether Josephus, from 2 Chronicles 35:25, here means the book of the Lamentations of Jeremiah, still extant, which chiefly belongs to the destruction of Jerusalem under Nebuchadnezzar, or to any other like melancholy poem now lost, but extant in the days of Josephus, belonging peculiarly to Josiah, cannot now be determined.

who was the first person that wrote, and left behind him in writing two books concerning these events. Now these two prophets were priests by birth, but of them Jeremiah dwelt in Jerusalem, from the thirteenth year of the reign of Josiah, until the city and temple were utterly destroyed. However, as to what befell this prophet, we will relate it in its proper place.

2. Upon the death of Josiah, which we have already mentioned, his son, Jehoahaz by name, took the kingdom, being about twenty-three years old. He reigned in Jerusalem; and his mother was Hamutal, of the city Libhah. He was an impious man, and impure in his course of life; but as the king of Egypt returned from the battle, he sent for Jehoahaz to come to him, to the city called Hamath[12] which belongs to Syria; and when he was come, he put him in bands, and delivered the kingdom to a brother of his, by the father's side, whose name was Eliakim, and changed his name to Jehoiakim and laid a tribute upon the land of a hundred talents of silver, and a talent of gold; and this sum of money Jehoiakim paid by way of tribute; but Neco carried away Jehoahaz into Egypt, where he died when he had reigned three months and ten days. Now Jehoiakim's mother was called Zebudah, of the city Rumah. He was of a wicked disposition, and ready to do mischief; nor was he either religions towards God, or good-natured towards men.

6   *How Nebuchadnezzar, When He Had Conquered the King of Egypt Made an Expedition Against the Jews, and Slew Jehoiakim, and Made Jeholachin His Son King*

1. NOW in the fourth year of the reign of Jehoiakim, one whose name was Nebuchadnezzar took the government over the Babylonians, who at the same time went up with a great army to the city Carchemish, which was at Euphrates, upon a resolution he had taken to fight with Neco king of Egypt, under whom all Syria then was. And when Neco understood the intention of the king of Babylon, and that this

---

12. This ancient city Hamath, which is joined with Arpad, or Aradus, and with Damascus, 2 Kings 18:34; Isaiah 36:19; Jeremiah 49:23, cities of Syria and Phoenicia, near the borders of Judea, was also itself evidently near the same borders, though long ago utterly destroyed.

expedition was made against him, he did not despise his attempt, but made haste with a great band of men to Euphrates to defend himself from Nebuchadnezzar; and when they had joined battle, he was beaten, and lost many ten thousands [of his soldiers] in the battle. So the king of Babylon passed over Euphrates, and took all Syria, as far as Pelusium, excepting Judea. But when Nebuchadnezzar had already reigned four years, which was the eighth of Jehoiakim's government over the Hebrews, the king of Babylon made an expedition with mighty forces against the Jews, and required tribute of Jehoiakim, and threatened upon his refusal to make war against him. He was aftrighted at his threatening, and bought his peace with money, and brought the tribute he was ordered to bring for three years.

2. But on the third year, upon hearing that the king of the Babylonians made an expedition against the Egyptians, he did not pay his tribute; yet was he disappointed of his hope, for the Egyptians durst not fight at this time. And indeed the prophet Jeremiah foretold every day, how vainly they relied on their hopes from Egypt, and how the city would be overthrown by the king of Babylon, and Jehoiakim the king would be subdued by him. But what he thus spake proved to be of no advantage to them, because there were none that should escape; for both the multitude and the rulers, when they heard him, had no concern about what they heard; but being displeased at what was said, as if the prophet were a diviner against the king, they accused Jeremiah, and bringing him before the court, they required that a sentence and a punishment might be given against him. Now all the rest gave their votes for his condemnation, but the elders refused, who prudently sent away the prophet from the court of [the prison], and persuaded the rest to do Jeremiah no harm; for they said that he was not the only person who foretold what would come to the city, but that Micah signified the same before him, as well as many others, none of which suffered any thing of the kings that then reigned, but were honored as the prophets of God. So they mollified the multitude with these words, and delivered Jeremiah from the punishment to which he was condemned. Now when this prophet had written all his prophecies, and the people were fasting, and assembled at the temple, on the ninth month of the fifth year of Jehoiakim, he read the book he had composed of his predictions of what was to befall the city, and the temple, and the multitude. And when the rulers heard of it, they

took the book from him, and bid him and Baruch the scribe to go their ways, lest they should be discovered by one or other; but they carried the book, and gave it to the king; so he gave order, in the presence of his friends, that his scribe should take it, and read it. When the king heard what it contained, he was angry, and tore it, and cast it into the fire, where it was consumed. He also commanded that they should seek for Jeremiah, and Baruch the scribe, and bring them to him, that they might be punished. However, they escaped his anger.

3. Now, a little time afterwards, the king of Babylon made an expedition against Jehoiakim, whom he received [into the city], and this out of fear of the foregoing predictions of this prophet, as supposing he should suffer nothing that was terrible, because he neither shut the gates, nor fought against him; yet when he was come into the city, he did not observe the covenants he had made, but he slew such as were in the flower of their age, and such as were of the greatest dignity, together with their king Jehoiakim, whom he commanded to be thrown before the walls, without any burial; and made his son Jehoiachin king of the country, and of the city: he also took the principal persons in dignity for captives, three thousand in number, and led them away to Babylon; among which was the prophet Ezekiel, who was then but young. And this was the end of king Jehoiakim, when he had lived thirty-six years, and of them reigned eleven. But Jehoiachin succeeded him in the kingdom, whose mother's name was Nehushta; she was a citizen of Jerusalem. He reigned three months and ten days.

7   *That the King of Babylon Repented of Making Jehoiachin King, and Took Him Away to Babylon and Delivered the Kingdom to Zedekiah. This King Would Not Relieve What Was Predicted by Jeremiah and Ezekiel but Joined Himself to the Egyptians; Who When They Came into Judea, Were Vanquished by the King of Babylon; as Also What Befell Jeremiah*

1. BUT a terror seized on the king of Babylon, who had given the kingdom to Jehoiachin, and that immediately; he was afraid that he should bear him a grudge, because of his killing his father, and thereupon should make the country revolt from him; wherefore he

sent an army, and besieged Jehoiachin in Jerusalem; but because he was of a gentle and just disposition, he did not desire to see the city endangered on his account, but he took his mother and kindred, and delivered them to the commanders sent by the king of Babylon, and accepted of their oaths, that neither should they suffer any harm, nor the city; which agreement they did not observe for a single year, for the king of Babylon did not keep it, but gave orders to his generals to take all that were in the city captives, both the youth and the handicraftsmen, and bring them bound to him; their number was ten thousand eight hundred and thirty-two; as also Jehoiachin, and his mother and friends. And when these were brought to him, he kept them in custody, and appointed Jehoiachin's uncle, Zedekiah, to be king; and made him take an oath, that he would certainly keep the kingdom for him, and make no innovation, nor have any league of friendship with the Egyptians.

2. Now Zedekiah was twenty and one year's old when he took the government; and had the same mother with his brother Jehoiakim, but was a despiser of justice and of his duty, for truly those of the same age with him were wicked about him, and the whole multitude did what unjust and insolent things they pleased; for which reason the prophet Jeremiah came often to him, and protested to him, and insisted, that he must leave off his impieties and transgressions, and take care of what was right, and neither give ear to the rulers, (among whom were wicked men,) nor give credit to their false prophets, who deluded them, as if the king of Babylon would make no more war against them, and as if the Egyptians would make war against him, and conquer him, since what they said was not true, and the events would not prove such [as they expected]. Now as to Zedekiah himself, while he heard the prophet speak, he believed him, and agreed to every thing as true, and supposed it was for his advantage; but then his friends perverted him, and dissuaded him from what the prophet advised, and obliged him to do what they pleased. Ezekiel also foretold in Babylon what calamities were coming upon the people, which when he heard, he sent accounts of them unto Jerusalem. But Zedekiah did not believe their prophecies, for the reason following: It happened that the two prophets agreed with one another in what they said as in all other things, that the city should be taken, and Zedekiah himself should be taken captive; but Ezekiel disagreed with him, and said that

Zedekiah should not see Babylon, while Jeremiah said to him, that the king of Babylon should carry him away thither in bonds. And be—3. Now when Zedekiah had preserved the league of mutual assistance he had made with the Babylonians for eight years, he brake it, and revolted to the Egyptians, in hopes, by their assistance, of overcoming the Babylonians. When the king of Babylon knew this, he made war against him: he laid his country waste, and took his fortified towns, and came to the city Jerusalem itself to besiege it. But when the king of Egypt heard what circumstances Zedekiah his ally was in, he took a great army with him, and came into Judea, as if he would raise the siege; upon which the king of Babylon departed from Jerusalem, and met the Egyptians, and joined battle with them, and beat them; and when he had put them to flight, he pursued them, and drove them out of all Syria. Now as soon as the king of Babylon was departed from Jerusalem, the false prophets deceived Zedekiah, and said that the king of Babylon would not any more make war against him or his people, nor remove them out of their own country into Babylon; and that those then in captivity would return, with all those vessels of the temple of which the king of Babylon had despoiled that temple. But Jeremiah came among them, and prophesied what contradicted those predictions, and what proved to be true, that they did ill, and deluded the king; that the Egyptians would be of no advantage to them, but that the king of Babylon would renew the war against Jerusalem, and besiege it again, and would destroy the people by famine, and carry away those that remained into captivity, and would take away what they had as spoils, and would carry off those riches that were in the temple; nay, that, besides this, he would burn it, and utterly overthrow the city, and that they should serve him and his posterity seventy years; that then the Persians and the Medes should put an end to their servitude, and overthrow the Babylonians; "and that we shall be dismissed, and return to this land, and rebuild the temple, and restore Jerusalem." When Jeremiah said this, the greater part believed him; but the rulers, and those that were wicked, despised him, as one disordered in his senses. Now he had resolved to go elsewhere, to his own country, which was called Anathoth, and was twenty furlongs distant from Jerusalem;[13] and as he was going, one of the rulers met him, and seized upon him, and accused him falsely, as though he were going as a deserter to the Babylonians; but Jeremiah said that he accused him falsely, and added, that he was only going to his own country; but the other would not believe him, but seized upon him, and led him away to the rulers, and laid an accusation against him, under whom he endured all sorts of torments and tortures, and was reserved to be punished; and this was the condition he was in for some time, while he suffered what I have already described unjustly.

4. Now in the ninth year of the reign of Zedekiah, on the tenth day of the tenth month, the king of Babylon made a second expedition against Jerusalem, and lay before it eighteen months, and besieged it with the utmost application. There came upon them also two of the greatest calamities at the same time that Jerusalem was besieged, a famine and a pestilential distemper, and made great havoc of them. And though the prophet Jeremiah was in prison, he did not rest, but cried out, and proclaimed aloud, and exhorted the multitude to open their gates, and admit the king of Babylon, for that if they did so, they should be preserved, and their whole families; but if they did not so, they should be destroyed; and he foretold, that if any one staid in the city, he should certainly perish by one of these ways,—either be consumed by the famine, or slain by the enemy's sword; but that if he would flee to the enemy, he should escape death. Yet did not these rulers who heard believe him, even when they were in the midst of their sore calamities; but they came to the king, and in their anger informed him what Jeremiah had said, and accused him, and complained of the prophet as of a madman, and one that disheartened their minds, and by the denunciation of miseries weakened the alacrity of the multitude, who were otherwise ready to expose themselves to dangers for him, and for their country, while he, in a way of

13. Josephus says here that Jeremiah prophesied not only of the return of the Jews from the Babylonian captivity, and this under the Persians and Medes, as in our other copies; but of cause they did not both say the same thing as to this circumstance, he disbelieved what they both appeared to agree in, and condemned them as not speaking truth therein, although all the things foretold him did come to pass according to their prophecies, as we shall show upon a fitter opportunity their rebuilding the temple, and even the city Jerusalem, which do not appear in our copies under his name. See the note on Antiq. B. XI. ch. 1. sect. 3.

threatening, warned them to flee to the enemy, and told them that the city should certainly be taken, and be utterly destroyed.

5. But for the king himself, he was not at all irritated against Jeremiah, such was his gentle and righteous disposition; yet, that he might not be engaged in a quarrel with those rulers at such a time, by opposing what they intended, he let them do with the prophet whatsoever they would; whereupon, when the king had granted them such a permission, they presently came into the prison, and took him, and let him down with a cord into a pit full of mire, that he might be suffocated, and die of himself. So he stood up to the neck in the mire which was all about him, and so continued; but there was one of the king's servants, who was in esteem with him, an Ethiopian by descent, who told the king what a state the prophet was in, and said that his friends and his rulers had done evil in putting the prophet into the mire, and by that means contriving against him that he should suffer a death more bitter than that by his bonds only. When the king heard this, he repented of his having delivered up the prophet to the rulers, and bid the Ethiopian take thirty men of the king's guards, and cords with them, and whatsoever else they understood to be necessary for the prophet's preservation, and to draw him up immediately. So the Ethiopian took the men he was ordered to take, and drew up the prophet out of the mire, and left him at liberty [in the prison].

6. But when the king had sent to call him privately, and inquired what he could say to him from God, which might be suitable to his present circumstances, and desired him to inform him of it, Jeremiah replied, that he had somewhat to say; but he said withal, he should not be believed, nor, if he admonished them, should be hearkened to; "for," said he, "thy friends have determined to destroy me, as though I had been guilty of some wickedness; and where are now those men who deceived us, and said that the king of Babylon would not come and fight against us any more? but I am afraid now to speak the truth, lest thou shouldst condemn me to die." And when the king had assured him upon oath, that he would neither himself put him to death, nor deliver him up to the rulers, he became bold upon that assurance that was given him, and gave him this advice: That he should deliver the city up to the Babylonians; and he said that it was God who prophesied this by him, that [he must do so] if he would be preserved, and escape out of the danger he was in, and that then neither should

the city fall to the ground, nor should the temple be burned; but that [if he disobeyed] he would be the cause of these miseries coming upon the citizens, and of the calamity that would befall his whole house. When the king heard this, he said that he would willingly do what he persuaded him to, and what he declared would be to his advantage, but that he was afraid of those of his own country that had fallen away to the Babylonians, lest he should be accused by them to the king of Babylon, and be punished. But the prophet encouraged him, and said he had no cause to fear such punishment, for that he should not have the experience of any misfortune, if he would deliver all up to the Babylonians, neither himself, nor his children, nor his wives, and that the temple should then continue unhurt. So when Jeremiah had said this, the king let him go, and charged him to betray what they had resolved on to none of the citizens, nor to tell any of these matters to any of the rulers, if they should have learned that he had been sent for, and should inquire of him what it was that he was sent for, and what he had said to him; but to pretend to them that he besought him that he might not be kept in bonds and in prison. And indeed he said so to them; for they came to the, prophet, and asked him what advice it was that he came to give the king relating to them. And thus I have finished what concerns this matter.

8   *How the King of Babylon Took Jerusalem and Burnt the Temple and Removed the People of Jerusalem and Zedekiah to Babylon. as Also, Who They Were That Had Succeeded in the High Priesthood under the Kings*

1. NOW the king of Babylon was very intent and earnest upon the siege of Jerusalem; and he erected towers upon great banks of earth, and from them repelled those that stood upon the walls; he also made a great number of such banks round about the whole city, whose height was equal to those walls. However, those that were within bore the siege with courage and alacrity, for they were not discouraged, either by the famine, or by the pestilential distemper, but were of cheerful minds in the prosecution of the war, although those miseries within oppressed them also, and they did not suffer themselves to be terrified, either by the contrivances of the enemy, or

by their engines of war, but contrived still different engines to oppose all the other withal, till indeed there seemed to be an entire struggle between the Babylonians and the people of Jerusalem, which had the greater sagacity and skill; the former party supposing they should be thereby too hard for the other, for the destruction of the city; the latter placing their hopes of deliverance in nothing else but in persevering in such inventions in opposition to the other, as might demonstrate the enemy's engines were useless to them. And this siege they endured for eighteen months, until they were destroyed by the famine, and by the darts which the enemy threw at them from the towers.

2. Now the city was taken on the ninth day of the fourth month, in the eleventh year of the reign of Zedekiah. They were indeed only generals of the king of Babylon, to whom Nebuchadnezzar committed the care of the siege, for he abode himself in the city of Riblah. The names of these generals who ravaged and subdued Jerusalem, if any one desire to know them, were these: Nergal Sharezer, Samgar Nebo, Rabsaris, Sorsechim, and Rabmag. And when the city was taken about midnight, and the enemy's generals were entered into the temple, and when Zedekiah was sensible of it, he took his wives, and his children, and his captains, and his friends, and with them fled out of the city, through the fortified ditch, and through the desert; and when certain of the deserters had informed the Babylonians of this, at break of day, they made haste to pursue after Zedekiah, and overtook him not far from Jericho, and encompassed him about. But for those friends and captains of Zedekiah who had fled out of the city with him, when they saw their enemies near them, they left him, and dispersed themselves, some one way, and some another, and every one resolved to save himself; so the enemy took Zedekiah alive, when he was deserted by all but a few, with his children and his wives, and brought him to the king. When he was come, Nebuchadnezzar began to call him a wicked wretch, and a covenant-breaker, and one that had forgotten his former words, when he promised to keep the country for him. He also reproached him for his ingratitude, that when he had received the kingdom from him, who had taken it from Jehoiachin, and given it to him, he had made use of the power he gave him against him that gave it; "but," said he, "God is great, who hated that conduct of thine, and hath brought thee under us." And when he had used these words to Zedekiah, he commanded his sons and his friends to be slain,

while Zedekiah and the rest of the captains looked on; after which he put out the eyes of Zedekiah, and bound him, and carried him to Babylon. And these things happened to him,[14] as Jeremiah and Ezekiel had foretold to him, that he should be caught, and brought before the king of Babylon, and should speak to him face to face, and should see his eyes with his own eyes; and thus far did Jeremiah prophesy. But he was also made blind, and brought to Babylon, but did not see it, according to the prediction of Ezekiel.

3. We have said thus much, because it was sufficient to show the nature of God to such as are ignorant of it, that it is various, and acts many different ways, and that all events happen after a regular manner, in their proper season, and that it foretells what must come to pass. It is also sufficient to show the ignorance and incredulity of men, whereby they are not permitted to foresee any thing that is future, and are, without any guard, exposed to calamities, so that it is impossible for them to avoid the experience of those calamities.

4. And after this manner have the kings of David's race ended their lives, being in number twenty-one, until the last king, who all together reigned five hundred and fourteen years, and six months, and ten days; of whom Saul, who was their first king, retained the government twenty years, though he was not of the same tribe with the rest.

5. And now it was that the king of Babylon sent Nebuzaradan, the general of his army, to Jerusalem, to pillage the temple, who had it also in command to burn it and the royal palace, and to lay the city even with the ground, and to transplant the people into Babylon. Accordingly, he came to Jerusalem in the eleventh year of king Zedekiah, and pillaged the temple, and carried out the vessels of God, both gold and silver, and particularly that large laver which Solomon dedicated, as also the pillars of brass, and their chapiters, with the golden tables and the candlesticks; and when he had carried these off, he set fire to the temple in the fifth month, the first day

---

14. This observation of Josephus about the seeming disagreement of Jeremiah, ch. 32:4, and 34:3, and Ezekiel 12:13, but real agreement at last, concerning the fate of Zedekiah, is very true and very remarkable. See ch. 7. sect. 2. Nor is it at all unlikely that the courtiers and false prophets might make use of this seeming contradiction to dissuade Zedekiah from believing either of those prophets, as Josephus here intimates he was dissuaded thereby.

of the month, in the eleventh year of the reign of Zedekiah, and in the eighteenth year of Nebuchadnezzar: he also burnt the palace, and overthrew the city. Now the temple was burnt four hundred and seventy years, six months, and ten days after it was built. It was then one thousand and sixty-two years, six months, and ten days from the departure out of Egypt; and from the deluge to the destruction of the temple, the whole interval was one thousand nine hundred and fifty-seven years, six months, and ten days; but from the generation of Adam, until this befell the temple, there were three thousand five hundred and thirteen years, six months, and ten days; so great was the number of years hereto belonging. And what actions were done during these years we have particularly related. But the general of the Babylonian king now overthrew the city to the very foundations, and removed all the people, and took for prisoners the high priest Seraiah, and Zephaniah the priest that was next to him, and the rulers that guarded the temple, who were three in number, and the eunuch who was over the armed men, and seven friends of Zedekiah, and his scribe, and sixty other rulers; all which, together with the vessels which they had pillaged, he carried to the king of Babylon to Riblah, a city of Syria. So the king commanded the heads of the high priest and of the rulers to be cut off there; but he himself led all the captives and Zedekiah to Babylon. He also led Josedek the high priest away bound. He was the son of Seraiah the high priest, whom the king of Babylon had slain in Riblah, a city of Syria, as we just now related.

6. And now, because we have enumerated the succession of the kings, and who they were, and how long they reigned, I think it necessary to set down the names of the high priests, and who they were that succeeded one another in the high priesthood under the Kings. The first high priest then at the temple which Solomon built was Zadok; after him his son Achimas received that dignity; after Achimas was Azarias; his son was Joram, and Joram's son was Isus; after him was Axioramus; his son was Phidens, and Phideas's son was Sudeas, and Sudeas's son was Juelus, and Juelus's son was Jotham, and Jotham's son was Urias, and Urias's son was Nerias, and Nerias's son was Odeas, and his son was Sallumus, and Sallumus's son was

Elcias, and his son [was Azarias, and his son] was Sareas,[15] and his son was Josedec, who was carried captive to Babylon. All these received the high priesthood by succession, the sons from their father.

7. When the king was come to Babylon, he kept Zedekiah in prison until he died, and buried him magnificently, and dedicated the vessels he had pillaged out of the temple of Jerusalem to his own gods, and planted the people in the country of Babylon, but freed the high priest from his bonds.

9 *How Nebuzaradan Set Gedaliah over the Jews That Were Left in Judea Which Gedaliah Was a Little Afterward Slain by Ishmael; and How Johanan After Ishmael Was Driven Away Went Down into Egypt with the People Which People Nebuchadnezzar When He Made an Expedition Against the Egyptians Took Captive and Brought Them Away to Babylon*

1. NOW the general of the army, Nebuzaradan, when he had carried the people of the Jews into captivity, left the poor, and those that had deserted, in the country, and made one, whose name was Gedaliah, the son of Ahikam, a person of a noble family, their governor; which Gedaliah was of a gentle and righteous disposition. He also commanded them that they should cultivate the ground, and pay an appointed tribute to the king. He also took Jeremiah the prophet out of prison, and would have persuaded him to go along with him to Babylon, for that he had been enjoined by the king to supply him with whatsoever he wanted; and if he did not like to do so, he desired him to inform him where he resolved to dwell, that he might signify the same to the king. But the prophet had no mind to follow him, nor to dwell any where else, but would gladly live in the ruins of his country,

---

15. I have here inserted in brackets this high priest Azarias, though he be omitted in all Josephus's copies, out of the Jewish chronicle, Seder Olam, of how little authority soever I generally esteem such late Rabbinical historians, because we know from Josephus himself, that the number of the high priests belonging to this interval was eighteen, Antiq. B. XX. ch. 10., whereas his copies have here but seventeen. Of this character of Baruch, the son of Neriah, and the genuineness of his book, that stands now in our Apocrypha, and that it is really a canonical book, and an appendix to Jeremiah, see Authent. Rec. Part I. p. 1—11.

and in the miserable remains of it. When the general understood what his purpose was, he enjoined Gedaliah, whom he left behind, to take all possible care of him, and to supply him with whatsoever he wanted. So when he had given him rich presents, he dismissed him. Accordingly, Jeremiah abode in a city of that country, which was called Mispah; and desired of Nebuzaradan that he would set at liberty his disciple Baruch, the son of Neriah, one of a very eminent family, and exceeding skillful in the language of his country.

2. When Nebuzaradan had done thus, he made haste to Babylon. But as to those that fled away during the siege of Jerusalem, and had been scattered over the country, when they heard that the Babylonians were gone away, and had left a remnant in the land of Jerusalem, and those such as were to cultivate the same, they came together from all parts to Gedaliah to Mispah. Now the rulers that were over them were Johanan, the son of Kareah, and Jezaniah, and Seraiah, and others beside them. Now there was of the royal family one Ishmael, a wicked man, and very crafty, who, during the siege of Jerusalem, fled to Baalis, the king of the Ammonites, and abode with him during that time; and Gedaliah persuaded them, now they were there, to stay with him, and to have no fear of the Babylonians, for that if they would cultivate the country, they should suffer no harm. This he assured them of by oath; and said that they should have him for their patron, and that if any disturbance should arise, they should find him ready to defend them. He also advised them to dwell in any city, as every one of them pleased; and that they would send men along with his own servants, and rebuild their houses upon the old foundations, and dwell there; and he admonished them beforehand, that they should make preparation, while the season lasted, of corn, and wine, and oil, that they might have whereon to feed during the winter. When he had thus discoursed to them, he dismissed them, that every one might dwell in what place of the country he pleased.

3. Now when this report was spread abroad as far as the nations that bordered on Judea, that Gedaliah kindly entertained those that came to him, after they had fled away, upon this [only] condition, that they should pay tribute to the king of Babylon, they also came readily to Gedaliah, and inhabited the country. And when Johanan, and the rulers that were with him, observed the country, and the humanity of Gedaliah, they were exceedingly in love with him, and told him

that Baalis, the king of the Ammonites, had sent Ishmael to kill him by treachery, and secretly, that he might have the dominion over the Israelites, as being of the royal family; and they said that he might deliver himself from this treacherous design, if he would give them leave to slay Ishmael, and nobody should know it, for they told him they were afraid that, when he was killed by the other, the entire ruin of the remaining strength of the Israelites would ensue. But he professed that he did not believe what they said, when they told him of such a treacherous design, in a man that had been well treated by him; because it was not probable that one who, under such a want of all things, had failed of nothing that was necessary for him, should be found so wicked and ungrateful towards his benefactor, that when it would be an instance of wickedness in him not to save him, had he been treacherously assaulted by others, to endeavor, and that earnestly, to kill him with his own hands: that, however, if he ought to suppose this information to be true, it was better for himself to be slain by the other, than to destroy a man who fled to him for refuge, and intrusted his own safety to him, and committed himself to his disposal.

4. So Johanan, and the rulers that were with him, not being able to persuade Gedaliah, went away. But after the interval of thirty days was over, Ishmael came again to Gedaliah, to the city Mispah, and ten men with him; and when he had feasted Ishmael, and those that were with him, in a splendid manner at his table, and had given them presents, he became disordered in drink, while he endeavored to be very merry with them; and when Ishmael saw him in that case, and that he was drowned in his cups to the degree of insensibility, and fallen asleep, he rose up on a sudden, with his ten friends, and slew Gedaliah, and those that were with him at the feast; and when he had slain them, he went out by night, and slew all the Jews that were in the city, and those soldiers also which were left therein by the Babylonians. But the next day fourscore men came out of the country with presents to Gedaliah, none of them knowing what had befallen him; when Ishmael saw them, he invited them in to Gedaliah, and when they were come in, he shut up the court, and slew them, and cast their dead bodies down into a certain deep pit, that they might not be seen; but of these fourscore men Ishmael spared those that entreated him not to kill them, till they had delivered up to him what riches they had concealed in the fields, consisting of their furniture, and garments,

and corn: but he took captive the people that were in Mispah, with their wives and children; among whom were the daughters of king Zedekiah, whom Nebuzaradan, the general of the army of Babylon, had left with Gedaliah. And when he had done this, he came to the king of the Ammonites.

5. But when Johanan and the rulers with him heard of what was done at Mispah by Ishmael, and of the death of Gedaliah, they had indignation at it, and every one of them took his own armed men, and came suddenly to fight with Ishmael, and overtook him at the fountain in Hebron. And when those that were carried away captives by Ishmael saw Johanan and the rulers, they were very glad, and looked upon them as coming to their assistance; so they left him that had carried them captives, and came over to Johanan: then Ishmael, with eight men, fled to the king of the Ammonites; but Johanan took those whom he had rescued out of the hands of Ishmael, and the eunuchs, and their wives and children, and came to a certain place called Mandra, and there they abode that day, for they had determined to remove from thence and go into Egypt, out of fear, lest the Babylonians should slay them, in case they continued in the country, and that out of anger at the slaughter of Gedaliah, who had been by them set over it for governor.

6. Now while they were under this deliberation, Johanan, the son of Kareah, and the rulers. that were with him, came to Jeremiah the prophet, and desired that he would pray to God, that because they were at an utter loss about what they ought to do, he would discover it to them, and they sware that they would do whatsoever Jeremiah should say to them. And when the prophet said he would be their intercessor with God, it came to pass, that after ten days God appeared to him, and said that he should inform Johanan, and the other rulers, and all the people, that he would be with them while they continued in that country, and take care of them, and keep them from being hurt by the Babylonians, of whom they were afraid; but that he would desert them if they went into Egypt, and, out of this wrath against them, would inflict the same punishments upon them which they knew their brethren had already endured. So when the prophet had informed Johanan and the people that God had foretold these things, he was not believed, when he said that God commanded them to continue in the country; but they imagined that he said so to gratify Baruch, his own

disciple, and belied God, and that he persuaded them to stay there, that they might be destroyed by the Babylonians. Accordingly, both the people and Johanan disobeyed the counsel of God, which he gave them by the prophet, and removed into Egypt, and carried Jeremiah and Barnch along with him.

7. And when they were there, God signified to the prophet that the king of Babylon was about making an expedition against the Egyptians, and commanded him to foretell to the people that Egypt should be taken, and the king of Babylon should slay some of them and, should take others captive, and bring them to Babylon; which things came to pass accordingly; for on the fifth year after the destruction of Jerusalem, which was the twenty-third of the reign of Nebuchadnezzar, he made an expedition against Celesyria; and when he had possessed himself of it, he made war against the Ammonites and Moabites; and when he had brought all these nations under subjection, he fell upon Egypt, in order to overthrow it; and he slew the king that then reigned[16] and set up another; and he took those Jews that were there captives, and led them away to Babylon. And such was the end of the nation of the Hebrews, as it hath been delivered down to us, it having twice gone beyond Euphrates; for the people of the ten tribes were carried out of Samaria by the Assyrians, in the days of king Hoshea; after which the people of the two tribes that remained after Jerusalem was taken [were carried away] by Nebuchadnezzar, the king of Babylon and Chaldea. Now as to Shalmanezer, he removed the Israelites out of their country, and placed therein the nation of the Cutheans, who had formerly belonged to the inner parts of Persia and Media, but were then called *Samaritans,* by taking the name of the country to which they were removed; but the king of Babylon, who brought out the two tribes,[17] placed no other nation in their country,

---

16. Herodotus says, this king of Egypt [Pharaoh Hophra, or Apries] was slain by the Egyptians, as Jeremiah foretold his slaughter by his enemies, Jeremiah 44:29, 30, and that as a sign of the destruction of Egypt [by Nebuchadnezzar]. Josephus says, this king was slain by Nebuchadnezzar himself.

17. We see here that Judea was left in a manner desolate after the captivity of the two tribes and was not I with foreign colonies, perhaps as an indication of Providence that the Jews were to repeople it without opposition themselves. I also esteem the latter and present desolate condition of the same country, without being repeopled by foreign colonies, to be a like indication, that the same Jews are hereafter to repeople it again themselves, at their so long expected future restoration.

by which means all Judea and Jerusalem, and the temple, continued to be a desert for seventy years; but the entire interval of time which passed from the captivity of the Israelites, to the carrying away of the two tribes, proved to be a hundred and thirty years, six months, and ten days.

10   *Concerning Daniel and What Befell Him at Babylon,*

1. BUT now Nebuchadnezzar, king of Babylon, took some of the most noble of the Jews that were children, and the kinsmen of Zedekiah their king, such as were remarkable for the beauty of their bodies, and the comeliness of their countenances, and delivered them into the hands of tutors, and to the improvement to be made by them. He also made some of them to be eunuchs; which course he took also with those of other nations whom he had taken in the flower of their age, and afforded them their diet from his own table, and had them instructed in the institutes of the country, and taught the learning of the Chaldeans; and they had now exercised themselves sufficiently in that wisdom which he had ordered they should apply themselves to. Now among these there were four of the family of Zedekiah, of most excellent dispositions, one of whom was called Daniel, another was called Ananias, another Misael, and the fourth Azarias; and the king of Babylon changed their names, and commanded that they should make use of other names. Daniel he called Baltasar; Ananias, Shadrach; Misael, Meshach; and Azarias, Abednego. These the king had in esteem, and continued to love, because of the very excellent temper they were of, and because of their application to learning, and the profess they had made in wisdom.

2. Now Daniel and his kinsmen had resolved to use a severe diet, and to abstain from those kinds of food which came from the king's table, and entirely to forbear to eat of all living creatures. So he came to Ashpenaz, who was that eunuch to whom the care of them was committed,[18] and desired him to take and spend what was brought for them from the king, but to give them pulse and dates for their

---

18. That Daniel was made one of these eunuchs of which Isaiah prophesied, Isaiah 39:7, and the three children his companions also, seems to me plain, both here in Josephus, and in our copies of Daniel, Daniel 1:3, 6–11, 18, although it must be granted

food, and any thing else, besides the flesh of living creatures, that he pleased, for that their inclinations were to that sort of food, and that they despised the other. He replied, that he was ready to serve them in what they desired, but he suspected that they would be discovered by the king, from their meagre bodies, and the alteration of their countenances, because it could not be avoided but their bodies and colors must be changed with their diet, especially while they would be clearly discovered by the finer appearance of the other children, who would fare better, and thus they should bring him into danger, and occasion him to be punished; yet did they persuade Arioch, who was thus fearful, to give them what food they desired for ten days, by way of trial; and in case the habit of their bodies were not altered, to go on in the same way, as expecting that they should not be hurt thereby afterwards; but if he saw them look meagre, and worse than the rest, he should reduce them to their former diet. Now when it appeared that they were so far from becoming worse by the use of this food, that they grew plumper and fuller in body than the rest, insomuch that he thought those who fed on what came from the king's table seemed less plump and full, while those that were with Daniel looked as if they had lived in plenty, and in all sorts of luxury. Arioch, from that time, securely took himself what the king sent every day from his supper, according to custom, to the children, but gave them the forementioned diet, while they had their souls in some measure more pure, and less burdened, and so fitter for learning, and had their bodies in better tune for hard labor; for they neither had the former oppressed and heavy with variety of meats, nor were the other effeminate on the same account; so they readily understood all the learning that was among the Hebrews, and among the Chaldeans, as especially did Daniel, who being already sufficiently skillful in wisdom, was very busy about the interpretation of dreams; and God manifested himself to him.

3. Now two years after the destruction of Egypt, king Nebuchadnezzar saw a wonderful dream, the accomplishment of which God showed him in his sleep; but when he arose out of his bed, he forgot the accomplishment. So he sent for the Chaldeans and magicians, and

---

that some married persons, that had children, were sometimes called eunuchs, in a general acceptation for courtiers, on account that so many of the ancient courtiers were real eunuchs. See Genesis 39:1.

the prophets, and told them that he had seen a dream, and informed them that he had forgotten the accomplishment of what he had seen, and he enjoined them to tell him both what the dream was, and what was its signification; and they said that this was a thing impossible to be discovered by men; but they promised him, that if he would explain to them what dream he had seen, they would tell him its signification. Hereupon he threatened to put them to death, unless they told him his dream; and he gave command to have them all put to death, since they confessed they could not do what they were commanded to do. Now when Daniel heard that the king had given a command, that all the wise men should be put to death, and that among them himself and his three kinsmen were in danger, he went to Arioch, who was captain of the king's guards, and desired to know of him what was the reason why the king had given command that all the wise men, and Chaldeans, and magicians should be slain. So when he had learned that the king had had a dream, and had forgotten it, and that when they were enjoined to inform the king of it, they had said they could not do it, and had thereby provoked him to anger, he desired of Arioch that he would go in to the king, and desire respite for the magicians for one night, and to put off their slaughter so long, for that he hoped within that time to obtain, by prayer to God, the knowledge of the dream. Accordingly, Arioch informed the king of what Daniel desired. So the king bid them delay the slaughter of the magicians till he knew what Daniel's promise would come to; but the young man retired to his own house, with his kinsmen, and besought God that whole night to discover the dream, and thereby deliver the magicians and Chaldeans, with whom they were themselves to perish, from the king's anger, by enabling him to declare his vision, and to make manifest what the king had seen the night before in his sleep, but had forgotten it. Accordingly, God, out of pity to those that were in danger, and out of regard to the wisdom of Daniel, made known to him the dream and its interpretation, that so the king might understand by him its signification also. When Daniel had obtained this knowledge from God, he arose very joyful, and told it his brethren, and made them glad, and to hope well that they should now preserve their lives, of which they despaired before, and had their minds full of nothing but the thoughts of dying. So when he had with them returned thanks to God, who had commiserated their youth, when it was day he came to Arioch, and desired him to bring him to the king, because he would discover to him that dream which he had seen the night before.

4. When Daniel was come in to the king, he excused himself first, that he did not pretend to be wiser than the other Chaldeans and magicians, when, upon their entire inability to discover his dream, he was undertaking to inform him of it; for this was not by his own skill, or on account of his having better cultivated his understanding than the rest; but he said, "God hath had pity upon us, when we were in danger of death, and when I prayed for the life of myself, and of those of my own nation, hath made manifest to me both the dream, and the interpretation thereof; for I was not less concerned for thy glory than for the sorrow that we were by thee condemned to die, while thou didst so unjustly command men, both good and excellent in themselves, to be put to death, when thou enjoinedst them to do what was entirely above the reach of human wisdom, and requiredst of them what was only the work of God. Wherefore, as thou in thy sleep wast solicitous concerning those that should succeed thee in the government of the whole world, God was desirous to show thee all those that should reign after thee, and to that end exhibited to thee the following dream: Thou seemedst to see a great image standing before thee, the head of which proved to be of gold, the shoulders and arms of silver, and the belly and the thighs of brass, but the legs and the feet of iron; after which thou sawest a stone broken off from a mountain, which fell upon the image, and threw it down, and brake it to pieces, and did not permit any part of it to remain whole; but the gold, the silver, the brass, and the iron, became smaller than meal, which, upon the blast of a violent wind, was by force carried away, and scattered abroad, but the stone did increase to such a degree, that the whole earth beneath it seemed to be filled therewith. This is the dream which thou sawest, and its interpretation is as follows: The head of gold denotes thee, and the kings of Babylon that have been before thee; but the two hands and arms signify this, that your government shall be dissolved by two kings; but another king that shall come from the west, armed with brass, shall destroy that government; and another government, that shall be like unto iron, shall put an end to the power of the former, and shall have dominion over all the earth, on account of the nature of iron, which is stronger than that of gold, of silver, and of brass." Daniel did also declare the meaning of the stone

to the king[19] but I do not think proper to relate it, since I have only undertaken to describe things past or things present, but not things that are future; yet if any one be so very desirous of knowing truth, as not to wave such points of curiosity, and cannot curb his inclination for understanding the uncertainties of futurity, and whether they will happen or not, let him be diligent in reading the book of Daniel, which he will find among the sacred writings.

5. When Nebuchadnezzar heard this, and recollected his dream, he was astonished at the nature of Daniel, and fell upon his knee; and saluted Daniel in the manner that men worship God, and gave command that he should be sacrificed to as a god. And this was not all, for he also imposed the name, of his own god upon him, [Baltasar,] and made him and his kinsmen rulers of his whole kingdom; which kinsmen of his happened to fall into great danger by the envy and malice [of their enemies]; for they offended the king upon the occasion following: he made an image of gold, whose height was sixty cubits, and its breadth six cubits, and set it in the great plain of Babylon; and when he was going to dedicate the image, he invited the principal men out of all the earth that was under his dominions, and commanded them, in the first place, that when they should hear the sound of the trumpet, they should then fall down and worship the image; and he threatened, that those who did not so, should be cast into a fiery furnace. When therefore all the rest, upon the hearing of the sound of the trumpet, worshipped the image, they relate that Daniel's kinsmen did not do it, because they would not transgress the laws of their country. So these men were convicted, and cast immediately into the fire, but were saved by Divine Providence, and after a surprising manner escaped death, for the fire did not touch them; and I suppose that it touched them not, as if it reasoned with itself, that they were cast into it without any fault of theirs, and that therefore it was too weak

---

19. Of this most remarkable passage in Josephus concerning the "stone cut out of the mountain, and destroying the image," which he would not explain, but intimated to be a prophecy of futurity, and probably not safe for him to explain, as belonging to the destruction of the Roman empire by Jesus Christ, the true Messiah of the Jews, take the words of Hayercamp, ch. 10. sect. 4: "Nor is this to be wondered at, that he would not now meddle with things future, for he had no mind to provoke the Romans, by speaking of the destruction of that city which they called the Eternal City."

to burn the young men when they were in it. This was done by the power of God, who made their bodies so far superior to the fire, that it could not consume them. This it was which recommended them to the king as righteous men, and men beloved of God, on which account they continued in great esteem with him.

6. A little after this the king saw in his sleep again another vision; how he should fall from his dominion, and feed among the wild beasts, and that when he halt lived in this manner in the desert for seven years,[20] he should recover his dominion again. When he had seen this dream, he called the magicians together again, and inquired of them about it, and desired them to tell him what it signified; but when none of them could find out the meaning of the dream, nor discover it to the king, Daniel was the only person that explained it; and as he foretold, so it came to pass; for after he had continued in the wilderness the forementioned interval of time, while no one durst attempt to seize his kingdom during those seven years, he prayed to God that he might recover his kingdom, and he returned to it. But let no one blame me for writing down every thing of this nature, as I find it in our ancient books; for as to that matter, I have plainly assured those that think me defective in any such point, or complain of my management, and

---

20. Since Josephus here explains the seven prophetic times which were to pass over Nebuchadnezzar (Daniel 4:16) to be seven years, we thence learn how he most probably must have understood those other parallel phrases, of "a time, times, and a half," Antiq. B. VII. ch. 25., of so many prophetic years also, though he withal lets us know, by his hint at the interpretation of the seventy weeks, as belonging to the fourth monarchy, and the destruction of Jerusalem by the Romans in the days of Josephus, ch. 2. sect. 7, that he did not think those years to be bare years, but rather days for years; by which reckoning, and by which alone, could seventy weeks, or four hundred and ninety days, reach to the age of Josephus. But as to the truth of those seven years' banishment of Nebuchadnezzar from men, and his living so long among the beasts, the very small remains we have any where else of this Nebuchadnezzar prevent our expectation of any other full account of it. So far we knew by Ptolemy's canon, a contemporary record, as well as by Josephus presently, that he reigned in all forty-three years, that is, eight years after we meet with any account of his actions; one of the last of which was the thirteen years' siege of Tyre, Antiq. B. XI. ch. 11., where yet the Old Latin has but three years and ten months: yet were his actions before so remarkable, both in sacred and profane authors, that a vacuity of eight years at the least, at the latter end of his reign, must be allowed to agree very well with Daniel's accounts; that after a seven years' brutal life, he might return to his reason, and to the exercise of his royal authority, for one whole year at least before his death.

have told them in the beginning of this history, that I intended to do no more than translate the Hebrew books into the Greek language, and promised them to explain those facts, without adding any thing to them of my own, or taking any thing away from there.

11   *Concerning Nebuchadnezzar and His Successors and How Their Government Was Dissolved by the Persians; and What Things Befell Daniel in Media; and What Prophecies He Delivered There*

1. NOW when king Nebuchadnezzar had reigned forty-three years,[21] he ended his life. He was an active man, and more fortunate than the kings that were before him. Now Berosus makes mention of his actions in the third book of his Chaldaic History, where he says thus: "When his father Nebuchodonosor [Nabopollassar] heard that the governor whom he had set over Egypt, and the places about Coelesyria and Phoenicia, had revolted from him, while he was not himself able any longer to undergo the hardships [of war], he committed to his son Nebuchadnezzar, who was still but a youth, some parts of his army, and sent them against him. So when Nebuchadnezzar had given battle, and fought with the rebel, he beat him, and reduced the country from under his subjection, and made it a branch of his own kingdom; but about that time it happened that his father Nebuchodonosor [Nabopollassar] fell ill, and ended his life in the city Babylon, when he had reigned twenty-one years;[22] and when he was made sensible, as he was in a little time, that his father Nebuchodonosor [Nabopollassar] was dead, and having settled the

---

21. These forty-three years for the duration of the reign of Nebuchadnezzar are, as I have just now observed, the very same number in Ptolemy's canon. Moses Chorenensis does also confirm this captivity of the Jews under Nebuchadnezzar, and adds, what is very remarkable, that sale of those Jews that were carried by him into captivity got away into Armenia, and raised the great family of the Bagratide there.

22. These twenty-one years here ascribed to one named Naboulassar, in the first book against Apion, or to Nabopollassar, the father of the great Nebuchadnezzar, are also the very same with those given him in Ptolemy's canon. And note here, that what Dr. Prideaux says, at the year, that Nebuchadnezzar must have been a common name of other kings of Babylon, besides the great Nebuchadnezzar himself is a groundless mistake of some modern chronologers rely, and destitute of all proper original authority.

affairs of Egypt, and the other countries, as also those that concerned the captive Jews, and Phoenicians, and Syrians, and those of the Egyptian nations; and having committed the conveyance of them to Babylon to certain of his friends, together with the gross of his army, and the rest of their ammunition and provisions, he went himself hastily, accompanied with a few others, over the desert, and came to Babylon. So he took upon him the management of public affairs, and of the kingdom which had been kept for him by one that was the principal of the Chaldeans, and he received the entire dominions of his father, and appointed, that when the captives came, they should be placed as colonies, in the most proper places of Babylonia; but then he adorned the temple of Belus, and the rest of the temples, in a magnificent manner, with the spoils he had taken in the war. He also added another city to that which was there of old, and rebuilt it, that such as would besiege it hereafter might no more turn the course of the river, and thereby attack the city itself. He therefore built three walls round about the inner city, and three others about that which was the outer, and this he did with burnt brick. And after he had, after a becoming manner, walled the city, and adorned its gates gloriously, he built another palace before his father's palace, but so that they joined to it; to describe whose vast height and immense riches it would perhaps be too much for me to attempt; yet as large and lofty as they were, they were completed in fifteen days.[23] He also erected elevated places for walking, of stone, and made it resemble mountains, and built it so that it might be planted with all sorts of trees. He also erected what was called a pensile paradise, because his wife was desirous to have things like her own country, she having been bred up in the palaces of Media." Megasthenes also, in his fourth book of his Accounts of India, makes mention. of these things, and

---

23. These fifteen days for finishing such vast buildings at Babylon, in Josephus's copy of Berosus, would seem too absurd to be supposed to be the true number, were it not for the same testimony extant also in the first book against Apion, sect. 19, with the same number. It thence indeed appears that Josephus's copy of Berosus had this small number, but that it is the true number I still doubt. Josephus assures us, that the walls of so much a smaller city as Jerusalem were two years and four months in building by Nehemiah, who yet hastened the work all he could, Antiq. B. XI. ch. 5. sect. 8. I should think one hundred and fifteen days, or a year and fifteen days, much more proportionable to so great a work.

thereby endeavors to show that this king [Nebuchadnezzar] exceeded Hercules in fortitude, and in the greatness of his actions; for he saith that he conquered a great part of Libya and Iberia. Diocles also, in the second book of his Accounts of Persia, mentions this king; as does Philostrates in his Accounts both of India and of Phoenicia, say, that this king besieged Tyre thirteen years, while at the same time Ethbaal reigned at Tyre. These are all the histories that I have met with concerning this king.

2. But now, after the death of Nebuchadnezzar, Evil-Merodach his son succeeded in the kingdom, who immediately set Jeconiah at liberty, and esteemed him among his most intimate friends. He also gave him many presents, and made him honorable above the rest of the kings that were in Babylon; for his father had not kept his faith with Jeconiah, when he voluntarily delivered up himself to him, with his wives and children, and his whole kindred, for the sake of his country, that it might not be taken by siege, and utterly destroyed, as we said before. When Evil-Mcrodach was dead, after a reign of eighteen years, Niglissar his son took the government, and retained it forty years, and then ended his life; and after him the succession in the kingdom came to his son Labosordacus, who continued in it in all but nine months; and when he was dead, it came to Baltasar,[24] who by the Babylonians was called Naboandelus; against him did Cyrus, the king of Persia, and Darius, the king of Media, make war;

---

24. It is here remarkable that Josephus, without the knowledge of Ptolemy's canon, should call the same king whom he himself here (Bar. i. 11, and Daniel 5:1, 2, 9, 12, 22, 29, 39) styles Beltazar, or Belshazzar, from the Babylonian god Bel, Naboandelus also; and in the first book against Apion, sect. 19, vol. iii., from the same citation out of Berosus, Nabonnedon, from the Babylonian god Nabo or Nebo. This last is not remote from the original pronunciation itself in Ptolemy's canon, Nabonadius; for both the place of this king in that canon, as the last of the Assyrian or Babylonian kings, and the number of years of his reign, seventeen, the same in both demonstrate that it is one and the same king that is meant by them all. It is also worth noting, that Josephus knew that Darius, the partner of Cyrus, was the son of Astyages, and was called by another name among the Greeks, though it does not appear he knew what that name was, as having never seen the best history of this period, which is Xenophon's. But then what Josephus's present copies say presently, sect. 4, that it was only within no long time after the hand-writing on the wall that Baltasar was slain, does not so well agree with our copies of Daniel, which say it was the same night, Daniel 5:30.

and when he was besieged in Babylon, there happened a wonderful and prodigious vision. He was sat down at supper in a large room, and there were a great many vessels of silver, such as were made for royal entertainments, and he had with him his concubines and his friends; whereupon he came to a resolution, and commanded that those vessels of God which Nebuchadnezzar had plundered out of Jerusalem, and had not made use of, but had put them into his own temple, should be brought out of that temple. He also grew so haughty as to proceed to use them in the midst of his cups, drinking out of them, and blaspheming against God. In the mean time, he saw a hand proceed out of the wall, and writing upon the wall certain syllables; at which sight, being disturbed, he called the magicians and Chaldeans together, and all that sort of men that are among these barbarians, and were able to interpret signs and dreams, that they might explain the writing to him. But when the magicians said they could discover nothing, nor did understand it, the king was in great disorder of mind, and under great trouble at this surprising accident; so he caused it to be proclaimed through all the country, and promised, that to him who could explain the writing, and give the signification couched therein, he would give him a golden chain for his neck, and leave to wear a purple garment, as did the kings of Chaldea, and would bestow on him the third part of his own dominions. When this proclamation was made, the magicians ran together more earnestly, and were very ambitious to find out the importance of the writing, but still hesitated about it as much as before. Now when the king's grandmother saw him cast down at this accident,[25] she began to encourage him, and to say, that there was a certain captive who came from Judea, a Jew by birth, but brought away thence by Nebuchadnezzar when he had destroyed Jerusalem, whose name was Daniel, a wise man, and one of great sagacity in finding out what was impossible for others to discover, and what was known to God alone, who brought to light and answered such questions to Nebuchadnezzar as no one else was able to answer when they were consulted. She therefore desired that

---

25. This grandmother, or mother of Baltasar, the queen dowager of Babylon, (for she is distinguished from his queen, Daniel 5:10, 13,) seems to have been the famous Nitocris, who fortified Babylon against the Medes and Persians, and, in all probability governed under Baltasar, who seems to be a weak and effeminate prince.

he would send for him, and inquire of him concerning the writing, and to condemn the unskilfulness of those that could not find their meaning, and this, although what God signified thereby should be of a melancholy nature.

3. When Baltasar heard this, he called for Daniel; and when he had discoursed to him what he had learned concerning him and his wisdom, and how a Divine Spirit was with him, and that he alone was fully capable of finding out what others would never have thought of, he desired him to declare to him what this writing meant; that if he did so, he would give him leave to wear purple, and to put a chain of gold about his neck, and would bestow on him the third part of his dominion, as an honorary reward for his wisdom, that thereby he might become illustrious to those who saw him, and who inquired upon what occasion he obtained such honors. But Daniel desired that he would keep his gifts to himself; for what is the effect of wisdom and of Divine revelation admits of no gifts, and bestows its advantages on petitioners freely; but that still he would explain the writing to him; which denoted that he should soon die, and this because he had not learnt to honor God, and not to admit things above human nature, by what punishments his progenitor had undergone for the injuries he had offered to God; and because he had quite forgotten how Nebuchadnezzar was removed to feed among wild beasts for his impieties, and did not recover his former life among men and his kingdom, but upon God's mercy to him, after many supplications and prayers; who did thereupon praise God all the days of his life, as one of almighty power, and who takes care of mankind. [He also put him in mind] how he had greatly blasphemed against God, and had made use of his vessels amongst his concubines; that therefore God saw this, and was angry with him, and declared by this writing beforehand what a sad conclusion of his life he should come to. And he explained the writing thus:" MANEH. This, if it be expounded in the Greek language, may signify a *Number,* because God hath numbered so long a time for thy life, and for thy government, and that there remains but a small portion. THEKEL This signifies a *weight,* and means that God hath weighed thy kingdom in a balance, and finds it going down already.—PHARES. This also, in the Greek tongue, denotes a *fragment,.* God will therefore break thy kingdom in pieces, and divide it among the Medes and Persians."

4. When Daniel had told the king that the writing upon the wall signified these events, Baltasar was in great sorrow and affliction, as was to be expected, when the interpretation was so heavy upon him. However, he did not refuse what he had promised Daniel, although he were become a foreteller of misfortunes to him, but bestowed it all upon him; as reasoning thus, that what he was to reward was peculiar to himself, and to fate, and did not belong to the prophet, but that it was the part of a good and a just man to give what he had promised, although the events were of a melancholy nature. Accordingly, the king determined so to do. Now, after a little while, both himself and the city were taken by Cyrus, the king of Persia, who fought against him; for it was Baltasar, under whom Babylon was taken, when he had reigned seventeen years. And this is the end of the posterity of king Nebuchadnezzar, as history informs us; but when Babylon was taken by Darius, and when he, with his kinsman Cyrus, had put an end to the dominion of the Babylonians, he was sixty-two years old. He was the son of Astyages, and had another name among the Greeks. Moreover, he took Daniel the prophet, and carried him with him into Media, and honored him very greatly, and kept him with him; for he was one of the three presidents whom he set over his three hundred and sixty provinces, for into so many did Darius part them.

5. However, while Daniel was in so great dignity, and in so great favor with Darius, and was alone intrusted with every thing by him, a having somewhat divine in him, he was envied by the rest; for those that see others in greater honor than themselves with kings envy them; and when those that were grieved at the great favor Daniel was in with Darius sought for an occasion against him, he afforded them no occasion at all, for he was above all the temptations of money, and despised bribery, and esteemed it a very base thing to take any thing by way of reward, even when it might be justly given him; he afforded those that envied him not the least handle for an accusation. So when they could find nothing for which they might calumniate him to the king, nothing that was shameful or reproachful, and thereby deprive him of the honor he was in with him, they sought for some other method whereby they might destroy him. When therefore they saw that Daniel prayed to God three times a day, they thought they had gotten an occasion by which they might ruin him; so they came to Darius and told him that the princes and governors had thought

proper to allow the multitude a relaxation for thirty days, that no one might offer a petition or prayer either to himself or to the gods, but that he who shall transgress this decree shall be east into the den of lions, and there perish."

6. Whereupon the king, not being acquainted with their wicked design, nor suspecting that it was a contrivance of theirs against Daniel, said he was pleased with this decree of theirs, and he promised to confirm what they desired; he also published an edict to promulgate to the people that decree which the princes had made. Accordingly, all the rest took care not to transgress those injunctions, and rested in quiet; but Daniel had no regard to them, but, as he was wont, he stood and prayed to God in the sight of them all; but the princes having met with the occasion they so earnestly sought to find against Daniel, came presently to the king, and accused him, that Daniel was the only person that transgressed the decree, while not one of the rest durst pray to their gods. This discovery they made, not because of his impiety, but because they had watched him, and observed him out of envy; for supposing that Darius did thus out of a greater kindness to him than they expected, and that he was ready to grant him pardon for this contempt of his injunctions, and envying this very pardon to Daniel, they did not become more honorable to him, but desired he might be cast into the den of lions according to the law. So Darius, hoping that God would deliver him, and that he would undergo nothing that was terrible by the wild beasts, bid him bear this accident cheerfully. And when he was cast into the den, he put his seal to the stone that lay upon the mouth of the den, and went his way, but he passed all the night without food and without sleep, being in great distress for Daniel; but when it was day, he got up, and came to the den, and found the seal entire, which he had left the stone sealed withal; he also opened the seal, and. cried out, and called to Daniel, and asked him if he were alive. And as soon as he heard the king's voice, and said that he had suffered no harm, the king gave order that he should be drawn up out of the den. Now when his enemies saw that Daniel had suffered nothing which was terrible, they would not own that he was preserved by God, and by his providence; but they said that the lions had been filled full with food, and on that account it was, as they supposed, that the lions would not touch Daniel, nor come to him; and this they alleged to the king. But the king, out of an

abhorrence of their wickedness, gave order that they should throw in a great deal of flesh to the lions; and when they had filled themselves, he gave further order that Daniel's enemies should be cast into the den, that he might learn whether the lions, now they were full, would touch them or not. And it appeared plain to Darius, after the princes had been cast to the wild beasts, that it was God who preserved[26] for the lions spared none of them, but tore them all to pieces, as if they had been very hungry, and wanted food. I suppose therefore it was not their hunger, which had been a little before satisfied with abundance of flesh, but the wickedness of these men, that provoked them [to destroy the princes]; for if it so please God, that wickedness might, by even those irrational creatures, be esteemed a plain foundation for their punishment.

7. When therefore those that had intended thus to destroy Daniel by treachery were themselves destroyed, king Darius sent [letters] over all the country, and praised that God whom Daniel worshipped, and said that he was the only true God, and had all power. He had also Daniel in very great esteem, and made him the principal of his friends. Now when Daniel was become so illustrious and famous, on account of the opinion men had that he was beloved of God, he built a tower at Ecbatana, in Media: it was a most elegant building, and wonderfully made, and it is still remaining, and preserved to this day; and to such as see it, it appears to have been lately built, and to have been no older than that very day when any one looks upon it, it is so fresh[27] flourishing, and beautiful, and no way grown old in so long

---

26. It is no way improbable that Daniel's enemies might suggest this reason to the king why the lions did not meddle with him and that they might suspect the king's kindness to Daniel had procured these lions to be so filled beforehand, and that thence it was that he encouraged Daniel to submit to this experiment, in hopes of coming off safe; and that this was the true reason of making so terrible an experiment upon those his enemies, and all their families, Daniel 6:21, though our other copies do not directly take notice of it

27. What Josephus here says, that the stones of the sepulchers of the kings of Persia at this tower, or those perhaps of the same sort that are now commonly called the ruins of Persepolis, continued so entire and unaltered in his days, as if they were lately put there, "I (says Reland) here can show to be true, as to those stones of the Persian mansoleum, which Com. Brunius brake off and gave me." He ascribed this to the hardness of the stones, which scarcely yields to iron tools, and proves frequently too hard for cutting by the chisel, but oftentimes breaks it to pieces.

time; for buildings suffer the same as men do, they grow old as well as they, and by numbers of years their strength is dissolved, and their beauty withered. Now they bury the kings of Media, of Persia, and Parthia in this tower to this day, and he who was entrusted with the care of it was a Jewish priest; which thing is also observed to this day. But it is fit to give an account of what this man did, which is most admirable to hear, for he was so happy as to have strange revelations made to him, and those as to one of the greatest of the prophets, insomuch, that while he was alive he had the esteem and applause both of the kings and of the multitude; and now he is dead, he retains a remembrance that will never fail, for the several books that he wrote and left behind him are still read by us till this time; and from them we believe that Daniel conversed with God; for he did not only prophesy of future events, as did the other prophets, but he also determined the time of their accomplishment. And while prophets used to foretell misfortunes, and on that account were disagreeable both to the kings and to the multitude, Daniel was to them a prophet of good things, and this to such a degree, that by the agreeable nature of his predictions, he procured the goodwill of all men; and by the accomplishment of them, he procured the belief of their truth, and the opinion of [a sort of] divinity for himself, among the multitude. He also wrote and left behind him what made manifest the accuracy and undeniable veracity of his predictions; for he saith, that when he was in Susa, the metropolis of Persia, and went out into the field with his companions, there was, on the sudden, a motion and concussion of the earth, and that he was left alone by himself, his friends fleeing away from him, and that he was disturbed, and fell on his face, and on his two hands, and that a certain person touched him, and, at the same time, bid him rise, and see what would befall his countrymen after many generations. He also related, that when he stood up, he was shown a great rain, with many horns growing out of his head, and that the last was higher than the rest: that after this he looked to the west, and saw a he-goat carried through the air from that quarter; that he rushed upon the ram with violence, and smote him twice with his horns, and overthrew him to the ground, and trampled upon him: that afterward he saw a very great horn growing out of the head of the he-goat, and that when it was broken off, four horns grew up that were exposed to each of the four winds, and he wrote that out of them arose another lesser horn, which, as he said, waxed great; and that God showed to him that it should fight against his nation, and take their city by force, and bring the temple worship to confusion, and forbid the sacrifices to be offered for one thousand two hundred and ninety-six days. Daniel wrote that he saw these visions in the Plain of Susa; and he hath informed us that God interpreted the appearance of this vision after the following manner: He said that the ram signified the kingdoms of the Medes and Persians, and the horns those kings that were to reign in them; and that the last horn signified the last king, and that he should exceed all the kings in riches and glory: that the he-goat signified that one should come and reign from the Greeks, who should twice fight with the Persian, and overcome him in battle, and should receive his entire dominion: that by the great horn which sprang out of the forehead of the he-goat was meant the first king; and that the springing up of four horns upon its falling off, and the conversion of every one of them to the four quarters of the earth, signified the successors that should arise after the death of the first king, and the partition of the kingdom among them, and that they should be neither his children, nor of his kindred, that should reign over the habitable earth for many years; and that from among them there should arise a certain king that should overcome our nation and their laws, and should take away their political government, and should spoil the temple, and forbid the sacrifices to be offered for three years' time. And indeed it so came to pass, that our nation suffered these things under Antiochus Epiphanes, according to Daniel's vision, and what he wrote many years before they came to pass. In the very same manner Daniel also wrote concerning the Roman government, and that our country should be made desolate by them. All these things did this man leave in writing, as God had showed them to him, insomuch that such as read his prophecies, and see how they have been fulfilled, would wonder at the honor wherewith God honored Daniel; and may thence discover how the Epicureans are in an error, who cast Providence out of human life, and do not believe that God takes care of the affairs of the world, nor that the universe is governed and continued in being by that blessed and immortal nature, but say that the world is carried along of its own accord, without a ruler and a curator; which, were it destitute of a guide to conduct it, as they imagine, it would be like ships without pilots, which we see drowned by the winds, or like chariots without drivers, which are overturned; so would the world be dashed to pieces by its being carried without a Providence, and so perish, and come to nought. So that, by the forementioned predictions of Daniel, those men seem to me very much to err from the truth, who determine that God exercises no providence over human affairs; for if that were the case, that the world went on by mechanical necessity, we should not see that all things would come to pass according to his prophecy. Now as to myself, I have so described these matters as I have found them and read them; but if any one is inclined to another opinion about them, let him enjoy his different sentiments without any blame from me.